The Economics of
Artificial Intelligence

**National Bureau of
Economic Research
Conference Report**

The Economics of Artificial Intelligence: An Agenda

Edited by **Ajay Agrawal, Joshua Gans, and Avi Goldfarb**

The University of Chicago Press

Chicago and London

The University of Chicago Press, Chicago 60637
The University of Chicago Press, Ltd., London
© 2019 by the National Bureau of Economic Research, Inc.
Published 2019
Printed in the United States of America

28 27 26 25 24 23 22 21 20   4 5

ISBN-13: 978-0-226-61333-8 (cloth)
ISBN-13: 978-0-226-61347-5 (e-book)
DOI: https://doi.org/10.7208/chicago/9780226613475.001.0001

Library of Congress Cataloging-in-Publication Data

Names: Agrawal, Ajay, editor. | Gans, Joshua, 1968– editor. | Goldfarb,
    Avi, editor.
Title: The economics of artificial intelligence : an agenda / Ajay
    Agrawal, Joshua Gans, and Avi Goldfarb, editors.
Other titles: National Bureau of Economic Research conference report.
Description: Chicago ; London : The University of Chicago Press,
    2019. | Series: National Bureau of Economic Research conference
    report | Includes bibliographical references and index.
Identifiers: LCCN 2018037552 | ISBN 9780226613338 (cloth : alk.
    paper) | ISBN 9780226613475 (ebook)
Subjects: LCSH: Artificial intelligence—Economic aspects.
Classification: LCC TA347.A78 E365 2019 | DDC 338.4/70063—dc23
LC record available at https://lccn.loc.gov/2018037552

♾ This paper meets the requirements of ANSI/NISO Z39.48-1992
(Permanence of Paper).

Relation of the Directors to the
Work and Publications of the
National Bureau of Economic Research

1. The object of the NBER is to ascertain and present to the economics profession, and to the public more generally, important economic facts and their interpretation in a scientific manner without policy recommendations. The Board of Directors is charged with the responsibility of ensuring that the work of the NBER is carried on in strict conformity with this object.

2. The President shall establish an internal review process to ensure that book manuscripts proposed for publication DO NOT contain policy recommendations. This shall apply both to the proceedings of conferences and to manuscripts by a single author or by one or more co-authors but shall not apply to authors of comments at NBER conferences who are not NBER affiliates.

3. No book manuscript reporting research shall be published by the NBER until the President has sent to each member of the Board a notice that a manuscript is recommended for publication and that in the President's opinion it is suitable for publication in accordance with the above principles of the NBER. Such notification will include a table of contents and an abstract or summary of the manuscript's content, a list of contributors if applicable, and a response form for use by Directors who desire a copy of the manuscript for review. Each manuscript shall contain a summary drawing attention to the nature and treatment of the problem studied and the main conclusions reached.

4. No volume shall be published until forty-five days have elapsed from the above notification of intention to publish it. During this period a copy shall be sent to any Director requesting it, and if any Director objects to publication on the grounds that the manuscript contains policy recommendations, the objection will be presented to the author(s) or editor(s). In case of dispute, all members of the Board shall be notified, and the President shall appoint an ad hoc committee of the Board to decide the matter; thirty days additional shall be granted for this purpose.

5. The President shall present annually to the Board a report describing the internal manuscript review process, any objections made by Directors before publication or by anyone after publication, any disputes about such matters, and how they were handled.

6. Publications of the NBER issued for informational purposes concerning the work of the Bureau, or issued to inform the public of the activities at the Bureau, including but not limited to the NBER Digest and Reporter, shall be consistent with the object stated in paragraph 1. They shall contain a specific disclaimer noting that they have not passed through the review procedures required in this resolution. The Executive Committee of the Board is charged with the review of all such publications from time to time.

7. NBER working papers and manuscripts distributed on the Bureau's web site are not deemed to be publications for the purpose of this resolution, but they shall be consistent with the object stated in paragraph 1. Working papers shall contain a specific disclaimer noting that they have not passed through the review procedures required in this resolution. The NBER's web site shall contain a similar disclaimer. The President shall establish an internal review process to ensure that the working papers and the web site do not contain policy recommendations, and shall report annually to the Board on this process and any concerns raised in connection with it.

8. Unless otherwise determined by the Board or exempted by the terms of paragraphs 6 and 7, a copy of this resolution shall be printed in each NBER publication as described in paragraph 2 above.

Contents

Acknowledgments

This volume contains chapters and ideas discussed at the first NBER Conference on the Economics of Artificial Intelligence, held in September 2017 in Toronto. We thank all the authors and discussants for their contributions. Funds for the conference and book project were provided by the Sloan Foundation, the Canadian Institute for Advanced Research, and the Creative Destruction Lab at the University of Toronto. At the Sloan Foundation, Danny Goroff provided guidance that improved the overall agenda. The NBER digitization initiative, under the leadership of Shane Greenstein, was a key early supporter. We thank our dean, Tiff Macklem. In addition, Jim Poterba at the NBER has been generous, giving us the flexibility needed to bring this project together. Special thanks are due to Rob Shannon, Denis Healy, Carl Beck, and Dawn Bloomfield for managing the conference and logistics and to Helena Fitz-Patrick for guiding the book through the editorial process. Finally we thank our families, Gina, Natalie, Rachel, Amelia, Andreas, Belanna, Ariel, Annika, Anna, Sam, and Ben.

Introduction

Ajay Agrawal, Joshua Gans, and Avi Goldfarb

Artificial intelligence (AI) technologies have advanced rapidly over the last several years. As the technology continues to improve, it may have a substantial impact on the economy with respect to productivity, growth, inequality, market power, innovation, and employment. In 2016, the White House put out several reports emphasizing this potential impact. Despite its importance, there is little economics research on the topic. The research that exists is derived from past technologies (such as factory robots) that capture only part of the economic reach of AI. Without a better understanding of how AI might impact the economy, we cannot design policy to prepare for these changes.

To address these challenges, the National Bureau of Economic Research held its first conference on the Economics of Artificial Intelligence in September 2017 in Toronto, with support from the NBER Economics Digitization Initiative, the Sloan Foundation, the Canadian Institute for Advanced Research, and the University of Toronto's Creative Destruction Lab. The purpose of the conference was to set the research agenda for economists working on AI. The invitation emphasized these points as follows:

Ajay Agrawal is the Peter Munk Professor of Entrepreneurship at the Rotman School of Management, University of Toronto, and a research associate of the National Bureau of Economic Research. Joshua Gans is professor of strategic management and holder of the Jeffrey S. Skoll Chair of Technical Innovation and Entrepreneurship at the Rotman School of Management, University of Toronto (with a cross appointment in the Department of Economics), and a research associate of the National Bureau of Economic Research. Avi Goldfarb holds the Rotman Chair in Artificial Intelligence and Healthcare and is professor of marketing at the Rotman School of Management, University of Toronto, and a research associate of the National Bureau of Economic Research.

For acknowledgments, sources of research support, and disclosure of the authors' material financial relationships, if any, please see http://www.nber.org/chapters/c14005.ack.

The context is this: imagine back to 1995 when the internet was about to begin transforming industries. What would have happened to economic research into that revolution had the leading economists gathered to scope out a research agenda at that time? Today, we are facing the same opportunity with regard to AI. This time around we are convening a group of 30 leading economists to scope out the research agenda for the next 20 years into the economics of AI.

Scholars who accepted the invitation were asked to write up and present ideas around a specific topic related to their expertise. For each paper, a discussant was assigned. Throughout the conference, in presentations, discussions, and debates, participants weighed in with their ideas for what the key questions will be, what research has already shown, and where the challenges will lie. Pioneering AI researchers Geoffrey Hinton, Yann LeCun, and Russ Salakhutdinov attended, providing useful context and detail about the current and expected future capabilities of the technology. The conference was unique because it emphasized the work that still needs to be done, rather than the presentation of standard research papers. Participants had the freedom to engage in informed speculation and healthy debate about the most important areas of inquiry.

This volume contains a summary of the proceedings of the conference. We provided authors with few constraints. This meant diversity in topics and chapter style. Many of the chapters contained herein are updated versions of the original papers and presentations at the conference. Some discussants commented directly on the chapters while others went further afield, emphasizing concepts that did not make it into the formal presentations but instead arose as part of debate and discussion. The volume also contains a small number of chapters that were not presented at the conference, but nevertheless represent ideas that came up in the general discussion and that warranted inclusion in a volume describing the proceedings of the conference.

We categorize the chapters into four broad themes. First, several chapters emphasize the role of AI as a general purpose technology (GPT), building on the existing literature on general purpose technologies from the steam engine to the internet. Second, many chapters highlight the impact of AI on growth, jobs, and inequality, focusing on research and tools from macro and labor economics. Third, five chapters discuss machine learning and economic regulation, with an emphasis on microeconomic consequences and industrial organization. The final set of chapters explores how AI will affect research in economics.

Of course, these themes are not mutually exclusive. Discussion of AI as a GPT naturally leads to discussions of economic growth. Regulation can enhance or reduce inequality. And AI's impact on economics is a consequence of it being a general purpose technology for scientific discovery (as emphasized in chapter 4 by Cockburn, Henderson, and Stern). Furthermore, a handful of concepts cut across the various parts, most notably the role of humans as AI improves and the interaction between technological advance and political economy.

Below, we summarize these four broad themes in detail. Before doing so, we provide a definition of the technology that brings together the various themes.

What Is Artificial Intelligence?

The Oxford English Dictionary defines artificial intelligence as "the theory and development of computer systems able to perform tasks normally requiring human intelligence." This definition is both broad and fluid. There is an old joke among computer scientists that artificial intelligence defines what machines cannot yet do. Before a machine could beat a human expert at chess, such a win would mean artificial intelligence. After the famed match between IBM's Deep Blue and Gary Kasparov, playing chess was called computer science and other challenges became artificial intelligence.

The chapters in this volume discuss three related, but distinct, concepts of artificial intelligence. First, there is the technology that has driven the recent excitement around artificial intelligence: machine learning. Machine learning is a branch of computational statistics. It is a tool of prediction in the statistical sense, taking information you have and using it to fill in information you do not have. Since 2012, the uses of machine learning as a prediction technology have grown substantially. One set of machine-learning algorithms, in particular, called "deep learning," has been shown to be useful and commercially viable for a variety of prediction tasks from search engine design to image recognition to language translation. The chapter in the book authored by us—Agrawal, Gans, and Goldfarb—emphasizes that rapid improvements in prediction technology can have a profound impact on organizations and policy (chapter 3). The chapter by Taddy (chapter 2) defines prediction with machine learning as one component of a true artificial intelligence and provides detail on the various machine-learning technologies.

While the recent interest in AI is driven by machine learning, computer scientists and philosophers have emphasized the feasibility of a true artificial general intelligence that equals or exceeds human intelligence (Bostrom 2014; Kaplan 2016). The closing sentence of this volume summarizes this possibility bluntly. Daniel Kahneman writes, "I do not think that there is very much that we can do that computers will not eventually be programmed to do." The economic and societal impact of machines that surpass human intelligence would be extraordinary. Therefore—whether such an event occurs imminently, in a few decades, in a millennium, or never—it is worth exploring the economic consequences of such an event. While not a focal aspect of any chapter, several of the chapters in this volume touch on the economic consequences of such superintelligent machines.

A third type of technology that is often labeled "artificial intelligence" is better seen as a process: automation. Much of the existing empirical work on the impact of artificial intelligence uses data on factory automation through robotics. Daron Acemoglu and Pascual Restrepo use data on factory robots to explore the impact of AI and automation on work (chapter 8). Automation is a potential consequence of artificial intelligence, rather than artificial intelligence per se. Nevertheless, discussions of the consequences of artificial intelligence and automation are tightly connected.

While most chapters in the book focus on the first definition—artificial intelligence as machine learning—a prediction technology, the economic implications of artificial general intelligence and automation receive serious attention.

AI as a GPT

A GPT is characterized by pervasive use in a wide range of sectors combined with technological dynamism (Bresnahan and Trajtenberg 1995). General purpose technologies are enabling technologies that open up new opportunities. While electric motors did reduce energy costs, the productivity impact was largely driven by increased flexibility in the design and location of factories (David 1990). Much of the interest in artificial intelligence and its impact on the economy stems from its potential as a GPT. Human intelligence is a general purpose tool. Artificial intelligence, whether defined as prediction technology, general intelligence, or automation, similarly has potential to apply across a broad range of sectors.

Brynjolfsson, Rock, and Syverson (chapter 1) argue the case for AI as a GPT. They focus on machine learning and identify a variety of sectors in which machine learning is likely to have a broad impact. They note expected continual technological progress in machine learning and a number of complementary innovations that have appeared along with machine learning. By establishing AI as a GPT, they can turn to the general lessons of the productivity literature on GPTs with respect to initially low rates of productivity growth, organizational challenges, and adjustment costs. They propose four potential explanations for the surprisingly low measured productivity growth given rapid innovation in AI and related technologies—false hopes, mismeasurement, redistribution, and implementation lags—and conclude that lags due to missing complementary innovations are most likely the primary source of missing productivity growth: "an underrated area of research involves the complements to the new AI technologies, not only in areas of human capital and skills, but also new processes and business models. The intangible assets associated with the last wave of computerization were about ten times as large as the direct investments in computer hardware itself."

Henderson's comment emphasizes the impact of a GPT on employment and the distribution of income, directly linking the discussion of AI as a

GPT to questions addressed in the section on Growth, Jobs, and Inequality. She agrees with the central thesis "One of the reasons I like the paper so much is that it takes seriously an idea that economists long resisted— namely, that things as nebulous as 'culture' and 'organizational capabilities' might be (a) very important, (b) expensive, and (c) hard to change." At the same time, she adds emphasis on additional implications: "I think that the authors may be underestimating the implications of this dynamic in important ways. . . . I'm worried about the transition problem at the societal level quite as much as I'm worried about it at the organizational level."

The next chapters provide micro-level detail on the nature of AI as a technology. Taddy (chapter 2) provides a broad overview of the meaning of intelligence in computer science. He then provides some technical detail on two key machine-learning techniques, deep learning and reinforcement learning. He explains the technology in a manner intuitive to economists: "Machine learning is a field that thinks about how to automatically build robust predictions from complex data. It is closely related to modern statistics, and indeed many of the best ideas in ML have come from statisticians (the lasso, trees, forests, etc.). But whereas statisticians have often focused on *model inference*—on understanding the parameters of their models (e.g., testing on individual coefficients in a regression)—the ML community has been more focused on the single goal of maximizing predictive performance. The entire field of ML is calibrated against 'out-of-sample' experiments that evaluate how well a model trained on one data set will predict new data."

Building on ideas in Agrawal, Gans, and Goldfarb (2018), we argue in chapter 3 that the current excitement around AI is driven by advances in prediction technology. We then show that modeling AI as a drop in the cost of prediction provides useful insight into the microeconomic impact of AI on organizations. We emphasize that AI is likely to substitute for human prediction, but complement other skills such as human judgment—defined as knowing the utility or valuation function: "a key departure from the usual assumptions of rational decision-making is that the decision-maker does not know the payoff from the risky action in each state and must apply *judgment* to determine the payoff. . . . Judgment does not come for free."

Prat's comment emphasizes that economists typically assume that the valuation function is given, and that loosening that assumption will lead to a deeper understanding of the impact of AI on organizations. He offers an example to illustrate: "Admissions offices of many universities are turning to AI to choose which applicants to make offers to. Algorithms can be trained on past admissions data. We observe the characteristics of applicants and the grades of past and present students. . . . The obvious problem is that we do not know how admitting someone who is likely to get high grades is going to affect the long-term payoff of our university. . . . Progress in AI should induce our university leaders to ask deeper questions about the relationship between student quality and the long-term goals of our higher-learning institutions. These questions cannot be answered with AI, but rather with more theory-driven retrospective approaches or perhaps more qualitative methodologies."

The next chapters explore AI as a GPT that will enhance science and innovation. After reviewing the history of artificial intelligence, Cockburn, Henderson, and Stern (chapter 4) provide empirical support for the widespread application of machine learning in general, and deep learning in particular, in scientific fields outside of computer science: "we develop what we believe is the first systematic database that captures the corpus of scientific paper and patenting activity in artificial intelligence . . . we find striking evidence for a rapid and meaningful shift in the application orientation of learning-oriented publications, particularly after 2009." The authors make a compelling case for AI as a general purpose tool in the method of invention. The chapter concludes by discussing the implications for innovation policy and innovation management: "the potential commercial reward from mastering this mode of research is likely to usher in a period of racing, driven by powerful incentives for individual companies to acquire and control critical large data sets and application-specific algorithms."

Mitchell's comment emphasizes the regulatory effects of AI as a GPT for science and innovation—in terms of intellectual property, privacy, and competition policy: "It is not obvious whether AI is a general purpose technology for innovation or a very efficient method of imitation. The answer has a direct relevance for policy. A technology that made innovation cheaper would often (but not always) imply less need for strong IP protection, since the balance would swing toward limiting monopoly power and away from compensating innovation costs. To the extent that a technology reduces the cost of imitation, however, it typically necessitates greater protection." Several later chapters detail these and other regulatory issues.

Agrawal, McHale, and Oettl (chapter 5) provide a recombinant growth model that explores how a general purpose technology for innovation could affect the rate of scientific discovery: "instead of emphasising the potential substitution of machines for workers in existing tasks, we emphasise the importance of AI in overcoming a specific problem that impedes human researchers—finding useful combinations in complex discovery spaces . . . we develop a relatively simple combinatorial-based knowledge production function that converges in the limit to the Romer/Jones function. . . . If the curse of dimensionality is both the blessing and curse of discovery, then advances in AI offer renewed hope of breaking the curse while helping to deliver on the blessing." This idea of AI as an input into innovation is a key component of Cockburn, Henderson, and Stern (chapter 4), as well as in several later chapters. It is an important element of Aghion, Jones, and Jones's model of the impact of AI on economic growth (chapter 9), emphasizing endogenous growth through AI (self-)improvements. It also underlies the chapters focused on how AI will impact the way economics research is conducted (chapters 21 through 24).

The section on AI as a general purpose technology concludes with Manuel Trajtenberg's discussion of political and societal consequences (chapter 6). At the conference, Trajtenberg discussed Joel Mokyr's paper "The Past and Future of Innovation: Some Lessons from Economic History," which will be published elsewhere. The chapter therefore sits between a stand-alone chapter and a discussion. Trajtenberg's chapter does not comment directly on Mokyr, but uses Mokyr's paper as a jumping-off point to discuss how technology creates winners and losers, and the policy challenges associated with the political consequences of the diffusion of a GPT. "The sharp split between winners and losers, if left to its own, may have serious consequences far beyond the costs for the individuals involved: when it coincides with the political divide, it may threaten the very fabric of democracy, as we have seen recently both in America and in Europe. Thus, if AI bursts onto the scene and triggers mass displacement of workers, and demography plays out its fateful hand, the economy will be faced with a formidable dual challenge, that may require a serious reassessment of policy options . . . we need to anticipate the required institutional changes, to experiment in the design of new policies, particularly in education and skills development, in the professionalization of service occupations, and in affecting the direction of technical advance. Furthermore, economists possess a vast methodological arsenal that may prove very useful for that purpose—we should not shy away from stepping into this area, since its importance for the economy cannot be overstated." The next set of chapters also emphasize the distributional challenges of economic growth driven by rapid technological change.

Growth, Jobs, and Inequality

Much of the popular discussion around AI focuses on the impact on jobs. If machines can do what humans do, then will there still be work for humans in the future? The chapters in this section dig into the consequences of AI for jobs, economic growth, and inequality. Almost all chapters emphasize that technological change means an increase in wealth for society. As Jason Furman puts it in chapter 12, "We need more artificial intelligence." At the same time, it is clear that the impact of AI on society will depend on how the increased income from AI is distributed. The most recent GPTs to diffuse, computers and the internet, likely led to increased inequality due to skill-bias (e.g., Autor, Katz, and Krueger 1998; Akerman, Gaarder, and Mogstad 2015) and to an increased capital share (e.g., Autor et al. 2017). This section brings together those chapters that emphasize (largely macroeconomic) ideas related to growth, inequality, and jobs. If the impact of AI will be like these other technologies, then what will the consequences look like for inequality, political economy, economic growth, jobs, and the meaning of work?

Stevenson (chapter 7) outlines many of the key issues. She emphasizes that economists generally agree that in the long run society will be wealthier. She highlights issues with respect to the short run and income distribution. Summarizing both the tension in the public debate and the key themes in several other chapters, she notes, "In the end, there's really two separate questions: there's an employment question, in which the fundamental question is can we find fulfilling ways to spend our time if robots take our jobs? And there's an income question, can we find a stable and fair distribution of income?"

Acemoglu and Restrepo (chapter 8) examine how AI and automation might change the nature of work. They suggest a task-based approach to understanding automation, emphasizing the relative roles of labor and capital in the economy. "At the heart of our framework is the idea that automation and thus AI and robotics replace workers in tasks that they previously performed, and via this channel, create a powerful *displacement effect*." This will lead to a lower labor share of economic output. At the same time, productivity will increase and capital will accumulate, thereby increasing the demand for labor. More importantly, "we argue that there is a more powerful countervailing force that increases the demand for labor as well as the share of labor in the national income: the *creation of new tasks*, functions, and activities in which labor has a comparative advantage relative to machines. The creation of new tasks generates a *reinstatement effect* directly counterbalancing the *displacement effect*." Like Stevenson, the long-run message is optimistic; however, a key point is that adjustment costs may be high. New skills are a necessary condition of the long-run optimistic forecast, and there is likely to be a short- and medium-term mismatch between skills and technologies. They conclude with a discussion of open questions about which skills are needed, the political economy of technological change (reinforcing ideas highlighted in the earlier chapter by Trajtenberg), and the interaction between inequality and the type of innovation enabled by automation going forward.

Aghion, Jones, and Jones (chapter 9) build on the task-based model, focusing on the impact on economic growth. They emphasize Baumol's cost disease: "Baumol (1967) observed that sectors with rapid productivity growth, such as agriculture and even manufacturing today, often see their share of GDP decline while those sectors with relatively slow productivity growth—perhaps including many services—experience increases. As a consequence, economic growth may be constrained not by what we do well, but rather by what is essential and yet hard to improve. We suggest that combining this feature of growth with automation can yield a rich description of the growth process, including consequences for future growth and income distribution." Thus, even in the limit where there is an artificial general intelligence that creates a singularity or intelligence explosion with a self-improving AI, cost disease forces may constrain growth. This link between technological advance and Baumol's cost disease provides a fundamental limit to the most optimistic and the most pessimistic views. Scarcity limits both growth and the downside risk. The chapter also explores how AI might reduce economic growth if it makes it easier to imitate a rival's innovations, returning to issues of intellectual property highlighted in Mitchell's comment. Finally, they discuss inequality within and across firms. They note that AI will increase wages of the least skilled employees of technologically advanced firms, but also increasingly outsource the tasks undertaken by such employees.

Francois's comment takes this emphasis on cost disease as a starting point, asking what those tasks will be that humans are left to do. "But it is when we turn to thinking about what are the products or services where humans will remain essential in production that we start to run into problems. What if humans can't do anything better than machines? Many discussions at the conference centered around this very possibility. And I must admit that I found the scientists' views compelling on this. . . . The point I wish to make is that even in such a world where machines are better at all tasks, there will still be an important role for human 'work.' And that work will become the almost political task of managing the machines." He argues that humans must tell the machines what to optimize. Bostrom (2014) describes this as the value-loading problem. Francois emphasizes that this is largely a political problem, and links the challenges in identifying values with Arrow's ([1951] 1963) impossibility theorem. He identifies key questions around ownership of the machines, length of time that rents should accrue to those owners, and the political structure of decision-making. In raising these questions, he provides a different perspective on issues highlighted by Stevenson on the meaning of work and Trajtenberg on the political economy of technological change.

The discussion of the meaning of work is a direct consequence of concerns about the impact of AI on jobs. Jobs have been the key focus of public discussion on AI and the economy. If human tasks get automated, what is left for humans to do? Bessen (chapter 10) explores this question, using data about other technological advances to support his arguments. He emphasizes that technological change can lead to an increase in demand and so the impact of automation on jobs is ambiguous, even within a sector. "The reason automation in textiles, steel, and automotive manufacturing led to strong job growth has to do with the effect of technology on demand. . . . New technologies do not just replace labor with machines, but in a competitive market, automation will reduce prices. In addition, technology may improve product quality, customization, or speed of delivery. All of these things can increase demand. If demand increases sufficiently, employment will grow even though the labor required per unit of output declines."

Like Bessen, Goolsbee (chapter 11) notes that much of the popular discussion around AI relates to labor market consequences. Recognizing that those consequences matter, his chapter mostly emphasizes the positive: growth and productivity are good. Artificial Intelligence has potential to increase our standard of living. Like Acemoglu and Restrepo, he notes that the short-term displacement effects could be substantial. One frequently cited solution to the displacement effects of AI is a universal basic income, in which all members of society receive a cash transfer from the government. He then discusses the economics of such a policy and the numerous challenges to making it work. "First . . . in a world where AI-induced unemployment is already high, separating work and income is an advantage. In a world like the one we are in now, offering a basic income will likely cause a sizable drop in the labor market participation by low-wage groups. . . . Second, for a given amount of money to be used on redistribution, UBI likely shifts money away from the very poor. . . . Third, . . . converting things to a UBI and getting rid of the in-kind safety net will lead to a situation in which, even if among a small share of UBI recipients, SOME people will blow their money in unsympathetic ways—gambling, drugs, junk food, Ponzi schemes, whatever. And now those people will come to the emergency room or their kids will be hungry and by the rules, they will be out of luck. That's what they were supposed to have used their UBI for." Before concluding, he touches on a variety of regulatory issues that receive more detailed discussion in chapters 16 through 20. His conclusion mirrors that of Francois, emphasizing the importance of humans in determining policy direction, even if AI improves to the point where it surpasses human intelligence.

Furman (chapter 12) is similarly optimistic, emphasizing that we need more, not less AI. "AI is a critical area of innovation in the U.S. economy right now. At least to date, AI has not had a large impact on the aggregate performance of the macroeconomy or the labor market. But it will likely become more important in the years to come, bringing substantial opportunities – and our first impulse should be to embrace it fully." Referencing data on productivity growth and on the diffusion of industrial robots, he then discusses potential negative effects on the economy as AI diffuses, particularly with respect to inequality and reduced labor force participation. The issues around labor force participation highlight the importance of Stevenson's questions on the meaning of work. Like Goolsbee, Furman notes several challenges to implementing a universal basic income as a solution to these negative effects. He concludes that policy has an important role to play in enabling society to fully reap the benefits of technological change while minimizing the disruptive effects.

Returning to the question of labor share highlighted by Acemoglu and Restrepo, Sachs (chapter 13) emphasizes that the income share going to capital grows with automation: "Rather than Solow-era stylized facts, I would therefore propose the following alternative stylized facts: (a) the share of national income accruing to capital rises over time in sectors experiencing automation, especially when capital is measured to include human capital; (b) the share of national income accruing to low-skill labor drops while the share accruing to high-skill labor rises; (c) the dynamics across sectors vary according to the differential timing of automation, with automation spreading from low-skilled and predictable tasks toward high-skilled and less predictable tasks; (d) automation reflects the rising intensity of science and technology throughout the economy . . ., and (e) future technological changes associated with AI are likely to shift national income from medium-skilled and high-skilled toward owners of business capital." The chapter concludes with a list of key open questions about the dynamics of automation, the role of monopoly rents, and the consequences for income distribution and labor force participation.

Korinek and Stiglitz (chapter 14) also emphasize income distribution, discussing the implications of AI-related innovation for inequality. They show that, in a first-best economy, contracts can be specified in advance that make innovation Pareto improving. However, imperfect markets and costly redistribution can imply a move away from the first-best. Innovation may then drive inequality directly by giving innovators a surplus, or indirectly by changing the demand for different types of labor and capital. They discuss policies that could help reduce the increase in inequality, emphasizing different taxation tools. Related to the ideas introduced in Mitchell's comment, they also explore IP policies: "If outright redistribution is infeasible, there may be other institutional changes that result in market distributions that are more favorable to workers. For example, intervention to steer technological progress may act as a second-best device . . . we provide an example in which a change in intellectual property rights—a shortening of the term of patent protection—effectively redistributes some of the innovators' surplus to workers (consumers) to mitigate the pecuniary externalities on wages that they experience, with the ultimate goal that the benefits of the innovation are more widely shared." Stiglitz and Korinek conclude with a more speculative discussion of artificial general intelligence (superhuman artificial intelligence), emphasizing that such a technological development will likely further increase inequality.

The final chapter in the section on growth, jobs, and inequality calls for a different emphasis. Cowen (chapter 15) emphasizes consumer surplus, international effects, and political economy. With respect to consumer surplus, he writes, "Imagine education and manufactured goods being much cheaper because we produced them using a greater dose of smart software. The upshot is that even if a robot puts you out of a job or lowers your pay, there will be some recompense on the consumer side." Cowen also speculates that AI might hurt developing countries much more than developed, as automation means that labor cost reasons to offshore decline. Finally, like Trajtenberg and Francois, he emphasizes the political economy of AI, highlighting questions related to income distribution.

Taken together, the chapters in this section highlight several key issues and provide models that identify challenges related to growth, jobs, inequality, and politics. These models set up a number of theoretical and empirical questions about how AI will impact economic outcomes within and across countries.

The discussions are necessarily speculative because AI has not yet diffused widely, so research must either be entirely theoretical or it must use related technologies (such as factory robots) as a proxy for AI. The discussions are also speculative because of the challenges in measuring the relevant variables. In order to determine the impact of AI on the economy, we need consistent measures of AI, productivity, intangible capital, and growth across sectors, regions, and contexts. Going forward, to the extent that progress occurs against the proposed research agenda, it will depend on advances in measurement.

Machine Learning and Regulation

Industry will be a key innovator and adopter of artificial intelligence. A number of regulatory issues arise. The regulatory issues related to truly intelligent machines are touched on by Trajtenberg, Francois, Goolsbee, and Cowen. Mitchell's comment of Cockburn, Henderson, and Stern emphasizes intellectual property regulation. This section focuses on other regulatory challenges with respect to advances in machine learning.

Varian (chapter 16) sets up the issues by describing the key models from industrial organization that are relevant to understanding the impact of machine learning on firms. He highlights the importance of data as a scarce resource, and discusses the economics of data as an input: it is nonrival and it exhibits decreasing returns to scale in a technical sense (because prediction accuracy increases in the square root of N). He discusses the structure of ML-using industries including vertical integration, economies of scale, and the potential for price discrimination. He emphasizes the difference between learning by doing and data network effects: "There is a concept that is circulating among lawyers and regulators called 'data network effects.' The model is that a firm with more customers can collect more data and use this data to improve its product. This is often true—the prospect of improving operations is what makes ML attractive—but it is hardly novel. And it is certainly not a network effect! This is essentially a supply-side effect known as 'learning by doing.'. . . A company can have huge amounts of data, but if it does nothing with the data, it produces no value. In my experience, the problem is not lack of resources, but is lack of skills. A company that has data but no one to analyze it is in a poor position to take advantage of that data." He concludes by highlighting policy questions related to algorithmic collusion (which was discussed at the conference as "economist catnip," interesting and fun but unlikely to be of first-order importance), security, privacy, and transparency.

Chevalier's comment builds on Varian's emphasis on the importance of data, exploring the potential of antitrust policy aimed at companies that use machine learning. Legal scholars and policymakers have asked whether antitrust essential facilities doctrine should be applied to data ownership. She emphasizes the trade-off between static and dynamic considerations for such a policy: "In evaluating antitrust policies in innovative industries, it is important to recognize that consumer benefits from new technologies arise not just from obtaining goods and services at competitive prices, but also from the flow of new and improved products and services that arise from innovation. Thus, antitrust policy should be evaluated not just in terms of its effect on prices and outputs, but also on its effect on the speed of innovation. Indeed, in the high technology industries, it seems likely that these dynamic efficiency considerations dwarf the static efficiency considerations." She also explores several practical challenges.

Another regulatory issue that arises from the importance of data is privacy. Tucker (chapter 17) notes that machine learning uses data to make predictions about what individuals may desire, be influenced by, or do. She emphasizes that privacy is challenging for three reasons: cheap storage means that data may persist longer than the person who generated the data intended, nonrivalry means that data may be repurposed for uses other than originally intended, and externalities caused by data created by one individual that contains information about others: "For example, in the case of genetics, the decision to create genetic data has immediate consequences for family members, since one individual's genetic data is significantly similar to the genetic data of their family members. . . . There may also be spillovers across a person's decision to keep some information secret, if such secrecy predicts other aspects of that individual's behavior that AI might be able to project from." She discusses potential negative impacts of these three challenges, concluding with some key open questions.

Jin (chapter 18) also focuses on the importance of data as an input into machine learning. She emphasizes that reduced privacy creates security challenges, such as identity theft, ransomware, and misleading algorithms (such as Russian-sponsored posts in the 2016 US election): "In my opinion, the leading concern is that firms are not fully accountable for the risk they bring to consumer privacy and data security. To restore full accountability, one needs to overcome three obstacles, namely (a) the difficulty to observe firms' actual action in data collection, data storage, and data use; (b) the difficulty to quantify the consequence of data practice, especially before low-probability adverse events realize themselves; and (c) the difficulty to draw a causal link between a firm's data practice and its consequence." Combined, Tucker and Jin's chapters emphasize that any discussion of growth and impact of AI requires an understanding of the privacy framework. Access to data drives innovation, underlies the potential for economic growth, and frames the antitrust debate.

The economics of data also create challenges with respect to the rules governing international trade. Goldfarb and Trefler (chapter 19) argue that economies of scale in data through feedback loops, along with economies of scope and knowledge externalities in AI innovation, could create the opportunity for country-level rents and strategic trade policy. At the same time, they emphasize that the geographic constraints on data and knowledge would have to be high for such a policy to be optimal at the country level. They highlight the rise of China: "China has become the focal point for much of the international discussion. The US narrative has it that Chinese protection has reduced the ability of dynamic US firms such as Google and Amazon to penetrate Chinese markets. This protection has allowed China to develop significant commercial AI capabilities, as evidenced by companies such as Baidu (a search engine like Google), Alibaba (an e-commerce web portal like Amazon), and Tencent (the developer of WeChat, which can be seen as combining the functions of Skype, Facebook, and Apple Pay) . . . we collected time-series data on the institutional affiliation of all authors of papers presented at a major AI research conference . . . we compare the 2012 and 2017 conferences. . . . While these countries all increased their absolute number of participants, in relative terms they all lost ground to China, which leapt from 10 percent in 2012 to 23 percent in 2017." The authors discuss the international dimensions of domestic regulation related to privacy, access to government data, and industrial standards.

The final regulatory issue highlighted in this section is tort liability. Galasso and Luo (chapter 20) review prior literature on the relationship between liability and innovation. They emphasize the importance of getting the balance right between consumer protection and innovation incentives: "A central question in designing a liability system for AI technologies is how liability risk should be allocated between producers and consumers, and how this allocation might affect innovation. . . . A key promise of AI technologies is to achieve autonomy. With less room for consumers to take precautions, the relative liability burden is likely to shift toward producers, especially in situations in which producers are in a better position than individual users to control risk. . . . On the other hand, during the transitional period of an AI technology, substantial human supervision may still be required. . . . In many of these situations, it may be impractical or too costly for producers to monitor individual users and to intervene. Therefore, it would be important to maintain consumer liability to the extent that users of AI technologies have sufficient incentives to take precautions and invest in training, thus internalizing potential harm to others."

Broadly, regulation will affect the speed at which AI diffuses. Too much regulation, and industry will not have incentives to invest. Too little regulation, and consumers will not trust the products that result. In this way, getting the regulatory balance right is key to understanding when and how any impact of AI on economic growth and inequality will arise.

Impact on the Practice of Economics

Cockburn, Henderson, and Stern emphasize that machine learning is a general purpose technology for science and innovation. As such, it is likely to have an impact on research in a variety of disciplines, including economics. Athey (chapter 21) provides an overview of the various ways in which machine learning is likely to affect the practice of economics. For example: "I believe that machine learning (ML) will have a dramatic impact on the field of economics within a short time frame. . . . ML does not add much to questions about identification, which concern when the object of interest, for example, a causal effect, can be estimated with infinite data, but rather yields great improvements when the goal is semiparametric estimation or when there are a large number of covariates relative to the number of observations . . . a key advantage of ML is that ML views empirical analysis as "algorithms" that estimate and compare many alternative models . . . 'outsourcing' model selection to algorithms works very well when the problem is 'simple'—for example, prediction and classification tasks, where performance of a model can be evaluated by looking at goodness of fit in a held-out test set." She emphasizes the usefulness of machine-learning techniques for policy problems related to prediction (as in Kleinberg et al. 2015). The chapter then details recent advances in using machine-learning techniques in causal inference, which she views as a fundamental new tool kit for empirical economists. She concludes with a list of sixteen predictions of how machine learning will impact economics, emphasizing new econometric tools, new data sets and measurement techniques, increased engagement of economists as engineers (and plumbers), and, of course, increased study of the economic impact of machine learning on the economy as a whole.

Lederman's comment emphasizes the usefulness of machine learning to create new variables for economic analysis, and how the use of machine learning by organizations creates a new kind of endogeneity problem: "We develop theoretical models to help us understand the data-generation process which, in turn, informs both our concerns about causality as well as the identification strategies we develop. . . . Overall, as applied researchers working with real-world data sets, we need to recognize that increasingly the data we are analyzing is going to be the result of decisions that are made by algorithms in which the decision-making process may or may not resemble the decision-making processes we model as social scientists."

If the study of AI is going to be a key question for economists going forward, Raj and Seamans (chapter 22) emphasize that we need better data: "While there is generally a paucity of data examining the adoption, use, and effects of both AI and robotics, there is currently less information available regarding AI. There are no public data sets on the utilization or adoption of AI at either the macro or micro level. The most complete source of information, the McKinsey Global Institute study, is proprietary and inaccessible to the general public or the academic community. The most comprehensive and widely used data set examining the diffusion of robotics is the International Federation of Robotics (IFR) Robot Shipment Data . . . the IFR does not collect any information on dedicated industrial robots that serve one purpose. Furthermore, some of the robots are not classified by industry, detailed data is only available for industrial robots (and not robots in service, transportation, warehousing, or other sectors), and geographical information is often aggregated" They provide a detailed discussion of data-collection opportunities by government and by academic researchers. If the agenda set up in the other chapters is to be answered, it is important to have a reliable data set that defines AI, measures its quality, and tracks its diffusion.

Related to Athey's emphasis of increased engagement of economists as engineering, Milgrom and Tadelis (chapter 23) describe how machine learning is already affecting market-design decisions. Using specific examples from online marketplaces and telecommunications auctions, they emphasize the potential of AI to improve efficiency by predicting demand and supply, overcoming computational barriers, and reducing search frictions: "AI and machine learning are emerging as important tools for market design. Retailers and marketplaces such as eBay, Taobao, Amazon, Uber, and many others are mining their vast amounts of data to identify patterns that help them create better experiences for their customers and increase the efficiency of their markets . . . two-sided markets such as Google, which match advertisers with consumers, are not only using AI to set reserve prices and segment consumers into finer categories for ad targeting, but they also develop AI-based tools to help advertisers bid on ads. . . . Another important application of AI's strength in improving forecasting to help markets operate more efficiently is in electricity markets. To operate efficiently, electricity market makers . . . must engage in demand and supply forecasting." The authors argue that AI will play a substantial role in the design and implementation of markets over a wide range of applications.

Camerer (chapter 24) also emphasizes the role of AI as a tool for predicting choice: "Behavioral economics can be defined as the study of natural limits on computation, willpower, and self-interest, and the implications of those limits for economic analysis (market equilibrium, IO, public finance, etc.). A different approach is to define behavioral economics more generally, as simply being open-minded about what variables are likely to influence economic choices. . . . In a general ML approach, predictive features could be—and *should* be—any variables that predict. . . . If behavioral economics is recast as open-mindedness about what variables might predict, then ML is an ideal way to do behavioral economics because it can make use of a wide set of variables and select which ones predict." He argues that firms, policymakers, and market designers can implement AI as either a "bionic patch" that improves human decision-making or "malware" that exploits human weaknesses. In this way, AI could reduce or exacerbate the political economy and inequality issues highlighted in earlier chapters. In addition, Camerer explores two other ways in which AI and behavioral economics will interact. He hypothesizes that machine learning could help predict human behavior in a variety of settings including bargaining, risky choice, and games, helping to verify or reject theory. He also emphasizes that (poor) implementation of AI might provide insight into new ways to model biases in human decision-making.

The book concludes with Kahneman's brief and insightful comment. Kahneman begins with a discussion of Camerer's idea of using prediction to verify theory, but continues with a broader discussion of a variety of themes that arose over the course of the conference. With an optimistic tone, he emphasizes that there are no obvious limits to what artificial intelligence may be able to do: "Wisdom is breadth. Wisdom is not having too narrow a view. That is the essence of wisdom; it is broad framing. A robot will be endowed with broad framing. When it has learned enough, it will be wiser than we people because we do not have broad framing. We are narrow thinkers, we are noisy thinkers, and it is very easy to improve upon us. I do not think that there is very much that we can do that computers will not eventually be programmed to do."

The Future of Research on the Economics of Artificial Intelligence

The chapters in this book are the beginning. They highlight key questions, recognize the usefulness of several economic models, and identify areas for further development. We can leverage what we know about GPTs to anticipate the impact of AI as it diffuses, recognizing that no two GPTs are identical. If AI is a general purpose technology, it is likely to lead to increased economic growth. A common theme in these chapters is that slowing down scientific progress—even if it were possible—would come at a significant cost. At the same time, many attendees emphasized that the distribution of the benefits of AI might not be even. It depends on who owns the AI, the effect on jobs, and the speed of diffusion.

The task given to the conference presenters was to scope out the research agenda. Perhaps more than anything, this volume highlights all that we do not know. It emphasizes questions around growth, inequality, privacy, trade, innovation, political economy, and so forth. We do not have answers yet. Of course, the lack of answers is a consequence of the early stage of AI's diffusion. We cannot measure the impact until AI is widespread.

With the current state of measurement, however, we may never get answers. As highlighted in the chapter by Raj and Seamans, we do not have good measures of AI. We also do not have a good measure of improvement to AI. What is the AI equivalent to the computational speed of a microchip or the horsepower of an internal combustion engine that will allow for quality-adjusted prices and measurement? We also do not have good measures of productivity growth when that growth is primarily driven by intangible capital. To answer these questions, the gross domestic product (GDP) measurement apparatus needs to focus on adjusting for intangible capital, software, and changes to the innovation process (Haskel and Westlake 2017). Furthermore, to the extent that the benefits of AI generate heterogeneous benefits to people as consumers and as workers, measurement of the benefit of AI will be tricky. For example, if AI enables more leisure and people choose to take more leisure, should that be accounted for in measures of inequality? If so, how?

While each chapter has its own take on the agenda, several themes cut across the volume as key aspects of the research agenda going forward. To the extent there is consensus on the questions, the consensus focuses on the potential of AI as a GPT, and the associated potential consequences on growth and inequality. A second consistent theme is the role of regulation in accelerating or constraining the diffusion of the technology. A third theme is that AI will change the way we do our work as economists. Finally, a number of issues appear in many chapters that are somewhat outside the standard economic models of technology's impact. How do people find meaning if AI replaces work with leisure? How can economists inform the policy debate on solutions proposed by technologists in the popular press such as taxing robots or a universal basic income? How does a technology's diffusion affect the political environment, and vice versa?

This book highlights the questions and provides direction. We hope readers of this book take it as a starting point for their own research into this new and exciting area of study.

References

Agrawal, Ajay, Joshua Gans, and Avi Goldfarb. 2018. *Prediction Machines: The Simple Economics of Artificial Intelligence.* Boston, MA: Harvard Business Review Press.
Akerman, Anders, Ingvil Gaarder, and Magne Mogstad. 2015. "The Skill Complementarity of Broadband Internet." *Quarterly Journal of Economics* 130 (4): 1781–824.
Arrow, Kenneth. (1951) 1963. *Social Choice and Individual Values,* 2nd ed. New York: John Wiley and Sons.
Autor, David, David Dorn, Lawrence F. Katz, Christina Patterson, and John Van Reenen. 2017. "The Fall of the Labor Share and the Rise of Superstar Firms." Working paper, Massachusetts Institute of Technology.
Autor, David H., Lawrence F. Katz, and Alan B. Krueger. 1998. "Computing

Inequality: Have Computers Changed the Labor Market?" *Quarterly Journal of Economics* 113 (4): 1169–213.

Bostrom, Nick. 2014. *Superintelligence: Paths, Dangers, Strategies*. Oxford: Oxford University Press.

Bresnahan, Timothy F., and M. Trajtenberg. 1995. "General Purpose Technologies 'Engines of Growth'?" *Journal of Econometrics* 65:83–108.

David, Paul A. 1990. "The Dynamo and the Computer: An Historical Perspective on the Modern Productivity Paradox." *American Economic Review Papers and Proceedings* 80 (2): 355–61.

Haskel, Jonathan, and Stian Westlake. 2017. *Capitalism without Capital: The Rise of the Intangible Economy*. Princeton, NJ: Princeton University Press.

Kaplan, Jerry. 2016. *Artificial Intelligence: What Everyone Needs to Know*. Oxford: Oxford University Press.

Kleinberg, Jon, Jens Ludwig, Sendhil Mullainathan, and Ziad Obermeyer. 2015. "Prediction Policy Problems." *American Economic Review* 105 (5): 491–95.

I

AI as a GPT

1

Artificial Intelligence and the Modern Productivity Paradox
A Clash of Expectations and Statistics

Erik Brynjolfsson, Daniel Rock, and Chad Syverson

The discussion around the recent patterns in aggregate productivity growth highlights a seeming contradiction. On the one hand, there are astonishing examples of potentially transformative new technologies that could greatly increase productivity and economic welfare (see Brynjolfsson and McAfee 2014). There are some early concrete signs of these technologies' promise, recent leaps in artificial intelligence (AI) performance being the most prominent example. However, at the same time, measured productivity growth over the past decade has slowed significantly. This deceleration is large, cutting productivity growth by half or more in the decade preceding the slowdown. It is also widespread, having occurred throughout the Organisation for Economic Co-operation and Development (OECD) and, more recently, among many large emerging economies as well (Syverson 2017).[1]

Erik Brynjolfsson is director of the MIT Initiative on the Digital Economy, the Schussel Family Professor of Management Science and professor of information technology at the MIT Sloan School of Management, and a research associate of the National Bureau of Economic Research. Daniel Rock is a PhD candidate at the MIT Sloan School of Management and a researcher at the MIT Initiative on the Digital Economy. Chad Syverson is the Eli B. and Harriet B. Williams Professor of Economics at the University of Chicago Booth School of Business and a research associate of the National Bureau of Economic Research.

We thank Eliot Abrams, Ajay Agrawal, David Autor, Seth Benzell, Joshua Gans, Avi Goldfarb, Austan Goolsbee, Andrea Meyer, Guillaume Saint-Jacques, Manuel Tratjenberg, and numerous participants at the NBER Workshop on AI and Economics in September 2017. In particular, Rebecca Henderson provided detailed and very helpful comments on an earlier draft and Larry Summers suggested the analogy to the J-curve. Generous funding for this research was provided in part by the MIT Initiative on the Digital Economy. This is a minor revision of NBER Working Paper no. 24001. For acknowledgments, sources of research support, and disclosure of the authors' material financial relationships, if any, please see http://www.nber.org/chapters/c14007.ack.

1. A parallel, yet more pessimistically oriented debate about potential technological progress is the active discussion about robots taking jobs from more and more workers (e.g., Brynjolfsson and McAfee 2011; Acemoglu and Restrepo 2017; Bessen 2017; Autor and Salomons 2017).

We thus appear to be facing a redux of the Solow (1987) paradox: we see transformative new technologies everywhere but in the productivity statistics.

In this chapter, we review the evidence and explanations for the modern productivity paradox and propose a resolution. Namely, there is no inherent inconsistency between forward-looking technological optimism and backward-looking disappointment. Both can simultaneously exist. Indeed, there are good conceptual reasons to *expect* them to simultaneously exist when the economy undergoes the kind of restructuring associated with transformative technologies. In essence, the forecasters of future company wealth and the measurers of historical economic performance show the greatest disagreement during times of technological change. In this chapter, we argue and present some evidence that the economy is in such a period now.

1.1 Sources of Technological Optimism

Paul Polman, Unilever's CEO, recently claimed that "The speed of innovation has never been faster." Similarly, Bill Gates, Microsoft's cofounder, observes that "Innovation is moving at a scarily fast pace." Vinod Khosla of Khosla Ventures sees "the beginnings of . . . [a] rapid acceleration in the next 10, 15, 20 years." Eric Schmidt of Alphabet Inc., believes "we're entering . . . the age of abundance [and] during the age of abundance, we're going to see a new age . . . the age of intelligence."[2] Assertions like these are especially common among technology leaders and venture capitalists.

In part, these assertions reflect the continuing progress of information technology (IT) in many areas, from core technology advances like further doublings of basic computer power (but from ever larger bases) to successful investment in the essential complementary innovations like cloud infrastructure and new service-based business models. But the bigger source of optimism is the wave of recent improvements in AI, especially machine learning (ML). Machine learning represents a fundamental change from the first wave of computerization. Historically, most computer programs were created by meticulously codifying human knowledge, mapping inputs to outputs as prescribed by the programmers. In contrast, machine-learning systems use categories of general algorithms (e.g., neural networks) to figure out relevant mappings on their own, typically by being fed very large sample data sets. By using these machine-learning methods that leverage the growth in total data and data-processing resources, machines have made impressive gains in perception and cognition, two essential skills for most

---

2. http://www.khoslaventures.com/fireside-chat-with-google-co-founders-larry-page-and -sergey-brin; https://en.wikipedia.org/wiki/Predictions_made_by_Ray_Kurzweil#2045:_The _Singularity; https://www.theguardian.com/small-business-network/2017/jun/22/alphabets -eric-schmidt-google-artificial-intelligence-viva-technology-mckinsey.

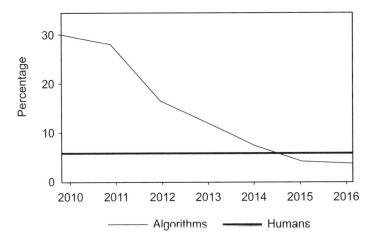

Fig. 1.1   AI versus human image recognition error rates

types of human work. For instance, error rates in labeling the content of photos on ImageNet, a data set of over ten million images, have fallen from over 30 percent in 2010 to less than 5 percent in 2016, and most recently as low as 2.2 percent with SE-ResNet152 in the ILSVRC2017 competition (see figure 1.1).[3] Error rates in voice recognition on the Switchboard speech recording corpus, often used to measure progress in speech recognition, have decreased to 5.5 percent from 8.5 percent over the past year (Saon et al. 2017). The 5 percent threshold is important because that is roughly the performance of humans on each of these tasks on the same test data.

Although not at the level of professional human performance yet, Facebook's AI research team recently improved upon the best machine language translation algorithms available using convolutional neural net sequence prediction techniques (Gehring et al. 2017). Deep learning techniques have also been combined with reinforcement learning, a powerful set of techniques used to generate control and action systems whereby autonomous agents are trained to take actions given an environment state to maximize future rewards. Though nascent, advances in this field are impressive. In addition to its victories in the game of Go, Google DeepMind has achieved superhuman performance in many Atari games (Fortunato et al. 2017).

These are notable technological milestones. But they can also change the economic landscape, creating new opportunities for business value creation and cost reduction. For example, a system using deep neural networks was tested against twenty-one board-certified dermatologists and matched their

---

3. http://image-net.org/challenges/LSVRC/2017/results. ImageNet includes labels for each image, originally provided by humans. For instance, there are 339,000 labeled as flowers, 1,001,000 as food, 188,000 as fruit, 137,000 as fungus, and so on.

performance in diagnosing skin cancer (Esteva et al. 2017). Facebook uses neural networks for over 4.5 billion translations each day.[4]

An increasing number of companies have responded to these opportunities. Google now describes its focus as "AI first," while Microsoft's CEO Satya Nadella says AI is the "ultimate breakthrough" in technology. Their optimism about AI is not just cheap talk. They are making heavy investments in AI, as are Apple, Facebook, and Amazon. As of September 2017, these companies comprise the five most valuable companies in the world. Meanwhile, the tech-heavy NASDAQ composite index more than doubled between 2012 and 2017. According to CBInsights, global investment in private companies focused on AI has grown even faster, increasing from $589 million in 2012 to over $5 billion in 2016.[5]

1.2   The Disappointing Recent Reality

Although the technologies discussed above hold great potential, there is little sign that they have yet affected aggregate productivity statistics. Labor productivity growth rates in a broad swath of developed economies fell in the middle of the first decade of the twenty-first century and have stayed low since then. For example, aggregate labor productivity growth in the United States averaged only 1.3 percent per year from 2005 to 2016, less than half of the 2.8 percent annual growth rate sustained from 1995 to 2004. Fully twenty-eight of the twenty-nine other countries for which the OECD has compiled productivity growth data saw similar decelerations. The unweighted average annual labor productivity growth rate across these countries was 2.3 percent from 1995 to 2004, but only 1.1 percent from 2005 to 2015.[6] What's more, real median income has stagnated since the late 1990s and noneconomic measures of well-being, like life expectancy, have fallen for some groups (Case and Deaton 2017).

Figure 1.2 replicates the Conference Board's analysis of its country-level Total Economy Database (Conference Board 2016). It plots highly smoothed annual productivity growth rate series for the United States, other mature economies (which combined match much of the OECD sample cited above), emerging and developing economies, and the world overall. The aforementioned slowdowns in the United States and other mature economies are clear in the figure. The figure also reveals that the productivity growth acceleration in emerging and developing economies during the first decade of the twenty-

4. https://code.facebook.com/posts/289921871474277/transitioning-entirely-to-neural -machine-translation/.
5. And the number of deals increased from 160 to 658. See https://www.cbinsights.com /research/artificial-intelligence-startup-funding/.
6. These slowdowns are statistically significant. For the United States, where the slowdown is measured using quarterly data, equality of the two periods' growth rates is rejected with a t-statistic of 2.9. The OECD numbers come from annual data across the thirty countries. Here, the null hypothesis of equality is rejected with a t-statistic of 7.2.

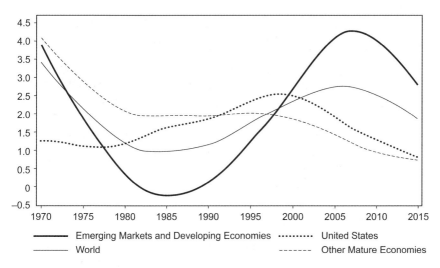

Fig. 1.2   Smoothed average annual labor productivity growth (percent) by region
Source: The Conference Board Total Economy Database™ (adjusted version), November 2016.
Note: Trend growth rates are obtained using HP filter, assuming a 1 = 100.

first century ended around the time of the Great Recession, causing a recent decline in productivity growth rates in these countries too.

These slowdowns do not appear to simply reflect the effects of the Great Recession. In the OECD data, twenty-eight of the thirty countries still exhibit productivity decelerations if 2008–2009 growth rates are excluded from the totals. Cette, Fernald, and Mojon (2016), using other data, also find substantial evidence that the slowdowns began before the Great Recession.

Both capital deepening and total factor productivity (TFP) growth lead to labor productivity growth, and both seem to be playing a role in the slowdown (Fernald 2014; OECD 2015). Disappointing technological progress can be tied to each of these components. Total factor productivity directly reflects such progress. Capital deepening is indirectly influenced by technological change because firms' investment decisions respond to improvements in capital's current or expected marginal product.

These facts have been read by some as reasons for pessimism about the ability of new technologies like AI to greatly affect productivity and income. Gordon (2014, 2015) argues that productivity growth has been in long-run decline, with the IT-driven acceleration of 1995 to 2004 being a one-off aberration. While not claiming technological progress will be nil in the coming decades, Gordon essentially argues that we have been experiencing the new, low-growth normal and should expect to continue to do so going forward. Cowen (2011) similarly offers multiple reasons why innovation may be slow, at least for the foreseeable future. Bloom et al. (2017) document that in many fields of technological progress research productivity has been falling, while Nordhaus (2015) finds that the hypothesis of an acceleration of technology-driven growth fails a variety of tests.

This pessimistic view of future technological progress has entered into long-range policy planning. The Congressional Budget Office, for instance, reduced its ten-year forecast for average US annual labor productivity growth from 1.8 percent in 2016 (CBO 2016) to 1.5 percent in 2017 (CBO 2017). Although perhaps modest on its surface, that drop implies US gross domestic product (GDP) will be considerably smaller ten years from now than it would in the more optimistic scenario—a difference equivalent to almost $600 billion in 2017.

1.3   Potential Explanations for the Paradox

There are four principal candidate explanations for the current confluence of technological optimism and poor productivity performance: (a) false hopes, (b) mismeasurement, (c) concentrated distribution and rent dissipation, and (d) implementation and restructuring lags.[7]

1.3.1   False Hopes

The simplest possibility is that the optimism about the potential technologies is misplaced and unfounded. Perhaps these technologies won't be as transformative as many expect, and although they might have modest and noteworthy effects on specific sectors, their aggregate impact might be small. In this case, the paradox will be resolved in the future because realized productivity growth never escapes its current doldrums, which will force the optimists to mark their beliefs to market.

History and some current examples offer a quantum of credence to this possibility. Certainly one can point to many prior exciting technologies that did not live up to initially optimistic expectations. Nuclear power never became too cheap to meter, and fusion energy has been twenty years away for sixty years. Mars may still beckon, but it has been more than forty years since Eugene Cernan was the last person to walk on the moon. Flying cars never got off the ground,[8] and passenger jets no longer fly at supersonic speeds. Even AI, perhaps the most promising technology of our era, is well behind Marvin Minsky's 1967 prediction that "Within a generation the problem of creating 'artificial intelligence' will be substantially solved" (Minsky 1967, 2).

On the other hand, there remains a compelling case for optimism. As we outline below, it is not difficult to construct back-of-the-envelope scenarios

---

7. To some extent, these explanations parallel the explanations for the Solow paradox (Brynjolfsson 1993).
8. But coming soon? https://kittyhawk.aero/about/.

I

AI as a GPT

in which even a modest number of currently existing technologies could combine to substantially raise productivity growth and societal welfare. Indeed, knowledgeable investors and researchers are betting their money and time on exactly such outcomes. Thus, while we recognize the potential for overoptimism—and the experience with early predictions for AI makes an especially relevant reminder for us to be somewhat circumspect in this chapter—we judge that it would be highly preliminary to dismiss optimism at this point.

1.3.2   Mismeasurement

Another potential explanation for the paradox is mismeasurement of output and productivity. In this case, it is the pessimistic reading of the empirical past, not the optimism about the future, that is mistaken. Indeed, this explanation implies that the productivity benefits of the new wave of technologies are already being enjoyed, but have yet to be accurately measured. Under this explanation, the slowdown of the past decade is illusory. This "mismeasurement hypothesis" has been put forth in several works (e.g., Mokyr 2014; Alloway 2015; Feldstein 2015; Hatzius and Dawsey 2015; Smith 2015).

There is a prima facie case for the mismeasurement hypothesis. Many new technologies, like smartphones, online social networks, and downloadable media involve little monetary cost, yet consumers spend large amounts of time with these technologies. Thus, the technologies might deliver substantial utility even if they account for a small share of GDP due to their low relative price. Guvenen et al. (2017) also show how growing offshore profit shifting can be another source of mismeasurement.

However, a set of recent studies provide good reason to think that mismeasurement is not the entire, or even a substantial, explanation for the slowdown. Cardarelli and Lusinyan (2015), Byrne, Fernald, and Reinsdorf (2016), Nakamura and Soloveichik (2015), and Syverson (2017), each using different methodologies and data, present evidence that mismeasurement is not the primary explanation for the productivity slowdown. After all, while there is convincing evidence that many of the benefits of today's technologies are not reflected in GDP and therefore productivity statistics, the same was undoubtedly true in earlier eras as well.

1.3.3   Concentrated Distribution and Rent Dissipation

A third possibility is that the gains of the new technologies are already attainable, but that through a combination of concentrated distribution of those gains and dissipative efforts to attain or preserve them (assuming the technologies are at least partially rivalrous), their effect on average productivity growth is modest overall, and is virtually nil for the median worker. For instance, two of the most profitable uses of AI to date have been for targeting and pricing online ads, and for automated trading of financial instruments, both applications with many zero-sum aspects.

One version of this story asserts that the benefits of the new technologies are being enjoyed by a relatively small fraction of the economy, but the technologies' narrowly scoped and rivalrous nature creates wasteful "gold rush"-type activities. Both those seeking to be one of the few beneficiaries, as well as those who have attained some gains and seek to block access to others, engage in these dissipative efforts, destroying many of the benefits of the new technologies.[9]

Recent research offers some indirect support for elements of this story. Productivity differences between frontier firms and average firms in the same industry have been increasing in recent years (Andrews, Criscuolo, and Gal 2016; Furman and Orszag 2015). Differences in profit margins between the top and bottom performers in most industries have also grown (McAfee and Brynjolfsson 2008). A smaller number of superstar firms are gaining market share (Autor et al. 2017; Brynjolfsson et al. 2008), while workers' earnings are increasingly tied to firm-level productivity differences (Song et al. 2015). There are concerns that industry concentration is leading to substantial aggregate welfare losses due to the distortions of market power (e.g., De Loecker and Eeckhout 2017; Gutiérrez and Philippon 2017). Furthermore, growing inequality can lead to stagnating median incomes and associated socioeconomic costs, even when total income continues to grow.

Although this evidence is important, it is not dispositive. The aggregate effects of industry concentration are still under debate, and the mere fact that a technology's gains are not evenly distributed is no guarantee that resources will be dissipated in trying to capture them—especially that there would be enough waste to erase noticeable aggregate benefits.

1.3.4   Implementation and Restructuring Lags

Each of the first three possibilities, especially the first two, relies on explaining away the discordance between high hopes and disappointing statistical realities. One of the two elements is presumed to be somehow "wrong." In the misplaced optimism scenario, the expectations for technology by technologists and investors are off base. In the mismeasurement explanation, the tools we use to gauge empirical reality are not up to the task of accurately doing so. And in the concentrated distribution stories, the private gains for the few may be very real, but they do not translate into broader gains for the many.

But there is a fourth explanation that allows both halves of the seeming paradox to be correct. It asserts that there really is good reason to be optimistic about the future productivity growth potential of new technologies, while at the same time recognizing that recent productivity growth has been low. The core of this story is that it takes a considerable time—often more than

---

9. Stiglitz (2014) offers a different mechanism where technological progress with concentrated benefits in the presence of restructuring costs can lead to increased inequality and even, in the short run, economic downturns.

is commonly appreciated—to be able to sufficiently harness new technologies. Ironically, this is especially true for those major new technologies that ultimately have an important effect on aggregate statistics and welfare. That is, those with such broad potential application that they qualify as general purpose technologies (GPTs). Indeed, the more profound and far-reaching the potential restructuring, the longer the time lag between the initial invention of the technology and its full impact on the economy and society.

This explanation implies there will be a period in which the technologies are developed enough that investors, commentators, researchers, and policymakers can imagine their potentially transformative effects, even though they have had no discernable effect on recent productivity growth. It isn't until a sufficient stock of the new technology is built and the necessary invention of complementary processes and assets occurs that the promise of the technology actually blossoms in aggregate economic data. Investors are forward looking and economic statistics are backward looking. In times of technological stability or steady change (constant velocity), the disjoint measurements will seem to track each other. But in periods of rapid change, the two measurements can become uncorrelated.

There are two main sources of the delay between recognition of a new technology's potential and its measurable effects. One is that it takes time to build the stock of the new technology to a size sufficient enough to have an aggregate effect. The other is that complementary investments are necessary to obtain the full benefit of the new technology, and it takes time to discover and develop these complements and to implement them. While the fundamental importance of the core invention and its potential for society might be clearly recognizable at the outset, the myriad necessary coinventions, obstacles, and adjustments needed along the way await discovery over time, and the required path may be lengthy and arduous. Never mistake a clear view for a short distance.

This explanation resolves the paradox by acknowledging that its two seemingly contradictory parts are not actually in conflict. Rather, both parts are in some sense natural manifestations of the same underlying phenomenon of building and implementing a new technology.

While each of the first three explanations for the paradox might have a role in describing its source, the explanations also face serious questions in their ability to describe key parts of the data. We find the fourth—the implementation and restructuring lags story—to be the most compelling in light of the evidence we discuss below. Thus it is the focus of our explorations in the remainder of this chapter.

1.4   The Argument in Favor of the Implementation and Restructuring Lags Explanation

Implicit or explicit in the pessimistic view of the future is that the recent slowdown in productivity growth portends slower productivity growth in the future.

We begin by establishing one of the most basic elements of the story: that slow productivity growth today does not rule out faster productivity growth in the future. In fact, the evidence is clear that it is barely predictive at all.

Total factor productivity growth is the component of overall output growth that cannot be explained by accounting for changes in observable labor and capital inputs. It has been called a "measure of our ignorance" (Abramovitz 1956). It is a residual, so an econometrician should not be surprised if it is not very predictable from past levels. Labor productivity is a similar measure, but instead of accounting for capital accumulation, simply divides total output by the labor hours used to produce that output.

Figures 1.3 and 1.4 plot, respectively, US productivity indices since 1948 and productivity growth by decade. The data include average labor productivity (LP), average total factor productivity (TFP), and Fernald's (2014) utilization-adjusted TFP (TFPua).[10]

Productivity has consistently grown in the postwar era, albeit at different rates at different times. Despite the consistent growth, however, past productivity growth rates have historically been poor predictors of future productivity growth. In other words, the productivity growth of the past decade tells us little about productivity growth for the coming decade. Looking only at productivity data, it would have been hard to predict the decrease in productivity growth in the early 1970s or foresee the beneficial impact of IT in the 1990s.

As it turns out, while there is some correlation in productivity growth rates over short intervals, the correlation between adjacent ten-year periods is not statistically significant. We present below the results from a regression of different measures of average productivity growth on the previous period's average productivity growth for ten-year intervals as well as scatterplots of productivity for each ten-year interval against the productivity in the subsequent period. The regressions in table 1.1 allow for autocorrelation in error terms across years (1 lag). Table 1.2 clusters the standard errors by decade. Similar results allowing for autocorrelation at longer time scales are presented in the appendix.

In all cases, the R^2 of these regressions is low, and the previous decade's productivity growth does not have statistically discernable predictive power over the next decade's growth. For labor productivity, the R^2 is 0.009. Although the intercept in the regression is significantly different from zero (productivity growth is positive, on average), the coefficient on the previous period's growth is not statistically significant. The point estimate is economically small, too. Taking the estimate at face value, 1 percent higher annual labor productivity growth in the prior decade (around an unconditional mean of about 2 percent per year) corresponds to less than 0.1 percent

10. Available at http://www.frbsf.org/economic-research/indicators-data/total-factor -productivity-tfp/.

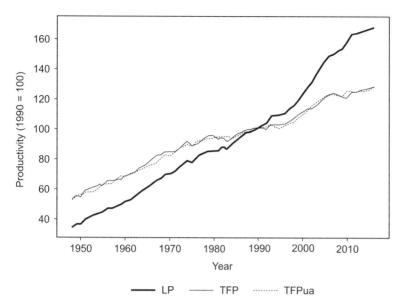

Fig. 1.3   US TFP and labor productivity indices, 1948–2016
Note: 1990 = 100.

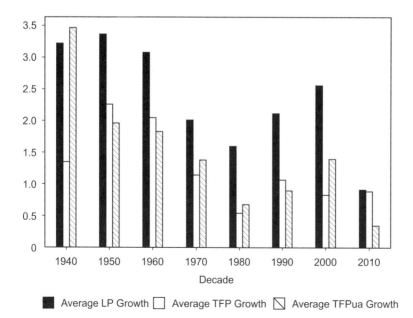

Fig. 1.4   US TFP and labor productivity growth (percent) by decade

Table 1.1   **Regressions with Newey-West standard errors**

Newey-West regressions (1 lag allowed) ten-year average productivity growth	(1) Labor productivity growth	(2) Total factor productivity growth	(3) Utilization-adjusted productivity growth
Previous ten-year average LP growth	0.0857 (0.177)		
Previous ten-year average TFP growth		0.136 (0.158)	
Previous ten-year average TFPua growth			0.158 (0.187)
Constant	1.949*** (0.398)	0.911*** (0.188)	0.910*** (0.259)
Observations	50	50	50
R-squared	0.009	0.023	0.030

Note: Standard errors in parentheses.
***Significant at the 1 percent level.
**Significant at the 5 percent level.
*Significant at the 10 percent level.

Table 1.2   **Regressions with standard errors clustered by decade**

Ten-year average productivity growth (SEs clustered by decade)	(1) Labor productivity growth	(2) Total factor productivity growth	(3) Utilization-adjusted productivity growth
Previous ten-year average LP growth	0.0857 (0.284)		
Previous ten-year average TFP growth		0.136 (0.241)	
Previous ten-year average TFPua growth			0.158 (0.362)
Constant	1.949** (0.682)	0.911** (0.310)	0.910 (0.524)
Observations	50	50	50
R-squared	0.009	0.023	0.030

Note: Robust standard errors in parentheses.
***Significant at the 1 percent level.
**Significant at the 5 percent level.
*Significant at the 10 percent level.

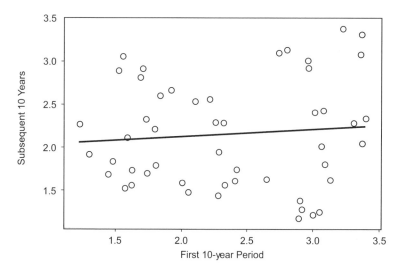

Fig 1.5   Labor productivity growth scatterplot

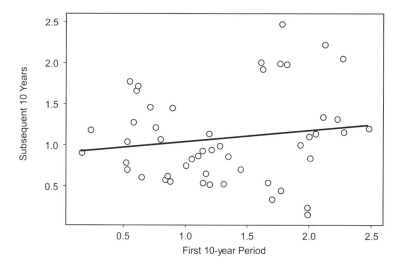

Fig. 1.6   Total factor productivity growth scatterplot

faster growth in the following decade. In the TFP growth regression, the R^2 is 0.023, and again the coefficient on the previous period's growth is insignificant. Similar patterns hold in the utilization-adjusted TFP regression (R^2 of 0.03). The lack of explanatory power of past productivity growth is also apparent in the scatterplots (see figures 1.5, 1.6, and 1.7).

The old adage that "past performance is not predictive of future results" applies well to trying to predict productivity growth in the years to come,

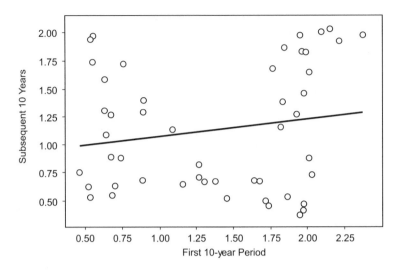

Fig. 1.7   **Utilization-adjusted total factor productivity growth scatterplot**

especially in periods of a decade or longer. Historical stagnation does not justify forward-looking pessimism.

1.5   A Technology-Driven Case for Productivity Optimism

Simply extrapolating recent productivity growth rates forward is not a good way to estimate the next decade's productivity growth. Does that imply we have no hope at all of predicting productivity growth? We don't think so.

Instead of relying only on past productivity statistics, we can consider the technological and innovation environment we expect to see in the near future. In particular, we need to study and understand the specific technologies that actually exist and make an assessment of their potential.

One does not have to dig too deeply into the pool of existing technologies or assume incredibly large benefits from any one of them to make a case that existing but still nascent technologies can potentially combine to create noticeable accelerations in aggregate productivity growth. We begin by looking at a few specific examples. We will then make the case that AI is a GPT, with broader implications.

First, let's consider the productivity potential of autonomous vehicles. According to the US Bureau of Labor Statistics (BLS), in 2016 there were 3.5 million people working in private industry as "motor vehicle operators" of one sort or another (this includes truck drivers, taxi drivers, bus drivers, and other similar occupations). Suppose autonomous vehicles were to reduce, over some period, the number of drivers necessary to do the current workload to 1.5 million. We do not think this is a far-fetched scenario given the potential of the technology. Total nonfarm private employment in mid-

2016 was 122 million. Therefore, autonomous vehicles would reduce the number of workers necessary to achieve the same output to 120 million. This would result in aggregate labor productivity (calculated using the standard BLS nonfarm private series) increasing by 1.7 percent (122/120 = 1.017). Supposing this transition occurred over ten years, this single technology would provide a direct boost of 0.17 percent to annual productivity growth over that decade.

This gain is significant, and it does not include many potential productivity gains from complementary changes that could accompany the diffusion of autonomous vehicles. For instance, self-driving cars are a natural complement to transportation-as-a-service rather than individual car ownership. The typical car is currently parked 95 percent of the time, making it readily available for its owner or primary user (Morris 2016). However, in locations with sufficient density, a self-driving car could be summoned on demand. This would make it possible for cars to provide useful transportation services for a larger fraction of the time, reducing capital costs per passenger-mile, even after accounting for increased wear and tear. Thus, in addition to the obvious improvements in labor productivity from replacing drivers, capital productivity would also be significantly improved. Of course, the speed of adoption is important for estimation of the impact of these technologies. Levy (2018) is more pessimistic, suggesting in the near term that long distance truck driver jobs will grow about 2 percent between 2014 and 2024. This is 3 percent less (about 55,000 jobs in that category) than they would have grown without autonomous vehicle technology and about 3 percent of total employment of long distance truck drivers. A second example is call centers. As of 2015, there were about 2.2 million people working in more than 6,800 call centers in the United States, and hundreds of thousands more work as home-based call center agents or in smaller sites.[11] Improved voice-recognition systems coupled with intelligence question-answering tools like IBM's Watson might plausibly be able to handle 60–70 percent or more of the calls, especially since, in accordance with the Pareto principle, a large fraction of call volume is due to variants on a small number of basic queries. If AI reduced the number of workers by 60 percent, it would increase US labor productivity by 1 percent, perhaps again spread over ten years. Again, this would likely spur complementary innovations, from shopping recommendation and travel services to legal advice, consulting, and real-time personal coaching. Relatedly, citing advances in AI-assisted customer service, Levy (2018) projects zero growth in customer service representatives from 2014 to 2024 (a difference of 260,000 jobs from BLS projections).

Beyond labor savings, advances in AI have the potential to boost total factor productivity. In particular, energy efficiency and materials usage could be improved in many large-scale industrial plants. For instance, a

---

11. https://info.siteselectiongroup.com/blog/how-big-is-the-us-call-center-industry-compared-to-india-and-philippines.

team from Google DeepMind recently trained an ensemble of neural networks to optimize power consumption in a data center. By carefully tracking the data already collected from thousands of sensors tracking temperatures, electricity usage, and pump speeds, the system learned how to make adjustments in the operating parameters. As a result, the AI was able to reduce the amount of energy used for cooling by 40 percent compared to the levels achieved by human experts. The algorithm was a general-purpose framework designed to account complex dynamics, so it is easy to see how such a system could be applied to other data centers at Google, or indeed, around the world. Overall, data center electricity costs in the United States are about $6 billion per year, including about $2 billion just for cooling.[12]

What's more, similar applications of machine learning could be implemented in a variety of commercial and industrial activities. For instance, manufacturing accounts for about $2.2 trillion of value added each year. Manufacturing companies like GE are already using AI to forecast product demand, future customer maintenance needs, and analyze performance data coming from sensors on their capital equipment. Recent work on training deep neural network models to perceive objects and achieve sensorimotor control have at the same time yielded robots that can perform a variety of hand-eye coordination tasks (e.g., unscrewing bottle caps and hanging coat hangers; Levine et al., [2016]). Liu et al. (2017) trained robots to perform a number of household chores, like sweeping and pouring almonds into a pan, using a technique called imitation learning.[13] In this approach, the robot learns to perform a task using a raw video demonstration of what it needs to do. These techniques will surely be important for automating manufacturing processes in the future. The results suggest that artificial intelligence may soon improve productivity in household production tasks as well, which in 2010 were worth as much as $2.5 trillion in nonmarket value added (Bridgman et al. 2012).[14]

Although these examples are each suggestive of nontrivial productivity gains, they are only a fraction of the set of applications for AI and machine learning that have been identified so far. James Manyika et al. (2017) analyzed 2,000 tasks and estimated that about 45 percent of the activities that people are paid to perform in the US economy could be automated using existing levels of AI and other technologies. They stress that the pace of

12. According to personal communication, August 24, 2017, with Jon Koomey, Arman Shehabi, and Sarah Smith of Lawrence Berkeley Lab.
13. Videos of these efforts available here: https://sites.google.com/site/imitationfrom observation/.
14. One factor that might temper the aggregate impact of AI-driven productivity gains is if product demand for the sectors with the largest productivity AI gains is sufficiently inelastic. In this case, these sectors' shares of total expenditure will shrink, shifting activity toward slower-growing sectors and muting aggregate productivity growth à la Baumol and Bowen (1966). It is unclear what the elasticities of demand are for the product classes most likely to be affected by AI.

automation will depend on factors other than technical feasibility, including the costs of automation, regulatory barriers, and social acceptance.

1.6   Artificial Intelligence Is a General Purpose Technology

As important as specific applications of AI may be, we argue that the more important economic effects of AI, machine learning, and associated new technologies stem from the fact that they embody the characteristics of general purpose technologies (GPTs). Bresnahan and Trajtenberg (1996) argue that a GPT should be pervasive, able to be improved upon over time, and be able to spawn complementary innovations.

The steam engine, electricity, the internal combustion engine, and computers are each examples of important general purpose technologies. Each of them increased productivity not only directly, but also by spurring important complementary innovations. For instance, the steam engine not only helped to pump water from coal mines, its most important initial application, but also spurred the invention of more effective factory machinery and new forms of transportation like steamships and railroads. In turn, these coinventions helped give rise to innovations in supply chains and mass marketing, to new organizations with hundreds of thousands of employees, and even to seemingly unrelated innovations like standard time, which was needed to manage railroad schedules.

Artificial intelligence, and in particular machine learning, certainly has the potential to be pervasive, to be improved upon over time, and to spawn complementary innovations, making it a candidate for an important GPT.

As noted by Agrawal, Gans, and Goldfarb (2017), the current generation of machine-learning systems is particularly suited for augmenting or automating tasks that involve at least some prediction aspect, broadly defined. These cover a wide range of tasks, occupations, and industries, from driving a car (predicting the correct direction to turn the steering wheel) and diagnosing a disease (predicting its cause) to recommending a product (predicting what the customer will like) and writing a song (predicting which note sequence will be most popular). The core capabilities of perception and cognition addressed by current systems are pervasive, if not indispensable, for many tasks done by humans.

Machine-learning systems are also designed to improve over time. Indeed, what sets them apart from earlier technologies is that they are designed to improve *themselves* over time. Instead of requiring an inventor or developer to codify, or code, each step of a process to be automated, a machine-learning algorithm can discover on its own a function that connects a set of inputs X to a set of outputs Y as long as it is given a sufficiently large set of labeled examples mapping some of the inputs to outputs (Brynjolfsson and Mitchell 2017). The improvements reflect not only the discovery of new algorithms and techniques, particularly for deep neural networks, but also their complementarities with vastly more powerful computer hardware and the availability of much larger digital data sets that can be used to train the systems (Brynjolfsson and McAfee 2017). More and more digital data is collected as a byproduct of digitizing operations, customer interactions, communications, and other aspects of our lives, providing fodder for more and better machine-learning applications.[15]

Most important, machine-learning systems can spur a variety of complementary innovations. For instance, machine learning has transformed the abilities of machines to perform a number of basic types of perception that enable a broader set of applications. Consider machine vision—the ability to see and recognize objects, to label them in photos, and to interpret video streams. As error rates in identifying pedestrians improve from one per 30 frames to about one per 30 million frames, self-driving cars become increasingly feasible (Brynjolfsson and McAfee 2017).

Improved machine vision also makes practical a variety of factory automation tasks and medical diagnoses. Gill Pratt has made an analogy to the development of vision in animals 500 million years ago, which helped ignite the Cambrian explosion and a burst of new species on earth (Pratt 2015). He also noted that machines have a new capability that no biological species has: the ability to share knowledge and skills almost instantaneously with others. Specifically, the rise of cloud computing has made it significantly easier to scale up new ideas at much lower cost than before. This is an especially important development for advancing the economic impact of machine learning because it enables cloud robotics: the sharing of knowledge among robots. Once a new skill is learned by a machine in one location, it can be replicated to other machines via digital networks. Data as well as skills can be shared, increasing the amount of data that any given machine learner can use.

This in turn increases the rate of improvement. For instance, self-driving cars that encounter an unusual situation can upload that information with a shared platform where enough examples can be aggregated to infer a pattern. Only one self-driving vehicle needs to experience an anomaly for many vehicles to learn from it. Waymo, a subsidiary of Google, has cars driving 25,000 "real" autonomous and about 19 million simulated miles each week.[16] All of the Waymo cars learn from the joint experience of the others. Similarly, a robot struggling with a task can benefit from sharing data and learnings with other robots that use a compatible knowledge-representation framework.[17]

When one thinks of AI as a GPT, the implications for output and welfare gains are much larger than in our earlier analysis. For example, self-driving cars could substantially transform many nontransport industries.

---

15. For example, through enterprise resource planning systems in factories, internet commerce, mobile phones, and the "Internet of Things."
16. http://ben-evans.com/benedictevans/2017/8/20/winner-takes-all.
17. Rethink Robotics is developing exactly such a platform.

Retail could shift much further toward home delivery on demand, creating consumer welfare gains and further freeing up valuable high-density land now used for parking. Traffic and safety could be optimized, and insurance risks could fall. With over 30,000 deaths due to automobile crashes in the United States each year, and nearly a million worldwide, there is an opportunity to save many lives.[18]

1.7 Why Future Technological Progress Is Consistent with Low Current Productivity Growth

Having made a case for technological optimism, we now turn to explaining why it is not inconsistent with—and in fact may even be naturally related to—low current productivity growth.

Like other GPTs, AI has the potential to be an important driver of productivity. However, as Jovanovic and Rousseau (2005) point out (with additional reference to David's [1991] historical example), "a GPT does not deliver productivity gains immediately upon arrival" (1184). The technology can be present and developed enough to allow some notion of its transformative effects even though it is not affecting current productivity levels in any noticeable way. This is precisely the state that we argue the economy may be in now.

We discussed earlier that a GPT can at one moment both be present and yet not affect current productivity growth if there is a need to build a sufficiently large stock of the new capital, or if complementary types of capital, both tangible and intangible, need to be identified, produced, and put in place to fully harness the GPT's productivity benefits.

The time necessary to build a sufficient capital stock can be extensive. For example, it was not until the late 1980s, more than twenty-five years after the invention of the integrated circuit, that the computer capital stock reached its long-run plateau at about 5 percent (at historical cost) of total nonresidential equipment capital. It was at only half that level ten years prior. Thus, when Solow pointed out his now eponymous paradox, the computers were *finally just then* getting to the point where they really could be seen everywhere.

David (1991) notes a similar phenomenon in the diffusion of electrification. At least half of US manufacturing establishments remained unelectrified until 1919, about thirty years after the shift to polyphase alternating current began. Initially, adoption was driven by simple cost savings in pro-

---

18. These latter two consequences of autonomous vehicles, while certainly reflecting welfare improvements, would need to be capitalized in prices of goods or services to be measured in standard GDP and productivity measures. We will discuss AI-related measurement issues in greater depth later. Of course, it is worth remembering that autonomous vehicles also hold the potential to create new economic costs if, say, the congestion from lower marginal costs of operating a vehicle is not counteracted by sufficiently large improvements in traffic management technology or certain infrastructure investments.

viding motive power. The biggest benefits came later, when complementary innovations were made. Managers began to fundamentally reorganize work by replacing factories' centralized power source and giving every individual machine its own electric motor. This enabled much more flexibility in the location of equipment and made possible effective assembly lines of materials flow.

This approach to organizing factories is obvious in retrospect, yet it took as many as thirty years for it to become widely adopted. Why? As noted by Henderson (1993, 2006), it is exactly *because* incumbents are designed around the current ways of doing things and so proficient at them that they are blind to or unable to absorb the new approaches and get trapped in the status quo—they suffer the "curse of knowledge."[19]

The factory electrification example demonstrates the other contributor to the time gap between a technology's emergence and its measured productivity effects: the need for installation (and often invention) of complementary capital. This includes both tangible and intangible investments. The timeline necessary to invent, acquire, and install these complements is typically more extensive than the time-to-build considerations just discussed. Consider the measured lag between large investments in IT and productivity benefits within firms. Brynjolfsson and Hitt (2003) found that while small productivity benefits were associated with firms' IT investments when one-year differences were considered, the benefits grew substantially as longer differences were examined, peaking after about seven years. They attributed this pattern to the need for complementary changes in business processes. For instance, when implementing large enterprise-planning systems, firms almost always spend several times more money on business process redesign and training than on the direct costs of hardware and software. Hiring and other human-resources practices often need considerable adjustment to match the firm's human capital to the new structure of production. In fact, Bresnahan, Brynjolfsson, and Hitt (2002) find evidence of three-way complementarities between IT, human capital, and organizational changes in the investment decisions and productivity levels. Furthermore, Brynjolfsson, Hitt, and Yang (2002) show each dollar of IT capital stock is correlated with about $10 of market value. They interpret this as evidence of substantial IT-related intangible assets and show that firms that combine IT investments with a specific set of organizational practices are not just more productive, they also have disproportionately higher market values than firms that invest in only one or the other. This pattern in the data is consistent with a long stream of research on the importance of organizational and even

19. Atkeson and Kehoe (2007) note manufacturers' reluctance to abandon their large knowledge stock at the beginning of the transition to electric power to adopt what was, initially, only a marginally superior technology. David and Wright (2006) are more specific, focusing on "the need for organizational and above all for *conceptual* changes in the ways tasks and products are defined and structured" (147, emphasis in original).

cultural change when making IT investments and technology investments more generally (e.g., Aral, Brynjolfsson, and Wu 2012; Brynjolfsson and Hitt 2000; Orlikowski 1996; Henderson 2006).

But such changes take substantial time and resources, contributing to organizational inertia. Firms are complex systems that require an extensive web of complementary assets to allow the GPT to fully transform the system. Firms that are attempting transformation often must reevaluate and reconfigure not only their internal processes but often their supply and distribution chains as well. These changes can take time, but managers and entrepreneurs will direct invention in ways that economize on the most expensive inputs (Acemoglu and Restrepo 2017). According to LeChatelier's principle (Milgrom and Roberts 1996), elasticities will therefore tend to be greater in the long run than in the short run as quasi-fixed factors adjust.

There is no assurance that the adjustments will be successful. Indeed, there is evidence that the modal transformation of GPT-level magnitude fails. Alon et al. (2017) find that cohorts of firms over five years old contribute little to aggregate productivity growth on net—that is, among established firms, productivity improvements in one firm are offset by productivity declines in other firms. It is hard to teach the proverbial old dog new tricks. Moreover, the old dogs (companies) often have internal incentives to not learn them (Arrow 1962; Holmes, Levine, and Schmitz 2012). In some ways, technology advances in industry one company death at a time.

Transforming industries and sectors requires still more adjustment and reconfiguration. Retail offers a vivid example. Despite being one of the biggest innovations to come out of the 1990s dot-com boom, the largest change in retail in the two decades that followed was not e-commerce, but instead the expansion of warehouse stores and supercenters (Hortaçsu and Syverson 2015). Only very recently did e-commerce become a force for general retailers to reckon with. Why did it take so long? Brynjolfsson and Smith (2000) document the difficulties incumbent retailers had in adapting their business processes to take full advantage of the internet and electronic commerce. Many complementary investments were required. The sector as a whole required the build out of an entire distribution infrastructure. Customers had to be "retrained." None of this could happen quickly. The potential of e-commerce to revolutionize retailing was widely recognized, and even hyped in the late 1990s, but its actual share of retail commerce was miniscule, 0.2 percent of all retail sales in 1999. Only after two decades of widely predicted yet time-consuming change in the industry, is e-commerce starting to approach 10 percent of total retail sales and companies like Amazon are having a first-order effect on more traditional retailers' sales and stock market valuations.

The case of self-driving cars discussed earlier provides a more prospective example of how productivity might lag technology. Consider what happens to the current pools of vehicle production and vehicle operation workers when autonomous vehicles are introduced. Employment on production side will initially increase to handle research and development (R&D), AI development, and new vehicle engineering. Furthermore, learning curve issues could well imply lower productivity in manufacturing these vehicles during the early years (Levitt, List, and Syverson 2013). Thus labor input in the short run can actually increase, rather than decrease, for the same amount of vehicle production. In the early years of autonomous vehicle development and production, the marginal labor added by producers exceeds the marginal labor displaced among the motor vehicle operators. It is only later when the fleet of deployed autonomous vehicles gets closer to a steady state that measured productivity reflects the full benefits of the technology.

1.8   Viewing Today's Paradox through the Lens of Previous General Purpose Technologies

We have indicated in the previous discussion that we see parallels between the current paradox and those that have happened in the past. It is closely related to the Solow paradox era circa 1990, certainly, but it is also tied closely to the experience during the diffusion of portable power (combining the contemporaneous growth and transformative effects of electrification and the internal combustion engine).

Comparing the productivity growth patterns of the two eras is instructive. Figure 1.8 is an updated version of an analysis from Syverson (2013). It overlays US labor productivity since 1970 with that from 1890 to 1940, the period after portable power technologies had been invented and were starting to be placed into production. (The historical series values are from Kendrick [1961].) The modern series timeline is indexed to a value of 100 in 1995 and

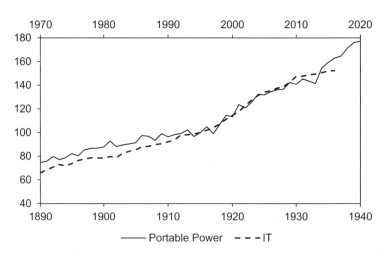

Fig. 1.8   Labor productivity growth in the portable power and IT eras

is labeled on the upper horizontal axis. The portable power era index has a value of 100 in 1915, and its years are shown on the lower horizontal axis.

Labor productivity during the portable power era shared remarkably similar patterns with the current series. In both eras, there was an initial period of roughly a quarter century of relatively slow productivity growth. Then both eras saw decade-long accelerations in productivity growth, spanning 1915 to 1924 in the portable power era and 1995 to 2004 more recently.

The late-1990s acceleration was the (at least partial) resolution of the Solow paradox. We imagine that the late 1910s acceleration could have similarly answered some economist's query in 1910 as to why one sees electric motors and internal combustion engines everywhere but in the productivity statistics.[20]

Very interesting, and quite relevant to the current situation, the productivity growth slowdown we have experienced after 2004 also has a parallel in the historical data, a slowdown from 1924 to 1932. As can be seen in the figure, and instructive to the point of whether a new wave of AI and associated technologies (or if one prefers, a second wave of IT-based technology) could reaccelerate productivity growth, labor productivity growth at the end of the portable power era rose again, averaging 2.7 percent per year between 1933 and 1940.

Of course this past breakout growth is no guarantee that productivity must speed up again today. However, it does raise two relevant points. First, it is another example of a period of sluggish productivity growth followed by an acceleration. Second, it demonstrates that productivity growth driven by a core GPT can arrive in multiple waves.

1.9   Expected Productivity Effects of an AI-Driven Acceleration

To understand the likely productivity effects of AI, it is useful to think of AI as a type of capital, specifically a type of intangible capital. It can be accumulated through investment, it is a durable factor of production, and its value can depreciate. Treating AI as a type of capital clarifies how its development and installation as a productive factor will affect productivity.

As with any capital deepening, increasing AI will raise labor productivity. This would be true regardless of how well AI capital is measured (which we might expect it won't be for several reasons discussed below) though there may be lags.

The effects of AI on TFP are more complex and the impact *will* depend on its measurement. If AI (and its output elasticity) were to be measured perfectly and included in both the input bundle in the denominator of TFP

---

20. We are not aware of anyone who actually said this, and of course today's system of national economic statistics did not exist at that time, but we find the scenario amusing, instructive, and in some ways plausible.

and the output bundle in the numerator, then measured TFP will accurately reflect true TFP. In this case, AI could be treated just like any other measurable capital input. Its effect on output could be properly accounted for and "removed" by the TFP input measure, leading to no change in TFP. This isn't to say that there would not be productive benefits from diffusion of AI; it is just that it could be valued like other types of capital input.

There are reasons why economists and national statistical agencies might face measurement problems when dealing with AI. Some are instances of more general capital measurement issues, but others are likely to be idiosyncratic to AI. We discuss this next.

1.10   Measuring AI Capital

Regardless of the effects of AI and AI-related technologies on actual output and productivity, it is clear from the productivity outlook that the ways AI's effects will be *measured* are dependent on how well countries' statistics programs measure AI capital.

The primary difficulty in AI capital measurement is, as mentioned earlier, that many of its outputs will be intangible. This issue is exacerbated by the extensive use of AI as an input in making other capital, including new types of software, as well as human and organizational capital, rather than final consumption goods. Much of this other capital, including human capital, will, like AI itself, be mostly intangible (Jones and Romer 2010).

To be more specific, effective use of AI requires developing data sets, building firm-specific human capital, and implementing new business processes. These all require substantial capital outlays and maintenance. The tangible counterparts to these intangible expenditures, including purchases of computing resources, servers, and real estate, are easily measured in the standard neoclassical growth accounting model (Solow 1957). On the other hand, the value of capital goods production for complementary intangible investments is difficult to quantify. Both tangible and intangible capital stocks generate a capital service flow yield that accrues over time. Realizing these yields requires more than simply renting capital stock. After purchasing capital assets, firms incur additional adjustment costs (e.g., business process redesigns and installation costs). These adjustment costs make capital less flexible than frictionless rental markets would imply. Much of the market value of AI capital specifically, and IT capital more generally, may be derived from the capitalized short-term quasi-rents earned by firms that have already reorganized to extract service flows from new investment.

Yet while the stock of tangible assets is booked on corporate balance sheets, expenditures on the intangible complements and adjustment costs to AI investment commonly are not. Without including the production and use of intangible AI capital, the usual growth accounting decompositions of changes in value added can misattribute AI intangible capital deepening to changes in TFP. As discussed in Hall (2000) and Yang and Brynjolfsson (2001), this constitutes an omission of a potentially important component of capital goods production in the calculation of final output. Estimates of TFP will therefore be inaccurate, though possibly in either direction. In the case where the intangible AI capital stock is growing faster than output, then TFP growth will be underestimated, while TFP will be overestimated if capital stock is growing more slowly than output.

The intuition for this effect is that in any given period t, the output of (unmeasured) AI capital stock in period $t + 1$ is a function the input (unmeasured) existing AI capital stock in period t. When AI stock is growing rapidly, the unmeasured outputs (AI capital stock created) will be greater than the unmeasured inputs (AI capital stock used).

Furthermore, suppose the relevant costs in terms of labor and other resources needed to create intangible assets are measured, but the resulting increases in intangible assets are not measured as contributions to output. In this case, not only will total GDP be undercounted but so will productivity, which uses GDP as its numerator. Thus periods of rapid intangible capital accumulation may be associated with *lower* measured productivity growth, even if true productivity is increasing.

With missing capital goods production, measured productivity will only reflect the fact that more capital and labor inputs are used up in producing measured output. The inputs used to produce unmeasured capital goods will instead resemble lost potential output. For example, a recent report from the Brookings Institution estimates that investments in autonomous vehicles have topped $80 billion from 2014 to 2017 with little consumer adoption of the technology so far.[21] This is roughly 0.44 percent of 2016 GDP (spread over three years). If all of the capital formation in autonomous vehicles was generated by equally costly labor inputs, this would lower estimated labor productivity by 0.1 percent per year over the last three years since autonomous vehicles have not yet led to any significant increase in measured final output. Similarly, according to the AI Index, enrollment in AI and ML courses at leading universities has roughly tripled over the past ten years, and the number of venture-back AI-related start-ups has more than quadrupled. To the extent that they create intangible assets beyond the costs of production, GDP will be underestimated.

Eventually the mismeasured intangible capital goods investments are expected to yield a return (i.e., output) by their investors. If and when measurable output is produced by these hidden assets, another mismeasurement effect leading to overestimation of productivity will kick in. When the output share and stock of mismeasured or omitted capital grows, the measured output increases produced by that capital will be incorrectly attributed to total factor productivity improvements. As the growth rate of investment in unmeasured capital goods decreases, the capital service flow from

21. https://www.brookings.edu/research/gauging-investment-in-self-driving-cars/.

unmeasured goods effect on TFP can exceed the underestimation error from unmeasured capital goods.

Combining these two effects produces a "J-curve" wherein early production of intangible capital leads to underestimation of productivity growth, but later returns from the stock of unmeasured capital creates measured output growth that might be incorrectly attributed to TFP.

Formally:

(1) $$Y + zI_2 = f(A, K_1, K_2, L)$$

(2) $$dY + zdI_2 = F_A dA + F_{K_1} dK_1 + F_L dL + F_{K_2} dK_2.$$

Output Y and unmeasured capital goods with price $z(zI_2)$ are produced with production function f. The inputs of $f(\cdot)$ are the total factor productivity A, ordinary capital K_1, unmeasured capital K_2, and labor L. Equation (2) describes the total differential of output as a function of the inputs to the production function. If the rental price of ordinary capital is r_1, the rental price of unmeasured capital is r_2, and the wage rate is w, we have

(3) $$\hat{S} = \frac{dY}{Y} - \left(\frac{r_1 K_1}{Y}\right)\left(\frac{dK_1}{K_1}\right) - \left(\frac{wL}{Y}\right)\left(\frac{dL}{L}\right)$$

and

(4) $$S^* = \frac{dY}{Y} - \left(\frac{r_1 K_1}{Y}\right)\left(\frac{dK_1}{K_1}\right) - \left(\frac{wL}{Y}\right)\left(\frac{dL}{L}\right) - \left(\frac{r_2 K_2}{Y}\right)\left(\frac{dK_2}{K_2}\right) + \left(\frac{zI_2}{Y}\right)\left(\frac{dI_2}{I_2}\right),$$

where $\hat{S}$ is the familiar Solow residual as measured and S^* is the correct Solow residual accounting for mismeasured capital investments and stock.

The mismeasurement is then

(5) $$\hat{S} - S^* = \left(\frac{r_2 K_2}{Y}\right)\left(\frac{dK_2}{K_2}\right) - \left(\frac{zI_2}{Y}\right)\left(\frac{dI_2}{I_2}\right) = \left(\frac{r_2 K_2}{Y}\right)g_{K_2} - \left(\frac{zI_2}{Y}\right)g_{I_2}.$$

The right side of the equation describes a hidden capital effect and a hidden investment effect. When the growth rate of new investment in unmeasured capital multiplied by its share of output is larger (smaller) than the growth rate of the stock of unmeasured capital multiplied by its share of output, the estimated Solow residual will underestimate (overestimate) the rate of productivity growth. Initially, new types of capital will have a high marginal product. Firms will accumulate that capital until its marginal rate of return is equal to the rate of return of other capital. As capital accumulates, the growth rate of net investment in the unmeasured capital will turn negative, causing a greater overestimate TFP. In steady state, neither net investment's share of output nor the net stock of unmeasured capital grows and the productivity mismeasurement is zero. Figure 1.9 provides an illustration.[22]

---

22. The price of new investment (z) and rental price of capital (r) are 0.3 and 0.12, respectively, in this toy economy. Other values used to create the figure are included in the appendix.

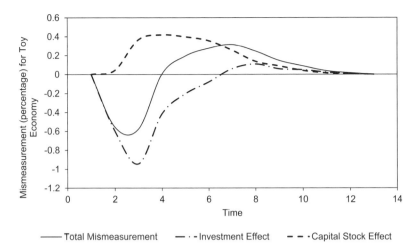

Fig. 1.9 **The mismeasurement J-curve for an economy accumulating a new kind of capital**

Looking forward, these problems may be particularly stark for AI capital, because its accumulation will almost surely outstrip the pace of ordinary capital accumulation in the short run. AI capital is a new category of capital—new in economic statistics, certainly, but we would argue practically so as well.

This also means that capital quantity indexes that are computed from within-type capital growth might have problems benchmarking size and effect of AI early on. National statistics agencies do not really focus on measuring capital types that are not already ubiquitous. New capital categories will tend to either be rolled into existing types, possibly with lower inferred marginal products (leading to an understatement of the productive effect of the new capital), or missed altogether. This problem is akin to the new goods problem in price indexes.

A related issue—once AI is measured separately—is how closely its units of measurement will capture AI's marginal product relative to other capital stock. That is, if a dollar of AI stock has a marginal product that is twice as high as the modal unit of non-AI capital in the economy, will the quantity indexes of AI reflect this? This requires measured relative prices of AI and non-AI capital to capture differences in marginal product. Measuring levels correctly is less important than measuring accurate proportional differences (whether intertemporally or in the cross section) correctly. What is needed in the end is that a unit of AI capital twice as productive as another should be twice as large in the capital stock.

It is worth noting that these are all classic problems in capital measurement and not new to AI. Perhaps these problems will be systematically worse for AI, but this is not obvious ex ante. What it does mean is that economists and national statistical agencies at least have experience in, if not quite a full solution for, dealing with these sorts of limitations. That said, some measurement issues are likely to be especially prevalent for AI. For instance, a substantial part of the value of AI output may be firm-specific. Imagine a program that figures out individual consumers' product preferences or price elasticities and matches products and pricing to predictions. This has different value to different companies depending on their customer bases and product selection, and knowledge may not be transferrable across firms. The value also depends on companies' abilities to implement price discrimination. Such limits could come from characteristics of a company's market, like resale opportunities, which are not always under firms' control, or from the existence in the firm of complementary implementation assets and/or abilities. Likewise, each firm will likely have a different skill mix that it seeks in its employees, unique needs in its production process, and a particular set of supply constraints. In such cases, firm-specific data sets and applications of those data will differentiate the machine-learning capabilities of one firm from another (Brynjolfsson and McAfee 2017).

1.11   Conclusion

There are plenty of both optimists and pessimists about technology and growth. The optimists tend to be technologists and venture capitalists, and many are clustered in technology hubs. The pessimists tend to be economists, sociologists, statisticians, and government officials. Many of them are clustered in major state and national capitals. There is much less interaction between the two groups than within them, and it often seems as though they are talking past each other. In this chapter, we argue that in an important sense, they are.

When we talk with the optimists, we are convinced that the recent breakthroughs in AI and machine learning are real and significant. We also would argue that they form the core of a new, economically important potential GPT. When we speak with the pessimists, we are convinced that productivity growth has slowed down recently and what gains there have been are unevenly distributed, leaving many people with stagnating incomes, declining metrics of health and well-being, and good cause for concern. People are uncertain about the future, and many of the industrial titans that once dominated the employment and market value leaderboard have fallen on harder times.

These two stories are not contradictory. In fact, in many ways they are consistent and symptomatic of an economy in transition. Our analysis suggests that while the recent past has been difficult, it is not destiny. Although it is always dangerous to make predictions, and we are humble about our ability to foretell the future, our reading of the evidence does provide some cause for optimism. The breakthroughs of AI technologies already demonstrated are not yet affecting much of the economy, but they portend bigger effects as they diffuse. More important, they enable complementary innovations that could multiply their impact. Both the AI investments and the complementary changes are costly, hard to measure, and take time to implement, and this can, at least initially, depress productivity as it is currently measured. Entrepreneurs, managers, and end-users will find powerful new applications for machines that can now learn how to recognize objects, understand human language, speak, make accurate predictions, solve problems, and interact with the world with increasing dexterity and mobility.

Further advances in the core technologies of machine learning would likely yield substantial benefits. However, our perspective suggests that an underrated area of research involves the complements to the new AI technologies, not only in areas of human capital and skills, but also new processes and business models. The intangible assets associated with the last wave of computerization were about ten times as large as the direct investments in computer hardware itself. We think it is plausible that AI-associated intangibles could be of a comparable or greater magnitude. Given the big changes in coordination and production possibilities made possible by AI, the ways that we organized work and education in the past are unlikely to remain optimal in the future.

Relatedly, we need to update our economic measurement tool kits. As AI and its complements more rapidly add to our (intangible) capital stock, traditional metrics like GDP and productivity can become more difficult to measure and interpret. Successful companies do not need large investments in factories or even computer hardware, but they do have intangible assets that are costly to replicate. The large market values associated with companies developing and/or implementing AI suggest that investors believe there is real value in those companies. In the case that claims on the assets of the firm are publicly traded and markets are efficient, the financial market will properly value the firm as the present value of its risk-adjusted discounted cash flows. This can provide an estimate of the value of both the tangible and intangible assets owned by the firm. What's more, the effects on living standards may be even larger than the benefits that investors hope to capture. It is also possible, even likely, that many people will not share in those benefits. Economists are well positioned to contribute to a research agenda of documenting and understanding the often intangible changes associated with AI and its broader economic implications.

Realizing the benefits of AI is far from automatic. It will require effort and entrepreneurship to develop the needed complements, and adaptability at the individual, organizational, and societal levels to undertake the associated restructuring. Theory predicts that the winners will be those with the lowest adjustment costs and that put as many of the right complements in place as possible. This is partly a matter of good fortune, but with the right road map, it is also something for which they, and all of us, can prepare.

Appendix

Table 1A.1   Regressions with Newey-West standard errors with longer time dependence

	(1) 1 lag allowed	(2) 2 lags allowed	(3) 3 lags allowed	(4) 4 lags allowed	(5) 10 lags allowed
Newey-West regressions, ten-year average, labor productivity growth					
Previous ten-year average productivity growth	0.0857	0.0857	0.0857	0.0857	0.0857
	(0.177)	(0.207)	(0.227)	(0.242)	(0.278)
Constant	1.949***	1.949***	1.949***	1.949***	1.949***
	(0.398)	(0.465)	(0.511)	(0.545)	(0.624)
Observations	50	50	50	50	50
R-squared	0.009	0.009	0.009	0.009	0.009
Newey-West regressions, ten-year average, TFP growth					
Previous ten-year average TFP growth	0.136	0.136	0.136	0.136	0.136
	(0.158)	(0.181)	(0.197)	(0.208)	(0.233)
Constant	0.911***	0.911***	0.911***	0.911***	0.911***
	(0.188)	(0.216)	(0.233)	(0.244)	(0.257)
Observations	50	50	50	50	50
R-squared	0.023	0.023	0.023	0.023	0.023
Newey-West regressions, ten-year average, TFP (util. adj.) growth					
Previous ten-year average TFPua growth	0.158	0.158	0.158	0.158	0.158
	(0.187)	(0.221)	(0.246)	(0.266)	(0.311)
Constant	0.910***	0.910***	0.910**	0.910**	0.910**
	(0.259)	(0.306)	(0.341)	(0.368)	(0.412)
Observations	50	50	50	50	50
R-squared	0.030	0.030	0.030	0.030	0.030

Note: Standard errors in parentheses.

***Significant at the 1 percent level.

**Significant at the 5 percent level.

*Significant at the 10 percent level.

Table 1A.2   **Parameters for the toy economy J-curve**

Time	Net investment	Net capital stock	Investment growth rate	Capital stock growth rate	Output
0.0	1.0	10.0			10,000.0
1.0	15.0	25.0	14.0	1.5	10,500.0
2.0	80.0	105.0	4.3	3.2	11,025.0
3.0	160.0	265.0	1.0	1.5	11,576.3
4.0	220.0	485.0	0.4	0.8	12,155.1
5.0	250.0	735.0	0.1	0.5	12,762.8
6.0	220.0	955.0	−0.1	0.3	13,401.0
7.0	140.0	1,095.0	−0.4	0.1	14,071.0
8.0	100.0	1,195.0	−0.3	0.1	14,774.6
9.0	50.0	1,245.0	−0.5	0.0	15,513.3
10.0	20.0	1,265.0	−0.6	0.0	16,288.9
11.0	10.0	1,275.0	−0.5	0.0	17,103.4
12.0	0.0	1,275.0	−1.0	0.0	17,958.6

References

Abramovitz, Moses. 1956. "Resource and Output Trends in the U.S. Since 1870." *American Economic Review, Papers and Proceedings* 46 (2): 5–23.

Acemoglu, D., and P. Restrepo. 2017. "The Race between Machine and Man: Implications of Technology for Growth, Factor Shares and Employment." NBER Working Paper no. 22252, Cambridge, MA.

Agrawal, Ajay, Joshua Gans, and Avi Goldfarb. 2017. "What to Expect from Artificial Intelligence." *Sloan Management Review*, Feb. 7. https://sloanreview.mit.edu /article/what-to-expect-from-artificial-intelligence/.

Alloway, Tracy. 2015. "Goldman: How 'Grand Theft Auto' Explains One of the Biggest Mysteries of the U.S. Economy." *Bloomberg Business*, May 26. http:// www.bloomberg.com/news/articles/2015-05-26/goldman-how-grand-theft-auto -explains-one-of-the-biggest-mysteries-of-the-u-s-economy.

Alon, Titan, David Berger, Robert Dent, and Benjamin Pugsley. 2017. "Older and Slower: The Startup Deficit's Lasting Effects on Aggregate Productivity Growth." NBER Working Paper no. 23875, Cambridge, MA.

Andrews, Dan, Chiara Criscuolo, and Peter Gal. 2016. "The Best *versus* the Rest: The Global Productivity Slowdown, Divergence across Firms and the Role of Public Policy." OECD Productivity Working Papers no. 5, Paris, OECD Publishing. Dec. 2.

Aral, Sinan, Erik Brynjolfsson, and Lynn Wu. 2012. "Three-Way Complementarities: Performance Pay, HR Analytics and Information Technology." *Management Science* 58 (5): 913–31.

Arrow, Kenneth. 1962. "Economic Welfare and the Allocation of Resources for Invention." In *The Rate and Direction of Inventive Activity: Economic and Social Factors*, edited by Richard R. Nelson, 609–26. Princeton, NJ: Princeton University Press.

Atkeson, Andrew, and Patrick J. Kehoe. 2007. "Modeling the Transition to a New

Economy: Lessons from Two Technological Revolutions." *American Economic Review* 97 (1): 64–88.

Autor, David, David Dorn, Lawrence F. Katz, Christina Patterson, and John Van Reenen. 2017. "Concentrating on the Fall of the Labor Share." *American Economic Review, Papers and Proceedings* 107 (5): 180–85.

Autor, David, and Anna Salomons. 2017. "Robocalypse Now–Does Productivity Growth Threaten Employment?" European Central Bank Conference Proceedings, June.

Baumol, William, and William Bowen. 1966. *Performing Arts, The Economic Dilemma: A Study of Problems Common to Theater, Opera, Music, and Dance.* New York: Twentieth Century Fund.

Bessen, James E. 2017. "AI and Jobs: The Role of Demand." Law and Economics Research Paper no. 17-46, Boston University School of Law.

Bloom, Nicholas, Charles I. Jones, John Van Reenen, and Michael Webb. 2017. "Are Ideas Getting Harder to Find?" NBER Working Paper no. 23782, Cambridge, MA.

Bresnahan, Timothy, Erik Brynjolfsson, and Lorin Hitt. 2002. "Information Technology, Workplace Organization, and the Demand for Skilled Labor: Firm-Level Evidence." *Quarterly Journal of Economics* 117 (1): 339–76.

Bresnahan, Timothy F., and Manuel Trajtenberg. 1996. "General Purpose Technologies: 'Engines of Growth'?" *Journal of Econometrics, Annals of Econometrics* 65 (1): 83–108.

Bridgman, B., A. Dugan, M. Lal, M. Osborne, and S. Villones. 2012. "Accounting for Household Production in the National Accounts, 1965–2010." *Survey of Current Business* 92 (5): 23–36.

Brynjolfsson, Erik. 1993. "The Productivity Paradox of Information Technology." *Communications of the ACM* 36 (12): 66–77.

Brynjolfsson, Erik, and Lorin Hitt. 2000. "Beyond Computation: Information Technology, Organizational Transformation and Business Performance." *Journal of Economic Perspectives* 14 (4): 23–48.

———. 2003. "Computing Productivity: Firm-Level Evidence." *Review of Economics and Statistics* 85 (4): 793–808.

Brynjolfsson, Erik, Lorin Hitt, and Shinkyu Yang. 2002. "Intangible Assets: Computers and Organizational Capital." *Brookings Papers on Economic Activity* 2002 (1). Brookings Institution. https://www.brookings.edu/bpea-articles/intangible -assets-computers-and-organizational-capital/.

Brynjolfsson, Erik, and Andrew McAfee. 2011. *Race against the Machine.* Lexington, MA: Digital Frontier.

———. 2014. *The Second Machine Age: Work, Progress, and Prosperity in a Time of Brilliant Technologies.* New York: W. W. Norton & Company.

———. 2017. "What's Driving the Machine Learning Explosion?" *Harvard Business Review* 18:3–11. July.

Brynjolfsson, Erik, Andrew McAfee, Michael Sorell, and Feng Zhu. 2008. "Scale without Mass: Business Process Replication and Industry Dynamics." HBS Working Paper no. 07–016, Harvard Business School. https://hbswk.hbs.edu/item/scale -without-mass-business-process-replication-and-industry-dynamics.

Brynjolfsson, Erik, and Tom Mitchell. 2017. "What Can Machine Learning Do? Workforce Implications." *Science* 358 (6370): 1530–34.

Brynjolfsson, Erik, and Michael D. Smith. 2000. "Frictionless Commerce? A Comparison of Internet and Conventional Retailers." *Management Science* 46 (4): 563–85.

Byrne, David M., John G. Fernald, and Marshall B. Reinsdorf. 2016. "Does the

United States Have a Productivity Slowdown or a Measurement Problem?" *Brookings Papers on Economic Activity* Spring:109–82.

Cardarelli, Roberto, and Lusine Lusinyan. 2015. "U.S. Total Factor Productivity Slowdown: Evidence from the U.S. States." IMF Working Paper no. WP/15/116, International Monetary Fund.

Case, Anne, and Angus Deaton. 2017. "Mortality and Morbidity in the 21st Century." *Brookings Papers on Economic Activity* Spring: 397_476.

Cette, Gilbert, John G. Fernald, and Benoit Mojon. 2016. "The Pre-Great Recession Slowdown in Productivity." *European Economic Review* 88:3–20.

Conference Board. 2016. "The Conference Board Total Economy Database: Summary Tables (November 2016)." New York, The Conference Board.

Congressional Budget Office (CBO). 2016. *The Budget and Economic Outlook: 2016 to 2026.* https://www.cbo.gov/publication/51129.

———. 2017. *The 2017 Long-Term Budget Outlook.* https://www.cbo.gov/publication /52480.

Cowen, Tyler. 2011. *The Great Stagnation: How America Ate All the Low-Hanging Fruit of Modern History, Got Sick, and Will (Eventually) Feel Better.* New York: Dutton.

David, Paul. 1991. "Computer and Dynamo: The Modern Productivity Paradox in a Not-Too-Distant Mirror." In *Technology and Productivity: The Challenge for Economic Policy,* 315–47. Paris: OECD Publishing.

David, Paul A., and Gavin Wright. 2006. "General Purpose Technologies and Surges in Productivity: Historical Reflections on the Future of the ICT Revolution." In *The Economic Future in Historical Perspective,* vol. 13, edited by Paul A. David and Mark Thomas. Oxford: Oxford University Press.

De Loecker, Jan, and Jan Eeckhout. 2017. "The Rise of Market Power and the Macroeconomic Implications." NBER Working Paper no. 23687, Cambridge, MA.

Esteva, A., B. Kuprel, R. A. Novoa, J. Ko, S. M. Swetter, H. M. Blau, and S. Thrun. 2017. "Dermatologist-Level Classification of Skin Cancer with Deep Neural Networks." *Nature* 542 (7639): 115–18.

Feldstein, Martin. 2015. "The U.S. Underestimates Growth." *Wall Street Journal,* May 18.

Fernald, John G. 2014. "A Quarterly, Utilization-Adjusted Series on Total Factor Productivity." FRBSF Working Paper no. 2012–19, Federal Reserve Bank of San Francisco. Updated March 2014. https://www.frbsf.org/economic-research/files /wp12-19bk.pdf.

Fortunato, Meire, Mohammad Gheshlaghi Azar, Bilal Piot, Jacob Menick, Ian Osband, Alex Graves, Vlad Mnih, et al. 2017. "Noisy Networks for Exploration." arXiv preprint arXiv:1706.10295. https://arxiv.org/abs/1706.10295.

Furman, Jason, and Peter Orszag. 2015. "A Firm-Level Perspective on the Role of Rents in the Rise in Inequality." Presentation at A Just Society Centennial Event in Honor of Joseph Stiglitz at Columbia University, Oct. 16.

Gehring, J., M. Auli, D. Grangier, D. Yarats, and Y. N. Dauphin. 2017. "Convolutional Sequence to Sequence Learning." arXiv preprint arXiv:1705.03122. https:// arxiv.org/abs/1705.03122.

Gordon, Robert J. 2014. "The Demise of US Economic Growth: Restatement, Rebuttal, and Reflections." NBER Working Paper no. 19895, Cambridge, MA.

———. 2015. *The Rise and Fall of American Growth: The U.S. Standard of Living since the Civil War.* Princeton, NJ: Princeton University Press.

Gutiérrez, Germán, and Thomas Philippon. 2017. "Declining Competition and Investment in the U.S." NBER Working Paper no. 23583, Cambridge, MA.

Guvenen, Fatih, Raymond J. Mataloni Jr., Dylan G. Rassier, and Kim J. Ruhl. 2017. "Offshore Profit Shifting and Domestic Productivity Measurement." NBER Working Paper no. 23324, Cambridge, MA.

Hall, Robert E. 2000. "E-Capital: The Link between the Stock Market and the Labor Market in the 1990s." *Brookings Papers on Economic Activity* Fall:73–118.

Hatzius, Jan, and Kris Dawsey. 2015. "Doing the Sums on Productivity Paradox v2.0." *Goldman Sachs U.S. Economics Analyst*, no. 15/30.

Henderson, Rebecca. 1993. "Underinvestment and Incompetence as Responses to Radical Innovation: Evidence from the Photolithographic Industry." *RAND Journal of Economics* 24 (2): 248–70.

———. 2006. "The Innovator's Dilemma as a Problem of Organizational Competence." *Journal of Product Innovation Management* 23:5–11.

Holmes, Thomas J., David K. Levine, and James A. Schmitz. 2012. "Monopoly and the Incentive to Innovate When Adoption Involves Switchover Disruptions." *American Economic Journal: Microeconomics* 4 (3): 1–33.

Hortaçsu, Ali, and Chad Syverson. 2015. "The Ongoing Evolution of US Retail: A Format Tug-of-War." *Journal of Economic Perspectives* 29 (4): 89–112.

Jones, C. I., and P. M. Romer. 2010. "The New Kaldor Facts: Ideas, Institutions, Population, and Human Capital." *American Economic Journal: Macroeconomics* 2 (1): 224–45.

Jovanovic, Boyan, and Peter L. Rousseau. 2005. "General Purpose Technologies." In *Handbook of Economic Growth*, vol. 1B, edited by Philippe Aghion and Steven N. Durlauf, 1181–224. Amsterdam: Elsevier B.V.

Kendrick, John W. 1961. *Productivity Trends in the United States*. National Bureau of Economic Research. Princeton, NJ: Princeton University Press.

Levine, S., C. Finn, T. Darrell, and P. Abbeel. 2016. "End-to-End Training of Deep Visuomotor Policies." *Journal of Machine Learning Research* 17 (39): 1–40.

Levitt, Steven D., John A. List, and Chad Syverson. 2013. "Toward an Understanding of Learning by Doing: Evidence from an Automobile Plant." *Journal of Political Economy* 121 (4): 643–81.

Levy, Frank. 2018. "Computers and Populism: Artificial Intelligence, Jobs, and Politics in the Near Term." *Oxford Review of Economic Policy* 34 (3): 393–417.

Liu, Y., A. Gupta, P. Abbeel, and S. Levine. 2017. "Imitation from Observation: Learning to Imitate Behaviors from Raw Video via Context Translation." arXiv preprint arXiv:1707.03374. https://arxiv.org/abs/1707.03374.

Manyika, James, Michael Chui, Mehdi Miremadi, Jacques Bughin, Katy George, Paul Willmott, and Martin Dewhurst. 2017. "Harnessing Automation for a Future That Works." *McKinsey Global Institute*, January. https://www.mckinsey.com/global-themes/digital-disruption/harnessing-automation-for-a-future-that-works.

McAfee, Andrew, and Erik Brynjolfsson. 2008. "Investing in the IT that Makes a Competitive Difference." *Harvard Business Review* July:98.

Milgrom, P., and J. Roberts. 1996. "The LeChatelier Principle." *American Economic Review* 86 (1): 173–79.

Minsky, Marvin. 1967. *Computation: Finite and Infinite Machines*. Upper Saddle River, NJ: Prentice-Hall.

Mokyr, J. 2014. "Secular Stagnation? Not in Your Life." *Geneva Reports on the World Economy* August:83–89.

Morris, David Z. 2016. "Today's Cars Are Parked 95 Percent of the Time." *Fortune*, Mar. 13.

Nakamura, Leonard, and Rachel Soloveichik. 2015. "Capturing the Productivity

Impact of the 'Free' Apps and Other Online Media." FRBP Working Paper no. 15–25, Federal Reserve Bank of Philadelphia.

Nordhaus, W. D. 2015. "Are We Approaching an Economic Singularity? Information Technology and the Future of Economic Growth." NBER Working Paper no. 21547, Cambridge, MA.

Organisation for Economic Co-operation and Development (OECD). 2015. *The Future of Productivity*. https://www.oecd.org/eco/growth/OECD-2015-The-future-of-productivity-book.pdf.

Orlikowski, W. J. 1996. "Improvising Organizational Transformation over Time: A Situated Change Perspective." *Information Systems Research* 7 (1): 63–92.

Pratt, Gill A. 2015. "Is a Cambrian Explosion Coming for Robotics?" *Journal of Economic Perspectives* 29 (3): 51–60.

Saon, G., G. Kurata, T. Sercu, K. Audhkhasi, S. Thomas, D. Dimitriadis, X. Cui, et al. 2017. "English Conversational Telephone Speech Recognition by Humans and Machines." arXiv preprint arXiv:1703.02136. https://arxiv.org/abs/1703.02136.

Smith, Noah. 2015. "The Internet's Hidden Wealth." *Bloomberg View*, June 6. http://www.bloombergview.com/articles/2015-06-10/wealth-created-by-the-internet-may-not-appear-in-gdp.

Solow, Robert M. 1957. "Technical Change and the Aggregate Production Function." *Review of Economics and Statistics* 39 (3): 312–20.

———. 1987. "We'd Better Watch Out." *New York Times Book Review*, July 12, 36.

Song, Jae, David J. Price, Fatih Guvenen, Nicholas Bloom, and Till von Wachter. 2015. "Firming Up Inequality." NBER Working Paper no. 21199, Cambridge, MA.

Stiglitz, Joseph E. 2014. "Unemployment and Innovation." NBER Working Paper no. 20670, Cambridge, MA.

Syverson, Chad. 2013. "Will History Repeat Itself? Comments on 'Is the Information Technology Revolution Over?'" *International Productivity Monitor* 25:37–40.

———. 2017. "Challenges to Mismeasurement Explanations for the US Productivity Slowdown." *Journal of Economic Perspectives* 31 (2): 165–86.

Yang, Shinkyu, and Erik Brynjolfsson. 2001. "Intangible Assets and Growth Accounting: Evidence from Computer Investments." Unpublished manuscript, Massachusetts Institute of Technology.

Comment   Rebecca Henderson

"Artificial Intelligence and the Modern Productivity Paradox" is a fabulous chapter. It is beautifully written, extremely interesting, and goes right to the heart of a centrally important question, namely, what effects will AI have on economic growth? The authors make two central claims. The first is that AI

Rebecca Henderson is the John and Natty McArthur University Professor at Harvard University, where she has a joint appointment at the Harvard Business School in the General Management and Strategy units, and a research associate of the National Bureau of Economic Research.

For acknowledgments, sources of research support, and disclosure of the author's material financial relationships, if any, please see http://www.nber.org/chapters/c14020.ack.

is a general purpose technology, or GPT, and as such is likely to have a dramatic impact on productivity and economic growth. The second is that the reason we do not yet see it in the productivity statistics is because—like all GPTs—this is a technology that will take time to diffuse across the economy.

More specifically, the authors argue that AI will take time to diffuse because its adoption will require mastering "adjustment costs, organizational changes, and new skills." They suggest that just as we did not see IT in the productivity statistics until firms had made the organizational changes and hired the human capital necessary to master it, so the adoption of AI will require not only the diffusion of the technology itself but also the development of the organizational and human assets that will be required to exploit its full potential.

This is a fascinating idea. One of the reasons I like the chapter so much is that takes seriously an idea that economists long resisted—namely, that things as nebulous as "culture" and "organizational capabilities" might be (a) very important, (b) expensive, and (c) hard to change. Twenty-five years ago, when I submitted a paper to the *RAND Journal of Economics* that suggested that incumbents were fundamentally disadvantaged compared to entrants because they were constrained by old ways of acting and perceiving, I got a letter from the editor that began "Dear Rebecca, you have written a paper suggesting that the moon is made of green cheese, and that economists have too little considered the motions of cheesy planetoids"

I like to think that few editors would respond that way today. Thanks to a wave of new work in organizational economics and the pioneering empirical research of scholars like Nick Bloom, John van Reenen, Raffaella Sadun, and the authors themselves, we now have good reason to believe that managerial processes and organizational structures have very real effects on performance and that they take a significant time to change. One of the most exciting things about this chapter is that it takes these ideas sufficiently seriously to suggest that the current slowdown in productivity is largely a function of organizational inertia—that a central macroeconomic outcome is a function of a phenomenon that thirty years ago was barely on the radar.

That's exciting. Is it true? And if it is, what are its implications?

My guess is that the deployment of AI will indeed be gated by the need to change organizational structures and processes. But I think that the authors may be underestimating the implications of this dynamic in important ways.

Take the case of accounting. A few months ago, I happened to meet the chief strategy officer for one of the world's largest accounting firms. He told me that his firm is the largest hirer of college graduates in the world—which may or may not be true, but which he certainly believed—and that his firm was planning to reduce the number of college graduates they hire by 75 percent over the next four to five years—largely because it is increasingly clear that AI is going to be able to take over much of the auditing work currently performed by humans. This shift will certainly be mediated by every accounting firm's ability to integrate AI into their procedures and to persuade their customers that it is worth paying for—examples of exactly the kinds of barriers that this chapter suggests are so important—but in principle it should dramatically increase the productivity of accounting services, exactly the effects that Erik and his coauthors are hoping for.

But I am worried about all the college graduates the accounting firms are not going to hire. More broadly, as AI begins to diffuse across the economy it seems likely that a lot of people will get pushed into new positions and a lot of people will be laid off. And just as changing organizational processes takes time, so it's going to take time to remake the social context in ways that will make it possible to handle these dislocations. Without these kinds of investments—one can imagine they might be in education, in relocation assistance, and the like—there is a real risk of a public backlash against AI that could dramatically reduce its diffusion rate.

For example, the authors are excited about the benefits that the widespread diffusion of autonomous vehicles are likely to bring. Productivity seems likely to skyrocket, while with luck tens of thousands of people will no longer perish in car crashes every year. But "driving" is one of the largest occupations there is. What will happen when millions of people begin to be laid off? I'm with the authors in believing that the diffusion of AI could be an enormous source of innovation and growth. But I can see challenges in the transition at the societal level, as well as at the organizational level. And there will also be challenges if too large a share of the economic gains from the initial deployment of the technology goes to the owners of capital rather than to the rest of society.

Which is to say that I am a little more pessimistic than Erik and his coauthors as to the speed at which AI will diffuse—and this is even before I start talking about the issues that Scott, Iain, and I touch on in our own chapter, namely, that we are likely to have significant underinvestment in AI relative to the social option, coupled with a fair amount of dissipative racing.

2

The Technological Elements
of Artificial Intelligence

Matt Taddy

2.1 Introduction

We have seen in the past decade a sharp increase in the extent that companies use data to optimize their businesses. Variously called the "Big Data" or "Data Science" revolution, this has been characterized by massive amounts of data, including unstructured and nontraditional data like text and images, and the use of fast and flexible machine learning (ML) algorithms in analysis. With recent improvements in deep neural networks (DNNs) and related methods, application of high-performance ML algorithms has become more automatic and robust to different data scenarios. That has led to the rapid rise of an artificial intelligence (AI) that works by combining many ML algorithms together—each targeting a straightforward prediction task—to solve complex problems.

In this chapter, we will define a framework for thinking about the ingredients of this new ML-driven AI. Having an understanding of the pieces that make up these systems and how they fit together is important for those who will be building businesses around this technology. Those studying the economics of AI can use these definitions to remove ambiguity from the conversation on AI's projected productivity impacts and data requirements. Finally, this framework should help clarify the role for AI in the practice of modern business analytics[1] and economic measurement.

This article was written while Matt Taddy was professor of econometrics and statistics at the University of Chicago Booth School of Business and a principal researcher at Microsoft Research New England. He is currently at Amazon.com.

For acknowledgments, sources of research support, and disclosure of the author's material financial relationships, if any, please see http://www.nber.org/chapters/c14021.ack.

1. This material has been adapted from a chapter in *Business Data Science*, forthcoming from McGraw-Hill.

2.2 What Is AI?

In figure 2.1, we show a breakdown of AI into three major and essential pieces. A full end-to-end AI solution—at Microsoft, we call this a *System of Intelligence*—is able to ingest human-level knowledge (e.g., via machine reading and computer vision) and use this information to automate and accelerate tasks that were previously only performed by humans. It is necessary here to have a well-defined task structure to engineer against, and in a business setting this structure is provided by business and economic domain expertise. You need a massive bank of data to get the system up and running, and a strategy to continue generating data so that the system can respond and learn. And finally, you need machine-learning routines that can detect patterns in and make predictions from the unstructured data. This section will work through each of these pillars, and in later sections we dive in detail into deep learning models, their optimization, and data generation.

Notice that we are explicitly separating ML from AI here. This is important: these are different but often confused technologies. Machine learning can do fantastic things, but it is basically limited to predicting a future that looks mostly like the past. These are tools for pattern recognition. In contrast, an AI system is able to solve complex problems that have been previously reserved for humans. It does this by breaking these problems into a bunch of simple prediction tasks, each of which can be attacked by a "dumb" ML algorithm. Artificial intelligence *uses* instances of machine learning as components of the larger system. These ML instances need to be organized within a structure defined by domain knowledge, and they need to be fed data that helps them complete their allotted prediction tasks.

This is not to down-weight the importance of ML in AI. In contrast to earlier attempts at AI, the current instance of AI is *ML driven*. Machine-learning algorithms are implanted in every aspect of AI, and below we describe the evolution of ML toward status as a general purpose technology. This evolution is the main driver behind the current rise of AI. However, ML algorithms are building blocks of AI within a larger context.

To make these ideas concrete, consider an example AI system from the Microsoft-owned company Maluuba that was designed to play (and win!) the video game Ms. Pac-Man on Atari (van Seijen et al. 2017).The system

AI = Domain Structure	+	Data Generation	+	General Purpose ML
Business Expertise		Reinforcement Learning		Deep Neural Nets
Structural Econom[etr]ics		Big Data Assets		Video/Audio/Text
Relaxations and Heuristics		Sensor/Video Tracking		OOS + SGD + GPUs

Fig. 2.1 AI systems are self-training structures of ML predictors that automate and accelerate human tasks

is illustrated in figure 2.2. The player moves Ms. Pac-Man on this game "board," gaining rewards for eating pellets while making sure to avoid getting eaten by one of the adversarial "ghosts." The Maluuba researchers were able to build a system that learned how to master the game, achieving the highest possible score and surpassing human performance.

A common misunderstanding of AI imagines that, in a system like Maluuba's, the player of the game *is* a deep neural network. That is, the system works by swapping out the human joystick operator for an artificial DNN "brain." That is not how it works. Instead of a single DNN that is tied to the Ms. Pac-Man avatar (which is how the human player experiences the game), the Maluuba system is broken down into 163 component ML tasks. As illustrated on the right panel of figure 2.2, the engineers have assigned a distinct DNN routine to each cell of the board. In addition, they have DNNs that track the game characters: the ghosts and, of course, Ms. Pac-Man herself. The direction that the AI system sends Ms. Pac-Man at any point in the game is then chosen through consideration of the advice from each of these ML components. Recommendations from the components that are close to Ms. Pac-Man's current board position are weighted more strongly than those of currently remote locations. Hence, you can think of the ML algorithm assigned to each square on the board as having a simple task to solve: when Ms. Pac-Man crosses over this location, which direction should she go next?

Learning to play a video or board game is a standard way for AI firms to demonstrate their current capabilities. The Google DeepMind system AlphaGo (Silver et al. 2016), which was constructed to play the fantastically complex board game "go," is the most prominent of such demonstrations. The system was able to surpass human capability, beating the world champion, Lee Sedol, four matches to one at a live-broadcast event in Seoul, South Korea, in March 2016. Just as Maluuba's system broke Ms. Pac-Man into a number of composite tasks, AlphaGo succeeded by breaking Go into an even larger number of ML problems: "value networks" that evaluate different board positions and "policy networks" that recommend moves. The key point here is that while the composite ML tasks can be attacked with relatively generic DNNs, the full combined system is constructed in a way that is highly specialized to the structure of the problem at hand.

In figure 2.1, the first listed pillar of AI is *domain structure*. This is the structure that allows you to break a complex problem into composite tasks that can be solved with ML. The reason that AI firms choose to work with games is that such structure is explicit: the rules of the game are codified. This exposes the massive gap between playing games and a system that could replace humans in a real-world business application. To deal with the real world, you need to have a theory as to the rules of the relevant game. For example, if you want to build a system that can communicate with customers, you might proceed by mapping out customer desires and intents in

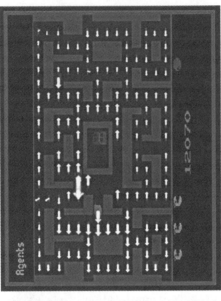

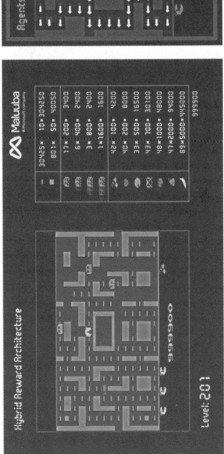

Fig. 2.2 Screenshots of the Maluuba system playing Ms. Pac-Man

Notes: On the left, we see the game board that contains a maze for Ms Pac-Man and the ghosts. On the right, the authors have assigned arrows showing the current direction for Ms. Pac-Man that is advised by different locations on the board, each corresponding to a distinct deep neural network. The full video is at https://youtu.be/zQyWMHFjewU .

such a way that allows different dialog-generating ML routines for each. Or, for any AI system that deals with marketing and prices in a retail environment, you need to be able to use the structure of an economic demand system to forecast how changing the price on a single item (which might, say, be the job of a single DNN) will affect optimal prices for other products and behavior of your consumers (who might themselves be modeled with DNNs).

The success or failure of an AI system is defined in a specific *context*, and you need to use the structure of that context to guide the architecture of your AI. This is a crucial point for businesses hoping to leverage AI and economists looking to predict its impact. As we will detail below, machine learning in its current form has become a *general purpose technology* (Bresnahan 2010). These tools are going to get cheaper and faster over time, due to innovations in the ML itself and above and below in the AI technology stack (e.g., improved software connectors for business systems above, and improved computing hardware like GPUs below). Macine learning has the potential to become a cloud-computing commodity.[2] In contrast, the domain knowledge necessary to combine ML components into an end-to-end AI solution will not be commoditized. Those who have expertise that can break complex human business problems into ML-solvable components will succeed in building the next generation of business AI, that which can do more than just play games.

In many of these scenarios, social science will have a role to play. Science is about putting structure and theory around phenomena that are observationally incredibly complex. Economics, as the social ccience closest to business, will often be relied upon to provide the rules for business AI. And since ML-driven AI relies upon measuring rewards and parameters inside its context, *econometrics* will play a key role in bridging between the assumed system and the data signals used for feedback and learning. The work will not translate directly. We need to build systems that allow for a certain margin of error in the ML algorithms. Those economic theories that apply for only a very narrow set of conditions—for example, at a knife's edge equilibrium—will be too unstable for AI. This is why we mention relaxations and heuristics in figure 2.1. There is an exciting future here where economists can contribute to AI engineering, and both AI and economics advance as we learn what recipes do or do not work for business AI.

Beyond ML and domain structure, the third pillar of AI in figure 2.1 is *data generation*. I am using the term "generation" here, instead of a more passive term like "collection," to highlight that AI systems require an active strategy to keep a steady stream of new and useful information flowing into the composite learning algorithms. In most AI applications there will

---

2. Amazon, Microsoft, and Google are all starting to offer basic ML capabilities like transcription and image classification as part of their cloud services. The prices for these services are low and mostly matched across providers.

be two general classes of data: fixed-size data assets that can be used to train the models for generic tasks, and data that is actively generated by the system as it experiments and improves performance. For example, in learning how to play Ms. Pac-Man the models could be initialized on a bank of data recording how humans have played the game. This is the fixed-size data asset. Then this initialized system starts to *play* the game of Ms. Pac-Man. Recalling that the system is broken into a number of ML components, as more games are played each component is able to experiment with possible moves in different scenarios. Since all of this is automated, the system can iterate through a massive number of games and quickly accumulate a wealth of experience.

For business applications, we should not underestimate the advantage of having large data assets to initialize AI systems. Unlike board or video games, real-world systems need to be able to interpret a variety of extremely subtle signals. For example, any system that interacts with human dialog must be able to understand the general domain language before it can deal with specific problems. For this reason, firms that have large banks of human interaction data (e.g., social media or a search engine) have a large technological advantage in conversational AI systems. However, this data just gets you started. The context-specific learning starts happening when, after this "warm start," the system begins interacting with real-world business events.

The general framework of ML algorithms actively choosing the data that they consume is referred to as reinforcement learning (RL).[3] It is a hugely important aspect of ML-driven AI, and we have a dedicated section on the topic. In some narrow and highly structured scenarios, researchers have build "zero-shot" learning systems where the AI is able to achieve high performance after starting without any static training data. For example, in subsequent research, Google DeepMind has developed the AlphaGoZero (Silver et al. 2017) system that uses zero-shot learning to replicate their earlier AlphaGo success. Noting that the RL is happening on the level of individual ML tasks, we can update our description of AI as being composed of many RL-driven ML components.

As a complement to the work on reinforcement learning, there is a lot of research activity around AI systems that can simulate "data" to appear as though it came from a real-world source. This has the potential to accelerate system training, replicating the success that the field has had with video and board games where experimentation is virtually costless (just play the game, nobody loses money or gets hurt). Generative adversarial networks (GANs; Goodfellow et al. 2014) are schemes where one DNN is simulating data and another is attempting to discern which data is real and which is simulated.

---

3. This is an old concept in statistics. In previous iterations, parts of reinforcement learning have been referred to as the sequential design of experiments, active learning, and Bayesian optimization.

For example, in an image-tagging application one network will generate captions for the image while the other network attempts to discern which captions are human versus machine generated. If this scheme works well enough, then you can build an image tagger while minimizing the number of dumb captions you need to show humans while training.

And finally, AI is pushing into physical spaces. For example, the Amazon Go concept promises a frictionless shopping checkout experience where cameras and sensors determine what you've taken from the shelves and charge you accordingly. These systems are as data intensive as any other AI application, but they have the added need to translate information from a physical to a digital space. They need to be able to recognize and track both objects and individuals. Current implementations appear to rely on a combination of object-based data sources via sensor and device networks (i.e., the IoT or Internet of Things), and video data from surveillance cameras. The sensor data has the advantage in that it is well structured and tied to objects, but the video data has the flexibility to look in places and at objects that you did not know to tag in advance. As computer vision technology advances, and as the camera hardware adapts and decreases in cost, we should see a shift in emphasis toward unstructured video data. We have seen similar patterns in AI development, for example, as use of raw conversation logs increases with improved machine reading capability. This is the progress of ML-driven AI toward general purpose forms.

2.3   General Purpose Machine Learning

The piece of AI that gets the most publicity—so much so that it is often confused with all of AI—is *general purpose* machine learning. Regardless of this slight overemphasis, it is clear that the recent rise of deep neural networks (DNNs; see section 2.5) is a main driver behind growth in AI. These DNNs have the ability to learn patterns in speech, image, and video data (as well as in more traditional structured data) faster, and more automatically, than ever before. They provide new ML capabilities and have completely changed the workflow of an ML engineer. However, this technology should be understood as a rapid evolution of existing ML capabilities rather than as a completely new object.

Machine learning is the field that thinks about how to automatically build robust predictions from complex data. It is closely related to modern statistics, and indeed many of the best ideas in ML have come from statisticians (the lasso, trees, forests, etc). But whereas statisticians have often focused *model inference*—on understanding the parameters of their models (e.g., testing on individual coefficients in a regression)—the ML community has been more focused on the single goal of maximizing *predictive performance*. The entire field of ML is calibrated against "out-of-sample" experiments that evaluate how well a model trained on one data set will predict new data.

And while there is a recent push to build more transparency into machine learning, wise ML practitioners will avoid assigning structural meaning to the parameters of their fitted models. These models are black boxes whose purpose is to do a good job in predicting a future that follows the same patterns as in past data.

Prediction is easier than model inference. This has allowed the ML community to quickly push forward and work with larger and more complex data. It also facilitated a focus on automation: developing algorithms that will work on a variety of different types of data with little or no tuning required. We have seen an explosion of general purpose ML tools in the past decade—tools that can be deployed on messy data and automatically tuned for optimal predictive performance.

The specific ML techniques used include high-dimensional ℓ_1 regularized regression (Lasso), tree algorithms and ensembles of trees (e.g., Random Forests), and neural networks. These techniques have found application in business problems under such labels as "data mining" and, more recently, "predictive analytics." Driven by the fact that many policy and business questions require more than just prediction, practitioners have added an emphasis on inference and incorporated ideas from statistics. Their work, combined with the demands and abundance of big data, coalesced together to form the loosely defined field of data science. More recently, as the field matures and as people recognize that not everything can be explicitly A/B tested, data scientists have discovered the importance of careful causal analysis. One of the most currently active areas of data science is combining ML tools with the sort of counterfactual inference that econometricians have long studied, hence now merging the ML and statistics material with the work of economists. See, for example, Athey and Imbens (2016), Hartford et al. (2017), and the survey in Athey (2017).

The push of ML into the general area of business analytics has allowed companies to gain insight from high-dimensional and unstructured data. This is only possible because the ML tools and recipes have become robust and usable enough that they can be deployed by nonexperts in computer science or statistics. That is, they can be used by people with a variety of quantitative backgrounds who have domain knowledge for their business use case. Similarly, the tools can be used by economists and other social scientists to bring new data to bear on scientifically compelling research questions. Again: the general usability of these tools has driven their adoption across disciplines. They come packaged as quality software and include validation routines that allow the user to observe how well their fitted models will perform in future prediction tasks.

The latest generation of ML algorithms, especially the deep learning technology that has exploded since around 2012 (Krizhevsky, Sutskever, and Hinton 2012), has increased the level of *automation* in the process of fitting and applying prediction models. This new class of ML is the *general purpose ML* (GPML) that we reference in the rightmost pillar of figure 2.1. The first component of GPML is deep neural networks: models made up of *layers* of nonlinear transformation *node* functions, where the output of each layer becomes input to the next layer in the network. We will describe DNNs in more detail in our Deep Learning section , but for now it suffices to say that they make it faster and easier than ever before to find patterns in unstructured data. They are also highly modular. You can take a layer that is optimized for one type of data (e.g., images) and combine it with other layers for other types of data (e.g., text). You can also use layers that have been pretrained on one data set (e.g., generic images) as components in a more specialized model (e.g., a specific recognition task).

Specialized DNN architectures are responsible for the key GPML capability of working on human-level data: video, audio, and text. This is essential for AI because it allows these systems to be installed on top of the same sources of knowledge that humans are able to digest. You don't need to create a new database system (or have an existing standard form) to feed the AI; rather, the AI can live on top of the chaos of information generated through business functions. This capability helps to illustrate why the new AI, based on GPML, is so much more promising than previous attempts at AI. Classical AI relied on hand-specified logic rules to mimic how a rational human might approach a given problem (Haugeland 1985). This approach is sometimes nostalgically referred to as GOFAI, or "good old-fashioned AI." The problem with GOFAI is obvious: solving human problems with logic rules requires an impossibly complex cataloging of all possible scenarios and actions. Even for systems able to learn from structured data, the need to have an explicit and detailed data schema means that the system designer must to know in advance how to translate complex human tasks into deterministic algorithms.

The new AI doesn't have this limitation. For example, consider the problem of creating a virtual agent that can answer customer questions (e.g., "why won't my computer start?"). A GOFAI system would be based on hand-coded dialog trees: if a user says *X*, answer *Y*, and so forth. To install the system, you would need to have human engineers understand and explicitly code for all of the main customer issues. In contrast, the new ML-driven AI can simply ingest all of your existing customer-support logs and learn to replicate how human agents have answered customer questions in the past. The ML allows your system to infer support patterns from the human conversations. The installation engineer just needs to start the DNN-fitting routine.

This gets to the last bit of GPML that we highlight in figure 2.1, the tools that facilitate model fitting on massive data sets: out-of-sample (OOS) validation for model tuning, stochastic gradient descent (SGD) for parameter optimization, and graphical processing units (GPUs) and other computer hardware for massively parallel optimization. Each of these pieces is essential for the success of large-scale GPML. Although they are commonly associated with deep learning and DNNs (especially SGD and GPUs), these tools have developed in the context of many different ML algorithms. The rise of DNNs over alternative ML modeling schemes is partly due to the fact that, through trial and error, ML researchers have discovered that neural network models are especially well suited to engineering within the context of these available tools (LeCun et al. 1998).

Out-of-sample validation is a basic idea: you choose the best model specification by comparing predictions from models estimated on data that was not used during the model "training" (fitting). This can be formalized as a cross-validation routine: you split the data into K "folds," and then K times fit the model on all data but the Kth fold and evaluate its predictive performance (e.g., mean squared error or misclassification rate) on the left-out fold. The model with optimal average OOS performance (e.g., minimum error rate) is then deployed in practice.

Machine learning's wholesale adoption of OOS validation as the arbitrator of model quality has freed the ML engineer from the need to *theorize* about model quality. Of course, this can create frustration and delays when you have nothing other than "guess-and-test" as a method for model selection. But, increasingly, the requisite model search is not being executed by humans: it is done by additional ML routines. This either happens explicitly, in *AutoML* (Feurer et al. 2015) frameworks that use simple auxiliary ML to predict OOS performance of the more complex target model, or implicitly by adding flexibility to the target model (e.g., making the tuning parameters part of the optimization objective). The fact that OOS validation provides a clear target to optimize against—a target which, unlike the in-sample likelihood, does not incentive over-fit—facilitates automated model tuning. It removes humans from the process of adapting models to specific data sets.

Stochastic gradient descent optimization will be less familiar to most readers, but it is a crucial part of GPML. This class of algorithms allows models to be fit to data that is only observed in small chunks: you can train the model on a *stream* of data and avoid having to do *batch* computations on the entire data set. This lets you estimate complex models on massive data sets. For subtle reasons, the engineering of SGD algorithms also tends to encourage robust and generalizable model fits (i.e., use of SGD discourages over-fit). We cover these algorithms in detail in a dedicated section.

Finally, the GPUs: specialized computer processors have made massive-scale ML a reality, and continued hardware innovation will help push AI to new domains. Deep neural network training with stochastic gradient descent involves massively *parallel* computations: many basic operations executed simultaneously across parameters of the network. Graphical processing units were devised for calculations of this type, in the context of video and computer graphics display where all pixels of an image need to be rendered simultaneously, in parallel. Although DNN training was originally a side use case for GPUs (i.e., as an aside from their main computer graphics mandate), AI applications are now of primary importance for GPU manufacturers. Nvidia, for example, is a GPU company whose rise in market value has been driven by the rise of AI.

The technology here is not standing still. The GPUs are getting faster and cheaper every day. We are also seeing the deployment of new chips that have been designed from scratch for ML optimization. For example, field-programmable gate arrays (FPGAs) are being used by Microsoft and Amazon in their data centers. These chips allow precision requirements to be set dynamically, thus efficiently allocating resources to high-precision operations and saving compute effort where you only need a few decimal points (e.g., in early optimization updates to the DNN parameters). As another example, Google's Tensor Processing Units (TPUs) are specifically designed for algebra with "tensors," a mathematical object that occurs commonly in ML.[4]

One of the hallmarks of a general purpose technology is that it leads to broad industrial changes, both above and below where that technology lives in the supply chain. This is what we are observing with the new general purpose ML. Below, we see that chip makers are changing the type of hardware they create to suit these DNN-based AI systems. Above, GPML has led to a new class of ML-driven AI products. As we seek more real-world AI capabilities—self-driving cars, conversational business agents, intelligent economic marketplaces—domain experts in these areas will need to find ways to resolve their complex questions into structures of ML tasks. This is a role that economists and business professionals should embrace, where the increasingly user-friendly GPML routines become basic tools of their trade.

2.4 Deep Learning

We have stated that deep neural networks are a key tool in GPML, but what exactly are they? And what makes them *deep*? In this section we will give a high-level overview of these models. This is not a user guide. For that, we recommend the excellent recent textbook by Goodfellow, Bengio, and Courville (2016). This is a rapidly evolving area of research, and new types of neural network models and estimation algorithms are being developed at a steady clip. The excitement in this area, and considerable media and business hype, makes it difficult to keep track. Moreover, the tendency of ML companies and academics to proclaim every incremental change as "completely brand new" has led to a messy literature that is tough for newcomers to navigate. But there is a general structure to deep learning, and a

---

4. A tensor is a multidimensional extension of a matrix—that is, a matrix is another name for a two-dimensional tensor.

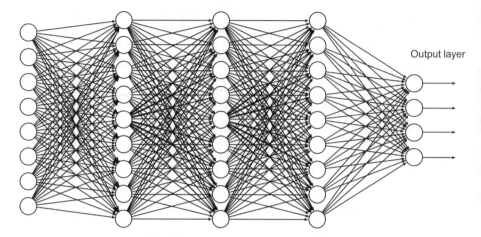

Fig. 2.3   A five-layer network
Source: Adapted from Nielsen (2015).

hype-free understanding of this structure should give you insight into the reasons for its success.

Neural networks are simple models. Indeed, their simplicity is a strength: basic patterns facilitate fast training and computation. The model has linear combinations of inputs that are passed through nonlinear activation functions called nodes (or, in reference to the human brain, neurons). A set of nodes taking different weighted sums of the same inputs is called a "layer," and the output of one layer's nodes becomes input to the next layer. This structure is illustrated in figure 2.3. Each circle here is a node. Those in the input (farthest left) layer typically have a special structure; they are either raw data or data that has been processed through an additional set of layers (e.g., convolutions as we will describe). The output layer gives your predictions. In a simple regression setting, this output could just be $\hat{y}$, the predicted value for some random variable y, but DNNs can be used to predict all sorts of high-dimensional objects. As it is for nodes in input layers, output nodes also tend to take application-specific forms.

Nodes in the interior of the network have a "classical" neural network structure. Say that $\eta_{hk}(\cdot)$ is the kth node in interior layer h. This node takes as input a weighted combination of the output of the nodes in the previous layer of the network, layer $h - 1$, and applies a *nonlinear* transformation to yield the output. For example, the ReLU (for "rectified linear unit") node is by far the most common functional form used today; it simply outputs the maximum of its input and zero, as shown in figure 2.4.[5] Say z_{ij}^{h-1} is output of

5. In the 1990s, people spent much effort choosing among different node transformation functions. More recently, the consensus is that you can just use a simple and computationally convenient transformation (like ReLU). If you have enough nodes and layers the specific transformation doesn't really matter, so long as it is nonlinear.

node j in layer $h - 1$ for observation i. Then the corresponding output for the kth node in the hth layer can be written

(1)
$$z_{ik}^{h} = \eta_{hk}\left(\omega_{h'}\mathbf{z}_{i}^{h-1}\right) = \max\left(0, \sum_{j}\omega_{hj}z_{ij}^{h-1}\right),$$

where ω_{hj} are the network *weights*. For a given network architecture—the structure of nodes and layers—these weights are the parameters that are updated during network training.

Neural networks have a long history. Work on these types of models dates back to the mid-twentieth century, for example, including Rosenblatt's Perceptron (Rosenblatt 1958). This early work was focused on networks as models that could mimic the actual structure of the human brain. In the late 1980s, advances in algorithms for *training* neural networks (Rumelhart et al. 1988) opened the potential for these models to act as general pattern-recognition tools rather than as a toy model of the brain. This led to a boom in neural network research, and methods developed during the 1990s are at the foundation of much of deep learning today (Hochreiter and Schmidhuber 1997; LeCun et al. 1998). However, this boom ended in bust. Due to the gap between promised and realized results (and enduring difficulties in training networks on massive data sets) from the late 1990s, neural networks became just one ML method among many. In applications they were supplanted by more robust tools such as Random Forests, high-dimensional regularized regression, and a variety of Bayesian stochastic process models.

In the 1990s, one tended to add network complexity by adding *width*. A couple of layers (e.g., a single hidden layer was common) with a large number of nodes in each layer were used to approximate complex functions.

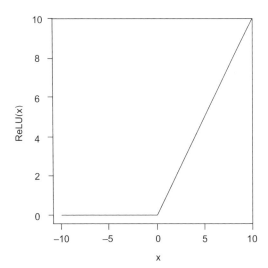

Fig. 2.4   The ReLU function

Researchers had established that such "wide" learning could approximate arbitrary functions (Hornik, Stinchcombe, and White 1989) if you were able to train on enough data. The problem, however, was that this turns out to be an inefficient way to learn from data. The wide networks are very *flexible*, but they need a ton of data to tame this flexibility. In this way, the wide nets resemble traditional *nonparametric* statistical models like series and kernel estimators. Indeed, near the end of the 1990s, Radford Neal showed that certain neural networks converge toward Gaussian Processes, a classical statistical regression model, as the number of nodes in a single layer grows toward infinity (Neal 2012). It seemed reasonable to conclude that neural networks were just clunky versions of more transparent statistical models.

What changed? A bunch of things. Two nonmethodological events are of primary importance: we got much more data (big data) and computing hardware became much more efficient (GPUs). But there was also a crucial methodological development: networks went *deep*. This breakthrough is often credited to 2006 work by Geoff Hinton and coauthors (Hinton, Osindero, and Teh 2006) on a network architecture that stacked many *pretrained* layers together for a handwriting recognition task. In this pretraining, interior layers of the network are fit using an *unsupervised* learning task (i.e., dimension reduction of the inputs) before being used as part of the supervised learning machinery. The idea is analogous to that of principal components regression: you first fit a low-dimensional representation of **x**, then use that low-D representation to predict some associated y. Hinton and colleague's scheme allowed researchers to train deeper networks than was previously possible.

This specific type of unsupervised pretraining is no longer viewed as central to deep learning. However, Hinton, Osindero, and Teh's (2006) paper opened many people's eyes to the potential for deep neural networks: models with many layers, each of which may have different structure and play a very different role in the overall machinery. That is, a demonstration that one *could* train deep networks soon turned into a realization that one *should* add depth to models. In the following years, research groups began to show empirically and theoretically that depth was important for learning efficiently from data (Bengio et al. 2007). The *modularity* of a deep network is key: each layer of functional structure plays a specific role, and you can swap out layers like Lego blocks when moving across data applications. This allows for fast application-specific model development, and also for *transfer learning* across models: an internal layer from a network that has been trained for one type of image recognition problem can be used to hot-start a new network for a different computer vision task.

Deep learning came into the ML mainstream with a 2012 paper by Krizhevsky, Sutskever, and Hinton (2012) that showed their DNN was able to smash current performance benchmarks in the well-known ImageNet computer vision contest. Since then, the race has been on. For example,

A	B	C
D	E	F
G	H	I

$\star$

ω_1	ω_2
ω_3	ω_4

$=$

$\omega_1 A + \omega_2 B + \omega_3 D + \omega_4 E$	$\omega_1 B + \omega_2 C + \omega_3 E + \omega_4 F$
$\omega_1 D + \omega_2 E + \omega_3 G + \omega_4 H$	$\omega_1 E + \omega_2 F + \omega_3 H + \omega_4 I$

Fig. 2.5   A basic convolution operation

Notes: The pixels A, B, and so forth, are multiplied and summed across kernel weights ω_k. The kernel here is applied to every 2×2 submatrix of our "image."

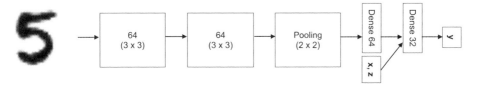

Fig. 2.6   The network architecture used in Hartford et al. (2017)

Notes: Variables x, z contain structured business information (e.g., product IDs and prices) that is mixed with images of handwritten digits in our network.

image classification performance has surpassed human abilities (He et al. 2016) and DNNs are now able to both recognize images and generate appropriate captions (Karpathy and Fei-Fei 2015).

The models behind these computer vision advances all make use of a specific type of *convolution* transformation. The raw image data (pixels) goes through multiple convolution layers before the output of those convolutions is fed into the more classical neural network architecture of equation (1) and figure 2.3. A basic image convolution operation is shown in figure 2.5: you use a *kernel* of weights to combine image pixels in a local area into a single output pixel in a (usually) lower-dimensional output image. So-called convolutional neural networks (CNNs; LeCun and Bengio 1995) illustrate the strategy that makes deep learning so successful: it is convenient to stack layers of different specializations such that image-specific functions (convolutions) can feed into layers that are good at representing generic functional forms. In a contemporary CNN, typically, you will have multiple layers of convolutions feeding into ReLU activations and, eventually, into a *max pooling* layer constructed of nodes that output the maximum of each input matrix.[6] For example, figure 2.6 shows the very simple architecture that we used in Hartford et al. (2017) for a task that mixed digit recognition with (simulated) business data.

This is a theme of deep learning: the models use early layer transformations that are specific to the input data format. For images, you use CNNs.

---

6. Convolutional neural networks are a huge and very interesting area. The textbook by Goodfellow, Bengio, and Courville (2016) is a good place to start if you want to learn more.

Fig. 2.7   A cartoon of a DNN, taking as input images, structured data $x_1 \ldots x_{\mathrm{big}}$**, and raw document text**

For text data, you need to *embed* words into a vector space. This can happen through a simple word2vec transformation (Mikolov et al. 2013) (a linear decomposition on the matrix of co-occurrence counts for words; for example, within three words of each other) or through a LSTM (long short-term memory) architecture (Hochreiter and Schmidhuber 1997)—models for sequences of words or letters that essentially mix a hidden Markov model (long) with an autoregressive process (short). And there are many other variants, with new architectures being developed every day.[7]

One thing should be clear: there is a lot of *structure* in DNNs. These models are *not* similar to the sorts of nonparametric regression models used by statisticians, econometricians, and in earlier ML. They are *semi-parametric*. Consider the cartoon DNN in figure 2.7. The early stages in the network provide dramatic, and often linear, dimension reduction. These early stages are highly parametric: it makes no sense to take a convolution model for image data and apply it to, say, consumer transaction data. The output of these early layers is then processed through a series of classical neural network nodes, as in equation (1). These later network layers work like a traditional nonparametric regression: they expand the output of early layers to approximate arbitrary functional forms in the response of interest. Thus, the DNNs combine restrictive dimension reduction with flexible function approximation. The key is that both components are learned jointly.

As warned at the outset, we have covered only a tiny part of the area of deep learning. There is a ton of exciting new material coming out of both industry and academia. (For a glimpse of what is happening in the

---

7. For example, the new *Capsule* networks of Sabour, Frosst, and Hinton (2017) replace the max-pooling of CNNs with more structured summarization functions.

field, browse the latest proceedings of NIPS [Neural Information Processing Systems, the premier ML conference] at https://papers.nips.cc/). You will see quickly the massive breadth of current research. One currently hot topic is on uncertainty quantification for deep neural networks, another is on understanding how imbalance in training data leads to potentially biased predictions. Topics of this type are gaining prominence as DNNs are moving away from academic competitions and into real-world applications. As the field grows, and DNN model construction moves from a scientific to an engineering discipline, we will see more need for this type of research that tells us when and how much we can trust the DNNs.

2.5   Stochastic Gradient Descent

To give a complete view of deep learning, we need to describe the one algorithm that is relied upon for training all of the models: SGD. Stochastic gradient descent optimization is a twist on gradient descent (GD), the previously dominant method for minimizing any function that you can differentiate. Given a minimization objective $\mathcal{L}(\Omega)$, where Ω is the full set of model parameters, each iteration of a gradient descent routine updates from current parameters Ω_t as

$$(2) \qquad \Omega_{t+1} = \Omega_t - C_t \nabla \mathcal{L} \mid_{\Omega_t},$$

where $\nabla \mathcal{L} \mid_{\Omega_t}$ is the gradient of $\mathcal{L}$ evaluated at the current parameters and C_t is a projection matrix that determines the size of the steps taken in the direction implied by $\nabla \mathcal{L}$.[8] We have the subscript t on C_t because this projection can be allowed to update during the optimization. For example, Newton's algorithm uses C_t equal to the matrix of objective second derivatives, $\nabla^2 \mathcal{L} \mid_{\Omega_t}$.

It is often stated that neural networks are trained through "back-propagation," which is not quite correct. Rather, they are trained through variants of gradient descent. Back-propagation (Rumelhart et al. 1988), or back-prop for short, is a method for calculating gradients on the parameters of a network. In particular, back-prop is just an algorithmic implementation of your chain rule from calculus. In the context of our simple neuron from equation (1), the gradient calculation for a single weight ω_{hj} is

$$(3) \qquad \frac{\partial \mathcal{L}}{\partial \omega_{hj}} = \sum_{i=1}^{n} \frac{\partial \mathcal{L}}{\partial z_{ij}^h} \frac{\partial z_{ij}^h}{\partial \omega_{hj}} = \sum_{i=1}^{n} \frac{\partial \mathcal{L}}{\partial z_{ij}^h} z_{ij}^{h-1} 1_{[0 < \Sigma_j \omega_{hj} z_{ij}^{h-1}]}.$$

Another application of the chain rule can be used to expand $\partial \mathcal{L} / \partial z_{ij}^h$ as $\partial \mathcal{L} / \partial z_{ij}^{h+1} * \partial z_{ij}^{h+1} / \partial z_{ij}^h$, and so on until you have written the full gradient as a product of layer-specific operations. The directed structure of the network lets you efficiently calculate all of the gradients by working backward layer

---

8. If $\Omega = [\omega_1 \ldots \omega_p]$, then $\nabla \mathcal{L}(\Omega) = [(\partial \mathcal{L}/\partial \omega_1) \ldots (\partial L/\partial \omega_p)]$. The *Hessian* matrix, $\nabla^2 \mathcal{L}$, has elements $[\nabla^2 \mathcal{L}]_{jk} = \partial L^2/\partial \omega_j \partial \omega_k)$.

by layer, from the response down to the inputs. This recursive application of the chain rule, and the associated computation recipes, make up the general back-prop algorithm.

In statistical estimation and ML model training, $\mathcal{L}$ typically involves a loss function that *sums* across data observations. For example, assuming an ℓ_2 (ridge) regularization penalty on the parameters, the *minimization* objective corresponding to regularized likelihood maximization over n independent observations d_i (e.g., $d_i = [\mathbf{x}_i, y_i]$ for regression) can be written as

$$(4) \qquad \mathcal{L}(\Omega) \equiv \mathcal{L}\left(\Omega; \{d_i\}_{i=1}^n\right) = \sum_{i=1}^n \left[-\log p(z_i \mid \Omega) + \lambda \| \Omega \|_2^2 \right],$$

where $\| \Omega \|_2^2$ is the sum of all squared parameters in Ω. More generally, $\mathcal{L}\left(\Omega; \{d_i\}_{i=1}^n\right)$ can consist of any loss function that involves summation over observations. For example, to model predictive uncertainty we often work with quantile loss. Define $\tau_q(\mathbf{x};\Omega)$ as the *quantile function*, parametrized by Ω, that maps from covariates $\mathbf{x}$ to the qth quantile of the response y:

$$(5) \qquad \mathrm{P}\left(y < \tau_q(\mathbf{x};\Omega) \mid \mathbf{x}\right) = q.$$

We fit τ_q to minimize the regularized quantile loss function (again assuming a ridge penalty):

$$(6) \qquad \mathcal{L}(\Omega; \{d_i\}_{i=1}^n) = \sum_{i=1}^n \left[(y_i - \tau_q(\mathbf{x}_i;\Omega))(q - 1_{[y_i < \tau_q(\mathbf{x}_i;\Omega)]}) + \lambda \| \Omega \|_2^2 \right].$$

The very common "sum of squared errors" criterion, possibly regularized, is another loss function that fits this pattern of summation over observations.

In all of these cases, the gradient calculations required for the updates in equation (2) involve sums over all n observations. That is, each calculation of $\nabla \mathcal{L}$ requires an order of n calculations. For example, in a ridge penalized linear regression where $\Omega = \boldsymbol{\beta}$, the vector of regression coefficients, the jth gradient component is

$$(7) \qquad \frac{\partial \mathcal{L}}{\partial \beta_j} = \sum_{i=1}^n \left[(y_i - \mathbf{x}_i \boldsymbol{\beta}) x_j + \lambda \beta_j \right].$$

The problem for massive data sets is that when n is really big these calculations become prohibitively expense. The issue is aggravated when, as it is for DNNs, Ω is high dimensional and there are complex calculations required in each gradient summand. GDGradient descent is the best optimization tool that we've got, but it becomes computationally infeasible for massive data sets.

The solution is to replace the actual gradients in equation (2) with *estimates* of those gradients based upon a subset of the data. This is the SGD algorithm. It has a long history, dating back to the Robbins-Monro (Robbins and Monro 1951) algorithm proposed by a couple of statisticians in 1951. In the most common versions of SGD, the full-sample gradient is simply replaced by the gradient on a smaller subsample. Instead of calculating gradients on the full-sample loss, $\mathcal{L}(\Omega;\{d_i\}_{i=1}^{n})$, we descend according to subsample calculations:

$$(8) \qquad \Omega_{t+1} = \Omega_t - C_t \nabla \mathcal{L}\left(\Omega;\{d_{i_b}\}_{b=1}^{B}\right)\big|_{\Omega_t},$$

where $\{d_{i_b}\}_{b=1}^{B}$ is a *mini-batch* of observations with $B \ll n$. The key mathematical result behind SGD is that, so long as the sequence of C_t matrices satisfy some basic requirements, the SGD algorithm will converge to a local optimum whenever $\nabla \mathcal{L}\left(\Omega;\{d_{i_b}\}_{b=1}^{B}\right)$ is an *unbiased* estimate of the full-sample gradient.[9] That is, SGD convergence relies upon

$$(9) \qquad E\left[\frac{1}{B}\nabla \mathcal{L}\left(\Omega;\{d_{i_b}\}_{b=1}^{B}\right)\right] = E\left[\frac{1}{n}\nabla \mathcal{L}\left(\Omega;\{d_i\}_{i=1}^{n}\right)\right] = E\nabla \mathcal{L}(\Omega;d),$$

where the last term here refers to the *population* expected gradient—that is, the average gradient for observation d drawn from the true data generating process.

To understand why SGD is so preferable to GD for machine learning, it helps to discuss how computer scientists think about the *constraints* on estimation. Statisticians and economists tend to view sample size (i.e., lack of data) as the binding constraint on their estimators. In contrast, in many ML applications the data is practically unlimited and continues to grow during system deployment. Despite this abundance, there is a fixed computational budget (or the need to update in near-real-time for streaming data), such that we can only execute a limited number of operations when crunching through the data. Thus, in ML, the binding constraint is the amount of computation rather than the amount of data.

Stochastic gradient descent trades faster updates for a slower per-update convergence rate. As nicely explained in a 2008 paper by Bottou and Bousquet (Bottou and Bousquet 2008), this trade is worthwhile when the faster updates allow you to expose your model to more data than would otherwise be possible. To see this, note that the mini-batch gradient $B^{-1}\nabla \mathcal{L}\left(\Omega;\{d_{i_b}\}_{b=1}^{B}\right)$ has a much higher variance than the full-sample gradient, $n^{-1}\nabla \mathcal{L}\left(\Omega;\{d_i\}_{i=1}^{n}\right)$. This variance introduces noise into the optimization updates. As a result, for a fixed data sample n, the GD algorithm will tend to take far fewer iterations than SGD to get to a minimum of the *in-sample* loss, $\mathcal{L}(\Omega;\{d_i\}_{i=1}^{n})$. However, in DNN training we don't really care about the in-sample loss. We really want to minimize future prediction loss—that is, we want to minimize the *population* loss function $E\mathcal{L}(\Omega;d)$. And the best way to understand the population loss is to see as much data as possible. Thus if the variance of the SGD updates is not too large, it is more valuable to spend computational

9. You can actually get away with biased gradients. In Hartford et al. (2017) we find that trading bias for variance can actually improve performance. But this is tricky business and in any case the bias must be kept very small.

effort streaming through more data than to spend it on minimizing the variance of each individual optimization update.

This is related to an important high-level point about SGD: the nature of the algorithm is such that engineering steps taken to improve *optimization* performance will tend to also improve *estimation* performance. The same tweaks and tricks that lower the variance of each SGD update will lead to fitted models that generalize better when predicting new unseen data. The "train faster, generalize better" paper by Hardt, Recht, and Singer (2016) explains this phenomenon within the framework of algorithm stability. For SGD to converge in fewer iterations means that the gradients on new observations (new mini-batches) are approaching zero more quickly. That is, faster SGD convergence means by definition that your model fits are generalizing better to unseen data. Contrast this with full-sample GD, for example, for likelihood maximization: faster convergence implies only quicker fitting on your current sample, potentially overfitting for future data. A reliance on SGD has made it relatively easy for deep learning to progress from a scientific to engineering discipline. Faster is better, so the engineers tuning SGD algorithms for DNNs can just focus on convergence speed.

On the topic of tuning SGD: real-world performance is very sensitive to the choice of C_t, the projection matrix in equation (8). For computational reasons, this matrix is usually diagonal (i.e., it has zeros off of the diagonal) such that entries of C_t dictate your *step-size* in the direction of each parameter gradient. Stochastic gradient descent algorithms have often been studied theoretically under a single step-size, such that $C_t = \gamma_t I$ where γ_t is a scalar and I is the identity matrix. Unfortunately, this simple specification will underperform and even fail to converge if γ_t is not going toward zero at a precise rate (Toulis, Airoldi, and Rennie 2014). Instead, practitioners make use of algorithms where $C_t = [\gamma_{1t} \cdots \gamma_{pt}]I$, with p the dimension of Ω, and each γ_{jt} is chosen to approximate $\partial^2 \mathcal{L} / \partial \omega_j^2$, the corresponding diagonal element of the Hessian matrix of loss-function second derivatives (i.e., what would be used in a Newton's algorithm). The ADAGRAD paper (Duchi, Hazan, and Singer 2011) provides a theoretical foundation for this approach and suggests an algorithm for specifying γ_{jt}. Most deep learning systems make use of ADAGRAD-inspired algorithms, such as ADAM (Kingma and Ba 2015), that combine the original algorithm with heuristics that have been shown empirically to improve performance.

Finally, there is another key trick to DNN training: *dropout*. This procedure, proposed by researchers (Srivastava et al. 2014) in Hinton's lab at the University of Toronto, involves introduction of random noise into each gradient calculation. For example, "Bernoulli dropout" replaces current estimates ω_{tj} with $w_{tj} = \omega_{tj} * \xi_{tj}$ where ξ_{tj} is a Bernoulli random variable with $p(\xi_{tj} = 1) = c$. Each SGD update from equation (8) then uses these parameter values when evaluating the gradient, such that

(10)
$$\Omega_{t+1} = \Omega_t - C_t \nabla f\left(\Omega; \{d_{i_b}\}_{b=1}^B\right)\big|_{W_t},$$

where W_t is the noised-up version of Ω_t, with elements w_{tj}.

Dropout is used because it has been observed to yield model fits that have lower out-of-sample error rates (so long as you tune c appropriately). Why does this happen? Informally, dropout acts as a type of implicit regularization. An example of explicit regularization is parameter penalization: to avoid over-fit, the minimization objective for DNNs almost always has a $\lambda \|\Omega\|_2^2$ ridge penalty term added to the data-likelihood loss function. Dropout plays a similar role. By forcing SGD updates to ignore a random sample of the parameters, it prevents over-fit on any individual parameter.[10] More rigorously, it has recently been established by a number of authors (Kendall and Gal 2017) that SGD with dropout corresponds to a type of "variational Bayesian Inference." That means that dropout SGD is solving to find the posterior *distribution* over Ω rather than a point estimate.[11] As interest grows around uncertainty quantification for DNNs, this interpretation of dropout is one option for bringing Bayesian inference into deep learning.

2.6   Reinforcement Learning

As our final section on the elements of deep learning, we will consider how these AI systems generate their own training data through a mix of experimentation and optimization. Reinforcement learning (RL) is the common term for this aspect of AI. Reinforcement learning is sometimes used to denote specific algorithms, but we are using it to refer to the full area of active data collection.

The general problem can be formulated as a reward-maximization task. You have some policy or "action" function, $d(x_t; \Omega)$, that dictates how the system responds to "event" t with characteristics x_t. The event could be a customer arriving on your website at a specific time, or a scenario in a video game, and so forth. After the event, you observe "response" y_t and the reward is calculated as $r(d(x_t; \Omega), y_t)$. During this process you are accumulating data and *learning* the parameters Ω, so we can write Ω_t as the parameters used at event t. The goal is that this learning converges to some optimal reward-maximizing parametrization, say $\Omega^{\mathring{a}}$, and that this happens after some T events where T is not too big—that is, so that you minimize *regret*,

(11)
$$\sum_{t=1}^{T}\left[r\left(d(x_t; \Omega^{\mathring{a}}), y_t\right) - r\left(d(x_t; \Omega_t), y_t\right)\right].$$

---

10. This seems to contradict our earlier discussion about minimizing the variance of gradient estimates. The distinction is that we want to minimize variance due to noise in the data, but here we are introducing noise in the parameters *independent* of the data.

11. It is a strange variational distribution, but basically the posterior distribution over Ω becomes that implied by W, with elements ω_j multiplied by random Bernoulli noise.

This is a very general formulation. We can map it to some familiar scenarios. For example, suppose that the event t is a user landing on your website. You would like to show a banner advertisement on the landing page, and you want to show the ad that has the highest probability of getting clicked by the user. Suppose that there are J different possible ads you can show, such that your action $d_t = d(x_t;\Omega_t) \in \{1, \ldots, J\}$ is the one chosen for display. The final reward is $y_t = 1$ if the user clicks the ad and $y_t = 0$ otherwise.[12]

This specific scenario is a *multi-armed bandit* (MAB) set-up, so named by analogy to a casino with many slot machines of different payout probabilities (the casino is the bandit). In the classic MAB (or simply "bandit") problem, there are no covariates associated with each ad and each user, such that you are attempting to optimize toward a single ad that has highest click probability across all users. That is, ω_j is $\pi(y_t = 1|d_t = j)$, the generic click probability for ad j, and you want to set d_t to the ad with highest ω_j. There are many different algorithms for bandit optimization. They use different heuristics to balance *exploitation* with *exploration*. A fully exploitive algorithm is greedy: it always takes the currently estimated best option without any consideration of uncertainty. In our simple advertising example, this implies always converging to the first ad that ever gets clicked on. A fully exploratory algorithm always randomizes the ads and it will never converge to a single optimum. The trick to bandit learning is finding a way to balance between these two extremes.

A classic bandit algorithm, and one which gives solid intuition into RL in general, is Thompson sampling (Thompson 1933). Like many tools in RL, Thompson sampling uses Bayesian inference to model the accumulation of knowledge over time. The basic idea is simple: at any point in the optimization process you have a probability distribution over the vector of click rates, $\omega = [\omega_1 \ldots \omega_J]$, and you want to show each ad j in proportion to the probability that ω_j is the largest click rate. That is, with $y^t = \{y_s\}_{s=1}^t$ denoting observed responses at time t, you want to have

$$(12) \qquad p(d_{t+1} = j) \propto p\left(\omega_j = \max\{\omega_k\}_{k=1}^J \mid y^t\right),$$

such that an ad's selection probability is equal to the posterior probability that it is the best choice. Since the probability in equation (12) is tough to calculate in practice (the probability of a maximum is not an easy object to analyze), Thompson sampling uses Monte Carlo estimation. In particular, you draw a sample of ad-click probabilities from the posterior distribution at time t,

$$(13) \qquad \omega_{t+1} \sim p(\omega \mid y^t),$$

---

12. This application, on the news website MSN.com with headlines rather than ads, motivates much of the RL work in Agarwal et al. (2014).

and set $d_{t+1} = \text{argmax}_j\, \omega_{t+1j}$. For example, suppose that you have a Beta(1,1) prior on each ad's click rate (i.e., a uniform distribution between zero and one). At time t, the posterior distribution for the jth ad's click rate is

$$(14) \qquad P(\omega_j | d^t, y^t) = \text{Beta}\left(1 + \sum_{s=1}^{t} 1_{[d_s = j]} y_s, 1 + \sum_{s=1}^{t} 1_{[d_s = j]}(1 - y_s)\right).$$

A Thompson sampling algorithm draws ω_{t+1j} from equation (14) for each j and then shows the ad with highest sampled click rate.

Why does this work? Think about scenarios where an ad j would be shown at time t—that is, when the sampled ω_{tj} is largest. This can occur if there is a lot of uncertainty about ω_j, in which case high probabilities have nontrivial posterior weight, or if the expected value of ω_j is high. Thus Thompson sampling will naturally balance between exploration and exploitation. There are many other algorithms for obtaining this balance. For example, Agarwal et al. (2014) survey methods that work well in the *contextual* bandit setting where you have covariates attached to events (such that action-payoff probabilities are event specific). The options considered include ε-greedy search, which finds a predicted optimal choice and explores within a neighborhood of that optimum, and a bootstrap-based algorithm that is effectively a nonparametric version of Thompson sampling.

Another large literature looks at so-called Bayesian optimization (Taddy et al. 2009). In these algorithms, you have an unknown function $r(x)$ that you would like to maximize. This function is modeled using some type of flexible Bayesian regression model, for example, a Gaussian process. As you accumulate data, you have a posterior over the "response surface" r at all potential input locations. Suppose that, after t function realizations, you have observed a maximal value $r_{\max}$. This is your current best option, but you want to continue exploring to see if you can find a higher maximum. The Bayesian optimization update is based on the *expected improvement* statistic,

$$(15) \qquad E\left[\max\left(0, r(x) - r_{\max}\right)\right],$$

the posterior expectation of improvement at new location x, thresholded below at *zero*. The algorithm evaluates equation (15) over a grid of potential x locations, and you choose to evaluate $r(x_{t+1})$ at the location x_{t+1} with highest expected improvement. Again, this balances exploitation with exploration: the statistic in equation (15) can be high if $r(x)$ has high variance or a high mean (or both).

These RL algorithms are all described in the language of optimization, but it is possible to map many learning tasks to optimization problems. For example, the term *active learning* is usually used to refer to algorithms that choose data to minimize some estimation variance (e.g., the average prediction error for a regression function over a fixed input distribution). Say $f(x; \Omega)$ is your regression function, attempting to predict response y. Then your *action* function is simply prediction, $d(x;\Omega) = f(x;\Omega)$, and your optimization goal could be to minimize the squared error—that is, to maximize $r(d(x;\Omega),y) = -(y - f(x;\Omega))^2$. In this way, active learning problems are special cases of the RL framework.

From a business and economic perspective, RL is interesting (beyond its obvious usefulness) for assigning a *value* to new data points. In many settings the rewards can be mapped to actual monetary value: for instance, in our advertising example where the website receives revenue-per-click. Reinforcement learning algorithms assign a dollar value to data observations. There is a growing literature on markets for data, for example, including the "data-is-labor" proposal in Lanier (2014). It seems useful for future study in this area to take account of how currently deployed AI systems assign relative data value. As a high-level point, the valuation of data in RL depends upon the *action* options and potential *rewards* associated with these actions. The value of data is only defined in a specific context.

The bandit algorithms described above are vastly simplified in comparison to the type of RL that is deployed as part of a deep learning system. In practice, when using RL with complex flexible functions like DNNs you need to be very careful to avoid over exploitation and early convergence (Mnih et al. 2015). It is also impossible to do a comprehensive search through the super high-dimensional space of optional values for the Ω that parametrizes a DNN. However, approaches such as that in van Seijen et al. (2017) and Silver et al. (2017) show that if you impose *structure* on the full learning problem then it can be broken into a number of simple composite tasks, each of which is solvable with RL. As we discussed earlier, there is an undeniable advantage to having large fixed data assets that you can use to hot-start your AI (e.g., data from a search engine or social media platform). But the exploration and active data collection of RL is essential when tuning an AI system to be successful in specific contexts. These systems are taking actions and setting policy in an uncertain and dynamic world. As statisticians, scientists, and economists are well aware, without constant experimentation it is not possible to learn and improve.

2.7   AI in Context

This chapter has provided a primer on the key ingredients of AI. We have also been pushing some general points. First, the current wave of ML-driven AI should be viewed as a new class of products growing up around a new general purpose technology: large-scale, fast, and robust machine learning. Artificial intelligence is not machine learning, but general purpose ML, specifically deep learning, is the electric motor of AI. These ML tools are going to continue to get better, faster, and cheaper. Hardware and big data resources are adapting to the demands of DNNs, and self-service ML solutions are available on all of the major cloud computing platforms. Trained

DNNs might become a commodity in the near-term future, and the market for deep learning could get wrapped up in the larger battle over market share in cloud computing services.

Second, we are still waiting for true end-to-end business AI solutions that drive a real increase in productivity. AI's current "wins" are mostly limited to settings with high amounts of explicit structure, like board and video games.[13] This is changing, as companies like Microsoft and Amazon produce semi-autonomous systems that can engage with real business problems. But there is still much work to be done, and the advances will be made by those who can impose structure on these complex business problems. That is, for business AI to succeed we need to combine the GPML and big data with people who know the rules of the "game" in their business domain.

Finally, all of this will have significant implications for the role of economics in industry. In many cases, the economists are those who can provide structure and rules around messy business scenarios. For example, a good structural econometrician (McFadden 1980; Heckman 1977; Deaton and Muellbauer 1980) uses economic theory to break a substantiative question into a set of *measurable* (i.e., identified) equations with parameters that can be estimated from data. In many settings, this is *exactly* the type of workflow required for AI. The difference is that, instead of being limited to basic linear regression, these measurable pieces of the system will be DNNs that can actively experiment and generate their own training data. The next generation of economists needs to be comfortable in knowing how to apply economic theory to obtain such structure, and how to translate this structure into recipes that can be automated with ML and RL. Just as big data led to data science, a new discipline combining statistics and computer science, AI will require interdisciplinary pioneers who can combine economics, statistics, and machine learning.

References

Agarwal, Alekh, Daniel Hsu, Satyen Kale, John Langford, Lihong Li, and Robert Schapire. 2014. "Taming the Monster: A Fast and Simple Algorithm for Contextual Bandits." In *Proceedings of the 31st International Conference on Machine Learning* 32:1638–46. http://proceedings.mlr.press/v32/agarwalb14.pdf.
Athey, Susan. 2017. "Beyond Prediction: Using Big Data for Policy Problems." *Science* 355:483–85.
Athey, Susan, and Guido Imbens. 2016. "Recursive Partitioning for Heterogeneous Causal Effects." *Proceedings of the National Academy of Sciences* 113:7353–60.
Bengio, Yoshua, and Yann LeCun. 2007. "Scaling Learning Algorithms towards AI." *Large-Scale Kernel Machines* 34 (5): 1–41.

---

13. The exception to this is web search, which has been effectively solved through AI.

Bottou, Léon, and Oliver Bousquet. 2008. "The Tradeoffs of Large Scale Learning." In *Advances in Neural Information Processing Systems*, 161–68. NIPS Foundation. http://books.nips.cc.

Bresnahan, Timothy. 2010. "General Purpose Technologies." *Handbook of the Economics of Innovation* 2:761–91.

Deaton, Angus, and John Muellbauer. 1980. "An Almost Ideal Demand System." *American Economic Review* 70:312–26.

Duchi, John, Elad Hazan, and Yoram Singer. 2011. "Adaptive Subgradient Methods for Online Learning and Stochastic Optimization." *Journal of Machine Learning Research* 12:2121–59.

Feurer, Matthias, Aaron Klein, Katharina Eggensperger, Jost Springenberg, Manuel Blum, and Frank Hutter. 2015. "Efficient and Robust Automated Machine Learning." In *Advances in Neural Information Processing Systems*, 2962–70. Cambridge, MA: MIT Press.

Goodfellow, Ian, Yoshua Bengio, and Aaron Courville. 2016. *Deep Learning*. Cambridge, MA: MIT Press.

Goodfellow, Ian, Jean Pouget-Abadie, Mehdi Mirza, Bing Xu, David Warde-Farley, Sherjil Ozair, Aaron Courville, and Yoshua Bengio. 2014. "Generative Adversarial Nets." In *Advances in Neural Information Processing Systems*, 2672–80. Cambridge, MA: MIT Press.

Hardt, Moritz, Ben Recht, and Yoram Singer. 2016. "Train Faster, Generalize Better: Stability of Stochastic Gradient Descent." In *Proceedings of the 33rd International Conference on Machine Learning* 48:1225–34. http://proceedings.mlr.press/v48/hardt16.pdf.

Hartford, Jason, Greg Lewis, Kevin Leyton-Brown, and Matt Taddy. 2017. "Deep IV: A Flexible Approach for Counterfactual Prediction." In *Proceedings of the 34th International Conference on Machine Learning* 70:1414–23. http://proceedings.mlr.press/v70/hartford17a.html.

Haugeland, John. 1985. *Artificial Intelligence: The Very Idea.* Cambridge, MA: MIT Press.

He, Kaiming, Xiangyu Zhang, Shaoqing Ren, and Jian Sun. 2016. "Deep Residual Learning for Image Recognition." In *Proceedings of the IEEE Conference on Computer Vision and Pattern Recognition*, 770–78. https://www.doi.org/10.1109/CVPR.2016.90.

Heckman, James J. 1977. "Sample Selection Bias as a Specification Error (with an Application to the Estimation of Labor Supply Functions)." NBER Working Paper no. 172, Cambridge, MA.

Hinton, Geoffrey E., Simon Osindero, and Yee-Whye Teh. 2006. "A Fast Learning Algorithm for Deep Belief Nets." *Neural Computation* 18 (7): 1527–54.

Hochreiter, Sepp, and Jürgen Schmidhuber. 1997. "Long Short-Term Memory." *Neural Computation* 9 (8): 1735–80.

Hornik, Kurt, Maxwell Stinchcombe, and Halbert White. 1989. "Multilayer Feedforward Networks are Universal Approximators." *Neural Networks* 2:359–66.

Karpathy, Andrej, and Li Fei-Fei. 2015. "Deep Visual-Semantic Alignments for Generating Image Descriptions." In *Proceedings of the IEEE Conference on Computer Vision and Pattern Recognition* 39: (4) 3128–37.

Kendall, Alex, and Yarin Gal. 2017. "What Uncertainties Do We Need in Bayesian Deep Learning for Computer Vision?" arXiv preprint arXiv:1703.04977. https://arxiv.org/abs/1703.04977.

Kingma, Diederik, and Jimmy Ba. 2015. "ADAM: A Method for Stochastic Optimization." In *Third International Conference on Learning Representations* (ICLR). https://arxiv.org/abs/1412.6980.

Krizhevsky, Alex, Ilya Sutskever, and Geoffrey E. Hinton. 2012. "Imagenet Classification with Deep Convolutional Neural Networks." In *Advances in Neural Information Processing Systems* 1:1097–105.

Lanier, Jaron. 2014. *Who Owns the Future?* New York: Simon & Schuster.

LeCun, Yann, and Yoshua Bengio. 1995. "Convolutional Networks for Images, Speech, and Time Series." In *The Handbook of Brain Theory and Neural Networks*, 255–58. Cambridge, MA: MIT Press.

LeCun, Yann, Léon Bottou, Yoshua Bengio, and Patrick Haffner. 1998. "Gradient-Based Learning Applied to Document Recognition." *Proceedings of the IEEE* 86:2278–324.

McFadden, Daniel. 1980. "Econometric Models for Probabilistic Choice among Products." *Journal of Business* 53 (3): S13–29.

Mikolov, Tomas, Ilya Sutskever, Kai Chen, Greg S. Corrado, and Jeff Dean. 2013. "Distributed Representations of Words and Phrases and Their Compositionality." In *Advances in Neural Information Processing Systems* 2:3111–19.

Mnih, Volodymyr, Koray Kavukcuoglu, David Silver, Andrei A. Rusu, Joel Veness, Marc G. Bellemare, Alex Graves, et al. 2015. "Human-Level Control through Deep Reinforcement Learning." *Nature* 518 (7540): 529–33.

Neal, Radford M. 2012. *Bayesian Learning for Neural Networks*, vol. 118. New York: Springer Science & Business Media.

Nielsen, Michael A. 2015. *Neural Networks and Deep Learning*. Determination Press. http://neuralnetworksanddeeplearning.com/.

Robbins, Herbert, and Sutton Monro. 1951. "A Stochastic Approximation Method." *Annals of Mathematical Statistics*, 22 (3): 400–407.

Rosenblatt, Frank. 1958. "The Perceptron: A Probabilistic Model for Information Storage and Organization in the Brain." *Psychological Review* 65:386.

Rumelhart, David E., Geoffrey E. Hinton, and Ronald J. Williams. 1988. "Learning Representations by Back-Propagating Errors." *Cognitive Modeling* 5 (3): 1.

Sabour, Sara, Nicholas Frosst, and Geoffrey E. Hinton. 2017. "Dynamic Routing between Capsules." In *Advances in Neural Information Processing Systems*, 3857–67.

Silver, David, Aja Huang, Chris J. Maddison, Arthur Guez, Laurent Sifre, George Van Den Driessche, Julian Schrittwieser, et al. 2016. "Mastering the Game of Go with Deep Neural Networks and Tree Search." *Nature* 529:484–89.

Silver, David, Julian Schrittwieser, Karen Simonyan, Ioannis Antonoglou, Aja Huang, Arthur Guez, et al. 2017. "Mastering the Game of Go without Human Knowledge." *Nature* 550:354–59.

Srivastava, Nitish, Geoffrey E. Hinton, Alex Krizhevsky, Ilya Sutskever, and Ruslan Salakhutdinov. 2014. "Dropout: A Simple Way to Prevent Neural Networks from Overfitting." *Journal of Machine Learning Research* 15 (1): 1929–58.

Taddy, Matt, Herbert K. H. Lee, Genetha A. Gray, and Joshua D Griffin. 2009. "Bayesian Guided Pattern Search for Robust Local Optimization." *Technometrics* 51 (4): 389–401.

Thompson, William R. 1933. "On the Likelihood That One Unknown Probability Exceeds Another in View of the Evidence of Two Samples." *Biometrika* 25:285–94.

Toulis, Panagiotis, Edoardo Airoldi, and Jason Rennie. 2014. "Statistical Analysis of Stochastic Gradient Methods for Generalized Linear Models." In *International Conference on Machine Learning*, 667–75.

van Seijen, Harm, Mehdi Fatemi, Joshua Romoff, Romain Laroche, Tavian Barnes, and Jeffrey Tsang. 2017. "Hybrid Reward Architecture for Reinforcement Learning." arXiv:1706.04208. https://arxiv.org/abs/1706.04208.

Prediction, Judgment, and Complexity
A Theory of Decision-Making and Artificial Intelligence

Ajay Agrawal, Joshua Gans, and Avi Goldfarb

3.1 Introduction

There is widespread discussion regarding the impact of machines on employment (see Autor 2015). In some sense, the discussion mirrors a long-standing literature on the impact of the accumulation of capital equipment on employment; specifically, whether capital and labor are substitutes or complements (Acemoglu 2003). But the recent discussion is motivated by the integration of software with hardware and whether the role of machines goes beyond physical tasks to mental ones as well (Brynjolfsson and McAfee 2014). As mental tasks were seen as always being present and essential, human comparative advantage in these was seen as the main reason why, at least in the long term, capital accumulation would complement employment by enhancing labor productivity in those tasks.

The computer revolution has blurred the line between physical and men-

Ajay Agrawal is the Peter Munk Professor of Entrepreneurship at the Rotman School of Management, University of Toronto, and a research associate of the National Bureau of Economic Research. Joshua Gans is professor of strategic management and holder of the Jeffrey S. Skoll Chair of Technical Innovation and Entrepreneurship at the Rotman School of Management, University of Toronto (with a cross appointment in the Department of Economics), and a research associate of the National Bureau of Economic Research. Avi Goldfarb holds the Rotman Chair in Artificial Intelligence and Healthcare and is professor of marketing at the Rotman School of Management, University of Toronto, and is a research associate of the National Bureau of Economic Research.

Our thanks to Andrea Prat, Scott Stern, Hal Varian, and participants at the AEA (Chicago), NBER Summer Institute (2017), NBER Economics of AI Conference (Toronto), Columbia Law School, Harvard Business School, MIT, and University of Toronto for helpful comments. Responsibility for all errors remains our own. The latest version of this chapter is available at joshuagans.com. For acknowledgments, sources of research support, and disclosure of the authors' material financial relationships, if any, please see http://www.nber.org/chapters /c14010.ack.

tal tasks. For instance, the invention of the spreadsheet in the late 1970s fundamentally changed the role of bookkeepers. Prior to that invention, there was a time-intensive task involving the recomputation of outcomes in spreadsheets as data or assumptions changed. That human task was substituted by the spreadsheet software that could produce the calculations more quickly, cheaply, and frequently. However, at the same time, the spreadsheet made the jobs of accountants, analysts, and others far more productive. In the accounting books, capital was substituting for labor, but the mental productivity of labor was being changed. Thus, the impact on employment critically depended on whether there were tasks the "computers cannot do."

These assumptions persist in models today. Acemoglu and Restrepo (2017) observe that capital substitutes for labor in certain tasks while at the same time technological progress creates new tasks. They make what they call a "natural assumption" that only labor can perform the new tasks as they are more complex than previous ones.[1] Benzell et al. (2015) consider the impact of software more explicitly. Their environment has two types of labor—high-tech (who can, among other things, code) and low-tech (who are empathetic and can handle interpersonal tasks). In this environment, it is the low-tech workers who cannot be replaced by machines while the high-tech ones are employed initially to create the code that will eventually displace their kind. The results of the model depend, therefore, on a class of worker who cannot be substituted directly for capital, but also on the inability of workers themselves to substitute between classes.

In this chapter, our approach is to delve into the weeds of what is happening currently in the field of artificial intelligence (AI). The recent wave of developments in AI all involve advances in machine learning. Those advances allow for automated and cheap prediction; that is, providing a forecast (or nowcast) of a variable of interest from available data (Agrawal, Gans and Goldfarb 2018b). In some cases, prediction has enabled full automation of tasks—for example, self-driving vehicles where the process of data collection, prediction of behavior and surroundings, and actions are all conducted without a human in the loop. In other cases, prediction is a standalone tool—such as image recognition or fraud detection—that may or may not lead to further substitution of human users of such tools by machines. Thus far, substitution between humans and machines has focused mainly on cost considerations. Are machines cheaper, more reliable, and more scalable (in their software form) than humans? This chapter, however, considers the role of prediction in decision-making explicitly and from that examines the complementary skills that may be matched with prediction within a task.

---

1. To be sure, their model is designed to examine how automation of tasks causes a change in factor prices that biases innovation toward the creation of new tasks that labor is more suited to.

Our focus, in this regard, is on what we term *judgment*. While judgment is a term with broad meaning, here we use it to refer to a very specific skill. To see this, consider a decision. That decision involves choosing an action, x, from a set, X. The payoff (or reward) from that action is defined by a function, $u(x, \theta)$ where θ is a realization of an uncertain state drawn from a distribution, $F(\theta)$. Suppose that, prior to making a decision, a *prediction* (or signal), s, can be generated that results in a posterior, $F(\theta|s)$. Thus, the decision maker would solve

$$\max_{x \in X} \int u\left(x, \theta\right) dF\left(\theta|s\right).$$

In other words, a standard problem of choice under uncertainty. In this standard world, the role of prediction is to improve decision-making. The payoff, or utility function, is known.

To create a role for judgment, we depart from this standard set-up in statistical decision theory and ask how a decision maker comes to know the function, $u(x, \theta)$? We assume that this is not simply given or a primitive of the decision-making model. Instead, it requires a human to undertake a costly process that allows the mapping from (x, θ) to a particular payoff value, u, to be discovered. This is a reasonable assumption given that beyond some rudimentary experimentation in closed environments, there is no current way for an AI to impute a utility function that resides with humans. Additionally, this process separates the costs of providing the mapping for each pair, (x, θ). (Actually, we focus, without loss in generality, on situations where $u(x, \theta) \neq u(x)$ for all θ and presume that if a payoff to an action is state independent that payoff is known.) In other words, while prediction can obtain a signal of the underlying state, judgment is the process by which the payoffs from actions that arise based on that state can be determined. We assume that this process of determining payoffs requires human understanding of the situation: it is not a prediction problem.

For intuition on the difference between prediction and judgment, consider the example of credit card fraud. A bank observes a credit card transaction. That transaction is either legitimate or fraudulent. The decision is whether to approve the transaction. If the bank knows for sure that the transaction is legitimate, the bank will approve it. If the bank knows for sure that it is fraudulent, the bank will refuse the transaction. Why? Because the bank knows the payoff of approving a legitimate transaction is higher than the payoff of refusing that transaction. Things get more interesting if the bank is uncertain about whether the transaction is legitimate. The uncertainty means that the bank also needs to know the payoff from refusing a legitimate transaction and from approving a fraudulent transaction. In our model, judgment is the process of determining these payoffs. It is a costly activity, in the sense that it requires time and effort.

As the new developments regarding AI all involve making prediction more readily available, we ask, how does judgment and its endogenous application change the value of prediction? Are prediction and judgment substitutes or complements? How does the value of prediction change monotonically with the difficulty of applying judgment? In complex environments (as they relate to automation, contracting, and the boundaries of the firm), how do improvements in prediction affect the value of judgment?

We proceed by first providing supportive evidence for our assumption that recent developments in AI overwhelmingly impact the costs of prediction. We then use the example of radiology to provide a context for understanding the different roles of prediction and judgment. Drawing inspiration from Bolton and Faure-Grimaud (2009), we then build the baseline model with two states of the world and uncertainty about payoffs to actions in each state. We explore the value of judgment in the absence of any prediction technology, and then the value of prediction technology when there is no judgment. We finish the discussion of the baseline model with an exploration of the interaction between prediction and judgment, demonstrating that prediction and judgment are complements as long as judgment isn't too difficult. We then separate prediction quality into prediction frequency and prediction accuracy. As judgment improves, accuracy becomes more important relative to frequency. Finally, we examine complex environments where the number of potential states is large. Such environments are common in economic models of automation, contracting, and boundaries of the firm. We show that the effect of improvements in prediction on the importance of judgment depend a great deal on whether the improvements in prediction enable automated decision-making.

3.2   AI and Prediction Costs

We argue that the recent advances in artificial intelligence are advances in the technology of prediction. Most broadly, we define prediction as the ability to take known information to generate new information. Our model emphasizes prediction about the state of the world.

Most contemporary artificial intelligence research and applications come from a field now called "machine learning." Many of the tools of machine learning have a long history in statistics and data analysis, and are likely familiar to economists and applied statisticians as tools for prediction and classification.[2] For example, Alpaydin's (2010) textbook *Introduction to Machine Learning* covers maximum likelihood estimation, Bayesian estimation, multivariate linear regression, principal components analysis, clustering, and nonparametric regression. In addition, it covers tools that may be less familiar, but also use independent variables to predict outcomes:

---

2. We define prediction as known information to generate new information. Therefore, classification techniques such as clustering are prediction techniques in which the new information to be predicted is the appropriate category or class.

regression trees, neural networks, hidden Markov models, and reinforcement learning. Hastie, Tibshirani, and Friedman (2009) cover similar topics. The 2014 *Journal of Economic Perspectives* symposium on big data covered several of these less familiar prediction techniques in articles by Varian (2014) and Belloni, Chernozhukov, and Hansen (2014).

While many of these prediction techniques are not new, recent advances in computer speed, data collection, data storage, and the prediction methods themselves have led to substantial improvements. These improvements have transformed the computer science research field of artificial intelligence. The Oxford English Dictionary defines artificial intelligence as "[t]he theory and development of computer systems able to perform tasks normally requiring human intelligence." In the 1960s and 1970s, artificial intelligence research was primarily rules-based, symbolic logic. It involved human experts generating rules that an algorithm could follow (Domingos 2015, 89). These are not prediction technologies. Such systems became very good chess players and they guided factory robots in highly controlled settings; however, by the 1980s, it became clear that rules-based systems could not deal with the complexity of many nonartificial settings. This led to an "AI winter" in which research funding artificial intelligence projects largely dried up (Markov 2015).

Over the past ten years, a different approach to artificial intelligence has taken off. The idea is to program computers to "learn" from example data or experience. In the absence of the ability to predetermine the decision rules, a data-driven prediction approach can conduct many mental tasks. For example, humans are good at recognizing familiar faces, but we would struggle to explain and codify this skill. By connecting data on names to image data on faces, machine learning solves this problem by predicting which image data patterns are associated with which names. As a prominent artificial intelligence researcher put it, "Almost all of AI's recent progress is through one type, in which some input data (A) is used to quickly generate some simple response (B)" (Ng 2016). Thus, the progress is explicitly about improvements in prediction. In other words, the suite of technologies that have given rise to the recent resurgence of interest in artificial intelligence use data collected from sensors, images, videos, typed notes, or anything else that can be represented in bits to fill in missing information, recognize objects, or forecast what will happen next.

To be clear, we do not take a position on whether these prediction technologies really do mimic the core aspects of human intelligence. While Palm Computing founder Jeff Hawkins argues that human intelligence is—in essence—prediction (Hawkins 2004), many neuroscientists, psychologists, and others disagree. Our point is that the technologies that have been given the label artificial intelligence are prediction technologies. Therefore, in order to understand the impact of these technologies, it is important to assess the impact of prediction on decisions.

3.3   Case: Radiology

Before proceeding to the model, we provide some intuition of how prediction and judgment apply in a particular context where prediction machines are expected to have a large impact: radiology. In 2016, Geoff Hinton—one of the pioneers of deep learning neural networks—stated that it was no longer worth training radiologists. His strong implication was that radiologists would not have a future. This is something that radiologists have been concerned about since 1960 (Lusted 1960). Today, machine-learning techniques are being heavily applied in radiology by IBM using its Watson computer and by a start-up, Enlitic. Enlitic has been able to use deep learning to detect lung nodules (a fairly routine exercise)[3] but also fractures (which is more complex). Watson can now identify pulmonary embolism and some other heart issues. These advances are at the heart of Hinton's forecast, but have also been widely discussed among radiologists and pathologists (Jha and Topol 2016). What does the model in this chapter suggest about the future of radiologists?

If we consider a simplified characterization of the job of a radiologist, it would be that they examine an image in order to characterize and classify that image and return an assessment to a physician. While often that assessment is a diagnosis (i.e., "the patient has pneumonia"), in many cases, the assessment is in the negative (i.e., "pneumonia not excluded"). In that regard, this is stated as a predictive task to inform the physician of the likelihood of the state of the world. Using that, the physician can devise a treatment.

These predictions are what machines are aiming to provide. In particular, it might provide a differential diagnosis of the following kind:

Based on Mr Patel's demographics and imaging, the mass in the liver has a 66.6 percent chance of being benign, 33.3 percent chance of being malignant, and a 0.1 percent of not being real.[4]

The action is whether some intervention is needed. For instance, if a potential tumor is identified in a noninvasive scan, then this will inform whether an invasive examination will be conducted. In terms of identifying the state of the world, the invasive exam is costly but safe—it can deduce a cancer with certainty and remove it if necessary. The role of a noninvasive exam is to inform whether an invasive exam should be forgone. That is, it is to make physicians more confident about abstaining from treatment and further analysis. In this regard, if the machine improves prediction, it will lead to fewer invasive examinations.

---

3. "You did not go to medical school to measure lung nodules." http://www.medscape.com /viewarticle/863127#vp_2.
4. http://www.medscape.com/viewarticle/863127#vp_3.

Judgment involves understanding the payoffs. What is the payoff to conducting a biopsy if the mass is benign, malignant, or not real? What is the payoff to not doing anything in those three states? The issue for radiologists in particular is whether a trained specialist radiologist is in the best position to make this judgment or will it occur further along the chain of decision-making or involve new job classes that merge diagnostic information such as a combined radiologist/pathologist (Jha and Topol 2016). Next, we formalize these ideas.

3.4   Baseline Model

Our baseline model is inspired by the "bandit" environment considered by Bolton and Faure-Grimaud (2009), although it departs significantly in the questions addressed and base assumptions made. Like them, in our baseline model, we suppose there are two states of the world, $\{\theta_1, \theta_2\}$ with prior probabilities of $\{\mu, 1 - \mu\}$. There are two possible actions: a state independent action with known payoff of S (safe) and a state dependent action with two possible payoffs, R or r, as the case may be (risky).

As noted in the introduction, a key departure from the usual assumptions of rational decision-making is that the decision maker does not know the payoff from the risky action in each state and must apply *judgment* to determine that payoff.[5] Moreover, decision makers need to be able to make a judgment for each state that might arise in order to formulate a plan that would be the equivalent of payoff maximization. In the absence of such judgment, the ex ante expectation that the risky action is optimal in any state is v (which is independent between states). To make things more concrete, we assume $R > S > r$.[6] Thus, we assume that v is the probability in any state that the risky payoff is R rather than r. This is not a conditional probability of the state. It is a statement about the payoff, given the state.

In the absence of knowledge regarding the specific payoffs from the risky action, a decision can only be made on the basis of prior probabilities. Then the safe action will be chosen if

$$\mu\big(vR + (1-v)r\big) + \big(1-\mu\big)\big(vR + (1-v)r\big) = vR + (1-v)r \leq S.$$

---

5. Bolton and Faure-Grimaud (2009) consider this step to be the equivalent of a thought experiment where thinking takes time. To the extent that our results can be interpreted as a statement about the comparative advantage of humans, we assume that only humans can do judgment.

6. Thus, we assume that the payoff function, u, can only take one of three values, $\{R, r, S\}$. The issue is which combinations of state realization and action lead to which payoffs. However, we assume that S is the payoff from the safe action regardless of state and so this is known to the decision maker. As it is the relative payoffs from actions that drive the results, this assumption is without loss in generality. Requiring this property of the safe action to be discovered would just add an extra cost. Implicitly, as the decision maker cannot make a decision in complete ignorance, we are assuming that the safe action's payoff can be judged at an arbitrarily low cost.

So that the payoff is: $V_0 = \max\{vR + (1 - v)r, S\}$. To make things simpler, we will focus our attention on the case where the safe action is—in the absence of prediction or judgment—the default. That is, we assume that

(A1)   **(Safe Default)** $vR + (1 - v)r \leq S$.

This assumption is made for simplicity only and will not change the qualitative conclusions.[7] Under (A1), in the absence of knowledge of the payoff function or a signal of the state, the decision maker would choose S.

3.4.1   Judgment in the Absence of Prediction

Prediction provides knowledge of the state. The process of judgment provides knowledge of the payoff function. Judgment therefore allows the decision maker to understand which action is optimal for a given state should it arise. Suppose that this knowledge is gained without cost (as it would be assumed to do under the usual assumptions of economic rationality). In other words, the decision maker has knowledge of optimal action in a given state. Then the risky action will be chosen (a) if it is the preferred action in both states (which arises with probability v^2); (b) if it is the preferred action in θ_1 but not θ_2 and $\mu R + (1 - \mu)r > S$ (with probability $v(1 - v)$); or (c) if it is the preferred action in θ_2 but not θ_1 and $\mu r + (1 - \mu)R > S$ (with probability $v(1 - v)$). Thus, the expected payoff is

$$v^2 R + v(1 - v)\max\left\{\mu R + (1 - \mu)r, S\right\}$$
$$+ \; v(1 - v)\max\left\{\mu r + (1 - \mu)R, S\right\} + (1 - v)^2 S.$$

Note that this is greater than V_0. The reason for this is that, when there is uncertainty, judgment is valuable because it can identify actions that are dominant or dominated—that is, that might be optimal across states. In this situation, any resolution of uncertainty does not matter as it will not change the decision made.

A key insight is that judgment itself can be consequential.

RESULT 1:   *If* $\max\{\mu R + (1 - \mu)r, \mu r + (1 - \mu)R\} > S$, *it is possible that judgment alone can cause the decision to switch from the default action (safe) to the alternative action (risky).*

As we are motivated by understanding the interplay between prediction and judgment, we want to make these consequential. Therefore, we make the following assumption to ensure prediction always has some value:

(A2) **(Judgment Insufficient)** $\max\{\mu R + (1 - \mu)r, \mu r + (1 - \mu)R\} \leq S$.

Under this assumption, if different actions are optimal in each state and this is known, the decision maker will not change to the risky action. This, of course, implies that the expected payoff is

---

7. Bolton and Faure-Grimaud (2009) make the opposite assumption. Here, as our focus is on the impact of prediction, it is better to consider environments where prediction has the effect of reducing uncertainty over riskier actions.

$$v^2R + (1 - v^2)S.$$

Note that, absent any cost, full judgment improves the decision maker's expected payoff.

Judgment does not come for free. We assume here that it takes time (although the formulation would naturally match with the notion that it takes costly effort). Suppose the discount factor is $\delta < 1$. A decision maker can spend time in a period determining what the optimal action is for a particular state. If they choose to apply judgment with respect to state θ_i, then there is a probability λ_i that they will determine the optimal action in that period and can make a choice based on that judgment. Otherwise, they can choose to apply judgment to that problem in the next period.

It is useful, at this point, to consider what judgment means once it has been applied. The initial assumption we make here is that the knowledge of the payoff function depreciates as soon as a decision is made. In other words, applying judgment can delay a decision (and that is costly) and it can improve that decision (which is its value) but it cannot generate experience that can be applied to other decisions (including future ones). In other words, the initial conception of judgment is the application of *thought* rather than the gathering of *experience*.[8] Practically, this reduces our examination to a static model. However, in a later section, we consider the experience formulation and demonstrate that most of the insights of the static model carry over to the dynamic model.

In summary, the timing of the game is as follows:

1. At the beginning of a decision stage, the decision maker chooses whether to apply judgment and to what state or whether to simply choose an action without judgment. If an action is chosen, uncertainty is resolved and payoffs are realized and we move to a new decision stage.

2. If judgment is chosen, with probability, $1 - \lambda_i$, they do not find out the payoffs for the risky action in that state, a period of time elapses and the game moves back to 1. With probability λ_i, the decision maker gains this knowledge. The decision maker can then take an action, uncertainty is resolved and payoffs are realized, and we move to a new decision stage (back to 1). If no action is taken, a period of time elapses and the current decision stage continues.

3. The decision maker chooses whether to apply judgment to the other state. If an action is chosen, uncertainty is resolved and payoffs are realized and we move to a new decision stage (back to 1).

4. If judgment is chosen, with probability, $1 - \lambda_{-i}$, they do not find out the payoffs for the risky action in that state, a period of time elapses and the game moves back to 1. With probability λ_{-i}, the decision maker gains this knowledge. The decision maker then chooses an action, uncertainty

---

8. The experience frame is considered in Agrawal, Gans, and Goldfarb (2018a).

Table 3.1   **Model parameters**

Parameter	Description
S	Known payoff from the safe action
R	Potential payoff from the risky action in a given state
r	Potential payoff from the risky action in a given state
θ_i	Label of state $i \in \{1,2\}$
μ	Probability of state 1
v	Prior probability that the payoff in a given state is R
λ_i	Probablilty that decision maker learns the payoff to the risky action θ_i if judgment is applied for one period
δ	Discount factor

is resolved and payoffs are realized, and we move to a new decision stage (back to 1).

When prediction is available, it will become available prior to the beginning of a decision stage. The various parameters are listed in table 3.1.

Suppose that the decision maker focuses on judging the optimal action (i.e., assessing the payoff) for θ_i. Then the expected present discount payoff from applying judgment is

$$\lambda_i\left(vR + (1-v)S\right) + (1-\lambda_i)\delta\lambda_i\left(vR + (1-v)S\right) + \sum_{t=2}^{\infty}(1-\lambda_i)^t\delta^t\lambda_i\left(vR + (1-v)S\right)$$

$$= \frac{\lambda_i}{1-(1-\lambda_i)\delta}\left(vR + (1-v)S\right).$$

The decision maker eventually can learn what to do and will earn a higher payoff than without judgment, but will trade this off against a delay in the payoff.

This calculation presumes that the decision maker knows the state—that θ_i is true—prior to engaging in judgment. If this is not the case, then the expected present discounted payoff to judgment on, say, θ_1 alone is

$$\frac{\lambda_1}{1-(1-\lambda_1)\delta}\left(\max\left\{v\left(\mu R + (1-\mu)(vR + (1-v)r)\right) + (1-v)\left(\mu r + (1-\mu)(vR + (1-v)r)\right), S\right\}\right)$$

$$= \frac{\lambda_1}{1-(1-\lambda_1)\delta}\left(\max\left\{v\left(\mu R + (1-\mu)(vR + (1-v)r)\right), S\right\} + (1-v)S\right),$$

where the last step follows from equation (A1). To make exposition simpler, we suppose that $\lambda_1 = \lambda_2 = \lambda$. In addition, let $\hat{\lambda} = \lambda / (1-(1-\lambda)\delta)$; $\hat{\lambda}$ can be given a similar interpretation to λ, the quality of judgment.

If the strategy were to apply judgment on one state only and then make a decision, this would be the relevant payoff to consider. However, because judgment is possible in both states, there are several cases to consider.

First, the decision maker might apply judgment to both states in sequence. In this case, the expected present discounted payoff is

$$\hat{\lambda}^2\Big(v^2R + v(1-v)\max\{\mu R + (1-\mu)r, S\}$$
$$+ v(1-v)\max\{\mu r + (1-\mu)R, S\} + (1-v)^2S\Big)$$
$$= \hat{\lambda}^2\big(v^2R + (1-v^2)S\big),$$

where the last step follows from equation (A1).

Second, the decision maker might apply judgment to, say, θ_1 first and then, contingent on the outcome there, apply judgment to θ_2. If the decision maker chooses to pursue judgment on θ_2 if the outcome for θ_1 is that the risky action is optimal, the payoff becomes

$$\hat{\lambda}\Big(v\hat{\lambda}\big(vR + (1-v)\max\{\mu R + (1-\mu)r, S\}\big)$$
$$+ (1-v)\max\{\mu r + (1-\mu)(vR + (1-v)r), S\}\Big)$$
$$= \hat{\lambda}\big(v\hat{\lambda}(vR + (1-v)S) + (1-v)S\big).$$

If the decision maker chooses to pursue judgment on θ_2 after determining that the outcome for θ_1 is that the safe action is optimal, the payoff becomes

$$\hat{\lambda}\Big(v\max\{\mu R + (1-\mu)(vR + (1-v)r), S\}$$
$$+ (1-v)\hat{\lambda}\big(v\max\{\mu r + (1-\mu)R, S\} + (1-v)S\big)\Big)$$
$$= \hat{\lambda}\big(v\max\{\mu R + (1-\mu)(vR + (1-v)r), S\} + (1-v)\hat{\lambda}S\big).$$

Note that this is option is dominated by not applying further judgment at all if the outcome for θ_1 is that the safe action is optimal.

Given this we can prove the following:

PROPOSITION 1:   *Under (A1) and (A2), and in the absence of any signal about the state, (a) judging both states and (b) continuing after the discovery that the safe action is preferred in a state are never optimal.*

PROOF: Note that judging two states is optimal if

$$\hat{\lambda} > \frac{S}{v\max\{\mu r + (1-\mu)R, S\} + (1-v)S}$$

$$\hat{\lambda} > \frac{\mu R + (1-\mu)\big(vR + (1-v)r\big)}{vR + (1-v)\max\{\mu R + (1-\mu)r, S\}}.$$

As (A2) implies that $\mu r + (1-\mu)R \le S$, the first condition reduces to $\hat{\lambda} > 1$. Thus, (a) judging two states is dominated by judging one state and continuing to explore only if the risk is found to be optimal in that state.

Turning to the strategy of continuing to apply judgment only if the safe action is found to be preferred in a state, we can compare this to the payoff from applying judgment to one state and then acting immediately. Note that

$$\hat{\lambda}\Big(v\max\big\{\mu R+(1-\mu)(vR+(1-v)r),S\big\}+(1-v)\hat{\lambda}S\Big)$$
$$> \hat{\lambda}\Big(v\max\big\{\mu R+(1-\mu)(vR+(1-v)r),S\big\}+(1-v)S\Big).$$

This can never hold, proving that (b) is dominated.

The intuition is similar to Propositions 1 and 2 in Bolton and Faure-Grimaud (2009). In particular, applying judgment is only useful if it is going to lead to the decision maker switching to the risky action. Thus, it is never worthwhile to unconditionally explore a second state as it may not change the action taken. Similarly, if judging one state leads to knowledge the safe action continues to be optimal in that state, in the presence of uncertainty about the state, even if knowledge is gained of the payoff to the risky action in the second state, that action will never be chosen. Hence, further judgment is not worthwhile. Hence, it is better to choose immediately at that point rather than delay the inevitable.

Given this proposition, there are only two strategies that are potentially optimal (in the absence of prediction). One strategy (we will term here J1) is where judgment is applied to one state and if the risky action is optimal, then that action is taken immediately; otherwise, the safe default is taken immediately. The state where judgment is applied first is the state most likely to arise. This will be state 1 if $\mu > 1/2$. This strategy might be chosen if

$$\hat{\lambda}\Big(v\max\big\{\mu R+(1-\mu)(vR+(1-v)r),S\big\}+(1-v)S\Big) > S$$

$$\Rightarrow \hat{\lambda} > \hat{\lambda}_{J1} \equiv \frac{S}{v\max\big\{\mu R+(1-\mu)(vR+(1-v)r),S\big\}+(1-v)S},$$

which clearly requires that $\mu R+(1-\mu)(vR+(1-v)r) > S$.

The other strategy (we will term here J2) is where judgment is applied to one state and if the risky action is optimal, then judgment is applied to the next state; otherwise, the safe default is taken immediately. Note that J2 is preferred to J1 if

$$\hat{\lambda}\Big(v\hat{\lambda}(vR+(1-v)S)+(1-v)S\Big)$$
$$> \hat{\lambda}\Big(v\max\big\{\mu R+(1-\mu)(vR+(1-v)r),S\big\}+(1-v)S\Big)$$
$$\Rightarrow \hat{\lambda}v(vR+(1-v)S) > v\max\big\{\mu R+(1-\mu)(vR+(1-v)r),S\big\}$$
$$\Rightarrow \hat{\lambda} > \frac{\max\big\{\mu R+(1-\mu)(vR+(1-v)r),S\big\}}{vR+(1-v)S}.$$

This is intuitive. Basically, it is only when the efficiency of judgment is sufficiently high that more judgment is applied. However, for this inequality to be relevant, J2 must also be preferred to the status quo yielding a payoff of S. Thus, J2 is not dominated if

$$\hat{\lambda} > \hat{\lambda}_{J2} \equiv \max \left\{ \frac{\max\left\{ \mu R + (1-\mu)(vR+(1-v)r), S \right\}}{vR + (1-v)S}, \frac{\sqrt{S(4v^2R+S(1+2v-3v^2))} - (1-v)S}{2v(vR+(1-v)S)} \right\},$$

where the first term is the range where J2 dominates J1, while the second term is where J2 dominates S alone; so for J2 to be optimal, it must exceed both. Note also that as $\mu \to (S-r)/(R-r)$ (its highest possible level consistent with [A1] and [A2]), then $\hat{\lambda}_{J2} \to 1$.

If $\mu R + (1-\mu)(vR + (1-v)r) > S$, note that

$$\hat{\lambda}_{J2} > \hat{\lambda}_{J1} \Rightarrow \frac{\mu R + (1-\mu)(vR+(1-v)r)}{vR+(1-v)S} > \frac{S}{v(\mu R + (1-\mu)(vR+(1-v)r)) + (1-v)S}$$

$$\Rightarrow (1-v)S(\mu R + (1-\mu)(vR+(1-v)r) - S) > v(RS - (\mu R + (1-\mu)(vR+(1-v)r))^2),$$

which may not hold for v sufficiently high. However, it can be shown that when $\hat{\lambda}_{J2} + \hat{\lambda}_{J1}$, then the two terms of $\hat{\lambda}_{J2}$ are equal and the second term exceeds the first when $\hat{\lambda}_{J2} \, \hat{\lambda}_{J1}$. This implies that in the range where $\hat{\lambda}_{J2} < \hat{\lambda}_{J1}$, J2 dominates J1.

This analysis implies there are two types of regimes with judgment only. If $\hat{\lambda}_{J2} > \hat{\lambda}_{J1}$, then easier decisions (with high $\hat{\lambda}$) involve using J2, the next tranche of decisions use J1 (with intermediate $\hat{\lambda}$) while the remainder involves no exercise of judgment at all. On the other hand, if $\hat{\lambda}_{J2} < \hat{\lambda}_{J1}$, then the easier decisions involve using J2 while the remainder do not involve judgment at all.

3.4.2 Prediction in the Absence of Judgment

Next, we consider the model with prediction but no judgment. Suppose that there exists an AI that can, if deployed, identify the state prior to a decision being made. In other words, prediction, if it occurs, is perfect; an assumption we will relax in a later section. Initially, suppose there is no judgment mechanism to determine what the optimal action is in each state.

Recall that, in the absence of prediction or judgment, (A1) ensures that the safe action will be chosen. If the decision maker knows the state, then the risky action in a given state is chosen if

$$vR + (1 - v)r > S.$$

This contradicts (A1). Thus, the expected payoff is

$$V_P = S,$$

which is the same outcome if there is no judgment or prediction.

3.4.3 Prediction and Judgment Together

Both prediction and judgment can be valuable on their own. The question we next wish to consider is whether they are complements or substitutes.

While perfect prediction allows you to choose an action based on the actual rather than expected state, it also affords the same opportunity with respect to judgment. As judgment is costly, it is useful not to waste considering what action might be taken in a state that does not arise. This was not possible when there was no prediction. But if you receive a prediction regarding the state, you can then apply judgment exclusively to actions in relation to that state. To be sure, that judgment still involves a cost, but at the same time does not lead to any wasted cognitive resources.

Given this, if the decision maker were the apply judgment after the state is predicted, their expected discounted payoff would be

$$V_{PJ} = \max\left\{\hat{\lambda}\big(vR + (1-v)S\big), S\right\}.$$

This represents the highest expected payoff possible (net of the costs of judgment). A necessary condition for both prediction and judgment to be optimal is that: $\hat{\lambda} \geq \hat{\lambda}_{PJ} \equiv s/[vR + (1-v)S]$. Note that $\hat{\lambda}_{PJ} \leq \hat{\lambda}_{J1}, \hat{\lambda}_{J2}$.

3.4.4   Complements or Substitutes?

To evaluate whether prediction and judgment are complements or substitutes, we adopt the following parameterization for the effectiveness of prediction: we assume that with probability e an AI yields a prediction, while otherwise, the decision must be made in its absence (with judgment only). With this parameterization, we can prove the following:

PROPOSITION 2:   *In the range of* λ *where* $\hat{\lambda} < \hat{\lambda}_{J2}$, *e and* λ *are complements, otherwise they are substitutes.*

PROOF: Step 1. Is $\hat{\lambda}_{J2} > R/[2(vR + (1-v)S)]$? First, note that

$$\frac{\max\left\{\mu R + (1-\mu)(vR + (1-v)r), S\right\}}{vR + (1-v)S} > \frac{R}{2(vR + (1-v)S)}$$

$$\Rightarrow \max\left\{\mu R + (1-\mu)(vR + (1-v)r), S\right\} > \frac{1}{2}R.$$

Note that by (A2) and since $\mu > (1/2)$, $S > \mu R + (1-\mu)r > (1/2)R$ so this inequality always holds.

Second, note that

$$\frac{\sqrt{S(4v^2 R + S(1 + 2v - 3v^2))} - (1-v)S}{2v(vR + (1-v)S)} > \frac{R}{2(vR + (1-v)S)}$$

$$\Rightarrow S(4v^2 R + S(1 + 2v - 3v^2)) > (vR + (1-v)S)^2$$

$$\Rightarrow S(S - 2R) > v(R^2 - 6RS + S^2),$$

which holds as the left-hand side is always positive while the right-hand side is always negative.

Step 2: Suppose that $\mu R + (1-\mu)(vR + (1-v)r) \leq S$; then J1 is never optimal. In this case, the expected payoff is

$$eV_{PJ} + (1-e)V_{J2} = e\hat{\lambda}(vR + (1-v)S) + (1-e)\hat{\lambda}(v\hat{\lambda}(vR + (1-v)S) + (1-v)S).$$

This mixed partial derivative with respect to $(e, \hat{\lambda})$ is $v(R - 2\hat{\lambda}(vR + (1-v)S))$. This is positive if $R/[2(vR + (1-v)S)] \geq \hat{\lambda}$. By Step 1, this implies that for $\hat{\lambda} < \hat{\lambda}_{J2}$, prediction and judgment are complements; otherwise, they are substitutes.

Step 3: Suppose that that $\mu R + (1-\mu)(vR + (1-v)r) > S$. Note that for $\hat{\lambda}_{J1} \hat{\lambda} < \hat{\lambda}_{J2}$, J1 is preferred to J2. In this case, the expected payoff to prediction and judgment is

$$e\hat{\lambda}(vR + (1-v)S) + (1-e)\hat{\lambda}(v \max\{\mu R + (1-\mu)(vR + (1-v)r), S\} + (1-v)S).$$

This mixed partial derivative with respect to $(e, \hat{\lambda})$ is $v(R - \max\{\mu R + (1-\mu)(vR + (1-v)r), S\}) > 0$. By Step 1, this implies that for $\hat{\lambda} < \hat{\lambda}_{J2}$, prediction and judgment are complements; otherwise, they are substitutes.

The intuition is as follows. When $\hat{\lambda} < \hat{\lambda}_{J2}$, then, in the absence of prediction either no judgment is applied or, alternatively, strategy J1 (with one round of judgment) is optimal; e parameterizes the degree of difference between the expected value with both prediction and judgment and the expected value without prediction with an increase in λ, increasing both. However, with one round of judgment, the increase when judgment is used alone is less than that when both are used together. Thus, when $\hat{\lambda} < \hat{\lambda}_{J2}$, prediction and judgment are complements.

By contrast, when $\hat{\lambda} > \hat{\lambda}_{J2}$, then strategy J2 (with two rounds of judgment) is used in the absence of prediction. In this case, increasing λ increases the expected payoff from judgment alone disproportionately more because judgment is applied on both states, whereas under prediction and judgment it is only applied on one. Thus, improving the quality of judgment reduces the returns to prediction. And so, when $\hat{\lambda} > \hat{\lambda}_{J2}$, prediction and judgment are substitutes.

3.5 Complexity

Thus far, the model illustrates the interplay between knowing the reward function (judgment) and prediction. While those results show that prediction and judgment can be substitutes, there is a sense in which they are more naturally complements. The reason is this: what prediction enables is a form of state-contingent decision-making. Without a prediction, a decision maker is forced to make the same choice regardless of the state that might arise. In the spirit of Herbert Simon, one might call this a heuristic. And in the absence of prediction, the role of judgment is to make that choice. Moreover, that choice is easier—that is, more likely to be optimal—when there exists dominant (or "near dominant") choices. Thus, when either the state space or the action space expand (as it may in more complex situations), it is less likely that there will exist a dominant choice. In that regard, faced with complexity, in the absence of prediction, the value of judgment diminishes and we are more likely to see decision makers choose default actions that, on average, are likely to be better than others.

Suppose now we add a prediction machine to the mix. While in our model such a machine, when it renders a prediction, can perfectly signal the state that will arise, let us consider a more convenient alternative that may arise in complex situations: the prediction machine can perfectly signal some states (should they arise), but for other states no precise prediction is possible except for the fact that one of those states is the correct one. In other words, the prediction machine can sometimes render a fine prediction and otherwise a coarse one. Here, an improvement in the prediction machine means an increase in the number of states in which the machine can render a fine prediction.

Thus, consider an N-state model where the probability of state i is μ_i. Suppose that states $\{1, \ldots, m\}$ can be finely predicted by an AI, while the remainder cannot be distinguished. Suppose that in the states that cannot be distinguished applying judgment is not worthwhile so that the optimal choice is the safe action. Also, assume that when a prediction is available, judgment is worthwhile; that is, $\hat{\lambda} \geq s/[vR + (1 - v)S]$. In this situation, the expected present discounted value when both prediction and judgment are available is

$$V_{PJ} = \hat{\lambda}\sum_{i=1}^{m}\mu_i\left(vR + (1 - v)S\right) + \sum_{i=m+1}^{N}\mu_i S.$$

Similarly, it is easy to see that $V_P = V_J = S = V_0$ as $vR + (1 - v)r \leq S$. Note that as m increases (perhaps because the prediction machine learns to predict more states), then the marginal value of better judgment increases. That is, $\hat{\lambda}\mu_m(vR + (1 - v)S) - \mu_m S$ is increasing in $\hat{\lambda}$.

What happens as the situation becomes more complex (that is, N increases)? An increase in N will weakly lead to a reduction in μ_i for any given i. Holding m fixed (and so the quality of the prediction machine does not improve with the complexity of the world), this will reduce the value of prediction and judgment as greater weight is placed on states where prediction is unavailable; that is, it is assumed that the increase in complexity does not, ceteris paribus, create a state where prediction is available. Thus, complexity appears to be associated with *lower* returns to both prediction and judgment. Put differently, an improvement in prediction machines would mean m increases with N fixed. In this case, the returns to judgment rise as greater weight is put on states where prediction is available.

This insight is useful because there are several places in the economics literature where complexity has interacted with other economic decisions. These include automation, contracting, and firm boundaries. We discuss each of these in turn, highlighting potential implications.

3.5.1 Automation

The literature on automation is sometimes synonymous with AI. This arises because AI may power new robots that are able to operate in open environments thanks to machine learning. For instance, while automated trains have been possible for some time since they run on tracks, automated cars are new because they need to operate in far more complex environments. It is prediction in those open environments that has allowed the emergence of environmentally flexible capital equipment. Note that leads to the implication that as AI improves, tasks in more complex environments can be handled by machines (Acemoglu and Restrepo 2017).

However, this story masks the message that emerges from our analysis that recent AI developments are all about prediction. Why prediction enables automated vehicles is because it is relatively straightforward to describe (and hence, program) what those vehicles should do in different situations. In other words, if prediction enables "state contingent decisions," then automated vehicles arise because someone knows what decision is optimal in each state. In other words, automation means that judgment can be encoded in machine behavior. Prediction added to that means that automated capital can be moved into more complex environments. In that respect, it is perhaps natural to suggest that improvements in AI will lead to a substitution of humans for machines as more tasks in more complex environments become capable of being programmed in a state-contingent manner.

That said, there is another dimension of substitution that arises in complex environments. As noted above, when states cannot be predicted (something that for a given technology is more likely to be the case in more complex environments), then the actions chosen are more likely to be defaults or the results of heuristics that perform, on average, well. Many, including Acemoglu and Restrepo (2017), argue that it is for more complex tasks that humans have a comparative advantage relative to machines. However, this is not at all obvious. If it is known that a particular default or heuristic should be used, then a machine can be programmed to undertake this. In this regard, the most complex tasks—precisely because little is known regarding how to take better actions given that the prediction of the state is coarse—may be more, not less, amenable to automation.

If we had to speculate, imagine that states were ordered in terms of diminished likelihood (i.e., $\mu_i \geq \mu_j$ for all $i < j$). The lowest index states might be ones that, because they arrive frequently, there is knowledge of what the optimal action is in each and so they can be programmed to be handled by a machine. The highest index states similarly, because the optimal action that cannot be determined can also be programmed. It is the intermediate states that arise less frequently but not infrequently where, if a reliable prediction existed, could be handled by humans applying judgment when those states arose. Thus, the payoff could be written

$$V_{PJ} = \sum_{i=1}^{k} \mu_i \left(vR + (1-v)S \right) + \hat{\lambda} \sum_{i=k+1}^{m} \mu_i \left(vR + (1-v)S \right) + \sum_{i=m+1}^{N} \mu_i S,$$

where tasks 1 through k are automated using prediction because there is knowledge of the optimal action. If this was the matching of tasks to machines and humans, then it is not at all clear whether an increase in complexity would be associated with more or less human employment.

That said, the issue for the automation literature is not subtleties over the term "complex tasks," but as AI becomes more prevalent, where might the substitution of machines for humans arise. As noted above, an increase in AI increases m. At this margin, humans are able to come into the marginal tasks and, because a prediction machine is available, use judgment to conduct state-contingent decisions in those situations. Absent other effects, therefore, an increase in AI is associated with more human labor on any given task. However, as the weight on those marginal tasks is falling in the level of complexity, it may not be the more complex tasks that humans are performing more of. On the other hand, one can imagine that in a model with a full labor market equilibrium that an increase in AI that enables more human judgment at the margin may also create opportunities to study that judgment to see if it can be programmed into lower index states and be handled by machines. So, while the AI does not necessarily cause more routine tasks to be handled by machines, it might create the economic conditions that lead to just that.

3.5.2   Contracting

Contracting shares much with programming. Here is Jean Tirole (2009, 265) on the subject:

> Its general thrust goes as follows. The parties to a contract (buyer, seller) initially avail themselves of an available design, perhaps an industry standard. This design or contract is the best contract under existing knowledge. The parties are unaware, however, of the contract's implications, but they realize that something may go wrong with this contract; indeed, they may exert cognitive effort in order to find out about what may go wrong and how to draft the contract accordingly: put differently, a *contingency* is foreseeable (perhaps at a prohibitively high cost), but not necessarily foreseen. To take a trivial example, the possibility that the price of oil increases, implying that the contract should be indexed on it, is perfectly foreseeable, but this does not imply that parties will think about this possibility and index the contract price accordingly.

Tirole argues that contingencies can be planned for in contracts using cognitive effort (akin to what we have termed here as judgment), while others may be optimally left out because the effort is too costly relative to the return given, say, the low likelihood that contingency arises.

This logic can assist us in understanding what prediction machines might do to contracts. If an AI becomes available then, in writing contracts, it is possible, because fine state predictions are possible, to incur cognitive costs to determine what the contingencies should be if those states should arise. For other states, the contract will be left incomplete—perhaps for a default action or alternatively some renegotiation process. A direct implication of this is that contracts may well become less incomplete.

Of course, when it comes to employment contracts, the effects may be different. As Herbert Simon (1951) noted, employment contracts differ from other contracts precisely because it is often not possible to specify what actions should be performed in what circumstance. Hence, what those contracts often allocate are different decision rights.

What is of interest here is the notion that contacts can be specified clearly—that is, programmed—but also that prediction can activate the use of human judgment. That latter notion means that actions cannot be easily contracted—by definition, contractibility is programming and needing judgment implies that programming was not possible. Thus, as prediction machines improve and more human judgment is optimal, then that judgment will be applied outside of objective contract measures—including objective performance measures. If we had to speculate, this would favor more subjective performance processes, including relational contracts (Baker, Gibbons, and Murphy 1999).[9]

3.5.3   Firm Boundaries

We now turn to consider what impact AI may have on firm boundaries (that is, the make or buy decision). Suppose that it is a buyer (B) who receives the value from a decision taken—that is, the payoff from the risky or safe action as the case may be. To make things simple, let's assume that $\mu_i = \mu$ for all i, so that $V = k(vR + (1-v)S) + \hat{\lambda}(m-k)(vR + (1-v)S) + (N-m)S$.

We suppose that the tasks are undertaken by a seller (S). The tasks $\{1, \ldots, k\}$ and $\{m+1, \ldots, N\}$ can be contracted upon, while the intermediate tasks require the seller to exercise judgment. We suppose that the cost of providing judgment is a function $c(\hat{\lambda})$, which is nondecreasing and convex. (We write this function in terms of $\hat{\lambda}$ just to keep the notation simple.) The costs can be anticipated by the buyer. So if one of the intermediate states arises, the buyer can choose to give the seller a fixed price contract (and bear none of the costs) or a cost-plus contract (and bear all of them).

Following Tadelis (2002), we assume that the seller market is competitive and so all surplus accrues to the buyer. In this case, the buyer return is

$$k\big(vR+(1-v)S\big)+\max\big\{\hat{\lambda}(m-k)\big(vR+(1-v)S\big),S\big\}+(N-m)S-p-zc(\hat{\lambda}),$$

while the seller return is: $p-(1-z)c(\hat{\lambda})$. Here $p+zc(\hat{\lambda})$ is the contract price and z is 0 for a fixed price contract and 1 for a cost-plus contract. Note that only with a cost-plus contract does the seller exercise any judgment. Thus, the buyer chooses a cost-plus over a fixed price contract if

$$k\big(vR+(1-v)S\big)+\max\big\{\hat{\lambda}(m-k)\big(vR+(1-v)S\big),S\big\}+(N-m)S-c(\hat{\lambda})$$
$$>k\big(vR+(1-v)S\big)+(N-k)S.$$

It is easy to see that as m rises (i.e., prediction becomes cheaper), a cost-plus contract is more likely to be chosen. That is, incentives fall as prediction becomes more abundant.

Now we can consider the impact of integration. We assume that the buyer can choose to make the decisions themselves, but at a higher cost. That is, $c(\hat{\lambda},I)>c(\hat{\lambda})$ where I denotes integration. We also assume that $\partial c(\hat{\lambda},I)/\partial\hat{\lambda}>\big(\partial c(\hat{\lambda})/\partial\hat{\lambda}\big)$. Under integration, the buyer's value is

$$k\big(vR+(1-v)S\big)+\hat{\lambda}^*(m-k)\big(vR+(1-v)S\big)+(N-m)S-c(\hat{\lambda}^*,I)$$

where $\hat{\lambda}^*$ maximizes the buyer payoff in this case. Given this, it can easily be seen that as m increases, the returns to integration rise.

By contrast, notice that as k increases, the incentives for a cost-plus contract are diminished and the returns to integration fall. Thus, the more prediction machines allow for the placement of contingencies in a contract (the larger m-k), the higher powered will seller incentives be and the more likely there is to be integration.

Forbes and Lederman (2009) showed that airlines are more likely to vertically integrate with regional partners when scheduling is more complex: specifically, where bad weather is more likely to lead to delays. The impact of prediction machines will depend on whether they lead to an increase in the number of states where the action can be automated in a state-contingent manner (k) relative to the increase in the number of states where the state becomes known but the action cannot be automated (m). If the former, then we will see more vertical integration with the rise of prediction machines. If the latter, we will see less. The difference is driven by the need for more costly judgment in the vertically integrated case as m-k rises.

3.6   Conclusions

In this chapter, we explore the consequences of recent improvements in machine-learning technology that have advanced the broader field of artificial intelligence. In particular, we argue that these advances in the ability of machines to conduct mental tasks are driven by improvements in machine prediction. In order to understand how improvements in machine prediction will impact decision-making, it is important to analyze how the payoffs of the model arise. We label the process of learning payoffs "judgment."

By modeling judgment explicitly, we derive a number of useful insights into the value of prediction. We show that prediction and judgment are generally complements, as long as judgment is not too difficult. We also show that improvements in judgment change the type of prediction quality that is most useful: better judgment means that more accurate predictions are valuable relative to more frequent predictions. Finally, we explore the role of complexity, demonstrating that, in the presence of complexity, the impact of improved prediction on the value of judgment depends on whether improved prediction leads to automated decision-making. Complexity is a key aspect of economic research in automation, contracting, and the boundaries of the firm. As prediction machines improve, our model suggests that the consequences in complex environments are particularly fruitful to study.

There are numerous directions research in this area could proceed. First, the chapter does not explicitly model the form of the prediction—including what measures might be the basis for decision-making. In reality, this is an important design variable and impacts on the accuracy of predictions and decision-making. In computer science, this is referred to as the choice of surrogates, and this appears to be a topic amenable for economic theoretical investigation. Second, the chapter treats judgment as largely a human-directed activity. However, we have noted that it can else be encoded, but have not been explicit about the process by which this occurs. Endogenising this—perhaps relating it to the accumulation of experience—would be an avenue for further investigation. Finally, this is a single-agent model. It would be interesting to explore how judgment and prediction mix when each is impacted upon by the actions and decisions of other agents in a game theoretic setting.

References

Acemoglu, Daron. 2003. "Labor- and Capital-Augmenting Technical Change." *Journal of the European Economic Association* 1 (1): 1–37.

Acemoglu, Daron, and Pascual Restrepo. 2017. "The Race between Machine and Man: Implications of Technology for Growth, Factor Shares, and Employment." Working paper, Massachusetts Institute of Technology.

Agrawal, Ajay, Joshua S. Gans, and Avi Goldfarb. 2018a. "Human Judgment and AI Pricing." *American Economic Association: Papers & Proceedings*, 108:58–63.

———. 2018b. *Prediction Machines: The Simple Economics of Artificial Intelligence.* Boston, MA: Harvard Business Review Press.

Alpaydin, Ethem. 2010. *Introduction to Machine Learning*, 2nd ed. Cambridge, MA: MIT Press.

Autor, David. 2015. "Why Are There Still So Many Jobs? The History and Future of Workplace Automation." *Journal of Economic Perspectives* 29 (3): 3–30.

Baker, George, Robert Gibbons, and Kevin Murphy. 1999. "Informal Authority in Organizations." *Journal of Law, Economics, and Organization* 15:56–73.

Belloni, Alexandre, Victor Chernozhukov, and Christian Hansen. 2014. "High-

Dimensional Methods and Inference on Structural and Treatment Effects." *Journal of Economic Perspectives* 28 (2): 29–50.

Benzell, Seth G., Laurence J. Kotlikoff, Guillermo LaGarda, and Jeffrey D. Sachs. 2015. "Robots Are Us: Some Economics of Human Replacement." NBER Working Paper no. 20941, Cambridge, MA.

Bolton, P., and A. Faure-Grimaud. 2009. "Thinking Ahead: The Decision Problem." *Review of Economic Studies* 76:1205–38.

Brynjolfsson, Erik, and Andrew McAfee. 2014. *The Second Machine Age*. New York: W. W. Norton.

Dogan, M., and P. Yildirim. 2017. "Man vs. Machine: When Is Automation Inferior to Human Labor?" Unpublished manuscript, The Wharton School of the University of Pennsylvania.

Domingos, Pedro. 2015. *The Master Algorithm*. New York: Basic Books.

Forbes, Silke, and Mara Lederman. 2009. "Adaptation and Vertical Integration in the Airline Industry." *American Economic Review* 99 (5): 1831–49.

Hastie, Trevor, Robert Tibshirani, and Jerome Friedman. 2009. *The Elements of Statistical Learning: Data Mining, Inference, and Prediction*, 2nd ed. New York: Springer.

Hawkins, Jeff. 2004. *On Intelligence*. New York: Times Books.

Jha, S., and E. J. Topol. 2016. "Adapting to Artificial Intelligence: Radiologists and Pathologists as Information Specialists." *Journal of the American Medical Association* 316 (22): 2353–54.

Lusted, L. B. 1960. "Logical Analysis in Roentgen Diagnosis." *Radiology* 74:178–93.

Markov, John. 2015. *Machines of Loving Grace*. New York: HarperCollins Publishers.

Ng, Andrew. 2016. "What Artificial Intelligence Can and Can't Do Right Now." *Harvard Business Review Online*. Accessed Dec. 8, 2016. https://hbr.org/2016/11/what-artificial-intelligence-can-and-cant-do-right-now.

Simon, H. A. 1951. "A Formal Theory of the Employment Relationship." *Econometrica* 19 (3): 293–305.

Tadelis, S. 2002. "Complexity, Flexibility and the Make-or-Buy Decision." *American Economic Review* 92 (2): 433–37.

Tirole, J. 2009. "Cognition and Incomplete Contracts." *American Economic Review* 99 (1): 265–94.

Varian, Hal R. 2014. "Big Data: New Tricks for Econometrics." *Journal of Economic Perspectives* 28 (2): 3–28.

Comment   Andrea Prat

One of the key activities of organizations is to collect, process, combine, and utilize information (Arrow 1974). A modern corporation exploits the vast amounts of data that it accumulates from marketing, operations, human resources, finance, and other functions to grow faster and be more

Andrea Prat is the Richard Paul Richman Professor of Business at Columbia Business School and professor of economics at Columbia University.

For acknowledgments, sources of research support, and disclosure of the author's material financial relationships, if any, please see http://www.nber.org/chapters/c14022.ack.

productive. This exploitation process depends on the kind of information technology (IT) that is available to the firm. If IT undergoes a revolution, we should expect deep structural changes in the way firms are organized (Milgrom and Roberts 1990).

Agrawal, Gans, and Goldfarb explore the effects that an IT revolution centered on artificial intelligence could have on organizations. Their analysis highlights an insightful distinction between *prediction*, the process of forecasting a state of the world θ given observable information, and *judgment*, the assessment of the effects of the state of the world and the possible action x the organization can take in response to it, namely, the value of the payoff function $u(\theta,x)$.

This is an important point of departure from existing work. Almost all economists—as well as computer scientists and decision scientists—assume that the payoff function $u(\theta,x)$ is known: the decision maker is presumed to have a good sense of how actions and states combine to create outcomes. This assumption, however, is highly unrealistic. The credit card fraud example supplied by the authors is convincing. What is the long-term cost to a bank of approving a fraudulent transaction or labeling a legitimate transaction a suspected fraud?

Organizations can spend resources to improve both their prediction precision and their judgment quality. Agrawal, Gans, and Goldfarb characterize the solution to this optimization problem. Their main result is that, under reasonable assumption, investment in prediction and investment in judgment are complementary (Proposition 2). Investing in prediction makes investment in judgment more beneficial in expected value.

This complementarity suggests that moving from a situation where prediction is prohibitively expensive to one where it is economical should increase the returns to judgment. In this perspective, the AI revolution will lead to an increase in the demand for judgment. However, judgment is an intrinsically different problem—one that cannot be solved through the analysis of big data.

Let me suggest an example. Admissions offices of many universities are turning to AI to choose which applicants to make offers to. Algorithms can be trained on past admissions data. We observe the characteristics of applicants and the grades of past and present students. Leaving aside the censored observations problem arising from the fact that we only see the grades of successful applicants who decide to enroll, we can hope that AI can provide a fairly accurate prediction of an applicant's future grades given his or her observable characteristics. The obvious problem is that we do not know how admitting someone who is likely to get high grades is going to affect the long-term payoff of our university. The latter is a highly complex object that depends on whether our alums become the kind of inspiring, successful, and ethical people that will add to the academic reputation and financial sustainability of our university. There is likely to be a connection between grades and this long-term goal, but we are not sure what it is. In this setting, Agrawal, Gans, and Goldfarb teach us an important lesson. Progress in AI should induce our university leaders to ask deeper questions about the relationship between student quality and the long-term goals of our higher-learning institutions. These questions cannot be answered within AI, but rather with more theory-driven retrospective approaches or perhaps more qualitative methodologies.

As an organizational economist, I am particularly interested in the implications of Agrawal, Gans, and Goldfarb's model for the study of organizations. First, this chapter highlights the importance of the dynamics of decision-making—a seriously underresearched topic. In a complex world, organizations are not going to immediately collect all the information they could possibly need about all possible contingencies they may face. Bolton and Faure-Grimaud (2009), a source of inspiration for Agrawal, Gans, and Goldfarb, model a decision maker who can "think ahead" about future states of the world in yet unrealized states of nature. They show that the typical decision maker does not want to think through a complete action plan, but rather focus on key short- and medium-term decisions. Agrawal, Gans, and Goldfarb show that Bolton and Faure-Grimaud's ideas are highly relevant for understanding how organizations are likely to respond to changes in information technology.

Second, Agrawal, Gans, and Goldfarb also speak to the organizational economics literature on mission. Dewatripont, Jewitt, and Tirole (1999) develop a model where organizational leaders are agents whose type is unknown, as in Holmstrom's (1999) career concerns paradigm. Each agent is assigned a mission, a set of measured variables that are used to evaluate and reward the agent. Dewatripont, Jewitt, and Tirole identify a tension between selecting a simple one-dimensional mission that will provide the agent with a strong incentive to perform well or a "fuzzy" multidimensional mission that will dampen the agent's incentive to work hard but will more closely mirror the true objective of the organization.

This tension is also present in Agrawal, Gans, and Goldfarb's world. Should we give the organization a mission that is close to a pure prediction problem, like admitting students who will get high grades? The pro is that it will be relatively easy to assess the leader's performance. The con is that the outcome may be weakly related to the organization's ultimate objective. Or should we give the organization a mission that also comprises the judgment problem, like furthering the long-term academic reputation of our university? This mission would be more representative of the organization's ultimate objective, but may make it hard to assess our leaders and give them a weak incentive to adopt new prediction technologies. One possible lesson from Agrawal, Gans, and Goldfarb is that, as the cost of adopting AI goes down, the moral hazard problem connected with judgment becomes relatively more important, thus militating in favor of incentive schemes that reward judgment rather than prediction.

Third, Agrawal, Gans, and Goldfarb's section on reliability touches on an important topic. Is it better to have a technology that returns accurate predictions with a low probability or less accurate predictions with a higher probability? The answer to this question depends on the available judgment technology. Better judgment technology increases the marginal benefit of prediction accuracy rather than prediction frequency. More broadly, this type of analysis can guide the design of AI algorithms. Given the mapping between states, actions, and outcomes, and given the cost of various prediction technologies, what prediction technology should the organization select? A general analysis of this question may require using information theoretical concepts, introduced to economics by Sims (2003).

Fourth, Agrawal, Gans, and Goldfarb show that economic theory can make important contributions to the debate over how AI will affect optimal organization. There is a related area where the interaction between economists and computer scientists can be beneficial. Artificial intelligence typically assumes a stable flow of instances. When a bank develops an AI-based system to detect fraud, it assumes that the available data, which is used to build and test the detection algorithm, comes from the same data-generating process as future data on which the algorithm will be applied. However, the underlying data-generating process is not an exogenously given natural phenomenon: it is the output of a set of human beings who are pursuing their own goals, like maximizing the chance of getting their nonfraudulent application accepted or maximizing their chance of defrauding the bank. These sentient creatures will in the long term respond to the fraud-detection algorithm by modifying their application strategy, for instance, by providing different information or by exerting effort to modify the reported variables. This means that the data-generating process will be subject to a structural change and that this change will be endogenous to the fraud-detection algorithm chosen by the bank. A similar phenomenon occurs in the university admission example discussed above: a whole consulting industry is devoted to understanding admissions criteria and advising applicants on how to maximize their success chances. A change in admissions practices is likely to be reflected in the choices that high school students make.

If the data-generating process is endogenous and depends on the prediction technology adopted by the organization, the judgment problem identified by Agrawal, Gans, and Goldfarb becomes even more complex. The organization must evaluate how other agents will respond to changes in the prediction technology. As, by definition, no data is available about not yet realized data-generating processes, the only way to approach this problem is by estimating a structural model that allows other agents to respond to changes in our prediction technology.

In conclusion, Agrawal, Gans, and Goldfarb make a convincing case that the AI revolution should increase the benefit of improving our judgment ability. They also provide us with a tractable yet powerful framework to understand the interaction between prediction and judgment. Future research should focus on further understanding the implications of improvements in prediction technology on the optimal structure of organizations.

References

Arrow, Kenneth. J. 1974. *The Limits of Organization*. New York: W. W. Norton.
Bolton, P., and A. Faure-Grimaud. 2009. "Thinking Ahead: The Decision Problem." *Review of Economic Studies* 76: 1205–38.
Dewatripont, Mathias, Ian Jewitt, and Jean Tirole. 1999. "The Economics of Career Concerns, Part II: Application to Missions and Accountability of Government Agencies." *Review of Economic Studies* 66 (1): 199–21.
Holmstrom, Bengt. 1999. "Managerial Incentive Problems: A Dynamic Perspective." *Review of Economic Studies* 66 (1): 169–82.
Milgrom, Paul, and John Roberts. 1990. "The Economics of Modern Manufacturing: Technology, Strategy, and Organization." *American Economic Review* June: 511–28.
Sims, Christopher. 2003. "Implications of Rational Inattention." *Journal of Monetary Economics* 50 (3): 665–90.

The Impact of Artificial Intelligence on Innovation
An Exploratory Analysis

Iain M. Cockburn, Rebecca Henderson, and Scott Stern

4.1 Introduction

Rapid advances in the field of artificial intelligence have profound implications for the economy as well as society at large. These innovations have the potential to directly influence both the production and the characteristics of a wide range of products and services, with important implications for productivity, employment, and competition. But, as important as these effects are likely to be, artificial intelligence also has the potential to change the innovation process itself, with consequences that may be equally profound, and which may, over time, come to dominate the direct effect.

Consider the case of Atomwise, a start-up firm that is developing novel technology for identifying potential drug candidates (and insecticides) by using neural networks to predict the bioactivity of candidate molecules. The company reports that its deep convolutional neural networks "far surpass" the performance of conventional "docking" algorithms. After appropriate training on vast quantities of data, the company's AtomNet product is described as being able to "recognize" foundational building blocks of

Iain M. Cockburn is the Richard C. Shipley Professor of Management at Boston University and a research associate of the National Bureau of Economic Research. Rebecca Henderson is the John and Natty McArthur University Professor at Harvard University, where she has a joint appointment at the Harvard Business School in the General Management and Strategy units, and a research associate of the National Bureau of Economic Research. Scott Stern is the David Sarnoff Professor of Management and chair of the Technological Innovation, Entrepreneurship, and Strategic Management Group at the MIT Sloan School of Management, and a research associate and director of the Innovation Policy Working Group at the National Bureau of Economic Research.

We thank Michael Kearney for extraordinary research assistance. For acknowledgments, sources of research support, and disclosure of the authors' material financial relationships, if any, please see http://www.nber.org/chapters/c14006.ack.

organic chemistry, and is capable of generating highly accurate predictions of the outcomes of real-world physical experiments (Wallach, Dzamba, and Heifels 2015). Such breakthroughs hold out the prospect of substantial improvements in the productivity of early stage drug screening. Of course, Atomwise's technology (and that of other companies leveraging artificial intelligence to advance drug discovery or medical diagnosis) is still at an early stage: though their initial results seem to be promising, no new drugs have actually come to market using these new approaches. But whether or not Atomwise delivers fully on its promise, its technology is representative of the ongoing attempt to develop a new innovation "playbook," one that leverages large data sets and learning algorithms to engage in precise prediction of biological phenomena in order to guide design-effective interventions. Atomwise, for example, is now deploying this approach to the discovery and development of new pesticides and agents for controlling crop diseases.

Atomwise's example illustrates two of the ways in which advances in artificial intelligence have the potential to impact innovation. First, though the origins of artificial intelligence are broadly in the field of computer science, and its early commercial applications have been in relatively narrow domains such as robotics, the learning algorithms that are now being developed suggest that artificial intelligence may ultimately have applications across a very wide range. From the perspective of the economics of innovation (among others, Bresnahan and Trajtenberg 1995), there is an important distinction between the problem of providing innovation incentives to develop technologies with a relatively narrow domain of application, such as robots purpose-built for narrow tasks, versus technologies with a wide   advocates might say almost limitless—domain of application, as may be true of the advances in neural networks and machine learning often referred to as "deep learning." As such, a first question to be asked is the degree to which developments in artificial intelligence are not simply examples of new technologies, but rather may be the kinds of "general purpose technologies" (GPTs) that have historically been such influential drivers of long-term technological progress.

Second, while some applications of artificial intelligence will surely constitute lower-cost or higher-quality inputs into many existing production processes (spurring concerns about the potential for large job displacements), others, such as deep learning, hold out the prospect of not only productivity gains across a wide variety of sectors, but also changes in the very nature of the innovation process within those domains. As articulated famously by Griliches (1957), by enabling innovation across many applications, the "invention of a method of invention" has the potential to have much larger economic impact than development of any single new product. Here we argue that recent advances in machine learning and neural networks, through their ability to improve both the performance of end-use technologies and the nature of the innovation process, are likely to have a particularly large impact on innovation and growth. Thus the incentives and obstacles that may shape the development and diffusion of these technologies are an important topic for economic research, and building an understanding of the conditions under which different potential innovators are able to gain access to these tools and to use them in a procompetitive way is a central concern for policy.

This chapter begins to unpack the potential impact of advances in artificial intelligence on innovation, and to identify the role that policy and institutions might play in providing effective incentives for innovation, diffusion, and competition in this area. We begin in section 4.2 by highlighting the distinctive economics of research tools, of which deep learning applied to research and development (R&D) problems is such an intriguing example. We focus on the interplay between the degree of generality of application of a new research tool and the role of research tools not simply in enhancing the efficiency of research activity, but in creating a new "playbook" for innovation itself. We then turn in section 4.3 to briefly contrast three key technological trajectories within artificial intelligence (AI)—robotics, symbolic systems, and deep learning. We propose that these often conflated fields will likely play very different roles in the future of innovation and technical change. Work in symbolic systems appears to have stalled and is likely to have relatively little impact going forward. And while developments in robotics have the potential to further displace human labor in the production of many goods and services, innovation in robotics technologies per se has relatively low potential to change the nature of innovation itself. By contrast, deep learning seems to be an area of research that is highly general purpose and has the potential to change the innovation process itself.

We explore whether this might indeed be the case through an examination of some quantitative empirical evidence on the evolution of different areas of artificial intelligence in terms of scientific and technical outputs of AI researchers as measured (imperfectly) by the publication of papers and patents from 1990 through 2015. In particular, we develop what we believe is the first systematic database that captures the corpus of scientific paper and patenting activity in artificial intelligence, broadly defined, and divides these outputs into those associated with robotics, symbolic systems, and deep learning. Though preliminary in nature (and inherently imperfect given that key elements of research activity in artificial intelligence may not be observable using these traditional innovation metrics), we find striking evidence for a rapid and meaningful shift in the application orientation of learning-oriented publications, particularly after 2009. The timing of this shift is informative, since it accords with qualitative evidence about the surprisingly strong performance of so-called "deep learning" multilayered neural networks in a range of tasks including computer vision and other prediction tasks.

Supplementary evidence (not reported here) based on the citation patterns to authors such as Geoffrey Hinton, who are leading figures in deep learning, suggests a striking acceleration of work in just the last few years that builds on a small number of algorithmic breakthroughs related to multi-layered neural networks.

Though not a central aspect of the analysis for this chapter, we further find that, whereas research on learning-oriented algorithms has had a slow and steady upward swing outside of the United States, US researchers have had a less sustained commitment to learning-oriented research prior to 2009, and have been in a "catch-up" mode ever since.

Finally, we begin to explore some of the organizational, institutional, and policy consequences of our analysis. We see machine learning as the "invention of a method of invention" whose application depends, in each case, on having access not just to the underlying algorithms, but also to large, granular data sets on physical and social behavior. Developments in neural networks and machine learning thus raise the question of, even if the underlying scientific approaches (i.e., the basic multilayered neural networks algorithms) are open, prospects for continued progress in this field—and commercial applications thereof—are likely to be significantly impacted by terms of access to complementary data. Specifically, if there are increasing returns to scale or scope in data acquisition (there is more learning to be had from the larger data set), it is possible that early or aggressive entrants into a particular application area may be able to create a substantial and long-lasting competitive advantage over potential rivals merely through the control over data rather than through formal intellectual property or demand-side network effects. Strong incentives to maintain data privately has the additional potential downside that data is not being shared across researchers, thus reducing the ability of all researchers to access an even larger set of data that would arise from public aggregation. As the competitive advantage of incumbents is reinforced, the power of new entrants to drive technological change may be weakened. Though this is an important possibility, it is also the case that, at least so far, there seems to be a significant amount of entry and experimentation across most key application sectors.

4.2   The Economics of New Research Tools: The Interplay between New Methods of Invention and the Generality of Innovation

At least since Arrow (1962) and Nelson (1959), economists have appreciated the potential for significant underinvestment in research, particularly basic research or domains of invention with low appropriability for the inventor. Considerable insight has been gained into the conditions under which the incentives for innovation may be more or less distorted, both in terms of their overall level and in terms of the direction of that research. As we consider the potential impact of advances in AI on innovation, two ideas from this literature seem particularly important—the potential for contracting problems associated with the development of a new broadly applicable research tool, and the potential for coordination problems arising from adoption and diffusion of a new "general purpose technology." In contrast to technological progress in relatively narrow domains, such as traditional automation and industrial robots, we argue that those areas of artificial intelligence evolving most rapidly—such as deep learning—are likely to raise serious challenges in both dimensions.

First, consider the challenge in providing appropriate innovation incentives when an innovation has potential to drive technological and organizational change across a wide number of distinct applications. Such general purpose technologies (David 1990; Bresnahan and Trajtenberg 1995) often take the form of core inventions that have the potential to significantly enhance productivity or quality across a wide number of fields or sectors. David's (1990) foundational study of the electric motor showed that this invention brought about enormous technological and organizational change across sectors as diverse as manufacturing, agriculture, retail, and residential construction. Such GPTs are usually understood to meet three criteria that distinguish them from other innovations: they have pervasive application across many sectors, they spawn further innovation in application sectors, and they themselves are rapidly improving.

As emphasized by Bresnahan and Trajtenberg (1995), the presence of a general purpose technology gives rise to both vertical and horizontal externalities in the innovation process that can lead not just to underinvestment but also to distortions in the direction of investment, depending on the degree to which private and social returns diverge across different application sectors. Most notably, if there are "innovation complementarities" between the general purpose technology and each of the application sectors, lack of incentives in one sector can create an indirect externality that results in a system-wide reduction in innovative investment itself. While the private incentives for innovative investment in each application sector depend on its the market structure and appropriability conditions, that sector's innovation enhances innovation in the GPT itself, which then induces subsequent demand (and further innovation) in other downstream application sectors. These gains can rarely be appropriated within the originating sector. Lack of coordination between the GPT and application sectors, as well as across application sectors, is therefore likely to significantly reduce investment in innovation. Despite these challenges, a reinforcing cycle of innovation between the GPT and a myriad of application sectors can generate a more systemic economy-wide transformation as the rate of innovation increases across all sectors. A rich empirical literature examining the productivity impacts of information technology (IT) point to the role of the microprocessor as a GPT as a way of understanding the impact of IT on the economy as a whole (among many others, Bresnahan and Greenstein 1999; Brynjolfsson and Hitt 2000; Bresnahan, Brynjolfsson, and Hitt 2002). Various aspects of artificial intelligence can certainly be understood as a GPT, and learning from examples such as the microprocessor are likely to be a useful foundation for thinking about both the magnitude of their impact on the economy and associated policy challenges.

A second conceptual framework for thinking about AI is the economics of research tools. Within the research sectors some innovations open up new avenues of inquiry, or simply improve productivity "within the lab." Some of these advances appear to have great potential across a broad set of domains beyond their initial application: as highlighted by Griliches (1957) in his classic studies of hybrid corn, some new research tools are inventions that do not just create or improve a specific product—instead, they constitute a new way of creating new products with much broader application. In Griliches's famous construction, the discovery of double-cross hybridization "was the invention of a method of inventing." (IMI) Rather than being a means of creating a single new corn variety, hybrid corn represented a widely applicable method for breeding many different new varieties. When applied to the challenge of creating new varieties optimized for many different localities (and even more broadly, to other crops), the invention of double-cross hybridization had a huge impact on agricultural productivity.

One of the important insights to be gained from thinking about IMIs, therefore, is that the economic impact of some types of research tools is not limited to their ability to reduce the costs of specific innovation activities—perhaps even more consequentially they enable a new approach to innovation itself, by altering the "playbook" for innovation in the domains where the new tool is applied. For example, prior to the systematic understanding of the power of "hybrid vigor," a primary focus in agriculture had been improved techniques for self-fertilization (i.e., allowing for more and more specialized natural varietals over time). Once the rules governing hybridization (i.e., heterosis) were systematized, and the performance advantages of hybrid vigor demonstrated, the techniques and conceptual approach for agricultural innovation was shifted, ushering in a long period of systematic innovation using these new tools and knowledge.

Advances in machine learning and neural networks appear to have great potential as a research tool in problems of classification and prediction. These are both important limiting factors in a variety of research tasks, and, as exemplified by the Atomwise example, application of "learning" approaches to AI hold out the prospect of dramatically lower costs and improved performance in R&D projects where these are significant challenges. But as with hybrid corn, AI-based learning may be more usefully understood as an IMI than as a narrowly limited solution to a specific problem. One the one hand, AI-based learning may be able to substantially "automate discovery" across many domains where classification and prediction tasks play an important role. On the other, that they may also "expand the playbook" is the sense of opening up the set of problems that can be feasibly addressed, and radically altering scientific and technical communities' conceptual approaches and framing of problems. The invention of optical lenses in the seventeenth century had important direct economic impact in applications such as spectacles. But optical lenses in the form of microscopes and telescopes also had enormous and long-lasting indirect effects on the progress of science, technological change, growth, and welfare: by making very small or very distant objects visible for the first time, lenses opened up entirely new domains of inquiry and technological opportunity. Leung et al. (2016), for example, evocatively characterize machine learning as an opportunity to "learn to read the genome" in ways that human cognition and perception cannot.

Of course, many research tools are neither IMIs nor GPTs, and their primary impact is to reduce the cost or enhance the quality of an existing innovation process. For example, in the pharmaceutical industry new kinds of materials promise to enhance the efficiency of specific research processes. Other research tools can indeed be thought of as IMIs but are nonetheless relatively limited in application. For example, the development of genetically engineered research mice (such as the OncoMouse) is an IMI that has had a profound impact on the conduct and playbook of biomedical research, but has no obvious relevance to innovation in areas such as information technology, energy, or aerospace. The challenge presented by advances in AI is that they appear to be research tools that not only have the potential to change the method of innovation itself, but also have implications across an extraordinarily wide range of fields. Historically, technologies with these characteristics—think of digital computing—have had large and unanticipated impacts across the economy and society in general. Mokyr (2002) points to the profound impact of IMIs that take the form not of tools per se, but innovations in the way research is organized and conducted, such as the invention of the university. General purpose technologies that are themselves IMIs (or vice versa) are particularly complex phenomena, whose dynamics are as yet poorly understood or characterized.

From a policy perspective, a further important feature of research tools is that it may be particularly difficult to appropriate their benefits. As emphasized by Scotchmer (1991), providing appropriate incentives for an upstream innovator that develops only the first "stage" of an innovation (such as a research tool) can be particularly problematic when contracting is imperfect and the ultimate application of the new products whose development is enabled by the upstream innovation is uncertain. Scotchmer and her coauthors emphasized a key point about a multistage research process: when the ultimate innovation that creates value requires multiple steps, providing appropriate innovation incentives are not only a question of whether and how to provide property rights in general, but also of how best to distribute property rights and incentives across the multiple stages of the innovation process. Lack of incentives for early stage innovation can therefore mean that the tools required for subsequent innovation do not even get invented; strong early stage property rights without adequate contracting opportunities may result in "hold-up" for later-stage innovators and so reduce the ultimate impact of the tool in terms of commercial application.

The vertical research spillovers created by new research tools (or IMIs) are not just a challenge for designing appropriate intellectual property policy.[1] They are also exemplars of the core innovation externality highlighted by endogenous growth theory (Romer 1990; Aghion and Howitt 1992); a central source of underinvestment in innovation is the fact that the intertemporal spillovers from innovators today to innovators tomorrow cannot be easily captured. While tomorrow's innovators benefit from "standing on the shoulders of giants," their gains are not easily shared with their predecessors. This is not simply a theoretical idea: an increasing body of evidence suggests that research tools and the institutions that support their development and diffusion play an important role in generating intertemporal spillovers (among others, Furman and Stern 2011; Williams 2013). A central insight of this work is that control—both in the form of physical exclusivity, as well as in the form of formal intellectual property rights—over tools and data can shape both the level and direction of innovative activity, and that rules and institutions governing control over these areas has a powerful influence on the realized amount and nature of innovation.

Of course, these frameworks cover only a subset of the key informational and competitive distortions that might arise when considering whether and how to provide optimal incentives for the type of technological change represented by some areas of AI. But these two areas in particular seem likely to be important for understanding the implications of the current dramatic advances in AI-supported learning. We therefore turn in the next section to a brief outline of the ways in which AI is changing, with an eye toward bringing the framework here to bear on how we might outline a research agenda exploring the innovation policy challenges that they create.

4.3   The Evolution of Artificial Intelligence: Robotics, Symbolic Systems, and Neural Networks

In his omnibus historical account of AI research, Nilsson (2010) defines AI as "that activity devoted to making machines intelligent, and intelligence is that quality that enables an entity to function appropriately and with foresight in its environment." His account details the contributions of multiple fields to achievements in AI, including but not limited to biology, linguistics, psychology and cognitive sciences, neuroscience, mathematics, philosophy

---

1. Challenges presented by AI-enabled invention for legal doctrine and the patent process are beyond the scope of this chapter.

and logic, engineering, and computer science. And, of course, regardless of their particular approach, artificial intelligence research has been united from the beginning by its engagement with Turing (1950) and his discussion of the possibility of mechanizing intelligence.

Though often grouped together, the intellectual history of AI as a scientific and technical field is usefully informed by distinguishing between three interrelated but separate areas: robotics, neural networks, and symbolic systems. Perhaps the most successful line of research in the early years of AI—dating back to the 1960s—falls under the broad heading of symbolic systems. Although early pioneers such as Turing had emphasized the importance of teaching a machine as one might a child (i.e., emphasizing AI as a learning process), the "symbol processing hypothesis" (Newell, Shaw, and Simon 1958; Newell and Simon 1976) was premised on the attempt to replicate the logical flow of human decision-making through processing symbols. Early attempts to instantiate this approach yielded striking success in demonstration projects, such as the ability of a computer to navigate elements of a chess game (or other board games) or engage in relatively simple conversations with humans by following specific heuristics and rules embedded into a program. However, while research based on the concept of a "general problem solver" has continued to be an area of significant academic interest, and there have been periodic explosions of interest in the use of such approaches to assist human decision-making (e.g., in the context of early stage expert systems to guide medical diagnosis), the symbolic systems approach has been heavily criticized for its inability to meaningfully impact real-world processes in a scalable way. It is, of course, possible that this field will see breakthroughs in the future, but it is fair to say that while symbolic systems continues to be an area of academic research, it has not been central to the commercial application of AI. Nor is it at the heart of the recent reported advances in AI that are associated with the area of machine learning and prediction.

A second influential trajectory in AI has been broadly in the area of robotics. While the concepts of "robots" as machines that can perform human tasks dates back at least to the 1940s, the field of robotics began to meaningfully flourish from the 1980s onward through a combination of the advances in numerically controlled machine tools and the development of more adaptive but still rules-based robotics that rely on the active sensing of a known environment. Perhaps the most economically consequential application of AI to date has been in this area, with large-scale deployment of "industrial robots" in manufacturing applications. These machines are precisely programmed to undertake a given task in a highly controlled environment. Often located in "cages" within highly specialized industrial processes (most notably automobile manufacturing), these purpose-built tools are perhaps more aptly described as highly sophisticated numerically controlled machines rather than as robots with significant AI content. Over the past twenty years, innovation in robotics has had an important impact on manufacturing and automation, most notably through the introduction of more responsive robots that rely on programmed response algorithms that can respond to a variety of stimuli. This approach, famously pioneered by Rod Brooks (1990), focused the commercial and innovation orientation of AI away from the modeling of human-like intelligence toward providing feedback mechanisms that would allow for practical and effective robotics for specified applications. This insight led, among other applications, to the Roomba and to other adaptable industrial robots that could interact with humans such as Rethink Robotics' Baxter. Continued innovation in robotics technologies (particularly in the ability of robotic devices to sense and interact with their environment) may lead to wider application and adoption outside industrial automation.

These advances are important, and the most advanced robots continue to capture public imagination when the term AI is invoked. But innovations in robotics are not, generally speaking, IMIs. The increasing automation of laboratory equipment certainly improves research productivity, but advances in robotics are not (yet) centrally connected to the underlying ways in which researchers themselves might develop approaches to undertake innovation itself across multiple domains. There are, of course, counterexamples to this proposition: robotic space probes have been a very important research tool in planetary science, and the ability of automated remote sensing devices to collect data at very large scale or in challenging environments may transform some fields of research. But robots continue to be used principally in specialized end-use "production" applications.

Finally, a third stream of research that has been a central element of AI since its founding can be broadly characterized as a "learning" approach. Rather than being focused on symbolic logic, or precise sense-and-react systems, the learning approach attempts to create reliable and accurate methods for the prediction of particular events (either physical or logical) in the presence of particular inputs. The concept of a neural network has been particularly important in this area. A neural network is a program that uses a combination of weights and thresholds to translate a set of inputs into a set of outputs, measures the "closeness" of these outputs to reality, and then adjusts the weights it uses to narrow the distance between outputs and reality. In this way, neural networks can learn as they are fed more inputs (Rosenblatt 1958, 1962). Over the course of the 1980s, Hinton and his coauthors further advanced the conceptual framework on which neural networks are based through the development of "back-propagating multilayer" techniques that further enhance their potential for supervised learning (Rumelhart, Hinton, and Williams 1986).

After being initially heralded as having significant promise, the field of neural networks has come in and out of fashion, particularly within the United States. From the 1980s through the middle of the first decade of the twenty-first century, their challenge seemed to be that there were significant limitations to the technology that could not be easily fixed by using larger training data sets or through the introduction of additional layers of "neurons." However, in the early twenty-first century, a small number of new algorithmic approaches demonstrated the potential to enhance prediction through back propagation through multiple layers. These neural networks increased their predictive power as they were applied to larger and larger data sets and were able to scale to an arbitrary level (among others, a key reference here is Hinton and Salakhutdinov [2006]). These advances exhibited a surprising level of performance improvement, notably in the context of the ImageNet visual recognition project competition pioneered by Fei-Fei Li at Stanford (Krizhevsky, Sutskever, and Hinton 2012).

4.4 How Might Different Fields within Artificial Intelligence Impact Innovation?

Distinguishing between these three streams of AI is a critical first step toward developing a better understanding of how AI is likely to influence the innovation process going forward, since the three differ significantly in their potential to be either GPTs or IMIs—or both.

First, though a significant amount of public discussion of AI focuses on the potential for AI to achieve superhuman performance over a wide range of human cognitive capabilities, it is important to note that, at least so far, the significant advances in AI have not been in the form of the "general problem solver" approaches that were at the core of early work in symbolic systems (and that were the motivation for considerations of human reasoning such as the Turing test). Instead, recent advances in both robotics and in deep learning are by and large innovations that require a significant level of human planning and that apply to a relatively narrow domain of problem-solving (e.g., face recognition, playing Go, picking up a particular object, etc.) While it is, of course, possible that further breakthroughs will lead to a technology that can meaningfully mimic the nature of human subjective intelligence and emotion, the recent advances that have attracted scientific and commercial attention are well removed from these domains.

Second, though most economic and policy analysis of AI draws out consequences from the last two decades of automation to consider the future economic impact of AI (e.g., in job displacement for an ever-increasing number of tasks), it is important to emphasize that there is a sharp difference between the advances in robotics that were a primary focus of applications of AI research during the first decade of the twenty-first century and the potential applications of deep learning that have come to the fore over the last few years.

As we suggested earlier, current advances in robotics are by and large associated with applications that are highly specialized and that are focused on end-user applications rather than on the innovation process itself, and these advances do not seem as of yet to have translated to a more generally applicable IMI. Robotics is therefore an area where we might focus on the impact of innovation (improved performance) and diffusion (more widespread application) in terms of job displacement versus job enhancement. We see limited evidence as yet of widespread applications of robotics outside industrial automation, or of the scale of improvements in the ability to sense, react to, and manipulate the physical environment that the use of robotics outside manufacturing probably requires. But there are exceptions: developments in the capabilities of "pick and place" robots and rapid progress in autonomous vehicles point to the possibility for robotics to escape manufacturing and become much more broadly used. Advances in robotics may well reveal this area of AI be a GPT, as defined by the classic criteria.

Some research tools/IMIs based on algorithms have transformed the nature of research in some fields, but have lacked generality. These types of algorithmic research tools, based on a static set of program instructions, are a valuable IMI, but do not appear to have wide applicability outside a specific domain and do not qualify as GPTs. For example, while far from perfect, powerful algorithms to scan brain images (so-called functional magnetic resonance imaging [MRI]) have transformed our understanding of the human brain, not only through the knowledge they have generated, but also by establishing an entirely new paradigm and protocol for brain research. However, despite its role as a powerful IMI, fMRI lacks the type of general purpose applicability that has been associated with the most important GPTs. In contrast, the latest advances in deep learning have the potential to be both a general purpose IMI and a classic GPT.

Table 4.1 summarizes these ideas.

How might the promise of deep learning as a general purpose IMI be realized? Deep learning promises to be an enormously powerful new tool that allows for the unstructured "prediction" of physical or logical events in contexts where algorithms based on a static set of program instructions (such as classic statistical methods) perform poorly. The development of this new approach to prediction enables a new approach to undertaking scientific and technical research. Rather than focusing on small well-characterized data sets or testing settings, it is now possible to proceed by identifying large pools of unstructured data that can be used to dynamically develop highly accurate predictions of technical and behavioral phenomena. In pioneering an unstructured approach to predictive drug candidate selection that brings together a vast array of previously disparate clinical and biophysical data, for example, Atomwise may fundamentally reshape the "ideas production function" in drug discovery.

If advances in deep learning do represent the arrival of a general purpose IMI, it is clear that there are likely to be very significant long-run economic, social, and technological consequences. First, as this new IMI diffuses across many application sectors, the resulting explosion in technological oppor-

Table 4.1   **General purpose technologies versus methods of invention**

		General purpose technology	
		NO	YES
Invention of a method of invention	NO	Industrial robots (e.g., Fanuc R2000)	"Sense & react robots (e.g., autonomous vehicles)
	YES	Statically coded algorithmic tools (e.g., fMRI)	**Deep learning**

tunities and increased productivity of research and development (R&D) seem likely to generate economic growth that can eclipse any near-term impact of AI on jobs, organizations, and productivity. A more subtle implication of this point is that "past is not prologue": even if automation over the recent past has resulted in job displacement (e.g., Acemoglu and Restrepo 2017), AI is likely to have at least as important an impact through its ability to enhance the potential for "new tasks" (as in Acemoglu and Restrepo 2018).

Second, the arrival of a general purpose IMI is a sufficiently uncommon occurrence that its impact could be profound for economic growth and its broader impact on society. There have been only a handful of previous general purpose IMIs and each of these has had an enormous impact, not primarily through their direct effects (e.g., spectacles, in the case of the invention of optical lenses), but through their ability to reshape the ideas production function itself (e.g., telescopes and microscopes). It would therefore be helpful to understand the extent to which deep learning is, or will, cause researchers to significantly shift or reorient their approach in order to enhance research productivity (in the spirit of Jones [2009]).

Finally, if deep learning does indeed prove to be a general purpose IMI, it will be important to develop institutions and a policy environment that is conductive to enhancing innovation through this approach, and to do so in a way that promotes competition and social welfare. A central concern here may be the interplay between a key input required for deep learning—large unstructured databases that provide information about physical or logical events—and the nature of competition. While the underlying algorithms for deep learning are in the public domain (and can and are being improved on rapidly), the data pools that are essential to generate predictions may be public or private, and access to them will depend on organizational boundaries, policy, and institutions. Because the performance of deep learning algorithms depends critically on the training data that they are created from, it may be possible, in a particular application area, for a specific company (either an incumbent or start-up) to gain a significant, persistent innovation advantage through their control over data that is independent of traditional economies of scale or demand-side network effects. This "competition for the market" is likely to have several consequences. First, it creates incentives for duplicative racing to establish a data advantage in particular application sectors (say, search, autonomous driving, or cytology) followed by the establishment of durable barriers to entry that may be of significant concern for competition policy. Perhaps even more important, this kind of behavior could result in a balkanization of data within each sector, not only reducing innovative productivity within the sector, but also reducing spillovers back to the deep learning GPT sector, and to other application sectors. This suggests that the proactive development of institutions and policies that encourage competition, data sharing, and openness is likely to be an important determinant of economic gains from the development and application of deep learning.

Our discussion so far has been largely speculative, and it would be useful to know whether our claim that deep learning may be both a general purpose IMI and a GPT, while symbolic logic and robotics are probably not, have any empirical basis. We turn in the next section to a preliminary examination of the evolution of AI as revealed by bibliometric data, with an eye toward answering this question.

4.5   Data

This analysis draws upon two distinct data sets, one that captures a set of AI publications from Thompson Reuters Web of Science, and another that identifies a set of AI patents issued by the US Patent and Trademark Office (USPTO). In this section, we provide detail on the assembly of these data sets and summary statistics for variables in the sample.

As previously discussed, peer-reviewed and public domain literature on AI points to the existence of three distinct fields within AI: robotics, learning systems, and symbol systems, each composed of numerous subfields. To track development of each of these using this data, we began by identifying the publications and patents falling into each of these three fields based on keywords. Appendix table 4A.1 lists the terms we used to define each field and identify the papers and patents belonging to it.[2] In short, the robotics field includes approaches in which a system engages with and responds to environmental conditions; the symbolic systems field attempts to represent complex concepts through logical manipulation of symbolic representations, and the learning systems field processes data through analytical programs modeled on neurologic systems.

4.5.1   Publication Sample and Summary Statistics

Our analysis focuses on journal articles and book publications through the Web of Science from 1955 to 2015. We conducted a keyword search utilizing the keywords described in appendix table 4A.1 (we tried several

---

2. Ironically enough, we relied upon human intelligence rather than machine learning to develop this classification system and apply it to this data set.

variants of these keywords and alternative algorithmic approaches, but this did not result in a meaningful difference in the publication set). We are able to gather detailed information about each publication, including publication year, journal information, topical information, as well as author and institutional affiliations.

This search yields 98,124 publications. We then code each publication into one of the three main fields of AI, as described earlier. Overall, relative to an initial data set of 98,124, we are able to uniquely classify 95,840 publications as symbolic systems, learning systems, robotics, or "general" AI (we drop papers that involve combinations of these three fields). Table 4.2 reports the summary statistics for this sample.

Of the 95,840 publications in the sample, 11,938 (12.5 percent) are classified as symbolic systems, 58,853 (61.4 percent) as learning, and 20,655 (21.6 percent) as robotics, with the remainder being in the general field of "artificial intelligence." To derive a better understanding of the factors that have shaped the evolution of AI, we create indicators for variables of interest including organization type (private versus academic), location type (US domestic versus international), and application type (computer science versus other application area, in addition to individual subject spaces, e.g., biology, materials science, medicine, physics, economics, etc.).

We identify organization type as academic if the organization of one of the authors on the publication is an academic institution; 81,998 publications (85.5 percent) and 13,842 (14.4 percent) are produced by academic and private-sector authors, respectively. We identify publication location as US domestic if one of the authors on the publication lists the United States as his or her primary location; 22,436 publications (25 percent of the sample) are produced domestically.

We also differentiate between subject matter. Forty-four percent of the publications are classified as computer science, with 56 percent classified as other applications. Summary statistics on the other applications are provided in table 4.3. The other subjects with the largest number of publications in the sample include telecommunications (5.5 percent), mathematics

Table 4.2   **Publication data summary statistics**

	Mean	Std. dev.	Min.	Max.
Publication year	2007	6.15	1990	2015
Symbolic systems	.12	.33	0	1
Learning systems	.61	.48	0	1
Robotics	.21	.41	0	1
Artificial intelligence	.06	.23	0	1
Computer science	.44	.50	0	1
Other applications	.56	.50	0	1
US domestic	.25	.43	0	1
International	.75	.43	0	1
Observations	95,840			

Table 4.3   Distribution of publications across subjects

	Mean	Std. dev.
Biology	.034	.18
Economics	.028	.16
Physics	.034	.18
Medicine	.032	.18
Chemistry	.038	.19
Mathematics	.042	.20
Materials science	.029	.17
Neurology	.038	.19
Energy	.015	.12
Radiology	.015	.12
Telecommunications	.055	.23
Computer science	.44	.50
Observations	95,840	

(4.2), neurology (3.8), chemistry (3.7), physics (3.4), biology (3.4), and medicine (3.1).

Finally, we create indicator variables to document publication quality including journal quality (top ten, top twenty-five, and top fifty journals by impact factor)[3] and a count variable for cumulative citation counts. Less than 1 percent of publications are in a top ten journal, with 2 percent and 10 percent in top twenty-five and top fifty journals, respectively. The average citation count for a publication in the sample is 4.9.

4.5.2   Patent Sample and Summary Statistics

We undertake a similar approach for gathering a data set of AI patents. We start with the public-use file of USPTO patents (Marco, Carley, et al. 2015; Marco, Myers, et al. 2015), and filter the data in two ways. First, we assemble a subset of data by filtering the USPTO Historical Masterfile on the US Patent Classification System (USPC) number.[4] Specifically, USPC numbers 706 and 901 represent "artificial intelligence" and "robots," respectively. Within USPC 706, there are numerous subclasses including "fuzzy logic hardware," "plural processing systems," "machine learning," and "knowledge processing systems," to name a few. We then use the USPC subclass to identify patents in AI fields of symbolic systems, learning systems, and robotics. We drop patents prior to 1990, providing a sample of 7,347 patents through 2014.

Second, we assemble another subset of AI patents by conducting a title

---

3. The rankings are collected from Guide2Research, found here: http://www.guide2research.com/journals/.

4. We utilized data from the Historical Patent Data Files. The complete (unfiltered) data sets from which we derived our data set are available here: https://www.uspto.gov/learning-and-resources/electronic-data-products/historical-patent-data-files.

Table 4.4   **Patent data summary statistics**

	Mean	Std. dev.	Min.	Max.
Application year	2003	6.68	1982	2014
Patent year	2007	6.98	1990	2014
Symbolic systems	.29	.45	0	1
Learning systems	.28	.45	0	1
Robotics	.41	.49	0	1
Artificial intelligence	.04	.19	0	1
Computer science	.77	.42	0	1
Other applications	.23	.42	0	1
US domestic firms	.59	.49	0	1
International firms	.41	.49	0	1
Org. type academic	.07	.26	0	1
Org. type private	.91	.29	0	1
Observations	13,615			

search on patents, with the search terms being the same keywords used to identify academic publications in AI.[5] This provides an additional 8,640 AI patents. We then allocate each patent into an AI field by associating the relevant search term with one of the overarching fields. For example, a patent that is found through the search term "neural network," is then classified as a "learning" patent. Some patents found through this search method will be duplicative of those identified by USPC search, that is, the USPC class will be 706 or 901. We drop those duplicates. Together these two subsets create a sample of 13,615 unique AI patents. Summary statistics are provided in table 4.4.

In contrast to the distribution of learning systems, symbolic systems, and robotics in the publication data, the three fields are more evenly distributed in the patent data: 3,832 (28 percent) learning system patents, 3,930 (29 percent) symbolic system patents, and 5,524 (40 percent) robotics patents. The remaining patents are broadly classified only as AI.

Using ancillary data sets to the USPTO Historical Masterfile, we are able to integrate variables of interest related to organization type, location, and application space. For example, patent assignment data tracks ownership of patents across time. Our interest in this analysis relates to upstream innovative work, and for this reason we capture the initial patent assignee by organization for each patent in our sample. This data enables the creation of indicator variables for organization type and location. We create an indicator for academic organization type by searching the name of the assignee for words relating to academic institutions, for example, "university," "college,"

5. We utilized data from the Document ID Dataset that is complementary to patent assignment data available on the USPTO website. The complete (unfiltered) data sets from which we derived our data set are available here: https://www.uspto.gov/learning-and-resources/electronic-data-products/patent-assignment-dataset.

or "institution." We do the same for private-sector organizations, searching for "corp.," "business," "inc.," or "co.," to name a few. We also search for the same words or abbreviations utilized in other languages, for example, "S.p.A." Only 7 percent of the sample is awarded to academic organizations, while 91 percent is awarded to private entities. The remaining patents are assigned to government entities, for example, the US Department of Defense.

Similarly, we create indicator variables for patents assigned to US firms and international firms, based on the country of the assignee. The international firm data can also be more narrowly identified by specific country (e.g., Canada) or region (e.g., European Union). Fifty-nine percent of our patent sample is assigned to US domestic firms, while 41 percent is assigned to international firms. Next to the United States, firms from non-Chinese, Asian nations account for 28 percent of patents in the sample. Firms from Canada are assigned 1.2 percent of the patents, and firms from China, 0.4 percent.

Additionally, the USPTO data includes NBER classification and subclassification for each patent (Hall, Jaffe, and Trajtenberg 2001; Marco, Carley, et al. 2015). These subclassifications provide some granular detail about the application sector for which the patent is intended. We create indicator variables for NBER subclassifications related to chemicals (NBER subclass 11, 12, 13, 14, 15, 19), communications (21), computer hardware and software (22), computer science peripherals (23), data and storage (24), business software (25), medical fields (31, 32, 33, and 39), electronics fields (41, 42, 43, 44, 45, 46, and 49), automotive fields (53, 54, 55), mechanical fields (51, 52, 59), and other fields (remaining). The vast majority of these patents (71 percent) are in NBER subclass 22, computer hardware and software. Summary statistics of the distribution of patents across application sectors are provided in table 4.5.

Table 4.5   Distribution of patents across application sectors

	Mean	Std. dev.
Chemicals	.007	.08
Communications	.044	.20
Computer hardware and software	.710	.45
Computer peripherals	.004	.06
Data and storage	.008	.09
Business software	.007	.09
All computer science	.773	.42
Medical	.020	.14
Electronics	.073	.26
Automotive	.023	.15
Mechanical	.075	.26
Other	.029	.16
Observations	13,615	

4.6   Deep Learning as a GPT: An Exploratory Empirical Analysis

These data allow us to begin examining the claim that the technologies of deep learning may be the nucleus of a general purpose invention for the method of invention.

We begin in figures 4.1A and 4.1B with a simple description of the evolution over time of the three main fields identified in the corpus of patents and

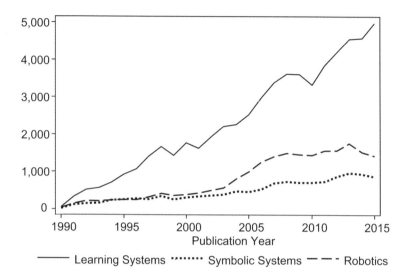

Fig. 4.1A   Publications by AI field over time

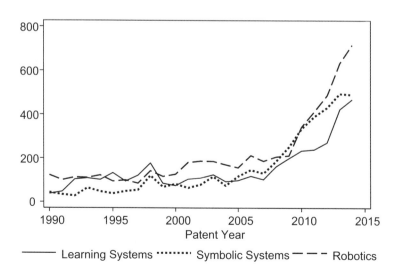

Fig. 4.1B   Patents by AI field over time

papers. The first insight is that the overall field of AI has experienced sharp growth since 1990. While there are only a small handful of papers (less than one hundred per year) at the beginning of the period, each of the three fields now generates more than one thousand papers per year. At the same time, there is a striking divergence in activity across fields: each start from a similar base, but there is a steady increase in the deep learning publications relative to robotics and symbolic systems, particularly after 2009. Interestingly, at least through the end of 2014, there is more similarity in the patterns for all three fields in terms of patenting, with robotics patenting continuing to hold a lead over learning and symbolic systems. However, there does seem to be an acceleration of learning-oriented patents in the last few years of the sample, and so there may be a relative shift toward learning over the last few years, which will manifest itself over time as publication and examination lags work their way through.

Within the publication data, there are striking variations across geographies. Figure 4.2A shows the overall growth in learning publications for the United States versus rest-of-world, and figure 4.2B maps the fraction of publications within each geography that are learning related. In the United States, learning is far more variable. Prior to 2000 the United States has a roughly equivalent share of learning-related publications, but the United States then falls significantly behind, only catching up again around 2013. This is consistent with the suggestion in qualitative histories of AI that learning research has had a "faddish" quality in the United States, with the additional insight that the rest of the world (notably Canada) seems to have taken advantage of this inconsistent focus in the United States to develop capabilities and comparative advantage in this field.

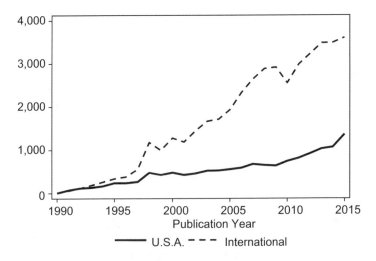

Fig. 4.2A   Academic institution publication fraction by AI field

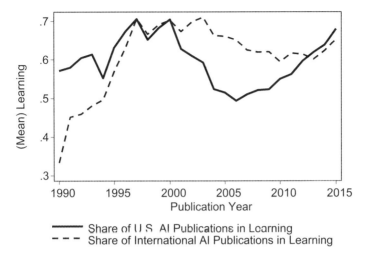

Fig. 4.2B   Fraction of learning publications by US versus world

With these broad patterns in mind, we turn to our key empirical exercise: whether late in the first decade of the twenty-first century deep learning shifted more toward "application-oriented" research than either robotics or symbolic systems. We begin in figure 4.3 with a simple graph that examines the number of publications over time (across all three fields) in computer science journals versus application-oriented outlets. While there has actually been a stagnation (even a small decline) in the overall number of AI publications in computer science journals, there has been a dramatic increase in the number of AI-related publications in application-oriented outlets. By the end of 2015, we estimate that nearly two-thirds of all publications in AI were in fields beyond computer science.

In figure 4.4 we then look at this division by field. Several patterns are worthy of note. First, as earlier, we can see the relative growth through 2009 of publications in learning versus the two other fields. Also, consistent with more qualitative accounts of the fields, we see the relative stagnation of symbolic systems research relative to robotics and learning. But, after 2009, there is a significant increase in application publications in both robotics and learning, but that the learning boost is both steeper and more long-lived. Over the course of just seven years, learning-oriented application publications more than double in number, and now represent just under 50 percent of *all* AI publications.[6]

These patterns are, if anything, even more striking if one disaggregates

6. The precise number of publications for 2015 is estimated from the experience of the first nine months (the Web of Science data run through September 30, 2015). We apply a linear multiplier for the remaining three months (i.e., estimating each category by 4/3).

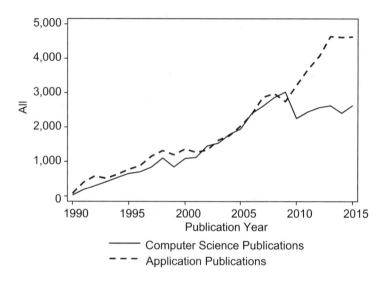

Fig. 4.3   Publications in computer science versus application journals

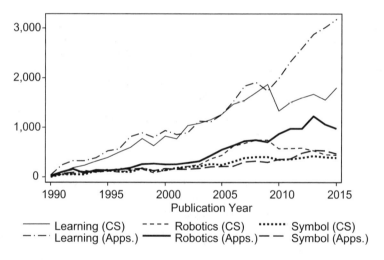

Fig. 4.4   Publications in computer science versus application journals by AI field

them by the geographic origin of the publication. In figure 4.5, we chart rates of publication in computer science versus applications for the United States as compared to the rest of the world. The striking upward swing in AI application papers that begins in 2009 turns out to be overwhelmingly driven by publications ex United States, though US researchers begin a period of catch-up at an accelerating pace toward the final few years of the sample.

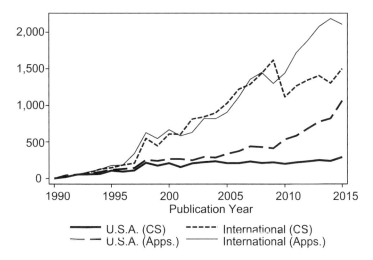

Fig. 4.5 **Learning publications in computer science versus applications by United States versus ROW**

Finally, we look at how publications have varied across application sectors over time. In table 4.6, we examine the number of publications by application field in each of the three areas of AI across two three-year cohorts (2004–2006 and 2013–2015). There are a number of patterns of interest. First and most important, in a range of application fields including medicine, radiology, and economics, there is a large relative increase in learning-oriented publications relative to robotics and symbolic systems. A number of other sectors, including neuroscience and biology, realize a large increase in both learning-oriented research as well as other AI fields. There are also some more basic fields such as mathematics that have experienced a relative decline in publications (indeed, learning-oriented publications in mathematics experienced a small absolute decline, a striking difference relative to most other fields in the sample). Overall, though it would be useful to identify more precisely the type of research that is being conducted and what is happening at the level of particular subfields, these results are consistent with our broader hypothesis that, alongside the overall growth of AI, learning-oriented research may represent a general purpose technology that is now beginning to be exploited far more systematically across a wide range of application sectors. (See table 4.7.)

Together, these preliminary findings provide some direct empirical evidence for at least one of our hypotheses: learning-oriented AI seems to have some of the signature hallmarks of a general purpose technology. Bibliometric indicators of innovation show that it is rapidly developing, and is being applied in many sectors—and these application sectors themselves include some of the most technologically dynamic parts of the economy.

Table 4.6 Publications across sectors by AI field, 2004–2006 versus 2013–2015

		Biology	Economics	Physics	Medicine	Chemistry	Math	Materials	Neuro.	Energy	Radiology	Telecom.	Comp. Sci.
Learning systems	2004–2006	258	292	343	231	325	417	209	271	172	94	291	3,889
	2013–2015	600	423	388	516	490	414	429	970	272	186	404	4582
	% growth	133	45	13	123	51	−1	105	258	58	98	39	18
Robotics	2004–2006	33	10	52	69	24	45	36	31	6	47	653	1,431
	2013–2015	65	12	122	83	92	80	225	139	18	25	401	1,322
	% growth	97	20	135	20	283	78	525	348	200	−47	−39	−8
Symbol systems	2004–2006	93	8	68	96	139	54	32	35	15	82	51	827
	2013–2015	105	10	125	84	149	60	101	73	22	56	88	1,125
	% growth	13	25	84	−13	7	11	216	109	47	−32	73	36

Table 4.7   **Herfindahl-Hirschman index for application sectors**

Application	$H = \sum \text{PatShare}^2$
Chemical applications	153.09
Communications	140.87
Hardware and software	86.99
Computer science peripherals	296
Data and storage	366.71
Computer science business models	222
Medical applications	290.51
Electronic applications	114.64
Automotive applications	197.03
Mechanical applications	77.51
Other	129.20

This preliminary analysis does not trace out the important knowledge spillovers between innovation in the GPT and innovation and application sectors, but it is probably far too early to look for evidence of this.

4.7   Deep Learning as a General Purpose Invention in the Method of Invention: Considerations for Organizations, Institutions, and Policy

With these results in mind, we now consider the potential implications for innovation and innovation policy if deep learning is indeed a general purpose technology (GPT) and/or a general purpose invention in the method of invention (IMI). If deep learning is merely a GPT, it is likely to generate innovation across a range of applications (with potential for spillovers both back to the learning GPT and also to other application sectors), but will not itself change the nature of the innovation production function. If it is also a general purpose IMI, we would expect it to have an even larger impact on economy-wide innovation, growth, and productivity as dynamics play out—and to trigger even more severe short-run disruptions of labor markets and the internal structure of organizations.

Widespread use of deep learning as a research tool implies a shift toward investigative approaches that use large data sets to generate predictions for physical and logical events that have previously resisted systematic empirical scrutiny. These data are likely to have three sources: prior knowledge (as in the case of "learning" of prior literatures by IBM's Watson), online transactions (e.g., search or online purchasing behavior), and physical events (e.g., the output from various types of sensors or geolocation data). What would this imply for the appropriate organization of innovation, the institutions we have for training and conducting research over time, and for policy, particularly, as we think about private incentives to maintain proprietary data sets and application-specific algorithms?

4.7.1 The Management and Organization of Innovation

Perhaps most immediately, the rise of general purpose predictive analytics using large data sets seems likely to result in a substitution toward capital and away from labor in the research production process. Many types of R&D and innovation more generally are effectively problems of labor-intensive search with high marginal cost per search (Evenson and Kislev [1976], among others). The development of deep learning holds out the promise of sharply reduced marginal search costs, inducing R&D organizations to substitute away from highly skilled labor toward fixed cost investments in AI. These investments are likely to improve performance in existing "search-intensive" research projects, as well as to open up new opportunities to investigate social and physical phenomena that have previously been considered intractable or even as beyond the domain of systematic scientific and empirical research.

It is possible that the ability to substitute away from specialized labor and toward capital (that in principle could be rented or shared) may lower the "barriers to entry" in certain scientific or research fields—particularly those in which the necessary data and algorithms are freely available—while erecting new barriers to entry in other areas (e.g., by restricting access to data and algorithms). As of yet, there are few, if any, organized markets for "trained" research tools or services based on deep learning, and few standards to evaluate alternatives. Our analysis suggests that the development of markets for shared AI services and the widespread availability of relevant data may be a necessary precursor to the broad adoption and dissemination of deep learning.

At the same time, the arrival of this new research paradigm is likely to require a significant shift in the management of innovation itself. For example, it is possible that the democratization of innovation will also be accompanied by a lack of investment by individual researchers in specialized research skills and specialized expertise in any given area, reducing the level of theoretical or technical depth in the workforce. This shift away from career-oriented research trajectories toward the ability to derive new findings based on deep learning may undermine long-term incentives for breakthrough research that can only be conducted by people who are at the research frontier. There is also the possibility that the large-scale replacement of skilled technical labor in the research sector by AI will "break science" in some fields by disrupting the career ladders and labor markets that support the relatively long periods of training and education required in many scientific and technical occupations.

Finally, it is possible that deep learning will change the nature of scientific and technical advance itself. Many fields of science and engineering are driven by a mode of inquiry that focuses on identifying a relatively small number of causal drivers of underlying phenomena built upon an underlying theory (the parsimony principle as restated by Einstein states that theory should be "as simple as possible but no simpler.") However, deep learning offers an alternative paradigm based on the ability to predict complex multicausal phenomena using a "black box" approach that abstracts away from underlying causes, but does allow for a singular prediction index that can yield sharp insight. De-emphasizing the understanding of causal mechanisms and abstract relationships may come at a cost: many major steps forward in science involve the ability to leverage an understanding of "big picture" theoretical structure to make sense of, or recognize the implications of, smaller discoveries. For example, it is easy to imagine a deep learning system trained on a large amount of x-ray diffraction data quickly "discovering" the double helix structure of DNA at very low marginal cost, but it would likely require human judgment and insight about a much broader biological context to notice that the proposed structure suggests a direct mechanism for heredity.

4.7.2   Innovation and Competition Policy and Institutions

A second area of impact, beyond the organization of individual research projects or the nature of what counts as "science" in a particular field, will be on the appropriate design and governance of institutions governing the innovation process. Three implications stand out.

First, as discussed earlier, research over the past two decades has emphasized the important role played by institutions that encourage cumulative knowledge production through low-cost independent access to research tools, materials, and data (Furman and Stern 2011; Murray and O'Mahony 2007). However, to date there has only been a modest level of attention to the questions of transparency and replicability within the deep learning community. Grassroots initiatives to encourage openness organized through online hubs and communities support knowledge production. But it is useful to emphasize that there is likely to be a significant gap between the private and social incentives to share and aggregate data—even among academic researchers or private-sector research communities. One implication of this divergence may be that to the degree any single research result depends on the aggregation of data from many sources, it will be important to develop rules of credit and attribution, as well as to develop mechanisms to replicate the results.

This implies that it will be particularly important to pay attention to the design and enforcement of formal intellectual property rights. On the one hand, it will be important to think carefully about the laws that currently surround the ownership of data. Should the data about, for example, my shopping and travel behavior belong to me or to the search engine or ride-sharing company that I use? Might consumers have a strong collective interest in ensuring that these data (suitably blinded, of course) are in the public domain so that many companies can use them in the pursuit of innovation?

On the other hand, the advent of deep learning has significant implications for the patent system. Though there has so far been relatively little patenting of deep learning innovations, historical episodes such as the discovery and attempted wholesale patenting of express sequence tags and other kinds of genetic data suggests that breakthroughs in research tools—often combined with a lack of capacity at patent offices and conflicting court decisions—can result in long periods of uncertainty that has hampered the issuing of new patents, and this in turn has led to lower research productivity and less competition. Deep learning also presents difficult questions of legal doctrine for patent systems that have been built around the idea of creative authors and inventors. For example, "inventorship" has a specific meaning in patent law, with very important implications for ownership and control of the claimed invention. Can an AI system be an inventor in the sense envisaged by the drafters of the US Constitution? Similarly, standards for determining the size of the inventive step required to obtain a patent are driven by a determination of whether the claimed invention would or would not be obvious to a "person having ordinary skill in the art." Who this "person" might be, and what constitutes "ordinary skill" in an age of deep learning systems trained on proprietary data are questions well beyond the scope of this chapter.

In addition to these traditional innovation policy questions, the prospect for deep learning raises a wide variety of other issues, including issues relating to privacy, the potential for bias (deep learning has been found to reinforce stereotypes already present in society), and consumer protection (related to areas such as search, advertising, and consumer targeting and monitoring). The key is that, to the extent that deep learning is general purpose, the issues that arise across each of these domains (and more) will play out across a wide variety of sectors and contexts and at a global rather than local level. Little analysis has been conducted that can help design institutions that will be responsive at the level of application sectors that also internalize the potential issues that may arise with the fact that deep learning is likely to be a GPT.

Finally, the broad applicability of deep learning (and possibly robotics) across many sectors is likely to engender a race within each sector to establish a proprietary advantage that leverages these new approaches. As such, the arrival of deep learning raises issues for competition policy. In each application sector there is the possibility of firms that are able to establish an advantage at an early stage, and in doing so position themselves to be able to generate more data (about their technology, about customer behavior, about their organizational processes), and will be able to erect a deep-learning-driven barrier to entry that will ensure market dominance over at least the medium term. This suggests that rules ensuring data accessibility are not only a matter of research productivity or aggregation, but also speak to the potential to guard against lock-in and anticompetitive conduct. At the present moment there seem to be a large number of individual companies attempting to take advantage of AI across a wide variety of domains (e.g., there are probably more than twenty firms engaging in significant levels of research in autonomous vehicles, and no firm has yet to show a decisive advantage), but this high level of activity likely reflects an expectation for the prospects for significant market power in the future. Ensuring that deep learning does not enhance monopolization and increase barriers to entry across a range of sectors will be a key topic going forward.

4.8   Concluding Thoughts

The purpose of this exploratory chapter has not been to provide a systematic account or prediction of the likely impact of AI on innovation, nor clear guidance for policy or the management of innovation. Instead, our goal has been to raise a specific possibility—that deep learning represents a new general purpose invention of a method of invention—and to draw out some preliminary implications of that hypothesis for management, institutions, and policy.

Our preliminary analysis highlights a few key ideas that have not been central to the economics and policy discussion so far. First, at least from the perspective of innovation, it is useful to distinguish between the significant and important advances in fields such as robotics from the potential of a general purpose method of invention based on application of multilayered neural networks to large amounts of digital data to be an invention in the method of invention. Both the existing qualitative evidence and our preliminary empirical analysis documents a striking shift since 2009 toward deep learning-based application-oriented research that is consistent with this possibility. Second, and relatedly, the prospect of a change in the innovation process raises key issues for a range of policy and management areas, ranging from how to evaluate this new type of science to the potential for prediction methods to induce new barriers to entry across a wide range of industries. Proactive analysis of the appropriate private and public policy responses toward these breakthroughs seems like an extremely promising area for future research.

Appendix

Table 4A.1   Artificial intelligence keyword allocation

Symbols	Learning	Robotics
Natural language processing	Machine learning	Computer vision
Image grammars	Neural networks	Robot
Pattern recognition	Reinforcement learning	Robots
Image matching	Logic theorist	Robot systems
Symbolic reasoning	Bayesian belief networks	Robotics
Symbolic error analysis	Unsupervised learning	Robotic
Pattern analysis	Deep learning	Collaborative systems
Symbol processing	Knowledge representation and reasoning	Humanoid robotics
Physical symbol system	Crowdsourcing and human computation	Sensor network
Natural languages	Neuromorphic computing	Sensor networks
Pattern analysis	Decision-making	Sensor data fusion
Image alignment	Machine intelligence	Systems and control theory
Optimal search	Neural network	Layered control systems
Symbolic reasoning		
Symbolic error analysis		

References

Acemoglu, D., and P. Restrepo. 2017. "Robots and Jobs: Evidence from US Labor Markets." NBER Working Paper no. 23285, Cambridge, MA.
———. 2018. "Artificial Intelligence, Automation and Work." NBER Working Paper no. 24196, Cambridge, MA.
Aghion, P., and P. Howitt. 1992. "A Model of Growth through Creative Destruction." *Econometrica* 60 (2): 323–51.
Arrow, K. 1962. "Economic Welfare and the Allocation of Resources for Invention." In *The Rate and Direction of Inventive Activity: Economic and Social Factors*, edited by R. R. Nelson. Princeton, NJ: Princeton University Press.
Bresnahan, T., E. Brynjolfsson, and L. Hitt. 2002. "Information Technology, Workplace Organization, and the Demand for Skilled Labor: Firm-Level Evidence." *Quarterly Journal of Economics* 117 (1): 339–76.
Bresnahan, T., and S. Greenstein. 1999. "Technological Competition and the Structure of the Computer Industry." *Journal of Industrial Economics* 47 (1): 1–40.
Bresnahan, T., and M. Trajtenberg. 1995. "General Purpose Technologies 'Engines of Growth'?" *Journal of Econometrics* 65:83–108.
Brooks, R. 1990. "Elephants Don't Play Chess." *Robotics and Autonomous Systems* 6:3–15.
Brynjolfsson, E., and L. M. Hitt. 2000. "Beyond Computation: Information Technology, Organizational Transformation and Business Performance." *Journal of Economic Perspectives* 14 (4): 23–48.
David, P. 1990. "The Dynamo and the Computer: An Historical Perspective on the Productivity Paradox." *American Economic Review* 80 (2): 355–61.

Evenson, R. E., and Y. Kislev. 1976. "A Stochastic Model of Applied Research." *Journal of Political Economy* 84 (2): 265–82.

Furman, J. L., and S. Stern. 2011. "Climbing atop the Shoulders of Giants: The Impact of Institutions on Cumulative Research." *American Economic Review* 101 (5): 1933–63.

Griliches, Z. 1957. "Hybrid Corn: An Exploration in the Economics of Technological Change." *Econometrica* 25 (4): 501–22.

Hall, B. H., A. B. Jaffe, and M. Trajtenberg. 2001. "The NBER Patent Citation Data File: Lessons, Insights and Methodological Tools." NBER Working Paper no. 8498, Cambridge, MA.

Hinton, G. E., and R. R. Salakhutdinov. 2006. "Reducing the Dimensionality of Data with Neural Networks." *Science* 313 (5786): 504–07.

Jones, B. F. 2009. "The Burden of Knowledge and the 'Death of the Renaissance Man': Is Innovation Getting Harder?" *Review of Economic Studies* 76 (1): 283–317.

Krizhevsky, A., I. Sutskever, and G. Hinton. 2012. "ImageNet Classification with Deep Convolutional Neural Networks." *Advances in Neural Information Processing* 25 (2). MIT Press. https://www.researchgate.net/journal/1049-5258 _Advances_in_neural_information_processing_systems.

Leung, M. K. K., A. Delong, B. Alipanahi, and B. J. Frey. 2016. "Machine Learning in Genomic Medicine: A Review of Computational Problems and Data Sets." *Proceedings of the IEEE* 104 (1): 176–97.

Marco, A., M. Carley, S. Jackson, and A. Myers. 2015. "The USPTO Historical Patent Data Files." USPTO Working Paper no. 2015–01, United States Patent and Trademark Office, 1–57.

Marco, A., A. Myers, S. Graham, P. D'Agostino, and K. Apple. 2015. "The USPTO Patent Assignment Dataset: Descriptions and Analysis." USPTO Working Paper no. 2015–02, United States Patent and Trademark Office, 1–53.

Mokyr, J. 2002. *Gifts of Athena*. Princeton, NJ: Princeton University Press.

Murray, F., and S. O'Mahony. 2007. "Exploring the Foundations of Cumulative Innovation: Implications for Organization Science." *Organization Science* 18 (6): 1006–21.

Nelson, Richard. 1959. "The Simple Economics of Basic Scientific Research." *Journal of Political Economy* 67 (3): 297–306.

Newell, A., J. C. Shaw, and H. A. Simon. 1958. "Elements of a Theory of Human Problem Solving." *Psychological Review* 6 (3): 151–66.

Newell, A., and H. A. Simon. 1976. "Computer Science as Empirical Inquiry: Symbols and Search." *Communications of the ACM* 19 (3): 113–26.

Nilsson, N. 2010. *The Quest for Artificial Intelligence: A History of Ideas and Achievements*. Cambridge: Cambridge University Press.

Romer, P. 1990. "Endogenous Technological Change." *Journal of Political Economy* 98 (5): S71–102.

Rosenblatt, F. 1958. "The Perceptron: A Probabilistic Model for Information Storage and Organization in the Brain." *Psychological Review* 65 (6): 386–408.

———. 1962. *The Principles of Neurodynamics*. New York: Spartan Books.

Rumelhart, D., G. Hinton, and R. Williams. 1986. "Learning Internal Representations by Error Propagation." In *Parallel Distributed Processing: Explorations in the Microstructure of Cognition, Volume 2: Psychological and Biological Models*, edited by J. McClelland and D. Rumelhart, 7–57. Cambridge, MA: MIT Press.

Scotchmer, S. 1991. "Standing on the Shoulders of Giants: Cumulative Research and the Patent Law." *Journal of Economic Perspectives* 5 (1): 29–41.

Turing, A. 1950. "Computing Machinery and Intelligence." *Mind* 59:433–60.

Wallach, I., M. Dzamba, and A. Heifels. 2015. "AtomNet: A Deep Convolutional Neural Network for Bioactivity Prediction in Structure-Based Drug Discovery." arXiv:1510.02855 [cs.LG]. https://arxiv.org/abs/1510.02855.
Williams, H. 2013. "Intellectual Property Rights and Innovation: Evidence from the Human Genome." *Journal of Political Economy* 121 (1): 1–27.

Comment   Matthew Mitchell

In their very interesting chapter, Cockburn, Henderson, and Stern make the case that artificial intelligence (AI) might serve as a general purpose technology in the production of innovations. My discussion centers on what this might mean for policy, and especially policies surrounding intellectual property (IP) protection. In particular, AI is likely to bring up new questions that are familiar from old IP debates about the balance between rewarding innovation and fears that this protection might in turn deter future innovation.

Is AI a Technology for Innovation or Imitation?

It is not obvious whether AI is a general purpose technology for innovation or a very efficient method of imitation. The answer has direct relevance for policy. A technology that made *innovation* cheaper would often (but not always) imply less need for strong IP protection, since the balance would swing toward limiting monopoly power and away from compensating innovation costs. To the extent that a technology reduces cost of *imitation*, however, it typically necessitates greater protection.

New technology is often useful for both innovation and imitation. For instance technologies like plastic molds, which can offer the possibility of new designs and therefore foster innovation, also lead to greater possibilities for reverse engineering. Machine learning is, in a sense, a sophisticated sort of mimicking; it sees what "works" (by some criterion) and finds ways to exploit that relationship. Therefore it seems that AI might be a general purpose technology for either innovation or imitation.

Consider a news aggregator. Many of these aggregators work because of some form of machine learning; they match the user to news stories that are predicted to be of interest. This is clearly a service that generates value, and would not exist in anything like its realized form in the absence of the underlying AI technology. But some news sites have argued that this constitutes infringement of their copyright. Semantically there is a question: Is the aggregator technology an innovation or is it imitation?

Matthew Mitchell is professor of economic analysis and policy at the University of Toronto.
For acknowledgments, sources of research support, and disclosure of the author's material financial relationships, if any, please see http://www.nber.org/chapters/c14023.ack.

Of course the answer is that it is both. It is much like the case of sequential innovations, where a later innovation builds on the earlier one, and at the same time uses and improves upon the prior. In those cases, to decide if the new innovation is a sufficient breakthrough on the old, words like "nonobvious" are employed in patent law. It is not completely clear how such words would apply to innovations that are made by machines; nonobviousness is designed in terms of a "person having ordinary skill in the art" and therefore is fundamentally about the human brain. How we will answer semantic questions like "what is obvious?" in a world where innovations are generated by machines will be central, and difficult, if we are to balance IP rewards and costs.

Situations like that of news aggregators have largely been managed, in practice, by the internet version of contracts. A news source can make its articles visible or invisible to the aggregator by blocking the content through a robots.txt file. That leaves only a competition concern: if news aggregators are few, they may still have monopoly power over creators of underlying content, making it difficult to solve problems simply by allowing content providers to opt out. The aggregator might control so much consumer attention that a news source cannot be viable without it.

Hammers That Make Nails

The aggregator example brings up the question of what policies might foster competition in a world where innovations are made using AI. Cockburn, Henderson, and Stern highlight the importance of data sharing and availability as an essential input in a world where the data itself is an input into the production of innovation by AI. This is clearly of critical importance. One issue that complicates policy is that the innovations may not only be produced *from* data, but also *generate* new data. Google's search engine generated data from users because it was a superior engine in the first place, but this can undoubtedly cement Google's market position. In a sense, asking the right questions or solving the right problems initially can generate users and data that lead to more innovations in the future. It is like a hammer that both needs nails to be productive, and also produces nails; being the first user of the hammer magnifies the advantage by creating more of the complementary input.

Here the economics literature on IP highlights two effects to balance: giving property rights to data (and not forcing the nails to be shared) is an encouragement to using the hammer in the first place (since it increases the value of the nails it produces) but also can make the hammer-nail technology less efficient for other firms (since they have less access to nails as an input). Striking the right balance on property rights for data strikes at the heart of the classic debate on how much competition is good for innovation.

Competition, Innovation, and Privacy

Whinston (2012) summarizes the classic forces of competition before and after innovation: Arrow (1962) suggests that ex ante competition is good for innovation, whereas Schumpeter (1942) argues that ex post competition is bad for innovation. Because today's innovations tend to lead to future innovations, for instance, through the data they generate if AI were involved, there is unfortunately no clear distinction between ex ante and ex post to serve as a rule. In the case of data, there is another force: privacy. It may be distasteful to enforce a data-sharing standard that would lead to multiple firms having the inputs necessary to attack the same problem. Goldfarb and Tucker (2012) point out that this means that privacy policy is connected to innovation policy more generally. Restrictions on data ownership will mean restrictions on a vital input into the innovation production process when innovations are produced with AI.

Since privacy concerns will likely mean less competition for innovation technologies built on AI, policymakers will have to be vigilant about insufficient competition. Since concern about insufficient competition harming innovation is largely about a lack of ex ante competition, the most important areas will be innovations in the early stage, relatively uncluttered areas of the technology space. Tailoring innovation policy in a new world of AI-generated innovations will require taking care to heed the general lessons of balancing benefits and costs of market power, while at the same time taking seriously the important new issues that are specific to the AI context. Cockburn, Henderson, and Stern's work helps us to better understand that context.

References

Arrow, K. 1962. "Economic Welfare and the Allocation of Resources to Invention." In *The Rate and Direction of Inventive Activity: Economic and Social Factors*, edited by Universities-National Bureau Committee for Economic Research and the Committee on Economic Growth of the Social Science Research Councils, 467–92. Princeton, NJ: Princeton University Press.

Goldfarb, Avi, and Catherine Tucker. 2012. "Privacy and Innovation." In *Innovation Policy and the Economy*, vol. 12, edited by Josh Lerner and Scott Stern, 65–89. Chicago: University of Chicago Press.

Schumpeter, Joseph. 1942. *Capitalism, Socialism and Democracy*. New York: Harper & Brothers.

Whinston, Michael D. 2012. "Comment on 'Competition and Innovation: Did Arrow Hit the Bull's Eye?'" In *The Rate and Direction of Inventive Activity Revisited*, edited by Josh Lerner and Scott Stern, 404–10. Chicago: University of Chicago Press.

5

Finding Needles in Haystacks
Artificial Intelligence and Recombinant Growth

Ajay Agrawal, John McHale, and Alexander Oettl

The potential for continued economic growth comes from the vast search space that we can explore. The curse of dimensionality is, for economic purposes, a remarkable blessing. To appreciate the potential for discovery, one need only consider the possibility that an extremely small fraction of the large number of potential mixtures may be valuable. (Romer 1993, 68–69)

Deep learning is making major advances in solving problems that have resisted the best attempts of the artificial intelligence community for years. It has turned out to be very good at discovering intricate structure in high-dimensional data and is therefore applicable to many domains of science, business, and government. (LeCun, Bengio, and Hinton 2015, 436)

5.1 Introduction

What are the prospects for technology-driven economic growth? Technological optimists point to the ever-expanding possibilities for combin-

Ajay Agrawal is the Peter Munk Professor of Entrepreneurship at the Rotman School of Management, University of Toronto, and a research associate of the National Bureau of Economic Research. John McHale is Established Professor of Economics and Dean of the College of Business, Public Policy, and Law at the National University of Ireland. Alexander Oettl is associate professor of strategy and innovation at the Georgia Institute of Technology and a research associate of the National Bureau of Economic Research.

We thank Kevin Bryan, Joshua Gans, and Chad Jones for thoughtful input on this chapter. We gratefully acknowledge financial support from Science Foundation Ireland, the Social Sciences Research Council of Canada, the Centre for Innovation and Entrepreneurship at the Rotman School of Management, and the Whitaker Institute for Innovation and Societal Development. For acknowledgments, sources of research support, and disclosure of the authors' material financial relationships, if any, please see http://www.nber.org/chapters/c14024.ack.

ing existing knowledge into new knowledge (Romer 1990, 1993; Weitzman 1998; Arthur 2009; Brynjolfsson and McAfee 2014). The counter case put forward by technological pessimists is primarily empirical: growth at the technological frontier has been slowing down rather than speeding up (Cowen 2011; Gordon 2016). Gordon (2016, 575) highlights this slowdown for the US economy. Between 1920 and 1970, total factor productivity grew at an annual average compound rate of 1.89 percent, falling to 0.57 percent between 1970 and 1994, then rebounding to 1.03 percent during the information technology boom between 1994 and 2004, before falling again to just 0.40 percent between 2004 and 2014. Even the maintenance of this lowered growth rate has only been possible due to exponential growth in the number of research workers (Jones 1995). Bloom et al. (2017) document that the total factor productivity in knowledge production itself has been falling both in the aggregate and in key specific knowledge domains such as transistors, health care, and agriculture.

Economists have given a number of explanations for the disappointing growth performance. Cowen (2011) and Gordon (2016) point to a "fishing out" or "low-hanging fruit" effect—good ideas are simply becoming harder to find. Jones (2009) points to the headwind created by an increased "burden of knowledge." As the technological frontier expands, it becomes harder for individual researchers to know enough to find the combinations of knowledge that produce useful new ideas. This is reflected in PhDs being awarded at older ages and a rise in team size as ever-more specialized researchers must combine their knowledge to produce breakthroughs (Agrawal, Goldfarb, and Teodoridis 2016). Other evidence points to the physical, social, and institutional constraints that limit access to knowledge, including the need to be physically close to the sources of knowledge (Jaffe, Trajtenberg, and Henderson 1993; Catalini 2017), the importance of social relationships in accessing knowledge (Mokyr 2002; Agrawal, Cockburn, and McHale 2006; Agrawal, Kapur, and McHale 2008), and the importance of institutions in facilitating—or limiting—access to knowledge (Furman and Stern 2011).

Despite the evidence of a growth slowdown, one reason to be hopeful about the future is the recent explosion in data availability under the rubric of "big data" and computer-based advances in capabilities to discover and process those data. We can view these technologies in part as "meta technologies"—technologies for the production of new knowledge. If part of the challenge is dealing with the combinatorial explosion in the potential ways that existing knowledge can be combined as the knowledge base grows, then meta technologies such as deep learning hold out the potential to partially overcome the challenges of fishing out, the rising burden of knowledge, and the social and institutional constraints on knowledge access.

Of course, meta technologies that aid in the discovery of new knowledge are nothing new. Mokyr (2002, 2017) gives numerous examples of how scientific instruments such as microscopes and x-ray crystallography significantly aided the discovery process. Rosenberg (1998) provides an account of how technology-embodied chemical engineering altered the path of discovery in the petrochemical industry. Moreover, the use of artificial intelligence (AI) for discovery is itself not new and has underpinned fields such as cheminformatics, bioinformatics, and particle physics for decades. However, recent breakthroughs in AI such as deep learning have given a new impetus to these fields.[1] The convergence of graphical processing unit (GPU)-accelerated computing power, exponential growth in data availability buttressed in part by open data sources, and the rapid advance in AI-based prediction technologies is leading to breakthroughs in solving many needle-in-a-haystack problems (chapter 3, this volume). If the curse of dimensionality is both the blessing and curse of discovery, advances in AI offer renewed hope of breaking the curse while helping to deliver on the blessing.

Understanding how these technologies could affect future growth dynamics is likely to require an explicitly combinatorial framework. Weitzman's (1998) pioneering development of a recombinant growth model has unfortunately not been well incorporated into the corpus of growth theory literature. Our contribution in this chapter is thus twofold. First, we develop a relatively simple combinatorial-based knowledge production function that converges in the limit to the Romer/Jones function. The model allows for the consideration of how existing knowledge is combined to produce new knowledge and also how researchers combine to form teams. Second, while this function can be incorporated into existing growth models, the specific combinatorial foundations mean that the model provides insights into how new metatechnologies such as artificial intelligence might matter for the path of future economic growth.

The starting point for the model we develop is the Romer/Jones knowledge production function. This function—a workhorse of modern growth theory—models the output of new ideas as a Cobb-Douglas function with the existing knowledge stock and labor resources devoted to knowledge production as inputs. Implicit in the Romer/Jones formulation is that new knowledge production depends on access to the existing knowledge stock and the ability to combine distinct elements of that stock into valuable new ideas. The promise of AI as a meta technology for new idea production is that it facilitates the search over complex knowledge spaces, allowing for both improved access to relevant knowledge and improved capacity to predict the value of new combinations. It may be especially valuable where the complexity of the underlying biological or physical systems has stymied technological advance, notwithstanding the apparent promise of new fields such as biotechnology or nanotechnology. We thus develop an explicitly combinatorial-based knowledge production function. Separate parameters

---

1. See, for example, the recent survey of the use of deep learning in computational chemistry by Garrett Goh, Nathan Hodas, and Abhinav Vishnu (2017).

control the ease of knowledge access, the ability to search the complex space of potential combinations, and the ease of forming research teams to pool knowledge access. An attractive feature of our proposed function is that the Romer/Jones function emerges as a limiting case. By explicitly delineating the knowledge access, combinatorial and collaboration aspects of knowledge production, we hope that the model can help elucidate how AI could improve the chances of solving needle-in-a-haystack-type challenges and thus influence the path of economic growth.

Our chapter thus contributes to a recent but rapidly expanding literature on the effects of AI on economic growth. Much of the focus of this new literature is on how increased automation substitutes for labor in the production process. Building on the pioneering work of Zeira (1998), Acemoglu and Restrepo (2017) develop a model in which AI substitutes for workers in existing tasks, but also creates new tasks for workers to do. Aghion, Jones, and Jones (chapter 9, this volume) show how automation can be consistent with relatively constant factor shares when the elasticity of substitution between goods is less than one. Central to their results is Baumol's "cost disease," which posits the ultimate constraint on growth to be from goods that are essential but hard to improve rather than goods whose production benefits from AI-driven technical change. In a similar vein, Nordhaus (2015) explores the conditions under which AI would lead to an "economic singularity" and examines the empirical evidence on the elasticity of substitution on both the demand and supply sides of the economy.

Our focus is different from these papers in that instead of emphasising the potential substitution of machines for workers in existing tasks, we emphasise the importance of AI in overcoming a specific problem that impedes human researchers—finding useful combinations in complex discovery spaces. Our chapter is closest in spirit to Cockburn, Henderson, and Stern (chapter 4, this volume), which examines the implications of AI—and deep learning in particular—as a general purpose technology (GPT) for invention. We provide a suggested formalization of this key idea. Nielsen (2012) usefully illuminates the myriad ways in which "big data" and associated technologies are changing the mechanisms of discovery in science. Nielsen emphasizes the increasing importance of "collective intelligence" in formal and informal networked teams, the growth of "data-driven intelligence" that can solve problems that challenge human intelligence, and the importance of increased technology facilitating access to knowledge and data. We incorporate all of these elements into the model developed in this chapter.

The rest of the chapter is organized as follows. In the next section, we outline some examples of how advances in artificial intelligence are changing both knowledge access and the ability to combine knowledge in high-dimensional data across a number of domains. In section 5.3, we develop an explicitly combinatorial-based knowledge production function and embed it in the growth model of Jones (1995), which itself is a modification of

Romer (1990). In section 5.4, we extend the basic model to allow for knowledge production by teams. We discuss our results in section 5.5 and conclude in section 5.6 with some speculative thoughts on how an "economic singularity" might emerge.

5.2   How Artificial Intelligence Is Impacting the Production of Knowledge: Some Motivating Examples

Breakthroughs in AI are already impacting the productivity of scientific research and technology development. It is useful to distinguish between such meta technologies that aid in the process of search (knowledge access) and discovery (combining existing knowledge to produce new knowledge). For search, we are interested in AIs that solve problems that meet two conditions: (a) potential knowledge relevant to the process of discovery is subject to an explosion of data that an individual researcher or team of researchers finds increasingly difficult to stay abreast of (the "burden of knowledge"); and (b) the AI predicts which pieces of knowledge will be most relevant to the researcher, typically through the input of search terms. For discovery, we also identify two conditions: (a) potentially combinable knowledge for the production of new knowledge is subject to combinatorial explosion, and (b) the AI predicts which combinations of existing knowledge will yield valuable new knowledge across a large number of domains. We now consider some specific examples of how AI-based search and discovery technologies may change the innovation process.

5.2.1   Search

Meta[α] produces AI-based search technologies for identifying relevant scientific papers and tracking the evolution of scientific ideas. The company was acquired by the Chan-Zuckerberg Foundation, which intends to make it available free of charge to researchers. This AI-based search technology meets our two conditions for a meta technology for knowledge access: (a) the stock of scientific papers is subject to exponential growth at an estimated 8–9 percent per year (Bornmann and Mutz 2015), and (b) the AI-based search technology helps scientists identify relevant papers, thereby reducing the "burden of knowledge" associated with the exponential growth of published output.

BenchSci is an AI-based search technology for the more specific task of identifying effective compounds used in drug discovery (notably antibodies that act as reagents in scientific experiments). It again meets our two conditions: (a) reports on compound efficacy are scattered through millions of scientific papers with little standardization in how these reports are provided, and (b) an AI extracts compound-efficacy information, allowing scientists to more effectively identify appropriate compounds to use in experiments.

5.2.2   Discovery

Atomwise is a deep learning-based AI for the discovery of drug molecules (compounds) that have the potential to yield safe and effective new drugs. This AI meets our two conditions for a meta technology for discovery: (a) the number of potential compounds is subject to combinatorial explosion, and (b) the AI predicts how basic chemical features combine into more intricate features to identify potential compounds for more detailed investigation.

Deep Genomics is a deep learning-based AI that predicts what happens in a cell when DNA is altered by natural or therapeutic genetic variation. It again meets our two conditions: (a) genotype-phenotype variations are subject to combinatorial explosion, and (b) the AI "bridges the genotype-phenotype divide" by predicting the results of complex biological processes that relate variations in the genotype to observable characteristics of an organism, thus helping to identify potentially valuable therapeutic interventions for further testing.

5.3   A Combinatorial-Based Knowledge Production Function

Figure 5.1 provides an overview of our modeling approach and how it relates to the classic Romer/Jones knowledge production function. The solid lines capture the essential character of the Romer/Jones function. Researchers use existing knowledge—the standing-on-shoulders effect—to produce

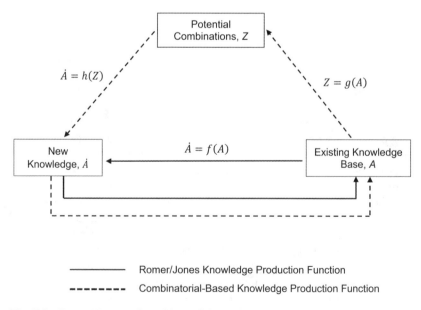

Romer/Jones Knowledge Production Function

Combinatorial-Based Knowledge Production Function

Fig. 5.1   Romer/Jones and combinatorial-based knowledge production functions

new knowledge. The new knowledge then becomes part of the knowledge base from which subsequent discoveries are made. The dashed lines capture our approach. The existing knowledge base determines the potential new combinations that are possible, the majority of which are likely to have no value. The discovery of valuable new knowledge is made by searching among the massive number of potential combinations. This discovery process is aided by meta technologies such as deep learning that allow researchers to identify valuable combinations in spaces where existing knowledge interacts in often highly complex ways. As with the Romer/Jones function, the new knowledge adds to the knowledge base—and thus the potential combinations of that knowledge base—which subsequent researchers have to work with. A feature of our new knowledge production function will be that the Romer/Jones function emerges as a limiting case both with and without team production of new knowledge. In this section, we first develop the new function without team production of new knowledge; in the next section, we extend the function to allow for team production.

The total stock of knowledge in the world is denoted as A, which we assume initially is measured discretely. An individual researcher has access to an amount of knowledge, A^ϕ (also assumed to be an integer), so that the share of the stock of knowledge available to an individual researcher is $A^{\phi-1}$.[2] We assume that $0 < \phi < 1$. This implies that the share of total knowledge accessible to an individual researcher is falling with the total stock of knowledge. This is a manifestation in the model of the "burden of knowledge" effect identified by Jones (2009)—it becomes more difficult to access all the available knowledge as the total stock of knowledge grows. The knowledge access parameter, ϕ, is assumed to capture not only what a researcher knows at a point in time, but also their ability to find existing knowledge should they require it. The value of the parameter will thus be affected by the extent to which knowledge is available in codified form and can be found as needed by researchers. The combination of digital repositories of knowledge and search technologies that can predict what knowledge will be most relevant to the researcher given the search terms they input—think of the ubiquitous Google as well as more specialized search technologies such as Meta$^\alpha$ and BenchSci—should increase the value of ϕ.

2. Paul Romer emphasized the importance of distinguishing between ideas (a nonrival good) and human capital (a rival good). "Ideas are . . . the critical input in the production of more valuable human and non-human capital. But human capital is also the most important input in the production of new ideas. . . . Because human capital and ideas are so closely related as inputs and outputs, it is tempting to aggregate them into a single type of good. . . . It is important, nevertheless, to distinguish ideas and human capital because they have different fundamental attributes as economic goods, with different implications for economic theory" (Romer 1993, 71). In our model, A^ϕ is a measure of a researcher's human capital. Clearly, human capital depends on the existing technological and other knowledge and the researcher's access to that knowledge. In turn, the production of new knowledge depends on the researcher's human capital.

Innovations occur as a result of combining existing knowledge to produce new knowledge. Knowledge can be combined a ideas at a time, where $a =$ 0, 1 . . . A^ϕ. For a given individual researcher, the total number of possible combinations of units of existing knowledge (including singletons and the null set)[3] given their knowledge access is

(1)
$$Z_i = \sum_{a=0}^{A^\phi} \binom{A^\phi}{a} = 2^{A^\phi}.$$

The total number of potential combinations, Z_i, grows exponentially with A^ϕ. Clearly, if A is itself growing exponentially, Z_i will be growing at a double exponential rate. This is the source of combinatorial explosion in the model. Since it is more convenient to work with continuously measured variables in the growth model, from this point on we treat A and Z_i as continuously measured variables. However, the key assumption is that the number of potential combinations grows exponentially with knowledge access.

The next step is to specify how potential combinations map to discoveries. We assume that a large share of potential combinations do not produce useful new knowledge. Moreover, of those combinations that are useful, many will have already been discovered and thus are already part of A. This latter feature reflects the fishing-out phenomenon. The per-period translation of potential combinations into valuable new knowledge is given by the (asymptotically) constant elasticity discovery function

(2)
$$\dot{A}_i = \beta\left(\frac{Z_i^\theta - 1}{\theta}\right) = \beta\left(\frac{(2^{A^\phi})^\theta - 1}{\theta}\right) \quad for < \theta \le 1$$

$$= \beta \ln Z_i = \beta \ln\left(2^{A^\phi}\right) = \beta \ln(2) A^\phi \quad for\ \theta = 0,$$

where β is a positively valued knowledge discovery parameter and use is made of L'Hôpital's rule for the limiting case of $\theta = 0$.[4]

For $\theta > 0$, the elasticity of new discoveries with respect to the number of possible combinations, Z_i, is

(3)
$$\frac{\partial \dot{A}}{\partial Z_i}\frac{Z_i}{\dot{A}} = \frac{\beta Z_i^{\theta-1}}{\beta\left[(Z_i^\theta - 1)/\theta\right]} = \left(\frac{Z_i^\theta}{Z_i^\theta - 1}\right)\theta,$$

---

3. Excluding the singletons and the null set, total number of potential combinations would be $2^{A^\phi} - A^\phi - 1$. As singletons and the null set are not true "combinations," we take equation (1) to be an approximation of the true number of potential combinations. The relative significance of this approximation will decline as the knowledge base grows, and we ignore it in what follows.

4. L'Hôpital's rule is often useful where a limit of a quotient is indeterminate. The limit of the term in brackets on the right-hand side of equation (2) as θ goes to zero is 0 divided by 0 and is thus indeterminate. However, by L'Hôpital's rule, the limit of this quotient is equal to the limit of the quotient produced by dividing the limit of the derivative of the numerator with respect to θ by the limit of the derivative of the denominator with respect to θ. This limit is equal to $\ln(2)A^\phi$.

which converges to θ as the number of potential combinations goes to infinity. For $\theta = 0$, the elasticity of new discoveries is

(4)
$$\frac{\partial \dot{A}}{\partial Z_i} \frac{Z_i}{\dot{A}} = \frac{\beta}{Z_i} \frac{Z_i}{\beta \ln Z_i} = \frac{1}{\ln Z_i},$$

which converges to zero as the number of potential combinations goes to infinity.

A number of factors seem likely to affect the value of the fishing-out/complexity parameter, θ. First are basic constraints relating to natural phenomena that limit what is physically possible in terms of combining existing knowledge to produce scientifically or technologically useful new knowledge. Pessimistic views on the possibilities for future growth tend to emphasize such constraints. Second is the ease of discovering new useful combinations that are physically possible. The potentially massive size and complexity of the space of potential combinations means that finding useful combinations can be a needle-in-the-haystack problem. Optimistic views of the possibilities for future growth tend to emphasize how the combination of AI (embedded in algorithms such as those developed by Atomwise and DeepGenomics) and increases in computing power can aid prediction in the discovery process, especially where it is difficult to identify patterns of cause and effect in high-dimensional data. Third, recognizing that future opportunities for discoveries are path dependent (see, e.g., Weitzman 1998), the value of θ will depend on the actual path that is followed. To the extent that AI can help identify productive paths, it will limit the chances of economies going down technological dead ends.

There are L_A researchers in the economy each working independently, where L_A is assumed to be measured continuously. (In section 5.4, we consider the case of team production in an extension of the model.) We assume that some researchers will duplicate each other's discoveries—the standing-on-toes effect. To capture this effect, new discoveries are assumed to take place "as if" the actual number of researchers is equal to L_A^λ, where $0 \leq \lambda \leq 1$. Thus the aggregate knowledge production function for $\theta > 0$ is given:

(5)
$$\dot{A} = \beta L_A^\lambda \left(\frac{\left(2^{A^\phi} \right)^\theta - 1}{\theta} \right).$$

At a point in time (with given values of A and L_A), how does an increase in θ affect the rate of discovery of new knowledge, $\dot{A}$? The partial derivative of $\dot{A}$ with respect to θ is

(6)
$$\frac{\partial \dot{A}}{\partial \theta} = \frac{\beta L_A^\lambda \left(\theta \ln(2) A^\phi - 1 \right) 2^{A^\phi \theta}}{\theta^2} + \frac{\beta L_A^\lambda}{\theta^2}.$$

A sufficient condition for this partial derivative to be positive is that that term in square brackets is greater than zero, which requires

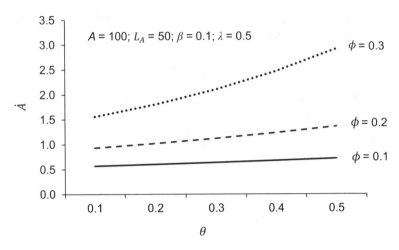

Fig. 5.2   Relationships between new knowledge production, θ, and ϕ

(7) $$A > \left(\frac{1}{\theta \ln(2)} \right)^{1/\phi}.$$

We assume this condition holds. Figure 5.2 shows an example of how $\dot{A}$ (and also the percentage growth of A given that A is assumed to be equal to 100) varies with θ for different assumed values of ϕ. Higher values of θ are associated with a faster growth rate. The figure also shows how θ and ϕ interact positively: greater knowledge access (as reflected in a higher value of ϕ) increases the gain associated with a given increase in the value of θ.

We assume, however, that θ itself evolves with A. A larger A means a bigger and more complex discovery search space. We further assume that this complexity will eventually overwhelm any discovery technology given the power of the combinatorial explosion as A grows. This is captured by assuming that θ is a declining function of A; that is, $\theta = \theta(A)$, where $\theta'(A) < 0$. In the limit as A goes to infinity, we assume that $\theta(A)$ goes to zero, or

(8) $$\lim_{A \to \infty} \theta(A) = 0.$$

This means that the discovery function converges asymptotically (given sustained growth in A) to

(9) $$\dot{A} = \beta \ln(2) L_A^\lambda A^\phi.$$

This mirrors the functional form of the Romer/Jones function and allows for decreasing returns to scale in the number of researchers, depending on the size of λ. While the form of the function is familiar by design, its combinatorial-based foundations have the advantage of providing richer motivations for the key parameters in the knowledge discovery function.

We use the fact that the functional form of equation (9) is the same as that used in Jones (1995) to solve for the steady state of the model. More precisely, given that the limiting behaviour of our knowledge production function mirrors the function used by Jones and all other aspects of the economy are assumed to be identical, the steady state along a balanced growth path with constant exponential growth will be the same as in that model.

As we have nothing to add to the other elements of the model, we here simply sketch the growth model developed by Jones (1995), referring the reader to the original for details. The economy is composed of a final goods sector and a research sector. The final goods sector uses labor, L_Y, and intermediate inputs to produce its output. Each new idea (or "blueprint") supports the design of an intermediate input, with each input being supplied by a profit-maximizing monopolist. Given the blueprint, capital, K, is transformed unit for unit in producing the input. The total labor force, L, is fully allocated between the final goods and research sectors, so that $L_Y + L_A = L$. We assume the labor force to be equal to the population and growing at rate $n(>0)$.

Building on Romer (1990), Jones (1995) shows that the production function for final goods can be written as

(10) $$Y = \left(AL_Y\right)^\alpha K^{1-\alpha},$$

where Y is final goods output. The intertemporal utility function of a representative consumer in the economy is given by

(11) $$U = \int_0^\infty u(c)e^{-\rho t}dt,$$

where c is per capita consumption and ρ is the consumer's discount rate. The instantaneous utility function is assumed to exhibit constant relative risk aversion, with a coefficient of risk aversion equal to σ and a (constant) intertemporal elasticity of substitution equal to $1/\sigma$.

Jones (1995) shows that the steady-state growth rate of this economy along a balanced growth path with constant exponential growth is given by

(12) $$g_A = g_y = g_c = g_k = \frac{\lambda n}{1-\phi},$$

where $g_A = \dot{A}/A$ is the growth rate of the knowledge stock, g_y is the growth rate of per capita output y, (where $y = Y/L$), g_c is the growth rate of per capita output c (where $c = C/L$), and g_k is the growth rate of the capital labor ratio (where $k = K/L$).

Finally, the steady-state share of labor allocated to the research sector is given by

(13) $$s = \frac{1}{1 + \left\{1 / \left[\lambda(\rho(1-\phi)/\lambda n) + (1/\sigma) - \phi\right]\right\}}.$$

We can now consider how changes in the parameters of knowledge production given by equation (5) will affect the dynamics of growth in the economy. We start with improvement in the availability of AI-based search technologies that improve a researcher's access to knowledge. In the context of the model, the availability of AI-based search technologies—for example, Google, Meta$^\alpha$, BenchSci, and so forth—should increase the value of ϕ and reduce the "burden of knowledge" effect. From equation (12), an increase in this parameter will increase the steady-state growth rate and also the growth rate and the level of per capital output along the transition path to the steady state.

We next consider AI-based technologies that increase the value of the discovery parameter, β. As β does not appear in the steady state in equation (12), the steady-state growth rate is unaffected. However, such an increase will raise the growth rate (and level) along the path to that steady state.

The most interesting potential changes to the possibilities for growth come about if we allow a change to the fishing-out/complexity parameter, θ. We assume that the economy is initially in a steady state and then experiences an increase in θ as the result of the discovery of a new AI technology. Recall that we assume that θ will eventually converge back to zero as the complexity that comes with combinatorial explosion eventually overwhelms the new AI. Thus, the steady state of the economy is unaffected. However, the transition dynamics are again quite different, with larger increases in knowledge for an given starting of the knowledge stock along the path back to the steady state.

Using Jones (1995) as the limiting case of the model is appealing because we avoid unbounded increases in the growth rate, which would lead to the breakdown of any reasonable growth model and indeed a breakdown in the normal operations of any actual economy. It is interesting to note, however, what happens to growth in the economy if instead of assuming that θ converges asymptotically to zero, it stays at some positive value (even if very small). Dividing both sides of equation (5) by A gives an expression for the growth rate of the stock of knowledge

$$(14) \qquad \frac{\dot{A}}{A} = \frac{\beta \ln(2) L_A^\lambda}{A} \left(\frac{(2^{A^\phi})^\theta - 1}{\theta} \right).$$

The partial derivative of this growth rate with respect to A is

$$(15) \qquad \frac{\partial(\dot{A}/A)}{\partial A} = \frac{L_A^\lambda \beta}{\theta A^2} \left[1 + \left(2^{A^\phi}\right)^\theta \left(\phi \theta \ln(2) A^\phi - 1\right) \right].$$

The key to the sign of this derivative is the sign of the term inside the last round brackets. This term will be positive for a large enough A. As A is growing over time (for any positive number of researchers and existing knowledge stock), the growth rate must eventually begin to rise once A exceeds some threshold value. Thus, with a fixed positive value of θ (or with θ converging asymptotically to a positive value), the growth rate will eventually begin to grow without bound.

A possible deeper foundation for our combinatorial-based knowledge production function is provided by the work on "rugged landscapes" (Kauffman 1993). Kauffman's NK model has been fruitfully applied to questions of organizational design (Levinthal 1997), strategy (Rivkin 2000) and science-driven technological search (Fleming and Sorenson 2004). In our setting, each potential combination of existing ideas accessible to a researcher is a point in the landscape represented by a binary string indicating whether each idea in the set of accessible knowledge is in the combination (a 1 in the string) or not (a 0 in the string). The complexity—or "ruggedness"—of the landscape depends on the total number of ideas that can be combined and also on the way that the elements of the binary string interact. For any given element, its impact on the value of the combination will depend on the value of X other elements.[5] The larger the value of X the more interrelated are the various elements of the string, creating a more rugged knowledge landscape and thus a harder the search problem for the innovator.

We can think of would-be innovators as starting from some already known valuable combination and searching for other valuable combinations in the vicinity of that combination (see, e.g., Nelson and Winter 1982). Purely local search can be thought of as varying one component of the binary string at a time for some given fraction of the total elements of the string. This implies that the total number of combinations that can be searched is a linear function of the innovator's knowledge. This is consistent with the Romer/Jones knowledge production function where the discovery of new knowledge is a linear function of knowledge access, A^f. Positive values of θ are then associated with the capacity to search a larger fraction of the space of possible combinations, which in turn increases the probability of discovering a valuable combination. Meta technologies such as deep learning can be thought of as expanding the capacity to search a given space of potential combinations—that is, as increasing the value of θ—thereby increasing the chance of new discoveries. Given its ability to deal with complex nonlinear spaces, deep learning may be especially valuable for search over highly rugged landscapes.

5.4   A Combinatorial-Based Knowledge Production
Function with Team Production: An Extended Model

Our basic model assumes that researchers working alone combine the knowledge to which they have access, A^ϕ, to discover new knowledge. In reality, new discoveries are increasingly being made by research teams (Jones 2009; Nielsen 2012; Agrawal, Goldfarb, and Teodoridis 2016). Assuming

---

5. K elements in Kauffman's original notation.

initially no redundancy in the knowledge that individual members bring to the team—that is, collective team knowledge is the sum of the knowledge of the individual team members—combining individual researchers into teams can greatly expand the knowledge base from which new combinations of existing knowledge can be made. This also opens up the possibility of a positive interaction between factors that facilitate the operation of larger teams and factors that raise the size of the fishing-out/complexity parameter, θ. New meta technologies such as deep learning can be more effective in a world where they are operating on a larger knowledge base due to the ability of researchers to more effectively pool their knowledge by forming larger teams.

We thus extend in this section the basic model to allow for new knowledge to be discovered by research teams. For a team with m members and no overlap in the knowledge of its members, the total knowledge access for the team is simply mA^ϕ. (We later relax the assumption of no knowledge overlap within a team.) Innovations occur as a result of the team combining existing knowledge to produce new knowledge. Knowledge can be combined by the team a ideas at a time, where $a = 0, 1 \ldots mA^\phi$. For a given team j with m members, the total number of possible combinations of units of existing knowledge (including singletons and the null set) given their combined knowledge access is

$$(16) \qquad Z_j = \sum_{a=0}^{mA^\phi} \binom{mA^\phi}{a} = 2^{mA^\phi}.$$

Assuming again for convenience that A^ϕ and Z can be treated as continuous, the per-period translation of potential combinations into valuable new knowledge by a team is again given by the (asymptotic) constant elasticity discovery function

$$(17) \qquad \dot{A}_j = \beta \left(\frac{Z_j^\theta - 1}{\theta} \right) = \beta \left(\frac{(2^{mA^\phi})^\theta - 1}{\theta} \right) \; for \; 0 < \theta \leq 1$$

$$= \beta \ln Z_j = \beta \ln(2^{mA^\phi}) = \beta \ln(2) mA^\phi \; for \; \theta = 0,$$

where use is again made of L'Hôpital's rule for the limiting case of $\theta = 0$.

The number of researchers in the economy at a point in time is again L_A (which we now assume is measured discretely). Research teams can potentially be formed from any possible combination of the L_A researchers. For each of these potential teams, a entrepreneur can coordinate the team. However, for a potential team with m members to form, the entrepreneur must have relationships with all m members. The need for a relationship thus places a constraint on feasible teams. The probability of a relationship existing between the entrepreneur and any given researcher is η, and thus the probability of relationships existing between all members of a team of size m is η^m. Using the formula for a binomial expansion, the expected total number of feasible teams is

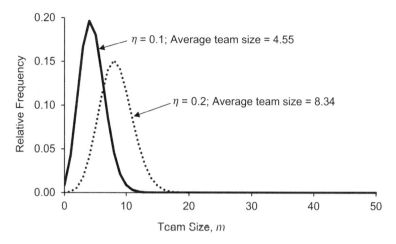

Fig. 5.3   Example of how the distribution of team size varies with η

(18)
$$S = \sum_{m=0}^{L_A} \binom{L_A}{m} \eta^m = (1 + \eta)^{L_A}.$$

The average feasible team size is then given by

(19)
$$\bar{m} = \frac{\sum_{m=0}^{L_A} \binom{L_A}{m} \eta^m m}{\sum_{m=0}^{L_A} \binom{L_A}{m} \eta^m}.$$

Factorizing the numerator and substituting in the denominator using equation (18), we obtain a simple expression for the average feasible team size:

(20)
$$\bar{m} = \frac{\sum_{m=0}^{L_A} \binom{L_A}{m} \eta^m m}{\sum_{m=0}^{L_A} \binom{L_A}{m} \eta^m} = \frac{(1 + \eta)^{L_A - 1} \eta L_A}{(1 + \eta)^{L_A}} = \left(\frac{\eta}{1 + \eta}\right) L_A.$$

Figure 5.3 shows an example of the full distribution of teams sizes (with $L_A = 50$) for two different values of η. An increase in η (i.e., an improvement in the capability to form teams) will push the distribution to the right and increase the average team size.

We can now write down the form that the knowledge production function would take if all possible research teams could form (ignoring for the moment any stepping-on-toes effects):

(21)
$$\dot{A} = \left(\sum_{m=0}^{L_A} \binom{L_A}{m} \eta^m \beta \frac{(2^{mA^\phi})^\theta - 1}{\theta}\right) \; for \; 0 < \theta \le 1.$$

We next allow for the fact that only a fraction of the feasible teams will actually form. Recognising obvious time constraints on the ability of a given researcher to be part of multiple research teams, we impose the constraint that each researcher can only be part of one team. However, we assume the size of any team that successfully forms is drawn from the same distribution over sizes as the potential teams. Therefore, the expected average team size is also given by equation (18). With this restriction, we can solve for the total number of teams, N, from the equation $L_A = N[\eta/(1 + \eta)]L_A$, which implies $N = (1 + \eta)/\eta$.

Given the assumption that the distribution of actual team sizes is drawn from the same distribution as the feasible team sizes, the aggregate knowledge production function (assuming $\theta > 0$) is then given by

$$(22) \qquad \dot{A} = \frac{(1+\eta)/\eta}{(1+\eta)^{L_A}}\left(\sum_{m=0}^{L_A} \binom{L_A}{m} \eta^m \beta \frac{(2^{mA^\phi})^\theta - 1}{\theta} \right)$$

$$= \frac{1}{(1+\eta)^{L_A-1}\eta}\left(\sum_{m=0}^{L_A} \binom{L_A}{m} \eta^m \beta \frac{(2^{mA^\phi})^\theta - 1}{\theta} \right),$$

where the first term is the actual number of teams as a fraction of the potentially feasible number of teams. For $\theta = 0$ the aggregate knowledge production function takes the form

$$(23) \qquad \dot{A} = \frac{1}{(1+\eta)^{L_A-1}\eta}\left(\sum_{m=0}^{L_A} \binom{L_A}{m} \eta^m m\beta\ln(2)A^\phi \right)$$

$$= \frac{1}{(1+\eta)^{L_A-1}\eta}\left((1+\eta)^{L_A-1}\eta L_A \beta\ln(2)A^\phi \right)$$

$$= \beta L_A \ln(2)A^\phi.$$

To see intuitively how an increase in η could affect aggregate knowledge discovery when $\theta > 0$, note that from equation (20) an increase in η will increase the average team size of the teams that form. From equation (16), we see that for a given knowledge access by an individual researcher, the number of potential combinations increases exponentially with the size of the team, m (see figure 5.4). This implies that combining two teams of size m' to create a team of size $2m'$ will more than double the new knowledge output of the team. Hence, there is a positive interaction between θ and η. On the other hand, when $\theta = 0$, combining the two teams will exactly double the new knowledge output given the linearity of the relationship between team size and knowledge output. In this case, the aggregate knowledge is invariant to the distribution of team sizes.

To see this formally, note that from equation (23) we know that when $\theta = 0$, the partial derivative of $\dot{A}$ with respect to η must be zero since η does not appear in the final form of the knowledge production function. This results

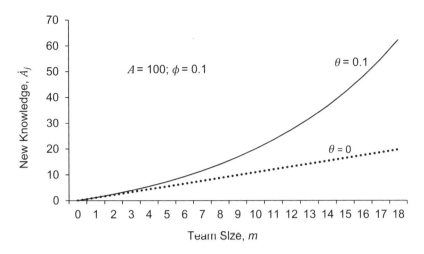

Fig. 5.4   Team knowledge production and team size

from the balancing of two effects as η increases. The first (negative) effect is that the number of teams as a share of the potentially possible teams falls. The second (positive) effect is that the amount of new knowledge production if all possible teams do form rises. We can now ask what happens if we raise θ to a strictly positive value. The first of these effects is unchanged. But that second effect will be stronger provided that the knowledge production of a team for any given team size rises with θ. A sufficient condition for this to be true is that

(24) $$A > \left(\frac{1}{\theta \ln(2)m} \right)^{1/\phi} \text{ for all } m > 0.$$

We assume that the starting size of the knowledge stock is large enough so that this condition holds. Moreover, the partial derivative of $\dot{A}$ with respect to η will be larger the larger is the value of θ. We show these effects for a particular example in figure 5.5.

The possibilities of knowledge overlap at the level of the team and duplication of knowledge outputs between teams creates additional complications. To allow for stepping-on-toes effects, it is useful to first rewrite equation (20) as

(25) $$\dot{A} = \left(\frac{1+\eta}{\eta} \right) \left(\frac{\eta}{1+\eta} \right) L_A \frac{1}{(1+\eta)^{L_A-1} \eta L_A} \left(\sum_{m=0}^{L_A} \binom{L_A}{m} \eta^m \beta \frac{(2^{mA^\phi})^\theta - 1}{\theta} \right).$$

We introduce two stepping-on-toes effects. First, we allow for knowledge overlap within teams to introduce the potential for redundancy of knowledge. A convenient way to introduce this effect is to assume that the overlap

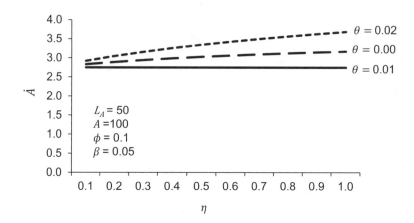

Fig. 5.5   Relationships between new knowledge production, η, and θ

reduces the *effective* average team size in the economy from the viewpoint of generating new knowledge. More specifically, we assume the effective team size is given by

$$(26) \qquad \bar{m}^e = \bar{m}^\gamma = \left(\left(\frac{\eta}{1+\eta} \right) L_A \right)^\gamma,$$

where $0 \le \gamma \le 1$. The extreme case of $\gamma = 0$ (full overlap) has each team acting as if it had effectively a single member; the opposite extreme of $\gamma = 1$ (no overlap) has no knowledge redundancy at the level of the team. Second, we allow for the possibility that new ideas are duplicated across teams. The effective number of non-idea-duplicating teams is given by

$$(27) \qquad N^e = N^{1-\psi} = \left(\frac{1+\eta}{\eta} \right)^{1-\psi},$$

where $0 \le \psi \le 1$. The extreme case of $\psi = 0$ (no duplication) implies that the effective number of teams is equal to the actual number of teams; the extreme case of $\psi = 1$ (full duplication) implies that a single team produces the same number of new ideas as the full set of teams.

We can now add the stepping-on-toes effects—knowledge redundancy within teams and discovery duplication between teams—to yield the general form of the knowledge production function for $\theta > 0$:

$$(28) \; \dot{A} = \left(\frac{1+\eta}{\eta} \right)^{1-\psi} \left(\left(\frac{\eta}{1+\eta} \right) L_A \right)^\gamma \frac{1}{(1+\eta)^{L_A-1} \eta L_A} \left(\sum_{m=0}^{L_A} \binom{L_A}{m} \eta^m \beta \frac{(2^{mA^\phi})^\theta - 1}{\theta} \right).$$

If we take the limit of equation (24) as θ goes to zero, we reproduce the limiting case of the knowledge production function. Ignoring integer constraints on L_A, this knowledge production function again has the form of the Romer/Jones function:

$$(29) \quad \dot{A} = \left(\frac{1+\eta}{\eta}\right)^{1-\psi} \left(\left(\frac{\eta}{1+\eta}\right)L_A\right)^{\gamma} \frac{1}{(1+\eta)^{L_A-1}\eta L_A} \left(\sum_{m=0}^{L_A}\binom{L_A}{m}\eta^m\beta\ln(2)mA^{\phi}\right)$$

$$= \left(\frac{1+\eta}{\eta}\right)^{1-\psi} \left(\left(\frac{\eta}{1+\eta}\right)L_A\right)^{\gamma} \frac{(1+\eta)^{L_A-1}\eta L_A}{(1+\eta)^{L_A-1}\eta L_A}\beta\ln(2)A^{\phi}$$

$$= \left(\frac{1+\eta}{\eta}\right)^{1-\psi} \left(\left(\frac{\eta}{1+\eta}\right)\right)^{\gamma} \beta\ln(2)L_A^{\gamma}A^{\phi}.$$

We note finally the presence of the relationship parameter η in the knowledge production equation. This can be taken to reflect in part the importance of (social) relationships in the forming of research teams. Advances in computer-based technologies such as email and file sharing (as well as policies and institutions) could also affect this parameter (see, e.g., Agrawal and Goldfarb [2008] on the effects of the introduction of precursors to today's internet on collaboration between researchers). Although not the main focus of this chapter, being able to incorporate the effects of changes in collaboration technologies increases the richness of the framework for considering the determinants of the efficiency of knowledge production.

5.5   Discussion

5.5.1   Something New under the Sun? Deep Learning as a New Tool for Discovery

Two key observations motivate the model developed above. First, using the analogy of finding a needle in a haystack, significant obstacles to discovery in numerous domains of science and technology result from highly nonlinear relationships of causes and effect in high-dimensional data. Second, advances in algorithms such as deep learning (combined with increased availability of data and computing power) offer the potential to find relevant knowledge and predict combinations that will yield valuable new discoveries.

Even a cursory review of the scientific and engineering literatures indicates that needle-in-the-haystack problems are pervasive in many frontier fields of innovation, especially in areas where matter is manipulated at the molecular or submolecular level. In the field of genomics, for example, complex genotype-phenotype interactions make it difficult to identify therapies that yield valuable improvements in human health or agricultural productivity. In the field of drug discovery, complex interactions between drug compounds and biological systems present an obstacle to identifying promising new drug therapies. And in the field of material sciences, including nanotechnology, complex interactions between the underlying physical and chemical mechanisms increases the challenge of predicting the performance of potential new materials with potential applications ranging from new materials to prevent traumatic brain injury to lightweight materials for use in transportation to reduce dependence on carbon-based fuels (National Science and Technology Council 2011).

The apparent speed with which deep learning is being applied in these and other fields suggests it represents a breakthrough general purpose meta technology for predicting valuable new combinations in highly complex spaces. Although an in-depth discussion of the technical advances underlying deep learning is beyond the scope of this chapter, two aspects are worth highlighting. First, previous generations of machine learning were constrained by the need to extract features (or explanatory variables) by hand before statistical analysis. A major advance in machine learning involves the use of "representation learning" to automatically extract the relevant features.[6] Second, the development and optimization of multilayer neural networks allows for substantial improvement in the ability to predict outcomes in high-dimensional spaces with complex nonlinear interactions (LeCun, Bengio, and Hinton 2015). A recent review of the use of deep learning in computational biology, for instance, notes that the "rapid increase in biological data dimensions and acquisition rates is challenging conventional analysis strategies," and that "[m]odern machine learning methods, such as deep learning, promise to leverage very large data sets for finding hidden structure within them, and for making accurate predictions" (Angermueller et al. 2016, 1). Another review of the use of deep learning in computational chemistry highlights how deep learning has a "ubiquity and broad applicability to a wide range of challenges in the field, including quantitative activity relationship, virtual screening, protein structure prediction, quantum chemistry, materials design and property prediction" (Goh, Hodas, and Vishu 2017).

Although the most publicized successes of deep learning have been in areas such as image recognition, voice recognition, and natural language processing, parallels to the way in which the new methods work on unstructured data are increasingly being identified in many fields with similar data challenges to produce research breakthroughs.[7] While these new general purpose research tools will not displace traditional mathematical models of

6. As described by LeCun, Bengio, and Hinton (2015, 436), "[c]onventional machine-learning techniques were limited in their ability to process natural data in their raw form. For decades, constructing a pattern-recognition or machine-learning system required careful engineering and considerable domain expertise to design a feature extractor that transformed the raw data (such as the pixel values of an image) into a suitable internal representation or feature vector from which the learning subsystem, often a classifier, could detect or classify patterns in the input. . . . Representation learning is a set of methods that allows a machine to be fed with raw data and to automatically discover the representations needed for detection or classification."

7. A recent review of deep-learning applications in biomedicine usefully draws out these parallels: "With some imagination, parallels can be drawn between biological data and the types of data deep learning has shown the most success with—namely image and voice data. A gene expression profile, for instance, is essentially a 'snapshot,' or image, of what is going on in a given cell or tissue in the same way that patterns of pixilation are representative of the objects in a picture" (Mamoshina et al. 2016, 1445).

cause and effect and careful experimental design, machine-learning methods such as deep learning offer a promising new tool for discovery—including hypothesis generation—where the complexity of the underlying phenomena present obstacles to more traditional methods.[8]

5.5.2   Meta Ideas, Meta Technologies, and General Purpose Technologies

We conceptualize AIs as general purpose meta technologies—that is, general purpose technologies (GPTs) for the discovery of new knowledge. Figure 5.6 summarises the relationship between Paul Romer's broader idea of meta ideas, meta technologies, and GPTs. Romer defines a meta idea as an idea that supports the production and transmission of other ideas (see, e.g., Romer 2008). He points to such ideas as the patent, the agricultural extension station, and the peer-review system for research grants as examples of meta ideas. We think of meta technologies as a subset of Romer's meta ideas (the area enclosed by the dashed lines in figure 5.6), where the idea for how to discover new ideas is embedded in a technological form such as an algorithm or measurement instrument.

Elhanan Helpman (1998, 3) argues that a "drastic innovation qualifies as a GPT if it has the potential for pervasive use in a wide range of sectors in ways that drastically change their mode of operation." He further notes two important features necessary to qualify as a GPT: "generality of purpose and innovational complementarities" (see also Bresnahan and Trajtenberg 1995). Not all meta technologies are general purpose in this sense. The set of general purpose meta technologies is given by the intersection of the two circles in figure 5.6. Cockburn, Henderson, and Stern (chapter 4, this volume) give the example of functional MRI as an example of a discovery tool that lacks the generality of purpose required for a GPT. In contrast, the range of application of deep learning as a discovery tool would appear to qualify it as a GPT. It is worth noting that some authors discuss GPTs as technologies that more closely align with our idea of a meta technology. Rosenberg (1998), for example, provides a fascinating examination of chemical engineering as an example of GPT. Writing of this branch of engineering, he argues that a "discipline that provides the concepts and methodologies to generate new or improved technologies over a wide range of downstream economic activity may be thought of as an even purer, or higher order, GPT" (Rosenberg 1998, 170).

---

8. A recent survey of the emerging use of machine learning in economics (including policy design) provides a pithy characterization of the power of the new methods: "The appeal of machine learning is that it manages to uncover generalizable patterns. In fact, the success of machine learning at intelligence tasks is largely due to its ability to discover complex structure that was not specified in advance. It manages to fit complex and very flexible functional forms to the data without simply overfitting; it finds functions that work well out of sample" (Mullainathan and Spiess 2017, 88).

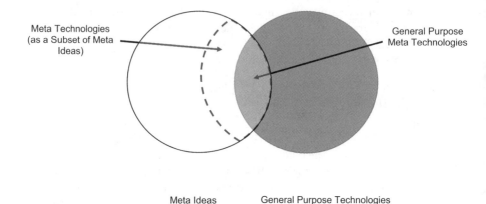

Fig. 5.6 Relationships between meta ideas, meta technologies, and general purpose technologies

Our concentration on general purpose meta technologies (GPMTs) parallels Cockburn, Henderson, and Stern's (chapter 4, this volume) idea of a general purpose invention of a method of invention. This idea combines the idea of a GPT with Zvi Griliches' (1957) idea of the "invention of a method of invention," or IMI. Such an invention has the "potential for a more influential impact than a single invention, but is also likely to be associated with a wide variation in the ability to adapt the new tool to particular settings, resulting in a more heterogeneous pattern of diffusion over time" (Cockburn, Henderson, and Stern, chapter 4, this volume). They see some emerging AIs such as deep learning as candidates for such general purpose IMIs and contrast these with AIs underpinning robotics that, while being GPTs, do not have the characteristic features of an IMI.

5.5.3 Beyond AI: Potential Uses of the New Knowledge Production Function

Although the primary motivation for this chapter is to explore how breakthroughs in AI could affect the path of economic growth, the knowledge production function we develop is potentially of broader applicability. By deriving the Romer/Jones knowledge production function as the limiting case of a more general function, our analysis may also contribute to providing candidate microfoundations for that function.[9] The key conceptual

9. In developing and applying the Romer/Jones knowledge production function, growth theorists have understood its potential combinatorial underpinnings and the limits of the Cobb-Douglas form. Charles Jones (2005) observes in his review chapter on "Growth and Ideas" for the *Handbook of Economic Growth*: "While we have made much progress in understanding economic growth in a world where ideas are important, there remain many open, interesting research questions. The first is 'What is the shape of the idea production function?' How do

change is to model discovery as operating on the space of potential combinations (rather than directly on the knowledge base itself). As in Weitzman (1998), our production function focuses attention explicitly on how new knowledge is discovered by combining existing knowledge, which is left implicit in the Romer/Jones formulation. While this shift in emphasis is motivated by the particular way in which deep learning can aid discovery—allowing researchers to uncover otherwise hard-to-find valuable combinations in highly complex spaces—the view of discovery as the innovative combination of what is already known has broader applicability. The more general function also has the advantage of providing a richer parameter space for mapping how meta technologies or policies could affect knowledge discovery. The ϕ parameter captures how access to knowledge at the individual researcher level determines the potential for new combinations to be made given the inherited knowledge base. The θ parameter captures how the available potential combinations (given the access to knowledge) map to new discoveries. Finally, the η parameter captures the ease of forming research teams and ultimately the average team size. To the extent that the capacity to bring the knowledge of individual researchers together through research teams directly affects the possible combinations, the ease of team formation can have an important effect on how the existing knowledge base is utilized for new knowledge discovery.

We hope this more general function will be of use in other contexts. In a recent commentary celebrating the twenty-fifth anniversary of the publication of Romer (1990), Joshua Gans (2015) observes that the Romer growth model has not been as influential on the design of growth policy as might have been expected despite its enormous influence on the subsequent growth theory literature. The reason he identifies is that it abstracts away "some of the richness of the microeconomy that give rise to new ideas and also their dissemination" (Gans 2015). By expanding the parameter space, our function allows for the inclusion of more of this richness, including the role that meta technologies such as deep learning can play in knowledge access and knowledge discovery, but potentially other policy and institutional factors that affect knowledge access, discovery rates, and team formation as well.

---

ideas get produced? The combinatorial calculations of Romer (1993) and Weitzman (1998) are fascinating and suggestive. The current research practice of modelling the idea production function as a stable Cobb-Douglas combination of research and the existing stock of ideas is elegant, but at this point we have little reason to believe it is correct. One insight that illustrates the incompleteness of our knowledge is that there is no reason why research productivity should be a smooth monotonic function of the stock of ideas. One can easily imagine that some ideas lead to domino-like unravelling of phenomena that were previously mysterious . . . Indeed, perhaps decoding of the human genome or the continued boom in information technology will lead to a large upward shift in the production function for ideas. On the other hand, one can equally imagine situations where research productivity unexpectedly stagnates, if not forever then at least for a long time" (Jones 2005, 1107).

5.6   Concluding Thoughts: A Coming Singularity?

We developed this chapter upon a number of prior ideas. First, the production of new knowledge is central to sustaining economic growth (Romer 1990, 1993). Second, the production of new ideas is fundamentally a combinatorial process (Weitzman 1998). Third, given this combinatorial process, technologies that predict what combinations of existing knowledge will yield useful new knowledge hold out the promise of improving growth prospects. Fourth, breakthroughs in AI represent a potential step change in the ability of algorithms to predict what knowledge is potentially useful to researchers and also to predict what combinations of existing knowledge will yield useful new discoveries (LeCun, Bengio, and Hinton 2015).

In a provocative recent paper, William Nordhaus (2015) explored the possibilities for a coming "economic singularity," which he defines as "[t]he idea . . . that rapid growth in computation and artificial intelligence will cross some boundary or singularity after which economic growth will accelerate sharply as an ever-accelerating pace of improvements cascade through the economy." Central to Nordhaus' analysis is that rapid technological advance is occurring in a relatively small part of the economy (see also Aghion, Jones, and Jones 2018). To generate more broadly based rapid growth, the products of the new economy need to substitute for products on either the demand- or supply-side of the economy. His review of the evidence—including, critically, the relevant elasticities of substitution—leads him to conclude that a singularity through this route is highly unlikely.

However, our chapter's analysis suggests an alternative route to an economic singularity—a broad-based alteration in the economy's knowledge production function. Given the centrality of new knowledge to sustained growth at the technological frontier, it seems likely that if an economic singularity were to arise, it would be because of some significant change to the knowledge production function affecting a number of domains outside of information technology itself. In a world where new knowledge is the result of combining existing knowledge, AI technologies that help ease needle-in-the-haystack discovery challenges could affect growth prospects, at least along the transition path to the steady state. It does not take an impossible leap of imagination to see how new meta technologies such as AI could alter—perhaps modestly, perhaps dramatically—the knowledge production function in a way that changes the prospects for economic growth.

References

Acemoglu, Daron, and Pascual Restrepo. 2017. "The Race between Machine and Man: Implications of Technology for Growth, Factor Shares and Employment." NBER Working Paper no. 22252, Cambridge, MA..

Agrawal, A., I. Cockburn, and J. McHale. 2006. "Gone But Not Forgotten: Knowledge Flows, Labor Mobility, and Enduring Social Relationships." *Journal of Economic Geography* 6 (5): 571–91.

Agrawal, Ajay, and Avi Goldfarb. 2008. "Restructuring Research: Communication Costs and the Democratization of University Innovation." *American Economic Review* 98 (4): 1578–90.

Agrawal, A., Avi Goldfarb, and Florenta Teodordis. 2016. "Understanding the Changing Structure of Scientific Inquiry." *American Economic Journal: Applied Economics* 8 (1): 100–28.

Agrawal, A., D. Kapur, and J. McHale. 2008. "How to Spatial and Social Proximity Influence Knowledge Flows: Evidence from Patent Data." *Journal of Urban Economics* 64: 258–69.

Angermueller, Christof, Tanel Pärnamaa, Leopold Parts, and Oliver Stegle. 2016. "Deep Learning for Computational Biology." *Molecular Systems Biology* 12 (878): 1–16.

Arthur, Brian W. 2009. *The Nature of Technology: What it Is and How it Evolves.* London: Penguin Books.

Bloom, Nicholas, Charles Jones, John Van Reenen, and Michael Webb. 2017. "Are Ideas Getting Harder to Find?" Working Paper, Stanford University.

Bornmann, Lutz, and Rüdiger Mutz. 2015. "Growth Rates of Modern Science: A Bibliometric Analysis Based on the Number of Publications and Cited References." *Journal of the Association for Information Science and Technology* 66 (11): 2215–22.

Bresnahan, Timothy, and Manuel Trajtenberg. 1995. "General Purpose Technologies 'Engines of Growth'?" *Journal of Econometrics* 65:83–108.

Brynjolfsson, Erik, and Andrew McAfee. 2014. *The Second Machine Age: Work Progress and Prosperity in a Time Of Brilliant Technologies.* New York: W. W. Norton.

Catalini, Christian. 2017. "Microgeography and the Direction of Inventive Activity." *Management Science* 64 (9). https://doi.org/10.1287/mnsc.2017.2798.

Cowen, Tyler. 2011. *The Great Stagnation: How America Ate All the Low-Hanging Fruit of Modern History, Got Sick, and Will (Eventually) Feel Better.* New York: Dutton, Penguin Group.

Fleming, Lee, and Olav Sorenson. 2004. "Science as a Map in Technological Search." *Strategic Management Journal* 25:909–28.

Furman, Jeffrey, and Scott Stern. 2011. "Climbing atop the Shoulders of Giants: The Impact of Institutions on Cumulative Research." *American Economic Review* 101:1933–63.

Gans, Joshua. 2015. "The Romer Model Turns 25." Digitopoly Blog. Accessed Aug. 21, 2017. https://digitopoly.org/2015/10/03/the-romer-model-turns-25/.

Goh, Garrett, Nathan Hodas, and Abhinav Vishnu. 2017. "Deep Learning for Computational Chemistry." *Journal of Computational Chemistry* 38 (16): 1291–307.

Gordon, Robert. 2016. *The Rise and Fall of American Growth: The U.S. Standard of Living Since the Civil War.* Princeton, NJ: Princeton University Press.

Griliches, Zvi. 1957. "Hybrid Corn: An Exploration in the Economics of Technical Change." *Econometrica* 25 (4): 501–22.

Helpman, Elhanan. 1998. "Introduction." In *General Purpose Technologies and Economic Growth*, edited by Elhanan Helpman. Cambridge, MA: MIT Press.

Jaffe, Adam, Manuel Trajtenberg, and Rebecca Henderson. 1993. "Geographic Localization of Knowledge Spillovers as Evidenced by Patent Citations." *Quarterly Journal of Economics* 108 (3): 577–98.

Jones, Benjamin. 2009. "The Burden of Knowledge and the 'Death of the Renaissance Man': Is Innovation Getting Harder." *Review of Economics and Statistics* 76 (1): 283–317.

Jones, Charles. 1995. "R&D-Based Models of Economic Growth." *Journal of Political Economy* 103 (4): 759–84.

———. 2005. "Growth and Ideas." *Handbook of Economic Growth*, vol. 1B, edited by Phillipe Aghion and Steven Durlauf. Amsterdam: Elsevier.

Kauffman, Stuart. 1993. *The Origins of Order*. Oxford: Oxford University Press.

LeCun, Yann, Yoshua Bengio, and Geoffrey Hinton. 2015. "Deep Learning." *Nature* 521:436–44.

Levinthal, Daniel. 1997. "Adaptation on Rugged Landscapes." *Management Science* 43:934–50.

Mamoshina, Polina, Armando Vieira, Evgeny Putin, and Alex Zhavoronkov. 2016. "Applications of Deep Learning in Biomedicine." *Molecular Pharmaceutics* 13:1445–54.

Mokyr, Joel. 2002. *The Gifts of Athena: Historical Origins of the Knowledge Economy*. Princeton, NJ: Princeton University Press.

———. 2017. "The Past and Future of Innovation: Some Lessons from Economic History." Paper presented at the NBER Conference on Research Issues in Artificial Intelligence, Toronto, Sept. 2017.

Mullainathan, Sendhil, and Jann Spiess. 2017. "Machine Learning: An Applied Econometric Approach." *Journal of Economic Perspectives* 31 (2): 87–106.

National Science and Technology Council. 2011. "Materials Genome Initiative for Global Competitiveness." Washington, DC.

Nelson, Richard, and Sidney Winter. 1982. *An Evolutionary Theory of Economic Change*. Cambridge, MA: Harvard University Press.

Nielsen, Michael. 2012. *Reinventing Discovery: The New Era of Networked Science*. Princeton, NJ: Princeton University Press.

Nordhaus, William. 2015. "Are We Approaching an Economic Singularity? Information Technology and the Future of Economic Growth." NBER Working Paper no. 21547, Cambridge, MA.

Rivkin, Jan. 2000. "Imitation of Complex Strategies." *Management Science* 46:824–44.

Romer, Paul. 1990. "Endogenous Technical Change." *Journal of Political Economy* 94: S71–102.

———. 1993. "Two Strategies for Economic Development: Using and Producing Ideas." In *Proceedings of the World Bank Annual Conference on Development Economics, 1992*. Washington, DC: The World Bank.

———. 2008. "Economic Growth." In *The Concise Encyclopaedia of Economics*, Library of Economic Liberty. http://www.econlib.org/library/Enc/EconomicGrowth.html.

Rosenberg, Nathan. 1998. "Chemical Engineering as a General Purpose Technology." In *General Purpose Technologies and Economic Growth*, edited by Elhanan Helpman. Cambridge, MA: MIT Press.

Weitzman, Martin. 1998. "Recombinant Growth." *Quarterly Journal of Economics* 113:331–60.

Zeira, Joseph. 1998. "Workers, Machines, and Economic Growth." *Quarterly Journal of Economics* 113 (4): 1091–117.

6

Artificial Intelligence as the Next GPT
A Political-Economy Perspective

Manuel Trajtenberg

6.1 Introduction

Artificial intelligence (AI) and related technologies are being heralded as "the next big thing," one that promises to revolutionize many areas of economic activity and thus to have a profound impact on economic growth. However, the rise of AI coincides with a recent wave of pessimism in terms of productivity growth, expressed forcefully by prominent economists such as Larry Summers (2016), and more thoroughly by Robert Gordon (2016).

Side by side with the gloom, the new "technology enthusiasts" envision a not-too-distant future in which AI will displace most (*all*?) human occupations while unleashing tremendous gains in productivity. This view poses once again disturbing questions about the future of employment, the distributional consequences of mass displacement, and so forth.

Nobody holds the crystal ball, hence rather than arguing about the inscrutable future, it is at least as important to inquire into what we can learn from history regarding episodes like this, that is, the appearance of a major new technology that is posed to have profound economic implications. Of course, the future is never a replay of the past, but it may provide a useful benchmark against which to assess the unfolding of the new technology.

Mokyr (2017) sounds a cautionary note in that regard: ever since the dawn of the Industrial Revolution in the late eighteenth century, both the pessimists and the enthusiasts have almost invariably been proven wrong.

Manuel Trajtenberg is a professor in the Eitan Berglas School of Economics at Tel Aviv University and a research associate of the National Bureau of Economic Research.

This is a follow-up to my discussion at this conference of Joel Mokyr's paper "The Past and the Future of Innovation: some lessons from Economic History." For acknowledgments, sources of research support, and disclosure of the author's material financial relationships, if any, please see http://www.nber.org/chapters/c14025.ack.

Moreover, Mokyr dismantles with solid historical and present day evidence Gordon's claim that technological advance is bound to slow down in a deterministic fashion (in particular, the claim that "all low-hanging scientific and technological fruit has already been picked").

However, nothing can be taken for granted—as Mokyr skillfully describes, institutions (including government policies) may play a key role enabling or retarding innovation. This is precisely the focus here: given that AI is poised to emerge as a powerful technological force, I discuss ways to mitigate the almost unavoidable ensuing disruption, and enhance AI's vast benign potential. This is particularly important in present times, in view of political-economic considerations that were mostly absent in previous historical episodes associated with the arrival of new general purpose technologies.

6.2   Is This Time Different? The Political Economy of Technological Disruptions

The presumption here, well argued in other papers in this conference,[1] is that AI has the potential of becoming a general purpose technology (GPT) in the foreseeable future,[2] thus bringing about a wave of complementary innovations in a wide and ever-expanding range of applications sectors. Such sweeping transformative processes always result in widespread economic disruption, with concomitant winners and losers.

The "winners" are primarily those associated with the emerging GPT sector itself, and those that are at the forefront of the deployment of the GTP in the main applications sectors. They tend to be young, entrepreneurial, and equipped both with the technical knowledge and the skills that are made relevant by the new GPT. The labor force composition of Silicon Valley offers a grand view of who are the winners in the present information and communication technologies (ICT)/internet era. There are further winners in those sectors that are ancillary to the core GTP circle, be it in services that directly benefit from the growth of the GPT (e.g., the venture capital (VC) industry, patent lawyers, designers, etc.), or in others that just ride on the localized boom (e.g., upscale restaurants and entertainment, gyms, tourism, etc.).

The "losers" are mostly those employed in sectors that structurally cannot benefit from the unfolding GPT ("laggards"), and those in industries where the adoption of the new GPT renders many existing competencies and skills obsolete, thus bringing about massive layoffs. They tend to be middle-aged, have lower than average educational levels, and reside in areas that do not have much diversified sources of employment.

As economists, we tend to view the big sweep of economic growth since

---

1. See Cockburn, Henderson, and Stern (chapter 5, this volume).
2. See Bresnahan and Trajtenberg (1995).

the Industrial Revolution as the very embodiment of the "Idea of Progress" (as conceived in the Enlightenment), and hence the rate of growth of gross domestic product (GDP) as an unequivocal uptick in the welfare of society as a whole. Sure, we do acknowledge that there are distributional conse-quences, and sure, ever since Pareto we know that we are not allowed to "sum-up utilities" (and thus the "minuses" of losers do not cancel out with the "pluses" of winners). But those half-hearted qualifications become just lip service—the truth is that we rarely dwell into the balance of winners and losers, and in particular we do not pay much attention to the later. Para-phrasing the well-known dictum of Isaac Newton, we may say that

> We enjoy today higher standards of living because we are standing on the broken backs of those that paved the way for technological progress, but did not live long enough to benefit from it.

Partly in response to these inequities, the post-World War II era saw the creation of the welfare state, including unemployment insurance, transfers to the disadvantaged, some form of health insurance, retraining programs, and so forth. These "safety nets" were supposed to provide a reasonable palliative to "losers," but the truth is that we still do not have effective mecha-nisms to prevent or ameliorate the costs of major technologically induced transformations.[3] Moreover, existing safety nets will quite likely fail to cope with the juxtaposition of two new and powerful phenomena: (a) much larger flows of GPT-displaced workers *and* (b) a new "great demographic transi-tion." Let us examine each in turn.

Regarding the extent of displacement: technological change always causes disruption, as brilliantly articulated by Schumpeter's notion of "creative destruction." Furthermore, there are inflection points as a new GPT starts working its way through the economy, when in relative short notice very many sectors, competencies, and skills became laggards and obsolete.

However, as clearly envisioned in this conference, AI in its various incar-nations seems to go much further, in that it has the potential to replace a very wide swath of human occupations. Many argued forcefully that there are *no* occupations that cannot be eventually replaced by AI, and that the *vast majority* of present occupations will indeed vanish within a generation.

The consensual view seems to be that a large proportion of employment as we know it today will give way to smart machines, and therefore that x percent of workers will be displaced, whereby x is thought to be *significantly larger than in previous GPTs.* At the same time, the extent to which new, pres-ently unforeseeable occupations may arise (denote them y percent) seems to be constrained by the very nature of AI: presumably AI will be able to

---

3. Typically, these safety nets function reasonably well when dealing with the consequences of not-too-pronounced business cycles or with small, *temporarily* deprived groups of the popula-tion. Not so when there are major structural transformations or when the underlying conditions that led to welfare dependency become permanent.

perform most of the new tasks, and hence they will not constitute a good enough counterbalance to the disappearing jobs, as has been the case in the past. The prevailing view is then that the net displacement of employment $(x - y)$ will turn out to be significantly larger for AI than in previous episodes of technological disruption, posing a serious challenge to traditional economic policies.

The second part of the challenge entails a steep drop in birth rates together with the extension of life expectancy (which has been steadily growing for well over a century). These powerful demographic forces have resulted in aging populations, with the concomitant increase in the dependency ratio and the looming threat on the long-term viability of the pension system. Notice that life expectancy is now increasing well past the retirement age, so that a typical person in her fifties contemplates a further stretch of twenty-five to thirty years of life. Thus, the prospect of being permanently laid off at that stage in life has dire consequences for the displaced individual as much as for society as a whole.

The joint effect of a large influx of displaced workers at the seemingly unique inflection point posed by AI, together with their longer life expectancy, may thus create a formidable challenge that even the most advanced welfare state will be hard pressed to cope with. Put differently, we cannot afford to have many more, and longer-lived, unemployed or underemployed people. This is what is at stake with the advent of AI.

There is yet another significant development that magnifies the challenge, and that is the *democratization of expectations*. The growth in income per capita involves not only a rise in material standards, but in other no less important dimensions of well-being, including reduced uncertainty and a concomitant heightened sense of control over our own lives, which entails also the expectation of having a voice in processes that affect us (Hirschman 1970). Not by coincidence, economic growth and expanding democracy have more often than not gone hand in hand within, as well as across, countries.

The Luddites of the early nineteenth century surely had their voice heard, as did their like-minded emulators over the following decades. However, they could hardly expect to make a dent on their fate: democracy was still highly limited and living standards still very low for the vast majority, so that most people were just consumed by the need to provide for their basic needs.

Much has changed since, and nowadays virtually every individual in advanced western countries has come to expect to be entitled, at least in principle, to full participation in every realm of society: the political, the economic, and the cultural. The expectation is not just to vote in periodic elections, but to have an influence via "participatory democracy"; not just to hold a job, but to partake in the benefits of economic growth—this is what constitutes "the democratization of expectations."

We claim that in such context it has become much harder to have some (many?) bear the costs of technological disruption (the losers), while others reap the benefits (the winners). Moreover, the losers have become much more skeptical of the vague promise that *eventually* the benefits will "trickle down" to them as well. With good reason: experience shows that the losers typically remain on the downside, even if the welfare state somehow softens their human costs. In advanced, democratic societies, people have become more impatient, more demanding of government, more intolerant of false promises, as well as of collective failures. Again, this should be surely considered a highly *positive* by-product of the rise in living standards.

The sharp split between winners and losers, if left to its own, may have serious consequences far beyond the costs for the individuals involved: when it coincides with the political divide, it may threaten the very fabric of democracy, as we have seen recently both in America and in Europe. Thus, if AI bursts into the scene and triggers mass displacement of workers, and demography plays out its fateful hand, the economy will be faced with a formidable dual challenge that may require a serious reassessment of policy options:

- Governments may have to assume a wider responsibility for navigating effective transitions from old to new GPTs, and not just for alleviating some of the costs. As said above, the democratization of expectations will not allow just for cosmetic adjustments—the political economy of it will eventually force real change.
- In so doing, governments may have to consider courses of action aimed *inter alia* at reducing significantly the number of those that fall in between the cracks during such transitions: actual and potential losers are bound to become much less tolerant of their fate. This should be done **not** by attempting to slow down the pace of technical change (that would be silly and ineffectual), but on the contrary, by making sure that many more can be brought to partake in it.

6.3   From Threat to Promise: Strategies for the AI-GPT Era

In order to meet the above-mentioned challenges, governments will have to design innovative strategies in the following key areas:

1. education: search for ways to provide for the changing nature of skills required for the AI era;

2. personal services: these are the fastest-growing occupations, but as defined at present cannot benefit from AI; and

3. direction of technical change: strive to human-enhancing innovations, not human replacing.

6.3.1   Education: The Upcoming Revolution

As already mentioned, the expectation is that AI will become the dominant GPT of the coming era, spreading throughout the economy, and displacing in the process a great many occupations. At the same time, the remaining occupations and new ones that may spring up as complementary to AI will require a new set of skills that are not quite those currently provided by the education system, at all levels.

This is not new: the first and second industrial revolutions in the course of the nineteenth century required, and were accompanied by, corresponding revolutions in education. The need to rely on a more skilled, educated workforce, as well as a more disciplined one, fed educational reforms first in Prussia (already in the late eighteenth century), then in the United Kingdom and in the United States, that led gradually to the institutionalization of free and universal education, with highly structured, government-set curriculums.

From the late nineteenth century to this day, this "factory model" of education spread widely, expanding *quantitatively* in all dimensions: more hours spent at school, more subjects covered, and more years of study. Thus, for example, the average years of schooling in the UK adult population was less than 1 in 1870, whereas at present it stands at over 13. Universal education now starts at age three to four in many countries, high school became compulsory in the second half of the twentieth century, and in the past three decades some form of tertiary education has become commonplace.

It is now widely accepted that this "factory model" needs to be revised and perhaps totally revamped in view of twin pervasive developments: first, the internet revolution, which in this context means the availability of information/knowledge on any subject, at all times and virtually at no cost; second, the rapidly changing requirements for meaningful employment.

In particular, the advent of AI as the new GPT, with its expected pervasive impact on employment, may call for a new education revolution, very much like the industrial revolutions of the nineteenth century. The key to it appears to be the shift away from imparting knowledge per se, to developing skills relevant for an AI-based economy. Likewise, such educational revolution will in all likelihood aim toward "personalized education," departing from the quest for uniformity that has characterized education systems ever since Prussian reforms.

What are likely to be the top skills required for employment in the upcoming AI era? There is a great deal of heated discussion in this area, but some agreement is emerging around a core set of skills, such as those listed in table 6.1.

There is a great deal of similarity between these three lists of skills, and in fact they can be classified into the following (nonexhaustive) main types:

- **Type I: analytical, creative, adaptive**
  - critical and creative thinking
  - analytical and research
  - sense-making

Table 6.1   **Skills sought for employment (from websites)**

UNICEF 10 life skills	MyStartJob.com	Top10onlinecolleges.org
1. Problem-solving	1. Communication skills	1. Sense-making
2. Critical thinking	2. Analytical and research	2. Social intelligence
3. Effective communication	3. Flexibility-adaptability	3. Novel adaptive thinking
4. Decision-making	4. Interpersonal abilities	4. Cross-cultural competency
5. Creative thinking	5. Decision-making	5. Computational thinking
6. Interpersonal relationships	6. Plan, organize, prioritize	6. New media literacy
7. Self-awareness	7. Wear multiple hats	7. Transdisciplinary
8. Empathy	8. Leadership/management	8. Design mind-set
9. Coping with stress	9. Attention to detail	9. Manage cognitive load
10. Coping with emotions	10. Self-confidence	10. Virtual collaboration

- novel adaptive thinking
- design mind-set
- **Type II: interpersonal, communication**
  - effective communication
  - interpersonal relationships/abilities
  - social intelligence
  - virtual collaboration
- **Type III: emotional, self-confidence**
  - self-awareness
  - empathy
  - coping with stress
  - manage cognitive load
  - coping with emotions

The important point to notice is that most of these skills are neither imparted in the current K–12 system, nor in academia. The whole system is still geared primarily toward the transmission of knowledge, highly structured and uniform, and not toward skills, let alone those skills. Pupils of all ages are now very aware of the fact that school-like information is available at the tip of their fingers, they are less receptive to frontal classes, their attention span is much shorter, and the sort of stimuli that makes them tick is different. This is also true at the tertiary level, and in addition, we are witnessing there the rise of the massive open online courses (MOOCS) and of other such online-based teaching tools.

In view of these trends, educational strategies may need to undergo equally significant changes away from the "factory system," and the fact that the incipient GPT may render many existing occupations obsolete, provides it with renewed urgency. These are some of the issues to tackle:

- Invert the pyramid: it is now widely recognized that critical skills, hard and soft, cognitive and social, are acquired very early on. Furthermore, failure to do so at the earliest stages may be hard (even impossible) to remedy later on (see, e.g., Heckman et al. 2014). Thus, we may have to consider investing much more in early childhood education, from birth to age six.

- Find ways to incorporate the development of skills (of the three types sketched above) as an integral part of teaching in every discipline and at all stages, including in academia.
- Effective educational methods are hard to come by, thus it is important to engage in bottom-up experimentation in pedagogy, school design, and social skills development in the context of flexible, creative, teaching environments.
- Reconsider the prevalent norm of uniform (typically government-mandated) curriculums and educational models, vis à vis diversity and open-innovation communities built around educational institutions.
- Foster research on the effectiveness of new educational models, their adequacy to shifting needs, the extent to which they promote equal opportunity, and so forth. This type of research will be crucial given the move away from "top-down" models and the emphasis on widespread experimentation.

6.3.2   Upgrading Personal Services

A Bureau of Labor Statistics (BLS) study[4] projects that virtually all of the employment gains in the decade to 2024 will be in services, and within the service sector particularly in health care and social assistance (see table 6.2).

Many of these occupations as performed today require little training and minimal educational attainment. Not surprisingly, most confer low wages, low status, and are supported by very little complementary technology. As the projections suggest, those occupations are at present not seriously threatened by AI—on the contrary, they will grow significantly. Thus, the overall prospects look rather gloomy when not only employment is considered by also wages: major upscale occupations are projected to remain stagnant or decline, whereas low-scale occupations are expected to grow.

Is this a deterministic outcome? Not necessarily, and the case of nursing may be quite instructive. After World War II, nursing was one of the lowest-ranking occupations in the United States: in 1946 the average wage of a nurse was just one-third that of female workers in the garment industry.[5] In 1964 Congress passed the Nurse Training Act, which essentially redefined the occupation and turned it into a profession requiring an academic

4. See: Occupational Employment Projections to 2024, Monthly Labor Review, US Bureau of Labor Statistics, Dec. 2015. Also in https://www.bls.gov/opub/mlr/2015/article/occupational -employment-projections-to-2024.htm.
5. In 1946, the average registered nurse (RN) earned about one dollar an hour—or $175 a month.

Table 6.2   US employment by major sector (millions)

Sector	2014	2024*	Change*	Percentage growth*
Goods producing	19	19	~	~0
Services	121	130	+ 9.3	+ 7
Of which: health care and social assistance	18	22	+ 3.8	+ 20
Other	10	11	+ 0.5	+ 1
Total	151	160	+ 9.8	+ 6

*Forecast

degree, with an upgraded curriculum. Since then the nursing profession has risen in every dimension—salaries, status, academic requirements, range of responsibilities, and so forth. These days, the nursing profession spans a range of specializations, whereby the upper echelon commands annual wages as high as $100,000. Moreover, nurses now use advanced technologies, and these in turn contribute to upgrade the profession.

It could have been otherwise had it not been for the legislation of 1964, and so it is for other occupations in personal services. Thus, we need to consider proactive strategies for the *professionalization of personal services*, particularly in health care and education, setting standards and academic requirements.

Take for example early childhood education: in most countries there are virtually no such standards for caregivers of children age one to three, precisely the ages that are crucial for their development. Suppose now that they were required to have specialized academic degrees, with a curriculum that would include psychology, brain development, testing for learning disabilities, and so forth. Not only would the status and wages of these workers increase, but they would be much more likely to benefit from complementary advanced technologies.

The advent of AI would probably not threaten these growing occupations, and furthermore, if they were upgraded in the way just described, AI could bestow significant benefits to them as well. For that to happen smart interfaces between the practitioners of these occupations and the AI machines will have to be developed. Thus, imagine, for example, professional caregivers using AI to test very young children for learning disabilities, and then for treating them with specially tailored AI-based games.

To sum up: BLS projections indicate that the bulk of job creation in the decade to 2024 will be in personal services, particularly in personal care. As currently practiced, most of these occupations are at the low end of the scale and rather impervious to technological advances. However, there are viable options to upgrade these occupations, particularly by setting academic standards and advanced curriculums. If that were to happen, then the changing composition of employment (i.e., more personal care, less of many others) would not adversely affect income distribution but perhaps to the contrary; furthermore, and more importantly here, AI may play a complementary role vis à vis these occupations, thus raising productivity in services and triggering a virtuous cycle.

6.3.3   The Direction of Technical Change: H-*Enhancing* or H-*Replacing*?

Although one of the seminal volumes in the economics of technological change is titled "The Rate and Direction of Inventive Activity," in fact the economic discipline has traditionally dealt much more with the "rate" than with the "direction." That may come as no surprise, since discussing direction requires getting into the guts of technology itself, and there is no reason to believe that economists have a comparative advantage in that regard.

Nevertheless, the extent and scope of technological advances that engulf us may require us to look more closely into the "black box" and try to understand, at the very least, what types of innovations we are facing and how they impact the economy. Furthermore, we would like to know whether there is room to affect the relative prevalence of the various types, in view of their differential economic effects.

Here is such an attempt: consider on the one hand innovations that mostly magnify, enhance, and extend sensory, motoric, analytical, and other human capabilities such as:

- In medicine: AI for diagnostics, for example, for reading and interpreting x-rays, CT scans and other imaging modalities; AI for robotic surgery (e.g., the da Vinci robot for prostate surgery); AI data mining of electronic medical records for follow-up evaluations of drug efficacy post-Food and Drug Administriation (FDA) approval, and so forth.
- In education: AI-based methods for "personalized teaching"; AI for online testing in MOOCS; (see also the above-mentioned applications for early childhood education), and so forth.

We label these "human-enhancing innovations" (HEI)—in medicine they do not replace doctors, but rather augment their human-bound capabilities (think of the precision and consistency of robot surgery), thus making better doctors. Similarly for teachers, eventually for judges (ruling with the aid of AI-based analysis), and so forth.

On the other hand, consider "human-replacing innovations" (HRI), that is, technical advances that *replace* human intervention, and furthermore that often leave for humans mostly "dumb" jobs that are not worth yet replacing given the very low wages that they command (and often are indeed difficult to replicate by machines, the proverbial one being janitors).

Some HRIs lead to cutting-edge, virtually human-free factories (best exemplified by Tesla's new facilities to produce batteries for its e-cars) that greatly improve productivity, even if reducing employment. Consider, however, the polar case of Walmart, the world's largest private employer (with over two million employees), having deployed advanced technologies along its whole chain of operations from logistics to retailing; it has turned a large proportion of its workers into "unthinking automatons," commanding very low wages with no prospect for improvement.

These then are two types of innovations (HEI and HRI) that have very different effects on key economic and social variables. It would seem that AI-based HEIs have the potential to unleash a new wave of *human creativity and productivity*, particularly in services (which to repeat are expected to be the fastest-growing occupations), whereas HRIs either decrease employment (e.g., Tesla), or create unworthy jobs.

Is it possible to design strategies to affect the direction of technical change in the sense of stimulating HEIs versus HRIs? It is hard to say, but it is certainly worthwhile investigating such possibility given the large impact that a change in direction may have on the economy. Incidentally, it would seem that in any case the traditional emphasis of economic policy on the "rate" of innovation, that is, on how much resources we devote to research and development (R&D), is misplaced—worldwide competition may be pushing us into too much investment in R&D, not too little (too many patents, too much replication, etc.). Some attention to the "direction" may bring much larger returns.

6.4   Concluding Remarks

The historical record suggests that dismal prophecies about the economic and social impact of great technological advances rarely come to pass. Thus, with AI poised to emerge as the new GPT, we should not necessarily envision a future whereby humans will be rendered obsolete and mass unemployment will be the "new normal." At the same time, as many occupations will indeed vanish, and many others will undergo significant changes, it is important to inquire into what sort of strategies may ameliorate the detrimental effects of AI and enhance the positive ones. This is all the more important given that in the twenty-first century the public at large has much less tolerance for bearing the costs of technical change and higher expectations for sharing into its benefits here and now.

Therefore, we need to anticipate the required institutional changes, experiment in the design of new policies (particularly in education and skills development) in the professionalization of service occupations, and in affecting the direction of technical advance. Furthermore, economists possess a vast methodological arsenal that may prove very useful for that purpose—we should not shy away from stepping into this area, since its importance for the economy cannot be overstated.

References

Bresnahan, Timothy, and Manuel Trajtenberg. 1995. "General Purpose Technologies 'Engines of Growth'?" *Journal of Econometrics* 65 (1): 83–108.

Gordon, Robert J. 2016. *The Rise and Fall of American Growth*. Princeton, NJ: Princeton University Press.

Heckman, James, Tim Kautz, Ron Diris, Bas ter Weel, and Lex Borghans. 2014. "Fostering and Measuring Skills: Improving Cognitive and Non-Cognitive Skills to Promote Lifetime Success." Report prepared for the Organisation of Economic Co-operation and Development, Paris. http://www.oecd.org/edu/ceri/Fostering-and-Measuring-Skills-Improving-Cognitive-and-NonCognitive-Skills-to-Promote-Lifetime-Success.pdf.

Hirschman, Albert. 1970. *Exit, Voice and Loyalty*. Cambridge, MA: Harvard University Press.

Mokyr, Joel. 2017. "The Past and the Future of Innovation: Some Lessons from Economic History." Paper presented at the conference on the Economics of Artificial Intelligence, Sept. 2017, Toronto.

Summers, Lawrence H. 2016. "The Age of Secular Stagnation: What It Is and What to Do About It." *Foreign Affairs*, Feb. 15. http://larrysummers.com/2016/02/17/the-age-of-secular-stagnation/.

II

Growth, Jobs, and Inequality

7

Artificial Intelligence, Income, Employment, and Meaning

Betsey Stevenson

The evolution of artificial intelligence (AI) evokes strong emotions in people. Some imagine a dystopia in which people are replaced by machines. Machines will develop the content we read, and the entertainment we enjoy. Artificial intelligence will pick our friends and our politicians, and ultimately take away any sense of human agency. And worst of all, those machines will deprive us of work. Human beings will lose meaning and income, and perhaps ultimately, be driven to extinction.

At the other end of the spectrum are those that envision the potential for utopia. With machines doing all the work, people will have plenty of income, yet very little unpleasant work to do. Instead, people will spend their days enjoying art and music. They will pursue their passions unburdened by the need to provide for their basic wants. They will feed their intellectual curiosity and fulfill the human demand for personal interactions. In short, people will be able to enjoy their lives with the freedom from time and money constraints that artificial intelligence provides.

So who is right?

7.1 Income Is Not the Problem

Economists think that we know the answer, or at least part of it. Most economists believe that automation promises a future of higher income that

Betsey Stevenson is associate professor of economics and public policy at the Gerald R. Ford School of Public Policy, University of Michigan; a visiting associate professor of economics at the University of Sydney; a research associate of the National Bureau of Economic Research; a research affiliate of the Centre for Economic Policy Research; and a research fellow of CESifo.

For acknowledgments, sources of research support, and disclosure of the author's material financial relationships, if any, please see http://www.nber.org/chapters/c14026.ack.

stems from the higher productivity that artificial intelligence will provide. In September 2017, the Chicago Booth IGM Forum's Economic Experts Panel asked forty-one economists from top universities in the United States whether they strongly agreed, agreed, were uncertain, disagreed, or strongly disagreed with the following statement: "Rising use of robots and artificial intelligence in advanced countries is likely to create benefits large enough that they could be used to compensate those workers who are substantially negatively affected for their lost wages."[1]

The answer was clear; no one disagreed with that statement. A few economists—10 percent—were uncertain, and the modal answer was agree, rather than strongly agree. Yet, it is clear that economists believe that artificial intelligence represents an opportunity for substantial economic gains. Indeed, productivity gains have been at the heart of improvements in living standards from the beginning of time. And so, it is difficult to imagine a world in which productivity gains do not generate benefits sufficiently large that we *could* compensate the losers.

Therefore, the relevant question is whether we *would* compensate the losers. Here economists are more skeptical. Economics tells us that there will be income gains, but our social and political structure help determine how they will be distributed.

7.2   Who Gets the Gains from Automation?

Much of the skepticism about being able to successfully redistribute income comes from a lack of trust that the political process will successfully manage redistribution in a world in which income is primarily generated by capital. The history of the last several decades has certainly not been encouraging on that front. The share of income held by the top 1 percent of the population has risen to nearly 20 percent, from around 10 percent in 1980, while the share going to the bottom 50 percent of the population has fallen to 12 percent from 20 percent in 1980.[2] Currently we are failing to redistribute the gains from technological advances, and so the concerns that distribution will be a challenge are supported by our recent past.

7.3   What Will We Do with Ourselves?

Yet, the concern runs deeper than wondering whether as a society we could manage to redistribute income. Most economists are concerned about how we will allocate jobs, and underneath that concern lies a belief that work matters independent of the earnings that are generated by the work.

1. IGM Economic Experts Panel (2017).
2. World Wealth and Income Database. http://wid.world/country/usa/.

Essentially, many people are skeptical that people could successfully find engaging and emotionally rewarding ways to spend their time if they were not working. One of the IGM Forum panelists, Robert Hall, expressed his concern most concretely: "Those not in the labor force are unhappy and inclined to opioids."

So economists are fearful about what will happen if people lose employment opportunities, yet economic history provides economists with optimism that employment will adapt. Which is why so many economists wonder what, if anything, will be different about artificial intelligence compared to the industrial revolution or other important periods of rapid technological change.

Economists' intuition around the impact of technological change on employment comes from considering how employment has adapted following previous periods of technological change. Here, once again, economists have a united view: technological change has not historically reduced employment. This view of economists is seen in a February 2014 question posed to the Chicago Booth IGM Forum's Economic Experts Panel. Forty-four economists from top universities in the United States were asked whether they strongly agreed, agreed, were uncertain, disagreed, or strongly disagreed with the following statement: "Advancing automation has not historically reduced employment in the United States."[3]

Economists are roughly united in agreeing with this statement, with only 4 percent disagreeing and 8 percent uncertain.[4]

Yet, when the IGM Economic Experts Panel was asked in September 2017 whether they strongly agreed, agreed, were uncertain, disagreed, or strongly disagreed with the following statement: "Holding labor market institutions and job training fixed, rising use of robots and artificial intelligence is likely to increase substantially the number of workers in advanced countries who are unemployed for long periods."

This is where economics lends a less clear answer and economists are divided on this question: 44 percent agree, 26 percent disagree, and 31 percent are uncertain. Is this a contradiction or a different view about artificial intelligence compared to other technologies? I don't think it is either. Instead, I believe these answers reflect the difference in what happens in the long run versus the short run. In the long run, technological change leads to prosperity and new jobs arise as we adjust to our new wealth, develop new skills, and come up with new ways to use human skills. In the short run, however, there is often a disruption.

---

3. IGM Economic Experts Panel (2014).
4. The figure of 88 percent is adjusted for respondents' confidence in their answer. Among all respondents, 76 percent agreed and 9 percent had no opinion.

7.4 The Long Run

One of the confusions around what will happen to employment and unemployment stems from not separating short-run versus long-run effects. When most of us think about artificial intelligence and increased automation, we are trying to think about what the long-run future holds, and our intuition comes from considering how growth has changed how people live across generations. It is not how it has changed our lives over the last five years, but instead contrasting how we live our lives—and if you are reading this it involves large periods of intellectual contemplation—with how our own family members ten generations back spent their lives. In the 1800s, the vast majority of Americans worked in agriculture and very few of them spent their time thinking about ideas. Today, 2 percent of Americans are directly employed in agriculture. There are more people employed in the public school system than in agriculture. In sum, few of us are in the jobs or careers that our great-great-great-great grandparents were in and many of us work in jobs today that did not exist a single generation ago.

One of the IGM panelists, Nancy Stokey, made it clear she was thinking about the long run: "If this had been true over the last two centuries, almost no one would be working anymore." When you take a really long-run view, it has to be true that automation has not reduced employment, at least not at as rapid a pace as the automation has itself occurred. In fact, many economists regard it as a puzzle that paid work has been remarkably stable even as nations have become increasingly prosperous, and its citizens might have been expected to use more of their higher income to choose to consume more leisure.

7.4.1 In the Long Run, Employment and Hours Worked Have Declined

Yet, despite our intuition, employment has tended to decline with technological progress. The difference between our beliefs about how technological progress has impacted employment and what has actually happened reflect two things. The first is that hours worked and employment has not declined by as much as one might have predicted. The second is that economists tend to think about employment in a model in which people who want to work can find jobs.

Hours of work have declined in most countries with productivity growth. Figure 7.1 shows average annual hours worked in a handful of developed countries since 1970. Annual hours worked declined fairly steadily in France, Germany, and Japan. The United States and the United Kingdom had smaller declines. Yet in each country, the annual hours worked fell.

To think more broadly about employment, childhood employment has been almost eliminated in developed countries. And employment of young adults, those age fifteen to twenty-five have declined as young people focus on investing in further human capital. On the other end of the life cycle, life

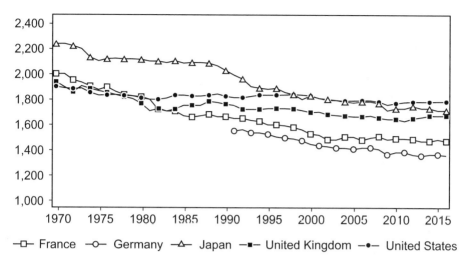

Fig. 7.1   Average annual hours worked
Source: OECD (2017).

expectancy has increased while retirement ages have fallen in most developed countries.

Work has declined in terms of the number and share of our life in terms of hours and days that we are going to spend working. The decline in work has occurred through the interaction of economic growth with government policies. For example, extended retirement has been facilitated by government pension and retirement programs. The dramatic reduction in child labor was facilitated by child labor laws. The demand for these programs and regulations is itself facilitated by the higher income that productivity growth creates.

Decreases in employment because of childhood education and retirement are thought to be improvements in living standards and not something we need or want to fix. However, they do require income redistribution. Older generations must support children, either through families or government redistribution (such as child tax credits, child allowances, child health care subsidies, etc.). Yet, most people agree that this is an improvement—few are trying to get kids back into the workforce to financially support themselves. Something similar is true at the other end of the life cycle. While the elderly can save for retirement, redistribution allows those who are retired to share in continued economic growth.

7.5   Short-Run Disruption

The real uncertainty with artificial intelligence is what will the disruption be like and how will we manage people through it. Most economists think there will be people who are hurt through decreased demand for their skills. There might be longer spells of unemployment and a larger need for worker retraining. There might be jobs that workers do not want or are not qualified to do. While we can prepare a new generation for a world in which robots do many of the jobs, preparing a generation midway through their lives is harder. People are resistant to starting over, they mourn what they have lost, and they resent a definition of progress that leaves them diminished in status and income.

The loss of income should be easier to solve than the loss of status. So how important is work and what do we know about it? Is work about the income that it generates or about the meaning and order it gives to our days? Much of the debate about the potential impact of automation on employment is really a debate about how we will spend our time. So it is useful to separate out the question of what will we do with our time if the robots take our jobs from the question of whether we can find a stable and fair distribution of income in such a scenario. And it is useful to realize that the answers in the long run may be very different to what happens in the short run. Yet, how we handle the short run will ultimately influence our long-run outcomes.

7.6   There Is Work outside of Employment

Work is a broader concept than paid labor. Paid labor is the result of a trade-off between leisure, home-produced goods, and market-produced goods. This matters from a measurement perspective because the 1970s was a period of very rapid substitution, with nonmarket-produced goods being substituted by market-produced goods. Women stopped making clothes and making pies and cakes from scratch, and started going to work, buying clothes, and buying pies and cake mixes. Technological change occurred in a way that crowded out homemade goods and crowded in women's labor force participation.[5] Should we think about this as increasing or decreasing work? One thing is clear, work shifted from outside our typical measurement scope to inside it. For example, I suspect that there are fewer childcare workers today than forty years ago if you count every stay-at-home mom with children as a childcare worker.

Yet, time-use surveys reveal that the decline in hours worked is smaller than measured hours of employment suggest, at least since the 1970s. If we look at time-use surveys, dads are working more hours, even though they are working less in the labor force.[6] Once we account for hours spent on childcare and housework, men work more hours than they did in the 1960s.

Why consider childcare and housework hours? If we want to think about really measuring what happens to work we need a more holistic sense of

5. Stevenson and Wolfers (2007).
6. Council of Economic Advisors (2014).

what work is. Particularly if the question is whether we can find meaningful ways to spend our time outside of paid work. Artificial intelligence won't replace the need for human connection, both in our personal lives and professionally. A robot may be able to care for an elderly bed-bound person, but it is unlikely to produce the joy and satisfaction of connecting with a human being. Will there be more paid jobs caring for one another? Undoubtedly. But will our higher incomes also allow us to choose to work less in order to provide more uncompensated care for our friends and family? I hope so.

7.7   Productivity Growth Ultimately Gives Us Better Lives and More Options

In the end, there are really two separate questions: there is an employment question, in which the fundamental question is, can we find fulfilling ways to spend our time if robots take our jobs? And there is an income question, can we find a stable and fair distribution of income?

The answer to both will depend on not just how technology changes, but how our institutions change in reaction to technological change. Do we embrace technology and increase funding for education, worker training, the arts, and community service? Or do we allow inequality to continue to grow unchecked, pitting workers against those investing in robots?

The challenge for society is to ensure that we solve both problems. That we help shape a society in which people can find fulfilling ways to spend their time. And to solve that problem, we must also solve the separate problem of finding a stable and fair distribution of income.

References

Council of Economic Advisors. 2014. "Eleven Facts about American Families and Work." https://obamawhitehouse.archives.gov/sites/default/files/docs/eleven_facts_about_family_and_work_final.pdf.
IGM Economic Experts Panel. 2014. Accessed Dec. 15, 2017. http://www.igmchicago.org/surveys/robots.
———. 2017. Accessed Dec. 15, 2017. http://www.igmchicago.org/surveys/robots-and-artificial-intelligence-2.
Organisation for Economic Co-operation and Development (OECD). 2017. "Hours Worked: Average Annual Hours Actually Worked." OECD Employment and Labour Market Statistics (database). Accessed Sept. 13, 2017. https://stats.oecd.org/Index.aspx?DataSetCode=ANHRS.
Stevenson, B., and J. Wolfers. 2007. "Marriage and Divorce: Changes and Their Driving Forces." *Journal of Economic Perspectives* 21 (2): 27–52.

Artificial Intelligence, Automation, and Work

Daron Acemoglu and Pascual Restrepo

8.1 Introduction

The last two decades have witnessed major advances in artificial intelligence (AI) and robotics. Future progress is expected to be even more spectacular, and many commentators predict that these technologies will transform work around the world (Brynjolfsson and McAfee 2014; Ford 2016; Boston Consulting Group 2015; McKinsey Global Institute 2017). Recent surveys find high levels of anxiety about automation and other technological trends, underscoring the widespread concerns about their effects (Pew Research Center 2017).

These expectations and concerns notwithstanding, we are far from a satisfactory understanding of how automation in general, and AI and robotics in particular, impact the labor market and productivity. Even worse, much of the debate in both the popular press and academic circles centers around a false dichotomy. On the one side are the alarmist arguments that the oncoming advances in AI and robotics will spell the end of work by humans, while many economists on the other side claim that because technological breakthroughs in the past have eventually increased the demand for labor and wages, there is no reason to be concerned that this time will be any different.

In this chapter, we build on Acemoglu and Restrepo (2016), as well as

Daron Acemoglu is the Elizabeth and James Killian Professor of Economics at the Massachusetts Institute of Technology and a research associate of the National Bureau of Economic Research. Pascual Restrepo is assistant professor of economics at Boston University.

We are grateful to David Autor for useful comments. We gratefully acknowledge financial support from Toulouse Network on Information Technology, Google, Microsoft, IBM, and the Sloan Foundation. For acknowledgments, sources of research support, and disclosure of the authors' material financial relationships, if any, please see http://www.nber.org/chapter/c14027.ack.

Zeira (1998) and Acemoglu and Autor (2011) to develop a framework for thinking about automation and its impact on tasks, productivity, and work.

At the heart of our framework is the idea that automation and thus AI and robotics replace workers in tasks that they previously performed, and via this channel, create a powerful *displacement effect*. In contrast to presumptions in much of macroeconomics and labor economics, which maintain that productivity-enhancing technologies always increase overall labor demand, the displacement effect can reduce the demand for labor, wages, and employment. Moreover, the displacement effect implies that increases in output per worker arising from automation will not result in a proportional expansion of the demand for labor. The displacement effect causes a decoupling of wages and output per worker, and a decline in the share of labor in national income.

We then highlight several countervailing forces that push against the displacement effect and may imply that automation, AI, and robotics could increase labor demand. First, the substitution of cheap machines for human labor creates a *productivity effect*: as the cost of producing automated tasks declines, the economy will expand and increase the demand for labor in nonautomated tasks. The productivity effect could manifest itself as an increase in the demand for labor in the same sectors undergoing automation or as an increase in the demand for labor in nonautomating sectors. Second, *capital accumulation* triggered by increased automation (which raises the demand for capital) will also raise the demand for labor. Third, automation does not just operate at the extensive margin—replacing tasks previously performed by labor—but at the intensive margin as well, increasing the productivity of machines in tasks that were previously automated. This phenomenon, which we refer to as *deepening of automation*, creates a productivity effect but no displacement, and thus increases labor demand.

Though these countervailing effects are important, they are generally insufficient to engender a "balanced growth path," meaning that even if these effects were powerful, ongoing automation would still reduce the share of labor in national income (and possibly employment). We argue that there is a more powerful countervailing force that increases the demand for labor as well as the share of labor in national income: the *creation of new tasks*, functions and activities in which labor has a comparative advantage relative to machines. The creation of new tasks generates a *reinstatement effect* directly counterbalancing the displacement effect.

Indeed, throughout history we have not just witnessed pervasive automation, but a continuous process of new tasks creating employment opportunities for labor. As tasks in textiles, metals, agriculture, and other industries were being automated in the nineteenth and twentieth centuries, a new range of tasks in factory work, engineering, repair, back-office, management, and finance generated demand for displaced workers. The creation of new tasks is not an autonomous process advancing at a predetermined rate, but one whose speed and nature are shaped by the decisions of firms, workers, and other actors in society, and might be fueled by new automation technologies. First, this is because automation, by displacing workers, may create a greater pool of labor that could be employed in new tasks. Second, the currently most discussed automation technology, AI itself, can serve as a platform to create new tasks in many service industries.

Our framework also highlights that even with these countervailing forces, the adjustment of an economy to the rapid rollout of automation technologies could be slow and painful. There are some obvious reasons for this related to the general slow adjustment of the labor market to shocks, for example, because of the costly process of workers being reallocated to new sectors and tasks. Such reallocation will involve both a slow process of searching for the right matches between workers and jobs, and also the need for retraining, at least for some of the workers.

A more critical, and in this context more novel, factor is a potential *mismatch between technology and skills*—between the requirements of new technologies and tasks and the skills of the workforce. We show that such a mismatch slows down the adjustment of labor demand, contributes to inequality, and also reduces the productivity gains from both automation and the introduction of new tasks (because it makes the complementary skills necessary for the operation of new tasks and technologies more scarce).

Yet another major factor to be taken into account is the possibility of *excessive automation*. We highlight that a variety of factors (ranging from a bias in favor of capital in the tax code to labor market imperfections create a wedge between the wage and the opportunity cost of labor) and will push toward socially excessive automation, which not only generates a direct inefficiency, but also acts as a drag on productivity growth. Excessive automation could potentially explain why, despite the enthusiastic adoption of new robotics and AI technologies, productivity growth has been disappointing over the last several decades.

Our framework underscores as well that the singular focus of the research and the corporate community on automation, at the expense of other types of technologies including the creation of new tasks, could be another factor leading to a productivity slowdown because it forgoes potentially valuable productivity growth opportunities in other domains.

In the next section, we provide an overview of our approach without presenting a formal analysis. Section 8.3 introduces our formal framework, though to increase readability, our presentation is still fairly nontechnical (and formal details and derivations are relegated to the appendix). Section 8.4 contains our main results, highlighting both the displacement effect and the countervailing forces in our framework. Section 8.5 discusses the mismatch between skills and technologies, potential causes for slow productivity growth and excessive automation, and other constraints on labor market adjustment to automation technologies. Section 8.6 concludes, and the appendix contains derivations and proofs omitted from the text.

8.2   Automation, Work, and Wages: An Overview

At the heart of our framework is the observation that robotics and current practice in AI are continuing what other automation technologies have done in the past: using machines and computers to substitute for human labor in a widening range of tasks and industrial processes.

Production in most industries requires the simultaneous completion of a range of tasks. For example, textile production requires production of fiber, production of yarn from fiber (e.g., by spinning), production of the relevant fabric from the yarn (e.g., by weaving or knitting), pretreatment (e.g., cleaning of the fabric, scouring, mercerizing and bleaching), dyeing and printing, finishing, as well as various auxiliary tasks including design, planning, marketing, transport, and retail.[1] Each one of these tasks can be performed by a combination of human labor and machines. At the dawn of the British Industrial Revolution, most of these tasks were heavily labor intensive. Many of the early innovations of that era were aimed at automating spinning and weaving by substituting mechanized processes for the labor of skilled artisans (Mantoux 1928).[2]

The mechanization of US agriculture offers another example of machines replacing workers in tasks they previously performed (Rasmussen 1982). In the first half of the nineteenth century, the cotton gin automated the labor-intensive process of separating the lint from the cotton seeds. In the second half of the nineteenth century, horse-powered reapers, harvesters, and plows replaced manual labor working with more rudimentary tools such as hoes, sickles, and scythes, and this process was continued with tractors in the twentieth century. Horse-powered threshing machines and fanning mills replaced workers employed in threshing and winnowing, two of the most labor-intensive tasks left in agriculture at the time. In the twentieth century, combine harvesters and a variety of other mechanical harvesters improved upon the horse-powered machinery, and allowed farmers to mechanically harvest several different crops.

Yet another example of automation comes from the development of the

---

1. See http://textileguide.chemsec.org/find/get-familiar-with-your-textile-production-processes/.

2. It was this displacement effect that motivated Luddites to smash textile machines and agricultural workers during the Captain Swing riots to destroy threshing machines. Though these workers often appear in history books as misguided, there was nothing misguided about their economic fears. They were quite right that they were going to be displaced. Of course, had they been successful, they might have prevented the Industrial Revolution from gaining momentum with potentially disastrous consequences for technological development and our subsequent prosperity.

factory system in manufacturing and its subsequent evolution. Beginning in the second half of the eighteenth century, the factory system introduced the use of machine tools such as lathes and milling machines, replacing the more labor-intensive production techniques relying on skilled artisans (Mokyr 1990). Steam power and later electricity greatly increased the opportunities for the substitution of capital for human labor. Another important turning point in the process of factory automation was the introduction of machines controlled via punch cards and then numerically controlled machines in the 1940s. Because numerically controlled machines were more precise, faster, and easier to operate than manual technologies, they enabled significant cost savings while also reducing the role of craft workers in manufacturing production. This process culminated in the widespread use of CNC (computer numerical control) machinery, which replaced the numerically controlled vintages (Groover 1983). A major new development was the introduction of industrial robots in the late 1980s, which automated many of the remaining labor-intensive tasks in manufacturing, including machining, welding, painting, palletizing, assembly, material handling, and quality control (Ayres and Miller 1983; Groover et al. 1986; Graetz and Michaels 2015; Acemoglu and Restrepo 2017).

Examples of automation are not confined to industry and agriculture. Computer software has already automated a number of tasks performed by white-collar workers in retail, wholesale, and business services. Software and AI-powered technologies can now retrieve information, coordinate logistics, handle inventories, prepare taxes, provide financial services, translate complex documents, write business reports, prepare legal briefs, and diagnose diseases. These technologies are set to become much better at these and other tasks during the next years (e.g., Brynjolfsson and McAfee 2014; Ford 2016).

As these examples illustrate, automation involves the substitution of machines for labor and leads to the displacement of workers from the tasks that are being automated. This displacement effect is not present—or present only incidentally—in most approaches to production functions and labor demand used in macroeconomics and labor economics. The canonical approach posits that production in the aggregate (or in a sector for that matter) can be represented by a function of the form $F(AL,BK)$, where L denotes labor and K is capital. Technology is assumed to take a "factor-augmenting" form, meaning that it multiplies these two factors of production as the parameters A and B do in this production function.

It might appear natural to model automation as an increase in B, that is, as capital-augmenting technological change. However, this type of technological change does not cause any displacement and always increases labor demand and wages (see Acemoglu and Restrepo 2016). Moreover, as our examples above illustrate, automation is not mainly about the development of more productive vintages of existing machines, but involves the introduction of new machinery to perform tasks that were previously the domain of human labor.

Labor-augmenting technological change, corresponding to an increase in A, does create a type of displacement if the elasticity of substitution between capital and labor is small. But in general, this type of technological change also expands labor demand, especially if capital adjusts over the long run (see Acemoglu and Restrepo 2016). Moreover, our examples make it clear that automation does not directly augment labor; on the contrary, it transforms the production process in a way that allows more tasks to be performed by machines.

8.2.1   Tasks, Technologies, and Displacement

We propose, instead, a task-based approach, where the central unit of production is a task as in the textile example discussed above.[3] Some tasks have to be produced by labor, while other tasks can be produced either by labor or by capital. Also, labor and capital have *comparative advantages* in different tasks, meaning that the relative productivity of labor varies across tasks. Our framework conceptualizes *automation* (or automation at the extensive margin) as an expansion in the set of tasks that can be produced with capital. If capital is sufficiently cheap or sufficiently productive at the margin, then automation will lead to the substitution of capital for labor in these tasks. This substitution results in a displacement of workers from the tasks that are being automated, creating the aforementioned displacement effect.

The displacement effect could cause a decline in the demand for labor and the equilibrium wage rate. The possibility that technological improvements that increase productivity can actually reduce the wage of *all* workers is an important point to emphasize because it is often downplayed or ignored.

With an elastic labor supply (or quasi-labor supply reflecting some labor market imperfections), a reduction in the demand for labor also leads to lower employment. In contrast to the standard approach based on factor-augmenting technological changes, a task-based approach immediately opens the way to productivity-enhancing technological developments that simultaneously reduce wages and employment.

8.2.2   Countervailing Effects

The presence of the displacement effect does not mean that automation will always reduce labor demand. In fact, throughout history, there are several periods where automation was accompanied by an expansion of

---

3. See Autor, Leavy, and Murnane (2003) and Acemoglu and Autor (2011). Different from these papers that develop a task-based approach focusing on inequality implications of technological change, we are concerned here with automation and the process of capital-replacing tasks previously performed by labor and their implications for wages and employment.

labor demand and even higher wages. There are a number of reasons why automation could increase labor demand.

1. *The Productivity Effect.* By reducing the cost of producing a subset of tasks, automation raises the demand for labor in nonautomated tasks (Autor 2015; Acemoglu and Restrepo 2016). In particular, automation leads to the substitution of capital for labor because at the margin, capital performs certain tasks more cheaply than labor used to. This reduces the prices of the goods and services whose production processes are being automated, making households effectively richer, and increasing the demand for all goods and services.

The productivity effect could manifest itself in two complementary ways. First, labor demand might expand in the same sectors that are undergoing automation.[4] A telling example of this process comes from the effects of the introduction of automated teller machines (ATMs) on the employment of bank tellers. Bessen (2016) documents that concurrent with the rapid spread of ATMs—a clear example of automating technology that enabled these new machines to perform tasks that were previously performed more expensively by labor—there was an expansion in the employment of bank tellers. Bessen suggests that this is because ATMs reduced the costs of banking and encouraged banks to open more branches, raising the demand for bank tellers who then specialized in tasks that ATMs did not automate.

Another interesting example of this process is provided by the dynamics of labor demand in spinning and weaving during the British Industrial Revolution as recounted by Mantoux (1928). Automation in weaving (most notably, John Kay's fly shuttle) made this task cheaper and increased the price of yarn and the demand for the complementary task of spinning. Later automation in spinning reversed this trend and increased the demand for weavers. In the words of John Wyatt, one of the inventors of the spinning machine, installing spinning machines would cause clothiers to "then want more hands in every other branch of the trade, viz. weavers, shearmen, scourers, combers, etc." (quoted in Mantoux 1928). This is also probably the reason why the introduction of Eli Whitney's cotton gin in 1793, which automated the labor-intensive process of separating the cotton lint from the seeds, appears to have led to greater demand for slave labor in southern plantations (Rasmussen 1982).

The productivity effect also leads to higher real incomes and thus to greater demand for all products, including those not experiencing automation. The greater demand for labor from other industries might then counteract the negative displacement effect of automation. The clearest historical example of this comes from the adjustment of the US and many European economies

---

4. This requires that the demand for the products of these sectors is elastic. Acemoglu and Restrepo (2017) refer to this channel as the price-productivity effect because it works by reducing the relative price of products that are being automated and restructuring production toward these sectors.

to the mechanization of agriculture. By reducing food prices, mechanization enriched consumers who then demanded more nonagricultural goods (Herrendorf, Rogerson, and Valentinyi 2013), and created employment opportunities for many of the workers dislocated by the mechanization process in the first place.[5]

This discussion also implies that, in contrast to the popular emphasis on the negative labor market consequences of "brilliant" and highly productive new technologies set to replace labor (e.g., Brynjolfsson and McAfee 2014; Ford 2016), the real danger for labor may come not from highly productive but from "so-so" automation technologies that are just productive enough to be adopted and cause displacement, but not sufficiently productive to bring about powerful productivity effects.

2. *Capital Accumulation.* As our framework in the next section clarifies, automation corresponds to an increase in the capital intensity of production. The high demand for capital triggers further accumulation of capital (e.g., by increasing the rental rate of capital). Capital accumulation then raises the demand for labor. This may have been an important channel of adjustment of the British economy during the Industrial Revolution and of the American economy in the first half of the twentieth century in the face of mechanization of agriculture, for in both cases there was rapid capital accumulation (Allen 2009; Olmstead and Rhode 2001).

As we discuss in the next section, under some (albeit restrictive) assumptions often adopted in neoclassical models of economic growth, capital accumulation can be sufficiently powerful that automation will always increase wages in the long run (see Acemoglu and Restrepo 2016), though the more robust prediction is that it will act as a countervailing effect.

3. *Deepening of Automation.* The displacement effect is created by automation at the extensive margin—meaning the expansion of the set of tasks that can be produced by capital. But what happens if technological improvements increase the productivity of capital in tasks that have already been automated? This will clearly not create additional displacement because labor was already replaced by capital in those tasks. But it will generate the same productivity effects we have already pointed out above. These productivity effects then raise labor demand. We refer to this facet of advances in automation technology as the deepening of automation (or as automation at the intensive margin because it is intensifying the productive use of machines).

A clear illustration of the role of deepening automation comes from the ˙introduction of new vintages of machinery replacing older vintages used in already automated tasks. For instance, in US agriculture the replacement of

---

5. Acemoglu and Restrepo (2017) refer to it as a "scale effect" because in their setting it acted in a homothetic manner, scaling up demand from all sectors, though in general it could take a nonhomothetic form.

horse-powered reapers and harvesters by diesel tractors increased productivity, presumably with limited additional substitution of workers in agricultural tasks.[6] In line with our account of the potential role of deepening automation, agricultural productivity and wages increased rapidly starting in the 1930s, a period that coincided with the replacement of horses by tractors (Olmstead and Rhode 2001; Manuelli and Seshadri 2014).

Another example comes from the vast improvements in the efficiency of numerically controlled machines used for metal cutting and processing (such as mills and lathes), as the early vintages controlled by punched cards were replaced by computerized models during the 1970s. The new computerized machines were used in the same tasks as the previous vintages, and so the additional displacement effects were probably minor. As a result, the transition to CNC (computer numerical control) machines increased the productivity of machinists, operators, and other workers in the industry (Groover 1983).

The three countervailing forces we have listed here are central for understanding why the implications of automation are much richer than the direct displacement effects might at first suggest, and why automation need not be an unadulterated negative force against the labor market fortunes of workers. Nevertheless, there is one aspect of the displacement effect that is unlikely to be undone by any of these four countervailing forces: as we show in the next section, automation necessarily makes the production process more capital intensive, reducing the share of labor in national income. Intuitively, this is because it entails the substitution of capital for tasks previously performed by labor, thus squeezing labor into a narrower set of tasks.

If, as we have suggested, automation has been ongoing for centuries, with or without powerful countervailing forces of the form listed here, we should have seen a "nonbalanced" growth process with the share of labor in national income declining steadily since the beginning of the Industrial Revolution. That clearly has not been the case (see, e.g., Kuznets 1966; Acemoglu 2009). This suggests that there have been other powerful forces making production more labor intensive and balancing the effects of automation. This is what we suggest in the next subsection.

8.2.3   New Tasks

As discussed in the introduction, periods of intensive automation have often coincided with the emergence of new jobs, activities, industries, and tasks. In nineteenth-century Britain, for example, there was a rapid expansion of new industries and jobs ranging from engineers, machinists, repairmen, conductors, back-office workers, and managers involved with

---

6. Nevertheless, the move from horse power to tractors contributed to a decline in agricultural employment via a different channel: tractors increased agricultural productivity, and because of inelastic demand, expenditure on agricultural products declined (Rasmussen 1982).

the introduction and operation of new technologies (e.g., Landes 1969; Chandler 1977; and Mokyr 1990). In early twentieth-century America, the mechanization of agriculture coincided with a large increase in employment in new industry and factory jobs (Kuznets 1966) among others in the burgeoning industries of farm equipment (Olmstead and Rhode 2001) and cotton milling (Rasmussen 1982). This is not just a historical phenomenon. As documented in Acemoglu and Restrepo (2016), from 1980 to 2010 the introduction and expansion of new tasks and job titles explains about half of US employment growth.

Our task-based framework highlights that the creation of new labor-intensive tasks (tasks in which labor has a comparative advantage relative to capital) may be the most powerful force balancing the growth process in the face of rapid automation. Without the demand for workers from new factory jobs, engineering, supervisory tasks, accounting, and managerial occupations in the second half of the nineteenth and much of the twentieth centuries, it would have been impossible to employ millions of workers exiting the agricultural sector and automated labor-intensive tasks.

In the same way that automation has a displacement effect, we can think of the creation of new tasks as engendering a *reinstatement effect*. In this way, the creation of new tasks has the opposite effect of automation. It always generates additional labor demand, which increases the share of labor in national income. Consequently, one powerful way in which technological progress could be associated with a balanced growth path is via the balancing of the impacts of automation by the creation of new tasks.

The creation of new tasks need not be an exogenous, autonomous process unrelated to automation, AI, and robotics for at least two reasons:

1. As emphasized in Acemoglu and Restrepo (2016), rapid automation may endogenously generate incentives for firms to introduce new labor-intensive tasks. Automation running ahead of the creation of new tasks reduces the labor share and possibly wages, making further automation less profitable and new tasks generating employment opportunities for labor more profitable for firms. Acemoglu and Restrepo (2016) show that this equilibrating force could be powerful enough to make the growth process balanced.

2. Some automation technology platforms, especially AI, may facilitate the creation of new tasks. A recent report by Accenture identified entirely new categories of jobs that are emerging in firms using AI as part of their production process (Accenture PLC 2017). These jobs include "trainers" (to train the AI systems), "explainers" (to communicate and explain the output of AI systems to customers), and "sustainers" (to monitor the performance of AI systems, including their adherence to prevailing ethical standards).

The applications of AI to education, health care, and design may also result in employment opportunities for new workers. Take education. Existing evidence suggests that many students, not least those with certain learning disabilities, will benefit from individualized education programs and personalized instruction (Kolb 1984). With current technology, it is prohibitively costly to provide such services to more than a small fraction of students. Applications of AI may enable the educational system to become more customized, and in the process create more jobs for education professionals to monitor, design, and implement individualized education programs. Similar prospects exist in health care and elderly care services.

8.2.4   Revisiting the False Dichotomy

The conceptual framework outlined above, which will be further elaborated in the next section, clarifies why the current debate is centered on a false dichotomy between disastrous and totally benign effects of automation.

Our task-based framework underscores that automation will always create a displacement effect. Unless neutralized by the countervailing forces, this displacement effect could reduce labor demand, wages, and employment. At the very least, this displacement effect implies that a falling share of output will accrue to labor. These possibilities push against the benign accounts emphasizing that technology always increases the demand for labor and benefits workers.

Our framework does not support the alarmist perspectives stressing the disastrous effects of automation for labor either. Rather, it highlights several countervailing forces that soften the impact of automation on labor. More important, as we have argued in the previous subsection, the creation of new labor-intensive tasks has been a critical part of the adjustment process in the face of rapid automation. The creation of new tasks is not just *manna* from heaven. There are good reasons why market incentives will endogenously lead to the creation of new tasks that gain strength when automation itself becomes more intensive. Also, some of the most defining automation technologies of our age, such as AI, may create a platform for the creation of new sets of tasks and jobs.

At the root of some of the alarmism is the belief that AI will have very different consequences for labor than previous waves of technological change. Our framework highlights that the past is also replete with automation technologies displacing workers, but this need not have disastrous effects for labor. Nor is it technologically likely that AI will replace labor in all or almost all of the tasks in which it currently specializes. This limited remit of AI can be best understood by contrasting the current nature and ambitions of AI with those of its first coming under the auspices of "cybernetics." The intellectual luminaries of cybernetics, such as Norbert Wiener, envisaged the production of *Human-Level Artificial Intelligence*—computer systems capable of thinking in a way that could not be distinguished from human intelligence—replicating all human thought processes and faculties (Nilsson 2009). In 1965, Herbert Simon predicted that "machines will be capable, within twenty years, of doing any work a man can do" (Simon 1965, 96). Marvin Minsky agreed, declaring in 1967 that "Within a generation, I am convinced, few compartments of intellect will remain outside the machine's realm" (Minsky 1967, 2).

Current practice in the field of AI, especially in its most popular and promising forms based on deep learning and various other "big data" methods applied to unstructured data, eschews these initial ambitions and aims at developing *applied artificial intelligence*—commercial systems specializing in clearly delineated tasks related to prediction, decision-making, logistics, and pattern recognition (Nilsson 2009). Though many occupations involve such tasks—and so AI is likely to have a displacement effect in these tasks— there are still many human skills that we still cannot automate, including complex reasoning, judgment, analogy-based learning, abstract problem-solving, and a mixture of physical activity, empathy, and communication skills. This reading of the current practice of AI suggests that the potential for AI and related technological advances to automate a vast set of tasks is limited.

8.2.5   Flies in the Ointment

Our framework so far has emphasized two key ideas. First, automation does create a potential negative impact on labor through the displacement effect and also by reducing the share of labor in national income. But second, it can be counterbalanced by the creation of new tasks (as well as the productivity effect, capital accumulation and the deepening of automation, which tend to increase the demand for labor, even though they do not generally restore the share of labor in national income to its preautomation levels).

The picture we have painted underplays some of the challenges of adjustment, however. The economic adjustment following rapid automation can be more painful than the process we have outlined for a number of reasons.

Most straightforward, automation changes the nature of existing jobs, and the reallocation of workers from existing jobs and tasks to new ones is a complex and often slow process. It takes time for workers to find new jobs and tasks in which they can be productive, and periods during which workers are laid off from their existing jobs can create a depressed local or national labor market, further increasing the costs of adjustment. These effects are visible in recent studies that have focused on the adjustment of local US labor markets to negative demand shocks, such as Autor, Dorn, and Hanson (2013), who study the slow and highly incomplete adjustment of local labor markets in response to the surge in Chinese exports, Mian and Sufi (2014), who investigate the implications of the collapse in housing prices on consumption and local employment, and perhaps more closely related to our focus, Acemoglu and Restrepo (2017), who find employment and wage declines in areas most exposed to one specific type of automation, the introduction of industrial robots in manufacturing.

The historical record also underscores the painful nature of the adjustment. The rapid introduction of new technologies during the British Industrial Revolution ultimately led to rising labor demand and wages, but this was only after a protracted period of stagnant wages, expanding poverty, and harsh living conditions. During an eighty-year period extending from the beginning of the Industrial Revolution to the middle of the nineteenth century, wages stagnated and the labor share fell, even as technological advances and productivity growth were ongoing in the British economy, a phenomenon which Allen (2009) dubs the "Engel's pause" (previously referred to as the "living standards paradox"; see Mokyr [1990]).

There should thus be no presumption that the adjustment to the changed labor market brought about by rapid automation will be a seamless, costless, and rapid process.

8.2.6 Mismatch between Skills and Technologies

It is perhaps telling that wages started growing in the nineteenth-century British economy only after mass schooling and other investments in human capital expanded the skills of the workforce. Similarly, the adjustment to the large supply of labor freed from agriculture in early twentieth-century America may have been greatly aided by the "high school movement," which increased the human capital of the new generation of American workers (Goldin and Katz 2010). The forces at work here are likely to be more general than these examples. New tasks tend to require new skills. But to the extent that the workforce does not possess those skills, the adjustment process will be hampered. Even more ominously, if the educational system is not up to providing those skills (and if we are not even aware of the types of new skills that will be required so as to enable investments in them), the adjustment will be greatly impeded. Even the most optimistic observers ought to be concerned about the ability of the current US educational system to identify and provide such skills.

At stake here is not only the speed of adjustment, but potential productivity gains from new technologies. If certain skills are complementary to new technologies, their absence will imply that the productivity of these new technologies will be lower than otherwise. Thus the mismatch between skills and technologies not only slows down the adjustment of employment and wages, but holds back potential productivity gains. This is particularly true for the creation of new tasks. The fact that while there is heightened concerns about job losses from automation, many employers are unable to find workers with the right skills for their jobs underscores the importance of these considerations (Deloitte and the Manufacturing Institute 2011).

8.2.7 Missing Productivity and Excessive Automation

The issues raised in the previous subsection are important not least because a deep puzzle in any discussion of the impact of new technologies is missing productivity growth—the fact that while so many sophisticated technologies are being adopted, productivity growth has been slow. As pointed out by Gordon (2016), US productivity growth since 1974 (with the exception of the period from 1995 to 2004) compares dismally to its postwar performance. While the annual rate of labor productivity growth of the US economy averaged 2.7 percent between 1947 and 1973, it only averaged 1.5 percent between 1974 and 1994. Average productivity growth rebounded to 2.8 percent between 1995 and 2004, and then fell again to only 1.3 percent between 2005 and 2015 (Syverson 2017). How can we make sense of this?

One line of attack argues that there is plenty of productivity growth, but it is being mismeasured. But, as pointed out by Syverson (2017), the pervasive nature of this slow down, and the fact that it is even more severe in industries that have made greater investments in information technology (Acemoglu et al. 2014), make the productivity mismeasurement hypothesis unlikely to account for all of the slowdown.

Our conceptual framework suggests some possible explanations. They center around the possibility of "excessive automation," meaning faster automation than socially desirable (Acemoglu and Restrepo 2016, 2018a). Excessive automation not only creates direct inefficiencies, but may also hold productivity growth down by wastefully using resources and displacing labor.

There are two broad reasons for excessive automation, both of which we believe to be important. The first is related to the biases in the US tax code, which subsidizes capital relative to labor. This subsidy takes the form of several different provisions, including additional taxes and costs employers have to pay for labor, subsidies in the form of tax credits and accelerated depreciation for capital outlays, and additional tax credit for interest rate deductions in case of debt-financed investments (AEI 2008; Tuzel and Zhang 2017). All of these distortions imply that at the margin, when a utilitarian social planner would be indifferent between capital and labor, the market would have an incentive to use machines, giving an inefficient boost to automation. This inefficiency could translate into slow productivity growth because the substitution of labor for machines worsens the misallocation of capital and labor.

Even absent such a fiscal bias, there are natural reasons for excessive automation. Labor market imperfections and frictions also tend to imply that the equilibrium wage is above the social opportunity cost of labor. Thus a social planner would use a lower shadow wage in deciding whether to automate a task than the market, creating another force toward excessive automation. The implications of this type of excessive automation would again include slower productivity growth than otherwise.

Finally, it is possible that automation has continued at its historical pace, or may have even accelerated recently, but the dismal productivity growth performance we are witnessing is driven by a slowdown in the creation of new tasks or investment in other productivity-enhancing technologies (see Acemoglu and Restrepo 2016). A deceleration in the creation of new tasks and technologies other than automation would also explain why the period of slow productivity growth coincided with poor labor market outcomes, including stagnant median wages and a decline in the labor share.

There are natural reasons why too much emphasis on automation may come at the cost of investments in other technologies, including the creation of new tasks. For instance, in a setting where technologies are developed endogenously using a common set of resources (e.g., scientists), there is a natural trade-off between faster automation and investments in other types of technologies (Acemoglu and Restrepo 2016). Though it is at the moment impossible to know whether the redirection of research resources away from the creation of new tasks and toward automation has played an important role in the productivity slowdown, the almost singular focus in the corporate sector and research community on AI, applications of deep learning, and other big data methods to automate various tasks makes it at least plausible that there may be too much attention devoted to automation at the expense of other technological breakthroughs.

8.3   A Model of Automation, Tasks, and the Demand for Labor

In the previous section, we provided an intuitive discussion of how automation in general, and robotics and AI in particular, is expected to impact productivity and the demand for labor. In this section, we outline a formal framework that underlines these conclusions. Our presentation will be somewhat informal and without any derivations, which are all collected in the appendix.

8.3.1   A Task-Based Framework

We start with a simplified version of the task-based framework introduced in Acemoglu and Restrepo (2016). Aggregate output is produced by combining the services of a unit measure of tasks $x \in [N-1, N]$ according to the following Cobb-Douglas (unit elastic) aggregator

$$(1) \qquad \ln Y = \int_{N-1}^{N} \ln y(x)dx,$$

where Y denotes aggregate output and $y(x)$ is the output of task x. The fact that tasks run between $N-1$ and N enables us to consider changes in the range of tasks, for example, because of the introduction of new tasks, without altering the total measure of tasks in the economy.

Each task can be produced by human labor, $\ell(x)$, or by machines, $m(x)$, depending on whether it has been (technologically) automated or not. In particular, tasks $x \in [N - 1, I]$ are technologically automated, so can be produced by either labor or machines, while the rest are not technologically automated, so must be produced with labor:

(2) $$y(x) = \begin{cases} \gamma_L(x)\ell(x) + \gamma_M(x)m(x) & \text{if } x \in [N - 1, I] \\ \gamma_L(x)\ell(x) & \text{if } x \in (I, N]. \end{cases}$$

Here, $\gamma_L(x)$ is the productivity of labor in task x and is assumed to be increasing, while $\gamma_M(x)$ is the productivity of machines in automated tasks. We assume that $\gamma_L(x)/\gamma_M(x)$ is increasing in x, and thus labor has a *comparative advantage* in higher-indexed tasks.[7]

The threshold I denotes the frontier of automation possibilities: it describes the range of tasks that can be automated using current available technologies in AI, industrial robots, various computer-assisted technologies, and other forms of "smart machines."

We also simplify the discussion by assuming that both the supply of labor, L, and the supply of machines, K, are fixed and inelastic. The fact that the supply of labor is inelastic implies that changes in labor demand impact the share of labor in national income and the wage, but not the level of employment. We outline below how this framework can be easily generalized to accommodate changes in employment and unemployment.

8.3.2   Types of Technological Change

Our framework incorporates four different types of technological advances. All advances increase productivity, but as we will see with a very different impact on the demand for labor and wages.

1. *Labor-augmenting technological advances*: Standard approaches in macroeconomics and labor economics typically focus on labor-augmenting technological advances. Such technological changes correspond to increases (or perhaps an equi-proportionate increase) in the function $\gamma_L(x)$. Our analysis will show that they are in fact quite special, and the implications of automation and AI are generally very different from those of labor-augmenting advances.

2. *Automation (at the extensive margin)*: We consider automation to be an expansion of the set of tasks that are technologically automated as represented by the parameter I.

---

7. Our theoretical framework builds on Zeira (1998) who develops a model where firms produce intermediates using labor-intensive or capital-intensive technologies. Zeira focuses on how wages affect the adoption of capital-intensive production methods and how this margin amplifies productivity differences across countries and over time. In contrast, we focus on the implications of automation—modeled here as an increase in the set of tasks that can be produced by machines, represented by I—for the demand for labor, wages, and employment, and we also study the implications of the introduction of new tasks. In Acemoglu and Restrepo (2016), we generalize Zeira's framework in a number of other dimensions and also endogenize the development of automation technologies and new tasks.

3. *Deepening of automation (or automation at the intensive margin)*: Another dimension of advances in AI and robotics technology will tend to increase the productivity of machines in tasks that are already automated, for example, by replacing existing machines with newer, more productive vintages. In terms of our model, this corresponds to an increase in the $\gamma_M(x)$ function for tasks $x < I$. We will see that this type of deepening of automation has very different implications for labor demand than automation (at the extensive margin).

4. *Creation of new tasks*: As emphasized in Acemoglu and Restrepo (2016), another important aspect of technological change is the creation of new tasks and activities in which labor has a comparative advantage. In our model this can be captured in the simplest possible way by an increase in N.

8.3.3   Equilibrium

Throughout, we denote the equilibrium wage rate by W and the equilibrium cost of machines (or the rental rate) by R. An equilibrium requires firms to choose the cost-minimizing way of producing each task and labor and capital markets to clear.

To simplify the discussion, we impose the following assumption

(A1)
$$\frac{\gamma_L(N)}{\gamma_M(N-1)} > \frac{W}{R} > \frac{\gamma_L(I)}{\gamma_M(I)}.$$

The second inequality implies that all tasks in $[N-1,I]$ will be produced by machines. The first inequality implies that the introduction of new tasks—an increase in N—will increase aggregate output. This assumption is imposed on the wage-to-rental rate ratio, which is an endogenous object; the appendix provides a condition on the stock of capital and labor that is equivalent to this assumption (see assumption [A2]).

We also show in the appendix that aggregate output (GDP) in the equilibrium takes the form

(3)
$$Y = B\left(\frac{K}{I-N+1}\right)^{I-N+1}\left(\frac{L}{N-I}\right)^{N-I},$$

where

(4)
$$B = \exp\left(\int_{N-1}^{I} \ln\gamma_M(x)dx + \int_{I}^{N} \ln\gamma_L(x)dx\right).$$

Aggregate output is given by a Cobb-Douglas aggregate of the capital stock and employment. This resulting aggregate production function in equation (3) is itself derived from the allocation of the two factors of production to tasks. More important, the exponents of capital and labor in this production function depend on the extent of automation, I, and the creation of new tasks, as captured by N.

Central to our focus is not only the impact of new technologies on productivity, but also on the demand for labor. The appendix shows that the demand for labor can be expressed as

(5)
$$W = (N - I)\frac{Y}{L}.$$

This equation is intuitive in view of the Cobb-Douglas production function in equation(3), since it shows that the wage (the marginal product of labor) is equal to the average product of labor—which we will also refer to as "productivity"—times the exponent of labor in the aggregate production function.

Equation (5) implies that the share of labor in national income is given by

(6)
$$s_L = \frac{WL}{Y} = N - I.$$

8.4   Technology and Labor Demand

8.4.1   The Displacement Effect

Our first result shows that automation (at the extensive margin) indeed creates a *displacement effect*, reducing labor demand as emphasized in section 8.2, but also that it is counteracted by a *productivity effect*, pushing toward greater labor demand.

Specifically, from equation (5) we directly obtain

(7)
$$\frac{d\ln W}{dI} = \underbrace{\frac{d\ln(N - I)}{dI}}_{\text{Displacement effect} < 0} + \underbrace{\frac{d\ln(Y / L)}{dI}}_{\text{Productivity effect} > 0}.$$

Without the productivity effect, automation would always reduce labor demand because it is directly replacing labor in tasks that were previously performed by workers. Indeed, if the productivity effect is limited, automation will reduce labor demand and wages.

8.4.2   Counteracting the Displacement Effect I: The Productivity Effects

The productivity effect, on the other hand, captures the important idea that by increasing productivity, automation raises labor demand in the tasks that are not automated. As highlighted in the previous section, there are two complementary manifestations of the productivity effect. The first works by increasing the demand for labor in nonautomated tasks in the industries where automation is ongoing. The second works by raising the demand for labor in other industries. The productivity effect shown in equation (7) combines these two mechanisms.

One important implication of the decomposition in equation (7) is that, in contrast to some popular discussions, the new AI and robotics technologies that are more likely to reduce the demand for labor are not those that are brilliant and highly productive, but those that are "so-so"—just productive enough to be adopted but not much more productive or cost-saving than the production processes that they are replacing. Interestingly, and related to our discussion on missing productivity, if new automation technologies are so-so, they would not bring major improvements in productivity either.

To elaborate further on this point and to understand the productivity implications of automation technologies better, let us also express the productivity effect in terms of the physical productivities of labor and machines and factor prices as follows:

$$\frac{d\ln(Y/L)}{dI} = \ln\left(\frac{W}{\gamma_L(I)}\right) - \ln\left(\frac{R}{\gamma_M(I)}\right) > 0.$$

The fact that this expression is positive, and that new automation technologies will be adopted, follows from assumption (A1). Using this expression, the overall impact on labor demand can be alternatively written as

$$(8) \qquad \frac{d\ln W}{dI} = -\underbrace{\frac{1}{N-I}}_{\text{Displacement effect<0}} + \underbrace{\ln\left(\frac{W}{\gamma_L(I)}\right) - \ln\left(\frac{R}{\gamma_M(I)}\right)}_{\text{Productivity effect > 0}}.$$

This expression clarifies that the displacement effect of automation will dominate the productivity effect and thus reduce labor demand (and wages) when $\gamma_M(I)/R \approx \gamma_L(I)/W$, which is exactly the case when new technologies are so-so—only marginally better than labor at newly automated tasks. In contrast, when $\gamma_M(I)/R \gg \gamma_L(I)/W$, automation will increase productivity sufficiently to raise the demand for labor and wages.

Turning next to the implications of automation for the labor share, equation (6) implies

$$(9) \qquad \frac{ds_L}{dI} = -1 < 0,$$

so that regardless of the magnitude of the productivity effect, automation always reduces the share of labor in national income. This negative impact on the labor share is a direct consequence of the fact that automation always increases productivity more than the wage, $d\ln(Y/L)/dI > d\ln W/dI$ (itself directly following from equation [7], which shows that the impact on wages is given by the impact on productivity minus the displacement effect).

The implications of standard labor-augmenting technological change, which corresponds to a (marginal) shift-up of the $\gamma_L(x)$ schedule, are very different from those of automation. Labor-augmenting technologies leave the form of the wage equation (5) unchanged, and increase average output per worker, Y/L, and the equilibrium wage, W, proportionately, and thus do not impact the share of labor in national income.[8]

8.4.3   Counteracting the Displacement Effect II: Capital Accumulation

We have so far emphasized the displacement effect created by new automation technologies. We have also seen that the productivity effect counteracts the displacement effects to some degree. In this and the next subsection, we discuss two additional countervailing forces.

The first force is capital accumulation. The analysis so far assumed that the economy has a fixed supply of capital that could be devoted to new machines (automation technologies). As a result, a further increase in automation (at the extensive margin) increases the demand for capital and thus the equilibrium rental rate, R. This may be understood as the short-run effect of automation.

Instead, we may envisage the "medium-run" effect as the impact of these technologies after the supply of machines used in newly automated tasks expands as well. Because machines and labor are q-complements, an increase in the capital stock, with the level of employment held constant at L, increases the real wage and reduces the rental rate. Equation (8) shows that this change in factor prices makes the productivity effect more powerful and the impact on the wage more likely to be positive.

In the limit, if capital accumulation fixes the rental rate at a constant level (which will be the case, for example, when we have a representative household with exponential discounting and time-separable preferences), the productivity effect will always dominate the displacement effect.[9]

Crucially, however, equation (6) still applies, and thus automation continues to reduce the labor share, even after the adjustment of the capital stock.

8.4.4   Counteracting the Displacement Effect III:
Deepening of Automation

Another potentially powerful force counteracting the displacement effect from automation at the extensive margin comes from the deepening of automation (or automation at the intensive margin), for example, because of improvements in the performance of already-existing automation technolo-

---

8. A small shift-up of $\gamma_L(x)$ does not violate assumption (A1) because at the margin it was strictly cost-saving to use machines. A larger labor-augmenting technological change may result in a violation of assumption (A1). At this point, only tasks below an endogenous threshold $\tilde{I} < I$ would be automated, and labor-augmenting technologies could also reduce $\tilde{I}$, increasing the labor share in national income.

9. Assuming that production exhibits constant returns to scale, the productivity gains from any technology accrue to both capital and labor. In particular, for any constant returns to scale production function, we have $d\ln Y|_{K,L} = s_L d\ln W + (1 - s_L)d\ln R$, where $d\ln Y|_{K,L} > 0$ denotes the productivity gains brought by technology holding the use of capital and labor constant, and s_L is the labor share. If the rental rate is constant in the long run, then $d\ln R = 0$ and all productivity gains accrue to the relatively inelastic factor, labor.

gies or the replacement of such technologies with newer, more productive vintages. This increase in the productivity of machines in tasks that are already automated corresponds in our model to an increase in the function $\gamma_M(x)$ in tasks below I.

To explore the implications of this type of change in the simplest possible way, let us suppose that $\gamma_M(x) = \gamma_M$ in all automated tasks, and consider an increase in the productivity of machines by $d\ln\gamma_M > 0$, with no change in the extensive margin of automation, I. The implications of this change in the productivity of machines on equilibrium wages and productivity can be obtained as

$$d\ln W = d\ln Y / L = \left(I - N + 1\right)d\ln\gamma_M > 0.$$

Hence, deepening of automation will tend to increase labor demand and wages, further counteracting the displacement effect. Note, however, that as with capital accumulation, in our model this has no impact on the share of labor in national income, as can be seen from the fact that wages and productivity increase by exactly the same amount.

8.4.5   New Tasks and the Comparative Advantage of Labor

Much more powerful than the countervailing effects of capital accumulation and the deepening of automation is the creation of new tasks in which labor has a comparative advantage. These tasks include both new, more complex versions of existing tasks and the creation of new activities, which are made possible by advances in technology. In terms of our framework, they correspond to increases in N.

An increase in N—the creation of new tasks—raises productivity by

$$\frac{d\ln Y / L}{dN} = \ln\left(\frac{R}{\gamma_M(N-1)}\right) - \ln\left(\frac{W}{\gamma_L(N)}\right) > 0,$$

which is positive from assumption (A1).

More important for our focus here, the creation of new tasks also increases labor demand and equilibrium wages by creating a *reinstatement effect* counteracting the displacement effect. In particular,

$$(10) \qquad \frac{d\ln W}{dN} = \underbrace{\ln\left(\frac{R}{\gamma_M(n-1)}\right) - \ln\left(\frac{W}{\gamma_L(N)}\right)}_{\text{Productivity effect}>0} + \underbrace{\frac{1}{N-I}}_{\text{Reinstatement effect}>0}.$$

In contrast to capital accumulation and the deepening of automation, which increase the demand for labor but do not affect the labor share, equation (6) implies that new tasks increase the labor share, that is,

$$\frac{ds_L}{dN} = 1.$$

The centrality of new tasks can be understood when viewed from a complementary historical angle. Automation is not a recent phenomenon. As we already discussed in section 8.2, the history of technology of the last two centuries is full of examples of automation, ranging from weaving and spinning machines to the mechanization of agriculture, as discussed in the previous section. Even with capital accumulation and the deepening of automation, if there were no other counteracting force, we would see the share of labor in national income declining steadily. Our conceptual framework highlights a major force preventing such a decline—the creation of new tasks in which labor has a comparative advantage.

This can be seen by putting together equations (7) and (10), which yields

$$
(11) \qquad d\ln W = \left[\ln\left(\frac{R}{\gamma_M(N-1)} \right) - \ln\left(\frac{W}{\gamma_L(N)} \right) \right] dN
$$

$$
+ \left[\ln\left(\frac{W}{\gamma_L(I)} \right) - \ln\left(\frac{R}{\gamma_M(I)} \right) \right] dI + \frac{1}{N-I}(dN - dI),
$$

and also from equation (6),

$$
ds_L = dN - dI.
$$

For the labor share to remain stable and for wages to increase in tandem with productivity, as has been the case historically, we need I—capturing the extensive margin of automation—to grow by the same amount as the range of new tasks, N. When that happens, equilibrium wages grow proportionately with productivity, and the labor share, s_L, remains constant, as can be seen from the fact that the first line of equation (11) is in this case equal to the increase in productivity or gross domestic product (GDP) per worker. Indeed, rewriting equation (11) imposing $dN = dI$, we have

$$
d\ln W = \left[\ln\left(\frac{\gamma_L(N)}{\gamma_M(N-1)} \right) - \ln\left(\frac{\gamma_L(I)}{\gamma_M(I)} \right) \right] dI > 0,
$$

which is strictly positive because of assumption (A1).

8.4.6   A False Dichotomy: Recap

With our conceptual framework exposited in a more systematic manner, we can now briefly revisit the false dichotomy highlighted in the introduction. Our analysis (in particular equation [7]) highlights that there is always a negative displacement effect on labor resulting from automation. Equation (11) reiterates that there is no presumption that this displacement effect could not reduce overall demand for labor.

However, several countervailing effects imply that a negative impact from automation on labor demand is not a forgone conclusion. Most important, the productivity effect could outweigh the displacement effect, leading to an expansion in labor demand and equilibrium wages from automation. The presence of the productivity effect as counterweight to the displacement created by automation highlights an important conceptual issue, however. In contrast to the emphasis in the popular discussions it is not the brilliant, superproductive automation technologies that threaten labor, but the "so-so" ones that create the displacement effect as they replace labor in tasks that it previously performed, but do not engender the countervailing productivity effect.

The productivity effect is supplemented by the capital accumulation that automation sets in motion and the deepening of automation, which increases the productivity of machines in tasks that have already been automated. But even with these countervailing effects, equation (9) shows that automation will always reduce the share of labor in national income. All the same, this does not signal the demise of labor either, because the creation of new tasks in which labor has a comparative advantage could counterbalance automation, which is our interpretation of why the demand for labor has kept up with productivity growth in the past despite several rapid waves of automation.

Our framework suggests that the biggest shortcoming of the alarmist and the optimist views is their failure to recognize that the future of labor depends on the balance between automation and the creation of new tasks. Automation will often lead to a healthy growth of labor demand and wages if it is accompanied with a commensurate increase in the set of tasks in which labor has a comparative advantage—a feature that alarmists seem to ignore. Even though there are good economic reasons for why the economy will create new tasks, this is neither a forgone conclusion nor something we can always count on—as the optimists seem to assume. Artificial intelligence and robotics could be permanently altering this balance, causing automation to pace ahead of the creation of new tasks with negative consequences for labor, at the very least in regard to the share of labor in national income.

8.4.7   Generalizations

Many of the features adopted in the previous subsection are expositional simplifications. In particular, the aggregate production function (1) can be taken to be any constant elasticity of substitution aggregate. One implication of this would be that aggregate output in equation (3) would be a constant elasticity aggregate itself. This does not affect any of our main conclusions, including the negative impact of automation on the labor share (see Acemoglu and Restrepo 2016).[10]

We also do not need assumption (A1) for any of the results. If the second

10. Recent work by Aghion, Jones, and Jones (2017) points out, however, that if the elasticity of substitution between tasks is less than one and there is an exogenous and high saving rate, the labor share might asymptote to a positive value even with continuously ongoing automation.

inequality in this assumption does not hold, changes in automation technology have no impact on the equilibrium because it is not cost effective to adopt all available automation technologies (for this reason, in the general case, Acemoglu and Restrepo [2016] distinguish technologically automated tasks from equilibrium automation). Given our focus here, there is no loss of generality in making this assumption.

A final feature that is worth commenting on is the fact that in the aggregate production function (1), the limits of integration are $N-1$ and N, ensuring that the total measure of tasks is one. This is useful for several reasons. First, when the introduction of new tasks expands the total measure of tasks, it becomes more challenging to obtain a balanced growth path (see Acemoglu and Restrepo 2016). Second, in this case some minor modifications are necessary so that an expansion in the total measure of tasks leads to productivity improvements. In particular, consider the general case where the elasticity of substitution between tasks is not necessarily equal to one. If it is greater than one, an increase in N leads to higher productivity, but not necessarily when it is less than or equal to one. In this latter case, we then need to introduce direct productivity gains from task variety. For example, in the present case where the elasticity of substitution between tasks is equal to one, we could modify (1) to $\ln Y = (1/N) \sum_0^N \ln[N^{1+\alpha} y(i)]$, where $\alpha \geq 0$ represents these productivity gains from task variety and ensures that the qualitative results explicit here continue to apply.

8.4.8   Employment and Unemployment

An additional generalization concerns the endogenous adjustment of employment in the face of new automation technologies. We have so far taken labor to be supplied inelastically for simplicity. There are two ways in which the level of employment responds to the arrival of new technologies. The first is via a standard labor supply margin. Acemoglu and Restrepo (2016) show that the endogenous adjustment of labor supply, including income effects and the substitution of consumption and leisure, links the level of employment to the share of labor in national income.

The second possibility is through labor market frictions, for example, as in Acemoglu and Restrepo (2018a). Under appropriate assumptions, the endogenous level of employment in this case is also a function of the share of labor in national income. Though both models with and without labor market frictions endogenize employment as a function of the labor share, their normative implications are potentially different, as we discuss below.

For now, however, the more important implication of such extensions is to link the level of employment (or unemployment) to labor demand. Automation, when it reduces labor demand, will also reduce the level of employment (or increase the level of unemployment). Moreover, because the supply of labor depends on the labor share, in our framework automation results in a reduction in employment (or an increase in unemployment). As such, our analysis so far also sheds light on (and clarifies the conditions for) the claims that new automation technologies will reduce employment. It also highlights, however, that the fact that automation has been ongoing does not condemn the economy to a declining path of employment. If automation is met by equivalent changes in the creation of new tasks, the share of labor in national income can remain stable and ensure a stable level of employment (or unemployment) in the economy.

8.5   Constraints and Inefficiencies

Even in the presence of the countervailing forces limiting the displacement effect from automation, there are potential inefficiencies and constraints limiting the smooth adjustment of the labor market and hindering the productivity gains from new technologies.

Here we focus on how the mismatch between skills and technologies not only increases inequality, but also hinders the productivity gains from automation and new tasks. We then explore the possibility that, concurrent with rapid automation, we are experiencing a slowdown in the creation of new tasks, which could result in slow productivity growth. Finally, we examine how a range of factors leads to excessive automation, which not only creates inefficiency but also hinders productivity.

8.5.1   Mismatch of Technologies and Skills

The emphasis on the creation of new tasks counterbalancing the potential negative effects of automation on the labor share and the demand for labor ignores an important caveat and constraint: the potential mismatch between the requirements of new technologies (tasks) and the skills of the workforce. To the extent that new tasks require skilled employees or even new skills to be acquired, the adjustment may be much slower than our analysis so far suggests.

To illustrate these ideas in the simplest possible fashion, we follow Acemoglu and Restrepo (2016) and assume that there are two types of workers, low-skill with supply L and high-skill with supply H, both of them supplied inelastically. We also assume that low-skill workers can only perform tasks below a threshold $S \in (I,N)$, while high-skill workers can perform all tasks. For simplicity, we assume that the productivity of both low-skill and high-skill workers in the tasks that they can perform is still given by $\gamma_L(x)$.[11] Low-skill workers earn a wage W_L and high-skill workers earn a wage W_H.

---

11. We can also introduce differential comparative advantages and also an absolute productivity advantage for high-skill workers, though we choose not to do so to increase transparency (see Acemoglu and Restrepo 2016). The more restrictive assumption here is that automation happens at the bottom of the range of tasks. In general, automation could take place in the middle range, and its impact would depend on whether automated tasks are competing predominantly against low-skill or high-skill workers (see Acemoglu and Autor 2011; Acemoglu and Restrepo 2018b).

In this simple extension of the framework presented so far, the threshold S can be considered as an inverse measure of the mismatch between new technologies and skills. A greater value of S implies that there are plenty of additional tasks for low-skill workers, while a low value of S implies the presence of only a few tasks left that low-skill workers can perform.

Assuming that in equilibrium $W_H > W_L$,[12] which implies that low-skill workers will perform all tasks in the range (I,S), equilibrium wages satisfy

$$W_H = \frac{Y}{H}(N - S) \text{ and } W_L = \frac{Y}{L}(S - I).$$

Thus, the impact of automation on inequality—defined here as the wage premium between high- and low-skill workers—is given by

$$\frac{d\ln W_H / W_L}{dI} = \frac{1}{S - I} > 0.$$

This equation shows that automation increases inequality. This is not surprising, since the tasks that are automated are precisely those performed by low-skill workers. But in addition, it also demonstrates that the impact of automation on inequality becomes worse when there is a severe skill mismatch—the threshold S is close to I. In this case, displaced workers will be squeezed into a very small range of tasks, and hence, each of these tasks will receive a large number of workers and will experience a substantial drop in price, which translates into a sharp decline in the wage of low-skill workers. In contrast, when S is large, displaced workers can spread across a larger set of tasks without depressing their wage as much.

A severe mismatch also affects the productivity gains from automation. In particular, we have

$$\frac{d\ln(Y / L)}{dI} = \ln\left(\frac{W_L}{\gamma_L(I)}\right) - \ln\left(\frac{R}{\gamma_M(I)}\right) > 0.$$

This equation shows that the productivity gains from automation depend positively on W_L / R: it is precisely when displaced workers have a high opportunity cost that automation raises productivity. Using the fact that $R = (Y/K)(I - N + 1)$, we obtain

$$\frac{W_L}{R} = \frac{S - I}{I - N + 1}\frac{K}{L}.$$

A worse mismatch (a lower S) reduces the opportunity cost of displaced workers further, and via this channel, it makes automation less profitable. This is because a severe mismatch impedes reallocation, reducing the productivity gains of freeing workers from automated tasks.

---

12. This is equivalent to $[(N - S)/(S - I)] > (H/L)$, so that high-skill workers are scarce relative to the range of tasks that only they can produce.

Equally important are the implications of a skill mismatch for the productivity gains from new tasks. Namely,

$$\frac{d\ln(Y/L)}{dN} = \ln\left(\frac{R}{\gamma_M(N-1)}\right) - \ln\left(\frac{W_H}{\gamma_H(N)}\right) > 0,$$

which depends negatively on W_H/R: it is precisely when high-skill workers have a relatively high wage that the gains from new tasks will be limited. With similar arguments to before, we also have

$$\frac{W_H}{R} = \frac{N-S}{1-N+1}\frac{K}{L},$$

which implies that in the presence of a worse mismatch (a lower S), the productivity gains from new tasks will be limited. This is because new tasks require high-skill workers who are scarce and expensive when S is low.

An important implication of this analysis is that to limit increasing inequality and to best deploy new tasks and harness the benefits of automation, society may need to simultaneously increase the supply of skills. A balanced growth process requires not only automation and the creation of new tasks to go hand-in-hand, but also the supply of high-skill workers to grow in tandem with these technological trends.

8.5.2   Automation at the Expense of New Tasks

As discussed in section 8.2, a puzzling aspect of recent macroeconomic developments has been the lack of robust productivity growth despite the bewildering array of new technologies. Our conceptual framework provides three novel (and at least to us, more compelling) reasons for slow productivity growth. The first was the skill mismatch discussed in the previous subsection.

The second one, discussed in this subsection, is that concurrent with the rapid introduction of new automation technologies, we may be experiencing a slowdown in the creation of new tasks and investments in other technologies that benefit labor.

This explanation comes in two flavors. First, we may be running out of good ideas to create new jobs, sectors, and products capable of expanding the demand for labor (e.g., Gordon 2016; Bloom et al. 2017), even if automation continues at a healthy or accelerating pace. Alternatively, the rapid introduction of new automation technologies may redirect resources that were devoted to other technological advances, in particular, the creation of new tasks (see Acemoglu and Restrepo 2016). To the extent that the recent enthusiasm—or even "frenzy"—about deep learning and some aspects of AI can be viewed as such a redirection, our framework pinpoints a potential powerful mechanism for slower productivity growth in the face of rapid automation.

Both explanations hinge on the redirection of research activity from the creation of new tasks to automation—in the first case exogenously and in the second for endogenous reasons. Recall from our analysis so far that the productivity gains from new tasks in our baseline framework are given by

$$\frac{d\ln(Y/L)}{dN} = \ln\left(\frac{R}{\gamma_M(N-1)}\right) - \ln\left(\frac{W}{\gamma_L(N)}\right) > 0,$$

while productivity gains from automation are

$$\frac{d\ln(Y/L)}{dI} = \ln\left(\frac{W}{\gamma_L(I)}\right) - \ln\left(\frac{R}{\gamma_M(I)}\right) > 0.$$

If the former expression is greater than the latter, then the redirection of research effort from the creation of new tasks toward automation, or a lower research efficiency in creating new tasks, will lead to a slowdown of productivity growth, even if advances in automation are accelerating and being adopted enthusiastically. This conclusion is strengthened if additional effort devoted to automation at the expense of the creation of new tasks runs into diminishing returns.

8.5.3 Excessive Automation

In this subsection, we highlight the third reason for why there may be modest productivity growth: socially excessive automation (see Acemoglu and Restrepo 2016, 2018a).

To illustrate why our framework can generate excessive automation, we modify the assumption that the supply of capital, K, is given, and instead suppose that machines used in automation are produced—as intermediate goods—using the final good at a fixed cost R. Moreover, suppose that because of subsidies to capital, accelerated depreciation allowances, tax credit for debt-financed investment or simply because of the tax cost of employing workers, capital receives a marginal subsidy of $\tau > 0$.

Given this subsidy, the rental rate for machines is $R(1-\tau)$, and assumption (A1) now becomes

$$\frac{\gamma_L(N)}{\gamma_M(N-1)} > \frac{W}{R(1-\tau)} > \frac{\gamma_L(I)}{\gamma_M(I)}.$$

Let us now compute GDP as value added, subtracting the cost of producing machines. This gives us

$$GDP = Y - RK.$$

Suppose next that there is an increase in automation. Then we have

$$\frac{d\text{GDP}}{dI} = \frac{dY}{dI}\bigg|_K + R(1-\tau)\frac{dK}{dI} - R\frac{dK}{dI},$$

which simplifies to

$$\frac{dGDP}{dI} = \underbrace{\ln\left(\frac{W}{\gamma_L(I)}\right) - \ln\left(\frac{R(1-\tau)}{\gamma_M(I)}\right)}_{\text{Productivity effect}>0} - \underbrace{R\tau\frac{dK}{dI}}_{\text{Excessive automation}<0}.$$

The first term is positive and captures the productivity increase generated by automation. However, when $\tau > 0$—so that the real cost of using capital is distorted—we have an additional negative effect originating from excessive automation.[13] At the root of this negative effect is the fact that subsidies induce firms to substitute capital for labor even when this is not socially cost-saving (though it is privately beneficial because of the subsidy).

This conclusion is further strengthened when there are also labor market frictions as pointed out in section 8.2. To illustrate this point in the simplest possible fashion, let us assume that there is a threshold $J \in (I,N)$ such that, when performing the tasks in $[I,J]$, workers earn rents $\omega > 0$ proportional to their wage in other tasks. In particular, workers are paid a wage W to produce tasks in $[J,N]$, and a wage $W(1 + \omega)$ to produce tasks in (I,J).[14] Let L_A denote the total amount of labor allocated to the tasks in (I,J), and note that these are the workers that will be displaced by automation, that is, by a small increase in I. Given this additional distortion, assumption (A1) now becomes

$$\frac{\gamma_L(N)}{\gamma_M(N-1)} > \frac{W}{R(1-\tau)} > \frac{1}{1+\omega}\frac{\gamma_L(I)}{\gamma_M(I)}.$$

The demand for labor in tasks where workers earn rents is now

$$L_A = \frac{Y}{W(1+\omega)}(J-I).$$

The demand for labor in tasks where workers do not earn rents is

$$L - L_A = \frac{Y}{W}(N-J).$$

Dividing these two expressions, we obtain the equilibrium condition for L_A,

$$\frac{L_A}{L-L_A} = \frac{1}{1+\omega}\frac{J-I}{N-J},$$

13. We show in the appendix that $K = (Y/R)(I - N + 1)$, which implies that K increases in I.

14. The assumption that there are rents only in a subset of tasks is adopted for simplicity. The same results apply (a) when there are two sectors and one of the sectors has higher rents/wages for workers and enables automation and (b) there is an endogenous margin between employment and nonemployment and labor market imperfections (such as search, bargaining, or efficiency wages) that create a wedge between wages and outside options. In both cases the automation decisions of firms fail to internalize the gap between the market wage and the opportunity cost of labor, leading to excessive automation (see Acemoglu and Restrepo 2018a).

which implies that the total number of workers earning rents declines with automation.

Moreover, the appendix shows that (gross) output is now given by

$$(12) \qquad Y = B\left(\frac{K}{I-N+1}\right)^{I-N+1} \left(\frac{L_A}{J-I}\right)^{J-I} \left(\frac{L-L_A}{N-J}\right)^{N-J},$$

and GDP is still given by $Y - RK$. Equation (12) highlights that there is now a misallocation of labor across tasks—output can be increased by allocating more workers to tasks (I,J) where their marginal product is greater (because of the rents they are earning).

Equation (12) further implies that the impact of automation on GDP is given by

$$\frac{d\text{GDP}}{dI} = \underbrace{\ln\left(\frac{W(1+\omega)}{\gamma_L(I)}\right) - \ln\left(\frac{R(1-\tau)}{\gamma_M(I)}\right)}_{\text{Productivity effect}>0} - \underbrace{R\tau\frac{dK}{dI}}_{\substack{\text{Excessive} \\ \text{automation}<0}} + \underbrace{W\omega\frac{dL_A}{dI}}_{\substack{\text{Excessive displacement} \\ \text{of labor}<0}}.$$

The new term $W\omega(dL_A/dI)$ captures the first-order losses from a decline in employment in tasks (I,J). These losses arise because by automating jobs where workers earn rents, firms are effectively displacing workers to other tasks in which they have a lower marginal product and earn a strictly lower wage, which increases the extent of misallocation.

The point highlighted here is much more general. Without labor market frictions, automation increases GDP (and net output), so at the very least it is possible to redistribute the gains that it creates to make workers—of different skill levels—better off. Labor market frictions change this picture. In the presence of such frictions, firms' automation decisions do not internalize the fact that the marginal product of labor is above its opportunity cost, or equivalently, do not recognize that there are first-order losses that workers will suffer as a result of automation. Consequently, equilibrium automation could reduce GDP and welfare and there may not be a way to make (all) workers better off, even with tools for costless redistribution. Under these circumstances, a utilitarian planner would choose a lower level of automation than the equilibrium.[15]

8.6   Concluding Remarks

Despite the growing concerns and intensifying debate about the implications of automation for the future of work, the economics profession and popular discussions lack a satisfactory conceptual framework. To us this

15. Naturally, if the planner could remove the rents, or the labor market frictions underpinning them, then the equilibrium would be restored to efficiency. Nevertheless, most sources of rents, including search, bargaining, and efficiency wages, would be present in the constrained efficient allocations as well.

lack of appropriate conceptual approach is also the key reason why much of the debate is characterized by a false dichotomy between the view that automation will spell the end of work for humans and the argument that technologies will always tend to increase the demand for labor as they have done in the past.

In this chapter, we summarized a conceptual framework that can help understand the implications of automation and bridge the opposite sides of this false dichotomy. At the center of our framework is a task-based approach, where automation is conceptualized as replacing labor in tasks that it used to perform. This type of replacement causes a direct displacement effect, reducing labor demand. If this displacement effect is not counterbalanced by other economic forces, it will reduce labor demand, wages, and employment. But our framework also emphasizes that there are several countervailing forces. These include the fact that automation will reduce the costs of production and thus create a productivity effect, the induced capital accumulation, and the deepening of automation—technological advances that increase the productivity of machines in tasks that have already been automated.

Our framework also emphasizes that these countervailing forces are generally insufficient to totally balance out the implications of automation. In particular, even if these forces are strong, the displacement effect of automation tends to cause a decline in the share of labor in national income. But we know from the history of technology and industrial development that despite several waves of rapid automation, the growth process has been more or less balanced, with no secular downward trend in the share of labor in national income. We argue this is because of another powerful force: the creation of new tasks in which labor has a comparative advantage, which fosters a countervailing reinstatement effect for labor. These tasks increase the demand for labor and tend to raise the labor share. When they go hand-in-hand with automation, the growth process is balanced and it need not imply a dismal scenario for labor.

Nevertheless, the adjustment process is likely to be slower and more painful than this account of balance between automation and new tasks at first suggests. This is because the reallocation of labor from its existing jobs and tasks to new ones is a slow process, in part owing to time-consuming search and other labor market imperfections. But even more ominously, new tasks require new skills. When the education sector does not keep up with the demand for new skills, the mismatch between skills and technologies is bound to complicate the adjustment process and hinder the productivity gains from new technologies.

Our framework further suggests that there are additional reasons for the productivity slowdown. At the center of these is a tendency for excessive automation because of the tax treatment of capital investments and labor market imperfections. Excessive automation directly reduces productivity, but may have even more powerful indirect effects because it redirects technological improvements away from productivity-enhancing activities that lead to the creation of new tasks to excessive efforts at the extensive margin of automation, a picture that receives informal support from the current singular focus on AI and deep learning.

We would like to conclude by pointing out a number of additional issues that may be important in understanding the full impact of AI and other automation technologies on future prospects of labor. We believe that these issues can be studied using simple extensions of the framework presented here.

First, we have emphasized the role of the productivity effect in partially counterbalancing the displacement effect created by automation. However, this countervailing effect works by increasing the demand for products. As we have also seen, automation tends to increase inequality. If, as a consequence of this distributional impact, the rise in real incomes resulting from automation ends up in the hands of a narrow segment of the population with much lower marginal propensity to consume than those losing incomes and their jobs, these countervailing forces would be weakened and might operate much more slowly. This imbalance in the distribution of the gains from automation might slow down the creation of new tasks as well.

Second, our analysis highlighted the negative consequences of a shortage of skills for realizing the productivity gains from automation and for inequality. In practice, the problem may be workers acquiring the wrong types of skills rather than a general lack of skills. For example, if AI and other new automation technologies necessitate a mix of numeracy, communication, and problem-solving skills different than those emphasized in current curricula, this would have implications similar to those of a shortage of skills, but it cannot be overcome by just increasing educational spending with current educational practices remaining intact. One important consideration in this respect is that there is little concrete information about what types of skills new technologies will complement, underscoring the importance of further empirical work in this area.

Third, government policies and labor market institutions may impact not just the speed of automation (and thus whether there is excessive automation), but what types of technologies will receive more investments. To the extent that some uses of AI may complement labor more or generate opportunities for more rapid creation of new tasks, an understanding of the impact of various policies, including support for academic and applied research, and social factors on the path of development of AI is critical.

Last but not least, the development and adoption of technologies that reinstate labor cannot be taken for granted. If we do not find a way of creating shared prosperity from the productivity gains generated by new technologies, there is a danger that the political reaction to these technologies may slow down or even completely stop their adoption and development. This underscores the importance of studying the distributional implications of AI and robotics, the political economy reactions to it, and the design of new and improved institutions for creating more broadly shared gains from these new technologies.

Appendix

Derivations for the Basic Model

Suppose that assumption (A1) holds. We first derive the demand for factors:

- Denote by $p(x)$ the price of task x. Assumption (A1) implies

$$(8A.1) \qquad p(x) = \begin{cases} \dfrac{R}{\gamma_M(x)} & \text{if } x \in \left[N-1, I\right] \\[2ex] \dfrac{W}{\gamma_L(x)} & \text{if } x \in \left(I, N\right]. \end{cases}$$

- In addition, the demand for task x is given by

$$y(x) = \frac{Y}{p(x)}.$$

- Thus, the demand for smart machines in task x is

$$k(x) = \begin{cases} \dfrac{Y}{R} & \text{if } x \in \left[N-1, I\right] \\[2ex] 0 & \text{if } x \in \left(I, N\right] \end{cases},$$

and the demand for labor in task x is

$$\ell(x) = \begin{cases} 0 & \text{if } x \in \left[N-1, I\right] \\[2ex] \dfrac{Y}{W} & \text{if } x \in \left(I, N\right]. \end{cases}$$

- Aggregating the demand for machines from this expression and setting it equal to the supply of capital, K, we have the following market-clearing condition for capital:

$$K = \frac{Y}{R}(I - N + 1).$$

Similarly, aggregating the demand for labor and setting it equal to its inelastic supply, L, we obtain the market-clearing condition for labor as

$$L = \frac{Y}{W}(N - I).$$

- Rearranging these two equations, the equilibrium rental rate and wage can be obtained as

(8A.2) $$R = \frac{Y}{K}(I - N + 1) \text{ and } W = \frac{Y}{L}(N - I),$$

which are the expressions used in the text.

We next turn to deriving the expression for aggregate output.

- Because we normalized the price of the final good to 1 as numeraire, we have

$$\int_{N-1}^{N} \ln p(x)dx = 0.$$

- Plugging in the expressions for $p(x)$ from equation (8A.1) yields

$$\int_{N-1}^{I} \left[\ln R - \ln \gamma_M(x) \right] dx + \int_{I}^{N} \left[\ln W - \ln \gamma_L(x) \right] dx = 0.$$

- Substituting the expressions for R and W from (8A.2), we obtain

$$\int_{N-1}^{I} \left[\ln Y - \ln\left(K/(I - N + 1)\right) - \ln \gamma_M(x) \right] dx$$
$$+ \int_{I}^{N} \left[\ln Y - \ln\left(L/(N - I)\right) - \ln \gamma_L(x) \right] dx = 0.$$

- This equation can be rearranged as

$$\ln Y = \int_{N-1}^{I} \left[\ln\left(\frac{K}{I - N + 1}\right) + \ln \gamma_M(x) \right] dx + \int_{I}^{N} \left[\ln\left(\frac{L}{N - 1}\right) + \ln \gamma_L(x) \right] dx$$

$$= \int_{N-1}^{I} \ln \gamma_M(x)dx + \int_{I}^{N} \ln \gamma_L(x)dx$$

$$+ (I - N + 1)\ln\left(\frac{K}{I - N + 1}\right) + (N - I)\ln\left(\frac{L}{N - I}\right),$$

which, after taking exponentials on both sides of the equation, yields the expression for aggregate output in equation (1) in the text.

Assumption (A1)

We now show that assumption (A1) is equivalent to the capital-labor ratio of the economy taking an intermediate value. In particular, there exist two positive thresholds $\underline{\kappa} < \bar{\kappa}$ such that assumption (A1) holds whenever

(A2)
$$\frac{K}{L} \in (\underline{\kappa}, \overline{\kappa}).$$

Equation (8A.2) shows that

$$\frac{W}{R} = \frac{K}{L}\frac{N-I}{I-N+1}.$$

Define

$$\underline{\kappa} = \frac{I-N+1}{N-I}\frac{\gamma_L(I)}{\gamma_M(I)}, \text{ and } \overline{\kappa} = \frac{I-N+1}{N-I}\frac{\gamma_L(N)}{\gamma_M(N-I)}.$$

Then equation (A2) is equivalent to assumption (A1).

Derivations in the Presence of Technology-Skill Mismatch

- Denote by $p(x)$ the price of task x. Assumption (A1) together with the fact that $W_H > W_L$ (see footnote 12) implies

$$p(x) = \begin{cases} \dfrac{R}{\gamma_M(x)} & \text{if } x \in \left[N-1, I\right] \\[2mm] \dfrac{W_L}{\gamma_L(x)} & \text{if } x \in (I, S) \\[2mm] \dfrac{W_H}{\gamma_L(x)} & \text{if } x \in S, N] \end{cases}.$$

- Following the same steps as in our baseline model, we obtain the market-clearing condition for capital,

$$K = \frac{Y}{R}(I - N + 1).$$

- The demand for low-skill labor in task x is given by

$$\ell(x) = \begin{cases} 0 & \text{if } x \in \left[N-1, I\right] \\[2mm] \dfrac{Y}{W_L} & \text{if } x \in (I, S) \\[2mm] 0 & \text{if } x \in S, N]. \end{cases}$$

- Aggregating the demand for low-skill labor and setting it equal to its inelastic supply, L, we obtain the market-clearing condition for low-skill labor as

$$L = \frac{Y}{W_L}(S - I),$$

which implies the expression for W_L given in the main text.

- The demand for high-skill labor in task x is given by

$$h(x) = \begin{cases} 0 & \text{if } x \in \left[N-1,I\right] \\ 0 & \text{if } x \in (I,S) \\ \dfrac{Y}{W_H} & \text{if } x \in S,N]. \end{cases}$$

- Aggregating the demand for high-skill labor and setting it equal to its supply, H, we obtain the market-clearing condition for high-skill labor as

$$H = \frac{Y}{W_H}(N - S),$$

which implies the expression for W_H given in the main text.

Derivations for the Model with Distortions

- Denote by $p(x)$ the price of task x. The variant of assumption (A1) introduced in section 8.5 implies

$$p(x) = \begin{cases} \dfrac{R(1-\tau)}{\gamma_M(x)} & \text{if } x \in \left[N-1,I\right] \\[2mm] \dfrac{W(1+\omega)}{\gamma_L(x)} & \text{if } x \in (I,J) \\[2mm] \dfrac{W}{\gamma_L(x)} & \text{if } x \in J,N]. \end{cases}$$

- Following the same steps as in the model with no distortions, we obtain the market-clearing condition for capital,

$$K = \frac{Y}{R(1-\tau)}(I - N + 1).$$

- The demand for labor in task x is

$$\ell(x) = \begin{cases} 0 & \text{if } x \in \left[N-1,I\right] \\[2mm] \dfrac{Y}{W(1+\omega)} & \text{if } x \in (I,J) \\[2mm] \dfrac{Y}{W} & \text{if } x \in J,N] \end{cases}$$

- The expression for $\ell(x)$ implies that the total amount of labor employed in tasks where labor gets rents is

$$L_A = \frac{Y}{W(1+\omega)}(J - I).$$

The total amount of labor employed in tasks where labor does not get rents is

$$L - L_A = \frac{Y}{W}(N - J).$$

To derive the expression for (gross) output we proceed as follows:

- Again from our choice of numeraire, we have

$$\int_{N-1}^{N} \ln p(x) dx = 0.$$

- Plugging in the expressions for $p(x)$ we obtain

$$\int_{N-1}^{I} \left[\ln R - \ln \gamma_M(x) \right] dx + \int_{I}^{J} \left[\ln W + \ln(1 + \omega) - \ln \gamma_L(x) \right] dx$$

$$+ \int_{J}^{N} \left[\ln W - \ln \gamma_L(x) \right] dx = 0.$$

- Substituting for factor prices using the expressions for K, L_A, and $L - L_A$, we obtain

$$\int_{N-1}^{I} \left[\ln Y - \ln\left(K / (I - N + 1) \right) - \ln \gamma_M(x) \right] dx$$

$$+ \int_{I}^{J} \left[\ln Y - \ln\left(L_A / (J - I) \right) - \ln \gamma_L(x) \right] dx$$

$$+ \int_{I}^{J} \left[\ln Y - \ln\left((L - L_A) / (N - J) \right) - \ln \gamma_L(x) \right] dx = 0.$$

- This equation can be rearranged as

$$\ln Y = \int_{N-1}^{I} \left[\ln\left(\frac{K}{I - N + 1} \right) + \ln \gamma_M(x) \right] dx + \int_{I}^{J} \left[\ln\left(\frac{L_A}{J - I} \right) + \ln \gamma_L(x) \right] dx$$

$$+ \int_{J}^{N} \left[\ln\left(\frac{L}{N - J} \right) + \ln \gamma_L(x) \right] dx$$

$$= \int_{N-1}^{I} \ln \gamma_M(x) dx + \int_{I}^{N} \ln \gamma_L(x) dx + (I - N + 1)\ln\left(\frac{K}{I - N + 1} \right)$$

$$+ (J - I)\ln\left(\frac{L_A}{J - I} \right) + (N - J)\ln\left(\frac{L - L_A}{N - J} \right),$$

which yields equation (12) in the text.

References

Accenture PLC. 2017. "How Companies Are Reimagining Business Processes With IT." https://sloanreview.mit.edu/article/will-ai-create-as-many-jobs-as-it -eliminates/.

Acemoglu, Daron. 2009. *Introduction to Modern Economic Growth*. Princeton, NJ: Princeton University Press.

Acemoglu, Daron, and David Autor. 2011. "Skills, Tasks and Technologies: Implications for Employment and Earnings." *Handbook of Labor Economics* 4:1043–171.

Acemoglu, Daron, David Autor, David Dorn, Gordon H. Hanson, and Brendan Price. 2014. "Return of the Solow Paradox? IT, Productivity, and Employment in US Manufacturing." *American Economic Review: Papers & Proceedings* 104 (5): 394–99.

Acemoglu, Daron, and Pascual Restrepo. 2016. "The Race between Machine and Man: Implications of Technology for Growth, Factor Shares and Employment." *American Economic Review* 108 (6): 1488–542.

———. 2017. "Robots and Jobs: Evidence from US Labor Markets." NBER Working Paper no. 23285, Cambridge, MA.

———. 2018a. "Excessive Automation: Technology Adoption and Worker Displacement in a Frictional World." Unpublished manuscript.

———. 2018b. "Low-Skill and High-Skill Automation." *Journal of Human Capital* 12 (2): 204–32.

Aghion, Philippe, Benjamin F. Jones, and Charles I. Jones. 2017. "Artificial Intelligence and Economic Growth." NBER Working Paper no. 23928, Cambridge, MA.

Allen, Robert C. 2009. "Engels' Pause: Technical Change, Capital Accumulation, and Inequality in the British Industrial Revolution." *Explorations in Economic History* 46 (4): 418–35.

American Enterprise Institute (AEI). 2008. "Taxing Capital." Report by the American Enterprise Institute. https://www.aei.org.

Autor, David H. 2015. "Why Are There Still So Many Jobs? The History and Future of Workplace Automation." *Journal of Economic Perspectives* 29 (3): 3–30.

Autor, David H., David Dorn, and Gordon H. Hanson. 2013. "The China Syndrome: Local Labor Market Effects of Import Competition in the United States." *American Economic Review* 103 (6): 2121–68.

Autor, David H., Frank Levy, and Richard J. Murnane. 2003. "The Skill Content of Recent Technological Change: An Empirical Exploration." *Quarterly Journal of Economics* 118 (4): 1279–333.

Ayres, Robert, and Steven M. Miller. 1983. *Robotics: Applications and Social Implications*. Pensacola, FL: Ballinger Publishing Company.

Bessen, James. 2016. *Learning by Doing: The Real Connection between Innovation, Wages, and Wealth*. New Haven, CT: Yale University Press.

Bloom, Nicholas, Charles I. Jones, John Van Reenen, and Michael Webb. 2017. "Are Ideas Getting Harder to Find?" NBER Working Paper no. 23782, Cambridge, MA.

Boston Consulting Group. 2015. "The Robotics Revolution: The Next Great Leap in Manufacturing." https://www.bcg.com/en-us/publications/2015/lean -manufacturing-innovation-robotics-revolution-next-great-leap-manufacturing .aspx.

Brynjolfsson, Erik, and Andrew McAfee. 2014. *The Second Machine Age: Work, Progress, and Prosperity in a Time of Brilliant Technologies*. New York: W. W. Norton & Company.

Chandler, Alfred D. 1977. *The Visible Hand: The Managerial Revolution in American Business*. Cambridge, MA: Harvard University Press.

Deloitte and The Manufacturing Institute. 2011. "Boiling Point? The Skills Gap in U.S. Manufacturing." Report. http://www.themanufacturinginstitute.org/~/media/A07730B2A798437D98501E798C2E13AA.ashx.

Ford, Martin. 2016. *The Rise of the Robots: Technology and the Threat of a Jobless Future*. New York: Basic Books.

Goldin, Claudia, and Larry Katz. 2010. *The Race between Education and Technology*. Cambridge, MA: Harvard University Press.

Gordon, Robert J. 2016. *The Rise and Fall of American Growth: The U.S. Standard of Living Since the Civil War*. Princeton, NJ: Princeton University Press.

Graetz, Georg, and Guy Michaels. 2015. "Robots at Work." CEP Discussion Paper no. 1335, Centre for Economic Performance.

Groover, Mikell. 1983. *CAD/CAM: Computer-Aided Design and Manufacturing*. Englewood Cliffs, NJ: Prentice Hall.

Groover, Mikell, Mitchell Weiss, Roger N. Nagel, and Nicholas G. Odrey. 1986. *Industrial Robotics: Technology, Programming and Applications*. New York: McGraw-Hill.

Herrendorf, Berthold, Richard Rogerson, and Ákos Valentinyi. 2013. "Two Perspectives on Preferences and Structural Transformation." *American Economic Review* 103 (7): 2752–89.

Kolb, David A. 1984. *Experiential Learning: Experience as the Source of Learning and Development*. Englewood Cliffs, NJ: Prentice Hall.

Kuznets, Simon. 1966. *Modern Economic Growth*. New Haven, CT: Yale University Press.

Landes, David. 1969. *The Unbound Prometheus*. New York: Cambridge University Press.

Mantoux, Paul. 1928. *The Industrial Revolution in the Eighteenth Century: An Outline of the Beginnings of the Modern Factory System in England*. New York: Harcourt.

Manuelli, Rodolfo E., and Ananth Seshadri. 2014. "Frictionless Technology Diffusion: The Case of Tractors." *American Economic Review* 104 (4): 1368–91.

McKinsey Global Institute. 2017. "Jobs Lost, Jobs Gained: Workforce Transitions in a Time of Automation." Report, McKinsey & Company. https://www.mckinsey.com/mgi/overview/2017-in-review/automation-and-the-future-of-work/jobs-lost-jobs-gained-workforce-transitions-in-a-time-of-automation.

Mian, Atif, and Amir Sufi. 2014. "What Explains the 2007–2009 Drop in Employment?" *Econometrica* 82 (6): 2197–223.

Minsky, Marvin. 1967. *Computation: Finite and Infinite Machines*. Englewood Cliffs, NJ: Prentice-Hall.

Mokyr, Joel. 1990. *The Lever of Riches: Technological Creativity and Economic Progress*. New York: Oxford University Press.

Nilsson, Nils J. 2009. *The Quest for Artificial Intelligence: A History of Ideas and Achievements*. Cambridge: Cambridge University Press.

Olmstead, Alan L., and Paul W. Rhode. 2001. "Reshaping the Landscape: The Impact and Diffusion of the Tractor in American Agriculture, 1910–1960." *Journal of Economic History* 61 (3): 663–98.

Pew Research Center. 2017. "Automation in Everyday Life." Online Report. http://www.pewinternet.org/2017/10/04/automation-in-everyday-life/.

Rasmussen, Wayne D. 1982. "The Mechanization of Agriculture." *Scientific American* 247 (3): 76–89.

Simon, Herbert A. 1965. *The Shape of Automation for Men and Management*. New York: Harper & Row.

Syverson, Chad. 2017. "Challenges to Mismeasurement Explanations for the US Productivity Slowdown." *Journal of Economic Perspectives* 31 (2): 165–86.

Tuzel, Selale, and Miao Ben Zhang. 2017. "Economic Stimulus at the Expense of Routine-Task Jobs." Unpublished manuscript, Marshall School of Business, University of Southern California.

Zeira, Joseph. 1998. "Workers, Machines, and Economic Growth." *Quarterly Journal of Economics* 113 (4): 1091–117.

Artificial Intelligence
and Economic Growth

Philippe Aghion, Benjamin F. Jones, and Charles I. Jones

9.1 Introduction

This chapter considers the implications of artificial intelligence for economic growth. Artificial intelligence (AI) can be defined as "the capability of a machine to imitate intelligent human behavior" or "an agent's ability to achieve goals in a wide range of environments."[1] These definitions immediately evoke fundamental economic issues. For example, what happens if AI allows an ever-increasing number of tasks previously performed by human labor to become automated? Artificial intelligence may be deployed in the ordinary production of goods and services, potentially impacting economic growth and income shares. But AI may also change the process by which we create new ideas and technologies, helping to solve complex problems and scaling creative effort. In extreme versions, some observers have argued that AI can become rapidly self-improving, leading to "singularities" that feature unbounded machine intelligence and/or unbounded economic growth in

Philippe Aghion is a professor at the Collège de France and at the London School of Economics. Benjamin F. Jones is the Gordon and Llura Gund Family Professor of Entrepreneurship, professor of strategy, and faculty director of the Kellogg Innovation and Entrepreneurship Initiative at Northwestern University, and a research associate of the National Bureau of Economic Research. Charles I. Jones is the STANCO 25 Professor of Economics at the Graduate School of Business at Stanford University and a research associate of the National Bureau of Economic Research.

We are grateful to Ajay Agrawal, Mohammad Ahmadpoor, Adrien Auclert, Sebastian Di Tella, Patrick Francois, Joshua Gans, Avi Goldfarb, Pete Klenow, Hannes Mahlmberg, Pascual Restrepo, Chris Tonetti, Michael Webb, and participants at the NBER Conference on Artificial Intelligence for helpful discussion and comments. For acknowledgments, sources of research support, and disclosure of the authors' material financial relationships, if any, please see http://www.nber.org/chapters/c14015.ack.

1. The former definition comes from the Merriam-Webster dictionary, while the latter is from Legg and Hutter (2007).

finite time (Good 1965; Vinge 1993; Kurzweil 2005). Nordhaus (2015) provides a detailed overview and discussion of the prospects for a singularity from the standpoint of economics.

In this chapter, we speculate on how AI may affect the growth process. Our primary goal is to help shape an agenda for future research. To do so, we focus on the following questions:

- If AI increases automation in the production of goods and services, how will it impact economic growth?
- Can we reconcile the advent of AI with the observed constancy in growth rates and capital share over most of the twentieth century? Should we expect such constancy to persist in the twenty-first century?
- Do these answers change when AI and automation are applied to the production of new ideas?
- Can AI drive massive increases in growth rates, or even a singularity, as some observers predict? Under what conditions, and are these conditions plausible?
- How are the links between AI and economic growth modulated by firm-level considerations, including market structure and innovation incentives? How does AI affect the internal organization of firms, and with what implications?

In thinking about these questions, we develop two main themes. First, we model AI as the latest form in a process of automation that has been ongoing for at least 200 years. From the spinning jenny to the steam engine to electricity to computer chips, the automation of aspects of production has been a key feature of economic growth since the Industrial Revolution. This perspective is taken explicitly in two key papers that we build upon: Zeira (1998) and Acemoglu and Restrepo (2016). We view AI as a new form of automation that may allow additional tasks to be automated that previously were thought to be out of reach from automation. These tasks may be nonroutine (to use the language of Autor, Levy, and Murnane [2003]), like self-driving cars, or they may involve high levels of skill, such as legal services, radiology, and some forms of scientific lab-based research. An advantage of this approach is that it allows us to use historical experience on economic growth and automation to discipline our modeling of AI.

A second theme that emerges in our chapter is that the growth consequences of automation and AI may be constrained by Baumol's "cost disease." Baumol (1967) observed that sectors with rapid productivity growth, such as agriculture and even manufacturing today, often see their share of gross domestic product (GDP) decline while those sectors with relatively slow productivity growth—perhaps including many services—experience increases. As a consequence, economic growth may be constrained not by what we do well but rather by what is essential and yet hard to improve. We suggest that combining this feature of growth with automation can yield a rich description of the growth process, including consequences for future growth and income distribution. When applied to a model in which AI automates the production of goods and services, Baumol's insight generates sufficient conditions under which one can get overall balanced growth with a constant capital share that stays well below 100 percent, even with near-complete automation. When applied to a model in which AI automates the production of ideas, these same considerations can prevent explosive growth.[2]

The chapter proceeds as follows. Section 9.2 begins by studying the role of AI in automating the production of goods and services. In section 9.3, we extend AI and automation to the production of new ideas. Section 9.4 then discusses the possibility that AI could lead to superintelligence or even a singularity. In section 9.5, we look at AI and firms, with particular attention to market structure, organization, reallocation, and wage inequality. In section 9.6, we examine sectoral evidence on the evolution of capital shares in tandem with automation. Finally, section 9.7 concludes.

9.2   Artificial Intelligence and Automation of Production

One way of looking at the last 150 years of economic progress is that it is driven by automation. The Industrial Revolution used steam and then electricity to automate many production processes. Relays, transistors, and semiconductors continued this trend. Perhaps artificial intelligence is the next phase of this process rather than a discrete break. It may be a natural progression from autopilots, computer-controlled automobile engines, and MRI machines to self-driving cars and AI radiology reports. While up until recently automation has mainly affected routine or low-skilled tasks, it appears that AI may increasingly automate nonroutine, cognitive tasks performed by high-skill workers.[3] An advantage of this perspective is that it allows us to use historical experience to inform us about the possible future effects of AI.

9.2.1   The Zeira (1998) Model of Automation and Growth

A clear and elegant model of automation is provided by Zeira (1998). In its simplest form, Zeira considers a production function like

(1) $$Y = AX_1^{\alpha_1} X_2^{\alpha_2} \cdot \ \ldots \ \cdot X_n^{\alpha_n} \text{ where } \sum_{i=1}^{n} \alpha_i = 1.$$

2. In the appendix we show that if some steps in the innovation process require human R&D, AI could possibly slow or even end growth by exacerbating business stealing, which in turn discourages human investments in innovation.

3. Autor, Levy, and Murnane (2003) discuss the effects of traditional software automating routine tasks. Webb et al. (2017) use the text of patent filings to study the different tasks that AI, software, and robotics are best positioned to automate.

While Zeira thought of the X_is as intermediate goods, we follow Acemoglu and Autor (2011) and refer to these as tasks; both interpretations have merit, and we will go back and forth between these interpretations. Tasks that have not yet been automated can be produced one-for-one by labor. Once a task is automated, one unit of capital can be used instead:

(2)
$$X_i = \begin{cases} L_i \text{ if not automated} \\ K_i \text{ if automated} \end{cases}.$$

If the aggregate capital K and labor L are assigned to these tasks optimally, the production function can be expressed (up to an unimportant constant) as

(3)
$$Y_t = A_t K_t^\alpha L_t^{1-\alpha},$$

where it is now understood that the exponent α reflects the overall share and importance of tasks that have been automated. For the moment, we treat α as a constant and consider comparative statics that increase the share of tasks that get automated.

Next, embed this setup into a standard neoclassical growth model with a constant investment rate; in fact, for the remainder of the chapter this is how we will close the capital/investment side of all our models. The share of factor payments going to capital is given by α and the long-run growth rate of $y \equiv Y/L$ is

(4)
$$g_y = \frac{g}{1 - \alpha},$$

where g is the growth rate of A. An increase in automation will therefore increase the capital share α and, because of the multiplier effect associated with capital accumulation, increase the long-run growth rate.

Zeira emphasizes that automation has been going on at least since the Industrial Revolution, and his elegant model helps us to understand that. However, its strong predictions that growth rates and capital shares should be rising with automation go against the famous Kaldor (1961) stylized facts that growth rates and capital shares are relatively stable over time. In particular, this stability is a good characterization of the US economy for the bulk of the twenieth century, for example, see Jones (2016). The Zeira framework, then, needs to be improved so that it is consistent with historical evidence.

Acemoglu and Restrepo (2016) provide one approach to solving this problem. Their rich environment allows for a constant elasticity of substitution (CES) production function and endogenizes the number of tasks as well as automation. In particular, they suppose that research can take two different directions: discovering how to automate an existing task or discovering new tasks that can be used in production. In their setting, a reflects the *fraction* of tasks that have been automated. This leads them to emphasize one possible resolution to the empirical shortcoming of Zeira: perhaps we are inventing new tasks just as quickly as we are automating old tasks. The fraction of tasks that are automated could be constant, leading to a stable capital share and a stable growth rate.

Several other important contributions to this rapidly expanding literature should also be noted. Peretto and Seater (2013) explicitly consider a research technology that allows firms to change the exponent in a Cobb-Douglas production function. While they do not emphasize the link to the Zeira model, with hindsight the connections to that approach to automation are interesting. The model of Hemous and Olsen (2016) is closely related to what follows in the next subsection. They focus on CES production instead of Cobb-Douglas, as we do below, but emphasize the implications of their framework for wage inequality between high-skill and low-skill workers. Agrawal, McHale, and Oettl (2017) incorporate artificial intelligence and the "recombinant growth" of Weitzman (1998) into an innovation-based growth model to show how AI can speed up growth along a transition path.

The next section takes a complementary approach, building on this literature and using the insights of Zeira and automation to understand the structural change associated with Baumol's cost disease.

9.2.2   Automation and Baumol's Cost Disease

The share of agriculture in GDP or employment is falling toward zero. The same is true for manufacturing in many countries of the world. Maybe automation increases the capital share in these sectors and also interacts with nonhomotheticities in production or consumption to drive the GDP shares toward zero. The aggregate capital share is then a balance of a rising capital share in agriculture/manufacturing/automated goods with a declining GDP share of these goods in the economy.

Looking toward the future, 3D printing techniques and nanotechnology that allow production to start at the molecular or even atomic level could someday automate all manufacturing. Could AI do the same thing in many service sectors? What would economic growth look like in such a world?

This section expands on the Zeira (1998) and Acemoglu and Restrepo (2016) models to develop a framework that is consistent with the large structural changes in the economy. Baumol (1967) observed that rapid productivity growth in some sectors relative to others could result in a "cost disease" in which the slow-growing sectors become increasingly important in the economy. We explore the possibility that automation is the force behind these changes.[4]

---

4. The growth literature on this structural transformation emphasizes a range of possible mechanisms, see Kongsamut, Rebelo, and Xie (2001), Ngai and Pissarides (2007), Herrendorf, Rogerson, and Valentinyi (2014), Boppart (2014), and Comin, Lashkari, and Mestieri (2015). The approach we take next has a reduced form that is similar to one of the special cases in Alvarez-Cuadrado, Long, and Poschke (2017).

Model

Gross domestic product is a CES combination of goods with an elasticity of substitution less than one:

$$(5) \qquad Y_t = A_t \left(\int_0^1 X_{it}^\rho di \right)^{1/\rho} \text{ where } \rho > 0,$$

where $A_t = A_0 e^{gt}$ captures standard technological change, which we take to be exogenous for now. Having the elasticity of substitution less than one means that tasks are gross complements. Intuitively, this is a "weak link" production function, where GDP is in some sense limited by the output of the weakest links. Here, these will be the tasks performed by labor, and this structure is the source of the Baumol effect.

As in Zeira, another part of technical change is the automation of production. Goods that have not yet been automated can be produced one-for-one by labor. When a good has been automated, one unit of capital can be used instead:

$$(6) \qquad X_{it} = \begin{cases} L_{it} \text{ if not automated} \\ K_{it} \text{ if automated} \end{cases}.$$

This division is stark to keep the model simple. An alternative would be to say that goods are produced with a Cobb-Douglas combination of capital and labor, and when a good is automated, it is produced with a higher exponent on capital.[5]

The remainder of the model is neoclassical:

$$(7) \qquad Y_t = C_t + I_t,$$

$$(8) \qquad \dot{K}_t = I_t - \delta K_t,$$

$$(9) \qquad \int_0^1 K_{it} di = K_t,$$

$$(10) \qquad \int_0^1 L_{it} di = L.$$

We assume a fixed endowment of labor for simplicity.

Let β_t be the fraction of goods that that have been automated as of date t. Here, and throughout the chapter, we assume that capital and labor are allocated symmetrically across tasks. Therefore, K_t / β_t units of capital are used in each automated task and $L/(1 - \beta_t)$ units of labor are used on each nonautomated task. The production function can then be written as

$$(11) \qquad Y_t = A_t \left[\beta_t \left(\frac{K_t}{\beta_t} \right)^\rho + (1 - \beta_t) \left(\frac{L}{1 - \beta_t} \right)^\rho \right]^{1/\rho}.$$

---

5. A technical condition is required, of course, so that tasks that have been automated are actually produced with capital instead of labor. We assume this condition holds.

Collecting the automation terms simplifies this to

$$(12) \qquad Y_t = A_t \left(\beta_t^{1-\rho} K_t^{\rho} + (1 - \beta_t)^{1-\rho} L^{\rho} \right)^{1/\rho}.$$

This setup therefore reduces to a particular version of the neoclassical growth model, and the allocation of resources can be decentralized in a standard competitive equilibrium. In this equilibrium, the share of automated goods in GDP equals the share of capital in factor payments:

$$(13) \qquad \alpha_{Kt} \equiv \frac{\partial Y_t}{\partial K_t} \frac{K_t}{Y_t} = \beta_t^{1-\rho} A_t^{\rho} \left(\frac{K_t}{Y_t} \right)^{\rho}.$$

Similarly, the share of nonautomated goods in GDP equals the labor share of factor payments:

$$(14) \qquad \alpha_{Lt} \equiv \frac{\partial Y_t}{\partial L_t} \frac{L_t}{Y_t} = \beta_t^{1-\rho} A_t^{\rho} \left(\frac{L_t}{Y_t} \right)^{\rho}.$$

Therefore the ratio of automated to nonautomated output—or the ratio of the capital share to the labor share—equals

$$(15) \qquad \frac{\alpha_{Kt}}{\alpha_{Lt}} = \left(\frac{\beta_t}{1 - \beta_t} \right)^{1-\rho} \left(\frac{K_t}{L_t} \right)^{\rho}.$$

We specified from the beginning that we are interested in the case in which the elasticity of substitution between goods is less than one, so that $\rho < 0$. From equation (15), there are two basic forces that move the capital share (or, equivalently, the share of the economy that is automated). First, an increase in the fraction of goods that are automated, β_t, will increase the share of automated goods in GDP and increase the capital share (holding K/L constant). This is intuitive and repeats the logic of the Zeira model. Second, as K/L rises, the capital share and the value of the automated sector as a share of GDP will decline. Essentially, with an elasticity of substitution less than one, the price effects dominate. The price of automated goods declines relative to the price of nonautomated goods because of capital accumulation. Because demand is relatively inelastic, the expenditure share of these goods declines as well. Automation and Baumol's cost disease are then intimately linked. Perhaps the automation of agriculture and manufacturing leads these sectors to grow rapidly and causes their shares in GDP to decline.[6]

The bottom line is that there is a race between these two forces. As more sectors are automated, β_t increases, and this tends to increase the share of automated goods and capital. But because these automated goods experience faster growth, their price declines, and the low elasticity of substitution means that their shares of GDP also decline.

Following Acemoglu and Restrepo (2016), we could endogenize automation by specifying a technology in which research effort leads goods to

---

6. Manuelli and Seshadri (2014) offer a systematic account of the how the tractor gradually replaced the horse in American agriculture between 1910 and 1960.

be automated. But it is relatively clear that depending on exactly how one specifies this technology, $\beta_t/(1 - \beta_t)$ can rise faster or slower than $(K_t/L_t)^\rho$ declines. That is, the result would depend on detailed assumptions related to automation, and currently we do not have adequate knowledge on how to make these assumptions. This is an important direction for future research. For now, however, we treat automation as exogenous and consider what happens when β_t changes in different ways.

Balanced Growth (Asymptotically)

To understand some of these possibilities, notice that the production function in equation (12) is just a special case of a neoclassical production function:

(16) $Y_t = A_t F\left(B_t K_t, C_t L_t\right)$ where $B_t \equiv \beta_t^{(1-\rho)/\rho}$ and $C_t \equiv (1 - \beta_t)^{(1-\rho)/\rho}$.

With $\rho < 0$, notice that $\uparrow \beta_t \Rightarrow \downarrow B_t$ and $\uparrow C_t$. That is, automation is equivalent to a combination of labor-augmenting technical change and capital-depleting technical change. This is surprising. One might have thought of automation as somehow capital augmenting. Instead, it is very different: it is labor augmenting and simultaneously *dilutes* the stock of capital. Notice that these conclusions would be reversed if the elasticity of substitution were greater than one; importantly, they rely on $\rho < 0$.

The intuition for this surprising result can be seen by noting that automation has two basic effects. These can be seen most easily by looking back at equation (11). First, capital can be applied to a larger number of tasks, which is a basic capital-augmenting force. However, this also means that a fixed amount of capital is spread more thinly, a capital-depleting effect. When the tasks are substitutes ($\rho > 0$), the augmenting effect dominates and automation is capital augmenting. However, when tasks are complements ($\rho < 0$), the depletion effect dominates and automation is capital depleting. Notice that for labor, the opposite forces are at work: automation concentrates a given quantity of labor onto a smaller number of tasks and hence is labor augmenting when $\rho < 0$.[7]

This opens up one possibility that we will explore next: what happens if the evolution of β_t is such that C_t grows at a constant exponential rate? This can occur if $1 - \beta_t$ falls at a constant exponential rate toward zero, meaning that $\beta_t \to 1$ in the limit and the economy gets ever closer to full automation (but never quite reaches that point). The logic of the neoclassical growth model suggests that this could produce a balanced growth path with constant factor shares, at least in the limit. (This requires A_t to be constant.)

In particular, we want to consider an exogenous time path for the fraction

---

7. In order for automation to increase output, we require a technical condition: $(K/\beta)^\rho <$ $[L/(1 - \beta)]^\rho$. For $\rho < 0$, this requires $K/\beta > L/1 - \beta$. That is, the amount of capital that we allocate to each task must exceed the amount of labor we allocate to each task. Automation raises output by allowing us to use our plentiful capital on more of the tasks performed by relatively scarce labor.

of tasks that are automated, β_t, such that $\beta_t \rightarrow 1$ but in a way that C_t grows at a constant exponential rate. This turns out to be straightfoward. Let $\gamma_t \equiv 1 - \beta_t$, so that $C_t = \gamma_t^{(1-\rho)/\rho}$. Because the exponent is negative ($\rho < 0$), if γ falls at a constant exponential rate, C_t will grow at a constant exponential rate. This occurs if $\dot{\beta}_t = \theta(1 - \beta_t)$, implying that $g_\gamma = -\theta$. Intuitively, a constant fraction, θ, of the tasks that have not yet been automated become automated each period.

Figure 9.1 shows that this example can produce steady exponential growth. We begin in year 0 with none of the goods being automated, and then have a constant fraction of the remainder being automated each year. There is obviously enormous structural change underlying—and generating—the stable exponential growth of GDP in this case. The capital share of factor payments begins at zero and then rises gradually over time, eventually asymptoting to a value around one-third. Even though an ever-vanishing fraction of the economy has not yet been automated, so labor has less and less to do. The fact that automated goods are produced with cheap capital combined with an elasticity of substitution less than one means that the automated share of GDP remains at one-third and labor still earns around two-thirds of GDP asymptotically. This is a consequence of the Baumol force: the labor tasks are the "weak links" that are essential and yet expensive, and this keeps the labor share elevated.[8]

Along such a path, however, sectors like agriculture and manufacturing exhibit a structural transformation. For example, let sectors on the interval [0,1/3] denote agriculture and the automated portion of manufacturing as of some year, such as 1990. These sectors experience a declining share of GDP over time, as their prices fall rapidly. The automated share of the economy will be constant only because new goods are becoming automated.

The analysis so far requires A_t to be constant, so that the only form of technical change is automation. This seems too extreme: surely technical progress is not only about substituting machines for labor, but also about creating better machines. This can be incorporated in the following way. Suppose A_t is *capital-augmenting* rather than Hicks-neutral, so that the production function in equation (16) becomes $Y_t = F(A_t B_t K_t, C_t L_t)$. In this case, one could get a balanced growth path (BGP) if A_t rises at precisely the rate that B_t declines, so that technological change is essentially purely labor-augmenting on net: better computers would decrease the capital share at precisely the rate that automation raises it, leading to balanced growth. At first, this seems like a knife-edge result that would be unlikely in practice. However, the logic of this example is somewhat related to the model in Grossman et al. (2017); that paper presents an environment in which it is optimal to have something similar to this occur. So perhaps this alternative

---

8. The neoclassical outcome here requires that θ not be too large (e.g., relative to the exogenous investment rate). If θ is sufficiently high, the capital share can asymptote to one and the model becomes "AK." We are grateful to Pascual Restrepo for working this out.

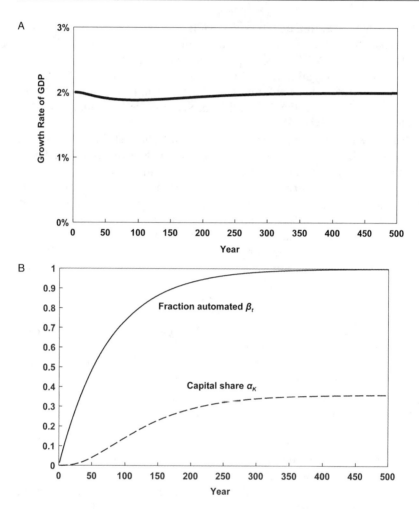

Fig. 9.1   Automation and asymptotic balanced growth. *A*, the growth rate of GDP over time; *B*, automation and the capital share

Note: This simulation assumes $\rho < 0$ and that a constant fraction of the tasks that have not yet been automated become automated each year. Therefore $C_t \equiv (1 - \beta)^{(1-\rho)/\rho}$ grows at a constant exponential rate (2 percent per year in this example), leading to an asymptotic balanced growth path (BGP). The share of tasks that are automated approaches 100 percent in the limit. Interestingly, the capital share of factor payments (and the share of automated goods in GDP) remains bounded, in this case at a value around one-third. With a constant investment rate of $\overline{s}$, the limiting value of the capital share is $(\overline{s}/g_Y + \delta)^\rho$.

approach could be given good microfoundations. We leave this possibility to future research.

Constant Factor Shares

Another interesting case worth considering is under what conditions can this model produce factor shares that are constant over time? Taking logs and derivatives of equation (15), the capital share will be constant if and only if

(17)
$$g_{\beta t} = \left(1 - \beta_t\right)\left(\frac{-\rho}{1-\rho}\right)g_{kt},$$

where g_{kt} is the growth rate of $k \equiv K/L$. This is very much a knife-edge condition. It requires the growth rate of β_t to slow over time at just the right rate as more and more goods get automated.

Figure 9.2 shows an example with this feature, in an otherwise neoclassical model with exogenous growth in A_t at 2 percent per year. That is, unlike the previous section, we allow other forms of technological change to make tractors and computers better over time, in addition to allowing automation. In this simulation, automation proceeds at just the right rate so as to keep the capital share constant for the first 150 years. After that time, we simply assume that β_t is constant and automation stops, so as to show what happens in that case as well.

The perhaps surprising result in this example is that the constant factor shares occur while the growth rate of GDP rises at an increasing rate. From the earlier simulation in figure 9.1, one might have inferred that a constant capital share would be associated with declining growth. However, this is not the case and instead growth rates increase. The key to the explanation is to note that with some algebra, we can show that the constant factor share case requires

(18)
$$g_{Yt} = g_A + \beta_t g_{Kt}.$$

First, consider the case with $g_A = 0$. We know that a true balanced growth path requires $g_Y = g_K$. This can occur in only two ways if $g_A = 0$: either $\beta_t = 1$ or $g_Y = g_K = 0$ if $\beta_t < 1$. The first case is the one that we explored in the previous example back in figure 9.1. The second case shows that if $g_A = 0$, then constant factor shares will be associated with zero exponential growth.

Now we can see the reconciliation between figures 9.1 and 9.2. In the absence of $g_A > 0$, the growth rate of the economy would fall to zero. Introducing $g_A > 0$ with constant factor shares *does* increases the growth rate. To see why growth has to accelerate, equation (18) is again useful. If growth were balanced, then $g_Y = g_K$. But then the rise in β_t would tend to raise g_Y and g_K. This is why growth accelerates.

Regime Switching

A final simulation shown in figure 9.3 combines aspects of the two previous simulations to produce results closer in spirit to our observed data, albeit in a highly stylized way. We assume that automation alternates between two regimes. The first is like figure 9.1, in which a constant fraction of the remaining tasks are automated each year, tending to raise the capital share and produce high growth. In the second, β_t is constant and no new automation occurs. In both regimes, A_t grows at a constant rate of 0.4 percent per

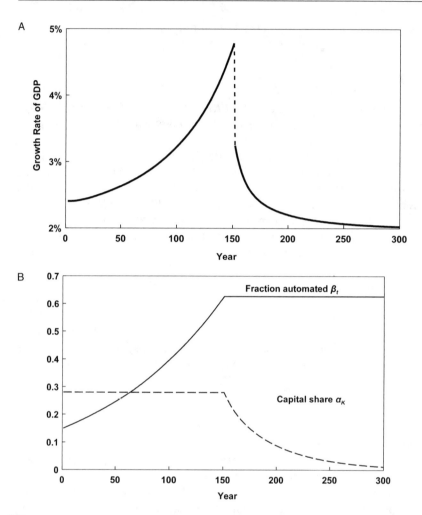

Fig. 9.2   Automation with a constant capital share. *A*, the growth rate of GDP over time; *B*, automation and the capital share

Note: This simulation assumes $\rho < 0$ and sets β_t so that the capital share is constant between year 0 and year 150. After year 150, we assume β_t stays at its constant value; A_t is assumed to grow at a constant rate of 2 percent per year throughout.

year, so that even when the fraction of tasks being automated is stagnant, the nature of automation is improving, which tends to depress the capital share. Regimes last for thirty years. Period 100 is highlighted with a black circle. At this point in time, the capital share is relatively high and growth is relatively low.

By playing with parameter values, including the growth rate of A_t and β_t, it is possible to get a wide range of outcomes. For example, the fact that

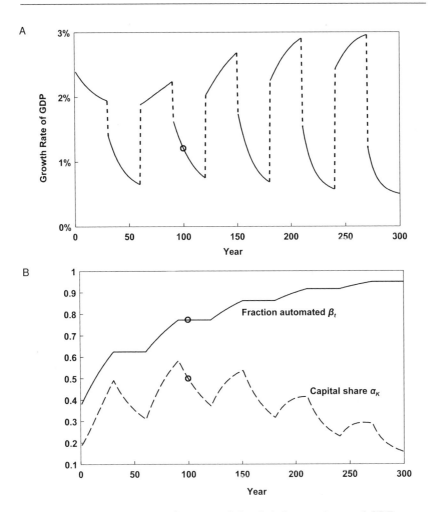

Fig. 9.3   Intermittent automation to match data? *A*, **the growth rate of GDP over time;** *B*, **automation and the capital share**

Note: This simulation combines aspects of the two previous simulations to produce results closer in spirit to our observed data. We assume that automation alternates between two regimes. In the first, a constant fraction of the remaining tasks are automated each year. In the second, β_t is constant and no new automation occurs. In both regimes, A_t grows at a constant rate of 0.4 percent per year. Regimes last for thirty years. Period 100 is highlighted with a black circle. At this point in time, the capital share is relatively high and growth is relatively low.

the capital share in the future is lower than in period 100 instead of higher can be reversed.

Summing Up

Automation—an increase in β_t—can be viewed as a "twist" of the capital- and labor-augmenting terms in a neoclassical production function. From

Uzawa's famous theorem, since we do not in general have purely labor-augmenting technical change, this setting will not lead to balanced growth. In this particular application (e.g., with $\rho < 0$), either the capital share or the growth rate of GDP will tend to increase over time, and sometimes both. We showed one special case in which all tasks are ultimately automated that produced balanced growth in the limit with a constant capital share less than 100 percent. A shortcoming of this case is that it requires automation to be the *only* form of technological change. If, instead, the nature of automation itself improves over time—consider the plow, then the tractor, then the combine-harvester, then GPS tracking—then the model is best thought of as featuring both automation and something like improvements in A_t. In this case, one would generally expect growth not to be balanced. However, a combination of periods of automation followed by periods of respite, like that shown in figure 9.3 does seem capable of producing dynamics at least superficially similar to what we have seen in the United States in recent years: a period of a high capital share with relatively slow economic growth.

9.3   Artificial Intelligence in the Idea Production Function

In the previous section, we examined the implications of introducing AI in the production function for goods and services. But what if the tasks of the innovation process themselves can be automated? How would AI interact with the production of new ideas? In this section, we introduce AI in the production technology for new ideas and look at how AI can affect growth through this channel.

A moment of introspection into our own research process reveals many ways in which automation can matter for the production of ideas. Research tasks that have benefited from automation and technological change include typing and distributing our papers, obtaining research materials and data (e.g., from libraries), ordering supplies, analyzing data, solving math problems, and computing equilibrium outcomes. Beyond economics, other examples include carrying out experiments, sequencing genomes, exploring various chemical reactions and materials. In other words, applying the same task-based model to the idea production function and considering the automation of research tasks seems relevant.

To keep things simple, suppose the production function for goods and services just uses labor and ideas:

(19)
$$Y_t = A_t L_t.$$

But suppose that various tasks are used to make new ideas according to

(20)
$$\dot{A}_t = A_t^{\phi} \left(\int_0^1 X_{it}^{\rho} di \right)^{1/\rho} \text{ where } \rho < 0.$$

Assuming some fraction β_t of tasks have been automated—using a similar setup to that in section 9.2—the idea production function can be expressed as

$$(21) \qquad \dot{A_t} = A_t^\phi \left((B_t K_t)^\rho + (C_t S_t)^\rho \right)^{1/\rho} \equiv A_t^\phi F\left(B_t K_t, C_t S_t \right),$$

where S_t is the research labor used to make ideas, and B_t and C_t are defined as before, namely, $B_t \equiv \beta_t^{(1-\rho)\rho}$ and $C_t \equiv (1 - \beta_t)^{(1-\rho)/\rho}$.

Several observations then follow from this setup. First, consider the case in which β_t is constant at some value but then increases to a higher value (recall that this leads to a one-time decrease in B_t and increase in C_t). The idea production function can then be written as

$$(22) \qquad \dot{A_t} = A_t^\phi S_t F\left(\frac{BK_t}{S_t}, C \right)$$

$$\sim A_t^\phi C S_t,$$

where the "~" notation means "is asymptotically proportional to." The second line follows if K_t / S_t is growing over time (i.e., if there is economic growth) and if the elasticity of substitution in $F(\cdot)$ is less than one, which we have assumed. In that case, the CES function is bounded by its scarcest argument, in this case researchers. Automation then essentially produces a level effect but leaves the long-run growth rate of the economy unchanged if $\phi < 1$. Alternatively, if $\phi = 1$—the classic endogenous growth case—then automation raises long-run growth.

Next, consider this same case of a one-time increase in β, but suppose the elasticity of substitution in $F(\cdot)$ equals one, so that $F(\cdot)$ is Cobb-Douglas. In this case, as in the Zeira model, it is easy to show that a one-time increase in automation will raise the long-run growth rate. Essentially, an accumulable factor in production (capital) becomes permanently more important, and this leads to a multiplier effect that raises growth.

Third, suppose now that the elasticity of substitution is greater than one. In this case, the argument given before reverses, and now the CES function asymptotically looks like the plentiful factor, in this case K_t. The model will then deliver explosive growth under fairly general conditions, with incomes becoming infinite in finite time.[9] But this is true even *without* any automation. Essentially, in this case researchers are not a necessary input and so standard capital accumulation is enough to generate explosive growth. This is one reason why the case of $\rho < 1$—that is, an elasticity of substitution less than one—is the natural case to consider. We focus on this case for the remainder of this section.

---

9. A closely related case is examined explicitly in the discussion surrounding equation (27) below.

9.3.1   Continuous Automation

We can now consider the special case in which automation is such that the newly automated tasks constitute a constant fraction, q, of the tasks that have not yet been automated. Recall that this was the case that delivered a balanced growth path back in the Balanced Growth section

In This Case, $B_t \rightarrow 1$ and $(\dot{C}_t / C_t) \rightarrow g_c = -[(1-\rho)/\rho] \cdot \theta > 0$ Asymptotically

The same logic that gave us equation (22) now implies that

$$(23) \qquad \dot{A}_t = A_t^\phi C_t S_t F\left(\frac{B_t K_t}{C_t S_t}, 1\right)$$

$$\sim A_t^\phi C_t S_t,$$

where the second line holds as long as $BK/CS \rightarrow \infty$, which holds for a large class of parameter values.[10]

This reduces to the Jones (1995) kind of setup, except that now "effective" research grows faster than the population because of AI. Dividing both sides of the last expression by A_t gives

$$(24) \qquad \frac{\dot{A}_t}{A_t} = \frac{C_t S_t}{A_t^{1-\phi}}.$$

In order for the left-hand side to be constant, we require that the numerator and denominator on the right side grow at the same rate, which then implies

$$(25) \qquad g_A = \frac{g_C + g_S}{1 - \phi}.$$

In Jones (1995), the expression was the same except $g_C = 0$. In that case, the growth rate of the economy is proportional to the growth rate of researchers (and ultimately, the population). Here, automation adds a second term and raises the growth rate: we can have exponential growth in research effort in the idea production function not only because of growth in the actual number of people, but also as a result of the automation of research implied by AI. Put another way, even with a constant number of researchers, the number of researchers per task $S/(1 - \beta_t)$ can grow exponentially: the fixed number of researchers is increasingly concentrated onto an exponentially declining number of tasks.[11]

---

10. Since $B \rightarrow 1$, we just require that $g_k > g_c$. This will hold—see below—for example if $\phi > 0$.
11. Substituting in for other solutions, the long-run growth rate of the economy is $g_y = \{-[(1-\rho)/\rho] \cdot \theta + n\}/(1-\phi)$, where n is the rate of population growth.

9.4   Singularities

To this point, we have considered the effects of gradual automation in the goods and idea production functions and shown how that can potentially raise the growth rate of the economy. However, many observers have suggested that AI opens the door to something more extreme—a "technological singularity" where growth rates will explode. John Von Neumann is often cited as first suggesting a coming singularity in technology (Danaylov 2012). I. J. Good and Vernor Vinge have suggested the possibility of a self-improving AI that will quickly outpace human thought, leading to an "intelligence explosion" associated with infinite intelligence in finite time (Good 1965; Vinge 1993). Ray Kurzweil in *The Singularity is Near* also argues for a coming intelligence explosion through nonbiological intelligence (Kurzweil 2005) and, based on these ideas, cofounded Singularity University with funding from prominent organizations like Google and Genentech.

In this section, we consider singularity scenarios in light of the production functions for both goods and ideas. Whereas standard growth theory is concerned with matching the Kaldor facts, including constant growth rates, here we consider circumstances in which growth rates may increase rapidly over time. To do so, and to speak in an organized way to the various ideas that borrow the phrase "technological singularity," we can characterize two types of growth regimes that depart from steady-state growth. In particular, we can imagine:

- a "Type I" growth explosion, where growth rates increase without bound but remain finite at any point in time; and
- a "Type II" growth explosion, where infinite output is achieved in finite time.

Both concepts appear in the singularity community. While it is common for writers to predict the singularity date (often just a few decades away), writers differ on whether the proposed date records the transition to the new growth regime of Type I or an actual singularity occurring of Type II.[12]

To proceed, we now consider examples of how the advent of AI could drive growth explosions. The basic finding is that complete automation of tasks by an AI can naturally lead to the growth explosion scenarios above. However, interestingly, one can even produce a singularity without relying on complete automation, and one can do it without relying on an intelligence explosion per se. Further below, we will consider several possible objections to these examples.

---

12. Vinge (1993), for example, appears to be predicting a Type II explosion, a case that has been examined mathematically by Solomonoff (1985), Yudkowsky (2013), and others. Kurzweil (2005), by contrast, who argues that the singularity will come around the year 2045, appears to be expecting a Type I event.

9.4.1   Examples of Technological Singularities

We provide four examples. The first two examples take our previous models to the extreme and consider what happens if everything can be automated—that is, if people can be replaced by AI in all tasks. The third example demonstrates a singularity through increased automation but without relying on complete automation. The final example looks directly at "superintelligence" as a route to a singularity.

Example 1: Automation of Goods Production

The Type I case can emerge with full automation in the production for goods. This is the well-known case of an AK model with ongoing technological progress. In particular, take the model of section 9.2, but assume that *all* tasks are automated as of some date t_0. The production function is thereafter $Y_t = A_t K_t$ and growth rates themselves grow exponentially with A_t. Ongoing productivity growth—for example, through the discovery of new ideas—would then produce ever-accelerating growth rates over time. Specifically, with a standard capital accumulation specification ($\dot{K}_t = \bar{s} Y_t - \delta K_t$) and technological progress proceeding at rate g, the growth rate of output becomes

$$(26) \qquad\qquad g_Y = g + \bar{s} A_t - \delta,$$

which grows exponentially with A_t.

Example 2: Automation of Ideas Production

An even stronger version of this acceleration occurs if the automation applies to the idea production function instead of (or in addition to) the goods production function. In fact, one can show that there is a mathematical singularity: a Type II event where incomes essentially become infinite in a finite amount of time.

To see this, consider the model of section 9.3. Once all tasks can be automated, that is, once AI replaces all people in the idea production function, the production of new ideas is given by

$$(27) \qquad\qquad \dot{A}_t = K_t A_t^\phi.$$

With $\phi > 0$, this differential equation is "more than linear." As we discuss next, growth rates will explode so fast that incomes become infinite in finite time.

The basic intuition for this result comes from noting that this model is essentially a two-dimensional version of the differential equation $\dot{A}_t = A_t^{1+\phi}$ (e.g., replacing the K with an A in equation [27]). This differential equation can be solved using standard methods to give

$$(28) \qquad\qquad A_t = \left(\frac{1}{A_0^{-\phi} - \phi t} \right)^{1/\phi}.$$

And it is easy to see from this solution that $A(t)$ exceeds any finite value before date $t^* = (1/\phi A_0^\phi)$. This is a singularity.

For the two dimensional system with capital in equation (27), the argument is slightly more complicated but follows this same logic. The system of differential equations is equation (27) together with the capital accumulation equation ($\dot{K}_t = \bar{s}Y_t - dK_t$, where $Y_t = A_t L$). Writing these in growth rates gives

$$(29) \qquad \frac{\dot{A}_t}{A_t} = \frac{K_t}{A_t} \cdot A_t^\phi,$$

$$(30) \qquad \frac{\dot{K}_t}{K_t} = \bar{s}L\frac{A_t}{K_t} - \delta.$$

First, we show that $(\dot{A}_t/A_t) > (\dot{K}_t/K_t)$. To see why, suppose they were equal. Then equation (30) implies that $(\dot{K}_t/K_t)$ is constant, but equation (29) would then imply that $(\dot{A}_t/A_t)$ is accelerating, which contradicts our original assumption that the growth rates were equal. So it must be that $(\dot{A}_t/A_t) > (\dot{K}_t/K_t)$.[13] Notice that from the capital accumulation equation, this means that the growth rate of capital is rising over time, and then the idea growth rate equation means that the growth rate of ideas is rising over time as well. Both growth rates are rising. The only question is whether they rise sufficiently fast to deliver a singularity.

To see why the answer is yes, set $\delta = 0$ and $\bar{s}L = 1$ to simplify the algebra. Now multiply the two growth rate equations together to get

$$(31) \qquad \frac{\dot{A}_t}{A_t} \cdot \frac{\dot{K}_t}{K_t} = A_t^\phi.$$

We have shown that $(\dot{A}_t/A_t) > (\dot{K}_t/K_t)$, so combining this with equation (31) yields

$$(32) \qquad \left(\frac{\dot{A}_t}{A_t}\right)^2 > A_t^\phi,$$

implying that

$$(33) \qquad \frac{\dot{A}_t}{A_t} > A_t^{\phi/2}.$$

That is, the growth rate of A grows at least as fast as $A_t^{\phi/2}$. But we know from the analysis of the simple differential equation given earlier—see equation (28)—that even if equation (33) held with equality, this would be enough to deliver the singularity. Because A grows faster than that, it also exhibits a singularity.

Because ideas are nonrival, the overall economy is characterized by increasing returns, à la Romer (1990). Once the production of ideas is fully

---

13. It is easy to rule out the opposite case of $(\dot{A}_t/A_t) < (\dot{K}_t/K_t)$.

automated, this increasing returns applies to "accumulable factors," which then leads to a Type II growth explosion, that is, a mathematical singularity.

Example 3: Singularities without Complete Automation

The above examples consider complete automation of goods production (Example 1) and ideas production (Example 2). With the CES case and an elasticity of substitution less than one, we require that *all* tasks are automated. If only a fraction of the tasks are automated, then the scarce factor (labor) will dominate, and growth rates do not explode. We show in this section that with Cobb-Douglas production, a Type II singularity can occur as long as a sufficient fraction of the tasks are automated. In this sense, the singularity might not even require full automation.

Suppose the production function for goods is $Y_t = A_t^\sigma K_t^\alpha L^{1-\alpha}$ (a constant population simplifies the analysis, but exogenous population growth would not change things). The capital accumulation equation and the idea production function are then specified as

$$(34) \qquad \dot{K}_t = \bar{s} L A_t^\sigma K_t^\alpha - \delta K_t,$$

$$(35) \qquad \dot{A}_t = K_t^\beta S^\lambda A_t^\phi,$$

where $0 < \alpha < 1$ and $0 < \beta < 1$, and where we also take S (research effort) to be constant. Following the Zeira (1998) model discussed earlier, we interpret α as the fraction of goods tasks that have been automated and β as the fraction of tasks in idea production that have been automated.

The standard endogenous growth result requires "constant returns to accumulable factors." To see what this means, it is helpful to define a key parameter:

$$(36) \qquad \gamma := \gamma \frac{\sigma}{1-\alpha} \cdot \frac{\beta}{1-\phi}.$$

In this setup, the endogenous growth case corresponds to $\gamma = 1$. Not surprisingly, then, the singularity case occurs if $\gamma > 1$. Importantly, notice that this can occur with both α and β less than one, that is, when tasks are not fully automated. For example, in the case in which $\alpha = \beta = \phi = 1/2$, then $\gamma = 2 \cdot \sigma$, so explosive growth and a singularity will occur if $\sigma > 1/2$. We show that $\gamma > 1$ delivers a Type II singularity in the remainder of this section. The argument builds on the argument given in the previous subsection.

In growth rates, the laws of motion for capital and ideas are

$$(37) \qquad \frac{\dot{K}_t}{K_t} = \bar{s} L^{1-\alpha} \frac{A_t^\sigma}{K_t^{1-\alpha}} - \delta,$$

$$(38) \qquad \frac{\dot{A}_t}{A_t} = S^\lambda \frac{K_t^\beta}{A_t^{1-\phi}}.$$

It is easy to show that these growth rates cannot be constant if $\gamma > 1$.[14]

If the growth rates are rising over time to infinity, then eventually either $g_{At} > g_{Kt}$, or the reverse, or the two growth rates are the same. Consider the first case, that is, $g_{At} > g_{Kt}$; the other cases follow the same logic. Once again, to simplify the algebra, set $\delta = 0$, $S = 1$, and $\bar{s}L^{1-\alpha} = 1$. Multiplying the growth rates together in this case gives

$$(39) \qquad \frac{\dot{A}_t}{A_t} \cdot \frac{\dot{K}_t}{K_t} = \frac{K_t^\beta}{A_t^{1-\phi}} \cdot \frac{A_t^\sigma}{K_t^{1-\alpha}}.$$

Since $g_A > g_K$, we then have

$$\left(\frac{\dot{A}_t}{A_t}\right)^2 > \frac{K_t^\beta}{A_t^{1-\phi}} \cdot \frac{A_t^\sigma}{K_t^{1-\alpha}}$$

$$> \frac{1}{K_t} \cdot \frac{K_t^\beta}{A_t^{1-\phi}} \cdot \frac{A_t^\upsilon}{K_t^{1-\sigma}} \qquad \text{(since } K_t > 1 \text{ eventually)}$$

$$> \frac{1}{K_t^{1-\beta}} \cdot \frac{1}{A_t^{1-\phi}} \cdot \frac{A_t^\sigma}{K_t^{1-\sigma}} \qquad \text{(rewriting)}$$

$$> \frac{1}{A_t^{1-\beta}} \cdot \frac{1}{A_t^{1-\phi}} \cdot \frac{A_t^\sigma}{A_t^{1-\alpha}} \qquad \text{(since } A_t > K_t \text{ eventually)}$$

$$> A_t^{\gamma-1} \qquad \text{(collecting terms).}$$

Therefore,

$$(40) \qquad \frac{\dot{A}_t}{A_t} > A_t^{(\gamma-1)/2}.$$

With $\gamma > 1$, the growth rate grows at least as fast as A_t raised to a positive power. But even if it grew just this fast we would have a singularity, by the same arguments given before. The case with $g_{Kt} > g_{At}$ can be handled in the same way, using Ks instead of As. QED.

Example 4: Singularities via Superintelligence

The examples of growth explosions above are based in automation. These examples can also be read as creating "superintelligence" as an artifact of automation, in the sense that advances of A_t across all tasks include, implicitly, advances across cognitive tasks, and hence a resulting singularity can be conceived of as commensurate with an intelligence explosion. It is interesting that automation itself can provoke the emergence of superintelligence. However, in the telling of many futurists, the story runs differently, where

---

14. If the growth rate of K is constant, then $\sigma g_A = (1 - \alpha)g_K$, so K is proportional to $A^{\sigma/(1-\alpha)}$. Making this substitution in equation (35) and using $\gamma > 1$ then implies that the growth rate of A would explode, and this requires the growth rate of K to explode.

an intelligence explosion occurs first and then, through the insights of this superintelligence, a technological singularity may be reached. Typically the AI is seen as "self-improving" through a recursive process.

This idea can be modeled using similar ideas to those presented above. To do so in a simple manner, divide tasks into two types: physical and cognitive. Define a common level of intelligence across the cognitive tasks by a productivity term $A_{\text{cognitive}}$, and further define a common productivity at physical tasks, A_{physical}. Now imagine we have a unit of AI working to improve itself, where progress follows

$$(41) \qquad \dot{A}_{\text{cognitive}} = A_{\text{cognitive}}^{1+\omega}.$$

We have studied this differential equation above, but now we apply it to cognition alone. If $\omega > 0$, then the process of self-improvement explodes, resulting in an unbounded intelligence in finite time.

The next question is how this superintelligence would affect the rest of the economy. Namely, would such superintelligence also produce an output singularity? One route to a singularity could run through the goods production function: to the extent that physical tasks are not essential (i.e., $\rho \geq 0$), then the intelligence explosion will drive a singularity in output. However, it seems noncontroversial to assert that physical tasks are essential to producing output, in which case the singularity will have potentially modest effects directly on the goods production channel.

The second route lies in the idea production function. Here the question is how the superintelligence would advance the productivity at physical tasks, A_{physical}. For example, if we write

$$(42) \qquad \dot{A}_{\text{physical}} = A_{\text{cognitive}}^{\gamma} F(K, L),$$

where $\gamma > 0$, then it is clear that A_{physical} will also explode with the intelligence explosion. That is, we imagine that the superintelligent AI can figure out ways to vastly increase the rate of innovation at physical tasks. In the above specification, the output singularity would then follow directly upon the advent of the superintelligence. Of course, the idea production functions (41) and (42) are particular, and there are reasons to believe they would not be the correct specifications, as we will discuss in the next section.

9.4.2   Objections to Singularities

The above examples show ways in which automation may lead to rapid accelerations of growth, including ever-increasing growth rates or even a singularity. Here we can consider several possible objections to these scenarios, which can broadly be characterized as "bottlenecks" that AI cannot resolve.

Automation Limits

One kind of bottleneck, which has been discussed above, emerges when some essential input(s) to production are not automated. Whether AI can ultimately perform all essential cognitive tasks, or more generally achieve human intelligence, is widely debated. If not, then growth rates may still be larger with more automation and capital intensity (sections 9.2 and 9.3), but the "labor free" singularities featured above (section 9.4.1) become out of reach.

Search Limits

A second kind of bottleneck may occur even with complete automation. This type of bottleneck occurs when the creative search process itself prevents especially rapid producitivy gains. To see this, consider again the idea production function. In the second example above, we allow for complete automation and show that a true mathematical singularity can ensue. But note also that this result depends on the parameter φ. In the differential equation

$$\dot{A}_t = A_t^{1+\phi}$$

we will have explosive growth only if $\phi > 0$. If $\phi \leq 0$, then the growth rate declines as A_t advances. Many models of growth and associated evidence suggest that, on average, innovation may be becoming harder, which is consistent with low values of ϕ on average.[15] Fishing out or burden of knowledge processes can point toward $\phi < 0$. Interestingly, the burden of knowledge mechanism (Jones 2009), which is based on the limits of human cognition, may not restrain an AI if an AI can comprehend a much greater share of the knowledge stock than a human can. Fishing-out processes, however, viewed as a fundamental feature of the search for new ideas (Kortum 1997), would presumably also apply to an AI seeking new ideas. Put another way, AI may resolve a problem with the fishermen, but it would not change what is in the pond. Of course, fishing-out search problems can apply not only to overall productivity but also to the emergence of a superintelligence, limiting the potential rate of an AI program's self-improvement (see equation [41]), and hence limiting the potential for growth explosions through the superintelligence channel.

Baumol Tasks and Natural Laws

A third kind of bottleneck may occur even with complete automation and even with a superintelligence. This type of bottleneck occurs when an essential input does not see much productivity growth. That is, we have another form of Baumol's cost disease.

To see this, generalize slightly the task-based production function (5) of section 9.2 as

$$Y = \left[\int_0^1 \left(a_{it} X_{it} \right)^\rho di \right]^{1/\rho}, \ \rho < 0,$$

15. See, for example, Jones (1995), Kortum (1997), Jones (2009), Gordon (2016), and Bloom et al. (2017).

where we have introduced task-specific productivity terms, a_{it}.

In contrast to our prior examples, where we considered a common technology term, A_t, that affected all of aggregate production, here we imagine that productivity at some tasks may be different than others and may proceed at different rates. For example, machine computation speeds have increased by a factor of about 10^{11} since World War II.[16] By contrast, power plants have seen modest efficiency gains and face limited prospects given constraints like Carnot's theorem. This distinction is important, because with $\rho < 0$, output and growth end up being determined not by what we are good at, but by what is essential but hard to improve.

In particular, let's imagine that some superintelligence somehow does emerge, but that it can only drive productivity to (effectively) infinity in a share θ of tasks, which we index from $i \in [0,\theta]$. Output thereafter will be

$$Y = \left[\int_\theta^1 (a_{it} Y_{it})^\rho \, di \right]^{1/\rho}.$$

Clearly, if these remaining technologies a_{it} cannot be radically improved, we no longer have a mathematical singularity (Type II growth explosion) and may not even have much future growth. We might still end up with an AK model, if all the remaining tasks can be automated at low cost, and this can produce at least accelerating growth if the a_{it} can be somewhat improved but, again, in the end we are still held back by the productivity growth in the essential things that we are worst at improving. In fact, Moore's Law, which stands in part behind the rise of artificial intelligence, may be a cautionary tale along these lines. Computation, in the sense of arithmetic operations per second, has improved at mind-boggling rates and is now mind-bogglingly fast. Yet economic growth has not accelerated, and may even be in decline.

Through the lens of essential tasks, the ultimate constraint on growth will then be the capacity for progress at the really hard problems. These constraints may in turn be determined less by the limits of cognition (i.e., traditionally human intelligence limits, which an AI superintelligence may overcome) and more by the limits of natural laws, such as the second law of thermodynamics, which constrain critical processes.[17]

Creative Destruction

Moving away from technological limits per se, the positive effect of AI (and super AI) on productivity growth may be counteracted by another

---

16. This ratio compares Beltchley Park's Colossus, the 1943 vacuum tube machine that made 5×10^5 floating point operations per second, with the Sunway TaihuLight computer, which in 2016 peaked at 9×10^{16} operations per second.

17. Returning to example 4 above, note that equation (42) assumes that all physical constraints can be overcome by superintelligence. However, one might alternatively specify $\max(A_{\text{physical}}) = c$, representing a firm physical constraint.

effect working through creative destruction and its impact on innovation incentives. Thus in the appendix we develop a Schumpeterian model in which: (a) new innovations displace old innovations; and (b) innovations involves two steps, where the first step can be performed by machines but the second step requires human inputs to research. In a singularity-like limit where successive innovations come with no time in between, the private returns to human research and development (R&D) falls down to zero and as a result innovation and growth taper off. More generally, the faster the first step of each successive innovation as a result of AI, the lower the return to human investment in stage-two innovation, which in turn counteracts the direct effect of AI and super-AI on innovation-led growth pointed out above.

9.4.3   Some Additional Thoughts

We conclude this section with additional thoughts on how AI and its potential singularity effects might affect growth and convergence.

A first idea is that new AI technologies might allow imitation/learning of frontier technologies to become automated. That is, machines would figure out in no time how to imitate frontier technologies. Then a main source of divergence might become credit constraints, to the extent that those might prevent poorer countries or regions from acquiring superintelligent machines whereas developed economies could afford such machines. Thus one could imagine a world in which advanced countries concentrate all their research effort on developing new product lines (i.e., on frontier innovation) whereas poorer countries would devote a positive and increasing fraction of their research labor on learning about the new frontier technologies as they cannot afford the corresponding AI devices. Overall, one would expect an increasing degree of divergence worldwide.

A second conjecture is that, anticipating the effect of AI on the scope and speed of imitation, potential innovators may become reluctant to patent their inventions, fearing that the disclosure of new knowledge in the patent would lead to straight imitation. Trade secrets may then become the norm, instead of patenting. Or alternatively innovations would become like what financial innovations are today, that is, knowledge creation with huge network effects and with very little scope for patenting.

Finally, with imitation and learning being performed mainly by super-machines in developed economies, then research labor would become (almost) entirely devoted to product innovation, increasing product variety or inventing new products (new product lines) to replace existing products. Then, more than ever, the decreasing returns to digging deeper into an existing line of product would be offset by the increased potential for discovering new product lines. Overall, ideas might end up being easier to find, if only because of the singularity effect of AI on recombinant idea-based growth.

9.5   Artificial Intelligence, Firms, and Economic Growth

To this point, we have linked artificial intelligence to economic growth emphasizing features of the production functions of goods and ideas. However, the advance of artificial intelligence and its macroeconomic effects will depend on the potentially rich behavior of firms. We have introduced one such view already in the prior section, where considerations of creative destruction provide an incentive-oriented mechanism that may be an important obstacle to singularities. In this section, we consider firms' incentives and behavior more generally to further outline the AI research agenda. We examine potentially first-order issues that emerge when introducing market structure, sectoral differences, and organizational considerations within firms.

9.5.1   Market Structure

Existing work on competition and innovation-led growth points to the existence of two counteracting effects: on the one hand, more intense product market competition (or imitation threat) induces neck-and-neck firms at the technological frontier to innovate in order to escape competition; on the other hand, more intense competition tends to discourage firms behind the current technology frontier to innovate and thereby catch-up with frontier firms. Which of these two effects dominates, in turn, depends upon the degree of competition in the economy, and/or upon how advanced the economy is. While the escape competition effect tends to dominate at low initial levels of competition and in more advanced economies, the discouragement effect may dominate for higher levels of competition or in less advanced economies.[18]

Can AI affect innovation and growth through potential effects it might have on product market competition? A first potential channel is that AI may facilitate the imitation of existing products and technologies. Here we particularly have in mind the idea that AI might facilitate reverse engineering, and thereby facilitate the imitation of leading products and technologies. If we follow the inverted-U logic of Aghion et al. (2005), in sectors with initially low levels of imitation, some AI-induced reverse engineering might stimulate innovation by virtue of the escape-competition effect. But too high (or too immediate) an imitation threat will end up discouraging innovation as potential innovators will face excessive expropriation. A related implication of AI is that its introduction may speed up the process by which each individual sector becomes congested over time. This in turn may translate into faster decreasing returns to innovating within any existing sector (see Bloom et al. 2014), but by the same token it may induce potential innovators to devote more resources to inventing new lines in

18. For example, see Aghion and Howitt (1992) and Aghion et al. (2005).

order to escape competition and imitation within current lines. The overall effect on aggregate growth will in turn depend upon the relative contributions of within-sector secondary innovation and fundamental innovation aimed at creating new product lines (see Aghion and Howitt 1996) to the overall growth process.

Another channel whereby AI and the digital revolution may affect innovation and growth through affecting the degree of product market competition is in relation to the development of platforms or networks. A main objective of platform owners is to maximize the number of participants to the platform on both sides of the corresponding two-sided markets. For example, Google enjoys a monopoly position as a search platform, Facebook enjoys a similar position as a social network with more than 1.7 billion users worldwide each month, and so does Booking.com for hotel reservations (more than 75 percent of hotel clients resort to this network). And the same goes for Uber in the area of individual transportation, Airbnb for apartment renting, and so on. The development of networks may in turn affect competition in at least two ways. First, data access may act as an entry barrier for creating new competing networks, although it did not prevent Facebook from developing a new network after Google. More important, networks can take advantage of their monopoly positions to impose large fees on market participants (and they do), which may discourage innovation by these participants, whether they are firms or self-employed individuals.

In the end, whether escape competition or discouragement effects dominate will depend upon the type of sector (frontier/neck-and-neck or older/lagging), the extent to which AI facilitates reverse engineering and imitation, and upon competition and/or regulatory policies aimed at protecting intellectual property rights while lowering entry barriers. Recent empirical work (e.g., see Aghion, Howitt, and Prantl 2015) points at patent protection and competition policy being complementary in inducing innovation and productivity growth. It would be interesting to explore how AI affects this complementarity between the two policies.

9.5.2   Sectoral Reallocation

A recent paper by Baslandze (2016) argues that the information technology (IT) revolution has produced a major knowledge diffusion effect, which in turn has induced a major sectoral reallocation from sectors that do not rely much on technological externalities from other fields or sectors (e.g., textile industries) to sectors that rely more heavily on technological externalities from other sectors. Her argument, which we believe applies to AI, rests on the following two counteracting effects of IT on innovation incentives: on the one hand, firms can more easily learn from each other and therefore benefit more from knowledge diffusion from other firms and sectors; on the other hand, the improved access to knowledge from other firms and sectors induced by IT (or AI) increases the scope for business stealing.

In high-tech sectors where firms benefit more from external knowledge, the former effect—knowledge diffusion—will dominate whereas in sectors that do not rely much on external knowledge the latter effect—competition or business stealing—will tend to dominate. Indeed in more knowledge dependent sectors firms see both their productive and their innovative capabilities increase to a larger extent than the capabilities of firms in sectors that rely less on knowledge from other sectors.

It then immediately follows that the diffusion of IT—and AI for our purpose—should lead to an expansion of sectors that rely more on external knowledge (in which the knowledge diffusion effect dominates) at the expense of the more traditional (and more self-contained) sectors where firms do not rely as much on external knowledge.

Thus, in addition to its direct effects on firms' innovation and production capabilities, the introduction of IT and AI involve a knowledge diffusion effect that is augmented by a sectoral reallocation effect at the benefit of high-tech sectors that rely more on knowledge externalities from other fields and sectors. The positive knowledge diffusion effect is partly counteracted by the negative business-stealing effect (Baslandze shows that the latter effect has been large in the United States and that without it the IT revolution would have yet induced a much higher acceleration in productivity growth for the whole US economy).

Based on her analysis, Baslandze (2016) responds to Gordon (2012) with the argument that Gordon only took into account the direct effect of IT and not its indirect knowledge diffusion and sectoral reallocation effects on aggregate productivity growth.

We believe that the same points can be made with respect to AI instead of IT, and one could try and reproduce Baslandze's calibration exercise to assess the relative importance of the direct and indirect effects of AI, to decompose the indirect effect of AI into its positive knowledge diffusion effect and its potentially negative competition effect, and to assess the extent to which AI affects overall productivity growth through its effects on sectoral reallocation.

9.5.3   Organization

How should we expect firms to adapt their internal organization, the skill composition of their workforce and their wage policies to the introduction of AI? In his recent book, *Economics for the Common Good*, Tirole (2017) spells out what one may consider to be "common wisdom" expectations on firms and AI. Namely, introducing AI should: (a) increase the wage gap between skilled and unskilled labor, as the latter is presumably more substitutable to AI than the former; (b) the introduction of AI allows firms to automate and dispense with middle men performing monitoring tasks (in other words, firms should become flatter, that is, with higher spans of control); (c) should encourage self-employment by making it easier for individuals to build their reputation. Let us revisit these various points in more detail. AI, skills, and wage premia: on AI and the increased gap between skilled and unskilled wage, the prediction brings us back to Krusell et al. (2000) based on an aggregate production function in which physical equipment is more substitutable to unskilled labor than to skilled labor, these authors argued that the observed acceleration in the decline of the relative price of production equipment goods since the mid-1970s could account for most of the variation in the college premium over the past twenty-five years. In other words, the rise in the college premium could largely be attributed to an increase in the rate of (capital-embodied) skill-biased technical progress. And, presumably, AI is an extreme form of capital-embodied, skill-biased technical change, as robots substitute for unskilled labor but require skilled labor to be installed and exploited. However, recent work by Aghion et al. (2017) suggests that while the prediction of a premium to skills may hold at the macroeconomic level, it perhaps misses important aspects of firms' internal organization and that the organization itself may evolve as a result of introducing AI. More specifically, Aghion et al. (2017) use matched employer-employee data from the United Kingdom, which they augment with information on R&D expenditures, to analyze the relationship between innovativeness and average wage income across firms.

A first, not surprising, finding is that more R&D-intensive firms pay higher wages on average and employ a higher fraction of high-occupation workers than less R&D-intensive firms (see figure 9.4).

This, in turn, is perfectly in line with the above prediction (a) but also with prediction (b) as it suggests that more innovative (or more "frontier") firms rely more on outsourcing for low-occupation tasks. However, a more surprising finding in Aghion et al. (2017) is that lower-skill (lower occupation) workers benefit more from working in more R&D-intensive firms (relative to working in a firm that does no R&D) than higher-skill workers. This finding is summarized by figure 9.5. In that figure, we first see that higher-skill workers earn more than lower-skill workers in any firm no matter how R&D intensive that firm is (the high-skill wage curve always lies strictly above the middle-skill curve, which itself always lies above the lower-skill curve). But, more interestingly, the lower-skill curve is steeper than the middle-skill and higher-skill curve. But the slope of each of these curves precisely reflects the premium for workers with the corresponding skill level to working in a more innovative firm.

Similarly, we should expect more AI-intensive firms to: (a) employ a higher fraction of (more highly paid) high-skill workers, (b) outsource an increasing fraction of low-occupation tasks, and (c) give a higher premium to those low-occupation workers they keep within the firm (unless we take the extreme view that all the functions to be performed by low-occupation workers could be performed by robots).

To rationalize the above findings and these latter predictions, let us fol-

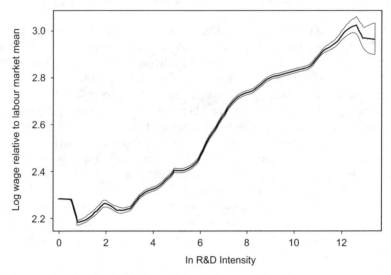

kernel = epanechnikov, degree = 0, bandwidth = .31, pwidth = .47

Fig. 9.4 Log hourly wage and R&D intensity

Source: Aghion et al. (2017).

Note: This figure plots the logarithm of total hourly income against the logarithm of total R&D expenditures (intramural + extramural) per employee (R&D intensity).

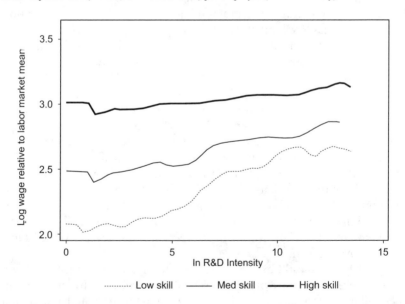

Fig. 9.5 Log hourly wage and R&D intensity

Source: Aghion et al. (2017).

Note: This figure plots the logarithm of total hourly income against the logarithm of total R&D expenditures (intramural + extramural) per employee (R&D intensity) for different skill groups.

low Aghion et al. (2017) who propose a model in which more innovative firms display a higher degree of complementarity between low-skill workers and the other production factors (capital and high-skill labor) within the firm. Another feature of their model is that high-occupation employees' skills are less firm-specific than low-skill workers: namely, if the firm was to replace a high-skill worker by another high-skill worker, the downside risk would be limited by the fact that higher-skill employees are typically more educated employees, whose market value is largely determined by their education and accumulated reputation, whereas low-occupation employees' quality is more firm-specific. This model is meant to capture the idea that low-occupation workers can have a potentially more damaging effect on the firm's value if the firm is more innovative (or more AI intensive for our purpose).

In particular, an important difference with the common wisdom, is that here innovativeness (or AI intensity) impacts on the organizational form of the firm and in particular on complementarity or substitutability between workers with different skill levels within the firm, whereas the common wisdom view takes this complementarity or substitutability as given. Think of a low-occupation employee (e.g., an assistant) who shows outstanding ability, initiative, and trustworthiness. That employee performs a set of tasks for which it might be difficult or too costly to hire a high-skill worker; furthermore, and perhaps more important, the low-occupation employee is expected to stay longer in the firm than higher-skill employees, which in turn encourages the firm to invest more in trust-building and firm-specific human capital and knowledge. Overall, such low-occupation employees can make a big difference to the firm's performance.

This alternative view of AI and firms is consistent with the work of theorists of the firm such as Luis Garicano. Thus in Garicano (2000) downstream, low-occupation employees are consistently facing new problems; among these new problems they sort out are those they can solve themselves (the easier problems) and the more difficult questions they pass on to upstream—higher-skill—employees in the firm's hierarchy. Presumably, the more innovative or more AI-intensive the firm is, the harder it is to solve the more difficult questions, and therefore the more valuable the time of upstream high-occupation employees becomes; this in turn makes it all the more important to employ downstream, low-occupation employees with higher ability to make sure that less problems will be passed on to the upstream, high-occupation employees within the firm so that these high-occupation employees will have more free time to concentrate on solving the most difficult tasks. Another interpretation of the higher complementarity between low-occupation and high-occupation employees in more innovative (or more AI-intensive) firms, is that the potential loss from unreliable low-occupation employees is bigger in such firms: hence the need to select out those low-occupation employees that are not reliable.

This higher complementarity between low-occupation workers and other production factors in more innovative (or more AI-intensive) firms in turn increases the bargaining power of low-occupation workers within the firm (it increases their Shapley Value if we follow Stole and Zwiebel [1996]). This in turn explains the higher payoff for low-occupation workers. It also predicts that job turnover should be lower (tenure should be higher) among low-occupation workers who work for more innovative (more AI-intensive) firms than for low-occupation workers who work for less innovative firms, whereas the turnover difference should be less between high-occupation workers employed by these two types of firms. This additional prediction is also confronted to the data in Aghion et al. (2017).

Note that so far R&D investment has been used as the measure of the firm's innovativeness or frontierness. We would like to test the same predictions, but using explicit measures of AI intensity as the RHS variable in the regressions (investment in robots, reliance on digital platforms). Artificial intelligence and firm organizational form: recent empirical studies (e.g., see Bloom et al. 2014) have shown that the IT revolution has led firms to eliminate middle-range jobs and move toward flatter organizational structure. The development of AI should reinforce that trend, while perhaps also reducing the ratio to low-occupation to high-occupation jobs within firms as we argued above.

A potentially helpful framework to think about firms' organizational forms is Aghion and Tirole (1997). There, a principal can decide whether or not to delegate authority to a downstream agent. She can delegate authority in two ways: (a) by formally allocating control rights to the agent (in that case we say that the principal delegates formal authority to the agent); or (b) informally through the design of the organization, for example, by increasing the span of control or by engaging in multiple activities: these devices enable the principal to commit to leave initiative to the agent (in that case we say that the principal delegates real authority to the agent). And agents' initiative particularly matters if the firm needs to be innovative, which is particularly the case for more frontier firms in their sectors. Whether she decides to delegate formal or only real authority to her agent, the principal faces the following trade-off: more delegation of authority to the agent induces the agent to take more initiative; on the other hand, this implies that the principal will lose some control over the firm, and therefore face the possibility that suboptimal decisions (from her viewpoint) be taken more often. Which of these two counteracting effects of delegation dominates, will in turn depend upon the degree of congruence between the principal's and the agent's preference, but also about the principal's ability to reverse suboptimal decisions.

How should the introduction of AI affect this trade-off between loss of control and initiative? To the extent that AI makes it easier for the principal to monitor the agent, more delegation of authority will be required in order to still elicit initiative from the agent. The incentive to delegate more authority to downstream agents, will also be enhanced by the fact that with AI, suboptimal decision-making by downstream agents can be more easily corrected and reversed: in other words, AI should reduce the loss of control involved in delegating authority downstream. A third reason for why AI may encourage decentralization in decision-making has to do with coordination costs: namely, it may be costly for the principal to delegate decision-making to downstream units if this prevents these units from coordinating within the firm (see Hart and Holmstrom 2010). But here again, AI may help overcome this problem by reducing the monitoring costs between the principal and its multiple downstream units, and thereby induce more decentralization of authority.

More delegation of authority in turn can be achieved through various means: in particular, by eliminating intermediate layers in the firm's hierarchy, by turning downstream units into profit centers or fully independent firms, or through horizontal integration that will commit the principal to spending time on other activities. Overall, one can imagine that the development of AI in more frontier sectors should lead to larger and more horizontally integrated firms, to flatter firms with more profit centers, which outsource an increasing number of tasks to independent self-employed agents. The increased reliance on self-employed independent agents will in turn be facilitated by the fact that, as well explained by Tirole (2017), AI helps agents to quickly develop individual reputations. This brings us to the third aspect of AI and organizations on self-employment. Artificial intelligence and self-employment: as stressed above, AI favors the development of self-employment for at least two reasons: first, it may induce AI intensive firms to outsource tasks, starting with low-occupation tasks; second, it makes it easier for independent agents to develop individual reputations. Does that imply that AI should result in the end of large integrated firms with individuals only interacting with each other through platforms? And which agents are more likely to become self-employed?

On the first question: Tirole (2017) provides at least two reasons for why firms should survive the introduction of AI. First, some activities involve large sunk costs and/or large fixed costs that cannot be borne by a single individual. Second, some activities involve a level of risk-taking that also may not be borne by one single agent. To this we should add the transaction cost argument that vertical integration facilitates relation-specific investments in situations of contractual incompleteness: Can we truly imagine that AI will by itself fully overcome contractual incompleteness?

On the second question: our above discussion suggests that low-skill activities involving limited risk and for which AI helps develop individual reputations (hotel or transport services, health assistance to the elder and/or handicapped, catering services, house cleaning) are primary candidates for increasingly becoming self-employment jobs as AI diffuses in the economy.

And indeed recent studies by Saez (2010), Chetty et al. (2011), and Kleven and Waseem (2013) point to low-income individuals being more responsive to tax or regulatory changes aimed at facilitating self-employment. Natural extensions of these studies would be to explore the extent to which such regulatory changes have had more impact in sectors with higher AI penetration.

The interplay between AI and self-employment also involves potentially interesting dynamic aspects. Thus it might be worth looking at whether self-employment helps individuals accumulate human capital (or at least protects them against the risk of human capital depreciation following the loss of a formal job), and the more so in sectors with higher AI penetration. Also interesting would be to look at how the interplay between self-employment and AI is itself affected by government policies and institutions, and here we have primarily in mind education policy and social or income insurance for the self-employed. How do these policies affect the future performance of currently self-employed individuals, and are they at all complemented by the introduction of AI? In particular, do currently self-employed individuals move back to working for larger firms, and how does the probability of moving back to a regular employment vary with AI, government policy, and the interplay between the two? Presumably, a more performing basic education system and a more comprehensive social insurance system should both encourage self-employed individuals to better take advantage of AI opportunities and support to accumulate skills and reputation and thereby improve their future career prospects. On the other hand, some may argue that AI will have a discouraging effect on self-employed individuals, if it lowers their prospects of ever reintegrating a regular firm in the future, as more AI-intensive firms reduce their demand for low-occupation workers.

9.6   Evidence on Capital Shares and Automation to Date

Models that conceptualize AI as a force of increasing automation suggest that an upswing in automation may be seen in the factor payments going to capital—the capital share. In recent years, the rise in the capital share in the United States and around the world has been a central topic of research. For example, see Karabarbounis and Neiman (2013), Elsby, Hobijn, and Şahin (2013), and Kehrig and Vincent (2017). In this section, we explore this evidence, first for industries within the United States, second for the motor vehicles industry in the United States and Europe, and finally by looking at how changes in capital shares over time correlate with the adoption of robots.

Figure 9.6 reports capital shares by industry from the US KLEMS data of Jorgenson, Ho, and Samuels (forthcoming); shares are smoothed using an HP filter with smoothing parameter 400 to focus on the medium- to long-run trends. It is well-known that the aggregate capital share has increased since at least the year 2000 in the US economy. Figure 9.6 shows that this aggregate trend holds up across a large number of sectors, including agriculture, construction, chemicals, computer equipment manufacturing, motor vehicles, publishing, telecommunications, and wholesale and retail trade. The main place where one does not see this trend is in services, including education, government, and health. In those sectors, the capital share is relatively stable or perhaps increasing slightly since 1990. But the big trend one sees in these data from services is a large downward trend between 1950 and 1980. It would be interesting to know more about what accounts for this trend.

While the facts are broadly consistent with automation (or an increase in automation), it is also clear that capital and labor shares involve many other economic forces as well. For example, Autor et al. (2017) suggest that a composition effect involving a shift toward superstar firms with high capital shares underlies the industry trends. That paper and Barkai (2017) propose that a rise in industry concentration and markups may underlie some of the increases in the capital share. Changes in unionization over time may be another contributing factor to the dynamics of factor shares. This is all to say that a much more careful analysis of factor shares and automation is required before any conclusions can be drawn.

Keeping that important caveat in mind, figure 9.7 shows evidence on the capital share in the manufacturing of transportation equipment for the United States and several European countries. As Acemoglu and Restrepo (2017) note (more on this below), the motor vehicles industry is by far the industry that has invested most heavily in industrial robots during the past two decades, so this industry is particularly interesting from the standpoint of automation.

The capital share in transportation equipment (including motor vehicles, but also aircraft and shipbuilding) shows a large increase in the United States, France, Germany, and Spain in recent decades. Interestingly, Italy and the United Kingdom exhibit declines in this capital share since 1995. The absolute level differences in the capital share for transportation equipment in 2014 are also interesting, ranging from a high of more than 50 percent in the United States to a low of around 20 percent in recent years in the United Kingdom. Clearly it would be valuable to better understand these large differences in levels and trends. Automation is likely only a part of the story.

Acemoglu and Restrepo (2017) use data from the International Federation of Robots to study the impact of the adoption of industrial robots on the US labor market. At the industry level, this data is available for the decade 2004 to 2014. Figure 9.8 shows data on the change in capital share by industry versus the change in the use of industrial robots.

Two main facts stand out from the figure. First, as noted earlier, the motor

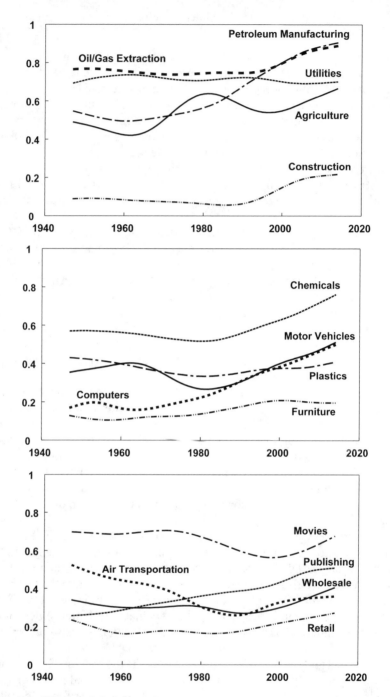

Fig. 9.6   US capital shares by industry

Source: The graph reports capital shares by industry from the U.S. KLEMS data of Jorgenson, Ho, and Samuels (2017).

Note: Shares are smoothed using an HP filter with smoothing parameter 400.

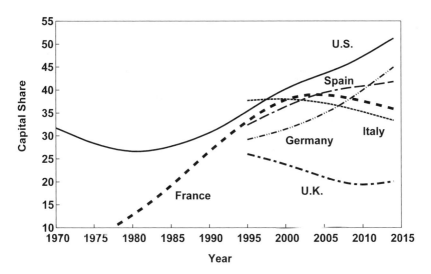

Fig. 9.7 **The capital share for transportation equipment**

Sources: Data for the European countries are from the EU-KLEMS project (http://www
.euklems.net/) for the "transportation equipment" sector, which includes motor vehicles, but
also aerospace and shipbuilding; see Jägger (2016). US data are from Jorgenson, Ho, and
Samuels (2017) for motor vehicles.

Note: Shares are smoothed using an HP filter with smoothing parameter 400.

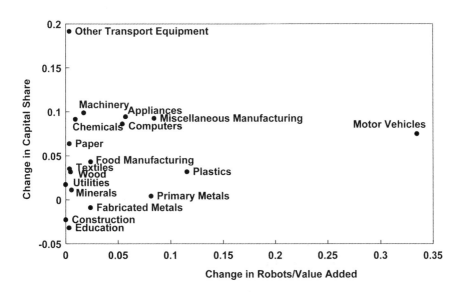

Fig. 9.8 **Capital shares and robots, 2004–2014**

Sources: The graph plots the change in the capital share from Jorgenson, Ho, and Samuels
(2017) against the change in the stock of robots relative to value added using the robots data
from Acemoglu and Restrepo (2017).

vehicles industry is by far the largest adopter of industrial robots. For example, more than 56 percent of new industrial robots purchased in 2014 were installed in the motor vehicles industry, the next highest share was under 12 percent in computers and electronic products.

Second, there is little correlation between automation as measured by robots and the change in the capital share between 2004 and 2014. The overall level of industrial robot penetration is relatively small, and as we discussed earlier, other forces including changes in market power, unionization, and composition effects are moving capital shares around in a way that makes it hard for a simple data plot to disentangle.

Graetz and Michaels (2017) conduct a more formal econometric study using the EU-KLEMS data and the International Federation of Robotics data from 1993 until 2007, studying the effect of robot adoption on wages and productivity growth. Similar to what we show in figure 9.8, they find no systematic relationship between robot adoption and factor shares. They do suggest that adoption is associated with boosts to labor productivity.

9.7   Conclusion

In this chapter, we discussed potential implications of AI for the growth process. We began by introducing AI in the production function of goods and services and tried to reconcile evolving automation with the observed stability in the capital share and per capita GDP growth over the last century. Our model, which introduces Baumol's "cost disease" insight into Zeira's model of automation, generates a rich set of possible outcomes. We thus derived sufficient conditions under which one can get overall balanced growth with a constant capital share that stays well below 100 percent, even with nearly complete automation. Essentially, Baumol's cost disease leads to a decline in the share of GDP associated with manufacturing or agriculture (once they are automated), but this is balanced by the increasing fraction of the economy that is automated over time. The labor share remains substantial because of Baumol's insight: growth is determined not by what we are good at but rather by what is essential and yet hard to improve. We also saw how this model can generate a prolonged period with high capital share and relatively low aggregate economic growth while automation keeps pushing ahead.

Next, we speculated on the effects of introducing AI in the production technology for new ideas. Artificial intelligence can potentially increase growth, either temporarily or permanently, depending on precisely how it is introduced. It is possible that ongoing automation can obviate the role of population growth in generating exponential growth as AI increasingly replaces people in generating ideas. Notably, in this chapter, we have taken automation to be exogenous and the incentives for introducing AI in various places clearly can have first-order effects. Exploring the details of endogenous automation and AI in this setup is a crucial direction for further research.

We then discussed the (theoretical) possibility that AI could generate some form of a singularity, perhaps even leading the economy to achieve infinite income in finite time. If the elasticity of substitution in combining tasks is less than one, this seems to require that all tasks be automated. But with Cobb-Douglas production, a singularity could occur even with less than full automation because the nonrivalry of knowledge gives rise to increasing returns. Nevertheless, here too the Baumol theme remains relevant: even if many tasks are automated, growth may remain limited due to areas that remain essential yet are hard to improve. Thus in the appendix we show that if some steps in the innovation process require human R&D, then super AI may end up slowing or even ending growth by exacerbating business-stealing, which in turn discourages human investments in innovation. Such possibilities, as well as other implications of "super-AI" (for example for cross-country convergence and property right protection), remain promising directions for future research.

The chapter next considered how firms may influence, and be influenced by, the advance of artificial intelligence, with further implications for understanding macroeconomic outcomes. We considered diverse issues of market structure, sectoral reallocations, and firms' organizational structure. Among the insights here we see that AI may in part discourage future innovation by speeding up imitation; similarly, rapid creative destruction, by limiting the returns to an innovation, may impose its own limit on the growth process. From an organizational perspective, we also conjectured that while AI should be skill-biased for the economy as a whole, more AI-intensive firms are likely to: (a) outsource a higher fraction of low-occupation tasks to other firms, and (b) pay a higher premium to the low-occupation workers they keep inside the firm.

Finally, we examined sectoral-level evidence regarding the evolution of capital shares in tandem with automation. Consistent with increases in the aggregate capital share, the capital share also appears to be rising in many sectors (especially outside services), which is broadly consistent with an automation story. At the same time, evidence linking these patterns to specific measures of automation at the sectoral level appears weak, and overall there are many economic forces at work in the capital share trends. Developing sharper measures of automation and investigating the role of automation in the capital share dynamics are additional, important avenues for further research.

Appendix

Artificial Intelligence in a Schumpeterian Model with Creative Destruction

In this appendix we describe and model a situation in which superintelligence (or "super-AI") may kill growth because it exacerbates creative destruction and thereby discourages any human investment into R&D. We first lay out a basic version of the Schumpeterian growth model. We then extend the model to introduce AI in the innovation technology.

Basics

Time is continuous and individuals are infinitely lived, there is a mass L of individuals who can decide between working in research or in production. Final output is produced according to

$$y = Ax^{\alpha},$$

where x is the flow of intermediate input and A is a productivity parameter measuring the quality of intermediate input x. Each innovation results in a new technology for producing final output and a new intermediate good to implement the new technology. It augments current productivity by the multiplicative factor $\gamma > 1$: $A_{t+1} = \gamma A_t$. Innovations in turn are the (random) outcome of research, and are assumed to arrive discretely with Poisson rate $\lambda.n$ where n is the current flow of research.

In a steady state the allocation of labor between research and manufacturing remains constant over time, and is determined by the arbitrage equation

(9A.1) $\omega = \lambda \gamma v,$

where the LHS of (A) is the productivity-adjusted wage rate $\omega = (w/A)$ which a worker earns by working in the manufacturing sector and $\lambda \gamma v$ is the expected reward from investing one unit flow of labor in research. The productivity-adjusted value v of an innovation is determined by the Bellman equation

$$rv = \tilde{\pi}(\omega) - \lambda nv,$$

where $\tilde{\pi}(\omega)$ denotes the productivity-adjusted flow of monopoly profits accruing to a successful innovator and where the term $(-\lambda nv)$ corresponds to the capital loss involved in being replaced by a subsequent innovator.

The above arbitrage equation, which can be reexpressed as

(9A.2) $\omega = \lambda \gamma \dfrac{\tilde{\pi}(\omega)}{r + \lambda n},$

together with the labor market-clearing equation

(9A.3) $$\tilde{x}(\omega) + n = L,$$

where $\tilde{x}(\omega)$ is the manufacturing demand for labor, jointly determine the steady-state amount of research n as a function of the parameters $\lambda, \gamma, L, r, \alpha$.

The average growth rate is equal to the size of each step, $\ln\gamma$, times the average number of innovations per unit of time, λn that is, $g = \lambda n \ln\gamma$.

A Schumpeterian Model with Artificial Intelligence

As before, there are L workers who can engage either in production of existing intermediate goods or in research aimed at discovering new intermediate goods. Each intermediate good is linked to a particular GPT. We follow Helpman and Trajtenberg (1994) in supposing that before any of the intermediate goods associated with GPT can be used profitably in the final goods sector, some minimal number of them must be available. We lose nothing essential by supposing that this minimal number is one. Once the good has been invented, its discoverer profits from a patent on its exclusive use in production, exactly as in the basic Schumpeterian model reviewed earlier.

Thus the difference between this model and the above basic model is that now the discovery of a new generation of intermediate goods comes in *two* stages. First a new GPT must come, and then the intermediate good must be invented that implements that GPT. Neither can come before the other. You need to see the GPT before knowing what sort of good will implement it, and people need to see the previous GPT in action before anyone can think of a new one. For simplicity we assume that no one directs R&D toward the discovery of a GPT. Instead, the discovery arrives as a serendipitous by-product of the collective experience of using the previous one.

Thus the economy will pass through a sequence of cycles, each having two phases; GPT_i arrives at time T_i. At that time the economy enters phase 1 of the ith cycle. During phase 1, the amount n of labor is devoted to research. Phase 2 begins at time $T_i + \Delta_i$ when this research discovers an intermediate good to implement GPT_i. During Phase 2 all labor is allocated to manufacturing until GPT_{i+1} arrives, at which time the next cycle begins.

A steady-state equilibrium is one in which people choose to do the same amount of research each time the economy is in Phase 1, that is, where n is constant from one GPT to the next. As before, we can solve for the equilibrium value of n using a research-arbitrage equation and a labor market-equilibrium curve. Let ω_j be the wage, and v_j the expected present value of the incumbent intermediate monopolist's future profits, when the economy is in phase j, each divided by the productivity parameter A of the GPT currently in use. In a steady state these productivity-adjusted variables will all be independent of which GPT is currently in use.

Because research is conducted in Phase 1 but pays off when the economy enters into Phase 2 with a productivity parameter raised by the factor γ, the usual arbitrage condition must hold in order for there to be a positive level of research in the economy

$$\omega_1 = \lambda\gamma v_2.$$

Suppose that once we are in Phase 2, the new GPT is delivered by a Poisson process with a constant arrival rate equal to m. Then the value of v_2 is determined by the Bellman equation

$$rv_2 = \tilde{\pi}(\omega_2) + \mu(v_1 - v_2).$$

By analogous reasoning, we have

$$rv_1 = \tilde{\pi}(\omega_1) - \lambda n v_1.$$

Combining the above equations yields the research-arbitrage equation

$$\omega_1 = \lambda\gamma\left[\tilde{\pi}(\omega_2) + \frac{\mu\tilde{\pi}(\omega_1)}{r + \lambda n}\right] / \left[r + \mu\right].$$

Because no one does research in Phase 2, we know that the value of ω_2 is determined independently of research, by the market-clearing condition $L = x(\omega_2)$ Thus we can take this value as given and regard the last equation as determining ω_1 as a function of n The value of n is determined, as usual, by this equation together with the labor-market equation

$$L - n = \tilde{x}(\omega_1).$$

The average growth rate will be the frequency of innovations times the size lng, for exactly the same reason as in the basic model. The frequency, however, is determined a little differently than before because the economy must pass through *two* phases. An innovation is implemented each time a full cycle is completed. The frequency with which this happens is the inverse of the expected length of a complete cycle. This in turn is just the expected length of Phase 1 plus the expected length of Phase 2:

$$1/\lambda n + 1/\mu = \frac{\mu + \lambda n}{\mu\lambda n}.$$

Thus we have the growth equation

$$g = \ln\gamma\frac{\mu\lambda n}{\mu + \lambda n},$$

where n satisfies

$$f(L - n) = \lambda\gamma\left[f(L) + \frac{\mu\tilde{\pi}(f(L - n))}{r + \lambda n}\right] / \left[r + \mu\right]$$

with

$$f(.) = \tilde{x}^{-1}(.)$$

as a decreasing function of its argument.

We are interested in the effect of μ on g and in particular by what happens when $\mu \to \infty$ as a result of AI in the production of ideas. Obviously, $n \to 0$ when $\mu \to \infty$ Thus $E = 1/\lambda n + 1/\mu \to \infty$ and therefore

$$g = \ln\gamma.\frac{1}{E} \to 0.$$

In other words, we have described and modeled a situation where superintelligence exacerbates creative destruction to a point that all human investments in to R&D are being deterred and as a result growth tapers off. However, two remarks can be made at this stage:

Remark 1: Here, we have assumed that the second innovation stage requires human research only. If instead AI allowed that stage to also be performed by machines, then AI will no longer taper off and can again become explosive as in our core analysis.

Remark 2: We took automation to be completely exogenous and costless. But suppose instead that it costs money to make μ increase to infinity: then, if creative destruction grows without limit as in our analysis above, the incentive to pay for increasing μ will go down to zero since the complementary human R&D for the stage-two innovation is also going to zero. But this goes against having $\mu \to \infty$ and therefore against having AI kill the growth process.[19]

References

Acemoglu, Daron, and David Autor. 2011. "Skills, Tasks and Technologies: Implications for Employment and Earnings." In *Handbook of Labor Economics*, vol. 4, edited by O. Ashenfelter and D. Card, 1043–171. Amsterdam: Elsevier.

Acemoglu, Daron, and Pascual Restrepo. 2016. "The Race between Man and Machine: Implications of Technology for Growth, Factor Shares and Employment." NBER Working Paper no. 22252, Cambridge, MA.

———. 2017. "Robots and Jobs: Evidence from US Labor Markets." NBER Working Paper no. 23285, Cambridge, MA.

Aghion, Philippe, and Peter Howitt. 1992. "A Model of Growth through Creative Destruction." *Econometrica* 60 (2): 323–51.

———. 1996. "Research and Development in the Growth Process." *Journal of Economic Growth* 1 (1): 49–73.

Aghion, Philippe, Peter Howitt, and Susanne Prantl. 2015. "Patent Rights, Product Market Reforms, and Innovation." *Journal of Economic Growth* 20 (3): 223–62.

Aghion, Philippe, Antonin Bergeaud, Richard Blundell, and Rachel Griffith. 2017. "The Innovation Premium to Low Skill Jobs." Unpublished manuscript.

Aghion, Philippe, Nick Bloom, Richard Blundell, Rachel Griffith, and Peter Howitt.

---

19. Of course, one could counterargue that super AI becomes increasingly costless in generating new innovation, in which case μ would again go to infinity and growth would again go down to zero.

2005. "Competition and Innovation: An Inverted-U Relationship." *Quarterly Journal of Economics* 120 (2): 701–28.

Aghion, Philippe, and Jean Tirole. 1997. "Formal and Real Authority in Organizations." *Journal of Political Economy* 105 (1): 1–29.

Agrawal, Ajay, John McHale, and Alex Oettl. 2017. "Artificial Intelligence and Recombinant Growth." Unpublished manuscript, University of Toronto.

Alvarez-Cuadrado, Francisco, Ngo Long, and Markus Poschke. 2017. "Capital-Labor Substitution, Structural Change and Growth." *Theoretical Economics* 12 (3): 1229–66.

Autor, David, David Dorn, Lawrence F. Katz, Christina Patterson, and John Van Reenen. 2017. "The Fall of the Labor Share and the Rise of Superstar Firms." NBER Working Paper no. 23396, Cambridge, MA.

Autor, David H., Frank Levy, and Richard J. Murnane. 2003. "The Skill Content Of Recent Technological Change: An Empirical Exploration." *Quarterly Journal of Economics* 118 (4): 1279–333.

Barkai, Simcha. 2017. "Declining Labor and Capital Shares." Unpublished manuscript, University of Chicago.

Baslandze, Salome. 2016. "The Role of the IT Revolution in Knowledge Diffusion, Innovation and Reallocation." Meeting Paper no. 1488, Society for Economic Dynamics.

Baumol, William J. 1967. "Macroeconomics of Unbalanced Growth: The Anatomy of Urban Crisis." *American Economic Review* 57:415–26.

Bloom, Nicholas, Charles I. Jones, John Van Reenen, and Michael Webb. 2017. "Are Ideas Getting Harder to Find?" Unpublished manuscript, Stanford University.

Bloom, Nicholas, Luis Garicano, Raffaella Sadun, and John Van Reenen. 2014. "The Distinct Effects of Information Technology and Communication Technology on Firm Organization." *Management Science* 60 (12): 2859–85.

Boppart, Timo. 2014. "Structural Change and the Kaldor Facts in a Growth Model with Relative Price Effects and Non???Gorman Preferences." *Econometrica* 82:2167–96.

Chetty, Raj, John N. Friedman, Tore Olsen, and Luigi Pistaferri. 2011. "Adjustment Costs, Firm Responses, and Micro vs. Macro Labor Supply Elasticities: Evidence from Danish Tax Records." *Quarterly Journal of Economics* 126 (2): 749–804.

Comin, Diego, Danial Lashkari, and Marti Mestieri. 2015. "Structural Transformations with Long-Run Income and Price Effects." Unpublished manuscript, Dartmouth College.

Danaylov, Nikola. 2012. "17 Definitions of the Technological Singularity." Singularity Weblog. https://www.singularityweblog.com/17-definitions-of-the-technological-singularity/.

Elsby, Michael W. L., Bart Hobijn, and Ayşegül Şahin. 2013. "The Decline of the U.S. Labor Share." *Brookings Papers on Economic Activity* 2013 (2): 1–63.

Garicano, Luis. 2000. "Hierarchies and the Organization of Knowledge in Production." *Journal of Political Economy* 108 (5): 874–904.

Good, I. J. 1965. "Speculations Concerning the First Ultraintelligent Machine." *Advances in Computers* 6: 31–88.

Gordon, Robert J. 2012. "Is U.S. Economic Growth Over? Faltering Innovation Confronts the Six Headwinds." NBER Working Paper no. 18315, Cambridge, MA.

———. 2016. *The Rise and Fall of American Growth: The US Standard of Living since the Civil War*. Princeton, NJ: Princeton University Press.

Graetz, Georg, and Guy Michaels. 2017. "Robots at Work." Unpublished manuscript, London School of Economics.

Grossman, Gene M., Elhanan Helpman, Ezra Oberfield, and Thomas Sampson.

2017. "Balanced Growth Despite Uzawa." *American Economic Review* 107 (4): 1293–312.

Hart, Oliver, and Bengt Holmstrom. 2010. "A Theory of Firm Scope." *Quarterly Journal of Economics* 125 (2): 483–513.

Helpman, Elhanan, and Manuel Trajtenberg. 1998. "A Time to Sow and a Time to Reap: Growth Based on General Purpose Technologies." In *General Purpose Technologies and Economic Growth*, edited by E. Helpman. Cambridge, MA: MIT Press.

Hemous, David, and Morten Olsen. 2016. "The Rise of the Machines: Automation, Horizontal Innovation and Income Inequality." Unpublished manuscript, University of Zurich.

Herrendorf, Berthold, Richard Rogerson, and Akos Valentinyi. 2014. "Growth and Structural Transformation." In *Handbook of Economic Growth*, vol. 2, 855–941. Amsterdam: Elsevier.

Jägger, Kirsten. 2016. "EU KLEMS Growth and Productivity Accounts 2016 release-Description of Methodology and General Notes." The Conference Board Europe.

Jones, Benjamin F. 2009. "The Burden of Knowledge and the Death of the Renaissance Man: Is Innovation Getting Harder?" *Review of Economic Studies* 76 (1): 283–317.

Jones, Charles I. 1995. "R&D-Based Models of Economic Growth." *Journal of Political Economy* 103 (4): 759–84.

———. 2016. "The Facts of Economic Growth." In *Handbook of Macroeconomics*, vol. 2, 3–69 Amsterdam: Elselvier.

Jorgenson, Dale W., Mun S. Ho, and Jon D. Samuels. Forthcoming. "Educational Attainment and the Revival of U.S. Economic Growth." *Education, Skills, and Technical Change: Implications for Future US GDP Growth*, edited by Charles Hulten and Valerie Ramey. Chicago: University of Chicago Press.

Kaldor, Nicholas. 1961. "Capital Accumulation and Economic Growth." In *The Theory of Capital*, edited by F. A. Lutz and D. C. Hague, 177–222. New York: St. Martins Press.

Karabarbounis, Loukas, and Brent Neiman. 2013. "The Global Decline of the Labor Share." *Quarterly Journal of Economics* 129 (1): 61–103.

Kehrig, Matthias, and Nicolas Vincent. 2017. "Growing Productivity without Growing Wages: The Micro-Level Anatomy of the Aggregate Labor Share Decline." Unpublished manuscript, Duke University.

Kleven, Henrik J., and Mazhar Waseem. 2013. "Using Notches to Uncover Optimization Frictions and Structural Elasticities: Theory and Evidence from Pakistan." *Quarterly Journal of Economics* 128 (2): 669–723.

Kongsamut, Piyabha, Sergio Rebelo, and Danyang Xie. 2001. "Beyond Balanced Growth." *Review of Economic Studies* 68 (4): 869–82.

Kortum, Samuel S. 1997. "Research, Patenting, and Technological Change." *Econometrica* 65 (6): 1389–419.

Krusell, Per, Lee E. Ohanian, José-Víctor Ríos-Rull, and Giovanni L. Violante. 2000. "Capital-Skill Complementarity and Inequality: A Macroeconomic Analysis." *Econometrica* 68 (5): 1029–53.

Kurzweil, Ray. 2005. *The Singularity is Near*. New York: Penguin.

Legg, Shane, and Marcus Hutter. 2007. "A Collection of Definitions of Intelligence." *Frontiers in Artificial Intelligence and Application* 157 (2007): 17–24.

Manuelli, Rodolfo E., and Ananth Seshadri. 2014. "Frictionless Technology Diffusion: The Case of Tractors." *American Economic Review* 104 (4): 1368–91.

Ngai, L. Rachel, and Christopher A. Pissarides. 2007. "Structural Change in a Multisector Model of Growth." *American Economic Review* 97 (1): 429–43.

Nordhaus, William D. 2015. "Are We Approaching an Economic Singularity? Information Technology and the Future of Economic Growth." NBER Working Paper no. 21547, Cambridge, MA.

Peretto, Pietro F., and John J. Seater. 2013. "Factor-Eliminating Technical Change." *Journal of Monetary Economics* 60 (4): 459–73.

Romer, Paul M. 1990. "Endogenous Technological Change." *Journal of Political Economy* 98 (5): S71–102.

Saez, Emmanuel. 2010. "Do Taxpayers Bunch at Kink Points?" *American Economic Journal: Economic Policy* 2 (3): 180–212.

Solomonoff, R. J. 1985. "The Time Scale of Artificial Intelligence: Reflections on Social Effects." *Human Systems Management* 5:149–53.

Stole, Lars, and Jeffrey Zwiebel. 1996. "Organizational Design and Technology Choice under Intrafirm Bargaining." 86 (1): 195–222.

Tirole, Jean. 2017. *Economics for the Common Good*. Princeton, NJ: Princeton University Press.

Vinge, Vernor. 1993. "The Coming Technological Singularity: How to Survive in the Post-Human Era." In *Vision-21: Interdisciplinary Science and Engineering in the Era of Cyberspace*, 11–22. Proceedings of a Symposium Coauthored by the NASA Lewis Research Center and the Ohio Aerospace Institute Held in Westlake, Ohio, Mar. 30–31.

Webb, Michael, Greg Thornton, Sean Legassick, and Mustafa Suleyman. 2017. "What Does Artificial Intelligence Do?" Unpublished manuscript, Stanford University.

Weitzman, Martin L. 1998. "Recombinant Growth." *Quarterly Journal of Economics* 113:331–60.

Yudkowsky, Eliezer. 2013. "Intelligence Explosion Microeconomics." Technical Report no. 2013–1, Machine Intelligence Research Institution.

Zeira, Joseph. 1998. "Workers, Machines, and Economic Growth." *Quarterly Journal of Economics* 113 (4): 1091–117.

Comment   Patrick Francois

The political economy of artificial intelligence (AI) was not included as a topic in this conference, but political economy arose in a number of conversations, including my discussion of this immensely thought-provoking chapter. So I want to discuss it further here. It is important for two reasons. One, if the scientists' predictions pan out, we are on the cusp of a world where humans will be largely redundant as an economic input. How we manage the relationship between the haves (who own the key inputs) and the have-nots (who only own labor) is going to be a key aspect of societal health. Successful ones will be inclusive in the sense of sharing rents owned by the haves with the have-nots. This is quite obvious. Less obviously, I am going to argue that

Patrick Francois is a professor at the Vancouver School of Economics of the University of British Columbia and a senior fellow at the Canadian Institute for Advanced Research.

For acknowledgments, sources of research support, and disclosure of the author's material financial relationships, if any, please see http://www.nber.org/chapters/c14028.ack.

managing the relationship between high-level human decision-making and our machines servants will involve humans at many levels, no matter how productive machines become. So, even in the limit where machines become better at doing *all* human production, there will still be work for humans in what could be broadly referred to as the political realm.

The chapter of Philippe Aghion, Benjamin Jones, and Charles Jones is a great starting point for the less structured discussion that I am about to set off on here. The chapter explores the growth implications of AI, where the aspect focused on is the increasing automation of production. That is, machines replacing labor at a continually increasing range of production, service, and creative tasks. Automation in this form is not new and has been going on since at least the Industrial Revolution. So any model written down projecting what will/might happen should not run afoul of the basic Kaldor facts. Accordingly, they build a model able to deliver a relatively stable labor share despite the continual displacement of labor from an increasing number of sectors.

In a nutshell this works as follows: with multiple sectors and low enough substitutability across the goods produced in them, consumers spend progressively more of real wealth on sectors not subject to automation. This leads to a protracted relative price increase of nonautomated goods' sectors. So two counteracting forces generate a force toward relative stability of the labor share in their model: (a), labor is usefully employed in fewer sectors—lowering its factor share; but (b), in the sectors where labor continues to work, relative prices are increasing—tending to raise the factor share. Essentially, though progressively fewer things remain useful for humans to do, these things become relatively well remunerated, and this can continue provided there remain *some* things that humans can do better than machines.

But it is when we turn to thinking about what are the products or services where humans will remain essential in production that we start to run into problems. What if humans cannot do anything better than machines? Many discussions at the conference centered around this very possibility. And I must admit that I found the scientists' views compelling on this. Though it has been the case that new services, which have been relatively labor intensive, have emerged as technology has mechanized the production of goods and services, and this has been demonstrated by others (Acemoglu and Restrepo 2016) to be another force that could stabilize the labor share. Even with this, the complete displacement of labor from production of goods and service will arise if machines dominate humans in the performance of *all* tasks.

Scientists disagree on how imminent this eventuality is, but few doubt that it will eventually occur. Though it may well be a limiting case reached only many generations down the track, from now on I will try to imagine what will happen in that limiting case. The one where machines can do everything better than humans. The point I wish to make is that even in such a world where machines are better at all tasks, there will still be an important role for human "work." And that work will involve what will become the almost political task of managing the machines.

The Political Economic Challenges That Machine-Superior Societies Will Face

But before I turn to that, a first challenge societies will face in a completely machine-superior world is: Who owns the machines? Capitalist societies succeed when they create incentives for investment. They reward innovators who come up with and implement good ideas, and thus encourage those ideas. Societies with the features that are well suited to pioneering the advance of machines today are also the economically successful societies, and generally the most healthy societies socially. Incentives for technological advance are greatest where property rights are best protected, and where the taxes on the successful are the lowest. So we predictably see the vanguard of this new world of machine superiority emerging from the most successful capitalist economies like the United States of America.

But everything changes when the machines reach the point of displacing human inputs in the task of innovation, what Aghion, Jones, and Jones term "AI in the idea production function." Here I'm again talking about the extreme case where machines do all of their own innovation much better than people, and without requiring any human input. At this point, the decisions on how to best improve the current technology, the risks to take, the directions to follow, and the implementation are all done by machines. Machines then improve themselves and enter in to a process of creating new and better machines without the need for human intervention.

Aghion, Jones, and Jones developed a fantastically interesting analysis of the almost science fiction-like possibility of singularities and productive extremes that can arise in that stage. I am going to, alternatively, focus on the political economic implications.

Presumably, at least at the start of this period, the human owners of these machines made improvements (and the stream of rents that those improvements generate)that are well identifiable. These are the owners of the machines that did the previous round of inventing. Similarly, as the next generation of improvements emerge, the machines that were earlier invented by the previous machines can be traced back to a primal machine inventor(s) with well-identified human inventor/owners, and so on. In a sense then, this last generation of human inventor/owners will have a claim to the rents generated by the machines from then on.

Should we, as a society, recognize that claim? The answer to that depends on where individuals, the political elites, and the economic elites in that society stand on the issue of inviolability of private property. At the point where machines become self-inventing, redistributing the ownership rents to all individuals in society will come without cost in terms of future growth because human incentives no longer play a role. This won't be easy for many of today's successful societies to do.

The social cost of not doing this will be human unrest on a massive scale. The degree of inequality in a society where the owners of the machines are the last generation of human/inventor/investors and the rest of society earns their incomes from labor will be extreme. Nationalizing ownership of the machines will be costless in terms of future growth, but the elite who own the machines may be (and if history is any guide, will be) extremely reluctant to give up their "hard-earned" rents, and their power, to the passive majority who did not have the foresight, hard work, and luck, to come up with these machines. The societies that will be most functional in this future will be those most willing to tax this last generation of productive inventor/investors to support the unlucky, less able, and perhaps even willingly slothful, who do not own a machine. Countries that, for the very reason of not heavily taxing innovation today will be in the vanguard of creating our technofuture, may have social values that will tend to make them somewhat poorly placed to manage it.

If the elite of such countries succeed in managing to control the political channels whereby rival elites may come to threaten them, or where the excluded masses who do not share ownership of the machines would be able to coordinate against them, they will be able to enjoy machine rents and become almost infinitely richer than the excluded. The autocratic elites of the Soviet Union employed just such methods of exclusion and disruption to rule their countries many decades after they had lost the cooperation of their masses. And they did not have super-smart robots to help them. If the future elite of countries that are willing to protect their rents from owning the economy's productive assets (machines) study history's successful autocrats well enough (or their machines do), this could go on for quite a while.

In contrast, where the machines are nationally owned, and where the rents are shared by all society's members, what I will call inclusive societies, there is no reason that we cannot have equality in consumption. The very good, incentive-based reasons for inequality to exist under capitalism will no longer apply.

The Political Economic Source of Future Human Work

What will humans do for work in a world where machines are better at doing everything than humans? It would seem that the obvious answer is nothing. We will have to learn to create meaning from non-work-related activities, and hopefully overcome our evolved proclivity toward equating personal value with social productivity. I am going to argue that this obvious answer is wrong. There will actually be vital and important work for humans to do in this world, and that the amount of it to be done will be greatest in the most inclusive societies.

Managing the Machines Will Be the Source of Human Work

Why would machines need managing? The machines will be self-replicating, self-maintaining, self-creating, self-repairing, self-improving, so what else needs to be done? What is not so clear is which ends the machines are pursuing.

Usually we tend to think in terms of well-defined human objectives, and for most of these it is a nonquestion as to what machines should do. For example, oncology machines will read MRIs, diagnose potential cancers, order more tests, or operations, or drugs, and so forth, based on protocols they have learned by being run millions of times on training data. They can learn what to do because objectives here are relatively simple, and success in meeting them can be used to determine optimal actions easily. So these machines with very narrow objectives need relatively little managing.

But machines will be producing all output and services in our economy, and while doing this will all the while continually reinvent and modify themselves in pursuit of objectives that were programmed in to them by their human masters. So we will have a complex set of evolving machines who are not only running all production, but doing all inventing as well. We could think of these machines as designed, but through the process of machine learning and machine-based innovation the designs would become far removed from anything imagined by the last generation of human designers that worked on them. Even understanding what they are doing will be difficult for us humans. Perhaps we will develop intuitions about them, a richer human language, or narratives about what they do that will give us some vague understandings of what they are about, but it is reasonable to suppose that no human will fully understand them.

The question is, Will we be willing to let this design direction simply continue without human interjection? I would argue that we will not. We (our societal "we") will be greatly concerned about the direction that this design takes, and managing this direction will require immense human oversight. The more so, the more inclusive a society is. But why would we need to manage it if we have already programmed in to these advanced machines a set of objectives that are human centred? If we have already delegated that to the machines? I am assuming that, as part of this programming, we will find fail-safes to short-circuit rogue machines following objectives that do not advance human welfare, as interestingly sketched by Nick Bostrom (2014), so I am explicitly excluding that particular dystopia.

But even with such fail-safes, additional human involvement will be required. This is because we cannot delegate a particular objective function to machines and be done with it, because whatever delegation that we implement at time t, based on an objective articulated with the knowledge we have at time t, may well be outdated by time $t' > t$ because either our knowledge or our values have changed by t'. We will need people (obviously greatly aided by machines) charged with working out what our social consensus is at time t', informing other citizens at t' what relevant information they need to make their decisions then, and then implementing those changes at time t'. These actions, which would of course be simple for machines to do since they will be so much smarter than us, will be inherently nonimplementable by the machines that are doing all our inventing and production at time t', because those machines will have been programmed with the objective functions of time t society, which is precisely what we wish to countenance changing at time t'.

The whole problem is that writing objectives at time t may lead machines to evolve capacities based on those objectives that become outdated at t'. In order for us to know whether they are outdated at t', we have to first develop a conception of what the machines should be doing at t', and how that differs from what we thought at t, and we need to somehow have a sense of what the machines are actually doing at t' and how it differs from t. All of these things are collective human decisions, and will require immense human effort.

For example, suppose we program in to these advanced machines an objective of maximizing human welfare defined in a utilitarian way in the year 2035. The designing machines will then set off to come up with machine improvements that advance our utilitarian human objectives. But in doing so, they may end up doing some violence to other objectives which, on the whole we were ready as a society to subordinate to sound utilitarian ones in 2035, but are no longer willing to countenance in 2050. For instance, it may be the case that the utilitarian-based inventing machines put no weight on animal welfare, other than how it indirectly advances the utilitarian goal. But it could be that our societal objectives, beliefs, views and so forth have evolved in the intervening years. Maybe we come to learn something more about animal neurology, or maybe we just change our values as we become richer. And then people, on the whole, start to want to privilege other mammals as much as ourselves. Or alternatively perhaps we become so impressed with the complexity of machines that we want to countenance nonorganic life as of value in itself. In either such case, we will need to, as human decision makers, understand enough of what machines are doing in pursuit of some of our earlier objectives to be able to see whether the societal objectives unstated in 2035 are being trammelled upon or not in 2050. They may not be, and in that case nothing much needs to change. But how will we know without checking?

That will be very complicated to do. It firstly requires some humans trying to understand just what it is that the machines are doing in 2050: How they are evolving and what they have been up to? We then need to work out what the relevant parts of that information are for our societal decision makers to know, and in inclusive societies "societal decision makers" are a lot of people. We then need to find a way of communicating this perhaps highly sophisticated information to these decisions makers, some, and perhaps many, of whom have very little technical training about machine function, so that they can make their decisions based on the knowledge and training that they do have.

This process also, of course, begs the question as to who "we" as a set of societal decision makers are in this context, and what "we" want. Some humans must be involved in making these ethical and social decisions. And here I do not mean decisions of the form whether a car should collide with and kill three old citizens instead of a pregnant mother, which is of course difficult, but which we at least implicitly grapple with every day. But I mean the more basic decisions as to what is the societal objective that the network of machines that are not only producing everything for us, but also designing and inventing everything for us are trying to attain. One could argue that we also implicitly engage in such decisions today as a society, for example, when we elect politicians or parties with competing platforms. However, in the future it will be much more explicit, as our collective stance on these things will be needed to determine precisely what direction we will orient our machine inventors to head towards every single day.

It will not be possible (or prudent if it were possible) to delegate this set of conversations and tasks to machines alone. Even though they may be demonstrably smarter and hence better at making those decisions given a well-defined objective function, the point is that there is and never will be such a well-defined social objective function (we have known this since Arrow's impossibility theorem). We need to modify it via our political processes in a continual way, and the objective function followed by the machines will need to be adjusted in reflection of a social conversation that occurs amongst humans. In inclusive societies, where presumably all citizens will have a voice in those decisions, this will involve a lot of people, all of whom will have to be informed so that they can weigh in on that social consensus.

Managing that conversation, reporting back to "us" what is relevant for that conversation emerging from the self-directed world of machines, and then adjusting the trajectory of the machines in light of what "we" decide via whatever social mechanisms we come up with to express as our collective will, must require humans at certain critical points. Human decision making will not be replicable or replaceable by machines here almost by definition.

So, to summarize, I am describing a world that we are admittedly far from today. A world in which most human labor is involved in the set of essentially political tasks related to managing the machines that will be doing all the production in our economy, and hence determining much of our societies' directions. A set of people will need to work at determining just what our current machines are doing and making that intelligible to social decision makers (which in inclusive societies will be a lot of citizens). Another set of people will need to work out how the diverse sets of opinions manifested by citizens maps back to a consensus about what our machines should be doing, and what directions they should be heading toward. All of these workers will be helped by machines, but the machines helping them will need human guidance since they will not be using objective protocols that could ever be unchanging. This is because it is the very protocols that the machines are using that we humans must be constantly discussing changing. Humans, though immeasurably dumber than machines, will be essential and nonsubstitutable in that process.

References

Acemoglu, Daron, and Pascual Restrepo. 2016. "The Race between Man and Machine: Implications of Technology for Growth, Factor Shares and Employment." Unpublished manuscript, Massachusetts Institute of Technology.

Bostrom, Nick. 2014. *Superintelligence: Paths, Dangers, Strategies.* Oxford: Oxford University Press.

10

Artificial Intelligence and Jobs
The Role of Demand

James Bessen

There is widespread concern today that artificial intelligence technologies will create mass unemployment during the next ten or twenty years. One recent paper concluded that new information technologies will put "a substantial share of employment, across a wide range of occupations, at risk in the near future" (Frey and Osborne 2017).

The example of manufacturing decline provides good reason to be concerned about technology and job losses. In 1958, the broadwoven textile industry in the United States employed over 300,000 production workers, and the primary steel industry employed over 500,000. By 2011, broadwoven textiles employed only 16,000, and steel employed only 100,000 production workers.[1] Some of these losses can be attributed to trade, especially since the mid-1990s. However, overall since the 1950s, most of the decline appears to come from technology and changing demand (Rowthorn and Ramaswamy 1999).

But the example of manufacturing also demonstrates that the effect of technology on employment is more complicated than a simple story of "automation causes job losses" in the affected industries. Indeed, figure 10.1 shows how textiles, steel, and automotive manufacturing all enjoyed strong employment growth during many decades that also experienced very rapid productivity growth. Despite persistent and substantial productivity growth, these industries have spent more decades with growing employment than

James Bessen is Executive Director of the Technology & Policy Research Initiative at Boston University School of Law.

For acknowledgments, sources of research support, and disclosure of the author's material financial relationships, if any, please see http://www.nber.org/chapters/c14029.ack.

1. These figures are for the broadwoven fabrics industry using cotton and manmade fibers, SIC 2211 and 2221, and the steel works, blast furnaces, and rolling mills industry, SIC 3312.

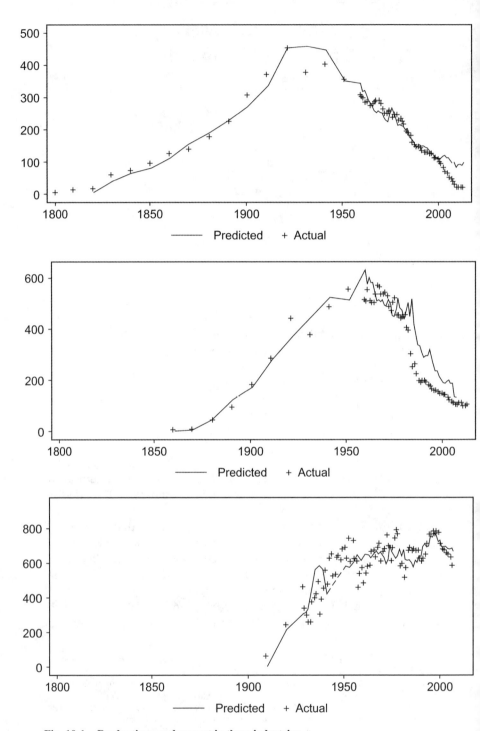

Fig. 10.1 Production employment in three industries

with job losses. This "inverted-U" pattern appears to be quite general for manufacturing industries (Buera and Kaboski 2009; Rodrik 2016).[2]

The reason automation in textiles, steel, and automotive manufacturing led to strong job growth has to do with the effect of technology on demand, as I explore below. New technologies do not just replace labor with machines, but, in a competitive market, automation will reduce prices. In addition, technology may improve product quality, customization, or speed of delivery. All of these things can increase demand. If demand increases sufficiently, employment will grow even though the labor required per unit of output declines.

Of course, job losses in one industry might be offset by employment growth in other industries. Such macroeconomic effects are covered by other articles in this volume (chapter 13, chapter 9). This chapter explores the effect of technology on employment in the affected industry itself. The rise and fall of employment poses an important puzzle. While a substantial literature has looked at structural change associated with technology, I argue that the most widely accepted explanations for deindustrialization are inconsistent with the observed historical pattern. To explain the inverted-U pattern, I present a very simple model that shows why demand for these products was highly elastic during the early years and why demand became inelastic over time. This model forecasts the rise and fall of employment in these industries with reasonable accuracy: the solid line in figure 10.1 shows those predictions. I then explore the implications of this model for the future impact of artificial intelligence over the next two decades.

10.1   Structural Change

The inverted-U pattern in figure 10.1 is also seen in the relative share of employment in the whole manufacturing sector, shown in figure 10.2. Logically, the rise and fall of the sector as a whole in this chart results from the aggregate rise and fall of separate manufacturing industries such as those in figure 10.1. Yet, explanations of this phenomenon based on broad sector-level factors face a challenge because individual industries show rather disparate patterns. For example, employment in the automotive industry appears to have peaked nearly a century after textile employment peaked. Data on individual industries are needed to analyze such disparate responses.

The literature on structural change provides two sorts of accounts for the relative size of the manufacturing sector, one based on differential rates of productivity growth, the other based on different income elasticities of demand.[3] Baumol (1967) showed that the greater rate of technical change

---

2. Other papers empirically analyzing the sector shifts include Dennis and Iscan (2009), Buera and Kaboski (2009), Kollmeyer (2009), Nickell, Redding, and Swaffield (2008), and Rowthorn and Ramaswamy (1999).

3. Acemoglu and Guerrieri (2008) also propose an explanation based on differences in capital deepening.

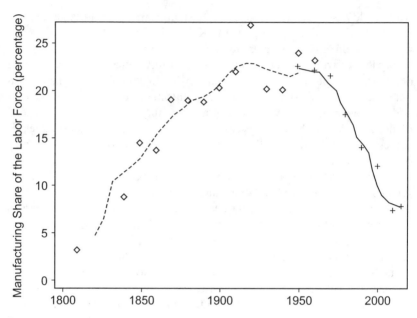

Fig. 10.2   **Manufacturing share of the labor force**
Sources: US Bureau of the Census 1975; BLS Current Employment Situation.
Note: Labor force includes agricultural laborers.

in manufacturing industries relative to services leads to a declining share of manufacturing employment under some conditions (see also Lawrence and Edwards 2013; Ngai and Pissarides 2007; Matsuyama 2009).

But differences in productivity growth rates do not seem to explain the initial rise in employment. For example, during the nineteenth century, the share of employment in agriculture fell while employment in manufacturing industries such as textiles and steel soared both in absolute and relative terms. But labor productivity in these manufacturing industries grew faster than labor productivity in agricultural. Parker and Klein (1966) find that labor productivity in corn, oats, and wheat grew 2.4 percent, 2.3 percent, and 2.6 percent per annum from 1840–1860 to 1900–10. In contrast, labor productivity in cotton textiles grew 3 percent per year from 1820 to 1900 and labor productivity in steel grew 3 percent from 1860 to 1900.[4] Nevertheless, employment in cotton textiles, and in primary iron and steel manufacturing, grew rapidly then.

The growth of manufacturing relative to agriculture surely involves some general equilibrium considerations, perhaps involving surplus labor in the agricultural sector (Lewis 1954). But at the industry level, rapid labor productivity growth along with job growth must mean a rapid growth in the

---

4. My estimates, data described below.

equilibrium level of demand—the amount consumed must increase sufficiently to offset the labor-saving effect of technology. For example, although labor productivity in cotton textiles increased nearly thirtyfold during the nineteenth century, consumption of cotton cloth increased one hundredfold. The inverted-U thus seems to involve an interaction between productivity growth and demand.

A long-standing literature sees sectoral shifts arising from differences in the income elasticity of demand. Clark (1940), building on earlier statistical findings by Engel (1857) and others, argued that necessities such as food, clothing, and housing have income elasticities that are less than one (see also Boppart 2014; Comin, Lashkari, and Mestieri 2015; Kongsamut, Rebelo, and Xie 2001; and Matsuyama 1992 for more general treatments of nonhomothetic preferences). The notion behind "Engel's Law" is that demand for necessities becomes satiated as consumers can afford more, so that wealthier consumers spend a smaller share of their budgets on necessities. Similarly, this tendency is seen playing out dynamically. As nations develop and their incomes grow, the relative demand for agricultural and manufactured goods falls and, with labor productivity growth, relative employment in these sectors falls even faster.

This explanation is also incomplete, however. While a low-income elasticity of demand might explain late twentieth century deindustrialization, it does not easily explain the rising demand for some of the same goods during the nineteenth century. By this account, cotton textiles are a necessity with an income elasticity of demand less than one. Yet, during the nineteenth century, the demand for cotton cloth grew dramatically as incomes rose. That is, cotton cloth must have been a "luxury" good then. Nothing in the theory explains why the supposedly innate characteristics of preferences for cloth changed.

It would seem that the nature of demand changed over time. Matsuyama (2002) introduced a model where the income elasticity of demand changes as incomes grow (see also Foellmi and Zweimüller 2008). In this model, consumers have hierarchical preferences for different products. As their incomes grow, consumer demand for existing products saturates and they progressively buy new products further down the hierarchy. Given heterogeneous incomes that grow over time, this model can explain the inverted-U pattern. It also corresponds, in a highly stylized way, to the sequence of growth across industries seen in figure 10.1.

Yet, there are two reasons that this model might not fit the evidence very well for individual industries. First, the timing of the growth of these industries seems to have much more to do with particular innovations that began eras of accelerated productivity growth than with the progressive saturation of other markets. Cotton textile consumption soared following the introduction of the power loom to US textile manufacture in 1814; steel consumption grew following the US adoption of the Bessemer steelmaking process in 1856, and Henry Ford's assembly line in 1913 initiated rapid growth in motor vehicles.

Second, there is the general problem of looking at the income elasticity of demand as the main driver of structural change: the data suggests that prices were often far more consequential for consumers than income. From 1810 to 2011, real gross domestic product (GDP) per capita rose thirtyfold, but output per hour in cotton textiles rose over eight hundredfold; inflation-adjusted prices correspondingly fell by three orders of magnitude. Similarly, from 1860 to 2011, real GDP per capita rose seventeenfold, but output per hour in steel production rose over 100 times and prices fell by a similar proportion. The literature on structural change has focused on the income elasticity of demand, often ignoring price changes. Yet these magnitudes suggest that low prices might substantially contribute to any satiation of demand. I develop a model that includes both income and price effects on demand, allowing both to have changing elasticities over time.

The inverted-U pattern in industry employment can be explained by a declining price elasticity of demand. If we assume that rapid productivity growth generated rapid price declines in competitive product markets, then these price declines would be a major source of demand growth. During the rising phase of employment, equilibrium demand had to increase proportionally faster than the fall in prices in response to productivity gains. During the deindustrialization phase, demand must have increased proportionally less than prices. Below I obtain estimates that show the price elasticity of demand falling in just this manner.

To understand why this may have happened, it is helpful to return to the origins of the notion of a demand curve. Dupuit (1844) recognized that consumers placed different values on goods used for different purposes. A decrease in the price of stone would benefit the existing users of stone, but consumers would also buy stone at the lower price for new uses such as replacing brick or wood in construction or for paving roads. In this way, Dupuit showed how the distribution of uses at different values gives rise to what we now call a demand curve, allowing for a calculation of consumer surplus.

This chapter proposes a parsimonious explanation for the rise and fall of industry employment based on a simple model where consumer preferences follow such a distribution function. The basic intuition is that when most consumers are priced out of the market (the upper tail of the distribution), demand elasticity will tend to be high for many common distribution functions. When, thanks to technical change, price falls or income rises to the point where most consumer needs are met (the lower tail), then the price and income elasticities of demand will be small. The elasticity of demand thus changes as technology brings lower prices to the affected industries and higher income to consumers generally.

10.2   Model

10.2.1   Simple Model of the Inverted-U

Consider production and consumption of two goods—cloth and a general composite good—in autarky. The model will focus on the impact of technology on employment in the textile industry under the assumption that the output and employment in the textile industry are only a small part of the total economy.

Production

Let the output of cloth be $q = A \cdot L$, where L is textile labor and A is a measure of technical efficiency. Changes in A represent labor-augmenting technical change. Note that this is distinct from those cases where automation completely replaces human labor. Bessen (2016) shows that such cases are rare, and that the main impact of automation consists of technology augmenting human labor.

I initially assume that product and labor markets are competitive so that the price of cloth is

(1) $$p = w/A,$$

where w is the wage. Below, I will test whether this assumption holds in the cotton and steel industries.

Then, given a demand function, $D(p)$, equating demand with output implies

$$D(p) = q = A \cdot L \qquad \text{or}$$

(2) $$L = D(p)/A.$$

We seek to understand whether an increase in A, representing technical improvement, results in a decrease or increase in employment L. That depends on the price elasticity of demand, ϵ, assuming income is constant. Taking the partial derivative of the log of equation (2) with respect to the log of A,

$$\frac{\partial \ln L}{\partial \ln A} = \frac{\partial \ln D(p)}{\partial \ln p}\frac{\partial \ln p}{\partial \ln A} - 1 = \epsilon - 1, \quad \epsilon \equiv -\frac{\partial \ln D(p)}{\partial \ln p}.$$

If the demand is elastic ($\epsilon > 1$), technical change will increase employment; if demand is inelastic ($\epsilon < 1$), jobs will be lost. In addition to this price effect, changing income might also affect demand as I develop below.

Consumption

Now, consider a consumer's demand for cloth. Suppose that the consumer places different values on different uses of cloth. The consumer's first set of clothing might be very valuable and the consumer might be willing to purchase even if the price is quite high. But cloth draperies might be a luxury that the consumer would not be willing to purchase unless the price is modest. Following Dupuit (1844) and the derivation of consumer surplus used in industrial organization theory, these different values can be represented by a distribution function. Suppose that the consumer has a number of uses for cloth that each give her value v, no more, no less. The total yards of cloth that these uses require can be represented as $f(v)$. That is, when the uses are ordered by increasing value, $f(v)$ is a scaled density function giving the yards of cloth for value v. If we suppose that our consumer will purchase cloth for all uses where the value received exceeds the price of cloth, $v > p$, then for price p, her demand is

$$D(p) = \int_p^\infty f(z)dz = 1 - F(p), \; F(p) \equiv \int_0^p f(z)dz,$$

where I have normalized demand so that maximum demand is 1. With this normalization, f is the density function and F is the cumulative distribution function. I assume that these functions are continuous, with continuous derivatives for $p > 0$.

The total value she receives from these purchases is then the sum of the values of all uses purchased,

$$U(p) = \int_p^\infty z \cdot f(z)dz.$$

This quantity measures the gross consumer surplus and can be related to the standard measure of net consumer surplus used in industrial organization theory (Tirole 1988, 8) after integrating by parts:

$$U(p) = \int_p^\infty z \cdot f(z)dz = -\int_p^\infty z \cdot D'(z)dz = p \cdot D(p) + \int_p^\infty D(z)dz.$$

In words, gross consumer surplus equals the consumer's expenditure plus net consumer surplus. I interpret U as the utility that the consumer derives from cloth.[5]

The consumer also derives utility from consumption of the general good, x, and from leisure time. Let the portion of time the consumer works be l so that leisure time is $1 - l$. Assume that the utility from these goods is additively separable from the utility of cloth so that total utility is

---

5. Note that in order to use this model of preferences to analyze demand over time, one of two assumptions must hold. Either there are no significant close substitutes for cloth or the prices of these close substitutes change relatively little. Otherwise, consumers would have to take the changing price of the potential substitute into account before deciding which to purchase. If there is a close substitute with a relatively static price, the value v can be reinterpreted as the value relative to the alternative. Below I look specifically at the role of close substitutes for cotton cloth, steel, and motor vehicles.

$$U(v) + G(x, 1 - l),$$

where G is a concave differentiable function. The consumer will select v, x, and l to maximize total utility subject to the budget constraint

$$wl \geq x + pD(v),$$

where the price of the composite good is taken as numeraire. The consumer's Lagrangean can be written

$$\mathcal{L}(v, x, l) = U(v) + G(x, 1 - l) + \lambda(wl - x - p \cdot D(v)).$$

Taking the first order conditions, and recalling that under competitive markets, $p = w/A$, we get

$$\hat{v} = G_l \frac{p}{w} = \frac{G_l}{A}, \; G_l \equiv \frac{\partial G}{\partial l};$$

G_l represents the marginal value of leisure time and the second equality results from applying assumption (1). In effect, the consumer will purchase cloth for uses that are at least as valuable as the real cost of cloth valued relative to leisure time. Note that if G_l is constant, the effect of prices and the effect of income are inversely related. This means that the price elasticity of demand will equal the income elasticity of demand. However, the marginal value of leisure time might very well increase or decrease with income; for example, if the labor supply is backward bending, greater income might decrease equilibrium G_l so that leisure time increases. To capture that notion, I parameterize $G_l = w^\alpha$ so that

(3) $$\hat{v} = w^\alpha / A = w^{\alpha-1} p, D(\hat{v}) = 1 - F(\hat{v}).$$

10.2.2 Elasticities

Using equation (3), the price elasticity of demand holding wages constant solves to

$$\epsilon = -\frac{\partial \ln D}{\partial \ln p} = \frac{\partial \ln D(\hat{v})}{\partial \ln \hat{v}} \frac{\partial \ln \hat{v}}{\partial \ln p} = \frac{pf(\hat{v})}{1 - F(\hat{v})} w^{\alpha-1},$$

and the income (wage) elasticity of demand holding price constant is

$$\rho = \frac{\partial \ln D}{\partial \ln w} = \frac{\partial \ln D(\hat{v})}{\partial \ln \hat{v}} \frac{\partial \ln \hat{v}}{\partial \ln w} = (1 - \alpha)\epsilon.$$

These elasticities change with prices and wages or alternatively with changes in labor productivity, A. The changes can create an inverted-U in employment. Specifically, if the price elasticity of demand, ϵ, is greater than 1 at high prices and lower than 1 at low prices, then employment will trace an inverted-U as prices decline with productivity growth. At high prices relative to income, productivity improvements will create sufficient demand to offset job losses; at low prices relative to income, they will not.

A preference distribution function with this property can generate a kind of industry life cycle as technology continually improves labor productivity over a long period of time. An early stage industry will have high prices and large unmet demand, so that price decreases result in sharp increases in demand; a mature industry will have satiated demand so further price drops only produce an anemic increase in demand.

A necessary condition for this pattern is that the price elasticity of demand must increase with price over some significant domain, so that it is smaller than 1 at low prices but larger than 1 at high prices. It turns out that many distribution functions have this property. This can be seen from the following propositions (proofs in the appendix):

PROPOSITION 1. *Single-peaked density functions. If the distribution density function, f, has a single peak at $p = \bar{p}$, then $(\partial \epsilon / \partial p) \geq 0 \forall p < \bar{p}$.*

PROPOSITION 2. *Common distributions. If the distribution is normal, lognormal, exponential or uniform, there exists a p^* such that for $0 < p < p^*, \epsilon < 1$, and for $p^* < p, \epsilon > 1$.*

These propositions suggest that the model of demand derived from distributions of preferences might be broadly applicable. The second proposition is sufficient to create the inverted-U curve in employment as long as the price starts above p^* and declines below it.

10.2.3   Empirical Estimates

This very simple model does not consider numerous factors that might influence demand. It does not consider the role of close substitutes or the effect of the business cycle on demand. New technology might create new products that generate new demand, altering the distribution, or new substitutes that decrease demand. Global trade might alter downstream industries, affecting the demand for intermediate goods such as cloth or steel. Nevertheless, the model appears to predict actual demand over a historical timeframe reasonably well.

Assuming that the preference distribution is lognormal, I estimate the per capita demand functions for these three commodities (see Bessen 2017 for details). The model fits the data quite closely, realizing R-squareds of .982 or higher. Using these predictions, I obtain very rough estimates of the price elasticity of demand at each end of the estimation sample (see table 10.1).

The demand was initially highly elastic but became highly inelastic.

Using estimated per capita demand, labor demand can be calculated incorporating population size, import penetration, labor productivity, and hours worked. These estimates are shown as the solid lines in figure 1. The estimates appear to be accurate over long periods of time. There are notable drops in employment during the Great Depression and excess employment in motor vehicles during World War II. Finally, employment falls below the

Table 10.1   **Rough estimates of elasticity of demand**

Cotton		Steel		Automotive	
Year	Elasticity	Year	Elasticity	Year	Elasticity
1810	2.13	1860	3.49	1910	6.77
1995	0.02	1982	0.16	2007	0.15

estimates when globalization takes a bite out of employment in textiles after 1995, and steel after 1982.

Thus, even though this overly simple model does not account for all of the factors that affect demand, it nevertheless provides a succinct explanation of the inverted-U in employment in these manufacturing industries.

10.3   Implication for AI

10.3.1   The Importance of Demand

Although the model presented here appears to provide a good explanation for how demand mediated the impact of technology in the past, what is the relevance of this analysis for new technologies? There is, of course, no guarantee that AI or other new technologies will be applied in markets with preference distributions similar to those of the textile, steel, and automotive industries.

The relevance of this history is more general. Specifically, the responsiveness of demand is key to understanding whether major new technologies will decrease or increase employment in affected industries. Productivity-enhancing technology will increase industry employment if product demand is sufficiently elastic. If the price elasticity of demand is greater than one, the increase in demand will more than offset the labor-saving effect of the technology. And demand will likely be sufficiently elastic if the technology is addressing large unmet needs affecting people with diverse preferences and uses for the technology. This situation corresponds to the upper tail of the distribution function. If, on the other hand, AI is targeted at more satiated markets, then jobs will be lost in the affected industries, although not necessarily in the economy as a whole.

The pace of change of a new technology is not sufficient by itself to determine the impact of that technology on employment. For example, a common view holds that faster technical change is more likely to eliminate jobs. Some people argue that because of Moore's Law, the rate of change will be fast for AI and this will cause unemployment (Ford 2015). However, my analysis highlights the importance of demand in mediating the impact of automation. If demand is sufficiently elastic and AI does not completely replace humans, then technical change will create jobs rather than destroy them. In this case, a faster rate of technical change will actually create *faster* employment growth rather than job losses.

The demand response to AI is, of course, an empirical question and, therefore, an important part of the AI research agenda.

10.3.2   Research Agenda

To understand the interaction between AI and demand over the next ten or twenty years, empirical researchers will need answers to several specific questions.

First, to what extent will AI replace humans and to what extent will it, instead, merely augment human capabilities? That is, to what extent will AI completely automate occupations and to what extent will it, instead, merely automate some, but not all, tasks performed by an occupation. If humans are completely replaced, demand no longer affects employment because there isn't any demand for humans. In the past, despite extensive productivity growth, technology has almost always only partially automated work. Consider what happened to the 271 detailed occupations used in the 1950 census by 2010. Most occupations listed then still exist in some form (sometimes grouped differently) today. Some occupations were eliminated for a variety of reasons. In many cases, demand for the occupational services declined (e.g., boardinghouse keepers); in some cases, demand declined because of technological obsolescence (e.g., telegraph operators). This, however, is not the same as automation. In only one case—elevator operators—can the decline and disappearance of an occupation be largely attributed to automation. Nevertheless, this sixty-year period witnessed extensive automation; it was just mostly partial automation.

This same pattern is likely to be true for AI over the next ten or twenty years for the simple reason that although AI can outperform humans on some tasks, today's AI fails miserably at other tasks that humans perform. A casual review of current developments suggests that over the near term AI may be able to completely automate some jobs of drivers and warehouse workers, but most AI applications are targeted toward automating just some subset of tasks performed by specific occupations. Nevertheless, a more rigorous empirical investigation is needed to measure the extent to which AI is bringing or will bring complete versus partial automation.

To the extent that automation continues to be partial rather than complete in the near term, demand will be key. This raises a second question: To what extent will the effect of AI on demand and employment during the next ten or twenty years be similar to the effect that AI and computer automation generally had over the last several decades? Computers have been used to automate work in activities such as accounting and loan making since the 1950s. The first fully automatic loan application system was installed in 1972. In 1987, an artificial intelligence system was first put into commercial operation in a system used to detect credit fraud. Since then, AI applications have been used to automate a variety of tasks in other industries and occupations, such as the electronic discovery of legal documents for litigation.

This means that we already have some evidence of the effects of AI and computer automation generally. It does not seem that computer automation or AI has so far led to significant job losses; the booming market for electronic discovery applications, for instance, has been associated with an increase in the employment of paralegals. A few studies have made estimates of the employment impact of computer technology (Gaggl and Wright 2017; Akerman, Gaarder, and Mogstad 2015), finding, if anything, a modest increase in employment following technology adoption.[6] Further studies could deepen our understanding of the impact of computer automation on employment, and how this impact differs across occupations and industries.

Also, we need to understand how AI applications in the near future will differ from those of the recent past. The model above provides a framework to analyze this question. In particular, to the extent that the new applications target the same services and industries as did the computer automation of the recent past, then we should expect the elasticity of demand to remain similar over the next ten or twenty years, perhaps with a modest decline. That is, the elasticity of demand is not likely to change very quickly. On the other hand, AI might introduce entirely new products and services that tap into otherwise unmet needs and wants. In this case, there may be new and unanticipated sources of employment growth. Research can help determine the extent of change in the sorts of applications, occupations, and industries affected by new AI applications that are also addressed by existing technologies. To the extent that AI creates wholly new applications, prediction will be more difficult. Indeed, in the past, predictions about technological unemployment have reliably failed to anticipate major new applications of technology and major new sources of demand.

A critical aspect of this research concerns the unevenness of the potential impact of AI. While AI might not create overall unemployment in the near future, it will likely eliminate jobs in some occupations while creating new jobs in others. The need to retrain and transition workers to new occupations, sometimes in new locations, might be highly disruptive even though the total employment rate remains high.

Finally, it is important to note that this analytical framework and research agenda are very much limited to the next ten or twenty years for two reasons. First, beyond a couple of decades, markets might well become saturated. Suppose, for example, that demand is highly elastic for many financial, health, and other services today so that information technology increases employment in these markets. If AI rapidly reduces costs or improves the

---

6. And, importantly, impacts that differed across skill groups.

quality of these services, the elasticity of demand will decline. That is, these markets might see the kind of reversals in employment growth seen in figure 10.1.

Second, in the future AI might very well be able to completely replace many more occupations. Then the effect of AI on demand will no longer matter for these occupations. For now, however, understanding how and where AI affects demand is critical to understanding employment effects.

Appendix

Propositions

To simplify notation, let the wage remain constant at 1. Then

$$\epsilon(p) = \frac{p\,f(p)}{1 - F(p)},$$

so that

$$\frac{\partial \epsilon(p)}{\partial p} = \frac{f'p}{1-F} + \frac{f^2 p}{(1-F)^2} + \frac{f}{1-F} = \epsilon\left(\frac{f'}{f} + \frac{f}{1-F} + \frac{1}{p}\right).$$

Note that the second and third terms in parentheses are positive for $p > 0$; the first term could be positive or negative. A sufficient condition for $(\partial \epsilon / \partial p) \geq 0$ is

(10A.1) $$\frac{f'}{f} + \frac{f}{1-F} \geq 0.$$

PROPOSITION 1. *For a single peaked distribution with mode $\bar{p}$, for $p < \bar{p}$, $f' \geq 0$ so that $(\partial \epsilon / \partial p) \geq 0$.*

PROPOSITION 2. *For each distribution, I will show that*

$$\frac{\partial \epsilon}{\partial p} \geq 0, \lim_{p \to 0} \epsilon = 0, \lim_{p \to \infty} \epsilon = \infty.$$

Taken together, these conditions imply that for sufficiently high price, $\epsilon > 1$, and for a sufficiently low price, $\epsilon < 1$.

Normal Distribution

$$f(p) = \frac{1}{\sigma}\varphi(x), F(p) = \Phi(x), \ \epsilon(p) = \frac{p}{\sigma}\frac{\varphi(x)}{(1-\Phi(x))}, x \equiv \frac{p-\mu}{\sigma},$$

where φ and Φ are the standard normal density and cumulative distribution functions respectively. Taking the derivative of the density function,

$$\frac{f'}{f} + \frac{f}{1 - F} = -\frac{x}{\sigma} + \frac{\varphi(x)}{\sigma(1 - \Phi(x))}.$$

A well-known inequality for the normal Mills' ratio (Gordon 1941) holds that for $x > 0$,[7]

(10A.2)
$$x \leq \frac{\varphi(x)}{1 - \Phi(x)}.$$

Applying this inequality, it is straightforward to show that (10A.1) holds for the normal distribution. This also implies that $\lim_{p \to \infty} \epsilon = \infty$. By inspection, $\epsilon(0) = 0$.

Exponential Distribution

$$f(p) \equiv \lambda e^{-\lambda p}, F(p) \equiv 1 - e^{-\lambda p}, \ \epsilon(p) = \lambda p, \ \lambda, \ p > 0.$$

Then,

$$\frac{f'}{f} + \frac{f}{1 - F} = -\lambda + \lambda = 0,$$

so (10A.1) holds. By inspection, $\epsilon(0) = 0$ and $\lim_{p \to \infty} \epsilon = \infty$.

Uniform Distribution

$$f(p) \equiv \frac{1}{b}, F(p) \equiv \frac{p}{b}, \ \epsilon(p) = \frac{p}{b - p}, 0 < p < b,$$

so that

$$\frac{f'}{f} + \frac{f}{1 - F} = \frac{1}{b - p} > 0.$$

By inspection, $\epsilon(0) = 0$ and $\lim_{p \to b} \epsilon = \infty$.

Lognormal Distribution

$$f(p) \equiv \frac{1}{p\sigma} \varphi(x), F(p) \equiv \Phi(x), \ \epsilon(p) = \frac{1}{\sigma} \frac{\varphi(x)}{(1 - \Phi(x))}, x \equiv \frac{\ln p - \mu}{\sigma},$$

so that

$$\frac{\partial \epsilon(p)}{\partial p} = \epsilon \left(\frac{f'}{f} + \frac{f}{1 - F} + \frac{1}{p} \right) = \epsilon \left(-\frac{1}{p} - \frac{x}{p\sigma} + \frac{\varphi}{p\sigma(1 - \Phi)} + \frac{1}{p} \right).$$

Canceling terms and using Gordon's inequality, this is positive. And taking the limit of Gordon's inequality, $\lim_{p \to \infty} \epsilon = \infty$. By inspection, $\lim_{p \to 0} \epsilon = 0$.

7. I present the inverse of Gordon's inequality.

References

Acemoglu, Daron, and Veronica Guerrieri. 2008. "Capital Deepening and Nonbalanced Economic Growth." *Journal of Political Economy* 116 (3): 467–98.

Akerman, Anders, Ingvil Gaarder, and Magne Mogstad. 2015. "The Skill Complementarity of Broadband Internet." *Quarterly Journal of Economics* 130 (4): 1781–824.

Baumol, William J. 1967. "Macroeconomics of Unbalanced Growth: The Anatomy of Urban Crisis." *American Economic Review* 57 (3): 415–26.

Bessen, James E. 2016. "How Computer Automation Affects Occupations: Technology, Jobs, and Skills." Law and Economics Research Paper no. 15-49, Boston University School of Law.

———. 2017. "Automation and Jobs: When Technology Boosts Employment." Law and Economics Research Paper no. 17-09, Boston University School of Law.

Boppart, Timo. 2014. "Structural Change and the Kaldor Facts in a Growth Model with Relative Price Effects and Non-Gorman Preferences." *Econometrica* 82 (6): 2167–96.

Buera, Francisco J., and Joseph P. Kaboski. 2009. "Can Traditional Theories of Structural Change Fit the Data?" *Journal of the European Economic Association* 7 (2–3): 469–77.

Clark, Colin. 1940. *The Conditions of Economic Progress.* London: Macmillan.

Comin, Diego A., Danial Lashkari, and Martí Mestieri. 2015. "Structural Change with Long-Run Income and Price Effects." NBER Working Paper no. 21595, Cambridge, MA.

Dennis, Benjamin N., and Talan B. İşcan. 2009. "Engel versus Baumol: Accounting for Structural Change Using Two Centuries of US Data." *Explorations in Economic History* 46 (2): 186–202.

Dupuit, Jules. 1844. "De la Mesure de L'utilité des Travaux Publics." *Annales des Ponts et Chaussées* 8 (2 sem): 332–75.

Engel, Ernst. 1857. "Die Productions- und Consumtionsverhältnisse des Königreichs Sachsen." Zeitschrift des Statistischen Bureaus des Königlich Sächsischen Ministerium des Inneren. 8–9:28–29.

Foellmi, Reto, and Josef Zweimüller. 2008. "Structural Change, Engel's Consumption Cycles and Kaldor's Facts of Economic Growth." *Journal of Monetary Economics* 55 (7): 1317–28.

Ford, Martin. 2015. *Rise of the Robots: Technology and the Threat of a Jobless Future.* New York: Basic Books.

Frey, Carl Benedikt, and Michael A. Osborne. 2017. "The Future of Employment: How Susceptible are Jobs to Computerisation?" *Technological Forecasting and Social Change* 114 (2017): 254–80.

Gaggl, Paul, and Greg C. Wright. 2017. "A Short-Run View of What Computers Do: Evidence from a UK Tax Incentive." *American Economic Journal: Applied Economics* 9 (3): 262–94.

Gordon, Robert D. 1941. "Values of Mills' Ratio of Area to Bounding Ordinate and of the Normal Probability Integral for Large Values of the Argument." *Annals of Mathematical Statistics* 12 (3): 364–66.

Kollmeyer, Christopher. 2009. "Explaining Deindustrialization: How Affluence, Productivity Growth, and Globalization Diminish Manufacturing Employment 1." *American Journal of Sociology* 114 (6): 1644–74.

Kongsamut, Piyabha, Sergio Rebelo, and Danyang Xie. 2001. "Beyond Balanced Growth." *Review of Economic Studies* 68 (4): 869–82.

Lawrence, Robert Z., and Lawrence Edwards. 2013. "US Employment Deindustrialization: Insights from History and the International Experience." Policy Brief no. 13–27, Peterson Institute for International Economics.

Lewis, W. Arthur. 1954. "Economic Development with Unlimited Supplies of Labour." *Manchester School* 22 (2): 139–91.

Matsuyama, Kiminori. 1992. "Agricultural Productivity, Comparative Advantage, and Economic Growth." *Journal of Economic Theory* 58 (2): 317–34.

———. 2009. "Structural Change in an Interdependent World: A Global View of Manufacturing Decline." *Journal of the European Economic Association* 7 (2–3): 478–86.

———. 2002. "The Rise of Mass Consumption Societies." *Journal of Political Economy* 110 (5): 1035–70.

Ngai, L. Rachel, and Christopher A. Pissarides. 2007. "Structural Change in a Multisector Model of Growth." *American Economic Review* 97 (1): 429–43.

Nickell, Stephen, Stephen Redding, and Joanna Swaffield. 2008. "The Uneven Pace of Deindustrialisation in the OECD." *World Economy* 31 (9): 1154–84.

Parker, William N., and Judith L. V. Klein. 1966. "Productivity Growth in Grain Production in the United States, 1840–60 and 1900–10." In *Output, Employment, and Productivity in the United States after 1800*, edited by Dorothy Brady, 523–82. Cambridge, MA: National Bureau of Economic Research.

Rodrik, Dani. 2016. "Premature Deindustrialization." *Journal of Economic Growth* 21 (1): 1–33.

Rowthorn, Robert, and Ramana Ramaswamy. 1999. "Growth, Trade, and Deindustrialization." *IMF Staff Papers* 46 (1): 18–41.

Tirole, Jean. 1988. *The Theory of Industrial Organization*. Cambridge, MA: MIT Press.

United States Bureau of the Census. 1975. Historical Statistics of the United States, Colonial Times to 1970, no. 93. US Department of Commerce, Bureau of the Census.

Public Policy in an AI Economy

Austan Goolsbee

11.1 Introduction

This conference has brought together a mix of technology and economics scholars to think broadly about the role of artificial intelligence (AI) in the economy, and this short chapter will present a few thoughts about the role of policy in a world where AI becomes ubiquitous.

Most of the public discussion about an AI-dominated economy has focused on robots and the future of work. Ruminations by public figures like Bill Gates, Stephen Hawking, and Elon Musk have stoked fears that robots will destroy our jobs (and, possibly, the world). Some of these same figures have called for various heterodox policy ideas, too, from moving to colonies in space to taxing the robots to providing a universal basic income (UBI) untethered to work.

As the research and comments in this volume suggest, economists have generally been less pessimistic when thinking about the role of AI on jobs. They often highlight the historical record of job creation despite job displacement, documented the way technological advances have eliminated jobs in some sectors but expanded jobs and increased wages in the economy overall, and highlighted the advantages that the new technologies will likely have in the future (some recent discussions include Autor 2015; Autor and Salomons 2018; Brynjolfsson and McAfee 2014; Mokyr 2014).

Austan Goolsbee is the Robert P. Gwinn Professor of Economics at the University of Chicago Booth School of Business and a research associate of the National Bureau of Economic Research.

I wish to thank the participants at the NBER Artificial Intelligence conference for helpful comments. For acknowledgments, sources of research support, and disclosure of the author's or authors' material financial relationships, if any, please see http://www.nber.org/chapters /c14030.ack.

The pessimistic case has come more from technology/business sector. Perhaps seeing the advances in technology up close, they worry that the machines may soon be so good that they could replace almost anyone. One major study across many industries by the McKinsey Global Institute (2017) argues that 73 million jobs may be destroyed by automation by 2030 because of the rise of the new technologies.

In many ways, it is unfortunate that labor market policy has dominated our thinking about the AI economy. The main economic impact of AI is not about jobs or, at least, is about much more than just jobs. The main economic impact of these technologies will be how good they are. If the recent advances continue, AI has the potential to improve the quality of our products and our standard of living. If AI helps us diagnose medical problems better, improves our highway safety, gives us back hours of our day that were spent driving in traffic, or even just improves the quality of our selfies, these are direct consumer benefits. These raise our real incomes and the economic studies valuing the improvements from quality and from new products tend to show their value is often extremely high (see the discussions in the volume of Bresnahan and Gordon [1997] or the discussions over valuing "free" goods like Goolsbee and Klenow [2006] and Varian [2013]).

That is a different way of saying that if AI succeeds, it will raise our productivity and higher productivity makes us rich. It is not a negative. Indeed, if AI succeeded in the way some fear, it would mean the exact reversal of the main problem facing growth in the last decade or more that productivity growth has been too slow. Indeed, it would decisively refute one of the central tenets of secular stagnationist thinkers like Gordon (2016), who argue that low productivity growth is a semi-permanent condition for the advanced economies because of the scarcity of path breaking ideas. Would that AI could change that equation.

This chapter will consider a few disparate thoughts about policy in an AI-intensive economy (interpreting AI broadly to include a cluster of information technology-based productivity improvements beyond just conventional artificial intelligence or machine learning). It will consider the speed of adoption of the technology—the impact on the job market and the implications for inequality across people and across places, discuss the challenges of enacting a universal basic income as a response to widespread AI adoption, discuss pricing, privacy and competition policy, and conclude with the question of whether AI will improve policy making itself.

11.2   The Speed of Adoption: Implications for the Job Market and for Inequality

Taking the issue of job displacement first, the basic conclusion of the economists is that for the last hundred years there have been massive amounts of job displacement, yet the structural unemployment rate has not seemed to rise, much less trend toward 100 percent. Over time, people adjust. They move. They get skills. The long-run impact of labor-saving technologies has overwhelming been positive for market economies. If the fear is that AI will replace low-skill jobs, it is a fact that tens or even hundreds of millions of low-skill jobs were displaced by technology in previous years in a process very similar to the one we describe today. If the fear is that AI is different this time around because it will begin to replace types of jobs that have never been automated before like higher-skill or white-collar jobs, the historical data indicate that those groups have been able to adjust to shocks and move to new sectors and new geographic areas easier than lower-skill workers have.

A critical issue is, of course, how fast the adjustment takes place/the speed of adoption of AI technology. The economy has proven quite capable of inventing new things for people to do over the long run. Obviously, if change happens all at once, the adjustment problem is worst. Spread out over time, however, the adjustment can be manageable. Take the much discussed case of autonomous cars. There were about 3.5 million truck, bus, and taxi drivers in 2015, and suppose that every one of them were lost due to advances in self-driving car technology. If this loss takes place over fifteen years, this would average a little over 19,000 per month, and compare that to the fact that in 2017 the Job Openings and Labor Turnover Survey (JOLTS) data show that the economy generated about 5.3 million jobs per month (with 5.1 million separations per month). The complete elimination of every job in the sector would increase the separation rate by less than four-tenths of a percent. It would force drivers into new sectors and be disruptive to their livelihoods. But as a macroeconomic phenomenon, the impact would be small. If that loss happened in two years, the impact would be quite significant. So it is worth considering what influences the speed of adoption and, certainly, a key determinant will be how good the AI actually is compared to people. But, many analysts seem to view that as the *only* thing that will determine adoption rates. It is worth considering at least two other factors: prices and adjustment costs.

First, many of these AI innovations involve significant capital outlays up front and that alone may slow their adoption for some time. Ride-share drivers, for example, by some measures can barely cover the cost of operating their cars (including depreciation, fuel, maintenance, and insurance) at the price of cars now. AI-enabled autonomous vehicles are likely to cost substantially more per car than conventional cars when they become available to the public. Will companies be willing to incur large upfront costs to bypass paying drivers? It really depends on prices that we do not yet know.

Second, "better" does not always mean faster adoption. Economists have shown automated stock picking through index funds superior to active management for decades, yet people still hold trillions in inefficient, high-fee funds. Millions of people have mortgages with higher than market interest rates that they do not refinance, cell phone data plans that do not match their usage, and so on. There are tens of millions of people that do not use the internet. Inertia is a powerful force slowing the adoption of technology products and is certainly worth remembering if we want to predict something like how fast people will give up common behaviors like driving for themselves.

Third, in an important sense, we know that AI can only be as good as its training sample and there are some very different types of customers in the country that may make the AI quality improvements much more fitting for certain types of customers than others. Microsoft created an AI program to learn from Twitter and see if it could create content that people would think was written by a human. They started it in the United States and had to shut it down almost immediately because it became so abusive and offensive. It mirrored what it saw online. Running the same program in China, where Twitter is heavily censored, it has performed well and not turned abusive. The attributes of the product and the "quality" of the product depend on how relevant the training sample is to that customer.

This is likely to influence the adoption rate of the AI technologies in different places. Again, think of the autonomous cars. Will we gather loads of information about driving in urban areas and on highways or in Silicon valley from the early adopters, tailor the product to their needs, but then find that it does not work as well for dirt roads or rural places or places without Bay Area weather?

Heterogeneous demand is the hobgoblin of the AI mind. Groups that differ most from the training sample will likely be the slowest to adopt the technology, in part, because it will be the least helpful to them. That may lead to another manifestation of the digital divide. In this sense, the rise of AI technologies is likely to make the problem of income and of geographic inequality even worse. To the extent that new AI technologies are expensive and tailored toward the training sample of adopters, it will be like having lower inflation and greater consumer surplus going to those groups (for discussions about differences in prices and innovation across income groups or for online buyers versus offline buyers, see Jaravel [2017] or Goolsbee and Klenow [2018]).

Government policy will face the potential of divisions along red state/ blue state or high-education/low-education locations or high-income/ low-income neighborhoods even more than it does today.

11.3   Challenges for Universal Basic Income as a Response to Job Market Displacement

Now suppose that the arguments above prove wrong. Nothing slows the speed of AI adoption and there is mass job displacement in a short time.

There has been a rising call among the believers in that scenario for universal basic income policy. Closely tied to the old Milton Friedman notion of a negative income tax, the UBI would grant some minimal level of income to people regardless of employment status as a new form of safety net and anyone could then work beyond that UBI level to earn more. In the purest libertarian concept, this UBI would replace the existing collection of safety net programs. The advantage of the UBI would be that people could survive in a world with few human jobs and alleviate poverty in a relatively efficient manner and without destroying all incentives in the private economy. It seeks to separate the notion of "making a living" from having a job. There are some small-scale experiments with the UBI in a few countries like Finland and New Zealand or funded by private individuals in the United States. There are a number of challenges associated with negative income taxes and UBIs as a policy solution to widespread AI adoption.

First, if you accept the economists' basic labor supply model (that people value leisure and so generally need to be paid to work) then there are likely to be some sizable number of people who are working only because they absolutely have to. In a world where AI-induced unemployment is already high, separating work and income might be an advantage. In a world like the one we are in now, though, offering a basic income will likely cause a sizable drop in labor market participation by low-wage earners. To the extent that nonparticipation in exactly that segment of the labor force is already viewed as a problem, the UBI would likely make things worse and risk angering the broader public.

Second, for a given amount of money to be used on redistribution, a UBI likely shifts money away from the very poor. To oversimplify, if you have $50 billion to alleviate poverty, the targeting approach followed in most countries today might use the $50 billion to help the poorest/sickest 25 million people and give them the equivalent of $25,000 of benefits each. With a broad-based UBI, the same $50 billion would be spread out. It might involve, say, 100 million people getting $5,000 each. Perhaps a UBI could change the total taste for redistribution in a society—leaving the most disadvantaged people with the same amount and upping the total amount spent—but for the UBI to not end up more regressive than the current system necessarily entails greater amounts of public funds.

Third, the conception of the UBI as a replacement for a myriad of other in-kind transfers and safety net programs forgets the historical origins of that safety net. Fundamentally, the in-kind safety net exists today because rich societies are not comfortable with grievously injured people coming into a hospital but being turned away if they do not have money or letting kids go hungry because their parents cannot afford to feed them, and so on. Converting to a UBI and abolishing the in-kind safety net will lead to a situation where some people will blow their UBI money in unsympathetic ways—gambling, drugs, junk food, Ponzi schemes, whatever. Those people will then come to emergency rooms or their kids will be hungry and by the rules, they will be out of luck. That is what their UBI income was supposed to cover. But the fact that advanced economies evolved an in-kind safety net in order to avoid this situation makes me think that enforcing "UBI discipline" and replacing the safety net with a straight transfer would require rather extraordinary changes in the psyche of people in the advanced economies.

11.4   Policy Responses to AI beyond Jobs: Pricing, Data Property Rights, and Antitrust

Just as the impact of AI goes far beyond just the impact on employment, the policy response to AI raises all sorts of other considerations, as well.

One is the perennial back-and-forth over the power of buyers versus the power of sellers in pricing. The same issue arose with the initial rise of ecommerce—the new online data on customers allowed new forms of price discrimination and market power but the ease of comparison shopping reduced search costs and promoted competition (e.g., Brown and Goolsbee 2002). So far, the power of the AI technology seems overwhelmingly to have been used by sellers. If they can individualize market and price discriminate with it, margins will likely rise. But consumers will likely push back. They may find technological solutions to use AI to thwart merchants. But a more straightforward response might be to follow past practice and start making various behaviors and practices illegal. This could include restrictions on consumer privacy and the ways that companies can use customer information. It might manifest as an argument over property rights in the sense of who owns the consumers' data and what level of consent it requires to use it, or might involve rules against various types of price discrimination. Regardless of the form, these issues of pricing and data seem like they will be a central area of policy in an AI-centric world.

The second thing about an AI economy is that the fixed-cost/economies of scale seem pretty significant, and in many cases there are also often network externalities and switching costs on the demand side of these industries. All of these seem to portend the possibility of many industries having a winner-take-all market structure or the continued rise of "platform" competition rather than conventional competition. If so, the rise of AI is likely to usher in a renewed emphasis on antitrust policy in much the same way the original Gilded Age consolidation of industry did before.

11.5   Conclusion: Will Robots Take Over Policy, Too?

The organizers of the volume also asked us to consider whether AI will enhance or even replace the jobs of policy makers—whether improvements in machine learning and AI could be used on the policy-making process itself. Personally, I do not think so because the most important policy matters are at their heart not issues of prediction. The technology may improve our ability to predict responses, but it does not help us balance interests or engage in politics. We already know, for example, a great deal about the fiscal implications for social security of the aging population. Artificial intelligence might improve our ability to predict revenue outcomes of various policy options, say. That has not been the problem with addressing social security. It has always been about choosing between options and making value judgments. The kinds of problems that AI helps with are those where large amounts of past data to inform the decision. Conditions with small samples or where the conditions are very different than in the past will be much less machine learnable. For small bore issues, AI may improve policy accuracy—what conditions should cause regulators to raise their estimated probability that a bank's loans will start to default, for example. For bigger issues, though, like whether the Federal Reserve should raise interest rates or whether we should cut high-income people's taxes—I have my doubts about what AI can contribute.

It is also sure to increase the attention paid to business practices of large AI platforms—their pricing, their use of personal data on customers, their behavior toward competitors, and the continuing consolidation of market power. Each of these is likely to become a major policy battleground of the future. For the time being, though, the job of policy makers themselves seem relatively safe . . . for now.

References

Autor, David. 2015. "Why Are There Still So Many Jobs? The History and Future of Workplace Automation." *Journal of Economic Perspectives* 29 (3): 3–30.

Autor, David, and A. M. Salomons. 2018. "Is Automation Labor-Displacing? Productivity Growth, Employment, and the Labor Share." *Brookings Papers on Economic Activity* 2018, Spring. https://www.brookings.edu/bpea-articles /is-automation-labor-displacing-productivity-growth-employment-and-the -labor-share/.

Bresnahan, Timothy, and Robert Gordon, eds. 1997. *The Economics of New Goods.* Chicago: University of Chicago Press.

Brown, Jeffrey, and Austan D. Goolsbee. 2002. "Does the Internet Make Markets More Competitive? Evidence from the Life Insurance Industry." *Journal of Political Economy* 110 (3): 481–507.

Brynjolfsson, Erik, and Andrew McAfee. 2014. *The Second Machine Age: Work, Progress, and Prosperity in a Time of Brilliant Technologies.* New York: W. W. Norton.

Goolsbee, Austan D., and Peter J. Klenow. 2006. "Valuing Consumer Goods by the Time Spent Using Them: An Application to the Internet." *American Economic Review, Papers and Proceedings* 96 (2): 108–13.

———. 2018. "Internet Rising, Prices Falling: Measuring Inflation in a World of E-Commerce." *American Economic Review, Papers and Proceedings* 108 (5): 488–92.

Gordon, Robert. 2016. *The Rise and Fall of American Growth: The US Standard of Living since the Civil War*. Princeton, NJ: Princeton University Press.

McKinsey Global Institute. 2017. *Jobs Lost, Jobs Gained: Workforce Transitions in a Time of Automation*. December. McKinsey & Co. Accessed Apr. 26, 2018. https://www.mckinsey.com/~/media/McKinsey/Global%20Themes/Future%20of%20Organizations/What%20the%20future%20of%20work%20will%20mean%20for%20jobs%20skills%20and%20wages/MGI-Jobs-Lost-Jobs-Gained-Report-December-6-2017.ashx.

Jaravel, Xavier. 2017. "The Unequal Gains from Product Innovations: Evidence from the US Retail Sector." Unpublished manuscript, London School of Economics. April.

Mokyr, Joel. 2014. "Secular Stagnation? Not in Your Life." In *Secular Stagnation: Facts Causes and Cures*, edited by Coen Teulings and Richard Baldwin, 83–89. London: CEPR Press.

Varian, Hal. 2013. "The Value of the Internet, Now and in the Future." *Economist*, Mar. 10. Accessed Apr. 26, 2018. https://www.economist.com/blogs/freeexchange/2013/03/technology-1.

12
Should We Be Reassured If Automation in the Future Looks Like Automation in the Past?

Jason Furman

Much of the debate about the economic impact of artificial intelligence (AI) centers on the question of whether this time will be different. Some optimists argue that AI is no different than technologies that came before it and that centuries of fears that machines will replace human labor have proven unfounded, with machines instead creating previously unimagined jobs and raising incomes. Others argue that AI is different—by replacing cognitive tasks, it could render much of human employment redundant, leading to mass unemployment in the eyes of the pessimists or historically unparalleled freedom for leisure in the eyes of the optimists.

The history of automation—and how the US economy has handled it over the last several decades—suggests that even if AI is similar to previous waves of automation, that should not be entirely comforting since technological advances in recent decades have brought tremendous benefits but have also contributed to increasing inequality and falling labor force participation. This outcome, however, is not inevitable because the effects of technological change on the workforce are mediated by a wide set of institutions, and as such, policy choices will have a major impact on actual outcomes. Artificial intelligence does not call for a completely new paradigm for economic policy—for example, as advocated by proponents of replacing the existing social safety net with a universal basic income (UBI)—but instead reinforces many of the steps that could already be justified by the goal of making sure that growth is shared more broadly.

To date, in fact, the problem we have faced is not *too much* automation

Jason Furman is professor of the practice of economic policy at Harvard Kennedy School and a nonresident senior fellow at the Peterson Institute for International Economics.

For acknowledgments, sources of research support, and disclosure of the author's material financial relationships, if any, please see http://www.nber.org/chapters/c14031.ack.

but *too little* automation—the issue I will address before considering some of the potentially harmful side effects that a faster pace of innovation can have for inequality and labor force participation. In the course of this discussion I will address the extent to which policy can advance AI while ensuring that more people share in the benefits of it, two goals that are ultimately complementary.

12.1   The Benefit of More Artificial Intelligence

Technologists see transformative change all around us but economists are a more sour bunch, focusing on productivity statistics that show that we are adding very little to output per hour. Measured productivity growth has slowed in thirty-five of thirty-six advanced economies, slowing from a 2.7 percent average annual growth rate from 1996 to 2006 to a 1.0 percent average annual growth rate from 2006 to 2016—with the slowdown in the G7 economies shown in figure 12.1.

There are many reasons to believe that the official statistics fail to capture the full range of productivity improvements, so the 1.0 percent estimate likely understates productivity growth from 2006 to 2016. But so, too, does the 2.7 percent figure understate productivity growth from 1996 to 2006, a period that witnessed the de facto invention of the World Wide Web and its associated uses for search, ecommerce, email, and much more—not to mention the widespread adoption of cellphones and invention of mobile

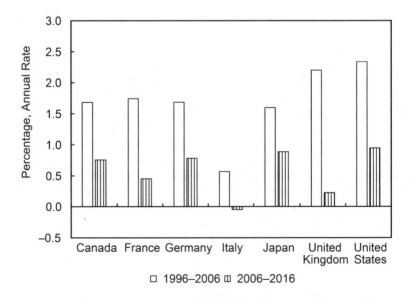

Fig. 12.1   Labor productivity growth, G-7 countries

Source: The Conference Board, Total Economy Database; author's calculations.

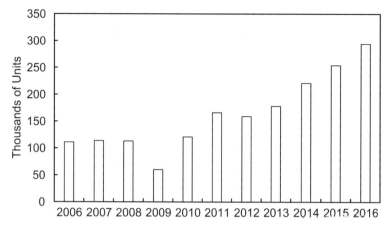

Fig. 12.2   Estimated worldwide annual supply of industrial robots, 2006–2016
Source: International Federation of Robotics, World Robotics (2016, 2017).

email. Recent research has confirmed that there is little reason to doubt the magnitude of the reduction in productivity growth, including pointing out that the slowdown has also occurred in well-measured industries (Byrne, Fernald, and Reinsdorf 2016; Syverson 2016).

This may seem counterintuitive given all the excitement around new innovations—including in robotics, AI, and automation more generally—but as exciting as these innovations may be, they still represent only a tiny fraction of our lives when compared to other sectors of the economy like housing, retail, education, and health—and, at least to date, the improvements they are making in these sectors are not dramatically different than the improvements we saw in previous eras of the economy.

That said, the technology sector of our economy is making important contributions to productivity growth. A 2015 study of robots in seventeen countries found that they added an estimated 0.4 percentage point on average to those countries' annual gross domestic product (GDP) growth between 1993 and 2007, accounting for a bit more than one-tenth of those countries' overall GDP growth during that time (Graetz and Michaels 2015). Moreover, since 2010, worldwide shipments of industrial robots have increased dramatically, as shown in figure 12.2, potentially signaling even more productivity growth in the future.

Relatedly, there has been dramatic progress in recent years in AI and its application in a diverse set of areas. For example, companies are using AI to analyze online customer transactions in order to detect and stop fraud, and, similarly, social networking sites are using it to detect when an account may have been hijacked. Thanks to AI, web search applications are now more accurate—for example, by correcting for manual entry error—thereby reducing costs associated with search. In radiology, where doctors must be able to examine radiological images for irregularities, AI's superior image processing techniques may soon be able to provide more accurate image analysis, expanding the potential for earlier detection of harmful abnormalities and reducing false positives, ultimately leading to better care. Artificial intelligence is also making inroads in the public sector as well. For example, predictive analytics has great potential to improve criminal justice procedures, although it must be used responsibly to avoid bias.

However, while AI research has been underway for decades, recent advances are still very new, and, as a result, AI has not had a large macroeconomic impact, at least not yet. The most recent major progress in AI has been in deep learning, a powerful method but one that must be applied in a customized way for each application. Even though we have not made as much progress recently on other areas of AI, such as logical reasoning, the advancements in deep-learning techniques may ultimately act as at least a partial substitute for these other areas.

While AI has an advantage over humans in many respects, humans still maintain a substantial advantage over AI for tasks that involve social intelligence, creativity, and general intelligence. For example, AI today can do decent translations but cannot come close to what a human can do with his or her knowledge of both languages, social and cultural context, and sense of the author's argument, emotional states, and intentions. As it stands, even the most popular machine translator still fails to reach the accuracy of a human translator.

It is possible that major new inventions like electricity have manifested themselves in the past in successive waves of added productivity growth, a pattern that could repeat itself in the future (Syverson 2013).

12.2 Past Innovations Have Sometimes Increased Inequality— and the Indications Suggest AI Could Be More of the Same

Advanced economies have seen vast amounts of innovation in the last three centuries. Most of the kinds of jobs that existed in the 1700s do not exist today, but jobs no one could have imagined then have taken their place. As a result, over long periods of time it has generally been the case that about 95 percent of the people in the United States who want a job at a given point in time can find one—despite massive changes in technology.

Although labor markets do not function like the stylized models for a commodity like wheat that populate economics textbooks, within broad parameters the basic operation of supply and demand is the mechanism that makes sure that just about everyone who wants a job can find one. For this to happen, however, wages need to adjust to make supply equal to demand. In recent decades, much of that adjustment in wages has been in the form of a large decline in wages for low-skill workers relative to high-skill workers.

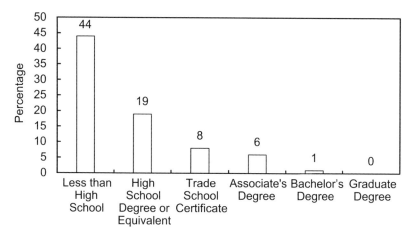

Fig. 12.3   Share of jobs with highly automatable skills by education
Source: Arntz, Gregory, and Zierahn (2016) calculations based on the Survey of Adult Skills (PIAAC 2012).

From 1975 until 2016, those with a high school degree watched their relative wages fall from over 70 percent of the amount earned by full-time, full-year workers with at least a college degree to just over 50 percent.

The worry is not that this time could be different when it comes to AI, but that this time could be the same as what we have experienced over the past several decades. The traditional argument that we do not need to worry about the robots taking our jobs still leaves us with the worry that the only reason we will still have our jobs is because we are willing to do them for lower wages.

The share of jobs that are threatened by future automation is fiercely debated, with estimates ranging from 9 percent by the Organisation for Economic Co-operation and Development ([OECD]; Arntz, Gregory, and Zierahn 2016, to 50 percent by Carl Frey and Michael Osborne 2013). While this question is important, there is less ambiguity on the wages/skills gradient of the jobs or tasks that are most likely to be substituted for by automation. The OECD researchers, for example, found that 44 percent of jobs with less than a high school degree had highly automatable skills, as compared to only 1 percent of jobs with a college degree, as shown in figure 12.3.

This is very similar to the gradient found in Frey and Osborne's work. The Council of Economic Advisers (Executive Office of the President 2016) sorted the Frey and Osborne occupations at risk of automation by wages and found that it ranged from 83 percent of occupations making less than $20 an hour to only 4 percent of occupations making more than $40 per hour, as shown in figure 12.4.

Since wages and skills are correlated, this means a large decline in the demand for lower-skill jobs and little decline in the demand for higher-skill jobs. This result points to a shift in the impact of automation on the labor market. At points in the past, automation led to a so-called polarization of the labor market because jobs requiring a moderate skill level—which historically included bookkeepers, clerks, and certain assembly-line workers—were easier to routinize, although more recently that process of polarization appears to have stopped (Autor 2014; Schmitt, Schierholz, and Mishel 2013). Conversely, higher-skill jobs that use problem-solving capabilities, intuition, and creativity, as well as lower-skill jobs that require situational adaptability and in-person interactions, were less easy to routinize. If anything, the new trends could put more pressure on earnings inequality. We are already seeing some of this play out—for example, when we go shopping and take our groceries to a kiosk instead of a cashier, or when we call a customer service help line and interact with an automated customer service representative.

It would be wrong, however, to believe that inequality is purely a function of technology. Relative wages do depend in part on the demand for labor, which is partially a function of technology. However, they also depend on the supply of different levels of skill—in other words, the distribution of educational attainment (Goldin and Katz 2008)—and also on institutional arrangements that affect wage setting, such as collective bargaining (Western and Rosenfeld 2011).

Technology, in other words, is *not* destiny. Many countries have experienced similar technological change as the United States, yet over the last four decades the United States has seen both a greater increase in income

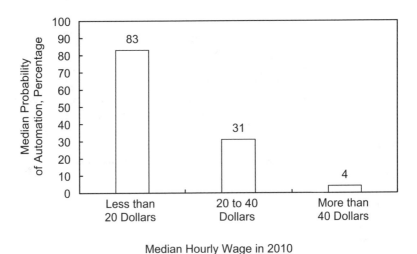

Fig. 12.4   Probability of automation by an occupation's median hourly wage
Source: Executive Office of the President (2016).

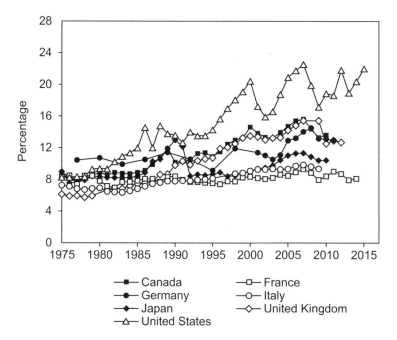

Fig. 12.5   Share of income earned by top 1 percent, 1975–2015
Source: World Wealth and Income Database.

inequality and higher overall levels of inequality than other major advanced economies, as shown in figure 12.5. When it comes to inequality—and, as I will note in a moment, to the labor market more broadly—institutions and policies can help determine whether and to what extent changes in technology shape economic outcomes.

12.3   The Long-Term Decline in the Labor Force Participation Rate Raises Other Concerns about the Potential Impact of AI

Moreover, the experience of the US labor market over the last half century raises questions around even this (relatively) optimistic view that we can avoid large-scale job losses at the expense of greater inequality. The fact that the labor force participation rate for men between the ages of twenty-five and fifty-four has declined steadily from a high of 98 percent in the 1950s to 89 percent in 2016 raises important doubts about the complacency about full employment as a general state of the economy. As discussed in detail in a report by the Council of Economic Advisers (2016), the decline in the labor force participation rate has been concentrated among men with a high school degree or less and has coincided with a decline in their relative wages. This decline suggests that decreasing labor force participation among this group is a manifestation of reduced labor demand, resulting in both fewer employment opportunities and lower wages for less-skilled men. Techno-logical advances, including the increasing use of automation, may partly account for this decline in demand for less-skilled labor, with globalization likely contributing as well.

(I focus on prime-age men because I believe their experience over the past six decades to be the best historical parallel for future effects of technological change on participation in the workforce for both men and women. In the second half of the twentieth century, prime-age women's participation rose sharply, as social and cultural changes in the decades following World War II swamped any negative effects on participation due to technological change. It is important to note, however, that prime-age women's participation has fallen in the last decade and a half—primarily for women with a high school degree or less—paralleling the earlier experience of prime-age men.)

The concern is not that robots will take human jobs and render humans unemployable. The traditional economic arguments against that are borne out by centuries of experience. Instead, the concern is that the process of turnover, in which workers displaced by technology find new employment as technology gives rise to new consumer demands and thus new jobs, could lead to sustained periods of time with a large fraction of people not work-ing. The traditional economic view is largely a statement about long-run equilibrium, not about what happens in the short-to-medium term. The fall in the labor force participation rate suggests that we must also think carefully about short-run dynamics as the economy moves toward this long-run equilibrium. In the short run, not all workers will have the training or ability to find the new jobs created by AI. Moreover, this "short run" (which is a description of where the economy is in relation to equilibrium, not a description of a definite length of time) could last for decades and, in fact, the economy could be in a series of "short runs" for even longer.

As a result, AI has the potential—just like other innovations we have seen in past decades—to contribute to further erosion in both the labor force participation rate and the employment rate. This does not mean that we will necessarily see a dramatically large share of jobs replaced by robots, but even continuing on the past trend of a nearly 0.2 percentage-point annual decline in the labor force participation rate for prime-age men would pose substantial problems for millions of people and for the economy as a whole.

As in the case of inequality, however, we should not interpret this as technological determinism. While most other advanced economies have seen declines in prime-age male labor force participation, the decline in the United States has been steeper than in almost every other advanced economy, as shown in figure 12.6. Part of the reason may be that US labor market institutions are less supportive of participation in the workforce than other countries' (CEA 2016).

There is no reason the economy cannot generate substantial levels of

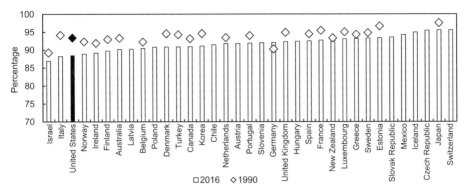

Fig. 12.6   Prime-age male labor force participation rates across the OECD
Source: Organisation for Economic Co-operation and Development.

employment at much higher levels of technology and productivity than we have today. What matters, however, is how our labor market institutions cope with these changes, help support the creation of new jobs, and successfully match workers to them. Some of the potential policies along these lines include expanding aggregate demand, increasing connective tissue in labor markets, reforming taxes to encourage work, and creating more flexibility for workers. Other possible policy responses include expanding education and training so more people have skills that complement and benefit from innovations, increasing the progressivity of the tax system to make sure that everyone shares in the overall benefits of the economy, and expanding institutional support for higher wages, including a higher minimum wage and stronger collective bargaining and other forms of worker voice.

12.4   The Costs of Replacing the Current Safety Net with a Universal Basic Income

Fears of mass job displacement as a result of automation and AI, among other motivations, have led some to propose deep changes to the structure of government assistance. One of the more common proposals has been to replace some or all of the current social safety net with a universal basic income (UBI): providing a regular, unconditional cash grant to every man, woman, and child in the United States, instead of, say, Temporary Assistance to Needy Families (TANF), the Supplemental Nutrition Assistance Program (SNAP), or Medicaid.

While the exact contours of various UBI proposals differ, the idea has been put forward from the right by Charles Murray (2006), the left by Andy Stern and Lee Kravitz (2016), and has been a staple of some technologists' policy vision for the future (Rhodes, Krisiloff, and Altman 2016). The different proposals have different motivations, including real and perceived deficiencies in the current social safety net, the belief in a simpler and more efficient system, and also the premise that we need to change our policies to deal with the changes that will be unleashed by AI and automation more broadly.

The issue is not that automation will render the vast majority of the population unemployable. Instead, it is that workers will either lack the skills or the ability to successfully match with the good, high-paying jobs created by automation. While a market economy will do much of the work to match workers with new job opportunities, it does not always do so successfully, as we have seen in the past half century. Fostering skills, training, job-search assistance, and other labor market institutions is a more direct approach to addressing the employment issues raised by AI than UBI.

Even with these changes, however, new technologies can increase inequality and potentially even poverty through changes in the distribution of wages. Nevertheless, replacing our current antipoverty programs with UBI would in any realistic design make the distribution of income worse, not better. Our tax and transfer system is largely targeted toward those in the lower half of the income distribution, which means that it works to reduce both poverty and income inequality. Replacing part or all of that system with a universal cash grant, which would go to all Americans *regardless of income*, would mean that relatively less of the system was targeted toward those at the bottom—increasing, not decreasing, income inequality. Unless one was willing to take in a much larger share of the economy in tax revenues than at present, it would be difficult both to provide a common amount to all individuals and to make sure that amount was sufficient to cover the needs of the poorest households. And for any additional investments in the safety net that one would want to make, one must confront the same targeting question.

Finally, some of the motivation for UBI has nothing to do with future technological developments. Instead, some UBI proponents have put forward the argument that it would be simpler, fairer, and less distortionary than the social assistance system we have today. This is not the space to go into great detail on this, but suffice it to say that today's system is imperfect. But at the same time, a wave of recent research has found that many of the common criticisms of these programs—for example, that they discourage work, or that they do little to reduce poverty—have been greatly overstated, and a number of programs—including nutritional assistance, Medicaid, and the Earned Income Tax Credit (EITC)—have important benefits for the long-run earnings, health, and educational attainment of children who grow up in recipient households.

This is not to say that we should not make the tax-and-transfer system more progressive—just that we need to match our ambitions to the revenue available and understand what is already successful in our social safety net.

12.5   Conclusion

Artificial intelligence is a critical area of innovation in the US economy right now. At least to date, AI has not had a large impact on the aggregate performance of the macroeconomy or the labor market. But it will likely become more important in the years to come—bringing substantial opportunities—and our first impulse should be to embrace it fully.

We need more productivity growth, including through more AI. Most of the innovation will be driven by the private sector, but government policies also have an impact through basic research and establishing a regulatory environment around privacy, cybersecurity, and competition.

At the same time, with or without AI we would have a lot to do if we want to address high levels of inequality and the falling labor force participation rate. To the degree that we are optimistic about AI, that should increase our motivation to undertake these changes. But there is little basis for believing that AI should dramatically change the overall direction or goals of our current policies.

Exogenous technological developments do not uniquely determine the future of growth, inequality, or employment. Public policy—including public policies to help workers displaced by technology find new and better jobs and a safety net that is responsive to need and ensures opportunity—will affect whether we are able to fully reap the benefits of AI while also minimizing its potentially disruptive effects on the economy and society. And in the process, such policies could also affect productivity growth—including advances in AI itself.

References

Arntz, Melanie, Terry Gregory, and Ulrich Zierahn. 2016. "The Risk of Automation for Jobs in OECD Countries: A Comparative Analysis." OECD Social, Employment and Migration Working Papers no. 189, Organisation for Economic Co-operation and Development.

Autor, David. 2014. "Polanyi's Paradox and the Shape of Employment Growth." NBER Working Paper no. 20485, Cambridge, MA.

Byrne, David, John Fernald, and Marshall Reinsdorf. 2016. "Does the United States Have a Productivity Slowdown or a Measurement Problem?" *Brookings Papers on Economic Activity*, Spring 2016. https://www.brookings.edu/wp-content/uploads/2016/03/byrnetextspring16bpea.pdf.

Council of Economic Advisers (CEA). 2016. "The Long-Term Decline in Prime-Age Male Labor Force Participation." Report, Executive Office of the President of the United States.

Executive Office of the President (EOP). 2016. "Artificial Intelligence, Automation, and the Economy." Report.

Frey, Carl, and Michael Osborne. 2013. "The Future of Employment: How Susceptible are Jobs to Computerization." Unpublished manuscript, Oxford University.
Goldin, Claudia, and Lawrence Katz. 2008. *The Race between Education and Tech-
nology*. Cambridge, MA: Harvard University Press.
Graetz, Georg, and Guy Michaels. 2015. "Robots at Work." CEPR Discussion Paper
no. DP10477, Centre for Economic Policy Research.
Murray, Charles. 2006. *In Our Hands: A Plan to Replace the Welfare State*. Wash-
ington, DC: AEI Press.
Rhodes, Elizabeth, Matt Krisiloff, and Sam Altman. 2016. "Moving Forward on
Basic Income." Blog, Y Combinator. May 31.
Schmitt, John, Heidi Schierholz, and Lawrence Mishel. 2013. "Don't Blame the
Robots. Assessing the Job Polarization Explanation of Growing Wage Inequality."
EPI Working Paper, Economic Policy Institute. https://www.epi.org/publication
/technology-inequality-dont-blame-the-robots//
Stern, Andy, and Lee Kravitz. 2016. *Raising the Floor: How a Universal Basic Income
Can Renew Our Economy and Rebuild the American Dream*. New York: Public-
Affairs.
Syverson, Chad. 2013. "Will History Repeat Itself? Comments on 'Is the Informa-
tion Technology Revolution Over?'" *International Productivity Monitor* 25 (2):
37–40.
———. 2016. "Challenges to Mismeasurement Explanations for the U.S. Productiv-
ity Slowdown." NBER Working Paper no. 21974, Cambridge, MA.
Western, Bruce, and Jake Rosenfeld. 2011. "Unions, Norms, and the Rise in U.S.
Wage Inequality." *American Sociological Review* 76 (4): 513–37.

R&D, Structural Transformation, and the Distribution of Income

Jeffrey D. Sachs

13.1 Introduction

Oh, for the days of balanced growth. In Solow's growth model, labor-augmenting technical change at a constant rate produces long-term growth in output per capita and wages at the same constant rate. The returns to capital are stable, as are the factor shares of national income going to labor and capital. In the heyday of the Solow model, these were viewed by Kaldor (1957) and others as the stylized facts of long-term economic growth.

These stylized facts have visibly broken down since around the year 2000. There has been a striking disconnect between the continued growth of labor productivity (gross domestic product [GDP] per worker) and the stagnation of compensation per worker, resulting in a discernible decline in the labor share of income, as shown in figure 13.1 for the nonfarm business sector (Elsby, Hobijn, and Şahin 2013; ILO and OECD 2015; Karabarbounis and Neiman 2013; Koh, Santaeulalia-Llopis, and Zheng 2015). The decline in labor share is widely, if not universally, attributed to automation—robots and other smart machines—displacing labor.

There are other possible culprits besides automation, including a conjectured rise in monopoly power, a fall in US union coverage and power, and the effects of global trade on the distribution of income. Of course, several factors may be at play. My view is that automation—the replacement of

Jeffrey D. Sachs is University Professor, the Quetelet Professor of Sustainable Development, and professor of health policy and management at Columbia University and a research associate of the National Bureau of Economic Research.

For acknowledgments, sources of research support, and disclosure of the author's material financial relationships, if any, please see http://www.nber.org/chapters/c14014.ack.

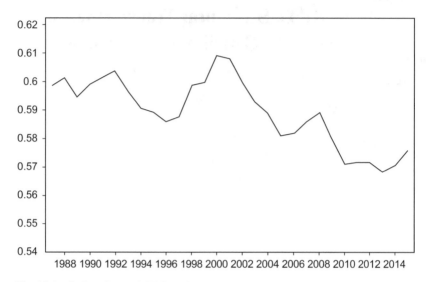

Fig. 13.1   Labor share of GDP at factor cost

Source: Data are from Components of Value Added by Industry, millions of dollars, Bureau of Economic Analysis, release date: November 3, 2016.

Note: The labor share is defined as compensation of employees divided by the sum of compensation of employees and operating surplus for the gross domestic product.

human labor by machines and code—is likely to be the most important of the factors.

Indeed, my argument is that the decline in the labor share via automation has been occurring well before the year 2000, but that it has been obscured in the macroeconomic data by offsetting structural changes. Balanced growth, in short, was always a mirage. The difference now is that the imbalances are now showing more vividly, and are likely to intensify.

One reason that unbalanced growth was underemphasized before the year 2000 is that different sectors of the economy were affected by automation in different, and indeed offsetting, ways. It is useful, I believe, to disaggregate GDP into five major sectors:

- goods-producing sectors: agriculture, mining, construction, and manufacturing;
- basic business services: utilities, wholesale trade, retail trade, transport, and warehousing;
- personal services: arts, leisure, food, and accommodations, other personal;
- professional services: information, finance, education, health, management, scientific and technical, other professional; and
- government services: federal, state, and local.

Table 13.1   **Required expertise and workflow predictability by sector**

Sector	Typical expertise/education	Typical workflow predictability
Goods producing	Low to moderate	High
Basic business services	Moderate	Moderate to high
Personal services	Low to moderate	Low to moderate
Professional services	High	Low
Government	Moderate to high	Moderate to high

These sectors are differentially susceptible to automation. Historically, there seem to have been two key dimensions to work tasks that determine their suitability for automation: degree of expertise required and repetitiveness/predictability of the task (Frey and Osborne 2013; Chui, Manyika, and Miremadi 2016; McKinsey Global Institute 2017). Tasks requiring high expertise (e.g., as measured by their educational requirements) and that have low predictability/repetitiveness in workflow have been less easily automated. Based on the occupational mix and production processes of the five sectors, we can place the sectors roughly as seen in table 13.1.

This suggests that the goods-producing sector has been easiest to automate and professional services the most difficult, with the other sectors somewhere in the middle, depending on the particular subsectors involved. As I describe later, artificial intelligence (AI) could change the character of automation in the future, leading to much more automation of high-skill tasks.

These differences in susceptibility to automation show up in the sector trends in labor share of value added (measured at factor cost) since 1987, shown in figure 13.2.

We see a large drop in the labor share of value added in the goods-producing sector, from 61.7 percent to 48.9 percent, consistent with the ease of automation in that sector, contrasted by an increase in the labor share of value added in professional services and government, consistent with the relative difficulty of automation in those two sectors. Basic business services also show a modest decline in the labor share, from 66.3 percent to 60.1 percent. The labor share of value added in personal services was unchanged, consistent with the relatively low workflow predictability of that sector, making it more difficult to automate.

Figure 13.2 makes clear that in the goods-producing and basic-business-service sectors, automation has been taking place for decades, but the trends have been somewhat obscured by the relative lack of automation in the other sectors, and by the fact that both output and employment have been shifting from goods production to professional services, that is, from the broad sectors experiencing the most automation to the ones experiencing the least automation.

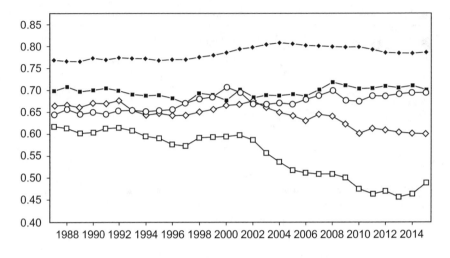

-□- Goods Producing   -◇- Basic Business Services   -○- Professional Services
-■- Personal Services   -♦- Government

Fig. 13.2   Labor share by sector

Source: Data source figure 13.1.

Notes: The labor share by sector is equal to the labor compensation for all subsectors divided by the sum of employee compensation and operating surplus for all subsectors. The sectors are as follows. Goods-producing sector: agriculture, forestry, fishing and hunting; mining; construction; and manufacturing. Basic business services: utilities, wholesale trade, retail trade, and transportation and warehousing. Professional services: information; finance and insurance; professional and business services; and educational services, health care, and social assistance. Personal services: arts, entertainment, recreation, accommodation, and food services. Government includes federal, state, and local government.

Even the significant observed decline in the labor share in the goods-producing sector understates the extent of structural change in that sector, since the composition of labor has also been shifting dramatically from production workers with relatively low levels of schooling to supervisory workers with higher levels of schooling. This too marks a rise in the share of capital income in value added, albeit the income earned by human capital rather than by business fixed capital.

Figure 13.3 offers a rough estimate of the overall share of labor income in the economy accounted for by different levels of educational attainment. For our purposes, I have grouped the educational attainment into three bins: low, compromising attainment up to some college including a two-year associate's degree; medium, comprising a bachelor's degree but no advanced degree; and high, comprising an advanced degree. Using census data on the mean income and number of workers at these levels of educational attainments, we can find the shares of labor income accruing to different categories, as shown in figure 13.3.

Labor income accruing to workers with less than a bachelor's degree

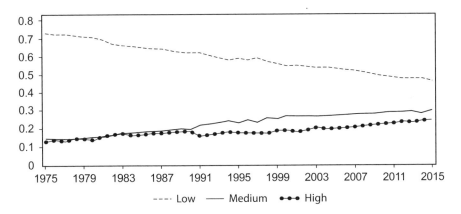

Fig. 13.3   Share of earnings by educational attainment
Source: Data are from the United States Census Bureau, table A-3, "Mean Earnings of Workers 18 Years and Over, by Educational Attainment, Race, Hispanic Origin, and Sex: 1975 to 2015," (https://census.gov/data/tables/2016/demo/education-attainment/cps-detailed-tables .html). Low education: not a high school graduate; high school graduate; some college or associate's degree; medium education: bachelor's degree; high education: advanced degree. Total income by level of educational attainment is the product of the number of workers with earnings and mean earnings.

plummeted from 72.7 percent to 46.1 percent. Workers with a bachelor's degree saw their share of labor income doubling from 14.3 percent to 29.6 percent, and workers with an advanced degree also saw their share of labor income doubling from 12.9 percent to 23.4 percent.

Real mean earnings per worker among these three categories shows a similar trend in figure 13.4. Earnings of low-skilled workers (defined here as all the way up to some college or an associate's degree) began to stagnate in the mid-1970s, and have not risen since then. Mean earnings for workers with a bachelor's or advanced degree continued to rise until around the year 2000 and have since been stagnant—or even falling, in real terms, in the case of those with advanced degrees.

The relative numbers of workers at each educational attainment has responded to the changing market incentives and to outlays for education by governments at all levels. As we see in figure 13.5, the proportion of all workers at less than a bachelor's degree declined from 83.4 percent to 64.3 percent, while those with a BA rose from 10.0 to 22.6 percent, and those with an advanced degree rose from 6.6 to 13.2 percent between 1975 and 2016.

What makes these trends especially important for us, I believe, is that the ability to automate tasks is likely to increase dramatically with the recent advances in big data, machine learning, and other forms of artificial intelligence. The trends to date—the falling share of labor income, rising share of earnings flowing to highly trained workers, and decline of real earnings of workers who are subject to automation—may soon be felt by a much wider swath of workers and sectors.

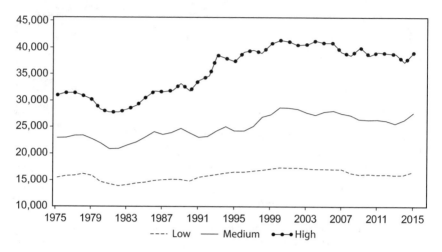

Fig. 13.4   Real mean earnings by education in $1982–1984

Source: Earnings data from source in figure 13.3.

Note: Real mean earnings for each education group are obtained by aggregating total earnings for the educational level, dividing by number of workers with earnings, and deflating by the Consumer Price Index.

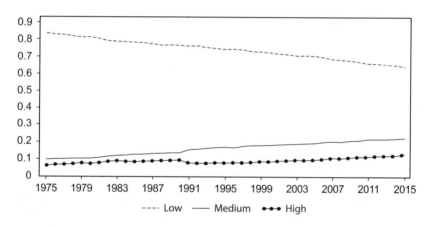

Fig. 13.5   Share of employment by education

Source: Employment data from the source in figure 13.3.

In a fundamental sense we are witnessing the gradual unfolding of a fundamental general purpose technology, digital information, that is at least as fundamental as the steam engine and electrification. Digital information began to unfold with the theoretical breakthroughs of Alan Turing, John von Neumann, Claude Shannon, and Norbert Weiner in the 1930s and 1940s, and then advanced dramatically with the first mainframe computers in the 1940s, the invention of the transistor in 1947, the invention of integrated circuits in the late 1950s, and the initiation of Moore's Law at the end of the 1950s. Of course, the digital revolution now engages a vast range of science and technology, including solid-state physics, nanotechnology, fiber optics, digital communication, and a startling range of applications across every domain of science and every sector of the economy.

The rising investments in research and development (R&D) are therefore a fundamental part of the story and the fundamental driver of structural transformation. Figure 13.6 shows the national accounts estimates of R&D annual outlays and the cumulative stock of intellectual property, both as a share of GDP. Research and development as a share of GDP roughly doubles from the early 1950s to today, from around 1.3 percent to 2.6 percent. The stock of intellectual property (IP) rises from around 4.5 percent to 14 percent of GDP. The point is that IP has risen far faster than GDP; the economy has become far more science intensive.

Rather than the Solow-era stylized facts, I would therefore propose the following alternative stylized facts:

1. The share of national income accruing to capital rises over time in sectors experiencing automation, especially when capital is measured to include human capital.

2. The share of national income accruing to low-skilled labor drops while the share accruing to high-skilled labor rises.

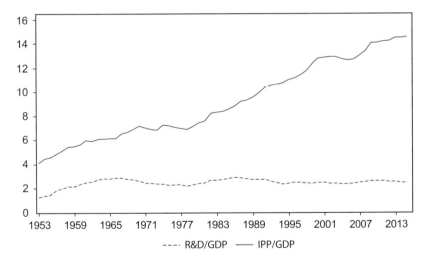

Fig. 13.6   R&D and intellectual property (percent GDP)
Source: The Net Stock of Intellectual Property Products is from the Bureau of Economic Analysis, table 2.1. Current-Cost Net Stock of Private Fixed Assets, Equipment, Structures, and Intellectual Property Products by Type, https://www.bea.gov/iTable/iTable.cfm?reqid=10 step=3 isuri=1 1003=18#reqid=10 step=3 isuri=1 1003=18. Investment in Intellectual Property Products is from Bureau of Economic Analysis, table 1.5. Investment in Fixed Assets and Consumer Durable Goods, https://www.bea.gov/iTable/iTable.cfm?ReqID=10 step=1#reqid=10 step=3 isuri=1 1003=96 1004=1950 1005=2016 1006=a 1011=0 1010=x.

3. The dynamics across sectors vary according to the differential timing of automation, with automation spreading from low-skill and predictable tasks toward higher-skill and less predictable tasks.

4. Automation reflects the rising intensity of science and technology throughout the economy, in terms of R&D, IP, and scientific expertise in the labor force.

5. Future technological changes associated with artificial intelligence (e.g., machine learning) are likely to shift national income from medium-skilled and high-skilled workers toward owners of business capital (fixed capital and intellectual property products).

There are, of course, many unsolved problems of both theory and measurement, but I will now try to lay out some basic concepts in more formal terms.

13.2   A Basic Model

Consider the goods-producing sector of the economy (agriculture, mining, construction, and manufacturing) the first to automate. Let Q be output. Output is produced by capital and labor. I will distinguish two kinds of physical capital, buildings (B) and machines (M), and two kinds of nonphysical capital, human capital and know-how embodied in machine technology.

Labor is organized into occupational tasks such as management, production, sales, and so forth. In general, these tasks require varying levels of expertise: unskilled (U), intermediate (I), and high (H), corresponding respectively to levels of education: less than a bachelor's degree, a bachelor's degree, and an advanced degree (masters, professional, or PhD). (Acemoglu and Autor 2011).

To illustrate, suppose that there are just two tasks for labor: production (P) and nonproduction (N). The production task requires basic skills. The nonproduction task requires intermediate skills. High skills are needed for three purposes: R&D, professional services such as medicine, and university education. Tasks requiring basic skills can also be carried out by workers with intermediate or high skills, and tasks requiring intermediate skills can also be carried out by workers with high educational attainment.

Machines M can substitute for labor while buildings B are complementary to tasks (see Sachs and Kotlikoff [2012] and Sachs, Benzell, and LaGarda [2015] for a similar approach). As a simple illustration, suppose that output Q is a Cobb-Douglas function of P, N, and B:

(1) $$Q = P^a N^b B^{(1-a-b)}.$$

Production P is produced either by labor L_P or machines M_P (such as assembly-line robots) assumed to be a perfect substitute, with t_P measuring the technological sophistication of the machines M_P:

(2)
$$P = L_P + t_P * M_P.$$

Similarly, nonproduction tasks can be produced by labor L_N or machines M_N:

(3)
$$N = L_N + t_N * M_N.$$

In the historical evolution of technology, it was easier to devise machines to carry out basic mechanical tasks (production) rather than intermediate tasks (nonproduction), so I start with the simplest assumption that $t_P > 0$ and $t_N = 0$. I note again, however, that as machines are getting "smarter," they are able to fulfill more nonproduction tasks.

Workers with basic education can work only in production, while workers with an intermediate education can work either in production or nonproduction tasks. Let L_U equal the number of workers with education U, and L_I the number of workers with educational attainment I. Then, with L_{ij} signifying the number of workers in task i (N, P) and skill j, full employment requires

(4)
$$L_U = L_{PU}$$
$$L_I = L_{NI} + L_{PI}.$$

The market equilibrium may involve a perfect sorting of tasks by skills (unskilled workers in production, intermediate-skilled workers in nonproduction, with $L_{PI} = 0$), or may involve some intermediate-skilled workers employed in basic-skill tasks, with $L_{PI} > 0$, a situation referred to as downskilling. In a dynamic context, the latter situation should be temporary, as workers will not generally invest in additional years of education for jobs that require a lower educational attainment.

In any period, the capital stock K is determined based on past savings and is allocated between buildings and machines in production tasks:

(5)
$$K = B + M_P.$$

Investors maximize their capital income by allocating K to equate the marginal products of buildings and machines, or by setting $M_P = 0$ at a corner solution (when the marginal product of buildings is higher than that of machines for $B = K$ and $M_P = 0$).

In the pure sorting equilibrium, the wages for LU and LI are given as follows:

(6)
$$W_U = a*(L_U + t_P * M_P)^{(a-1)} L_I^b S^{(1-a-b)}$$
$$W_I = b*(L_U + t_P * M_P)^a L_I^{b-1} S^{(1-a-b)},$$

and K receives the rate of return r:

(7)
$$r = (1 - a - b)*L_U^a L_I^b M_P^{-(a+b)}.$$

If t_P is below a threshold value t_P^T, then the entire capital stock K is allocated to buildings, so that $B = K$ and $M = 0$. In that case, there is no automation. If t_p is above t_p^T, then some capital is allocated to machines, with the added equilibrium condition

$$(8) \qquad\qquad\qquad r = t_p * W_U.$$

The threshold t_p^T can be found by equating $t_p^T * W_U$ with the marginal product of structures when $B = K$, specifically: $t_p^T * L_U^{(a-1)} L_I^b * K^{(1-a-b)} = (1 - a - b) * L_U^a L_I^b K^{-(a+b)}$. With a little algebra, we find that

$$(9) \qquad\qquad\qquad t_p^T = (1 - a - b) * \left(\frac{L_U}{K} \right).$$

The capital share of income KS is given simply as

$$(10) \qquad\qquad\qquad KS = \frac{(r * K)}{Q}.$$

Suppose now that the economy is operating in the range of automation, with $t_p > t_p^T$ and $M > 0$. The comparative static effects of a further rise in t_p are as follows:

$$(11) \qquad\qquad\qquad \frac{\partial r}{\partial t_p} > 0,$$

$$\frac{\partial W_B}{\partial t_p} < 0,$$

$$\frac{\partial W_I}{\partial t_p} > 0,$$

$$\frac{\partial M_P}{\partial t_p} > 0,$$

$$\frac{\partial KS}{\partial t_p} > 0.$$

The incremental improvement in machine technology (automation) leads to a rise in the return to capital (a), a fall in the wage of basic labor (b), a rise in the wage of intermediate labor (c), a rise in automation (d), and a rise in the share of capital income (e). This is simply a case of skill-biased technical change, in the form of technological change that induces the substitution of less educated workers by machines in the goods-producing sector.

13.3   Investing in Education

So far, we have taken the supplies of L_U and L_I as given, a reasonable assumption at a given moment of time but not in a dynamic context. The rise in the labor market returns to schooling, $[\partial(W_I - W_U)]/\partial t_p > 0$, will lead to a rise in investment in schooling, either by household outlays or public outlays. Remaining in a quasi-static context, suppose we start with initial levels of K, L_B, and L_I denoted by $K(0)$, $L_B(0)$, and $L_I(0)$ and assume a given flow of saving (SV) that may be allocated to fixed business investment F or education E_I for upgrading basic skills to intermediate skills:

(12)
$$SV = F + E_I,$$

$$K = K(0)*(1-d) + F,$$

$$L_I = L_I(0) + \frac{E_I}{c_I},$$

$$L_U = L_U(0) - \frac{E_I}{c_I}.$$

The parameter c_I is the unit cost of producing one intermediate-skilled worker from one low-skilled worker, taken here to be fixed. This cost includes both the direct education outlays (such as tuition) as well as the opportunity costs, notably the reduction of a student's labor market participation and earnings during the years of study.

Once again, the marginal returns to alternative investments should be set equal, so that the marginal product of fixed capital, equal to r, should be set equal to the returns to education, measured as $W_I - W_U$. In equilibrium,

(13)
$$r*c_I = W_I - W_U.$$

How, then, does a rise in t_P affect the investment in education? There are two effects. By raising the returns to fixed investment, r, the investment allocation can be shifted away from human capital to business fixed capital. On the other hand, by raising the wage of intermediate-skilled workers relative to basic-skilled workers, the net return to schooling is raised. In practice, the second effect is likely to dominate, especially if we also recognize that the rise in the return to capital will also likely increase the overall rate of saving SV.

If the education incentive effect indeed dominates, then the technological improvement increases the flow of students into higher education, thereby reducing the supply of basic-skilled workers and raising the supply of intermediate-skilled workers. The boost in the supply of skilled labor moderates the increase in wage inequality following the rise in t_P. In the extreme case that r remains constant, the wage differential would also remain unchanged by an offsetting increase in the skilled workforce sufficient to drive the wage differential back to the original level $r*c$.

13.4   Endogenous Growth

The model is greatly enriched by allowing the rate of technological advance to depend on the investments in R&D carried out by highly skilled scientists and engineers. Let us therefore now introduce a cadre of high-skilled professional workers in the number L_H. We will suppose that these workers are generally holders of advanced degrees in science, technology, engineering, and mathematics (STEM) fields.

The highly skilled workers L_H are employed in four major activities: (a) research and development, $L_{R\&D}$; (b) higher education, L_{ED}; (c) health care L_{HL} (medical doctors, medical equipment engineers, statisticians, etc.); and (d) professional consultancy services L_C. Other than health professionals and academic researchers, most workers with advanced degrees are employed in professional firms (engineering, consultancy, architecture, legal, etc.) that sell their research and consulting services to companies in other sectors, such as manufacturing:

$$(14) \qquad L_H = L_{R\&D} + L_{ED} + L_{HL} + L_C.$$

High-skilled professionals require an advanced degree, and therefore education at the postbachelor's level, denoted E_H. Thus, we revise the equations in (11) as follows:

$$(15) \qquad SV = F + E_I + E_H,$$

$$K = K(0)*(1-d) + F,$$

$$L_H = L_H(0) + \frac{E_H}{c_H},$$

$$L_I = L_I(0) + \frac{E_I}{c_I} - \frac{E_H}{c_H},$$

$$L_U = L_U(0) - \frac{E_I}{c_I}.$$

The benefit of investing in advanced training depends, of course, on the productivity of high-skilled workers in their four respective activities: R&D, education, health care, and consultancy. We need, therefore, to specify production functions for these four activities.

One of the main fruits of R&D will be to improve automation, meaning a rise in t_P. A plausible relationship might be something like

$$(16) \qquad t_P(t+1) = t_P(t)*(1-\text{dep}_{t_P}) + R\&D(t),$$

so that R&D(t) in turn would be produced with some combination of skilled labor, smart machines, and buildings in the R&D sector, such as

$$(17) \qquad R\&D(t) = (\Theta_{R\&D}*L_{R\&D})^g * B_{R\&D}^{(1-g)}.$$

The parameter $\Theta_{R\&D}$ signifies the efficiency of research by high-skilled workers. A high value of $\Theta_{R\&D}$ would signify a fruitful period for scientific research, for example, due to a significant breakthrough in scientific knowledge. The inventions of the transistor and integrated circuit in the 1940s and 1950s, and the design of modern computers around the same time, meant that the productivity of applied physicists and engineers rose markedly after World War II, ushering in the information revolution and a golden age for R&D that lasts till today, and that is indeed accelerating.

The parameter $t_{R\&D}$ signifies the possibility of artificial intelligence substituting for researchers in new R&D. This is of course already happening in areas such as drug discovery, where machine learning can scan through vast libraries of drug candidates for potential research targets. To date, advanced machines have mostly complemented rather than substituted for high-skilled researchers, yet it is not hard to envision the day soon when smart machines excel at research in biochemistry, genomics, code writing, and machine design. The inventors of ultrasmart machines will eventually put themselves out of business, or at least drastically lower their own wages as $t_{R\&D}$ rises significantly.

The health sector output HL would have a similar production function, such as

(18) $$HL(t) = (\Theta_{HL} * L_{HL} + t_{HL} * M_{HL})^g * S_{HL}^{(1-g)}.$$

A rise in Θ_{HL} would increase the supply of health services and the demand for health workers. But what of the demand for health services? We might suppose that the demand would also increase with Θ_{HL}. As health technology breakthroughs are made, these tend to become part of a minimum basic package of health services guaranteed by law and backed by public outlays. Thus, the public outlays on health services would tend to rise with Θ_{HL}.

13.5   Parameterizing the Model for the US Economy

The practical longer-term goal of this model will be to create a computable general equilibrium (CGE) model of the US economy that can analyze the past and future effects of technological change, especially artificial intelligence and robotics, on the distribution of incomes, wealth, jobs, and sectors. A primary purpose will be to analyze the likely progress of AI in substituting for many occupations that currently have high educational requirements, such as in health care (remote patient monitoring, advanced imaging, machine-led diagnostics), education (online education, expert systems for teacher training and pedagogy), and various areas of research and development. This is a work in progress.

At this stage, it will have to suffice to present some early simulation results of an illustrative model not yet parameterized for US conditions. I will present two such simulations, to examine: (a) a rise in the productivity of R&D, and (b) a rise in automation for middle-skilled tasks (jobs currently requiring BA-level workers).

13.6   Rise in R&D Productivity

What happens to the structure of an economy when the returns to R&D rise because of a new general purpose technology such as transistors and computers in the 1950s or machine learning and artificial intelligence in the 2020s. The experiment, to be precise, is a permanent, one-time step increase in $\Theta_{R\&D}$, the productivity of high-skilled R&D workers. In this first variant, I assume that only low-skilled workers face the competition from automation. In a sense, this illustration tracks the experience of the 1950s–2010s, when the breakthroughs of the digital revolution enabled the automation of low-skill tasks. The full model and specific parameters are available in the supplementary materials. For the purposes here, I emphasize the qualitative results.

In the numerical illustration, the rise in $\Theta_{R\&D}$ occurs in period 5 yet is anticipated from period 1. Even before the rise in R&D takes hold, workers begin to raise their educational attainment in anticipation of the widening gap between low-skill and higher-skill wages. After the rise in $\Theta_{R\&D}$ the shift in educational attainment is even stronger. The end result is a sharp decline in the proportion of low-skilled workers and a commensurate rise in middle-skilled and high-skilled workers, as shown in figure 13.7, which qualitatively tracks the same empirical pattern we saw for the US economy in figure 13.5.

Automation initially gives rise to a fall in wages for unskilled workers, and a rise in wages for the intermediate and high-skilled sectors. The wage gap between high-skilled and low-skilled workers therefore opens, but then leads to the shift in educational attainment in figure 13.7, thereby tending to restore the preshock relative wages across skill levels.

In the second simulation, the rise in $\Theta_{R\&D}$ for low-skill tasks (again starting in period 5) is now accompanied by a similar rise in R&D productivity for automation in intermediate-skill tasks (starting in period 10). Thus, automation replaces both low-skilled and intermediate-skilled workers. The

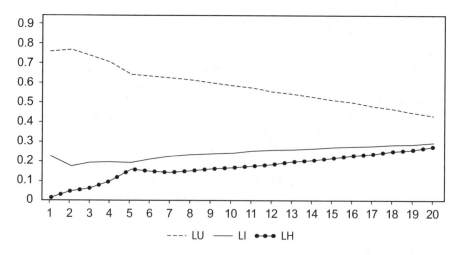

Fig. 13.7   Labor by educational attainment
Source: See appendixes A, B, and C.

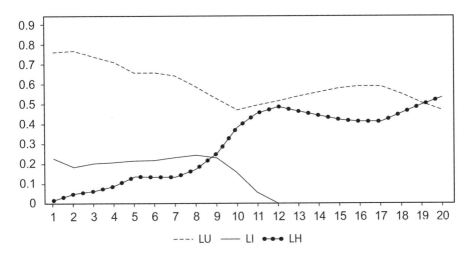

Fig. 13.8   Labor by educational attainment: automation for low-skill and intermediate-skill tasks
Source: See appendixes A, B, and C.

result, of course, is to give an added boost to the attainment of advanced degrees, so that both L_U and L_I decline, while L_H rises. The pattern is shown in figure 13.8, which may usefully be compared with figure 13.7.

In the case of automation of both unskilled and intermediate-skill tasks, the main result is that market forces induce those receiving a bachelor's degree to continue on to an advanced degree. The labor market ends up with just two kinds of labor, unskilled and highly skilled, with intermediate-skilled workers disappearing from the scene. Note that the model so far assumes that all workers are equally endowed with the skills needed for all levels of education; there is no "scarcity" value of STEM skills, for example, that would limit the supply of high-skilled workers. In a more realistic model, we would grapple with the obvious fact that not all students have the aptitude for an advanced degree for high-skill work. Instead of the wage differentials being offset by highly elastic shifts in educational attainment, a premium on higher education would be sustained in the long run as a kind of natural rent on high educational aptitude.

In both scenarios, the labor share of GDP declines markedly, as jobs are lost to automation. Figure 13.9 shows the time path of the labor share of GDP in the second scenario, in which automation for low-skilled workers takes off after period 5, and for intermediate-skilled workers after period 10. The labor share of income begins to dip around period 5, but then soars again around period 10 as the wages of skilled workers increases. Over time, as workers raise their educational attainment, wages decline and the overall labor share of income falls sharply under the pressures of automation.

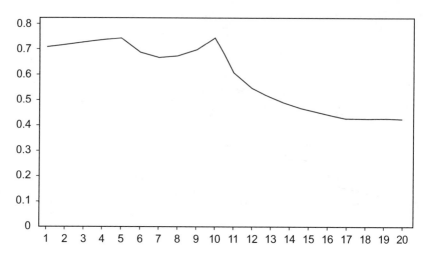

Fig. 13.9   Labor share of GDP
Source: See appendixes A, B, and C.

13.7   Next Steps

So far, the conclusions of the simulations are wholly qualitative. The next steps in modeling will be to parameterize the model according to the main structural features of the US economy. Of course, there are many difficult modeling and conceptual choices ahead, both in validating a parametrized model according to recent history and using the model to project the implications of future technological changes. Some of the difficulties are the following:

1. modeling the automation process with empirical detail, for example, by identifying the classes of machines that are complementarity to versus substitutional with various skills and occupations;

2. estimating the returns to automation-inducing R&D, and the implications for the earnings of advanced technical workers;

3. characterizing the supply and demand for higher education as a function of wage differential, borrowing costs, and educational aptitudes;

4. characterizing the relative roles of private and public financing in determining the investments in R&D and in education;

5. creating realistic scenarios for the future evolution of smart machines and their interaction with occupations at various skill levels;

6. modeling the intergenerational dynamics of automation as in Sachs and Kotlikoff (2012) and Benzell, Kotlikoff, LaGarda, and Sachs (2015);

7. accounting for monopoly rents on patents and other changes in market structure associated with smart machines and artificial intelligence;

8. accounting for the income distributional consequences of big data and network externalities, for example, for giants such as Google and Amazon;

9. accounting for the distributional implication of dematerialized production (ecommerce, ebooks, epayments) and the sharing economy (e.g., vehicles on demand); and

10. modeling the changes in past and future labor force participation and leisure time as the result of smart machines, artificial intelligence, and automation.

Appendix A
GAMS Equations

$Kf(tf)$. . .$K(tf) = e = K0$;
$Hf(tf)$. . .$H(tf) = e = H0$;
$Uf(tf)$. . .$U(tf) = e = U0$;
$Sf(tf)$. . .$S(tf) = e = S0$;
$IPPAf(tf)$. . .$IPPA(tf) = e = IPPA0$;
$IPPAIf(tf)$. . .$IPPAI(tf) = e = IPPAI0$;
Output(t). . .$Q(t) = e = TA(t)^{**}Alpha^*M(t)^{**}(1\text{-}Alpha)$;
BAprod(t). . .$BA(t) = e = MBA(t)^{**}.2^*SBA(t)^{**}.2^*HBA(t)^{**}.6$;
PROFprod(t). . .$PROF(t) = e = MPROF(t)^{**}.2^*ProdPROF(t)^*$
   $HPROF(t)^{**}.8$;
*PROFprod(t). . .$PROF(t) = e = ProdPROF(t)^*HProf(t)$;
Health(t). . .$HL(t) = e = MHL(t)^{**}.2^*LUHL(t)^{**}.1^*SHL(t)^{**}$
   $.2^*HHL(t)^{**}.5$;
*HealthD(t). . .$HL(t) = e = IILmin^*IPP(t)^{**}.2$;
HealthD(t). . .$HL(t) = e = .01$;
Capital(t). . .$K(t) = e = M(t) + MBA(t) + MPROF(t) + MHL(t) + RA(t)$
   $+ RAI(t)$;
Task(t). . .$TA(t) = e = (LU(t) + A(t))^{**}Beta^*(LS(t) + AI(t))^{**}(1\text{-}Beta)$;
Robot(t). . .$A(t) = e = ThetaA(t)^*HA(t)^{**}Gamma^*IPPA(t)^{**}$
   $Delta^*RA(t)^{**}(1\text{-}Gamma\text{-}Delta)$;
ArtInt(t). . .$AI(t) = e = ThetaAI(t)^*HAI(t)^{**}Gamma^*IPPAI(t)^{**}$
   $Delta^*RAI(t)^{**}(1\text{-}Gamma\text{-}Delta)$;
RDA($t + 1$). . .$IPPA(t + 1) = e = IPPA(t)^*(1\text{-}depRD) +$
   $PRODRDA(t)^*HRD(t)$;
RDAI($t + 1$). . .$IPPAI(t + 1) = e = IPPAI(t)^*(1\text{-}depRD) +$
   $PRODRDAI(t)^*HRD(t)$;
HighS(t). . .$H(t) = e = HAI(t) + HA(t) + HRD(t) + HBA(t) + HPROF(t)$
   $+ HHL(t)$;

KNext(t + 1). . .$K(t + 1) = e = K(t)$*(1-dep) + FINV(t);
Saving(t). . .$C(t) = e = Q(t)$—FINV(t) ;
UNext(t + 1). . .$U(t + 1) = e = U(t)$*(1-n)—BA(t) + n*($U(t) + S(t) + H(t)$) ;
SNext(t + 1). . .$S(t + 1) = e = S(t)$*(1-n) + BA(t)—PROF(t);
HNext(t + 1). . .$H(t + 1) = e = H(t)$*(1-n) + PROF(t);
LaborU(t). . .$U(t) = e = $ LU(t) + BA(t) + LUHL(t);
LaborS(t). . .$S(t) = e = $ LS(t) + 0.2*PROF(t) + SBA(t) + SHL(t);
Utils(t). . .Ut(t) $= e = $log($C(t)$));
KLast(tl). . .KL(tl) $= e = K(tl)$*(1-dep)+ FINV(tl);
CLast(tl). . .CL(tl) $= e = Q(tl)$—dep*KL(tl);
Utility. . .Util $= e = $ sum(t,disc(t)*$Ut(t)$) + sum(tl,disc(tl)*log(CL(tl))/
    Discrate);
* Output
Parameter WageU(t), WageS(t), WageH(t), Rrate(t), IPPArate(t),
    IPPAIrate(t), Lshare(t), Kshare(t), HAshare(t), RArate(t), Income(t),
    Lshare(t), LUshare(t), LSshare(t), LHshare(t);
Parameter Kshare(t), IPshare(t), LULF(t), LSLF(t), LHLF(t), LF(t);
WageU(t) = Alpha*Q.L(t)/TA.L(t) * Beta * TA.L(t)/(LU.L(t) + A.L(t));
WageS(t) = Alpha*Q.L(t)/TA.L(t) * (1-Beta) * TA.L(t)/(LS.L(t) +
    AI.L(t));
Rrate(t) = (1-Alpha)*Q.L(t)/M.L(t) ;
WageH(t) = ThetaA(t)*Gamma*(A.L(t)/HA.L(t))*WageU(t);
HAshare(t) = HA.L(t)/H.L(t);
RArate(t) = (1-Gamma-Delta)*(A.L(t)/RA.L(t))*WageU(t);
IPPArate(t) = Gamma*(A.L(t)/IPPA.L(t))*WageU(t);
IPPAIrate(t) = Gamma*(AI.L(t)/IPPAI.L(t))*WageS(t);
Income(t) = WageU(t)*LU.L(t) + WageS(t)*LS.L(t) + WageH(t)*H.L(t)
    + Rrate(t)*K.L(t) + IPPArate(t)*IPPA.L(t) + IPPAIrate(t)*IPPAI.L(t);
Lshare(t) = (WageU(t)*LU.L(t) + WageS(t)*S.l(t) + WageH(t)*H.L(t))/
    Income(t);
LUshare(t) = WageU(t)*LU.L(t)/Income(t);
LSshare(t) = WageS(t)*LS.L(t)/Income(t);
LHshare(t) = WageH(t)*H.L(t)/Income(t);
Kshare(t) = Rrate(t)*K.L(t)/Income(t);
IPshare(t) = (IPPArate(t)*IPPA.L(t) + IPPAIrate(t)*IPPAI.L(t))/
    Income(t);
LF(t) = LU.L(t) + LS.L(t) + H.L(t);
LULF(t) = LU.L(t)/LF(t);
LSLF(t) = LS.L(t)/LF(t);
LHLF(t) = H.L(t)/LF(t);

Appendix B
Parameter Values

Parameters Gamma, Alpha, Beta, Delta, Disc(t), dep, depRD, HLmin,
   Discrate;
Gamma = .5;
Alpha = .7;
Beta = .7;
Gamma = .3;
Delta = .3;
Discrate = .06;
Disc(t) = (1/(1+Discrate))**(ord(t)-1);
dep = 0.05;
depRD = .05;
HLmin = .1;
Parameters ThetaA, ThetaAI, tfpRA(t), tfpRAI(t);
ThetaA(t) = 1;
ThetaAI(t) = 1;
*tfpRA(t) = .01;
*tfpRA(t)\$(ord(t) ge 10) = 1;
*tfpRAI(t) = .01;
*tfpRAI(t)\$(ord(t) ge 15) = 1;
tfpRA(t) = 1;
tfpRAI(t) = 1;

Appendix C
Initial Values

Parameter K0, U0, S0, H0, ProdRDA(t), ProdRDAI(t), ProdPROF(t),
   IPPA0, IPPAI0, n, Start(t);
K0 = 21.9;
U0 = 7.3;
S0 = 2.25;
H0 = 0.15;
ProdRDA(t) = .01;
ProdRDAI(t) = .01;
*ProdRDAI(t)\$(ord(t) ge 10) = 1;
ProdPROF(t) = 2;
IPPA0 = 0.001;

IPPAI0 = 0.001;
n = 0.05;

References

Acemoglu, Daron, and David Autor. 2011. "Skills, Tasks and Technologies: Implications for Employment and Earnings." In *Handbook of Labor Economics*, vol. 4b, edited by Orley Ashenfelter and David E. Card. Amsterdam: Elsevier.

Benzell, Seth G., Laurence J. Kotlikoff, Guillermo LaGarda, and Jeffrey D. Sachs. 2015. "Robots Are Us: Some Economics of Human Replacement." NBER Working Paper no. 20941, Cambridge, MA.

Chui, Michael, James Manyika, and Mehdi Miremadi. 2016. "Where Machines Could Replace Humans and Where They Can't (Yet)." *McKinsey Quarterly* July 2016. https://www.mckinsey.com/business-functions/digital-mckinsey/our-insights/where-machines-could-replace-humans-and-where-they-cant-yet.

Elsby, Michael W. L., Bart Hobijn, and Ayşegül Şahin. 2013. "The Decline of the U.S. Labor Share." Federal Reserve Bank of San Francisco Working Paper Series no. 2013–27, Federal Reserve Bank of San Francisco, September.

Frey, Carl Benedikt, and Michael A. Osborne. 2013. "The Future of Employment: How Susceptible are Jobs to Computerization." Working Paper, Oxford Martin School, University of Oxford. September. https://www.oxfordmartin.ox.ac.uk/downloads/academic/The_Future_of_Employment.pdf.

International Labor Organization (ILO) and Organisation for Economic Co-operation and Development (OECD). 2015. "The Labor Share in the G20 Economies." G20 Employment Working Group, February.

Kaldor, Nicholas. 1957. "A Model of Economic Growth." *Economic Journal* 67 (268): 591–624.

Karabarbounis, Loukas, and Brent Neiman. 2013. "The Global Decline of the Labor Share." NBER Working Paper no. 19136, Cambridge, MA.

Koh, Dongya, Raul Santaeulalia-Llopis, and Yu Zheng. 2015. "Labor Share Decline and the Capitalization of Intellectual Property Products." Working Paper, January.

McKinsey Global Institute. 2017. "A Future that Works: Automation, Employment, and Productivity." Report, January. https://www.mckinsey.com/mgi/overview/2017-in-review/automation-and-the-future-of-work/a-future-that-works-automation-employment-and-productivity.

Sachs, Jeffrey D., Seth G. Benzell, and Guillermo LaGarda. 2015. "Robots: Curse or Blessing? A Basic Framework." NBER Working Paper no. 21091, Cambridge, MA.

Sachs, Jeffrey D., and Laurence J. Kotlikoff. 2012. "Smart Machines and Long-Term Misery." NBER Working Paper no. 18629, Cambridge, MA.

14

Artificial Intelligence and Its Implications for Income Distribution and Unemployment

Anton Korinek and Joseph E. Stiglitz

14.1 Introduction

The introduction of artificial intelligence (AI) is the continuation of a long process of automation. Advances in mechanization in the late nineteenth and early twentieth centuries automated much of the physical labor performed by humans. Advances in information technology in the mid- to late twentieth century automated much of the standardized data processing that used to be performed by humans. However, each of these past episodes of automation left large areas of work that could only be performed by humans.

Some propose that advances in AI are merely the latest wave in this long process of automation, and may in fact generate less economic growth than past technological advances (see, e.g., Gordon 2016). Others, by contrast, emphasize that AI critically differs from past inventions: as artificial intelligence draws closer and closer to human general intelligence, much of human labor runs the risk of becoming obsolete and being replaced by AI in all domains. In this view, progress in artificial intelligence is not only a continua-

Anton Korinek is associate professor of economics and business administration at the University of Virginia and Darden GSB and a research associate of the National Bureau of Economic Research. Joseph E. Stiglitz is University Professor at Columbia University and a research associate of the National Bureau of Economic Research.

This chapter was prepared as a background paper for the NBER conference The Economics of Artificial Intelligence. We would like to thank our discussant Tyler Cowan as well as Jayant Ray and participants at the NBER conference for helpful comments. We also acknowledge research assistance from Haaris Mateen as well as financial support from the Institute for New Economic Thinking (INET) and the Rewriting the Rules project at the Roosevelt Institute, supported by the Ford, Open Society, and the Bernard and Irene Schwartz Foundations. For acknowledgments, sources of research support, and disclosure of the authors' material financial relationships, if any, please see http://www.nber.org/chapters/c14018.ack.

tion, but the culmination of technological progress; it could lead to a course of history that is markedly different from the implications of previous waves of innovation, and may even represent what James Barrat (2013) has termed "Our Final Invention."

No matter what the long-run implications of AI are, it is clear that it has the potential to disrupt labor markets in a major way, even in the short and medium run, affecting workers across many professions and skill levels.[1] The magnitude of these disruptions will depend on two important factors: the speed and the factor bias of progress in AI.

On the first factor, measured productivity has increased rather slowly in recent years, even as the world seems to be captured by AI fever.[2] If AI-related innovations enter the economy at the same slow pace as suggested by recent productivity statistics, then the transition will be slower than, for example, the wave of mechanization in the 1950–1970s, and the resulting disruptions may not be very significant. However, there are three possible alternatives: First, some suggest that productivity is significantly undermeasured, for example, because quality improvements are not accurately captured. The best available estimates suggest that this problem is limited to a few tenths of a percentage point (see, e.g., the discussion in Groshen et al. [2017]). Furthermore, there are also unmeasured deteriorations in productivity, for example, declines in service quality as customer service is increasingly automated. Second, the aggregate implications of progress in AI may follow a delayed pattern, similar to what happened after the introduction of computers in the 1980s. Robert Solow (1987) famously quipped that "you can see the computer age everywhere but in the productivity statistics." It was not until the 1990s that a significant rise in aggregate productivity could be detected, after sustained investment in computers and a reorganization of business practices had taken place. Third, it is of course possible that a significant discontinuity in productivity growth occurs, as suggested, for example, by proponents of a technological singularity (see, e.g., Kurzweil 2005).

On the second factor, the disruptions generated by AI-related innovations depend on whether they are labor-saving, using the terminology of Hicks (1932), that is, whether at a given wage the innovations lead to less demand for labor. Some suggest that artificial intelligence will mainly *assist* humans in being more productive, and refer to such new technologies as *intelligence-assisting innovation* (IA), rather than AI. Although we agree that most AI-related innovations are likely to be complementary to at least some jobs, we believe that in taking a broader perspective, progress in AI

---

1. For example, Frey and Osborne (2017) warn that 47 percent of jobs in the US economy are at risk of being automated by advances in AI-related fields. Areas in which human intelligence has recently become inferior to artificial intelligence include many applications of radiology, trading in financial markets, paralegal work, underwriting, driving, and so forth.

2. For example, Google Trends reveals that search interest in the topic "artificial intelligence" has quadrupled over the past four years.

is more likely to substitute for human labor, or even to replace workers outright, as we will assume in some of our formal models below.

We believe that the primary economic challenge posed by the proliferation of AI will be one of income distribution. We economists set ourselves too easy a goal if we just say that technological progress *can make everybody better off*—we also have to say *how we can make this happen*. This chapter is an attempt to do so by discussing some of the key economic research issues that this raises.[3]

In section 14.2 of this chapter, we provide a general taxonomy of the relationship between technological progress and welfare. We first observe that in a truly first-best economy—in which complete risk markets are available before a veil of ignorance about innovations is lifted—all individuals will share in the benefits of technological progress. However, since the real world does not correspond to this ideal, redistribution is generally needed to ensure that technological progress generates Pareto improvements. If markets are perfect and redistribution is costless, it can always be ensured that technological progress makes everybody better off. The same result holds if the costs of redistribution are sufficiently low. In all these cases, there can be political unanimity about the desirability of technological progress. However, if redistribution is too costly, it may be impossible to compensate the losers of technological progress, and they will rationally oppose progress. Even worse, if the economy suffers from market imperfections, technological progress may actually move the Pareto frontier inwards, that is, some individuals may necessarily be worse off. Finally, we observe that the first welfare theorem does not apply to the process of innovation, and as a result, privately optimal innovation choices may move the Pareto frontier inward.

In section 14.3, we decompose the mechanisms through which innovation leads to inequality into two channels. First, inequality rises because innovators earn a surplus. Unless markets for innovation are fully contestable, the surplus earned by innovators is generally in excess of the costs of innovation and includes what we call innovator rents. We discuss policies that affect the sharing of such rents, such as antitrust policies and changes in intellectual property rights. The second channel is that innovations affect market prices; they change the demand for factors such as different types of labor and capital, which affects their prices and generates redistributions. For example, AI may reduce a wide range of human wages and generate a redistribution to entrepreneurs. From the perspective of our first-best benchmark with complete insurance markets, these factor price changes represent pecuniary externalities. We discuss policies to counter the effects of the resulting factor price changes.

---

3. An important, and maybe even more difficult, complementary question, which is beyond the scope of this chapter, is to analyze the political issues involved.

In section 14.4, we develop a simple formal model of worker-replacing technological change, that is, we introduce a machine technology that acts as a perfect substitute for human labor. We study the implications for wages and discuss policy remedies. In the short run, an additional unit of machine labor that is added to the economy earns its marginal product, but also generates a zero-sum redistribution from labor to traditional capital because it changes the relative supply of the two. In the long run, the machine technology turns labor into a reproducible factor. Thus, in the long run, growth will likely be limited by some other irreproducible factor, and all the benefits of technological progress will accrue to that factor. However, since it is in fixed supply, it can be taxed and the proceeds can be redistributed without creating distortions. Hence a Pareto improvement is easily achieved.

In a second model, we demonstrate how changes in patent length and capital taxation can act as a second-best device to redistribute if lump sum transfers between workers and innovators are not available. A longer patent life both delays how quickly innovations enter the public domain, lowering consumer prices, and increases the incentives of innovators to produce worker-replacing machines. However, the resulting losses for workers can be made up for by imposing a distortionary tax on capital and providing transfers, so long as the supply elasticity of capital is sufficiently low.

We also discuss the implications of endogenous factor bias in technological change. Worker-replacing technological progress should make capital-saving innovations more desirable, providing some relief to workers. We also note that our economy is developing more and more into a service economy, and that the large role of government in many service sectors (e.g., education, healthcare, etc.) creates ample scope for interventions to support workers.

In section 14.5, we observe two categories of reasons for why innovation may lead to technological unemployment. The first category of reasons arises because wages cannot adjust, even in the long run: efficiency wage theory implies that employers may find it efficient to pay wages above the market-clearing level so that workers have incentives to exert proper effort. If technological progress lowers the marginal product of workers, and hence their real wage declines below their cost of living, then classic nutritional efficiency wage theories apply: unemployment would result because (in the absence of government support) workers could not survive working for the market-clearing wage and it would pay employers to raise real wages above the market-clearing level because of the resulting increase in worker productivity. The second category of technological unemployment arises as a transition phenomenon, when jobs are replaced at a faster rate than workers can find new ones. We discuss a variety of factors that may slow down the adjustment process. Efficiency wage arguments may also play an important role as a transitional phenomenon, in particular if workers' notion of fair wages is sticky. Finally, we discuss that jobs may not only provide wages but also meaning and note that, unless societal attitudes change with the proliferation of AI, it may be welfare enhancing to subsidize jobs rather than simply redistributing resources.

In section 14.6, we take a longer-term perspective that is somewhat more speculative and discuss the potential implications of superhuman artificial intelligence. We consider two scenarios: one in which some humans use technology to enhance themselves and attain superhuman intelligence, and one in which autonomous machines that are completely separate from humans reach superhuman intelligence. In both cases, the superior productivity of superior intelligence will likely lead to vast increases in income inequality. From a Malthusian perspective, the superintelligent entities are likely to command a growing share of the scarce resources in the economy, creating the risk of pushing regular humans below their subsistence level. We discuss corrective actions that could be taken.

14.2   Technological Progress and Welfare: A Taxonomy

In 1930 Keynes wrote an essay on the "Economic Possibilities of our Grandchildren," in which he described how technological possibilities may translate into utility possibilities. He worried about the quality of life that would emerge in a world with excess leisure. And he thought all individuals might face that quandary. But what has happened in recent years has raised another possibility: innovation could lead to a few very rich individuals—who may face this challenge—whereas the vast majority of ordinary workers may be left behind, with wages far below what they were at the peak of the industrial age.

So let us start by considering the arrival of a new technology that partially (or fully) replaces workers and let us ask the question: *would their standard of living necessarily decline?* We will consider this question in a number of different settings, providing a taxonomy for how technological progress might affect the welfare of different groups in society depending on the environment.

14.2.1   First Best

We start with a first-best scenario in which we assume that all markets are perfect: this includes risk markets that are free of adverse incentive effects and that allow individuals to insure against the advent of innovations "behind the veil of ignorance," that is, before they know whether they will be workers or innovators. The main purpose for considering this idealized setting is to demonstrate that from an ex ante perspective, compensating workers for the losses imposed by technological progress is a question of economic efficiency not redistribution.

If risk markets were perfect and accessible to all agents before they knew their place in the economy, then all agents would be insured against any risk that might affect their well-being, including the risk of innovation reducing the value of their factor endowment. For example, workers would be insured against the risk of declining wages.[4] This leads us to the following observation:

OBSERVATION 1)   *Consider a first-best world in which all individuals have access to a perfect insurance market "behind the veil of ignorance," that is, before they know whether they will be innovators or workers. If an innovation occurs in such a world, the winners would compensate the losers as a matter of optimal risk sharing. As a result, technological progress always makes everybody better off, and there is political unanimity in supporting it.*

This is a powerful observation because it reminds us that if we had an ideal market, something that very much looks like redistribution would naturally emerge. In our first-best economy, there are no losers from technological progress. Losers only exist if risk markets are imperfect compared to this benchmark. In more technical language, worker-replacing technological progress imposes pecuniary externalities on workers, which lead to inefficiency when risk markets are imperfect (see, e.g., Stiglitz and Weiss 1981; Greenwald and Stiglitz 1986; Geanakoplos and Polemarchakis 1986; or more recently Dávila and Korinek 2018).

This implies that policy measures to mitigate or undo the pecuniary externalities arising from technological progress—for example, redistribution programs—make the economy's allocation more efficient from an ex ante perspective, rather than "interfering" with economic efficiency. They bring us closer to the allocation that a well-functioning risk market would achieve. Policymakers who oppose redistribution to compensate the losers of innovation because it interferes with the free market seem to—inappropriately, in our view—take an ex post perspective, after an innovation has taken place and after individuals know their place in the economy. Even though they may pretend to preach about idealized free markets, they clearly have not understood the full implications of how an idealized free market would work, that is, that such a market would provide precisely the type of insurance that they are opposing.

In practice, workers who might be replaced by technological progress cannot purchase insurance contracts against being replaced, so in the absence of adequate government assistance, they are in fact hurt by the innovation. Of course there are good reasons for why such idealized risk markets are not present in the real world.

First, the limited lifespan of humans makes it difficult to write insurance contracts that stretch over multiple generations. Workers would have had to obtain the described insurance a long time ago, before AI was well

---

4. We will discuss the reasons why this is typically not the case in practice below.

conceived and its implications were clear, when the associated insurance premium would have been commensurately low. Perhaps their farsighted ancestors could have written state-contingent contracts on their behalf. Today, obtaining insurance against AI-reducing wages would require workers to pay large amounts since the possibility is very real. In short, effective insurance would have had to take place behind a "veil of ignorance" about the likely advent of AI.

To put it another way, in this perspective the first "insurable damage" to the individual occurs at the time that the probability of an innovation becomes nonnegligible, for at that time the insurance premium required for income smoothing becomes significant, and her welfare is lowered. The individual would have wanted to buy insurance against the risk that her insurance premium would go up. Thus, in a perfect market, insurance markets would have to go back at least to a date at which there was a negligible probability that the innovation occurs. This presents a problem: it may be that at the moment that the concept of AI is formulated precisely enough to be an insurable event (and therefore becomes an insurable event), it has a non-zero probability.

Second, even for more limited time periods, risk markets with respect to technological change are clearly not perfect. Among the main reasons are information problems.

Describing the State Space. This starts with the basic problem alluded to earlier of how difficult it is to describe the future state space.[5] We cannot easily write a contract on something before it has been invented. Addressing this problem would require that an individual has to be insured against any technological event that leads to lower wages. But any such insurance contract would necessarily have adverse incentive effects.

More broadly, the curse of asymmetric information that inhibits insurance markets is as prevalent here as it is elsewhere.

Adverse Selection. Innovation leads to important adverse-selection problems. Some people in the market are more informed than others. In an ideal market, the winners of innovation would provide insurance to the losers, and the winners (e.g., entrepreneurs) would almost certainly be better informed than the losers (e.g., workers).

Moral Hazard. Innovation may also be subject to moral hazard problems, that is, the presence of insurance may affect the likelihood that the insured event occurs. Although workers are unlikely to affect the pace of innovation in AI, the actions of innovators may be, to some extent, affected. If they were to completely insure away all their returns from innovation, there

---

5. Interestingly, this type of information problem is easy to deal with after innovation has occurred, because then we know what has been invented and in which state we are, but very difficult to capture in ex ante contracts.

would be scant incentive to exert effort.[6] Since, in a perfect insurance world, the winners would insure the losers, full insurance would lead to stagnation.

Insurance and Redistribution

A natural counterpart to observation 1 is that in the absence of perfect insurance markets "behind the veil of ignorance," ensuring that progress leads to a Pareto improvement generally requires redistribution. If workers have access to some insurance against the risk of AI but not perfect insurance, this does not remove the need for redistributions.

For example, obtaining AI insurance today would require workers to pay a large premium. Of course, conceptually, if one went back in time, before AI was well conceived and its implications clear, one might argue that the premium would be low. But even that might not be so, since premiums for large events, even with small probability, can be high. In any case, at the very moment of conception of AI—the first possible moment that one could conceivably have written a policy—AI would still have distributional consequences; workers would have to pay a premium to divest themselves of this risk, and thus they would be worse off compared to the innovators, the winners.

14.2.2   Perfect Markets Ex Post and No Costs of Redistribution

Our next case pertains to a world that may be described as a second-best world without the perfect insurance markets referred to earlier, but in which, ex post, all markets are functioning well *and* there can be costless redistributions. This case covers several critical results that, although obvious at some level, often get lost in the debate about AI and technological progress more generally.

OBSERVATION 2)   *If redistribution is costless and appropriate redistributions are made, then technological progress is always desirable for all agents. In that case, there is political unanimity in supporting technological progress.*

For convenience, and in conformity to conventional usage, we will refer the world with costless redistribution but otherwise perfectly functioning markets, as first best ex post; though we remind the reader that the previous analysis suggested that in a true first-best, workers would have insurance against the risks from AI, such that they would commensurately share any gains from innovation. If the world is first-best ex post in the sense thus

6. Some might argue that this problem is equally hard to deal with before or after innovation has occurred. If we tax innovators ex post, it destroys incentives just as much as if we fully insure away all returns from innovation. However, in both cases, the significance of any adverse effects is not clear. Innovators are at least partially driven by non-pecuniary motives. And partial insurance or partial redistribution are always an option. If Bill Gates had been told, ex ante, that government would take away 50 percent of his returns over $10 billion, there is little reason to believe that it would have had any significant effect on innovation and investment. Ex post, taxing the winners in "winner takes all" games may have only small incentive effects.

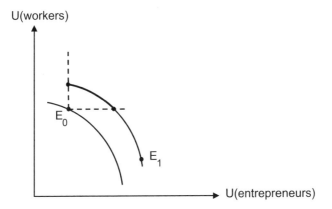

Fig. 14.1 **Pareto frontier before and after innovation with costless redistribution**

defined, then the utility possibilities curve (or Pareto frontier) moves out. We provide an example in figure 14.1, which depicts a utility possibilities frontier for two types of agents, workers, and entrepreneurs. In the example, technological progress increases the maximum utility level of entrepreneurs for any given level of utility of workers.[7] Innovation has increased production possibilities, and with lump sum redistributions, an expansion in production possibilities automatically implies an expansion in utility possibilities, that is, that everybody could be better off.

The fact that they *could* be better off does not mean that they *will* be better off. That depends on institutional arrangements. In figure 14.1, we denote the initial equilibrium by E_0 and the after-innovation equilibrium by E_1. We have deliberately not called it a competitive market equilibrium: markets do not exist in a vacuum (see e.g. Stiglitz et al. 2015). They are structured by rules and regulations, for example, concerning intellectual property rights and antitrust policies, and there may be tax and other policies in place. We thus simply refer to E_0 and E_1 as the before and after innovation (institution-given) equilibrium given the existing set of institutions. Note that in the example drawn in the figure, workers are worse off. That would normally be the case with what Hicks referred to as labor-saving innovations, that is, innovations that at a given wage lead to less demand for labor. Artificial intelligence appears to be a labor-saving innovation. In the simple formal models of worker-replacing innovations that we work out below, that is clearly the case.

This in turn has two important implications.

First, without adequate redistribution it makes sense for workers to resist the innovation. Luddism—the movement named after the possibly fictional

---

7. More generally, we could define a multidimensional utility possibilities frontier by adding any number of categories of individuals, or even naming the individuals.

character Ned Ludd that opposed automation in the textile sector in the late eighteenth and early nineteenth centuries in England—is a rational response for workers who are worse off from automation and who are not sufficiently compensated.

Second, in a democracy in which workers are in a majority it would make sense for enlightened innovators to support redistribution, to make sure that workers are at least not worse off. With redistribution, both innovators and workers *can* be better off. If appropriate redistribution is made so that everybody shares in the fruits of technological progress, there will again be political unanimity in supporting technological progress—progress will not be politically contentious.

There might be significant debate about how much compensation workers should receive, that is where in the "northeast corner of E_0" society should be. On the one hand, this debate concerns the distribution of the surplus generated by innovation. On the other hand, labor-saving innovation reduces wages, which generates a redistribution from workers to other factor owners like rentiers and capitalists, for which workers may seek compensation. This redistribution represents a pecuniary externality from the innovation, as we will discuss in further detail in section 14.3.2.

In figure 14.1, we have marked in bold that part of the postinnovation Pareto frontier that represents a Pareto improvement and lies to the northeast of E_0. A range of philosophical principles can be adduced for determining what is a "just" division of the fruits of innovation. Behavioral economics may provide insights into what kinds of divisions might be acceptable.[8]

Of course, the innovation may not be labor saving, and the equilibrium E_1 itself could be to the northeast of E_0. Although this case is easier, the distribution of the gains from innovation and any associated pecuniary externalities and rents may still be contentious, especially if they lead to large disparities in income. Distributive issues can also interact with production, as emphasized for example, by the efficiency wage theories that we consider in greater depth in section 14.5.

14.2.3 Perfect Markets but Costly Redistribution

There is another possibility—that as we try to redistribute, the new utility possibility curve may lie inside of the old utility possibilities frontier near the original equilibrium. This may be the case even in a world that is first-best

---

8. Consider a model in which workers and innovators have to agree on whether the innovation is acceptable. The innovator has the power to set the division of the gains (i.e., where along the curve Northeast of E_0 the new equilibrium lies), but the workers have the power to accept or reject. This is the standard ultimatum game, for which there is a large body of literature suggesting that at least some of the fruits of innovation have to be shared with workers. If they perceive the allocation of benefits to be unfair, they would rather be worse off (e.g., at the original point without the innovation) than at the point that just makes them indifferent to where they were before. See Fehr and Schmidt (2003).

ex post, that is, in which all the conditions for Pareto efficiency would be satisfied ex post after the innovation has taken place.

OBSERVATION 3)   *If the world is first-best ex-post, but redistribution is limited or costly, then a Pareto improvement may not be possible, and some groups in society may oppose technological progress. With a sufficiently inequality-averse social welfare function, societal welfare may be reduced.*

This case is illustrated in figure 14.2. The utility possibilities frontier is constrained by the costs imposed by redistribution. Even though it might appear that innovation could make everyone better off technologically, given the existing set of institutions of that economy, it actually can't—there may not be scope for avoiding utility losses for workers.

Some economists argue that the world looks like figure 14.2, and that if we try to transfer from innovators to workers, so much output is lost that workers are still worse off. If that is the case, then one cannot say that the innovation is a Pareto improvement. One hesitates to use the word "innovation." It is a change, perhaps a technological change, which has had the effect of making some people better off and others worse off. It is a distribution-inducing change and will be contentious.

A social welfare function that places no weight on inequality—which treats a dollar to rich innovators the same as a dollar to a poor worker—would, of course, conclude that the innovation is desirable. But with a more natural, inequality-averse social welfare function, the so-called innovation is welfare decreasing.

The workers who lose out would rationally oppose the innovation. If workers are in a majority and innovators wish to maintain their position, it would behoove the innovators to think harder about how to engage in redistribution. This is, of course, a collective action problem for innovators—for individual innovators, the contribution to economy-wide inequality is typi-

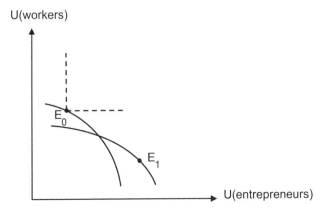

Fig. 14.2   Potential Pareto frontier with costly redistribution

cally limited, even if their collective behavior makes workers worse off. As a result, innovators often devote effort to actions that enhance their market power—lowering *real* incomes of workers still further—and to not paying taxes (both via clever tax avoidance using the existing legal framework, and via political lobbying to provide special exemptions from taxation for their industries). Disregarding, in our view unwisely, that their actions may stir up political opposition to innovation, some innovators go further and argue for weakening the progressivity of the tax system and a smaller state, so there are less public resources to provide for the well-being of the workers who are hurt by innovation.

According to a long-run version of "trickle-down" economics, repeated innovations will eventually increase the wealth of innovators so much that the benefits will trickle down to regular workers. In this view, a Pareto improvement is always possible in the long run, as in figure 14.1, even if an entire generation of workers is hurt in the short-to-medium run. This is a possibility and, in fact, the first industrial revolution may be an example. During the Industrial Revolution, workers eventually obtained enough human capital—which was publicly provided, as is in the interests of the innovators—so that the wages of almost all increased. In the current context, however, once machines are smart enough, innovators may no longer have incentives to support the public financing of human capital accumulation, and it may well be that workers' standards of living decrease. In particular, in a political system dominated by money, the innovators, increasingly rich, may use their economic and political influence to resist redistribution. Furthermore, even if long-run trickle-down economics was correct, it may lead to tremendous suffering and social upheaval in the short run. It may also—understandably—not be very credible if innovators promise that once they are rich enough, they will support workers, but that they are not quite rich enough yet.

This leads to the important question: *How costly is redistribution in practice?* As we noted earlier, markets do not exist in a vacuum. They are structured by laws and regulations and by how those laws and regulations are enforced. The outcome is the so-called "market" distribution of income, which is then subject to taxes and transfer, leading to an after-tax distribution of income. But this conventional distinction may not be quite accurate: the rules of the game concerning redistribution affect the market income distribution, and are themselves endogenous, affected by the rules of the political game, which in turn are affected by the distribution of wealth. (See Piketty, Saez, and Stantcheva (2014) and Stiglitz 2017.) The points that we have denoted E_0 and E_1 describe the initial outcome and the outcome after-technological change, *assuming that laws, regulations, institutions, and so forth remain unchanged.* But, of course, it is not reasonable to expect that they would remain unchanged with the advent of a change as significant as AI.

Setting aside the endogeneity of the rules themselves, each set of (feasible) laws, regulations, institutions, and so on defines a feasible utility possibilities frontier. We can think of the second-best utility possibilities frontier as the outer envelope of all these frontiers. As the outer envelope, the second-best utility possibilities frontier provides more flexibility for redistribution than does that associated with one particular set of rules, regulations, and institutions. This reflects that any changes in laws, regulations, or institutions, and so forth will also have redistributive effects. Given this additional flexibility, the likelihood that a Pareto improvement as in figure 14.1 can be achieved is greater. We provide further arguments for why this is likely to be the case in section 14.4 (although we cannot entirely rule out a situation like that depicted in figure 14.2 in which a Pareto improvement is not feasible).

14.2.4   Imperfect Markets

Let us also consider a fourth case, which does not necessarily reflect the specific situation with advances in artificial intelligence, but which is important to understand and keep in mind when we evaluate technological innovations.

OBSERVATION 4)   *If the economy is not first-best ex post, then the utility possibilities frontier may move inward in response to an expansion of production possibilities. Furthermore, this may even be true with costless redistribution.*

When we speak about an economy that is not first-best, we mean an economy that deviates from the Arrow-Debreu benchmark, that is, that exhibits market imperfections such as information problems, missing markets, and price and wage rigidities, which can result in aggregate demand problems, monopolies and monopsonies, and so forth. Typically, these mean that the market equilibrium is not Pareto efficient. The utility possibilities frontier represents the maximum utility of workers, given that of entrepreneurs, taking the market failures as given.

This case is illustrated in figure 14.3. The initial equilibrium is E_0, but the innovation, which would have led to greater efficiency in the absence of these market imperfections, makes workers worse off—and even with costless redistributions, there is no way that both workers and entrepreneurs can be better off.

An example, elaborated on by Delli Gatti et al. (2012a, 2012b), were the agricultural improvements at the end of the nineteenth century and beginning of the twentieth. The result was that agricultural prices plummeted, and so too did incomes on farms and in the rural sector. But mobility is costly—moving to the urban sector required capital, and many farmers saw their capital disappear as the value of their farms decreased. Those with loans often went bankrupt. Capital market imperfections (based on information asymmetries) meant that farmers could not borrow to move to the city to where the new jobs would be created. But as incomes in the rural sector plummeted, they could not buy the goods made by the manufacturing

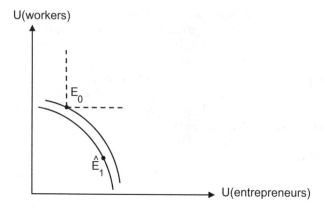

Fig. 14.3   Potential Pareto frontier with market imperfections

sector. Workers in both the rural and urban sector were worse off.[9] This provides one interpretation of the Great Depression—in the short run, the innovations at the time proved Pareto inferior.

Another example is given by the now-standard result that free trade may lead everyone to be worse off in the absence of good risk markets (Newbery and Stiglitz 1984). That result can be interpreted as one involving technological progress. Assume that there was no way of transporting goods between two countries. A technological advance allows goods to be transported freely. Then, under the quite plausible conditions postulated by Newbery-Stiglitz, welfare (of everyone!) in both countries could decrease.

The theory of the second-best (Meade 1955; Lipsey and Lancaster 1956) reminds us that in the presence of market imperfections, improving the functioning of one market may deteriorate overall welfare. There are reasons to believe that certain innovations in financial markets, for example, structured financial products and certain derivatives like credit default swaps, especially in the absence of appropriate regulations, contributed greatly to the Great Recession (Financial Crisis Inquiry Commission 2011).[10]

It is important to appreciate the result described in Observation 4 to understand how crucial our institutions and our market imperfections are in determining whether and how large a benefit society will derive from innovation.

9. In the central Delli Gatti et al. model, the agricultural sector has constant returns to scale and wages in the urban sector are rigid (e.g, because of efficiency wage considerations), so that the agricultural innovations are unambiguously welfare decreasing. In one variant of the model, where urban wages are flexible, wage decreases lead to still higher unemployment. Though it is possible that entrepreneurs gain more from the wage reductions than they lose from the loss of sales, social welfare is decreased with sufficiently inequality averse social welfare functions.

10. At a theoretical level, Simsek (2013) and Guzman and Stiglitz (2016a, 2016b) have shown that opening up new markets—through financial innovation—can lead to greater volatility in consumption.

14.2.5   Ascertaining Whether the Economy Is
             Best Described by Observation 1, 2, 3, or 4

It is not always easy to ascertain which of the four observations in the four subsections above best describes the economy. Typically, the only thing that we can observe is that an innovation has made some individuals better off and some worse off. (In our analysis of AI, we assume that it has made workers worse off and entrepreneurs better off.) The presumption is that risk markets for innovation are highly imperfect (so Observation 1 does not apply), redistributions are costly (so Observation 2 does not strictly apply), and markets are imperfect (so Observation 3 does not strictly apply.) But the costs of redistributions may be sufficiently low and the market imperfections sufficiently small that figure 14.1 still applies: everyone could be made better off. Alternatively, redistributions may be so costly that figure 14.2 applies. Or market failures may be sufficiently large and redistributions sufficiently costly that figure 14.3 applies.

We emphasize that which situation we are in depends not just on the possibilities of ex post redistribution, but on the institutional flexibility, which determines the ex ante distribution.

As we noted, the second-best utility possibilities frontier is the outer envelope of all conceivable constrained utility possibilities frontiers, which reflect all the conceivable institutional regimes in an economy and all the market imperfections that the economy may suffer from. By *institutional regimes* we mean all explicit tax and redistribution systems (from negative income tax systems to universal basic income to the regressive tax system currently in place), intellectual property regimes, job programs, education programs, but even social norms such as those related to charitable contributions. *Market imperfections* include all the market arrangements that differ from the Arrow-Debreu "optimal" benchmark, the conditions that ensure the Pareto efficiency of the market. As we noted earlier, the term embraces imperfections in information, competition, and risk and capital markets (including "missing" markets), but also rigidities in factor reallocation or in prices that determine how easily factors and products reallocate and which may be particularly important in the context of technological progress.

Changing any of these institutions or market imperfections has an effect on workers' welfare. In general, it may be desirable to use a package of changes to all these institutions to ensure Pareto improvements after technological change has occurred. For instance, in section 14.4.3, we show that a combination of a change in the intellectual property regime *and* a change in capital taxation can ensure that an innovation is a Pareto improvement.

Finally, we also note that the possibility of achieving a Pareto improvement depends on how broadly we define the classes of individuals that are affected by an innovation. Our earlier example differentiated society, for simplicity, into two categories, workers and entrepreneurs. More generally, different categories of workers, for example, skilled and unskilled workers, or workers in different sectors or tasks, are differentially affected by innovation. By the same token, different categories of entrepreneurs or innovators are differentially affected by innovation—for example, a given entrepreneur will generally be worse off if she is out-competed by another's innovation. In the limit, if we consider the welfare of every single agent in the economy, clear Pareto improvements in a strict sense will be very difficult to find. As a result, our scope of analysis has to be targeted at the level that is relevant for the question at hand.

From both a political and a macroeconomic perspective, it is desirable that our welfare analysis focuses on groups that are sufficiently broad so that they matter for the political or economic equilibrium. It may also be useful to focus on groups that can be targeted with specific policy measures. Having said that, there is also a useful role for social safety nets that insure single individuals that lose out—for example, an innovator who goes broke because he was outpaced by a competitor.

14.2.6 Endogenous Technological Progress

A fifth and last point to emphasize is that there is no first welfare theorem for endogenous innovation. Generally speaking, the private returns to innovation in an economy differ from the social returns.[11]

OBSERVATION 5)   *The privately optimal choice of innovation may move the utility possibilities frontier inward, even if redistribution is costless.*

This implies that there may be benefits from intervening in the innovation process to generate Pareto improvements, for example, by making it less labor saving (see e.g. Stiglitz 2014b). Again, this does not specifically refer to advances in artificial intelligence—it will probably not apply to most examples of innovation in AI—but it is easy to think of examples where privately optimal innovation may generate Pareto deteriorations, for example, in the context of high-frequency trading in financial markets (see, e.g., Stiglitz 2014c).

14.2.7 Relationship between Technological Progress and Globalization

Many of the effects of technological change in general, and AI in particular, are similar to those of globalization. Indeed, globalization can be viewed as a change in technology, that of trading with the rest of the world.

---

11. It is hard to know who first had this insight. Certainly, Thomas Jefferson, America's third president, recognized it when he said that knowledge is like a candle: when it lights another, the light of the first candle is not diminished. In the economics literature, it was clearly articulated by Arrow (1962) and Stiglitz (1987a). For a more recent statement of why social and private returns to innovation differ, see Stiglitz and Greenwald (2015). These results hold regardless of the intellectual property regime. Poorly designed intellectual property regimes can (and do) impair innovation. For a simple theoretical model, see Stiglitz (2014a); for empirical evidence, see Williams (2010).

In particular, trade of advanced countries with developing countries is "labor saving" (in the sense of Hicks): the demand for unskilled workers, or workers in general, decreases, at any given wage, implying that while the production possibilities curve moves out, and the utility possibilities curve may move out, the new equilibrium entails workers being worse off, as in figures 14.1 and 14.2. (In the absence of good risk markets, as we noted, everyone can be worse off, as in figure 14.3). Thus, the issue of whether globalization is welfare enhancing comes back to the question addressed in this chapter: is it possible to ensure, either through redistributive taxes or changes in institutions/rules, that workers are not made worse off. Again, there is a presumption that the gains to capital (or enterprises) could be taxed to provide the requisite redistributions.[12]

As we discuss in greater detail below, one of the side effects of innovation and intellectual property rights (IPR) is the creation of market power, resulting in ex post inefficient outcomes. Similarly, one of the consequences of globalization is to weaken the market power of workers. This is important because there is ample evidence that labor markets are far from perfectly competitive. The requisite compensation and/or offsetting changes in institutional rules to ensure that globalization represents a Pareto improvement may thus have to be all the greater.

14.3   Technological Progress and Channels of Inequality

There are two main channels through which technological progress may affect the distribution of resources and thus inequality: first, through the surplus earned by innovators and second, through effects on other agents in the economy.

14.3.1   Surplus Earned by Innovators

Technology is an information good, which implies that it is *nonrival*, but it may be *excludable*. Nonrival means that information can be used without being used up—in principle, many economic actors could use the same technology at the same time. If information about an innovation is widely shared, it can be used by all of society and provide welfare benefits to anybody who uses it. The excludable nature of information means, however, that others can be prevented from either obtaining or using a technology, for example, by withholding it from the public (e.g., as a business secret) or

---

12. Although a given country that opens up to trade is always made better off in a first-best world, ensuring a global Pareto improvement after a country reduces its trade barriers may be even more difficult than after technological progress has occurred, since changes in trade barriers affect international terms of trade and lead to redistributions across all other countries that can only be undone via cross-country transfers. (See, e.g., Korinek 2016). Furthermore, within each country, gains from trade inherently require changes in relative prices, which means that large redistributions are even more likely than in the case of technological progress.

by using social institutions such as intellectual property rights (e.g., copyrights or patents). This excludability may provide innovators with market power that enables them to charge a positive price for the innovation and earn a surplus.

Society faces a difficult trade-off in determining how to engineer the optimal level of innovation. In a first-best world, there are no agency problems in the process of innovation, and an optimal solution would be for the public to fund innovations and make them freely available to all (see, e.g., Arrow 1962). In fact, this model of financing innovation is common for basic research and has given rise to some very significant innovations in history, including the invention of the internet. A closely related solution is the production of innovations for nonpecuniary rewards, such as, for example, the prevalence of open source technology, which is widespread in the context of software and even artificial intelligence.[13]

However, in many circumstances, private agents are superior in producing innovation, and when they fund innovation, they expect to earn a return. The surplus earned by innovators then plays an important economic role because it rewards innovators for what they accomplish—it represents the economic return to innovation activity. However, as a result there is generally some market power associated with innovations, especially when there is a system of IPR in place, and this generally leads to inefficiencies compared to the first-best allocation in which innovations are distributed as public goods.[14]

We distinguish the following two cases, which determine whether innovators earn rents, that is, payoffs in excess of the cost of their innovative activity:

First, if entry into innovation activity is restricted, then the surplus or net income earned by innovators is generally greater than the costs of innovation activity. A natural example of such restrictions is when only a small number of people are endowed with special skills that enable them to innovate. These innovators then earn rents based on their exclusive abilities.

Restrictions to innovative activity may also arise from market structure: in markets with Bertrand competition, the first entrant who develops a costly innovation may enjoy a monopoly position because any potential competitor knows that if she enters, the incumbent will cut prices to marginal cost so that she cannot recoup the investment into an innovation.[15]

---

13. This approach relies on individuals or companies that are willing to innovate in exchange for nonpecuniary rewards such as prestige or, alternatively, on a calculated decision that providing free technology will steer potential customers or employees toward an innovator's platform, as seems to be the case in the field of AI.

14. For discussions of the merits of alternative ways of funding and incentivizing innovation, see Dosi and Stiglitz (2014), Baker, Jayadev, and Stiglitz (2017), Stiglitz (2008), and Korinek and Ng (2017).

15. See Stiglitz (1987b) and Dasgupta and Stiglitz (1988). When the number of firms is limited and there is Cournot competition, there will also be rents associated with innovation. For more general theoretical discussions of industrial structure and innovation, see Dasgupta and Stiglitz (1980a 1980b) and Stiglitz and Greenwald (2015, ch. 5).

Second, if innovative activity is contestable, that is, if there is a sufficiently large set of potential innovators with equal skills, then the expected rents to innovative activity are competed down to zero, that is, the marginal entrant into innovative activity is indifferent between innovating or not.[16] However, given that the payoffs to innovation are highly stochastic, there will be winners and losers ex post. In the context of new technologies, the distribution of payoffs seems to be increasingly skewed, with a small number of entrepreneurs earning gigantic payoffs and the vast majority earning little in return for their efforts. This gives rise to significant inequality even among innovators.[17]

In either case, the returns earned by an innovator may not correspond closely to the social returns to the innovation; in particular, some of the returns may reflect the capture of profits that would otherwise have gone to other entrepreneurs.

Policies to Share the Surplus of Innovators

There is a growing consensus that one of the sources of the growth of inequality is the growth of rents, including the rents that innovators earn in excess of the cost of innovation (see e.g. Korinek and Ng 2018). Taxing and redistributing such rents has an important role in ensuring that AI and other advances in technology are Pareto improving. Also, anti-trust policies may lower such rents, ensuring that the benefits of innovations are more widely shared, as more competition lowers consumer prices from which all benefit. From the perspective of low wage workers who lose from innovation, targeted expenditure programs financed by high rent taxes may be of greater benefit than the lowering of prices, the benefit of which will go disproportionately to those who have high spending power.

Moreover, changes in intellectual property rights (IPRs) affect who receives the benefits of innovation—and thus the "incidence" of innovation, since IPRs are instrumental in providing extended market power to innovators.[18]

Additionally, public research—with government or the public at large appropriating the returns, rather than allowing private firms to do so—together with stronger competition policies, might reduce the scope for

---

16. Given the difficulty of predicting the success of innovative activity or of even assigning success probabilities, it is questionable how efficiently this mechanism works in practice. For example, there may be excessive entry because of overoptimism by some potential entrepreneurs, or there may be insufficient entry because of imperfect insurance markets for risk averse entrepreneurs. If some are better at innovating than others (and know it), then these individuals will enjoy inframarginal innovation rents (on average.)

17. If there are diminishing returns to the allocation of resources to innovation, the efficient resource allocation will entail there being rents associated with innovation. Who captures these rents will be affected by the institutional (including tax) structure. In the absence of adequate mechanisms for the public capturing those rents, there may be excessive investments in innovation, a standard result in the economics of the commons.

18. Especially when there is Bertrand competition, the benefits of innovation may be quickly shared with consumers upon the termination of patents.

monopolies capturing large fractions of the returns to innovation, and thus enhance the likelihood that AI will be Pareto improving.

Workers may also note that the innovations that ultimately led to AI—including those created by private entrepreneurs—build on significant public support. Society as a whole, but not necessarily this generation of innovators, paid for this knowledge, and should therefore share in the surplus generated by the innovation. One proposal to ensure that workers share in the benefits of innovation—and are less likely to lose from it—is to give workers shares in enterprises to ensure that their welfare goes up in tandem with that of shareholders/innovators as a whole.

14.3.2   Effects on Others

Innovation also leads to large redistributions among others in the economy who are not directly involved in the process of innovation, for example, workers who experience a sudden increase or decline in the demand for their labor. These redistributions can thus be viewed as externalities from innovation, and they are one of the main reasons why innovation raises concerns about inequality. We distinguish two categories of such externalities, pecuniary and nonpecuniary externalities. We discuss both in detail in the following.

Pecuniary Externalities: Price and Wage Changes

Among the most prominent implications of technological change is that it affects the prices of factors of production (including wages) and of produced goods. Hicks (1932) already observed that innovations generally change the demand for factors and will, in equilibrium, lead to factor price changes, especially changes in wages. The price and wage changes that result from innovations represent pecuniary externalities. Traditional general equilibrium theory, following Arrow and Debreu, emphasized that pecuniary externalities are fully consistent with Pareto efficiency. However, the benchmark of Pareto efficiency is blind to the distribution of income. Even if the equilibrium reached after an innovation is Pareto efficient, the pecuniary externalities lead to redistributions and imply that there are winners and losers.[19]

If—as many technologists predict—artificial intelligence directly replaces human labor, the demand for human labor will go down, and so will wages. More generally, innovations typically reduce demand for specific types of labor with specific human capital. For example, self-driving cars will likely depress the wages of drivers, or radiology-reading AI may lower the wages of traditional radiologists. Conversely, AI has certainly led to an increase in demand for computer scientists and has greatly increased their wages, in par-

---

19. Greenwald and Stiglitz (1986) and Geanakoplos and Polemarchakis (1986) demonstrated that pecuniary externalities also matter for efficiency when there are market imperfections such as imperfect information and incomplete markets; market equilibrium will as a result not even be Pareto efficient.

ticular in subfields that are directly related to AI. Since AI is a general purpose technology, there are reasons to believe that advances in AI will reverberate throughout many different sectors and lead to significant changes in wages throughout the economy in coming decades. Similar arguments can be made about the demand for and the value of different types of specific capital, as well as the demand for and prices of particular products.

Even though there are frequently losers, technological progress by definition shifts out the production possibilities frontier. This implies that the total dollar gain of the winners of progress exceeds the dollar loss of the losers.[20] In section 14.4 below, we will use this property of technological progress to argue that under relatively broad conditions this should enable the redistribution that is necessary to ensure that innovation leads to a Pareto improvement: the gains that arise to some factor owners as a result of technological progress are excess returns that are like unearned rents and could be taxed away without introducing distortions into the economy.

Although we noted that pecuniary externalities are generally viewed as Pareto efficient, there are two reasons for why they are likely to be associated with inefficiency in practice. First, Greenwald and Stiglitz (1986) and Geanakoplos and Polemarchakis (1986) demonstrated that pecuniary externalities matter for efficiency when there are market imperfections such as imperfect information and incomplete markets; market equilibrium will as a result not be Pareto efficient. Compared to the benchmark of idealized insurance markets "behind the veil of ignorance" that we discussed in section 14.2, the pecuniary externalities from innovation are clearly inefficient. Additional market imperfections are likely to lead to additional inefficiencies. Second, if the pecuniary externalities from innovation give rise to the need for redistributive policies that are costly to perform, the policy response will generate additional inefficiencies.

Policies to Counter Wage Declines

Aside from lump sum transfers, there are a range of further policies to counter the wage declines that are experienced by workers who are displaced by machines, even for low-skill jobs. These include wage subsidies and earned income tax credits. If bargaining power in labor markets is biased toward employers, an increased minimum wage can also help ensure that no one who works full time is in poverty. Furthermore, ensuring high aggregate demand—and thus a low unemployment rate—also increases the bargaining power of workers and leads to higher wages.

Other policies aimed at increasing the demand for especially low-skill labor include any measures that raise the wages of workers that are substitutes, for example, higher wages in the public sector as well as an increase in

20. If lump sum transfers were feasible, the winners could compensate the losers. However, in the absence of such compensation, social welfare may be lower.

public investments and other public expenditures; all of these policies help to drive up wages in the economy more generally.

Policies that could be used to finance such measures include carbon taxes, which would encourage resource-saving innovation at the expense of labor-saving innovation. It would thus simultaneously address two of most serious global problems, global climate change and inequality.[21]

Furthermore, the elimination of tax deduction for interest and the imposition of a tax on capital would increase the cost of capital and induce more capital augmenting innovation rather than labor saving innovation.[22]

Non-Pecuniary Externalities

Innovation may also generate nonpecuniary externalities on agents other than the innovator. Classic examples for this are technological externalities—for example, if an innovation produces public goods or generates or alleviates pollution. In markets that deviate from the Arrow-Debreu benchmark, a variety of nonpecuniary effects may arise: for example, innovation may affect quantities demanded, or the probability of buying or selling a good or factor, including the probability of being unemployed.

Some effects are such that they can be interpreted either as pecuniary or nonpecuniary externalities. For example, product innovations can be interpreted as a price changes—the price of the newly invented good changes from infinity to some positive value—or as a change in the price of the consumption services provided by the good. Alternatively, they can also be interpreted in a nonpecuniary manner by viewing a product (such as a smartphone) as providing a bundle of services to consumers that can only be bought in fixed proportion (e.g., since we cannot separately purchase different functions of the smartphone). In that view, an innovation represents a change in the structure of incomplete markets because it changes the bundle of consumption service available from a product. Similarly, changes in job quality can be interpreted by viewing each job as a vector of transactions that are only available in predetermined bundles, and the innovation changes the elements in the bundle that are available. It is well known that changes in the degree of market incompleteness for such bundles give rise to externalities (a specific application of Greenwald and Stiglitz 1986).

14.4 Worker-Replacing Progress and Redistribution

This section considers a stark form of technological progress that we term worker-replacing technological progress. We develop two simple models

---

21. As we noted above, there is no first fundamental welfare theorem for innovation, and indeed, there is a presumption that the market is biased toward labor-saving innovation relative to innovations directed toward "saving the planet." (See Stiglitz 2014b.)

22. The allocation of resources to capital augmenting technological change depends on the after-tax share of capital. An increase in the relative cost of capital will increase the capital share if the elasticity of substitution is less than unity. Most of the empirical evidence suggests that this is the case.

to analyze the two channels generating inequality that we discussed in the previous section. In sections 14.4.1 and 14.4.2, we consider the pecuniary externalities (redistributions) generated by worker-replacing progress, both from a static and a dynamic perspective. In section 14.4.3., we focus on the distribution of the surplus accruing to innovators in a model in which the surplus is determined by the level of patent protection. Furthermore, in section 14.4.4 we discuss the implications of endogenous factor bias in technological progress.

14.4.1 Static Pecuniary Externalities of Worker-Replacing Progress

For sections 14.4.1 and 14.4.2, we consider the simple model of worker-replacing technological change of Korinek and Stiglitz (2017). We assume a production technology that combines capital and labor in a constant-returns-to-scale (CRS) function, but where labor consists of the sum of human and machine labor. Assuming that human and machine labor enter the production function additively means that they are perfect substitutes for each other. The details of the baseline model are presented in box 14.1.

We analyze three questions: What does worker-replacing technological change do to wages in the short run and in the long run? And what can policy do about it?

First, we look exclusively at the short run before any of the other factors have adjusted:

OBSERVATION 6)   *Machine Labor and Factor Earnings (in the short run): adding a marginal unit of machine labor reduces human wages, but increases returns of complementary factors in a zero-sum manner.*

Intuitively, what happens if we add one unit of machine labor is that first, that unit will earn its marginal return, but second, there is also a redistribution from labor to capital, which now becomes relatively scarcer. The gains of capital are exactly the losses of the existing stock of labor.

The redistribution generated by technological progress can be thought of as a pecuniary externality, as we emphasized earlier. The income losses of wage earners and the income gains of other factors owners are inefficient compared to the first-best benchmark considered in section 14.2.1. In the given example, the owners of capital have obtained windfall gains but have not done anything to earn these higher return. A compensatory transfer from capital owners to workers simply undoes these windfall gains and leaves them equally well off as they were before.

More generally, adding machine labor creates a redistribution away from human labor toward complementary factors. This result holds for any CRS production function no matter what the complementary factor, for instance, whether it is capital or land or unskilled versus skilled labor or entrepreneurial rents. Policy can undo these redistributions by taxing windfall gains while leaving the price system to work at the margin. The result also holds for decreasing-returns-to-scale production functions if we interpret the profits

Box 14.1

Machine Labor and Factor Earnings

Assume a constant-returns-to-scale production function that produces output Y by combining capital K with labor, consisting of the sum of human labor H and machine labor M:

$$Y = F(K, H + M).$$

In this formulation human labor and machine labor are perfect substitutes, so machine technology is what we call worker-replacing.

In the competitive equilibrium, the wage is determined by the marginal product of labor,

$$w = F_L.$$

Proposition 1: Machine Labor and Factor Earnings: adding a marginal unit of machine labor reduces human wages but increases the returns to capital in a zero-sum manner, in addition to increasing output by the marginal product of labor, which is equal to the wage.

Proof: Using Euler's Theorem, we rewrite the production function:

$$(H + M)F_L(\cdot) + KF_K(\cdot) = F(K, H + M).$$

We can now ascertain the effect of an additional unit of M:

$$F_L + (H + M)F_{LL} + KF_{KL} = F_L,$$

or, simplified, $\underbrace{(H + M)F_{LL}}_{\text{decline in wage bill}} + \underbrace{KF_{KL}}_{\text{increase in return to K}} = 0.$

Source: Korinek and Stiglitz (2017).

earned by the owner of the technology as compensation for the implicit factor "entrepreneurship," which takes part in the zero-sum redistribution.

Let us also emphasize that taxes on previously accumulated factors that suddenly earn an unexpected excess return are nondistortionary. This means that at least in principle, there is a role for implementing costless redistribution and generating a Pareto improvement. (In practice, there are some natural caveats to this result. For example, it relies on the assumption that we can distinguish between previously installed capital that earns windfall gains and new capital that would be distorted if it were taxed.)

14.4.2 Dynamic Implications of Worker-Replacing Progress

In the longer run, worker-replacing technological change will lead to significant economic change. It implies that the biggest constraint on output—the scarcity of labor—is suddenly relaxed. As a result, greater amounts of complementary factors, here capital, are accumulated.

OBSERVATION 7) *Machine Labor and Abundance of Labor: If not only capital, but also labor, is reproducible at sufficiently low cost, then the economy will grow exponentially in AK fashion, driven purely by factor accumulation, even in the absence of further technological change.*

In Korinek and Stiglitz (2017), we describe the dynamics of this transition as machines made by machines get increasingly efficient or, equivalently, as the cost of producing machines decreases. We identify a singularity point at which it becomes cost effective for machines to start to fully replace human labor.[23] In the simplest case, when complementary factors such as capital adjust without friction, the human wage may actually be unchanged because capital K grows in proportion to effective labor $(H + M)$ so that the marginal productivity of labor and the wage remain unchanged. In other words, investment is allocated between conventional machines and human-replacing robots in such a way that the return is equal to the intertemporal marginal rate of substitution. Under the assumption that workers only care about their absolute income, not their relative income, this outcome would not be too bad: in absolute terms, even though the human labor share would go to zero as an increasing fraction of the labor in the economy is performed by machines, workers are no worse off as a result of AI.

When factors are slow to adjust, the pattern of transition can be complex, with demand for human labor typically going down temporarily.[24] In general, the pattern of adjustment depends on how fast the capital stock versus the stock of labor adjust. (For example, if the capital stock rises in anticipation of an increased supply of machine labor in the future that has not yet materialized, then human wages may even go up at intermediate stages.)[25]

However, the following observation describes that in the long run, workers are actually worse off as a result of machine labor if there are nonreproducible complementary factors that are in scarce supply, such as land or other natural resources.

23. This singularity captures the important economic aspects of what technologists such as Vernor Vinge (1993) or Ray Kurzweil (2005) call the technological singularity. A similar point is also made in Aghion, Jones, and Jones (2017).

24. Berg, Buffie, and Zanna (2018) shows that it may actually take decades for the economy's complementary capital stock to adjust after major revolutions in labor-saving technology.

25. This assumes that capital is "putty-putty," that is, that capital investments made before AI arrives are equally productive after AI, as would be the case if humans and robots were in fact identical.

OBSERVATION 8)   *Machine Labor and Return of Scarcity: if there are non-reproducible complementary factors, they eventually limit growth; human real wages fall, and the owners of nonreproducible factors absorb all the rents.*

Intuitively, as the supply of effective labor proliferates due to the introduction of machine labor, agents in the economy will compete for scarce nonreproducible resources like land, driving up their price.

A similar argument holds for nonreproducible consumption goods: even if all factors in the production process are reproducible so that productive output in the economy exhibits AK-style growth and workers' product wages remain unchanged, competition for fixed resources that are part of their consumption basket, such as land used for housing, may lead workers to eventually be worse off. This may be particularly important in urban settings where, say, economic activity occurs at the center. Rich rentiers may occupy the more desirable locations near the center, with workers having to obtain less expensive housing at the periphery, spending more time commuting. The advent of AI will thus lower their utility.

However, just as in the earlier case, at the margin, the redistribution from workers to nonreproducible factor owners is zero sum. Since taxes on nonreproducible factors are by definition nondistortionary, there is scope for nondistortionary redistribution.

OBSERVATION 9)   *Nonreproducible Factors and Pareto Improvements: so long as nondistortionary taxes on factor rents are feasible, labor-replacing innovation can be a Pareto improvement.*

14.4.3   Redistributing the Innovators' Surplus via Changes in Institutions

If outright redistribution is not feasible or limited, there may be other institutional changes that result in market distributions that are more favorable to workers. For example, intervention to steer technological progress may act as a second-best device.

In this section, we provide an example in which a change in intellectual property rights—a shortening of the term of patent protection—effectively redistributes some of the innovators' surplus to workers (consumers) to mitigate the pecuniary externalities on wages that they experience, with the ultimate goal that the benefits of the innovation are more widely shared. If an innovation results in a lower cost of production, then the innovator enjoys the benefits of the innovation in the form of higher profits during the life of the patent; but after the expiration of the patent, society enjoys the benefits in terms of lower prices. The trade-off is that shortening the life of the patent may reduce the pace of innovation. But in the spirit of the theory of the second-best, there is generally an "optimal" patent life, in which there is still some innovation, but in which the well-being of workers is protected.

Box 14.2

Intellectual Property Regime and Redistribution

Consider an economy with a unit mass of workers $H = 1$, in which the capital stock supplied each period $K(\tau)$ is a function solely of a distortionary capital tax τ, the proceeds of which are distributed to workers, and the effective stock of machine labor $M(z)$ is an increasing function of patent life z.

A worker's total income I consists of her wage plus the revenue of the capital tax,

$$I = w + \tau\, K(\tau).$$

For any level of $M(z)$, we define $\tau(M)$ as the value of the capital tax that keeps workers just as well off as they were before the introduction of machine labor.

Proposition 1. As long as elasticity of capital supply is not too large, we can always increase z from $z = 0$ and compensate workers by raising the capital tax τ.

Steady-State Dynamics

Consider an intertemporal setting in which the growth rate $g = g(z, \tau)$ is a function of the length of the patent z and the tax rate τ, by which we now denote the tax rate on innovators. Assume that the share of output that is invested is a function of the growth rate $(i(g))$ and that the fraction of output not spent on investment that is appropriated by the innovator is $b(z, \tau)$. In steady state, the present discounted value of the income of workers can be approximated as

$$PDV = (1 - i(g))\,[1 - (1 - \tau)b(z, \tau)]/(r - g),$$

where r is the discount rate. If we choose $\{z, \tau\}$ to maximize the PDV, in general, the optimum will not be a corner solution in which any innovation hurts workers.

Proposition 2. In general, the optimal $\{z^*, \tau^*\}$ entails $g > 0$.

It is easy to write down sufficient conditions under which Proposition 2 holds: setting τ^* equal to zero, all that we require is that $|g_z|$ is not too large relative to $|b_z|$.

With network externalities the innovator may be able to maintain a dominant position even after the end of the patent, and may continue to earn the surplus from her innovation. With taxes on monopoly profits, it should be possible to ensure that the innovations are Pareto improving and that even human worker-replacing technological change can improve the well-being of workers.

14.4.4   Factor-Biased Technological Change

So far, we have simply assumed that technological change—the introduction of AI—is worker replacing. But advances in technology also make some machines more productive and others obsolete, affecting the (marginal) return to traditional capital.[26] It is thus useful to think of the world as having three groups: capitalists, workers, and innovators. Intellectual property rights (and antitrust laws) determine the returns to innovators, but the nature of technological change in a competitive market determines the division between workers and capitalists.

A long-standing literature, going back to Kennedy (1964), von Weizacker (1966), and Samuelson (1965), describes the endogenous determination of the factor bias of technological progress.[27] The central result is that as the share of labor becomes smaller, the bias shifts toward capital-augmenting technological progress. If the world works as these models suggest, this should limit the decline in the share of labor (at least in a stable equilibrium) and in inequality.[28] As the share of labor decreases, the incentive to produce worker-replacing innovation such as AI decreases. But the relevant discounted future wage share near the point of singularity—the point where it is cost effective for machines to fully replace human labor and produce more machines all by themselves—may be sufficiently great that there is nonetheless an incentive to pass the point of singularity.

Let us assume that land becomes the binding constraint once human labor is fully replaceable by machine labor. In that case, provided the elasticity of substitution between land and the other production factors—capital cum labor—is less than unity, the share of land increases over time, generating the result (analogous to that where labor is the binding constraint in the standard literature) that in the long run, all technological progress is land augmenting. If the production function is constant returns to scale in land,

26. As we noted earlier, IA (intelligence assisting) innovation may increase the productivity of humans, and thus increase the demand for humans if the elasticity of substitution is less than unity.

27. Important contributions were also made by Drandakis and Phelps (1965). More recently, there has been some revival of the literature, with work of Acemoglu (2002), Stiglitz (2006, 2014b) and Acemoglu and Restrepo (2018), among others.

28. One can describe dynamics with standard wage-setting mechanisms. The system is stable so long as the elasticity of substitution between factors is less than unity (Acemoglu 1998; Stiglitz 2006, 2014b).

labor (including machine labor) and traditional capital, then the long-run rate of growth is determined by the pace of land-augmenting technological change.

Role of the Service Sector

Currently, progress in AI focuses on certain sectors of the economy, like manufacturing. Partly because of the resulting lower cost of manufacturing, and partly because of the shape of preferences, the economy is evolving toward a service-sector economy. (If there is differential productivity across sectors, and the elasticity of demand for the innovation sector is not too high, then production factors will move out of that sector into other sectors. This is even more so if preferences are nonhomothetic, for example, demand for food and many manufactured goods having an income elasticity less than unity.) Among the key service sectors are education, health, the military, and other public services. The value of those services is in large part socially determined, that is, by public policies not just a market process. If we value those services highly—pay good wages, provide good working conditions, and create a sufficient number of jobs—this will limit increases in the inequality of market income. Governments typically play an important role in these sectors, and their employment policies will thus play an important role in the AI transition. Many of these service-sector jobs have limited skill requirements. However, higher public-sector wages will—through standard equilibrium effects—also raise wages in the private sector, will improve the bargaining position of workers, and will result in such jobs having higher "respect." All of this will, of course, require tax revenues. If the elasticity of entrepreneurial services is low, for example, if entrepreneurs are driven partly by nonpecuniary motives, we can impose high taxes to finance these jobs.

14.5   Technological Unemployment

Unemployment is one of the most problematic societal implications of technological progress—new technology often implies that old jobs are destroyed and workers need to find new jobs. Economists, of course, understand the "lump-of-labor fallacy"—the false notion that there is a fixed number of jobs, and that automating a given job means that there will forever be fewer jobs left in the economy. In a well-functioning economy, we generally expect that technological progress creates additional income, which in turn can support more jobs.

However, there are two sound economic reasons for why technological unemployment may arise: first, because wages do not adjust for some structural reason, as described, for example, by efficiency wage theories, and second as a transition phenomenon. The two phenomena may also interact in important ways, for example, when efficiency wage considerations slow down the transition to a new equilibrium. We discuss the two categories in turn in the following subsections.

The unemployment implications are especially problematic when technological progress is labor saving, which—by definition—requires that either wages have to fall or that other complementary factors like capital have to adjust enough for labor market equilibrium to be restored at or above the historic wage.

14.5.1   Efficiency Wage Theory and Nonadjustment of Wages

The first category of technological unemployment arises when wages do not adjust for structural reasons. Efficiency wage theory emphasizes that productivity depends on wages and so employers may have reasons to pay wages above the market-clearing level. The original efficiency wage paper (Stiglitz 1969) noted one of the reasons for this: that income disparities can weaken worker morale. Akerlof and Yellen (1990) have formalized this into the "fair wage hypothesis."

If fairness considerations are significant enough, and workers think that a decrease in their wages is "unfair" (e.g., because the income of entrepreneurs increases so entrepreneurs could easily "afford" pay increases), it means that the scope of labor-saving progress that shifts the utility possibilities curve out *without redistributions* is very limited. Similar results hold if workers' well-being and efforts are related to relative incomes. The new utility possibilities curve may lie outside the old one to the "north" of E_0, that is, there is scope for a Pareto improvement in principle; but it may lie inside of the old utility possibilities curve near E_1, that is, the utility possibilities of workers decrease for a given level of utility of entrepreneurs because workers reduce their effort so much that the effective labor supply declines—any gains from technology are more than offset by increased shirking. Shapiro and Stiglitz (1984) emphasize that paying a wage above the market-clearing level reduces shirking, leading to unemployment.

An even more daunting example of efficiency wages may arise if automation continues and the marginal product of labor for low-skill workers falls below their cost of living at what they view as their basic subsistence (even if they exert their best effort). Unless basic social services are provided to such workers, a nutritional efficiency wage model applies in that case, similar to what Stiglitz (1976) described for developing countries: employers could not pay a market-clearing wage because they know that this would be insufficient for their employees to provide for themselves and remain productive.[29] We will follow up on this theme in the final section of our chapter.

In traditional efficiency wage models, the unemployment effects of effi-

---

29. Even worse outcomes could emerge in the presence of imperfect capital markets, if expenditures on health and nutrition at one date affect productivity at later dates.

ciency wages are permanent, part of the long-run equilibrium. For example, if technological change leads to greater inequality (or better information about the existing level of inequality), morale effects and the resulting efficiency wage responses imply that the equilibrium level of unemployment rises.

However, efficiency wage arguments may also contribute to slowing down the transition to a new equilibrium after an innovation, as we will explore subsection 14.5.2.

Minimum Wages and Nonadjustment of Wages

An alternative reason why wages may not adjust to the market-clearing level are minimum wage laws. Basic economics implies that there will be unemployment if wages are set to an excessive level. Although this is a theoretical possibility, recent experience in the United States has repeatedly shown that modest increases in minimum wages from current levels have hardly any employment effects but raise the income of minimum wage workers, which may have positive aggregate demand effects since low-income workers have a high marginal propensity to consume (see, e.g., Schmitt 2013). From an economic theory perspective, these observations are possible because wages are not determined in a purely Walrasian manner—there is a significant amount of bargaining involved when prospective employers and employees match—and increases in minimum wages substitute for the lacking bargaining power of workers (see, e.g., Manning 2011).

14.5.2   Technological Unemployment as a Transition Phenomenon

The second category of technological unemployment is as a transition phenomenon, that is, when technological change makes workers redundant at a faster pace than they can find new jobs or that new jobs are created. This phenomenon was already observed by Keynes (1932). It is well understood that there is always a certain "natural" or "equilibrium" level of unemployment as a result of churning in the labor market. In benchmark models of search and matching to characterize this equilibrium level of unemployment (see Mortensen and Pissarides 1994, 1998), employment relationships are separated at random, and workers and employers need to search for new matches to replace them. The random shocks in this framework can be viewed as capturing, in reduced form, phenomena such as life cycle transitions but also technological progress in individual firms. In this view, an increase in the pace of technological progress corresponds to a higher job separation rate and results in a higher equilibrium level of unemployment.

The transition may be especially prolonged if technology implies that the old skills of workers become obsolete and they need to acquire new skills and/or find out what new jobs match their skills (see, e.g., Restrepo 2015).

Even if in the long run workers adjusted to AI, the transition may be difficult. Artificial intelligence will impact some sectors more than others, and there will be significant job dislocation. As a general lesson, markets on their own are not good at structural transformation. Often, the pace of job destruction is greater than the pace of job creation, especially as a result of imperfections in capital markets, inhibiting the ability of entrepreneurs to exploit quickly new opportunities as they are opened up.

The Great Depression as an Example of Transitional Unemployment

The Great Depression can be viewed as being caused by rapid pace of innovation in agriculture (see Delli Gatti et al. 2012a). Fewer workers were needed to produce the food that individuals demanded, resulting in marked decline in agriculture prices and income, leading to a decline in demand for urban products. In the late 1920s, these effects became so large that long-standing migration patterns were reversed.

What *might* have been a Pareto improvement turned out to be an immiserizing technological change, as both those in the urban and rural sector suffered.

The general result is that noted earlier: with mobility frictions and rigidities (themselves partly caused be capital market imperfections, as workers in the rural sector couldn't obtain funds to obtain the human capital required in the urban sector and to relocate) technological change can be welfare decreasing. The economy can be caught, for an extensive period of time, in a low-level equilibrium trap, with high unemployment and low output.

In the case of the Great Depression, government intervention (as a by-product of World War II) eventually enabled a successful structural transformation: the intervention was not only a Keynesian stimulus, but facilitated the move from rural farming areas to the cities where manufacturing was occurring at the time and facilitated the retraining of the labor force, helping workers acquire the skills necessary for success in an urban manufacturing environment, which were quite different from those that ensured success in a rural, farming environment. It was, in this sense, an example of a successful industrial policy.

There are clear parallels to the situation today in that a significant fraction of the workforce may not have the skills required to succeed in the age of AI.

Transitional Efficiency Wage Theory

Efficiency wage arguments may also slow down the transition to a new equilibrium after technological progress. For example, if worker morale depends on last period's wages, it may be difficult to reduce wages to the market-clearing level after a labor-saving innovation, and unemployment may persist for a long time.[30]

---

30. In the limiting case, employers may simply keep wages fixed to avoid negative morale effects, and unemployment would persist forever—or until some offsetting shock occurs.

14.5.3 Jobs and Meaning

The potentially widespread destruction of jobs can have large human consequences that go beyond just economics because jobs provide not only income but also other mental services such as meaning, dignity, and fulfillment to humans. Whether this is a legacy of our past, and whether individuals could find meaning in other forms of activities, mental or physical, is a matter of philosophical debate.

If workers derive a separate benefit from work in the form of meaning, then job subsidies are a better way of ensuring that technological advances are welfare enhancing than simply providing lump sum grants (e.g., through the provision of a universal basic income), as some are suggesting in response to the inequalities created by AI.

This discussion is, of course, a departure from the usual neoclassical formulation, where work only enters negatively into individual's well-being. There are some that claim that individuals' deriving dignity and meaning from work is an artifact of a world with labor scarcity. In a workerless AI world, individuals will have to get their identity and dignity elsewhere, for example, through spiritual or cultural values. The fact that most humans can find a meaningful life after retirement perhaps suggests that there are good substitutes for jobs in providing meaning.

14.6 Longer-Term Perspectives: AI and the Return of Malthus?

There is a final point that is worth discussing in a chapter on the implications of artificial intelligence for inequality. This point relates to a somewhat longer-term perspective. Currently, artificial intelligence is at the stage where it strictly dominates human intelligence in a number of specific areas, for instance playing chess or Go, identifying patterns in x-rays, driving, and so forth. This is commonly termed *narrow* artificial intelligence. By contrast, humans are able to apply their intelligence across a wide range of domains. This capacity is termed *general* intelligence.

If AI reaches and surpasses human levels of general intelligence, a set of radically different considerations apply. Some techno-optimists predict the advent of general artificial intelligence for as early as 2029 (see Kurzweil 2005), although the median estimate in the AI expert community is around 2040 to 2050, with most AI experts assigning a 90 percent probability to human-level general artificial intelligence arising within the current century (see Bostrom 2014). A minority believes that general artificial intelligence will never arrive. However, if human-level artificial general intelligence is reached, there is broad agreement that AI would soon after become super-intelligent, that is, more intelligent than humans, since technological progress would likely accelerate, aided by the intelligent machines. Given these predictions, we have to think seriously about the implications of artificial general intelligence for humanity and, in the context of this chapter, for what it implies for our economy as well as for inequality.

Assuming that our social and economic system will be maintained upon the advent of artificial general intelligence and superintelligence,[31] there are two main scenarios. One scenario is that man and machine will merge, that is, that humans will "enhance" themselves with ever more advanced technology so that their physical and mental capabilities are increasingly determined by the state of the art in technology and AI rather than by traditional human biology (see, e.g., Kurzweil, 2005). The second scenario is that artificially intelligent entities will develop separately from humans, with their own objectives and behavior (see, e.g., Bostrom 2014; Tegmark 2017). As we will argue below, it is plausible that the two scenarios might differ only in the short run.

First Scenario: Human Enhancement and Inequality

The scenario that humans will enhance themselves with machines may lead to massive increases in human inequality, unless policymakers recognize the threat and take steps to equalize access to human enhancement technologies.[32] Human intelligence is currently distributed within a fairly narrow range compared to the distance between the intelligence of humans and that of the next-closest species. If intelligence becomes a matter of ability to pay, it is conceivable that the wealthiest (enhanced) humans will become orders of magnitude more productive—"more intelligent"—than the unenhanced, leaving the majority of the population further and further behind. In fact, if intelligence enhancement becomes possible, then—unless preemptive actions are taken—it is difficult to imagine how to avoid such a dynamic. For those who can afford it, the incentive to purchase enhancements is great, especially since they are in competition with other wealthy humans who may otherwise leapfrog them. This is even more so in an economy which is, or is perceived to be, a winner-take-all economy and/or in which well-being is based on relative income. Those who cannot afford the latest technology will have to rely on what is in the public domain, and if the pace of innovation increases, the gap between the best technology and what is publicly available will increase.

A useful analogy is to compare human enhancement technology to health care—technology to *maintain* rather than *enhance* the human body. Dif-

---

31. Researchers who work on the topic of AI safety point out that there is also a risk of doomsday scenarios in which a sufficiently advanced artificial intelligence eradicates humanity because humans stand in the way of its goals. See, for example, Bostrom (2014) who elaborates on this using the example of a "paperclip maximizer"—an AI that has been programmed to produce as many paperclips as possible, without regard for other human goals, and who realizes that humans contain valuable raw materials that should better be transformed into paperclips.

32. In many respects, the issues are parallel to those associated with performance-enhancing drugs. In sports, these have been strictly regulated, but in other arenas, they have not.

ferent countries have chosen significantly different models for how to provide access to health care, with some regarding it as a basic human right and others allocating it more according to ability to pay. In the United States, for example, the expected life spans of the poor and the wealthy have diverged significantly in recent decades, in part because of unequal access to health care and ever more costly new technologies that are only available to those who can pay. The differences are even starker if we look at humanity across nations, with the expected life span in the richest countries being two-thirds longer than in the least developed countries (see, e.g., UN 2015). Like with health care, it is conceivable that different societies will make significantly different choices about access to human enhancement technologies.

Once the wealthiest enhanced humans have separated sufficiently far from the unenhanced, they can effectively be considered as a separate species of artificially intelligent agents. To emphasize the difference in productivities, Yuval Harari (2017) has dubbed the two classes that may result "the gods" and "the useless." In that case, the long-run implications of our first scenario coincide with the second scenario.

Second Scenario: Artificially Intelligent Agents and the Return of Malthus

We thus turn to the scenario that artificially intelligent entities develop separately from regular (or unenhanced) humans. One of the likely characteristics of any sufficiently intelligent entity—no matter what final objectives are programmed into it by evolution or by its creator—is that it will act by pursuing intermediate objectives or "basic drives" that are instrumental for any final objective (Omohundro 2008). These intermediate objectives include self-preservation, self-improvement, and resource accumulation, which all make it likelier and easier for the entity to achieve its final objectives.

It may be worthwhile pursuing the logic of what happens if humans do not or cannot assert ownership rights over artificially intelligent or superintelligent entities.[33] That would imply that sufficiently advanced AI is likely to operate autonomously.

To describe the resulting economic system, Korinek (2017) assumes that there are two types of entities, unenhanced humans and AI entities, which are in a Malthusian race and differ—potentially starkly—in how they are affected by technological progress. At the heart of Malthusian models is the notion that survival and reproduction requires resources, which are poten-

---

33. If humans and artificially intelligent entities are somewhat close in their levels of intelligence, it may still be possible for humans to assert ownership rights over the AI—in fact, throughout the history of mankind, those determining and exerting property rights have not always been the most intelligent. For example, humans could still threaten to turn off or destroy the computers on which AI entities are running. However, if the gap between humans and superintelligent AI entities grows too large, it may be impossible for humans to continue to exert control, just like a two-year-old would not be able to effectively exert property rights over adults.

tially scarce.[34] Formally, traditional Malthusian models capture this by describing how limited factor supplies interact with two related sets of technologies, a production and a consumption/reproduction technology: First, humans supply the factor labor, which is used in a production technology to generate consumption goods. Second, a consumption/reproduction technology converts consumption goods into the survival and reproduction of humans, determining the future supply of the factor labor.

Throughout human history Malthusian dynamics, in which scarce consumption goods limited the survival and reproduction of humans, provided a good description of the state of humanity, roughly until when Malthus (1798) published his *Essay on the Principle of Population* to describe the resulting Iron Law of Population. Over the past two centuries, humanity, at least in advanced countries, was lucky to escape its Malthusian constraints: capital accumulation and rapid labor-augmenting technological progress generated by the Industrial Revolution meant that our technology to produce consumption goods was constantly ahead of the consumption goods required to guarantee our physical survival. Moreover, human choices to limit physical reproduction meant that the gains of greater productivity were only partly dissipated in increased population. However, this state of affairs is not guaranteed to last forever.

Korinek (2017) compares the production and consumption/reproduction technologies of humans and AI entities and observes that they differ starkly: On the production side, the factor human labor is quickly losing ground to the labor provided by AI entities, captured by the notion of *worker-replacing technological progress* that we introduced earlier. In other words, AI entities are becoming more and more efficient in the production of output compared to humans. On the consumption/reproduction side, the human technology to convert consumption goods such as food and housing into future humans has experienced relatively little technological change—the basic biology of unenhanced humans is slow to change. By contrast, the reproduction technology of AI entities—to convert AI consumption goods such as energy, silicon, aluminum into future AI—is subject to exponential progress, as described, for example, by Moore's Law and its successors, which postulate that computing power per dollar (i.e., per unit of "AI consumption good") doubles roughly every two years.[35]

---

34. If AI directs its enhanced capabilities at binding resource constraints, it is conceivable that such constraints might successively be lifted, just as we seem to have avoided the constraints that might have been imposed by the limited supply of fossil fuels. At present, humans consume only a small fraction—about 0.1 percent—of the energy that earth receives from the sun. However, astrophysicists such as Tegmark (2017) note that according to the laws of physics as currently known, there will be an ultimate resource constraint on superintelligent AI given by the availability of energy (or, equivalently, matter, since $E = mc^2$) accessible from within our event horizon.

35. The original version of Moore's Law, articulated by the cofounder of Intel, Gordon Moore (1965), stated that the number of components that can be fit on an integrated circuit (IC) would double every year. Moore revised his estimate to every two years in 1975. In recent

Taken together, these two dynamics imply—unsurprisingly—that humans may lose the Malthusian race in the long run, unless counteracting steps are taken, to which we will turn shortly. In the following paragraphs we trace out what this might entail and how we might respond to it. (Fully following the discussion requires a certain suspension of disbelief. However, we should begin by recognizing that machines can already engage in a large variety of economic transactions—trading financial securities, placing orders, making payments, and so forth. It is not a stretch of the mind to assume that they could in fact engage in all of what we now view as economic activities. In fact, if an outside observer from a different planet were to witness the interactions among the various intelligent entities on earth, it might not be clear to her if, for example, artificially intelligent entities such as Apple or Google control what we humans do [via a plethora of control devices called smartphones that we carry with us] or whether we intelligent humans control what entities such as Apple and Google do. See also the discussion in Turing [1950].) The most interesting aspects of the economic analysis concern the transition dynamics and the economic mechanisms through which the Malthusian race plays out.

In the beginning, those lacking the skills that are useful in an AI-dominated world may find that they are increasingly at a disadvantage in competing for scarce resources, and they will see their incomes decline, as we noted earlier. The proliferation of AI entities will at first put only modest price pressure on scarce resources, and most of the scarce factors are of relatively little interest to humans (such as silicon), so humanity as a whole will benefit from the high productivity of AI entities and from large gains from trade. From a human perspective, this will look like AI leading to significant productivity gains in our world. Moreover, any scarce factors that are valuable for the reproduction and improvement of AI, such as human labor skilled in programming, or intellectual property, would experience large gains.

As time goes on, the superior production and consumption technologies of AI entities imply that they will proliferate. Their ever-increasing efficiency units will lead to fierce competition over any nonreproducible factors that are in limited supply, such as land and energy, pushing up the prices of such factors and making them increasingly unaffordable for regular humans, given their limited factor income. It is not hard to imagine an outcome where the AI entities, living for themselves, absorb (i.e., "consume") more and more of our resources.

Eventually, this may force humans to cut back on their consumption to the point where their real income is so low that they decline in numbers.

years, companies such as Intel have predicted that the literal version of Moore's Law may come to an end over the coming decade, as the design of traditional single-core ICs has reached its physical limits. However, the introduction of multidimensional ICs, multicore processors and other specialized chips for parallel processing implies that a broader version of Moore's Law, expressed in terms of computing power per dollar, is likely to continue for several decades to come. Quantum computing may extend this time span even further into the future.

Technologists have described several dystopian ways in which humans could survive for some time—ranging from uploading themselves into a simulated (and more energy-efficient) world,[36] to taking drugs that reduce their energy intake. The decline of humanity may not play out in the traditional way described by Malthus—that humans are literally starving—since human fertility is increasingly a matter of choice rather than nutrition. It is sufficient that a growing number of unenhanced humans decide that given the prices they face, they cannot afford sufficient offspring to meet the human replacement rate while providing their offspring with the space, education, and prospects that they aspire to.

One question that these observations bring up is whether it might be desirable for humanity to slow down or halt progress in AI beyond a certain point. However, even if such a move were desirable, it may well be technologically infeasible—progress may have to be stopped well short of the point where general artificial intelligence could occur. Furthermore it cannot be ruled out that a graduate student under the radar working in a garage will create the world's first superhuman AI.

If progress in AI cannot be halted, our description above suggests mechanisms that may ensure that humans can afford a separate living space and remain viable: because humans start out owning some of the factors that are in limited supply, if they are prohibited from transferring these factors, they could continue to consume them without suffering from their price appreciation. This would create a type of human "reservation" in an AI-dominated world. Humans would likely be tempted to sell their initial factor holdings, for two reasons: First, humans may be less patient than artificially intelligent entities. Second, superintelligent AI entities may earn higher returns on factors and thus be willing to pay more for them than other humans. That is why, for the future of humanity, it may be necessary to limit the ability of humans to sell their factor allocations to AI entities. Furthermore, for factors such as energy that correspond to a flow that is used up in consumption, it would be necessary to allocate permanent usage rights to humans. Alternatively, we could provide an equivalent flow income to humans that is adjusted regularly to keep pace with factor prices.[37]

14.7 Conclusions

The proliferation of AI and other forms of worker-replacing technological change can be unambiguously positive in a first-best economy in which individuals are fully insured against any adverse effects of innovation, or if it is coupled with the right form of redistribution. In the absence of such

36. See, for example, Hanson (2016). In fact, Aguiar et al. (2017) document that young males with low education have already shifted a considerable part of their time into the cyber world rather than supplying labor to the market economy—at wages that they deem unattractive.

37. All of this assumes that the superintelligent AI entities don't use their powers in one way or another to abrogate these property rights.

intervention, worker-replacing technological change may not only lead to workers getting a diminishing fraction of national income, but may actually make them worse off in absolute terms.

The scope for redistribution is facilitated by the fact that the changes in factor prices create windfall gains on the complementary factors, which should make it feasible to achieve Pareto improvements. If there are limits on redistribution, the calculus worsens and a Pareto improvement can no longer be ensured. This may lead to resistance from those in society who are losing. As a result, there is a case for using as broad of a set of second-best policies as possible, including changes in intellectual property rights, to maximize the likelihood that AI (or technological progress more generally) generate a Pareto improvement.

Artificial intelligence and other changes in technology necessitate large adjustments, and while individuals and the economy more broadly may be able to adjust to slow changes, this may not be so when the pace is rapid. Indeed, in such situations, outcomes can be Pareto inferior. The more willing society is to support the necessary transition and to provide support to those who are "left behind," the faster the pace of innovation that society can accommodate, and still ensure that the outcomes are Pareto improvements. A society that is not willing to engage in such actions should expect resistance to innovation, with uncertain political and economic consequences.

References

Acemoglu, Daron. 1998. "Why Do New Technologies Complement Skills? Directed Technical Change and Wage Inequality." *Quarterly Journal of Economics* 113 (4): 1055–89.
———. 2002. "Directed Technical Change." *Review of Economic Studies* 69 (4): 781–809.
Acemoglu, Daron, and Pascual Restrepo. 2018. "The Race between Machine and Man: Implications of Technology for Growth, Factor Shares and Employment." *American Economic Review* 108 (6): 1488–542.
Aghion, Philippe, Benjamin Jones, and Charles Jones. 2017. "Artificial Intelligence and Economic Growth." NBER Working Paper no. 23928, Cambridge, MA.
Aguiar, Mark, Mark Bils, Kerwin Kofi Charles, and Erik Hurst. 2017. "Leisure Luxuries and the Labor Supply of Young Men." NBER Working Paper no. 23552, Cambridge, MA.
Akerlof, George, and Janet Yellen. 1990. "The Fair Wage-Effort Hypothesis and Unemployment." *Quarterly Journal of Economics* 105 (2): 255–83.
Arrow, Kenneth. 1962. "Economic Welfare and the Allocation of Resources for Invention." In *The Rate and Direction of Inventive Activity: Economic and Social Factors*, edited by Richard R. Nelson, 609–26. Princeton, NJ: Princeton University Press.
Baker, Dean, Arjun Jayadev, and Joseph E. Stiglitz. 2017. "Innovation, Intellectual Property, and Development: A Better Set of Approaches for the 21st Century." AccessIBSA: Innovation & Access to Medicines in India, Brazil & South Africa.

Barrat, James. 2013. *Our Final Invention: Artificial Intelligence and the End of the Human Era*. New York: St. Martin's Press.

Berg, Andrew, Edward F. Buffie, and Luis-Felipe Zanna. 2018. "Should We Fear the Robot Revolution? (The Correct Answer is Yes)." *Journal of Monetary Economics* 97. www.doi.org/10.1016/j.jmoneco.2018.05.012.

Bostrom, Nick. 2014. *Superintelligence: Paths, Dangers, Strategies*. Oxford: Oxford University Press.

Dasgupta, Partha, and Joseph E. Stiglitz. 1980a. "Uncertainty, Industrial Structure and the Speed of R&D." *Bell Journal of Economics* 11 (1): 1–28.

———. 1980b. "Industrial Structure and the Nature of Innovative Activity." *Economic Journal* 90 (358): 266–93.

———. 1988. "Potential Competition, Actual Competition and Economic Welfare." *European Economic Review* 32:569–77.

Dávila, Eduardo, and Anton Korinek. 2018. "Pecuniary Externalities in Economies with Financial Frictions." *Review of Economic Studies* 85 (1): 352–95.

Delli Gatti, Domenico, Mauro Gallegati, Bruce C. Greenwald, Alberto Russo, and Joseph E. Stiglitz. 2012a. "Mobility Constraints, Productivity Trends, and Extended Crises." *Journal of Economic Behavior & Organization* 83 (3): 375–93.

———. 2012b. "Sectoral Imbalances and Long-run Crises." In *The Global Macro Economy and Finance*, edited by Franklin Allen, Masahiko Aoki, Jean-Paul Fitoussi, Nobuhiro Kiyotaki, Robert Gordon, and Joseph E. Stiglitz. International Economic Association Series. London: Palgrave Macmillan.

Dosi, Giovanni, and Joseph E. Stiglitz. 2014. "The Role of Intellectual Property Rights in the Development Process, with Some Lessons from Developed Countries: An Introduction." In *Intellectual Property Rights: Legal and Economic Challenges for Development*, edited by Mario Cimoli, Giovanni Dosi, Keith E. Maskus, Ruth L. Okediji, Jerome H. Reichman, and Joseph E. Stiglitz, 1–53. Oxford: Oxford University Press.

Drandakis, Emmanuel, and Edmund Phelps. 1965. "A Model of Induced Invention, Growth and Distribution." *Economic Journal* 76:823–40.

Fehr, Ernst, and Klaus M. Schmidt. 2003. "Theories of Fairness and Reciprocity—Evidence and Economic Applications." In *Advances in Economics and Econometrics*, Econometric Society Monographs, Eighth World Congress, vol. 1, edited by Mathias Dewatripont, Lars Peter Hansen, and Stephen J Turnovsky, 208–57. Cambridge: Cambridge University Press.

Financial Crisis Inquiry Commission. 2011. "The Financial Crisis Inquiry Report." Final Report of the National Commission. January. http://www.gpoaccess.gov/fcic/fcic.pdf.

Frey, Carl Benedikt, and Michael A. Osborne. 2017. "The Future of Employment: How Susceptible Are Jobs to Computerisation?" *Technological Forecasting and Social Change* 114:254–80.

Geanakoplos, John, and Herakles Polemarchakis. 1986. "Existence, Regularity, and Constrained Suboptimality of Competitive Allocations When the Asset Market Is Incomplete." In *Uncertainty, Information and Communication: Essays in Honor of KJ Arrow*, edited by W. Heller, R. Starr, and D. Starrett, 65–96. Cambridge: Cambridge University Press.

Gordon, Robert. 2016. *The Rise and Fall of American Growth: The U.S. Standard of Living since the Civil War*. Princeton, NJ: Princeton University Press.

Greenwald, Bruce, and Joseph E. Stiglitz. 1986. "Externalities in Economics with Imperfect Information and Incomplete Markets." *Quarterly Journal of Economics* 101 (2): 229–64.

Groshen, Erica L., Brian C. Moyer, Ana M. Aizcorbe, Ralph Bradley, and David M. Friedman. 2017. "How Government Statistics Adjust for Potential Biases from

Quality Change and New Goods in an Age of Digital Technologies: A View from the Trenches." *Journal of Economic Perspectives* 31 (2): 187–210.

Guzman, Martin, and Joseph E. Stiglitz. 2016a. "Pseudo-Wealth and Consumption Fluctuations." NBER Working Paper no. 22838, Cambridge, MA.

Guzman, Martin, and Joseph E. Stiglitz. 2016b. "A Theory of Pseudo-Wealth." In *Contemporary Issues in Macroeconomics: Lessons from The Crisis and Beyond,* edited by Joseph E. Stiglitz and Martin Guzman. IEA Conference Volume no. 155-II. Basingstoke, UK: Palgrave Macmillan.

Hanson, Robin. 2016. *The Age of Em.* Oxford: Oxford University Press.

Harari, Yuval N. 2017. *Homo Deus: A Brief History of Tomorrow.* New York: Harper.

Hicks, John. 1932. *The Theory of Wages.* London: Macmillan.

Kennedy, Charles. 1964. "Induced Bias in Innovation and the Theory of Distribution." *Economic Journal* LXXIV:541–47.

Keynes, John Maynard. 1932. "Economic Possibilities for our Grandchildren." In *Essays in Persuasion,* 358–73. San Diego, CA: Harcourt Brace.

Korinek, Anton. 2016. "Currency Wars or Efficient Spillovers? A General Theory of International Policy Cooperation." NBER Working Paper no. 23004, Cambridge, MA.

———. 2017. "The Rise of Artificially Intelligent Agents." Working paper, Johns Hopkins University.

Korinek, Anton, and Ding Xuan Ng. 2018. "Digitization and the Macroeconomics of Superstars." Working paper, Johns Hopkins University and University of Virginia.

Korinek, Anton, and Joseph E. Stiglitz. 2017. "Worker-Replacing Technological Progress." NBER Working Paper no. 24174, Cambridge, MA.

Kurzweil, Ray. 2005. *The Singularity Is Near: When Humans Transcend Biology.* New York: Viking.

Lipsey, Richard, and Kelvin Lancaster. 1956. "The General Theory of Second Best." *Review of Economic Studies* 24 (1): 11–32.

Malthus, Thomas Robert. 1798. *An Essay on the Principle of Population.* Project Gutenberg.

Manning, Alan. 2011. "Imperfect Competition in Labour Markets." In *Handbook of Labor Economics,* vol. 4, edited by O. Ashenfelter and D. Card. North-Holland: Amsterdam.

Meade, James E. 1955. *Trade and Welfare.* Oxford: Oxford University Press.

Moore, Gordon E. 1965. "Cramming More Components onto Integrated Circuits." *Electronics* 38 (8): 114:ff.

Mortensen, Dale T., and Christopher A. Pissarides. 1994. "Job Creation and Job Destruction in the Theory of Unemployment." *Review of Economic Studies* 61 (3): 397–415.

———. 1998. "Technological Progress, Job Creation, and Job Destruction." *Review of Economic Dynamics* 1 (4): 733–53.

Newbery, David, and Joseph E. Stiglitz. 1984. "Pareto Inferior Trade." *Review of Economic Studies* 51 (1): 1–12.

Omohundro, Stephen M. 2008. "The Basic AI drives." In *Artificial General Intelligence 2008: Proceedings of the First AGI Conference,* edited by Pei Wang, Ben Goertzel, and Stan Franklin, 483–92. Amsterdam: IOS.

Piketty, Thomas, Emmanuel Saez, and Stefanie Stantcheva. 2014. "Optimal Taxation of Top Labor Incomes: A Tale of Three Elasticities." *American Economic Journal: Economic Policy* 6 (1): 230–71.

Restrepo, Pascual. 2015. "Skill Mismatch and Structural Unemployment." Working paper, Massachusetts Institute of Technology.

Samuelson, Paul. 1965. "A Theory of Induced Innovations along Kennedy-Weisacker Lines." *Review of Economics and Statistics* XLVII:444–64.

Schmitt, John. 2013. *Why Does the Minimum Wage Have No Discernible Effect on Employment?* Washington, DC: Center for Economic and Policy Research.

Shapiro, Carl, and Joseph E. Stiglitz. 1984. "Equilibrium Unemployment as a Worker Discipline Device." *American Economic Review* 74 (3): 433–44.

Simsek, Alp. 2013. "Speculation and Risk Sharing with New Financial Assets." *Quarterly Journal of Economics* 128 (3): 1365–96.

Solow, Robert. 1987. "We'd Better Watch Out." *New York Times Book Review*, July 12, 36.

Stiglitz, Joseph E. 1969. "Distribution of Income and Wealth among Individuals." *Econometrica* 37 (3): 382–97.

———. 1976. "The Efficiency Wage Hypothesis, Surplus Labour and the Distribution of Income in LDCs." *Oxford Economic Papers* 28:185–207.

———. 1987a. "On the Microeconomics of Technical Progress." In *Technology Generation in Latin American Manufacturing Industries*, edited by Jorge M. Katz, 56–77. New York: St. Martin's Press.

———. 1987b. "Technological Change, Sunk Costs, and Competition." *Brookings Papers on Economic Activity* 3:883–947.

———.2006. "Samuelson and the Factor Bias of Technological Change." *Samuelsonian Economics and the Twenty-First Century*, edited by M. Szenberg et al., 235–51. New York: Oxford University Press.

———. 2008. "The Economic Foundations of Intellectual Property." *Duke Law Journal* 57 (6): 1693–724.

———. 2014a. "Intellectual Property Rights, the Pool of Knowledge, and Innovation." NBER Working Paper no. 20014, Cambridge, MA.

———. 2014b. "Unemployment and Innovation." NBER Working Paper no. 20670, Cambridge, MA.

———. 2014c. "Tapping the Brakes: Are Less Active Markets Safer and Better for the Economy?" Presentation at the Federal Reserve Bank of Atlanta 2014 Financial Markets Conference.

———. 2017. "Pareto Efficient Taxation and Expenditures: Pre- and Redistribution." NBER Working Paper no. 23892, Cambridge, MA.

Stiglitz, Joseph E., and Bruce Greenwald 2015. *Creating a Learning Society: A New Approach to Growth, Development, and Social Progress.* New York: Columbia University Press.

Stiglitz, Joseph E., with Nell Abernathy, Adam Hersh, Susan Holmberg, and Mike Konczal. 2015. *Rewriting the Rules of the American Economy,* A Roosevelt Institute Book. New York: W. W. Norton.

Stiglitz, Joseph E., and Andrew Weiss. 1981. "Credit Rationing in Markets with Imperfect Information." *American Economic Review* 71 (3): 393–410.

Tegmark, Max. 2017. *Life 3.0: Being Human in the Age of Artificial Intelligence.* New York: Knopf.

Turing, Alan M. 1950. "Computing Machinery and Intelligence." *Mind* 59 (236): 433–60.

United Nations Department of Economic and Social Affairs (UN). 2015. "United Nations World Population Prospects: 2015 Revision." https://esa.un.org/unpd/wpp/publications/files/key_findings_wpp_2015.pdf.

Vinge, Vernor. 1993. "The Coming Technological Singularity: How to Survive in the Post-Human Era." In *Proc. Vision 21: Interdisciplinary Science and Engineering in the Era of Cyberspace*, 11–22. NASA: Lewis Research Center.

von Weizacker, C. C. 1966. "Tentative Notes on a Two-Sector Model with Induced Technical Progress." *Review of Economic Studies* 33:245–51.

Williams, Heidi. 2010. "Intellectual Property Rights and Innovation: Evidence from the Human Genome." NBER Working Paper no. 16213, Cambridge, MA.

15

Neglected Open Questions in the Economics of Artificial Intelligence

Tyler Cowen

Many recent writings consider artificial intelligence (AI), or more broadly "smart software," as a transformative technology. Commonly, these writings focus on the substitution of capital for labor and the attendant domestic labor market effects. Without meaning to downplay the importance of that topic, I'd like to focus our attention on some other aspects of how artificial intelligence might affect our society.

15.1 The Distribution of Consumer Surplus

Most analyses of automation focus on the production function, but the new and cheaper outputs resulting from automation have distributional effects as well. For instance, the Industrial Revolution made food cheaper and more reliable in supply, in addition to mechanizing jobs in the factory and in the fields. A new, larger, cheaper and more diverse book market was created, and so on. Artificial intelligence, in turn, holds out the prospect of lowering prices for the outputs that can be produced by the next generation of automation. Imagine education and manufactured goods being much cheaper because we produced them using a greater dose of smart software. The upshot is that even if a robot puts you out of a job or lowers your pay, there will be some recompense on the consumer side. Internet goods such as Facebook already constitute a significant part of individuals' time allocation, and of course they are free or very cheap at the relevant margin.

It's worth thinking about whether the new AI-enabled outputs will be pro-

Tyler Cowen is professor of economics at George Mason University.

For acknowledgments, sources of research support, and disclosure of the author's material financial relationships, if any, please see http://www.nber.org/chapters/c14032.ack.

duced at constant, increasing, or declining cost. Usually software-intensive goods tend to be produced at declining cost; namely, there is an upfront investment in the software, but at the margin additional copies are quite cheap or possibly free.

The declining cost scenario seems to have some optimistic properties. If the marginal cost is zero or near-zero, in the longer run the output price should fall considerably. In some cases, such as with social networks, the price may be zero to begin with, or perhaps negative to encourage people to join the network. Once we consider these consumption side effects, the distributional implication of an AI revolution could be more egalitarian than the job displacement effects alone would indicate.

For instance, consider the role of smartphones and cell phones in Africa today. These items have a relatively low marginal cost, and they are sold in Africa quite cheaply. They have transformed some sectors of African economies by making it much easier to manage businesses, and they also allow Africans the pleasure of communicating with each other more easily. The substitution of labor for capital in smartphone manufacturing hasn't impacted African economies much at all because Africa is not a major part of the supply chain. The more that tech production is clustered, the more that the consumption effects will be the major effects for many parts of the world.

These distribution effects may be less egalitarian if hardware rather than software is the constraint for the next generation of AI. Hardware is more likely to exhibit constant or rising costs, and that makes it more difficult for suppliers to charge lower prices to poorer buyers. You might think it is obvious that future productivity gains will come in the software area—and maybe so—but the very best smart phones, such as iPhones, also embody significant innovations in the areas of materials. A truly potent AI device might require portable hardware at significant cost. At this point we don't know, but it would be unwise to assume that future innovations will be software-intensive to the same extent that recent innovations have been.

If future AI innovations lead to very low consumer prices, this may affect our policy recommendations. Often analysts who are worried about automation call for better education and job training. Those may still be good ideas, but another approach can pay off as well. To the extent productivity is very high and prices are very low, it may suffice for workers to own some capital or natural resources. That is, wealth can serve as a substitute for income, given the extremely high purchasing power resulting from the low prices. Giving everyone some land, a birthright grant or shares in a sovereign wealth fund are options to consider, on top of whatever changes might be made to education and labor markets.

Perhaps counterintuitively, the economics of natural resources would become significantly more relevant in such a world. The scarcity of labor would matter much less, and of course robots could be used to make more robots. You might even imagine software programs generating new products and ideas, and organizing their implementation. What would, in fact, constrain production? The answer is energy and possibly land. As scarce inputs, land and energy would determine which economies would do well and which not so well. In such a world the returns to education could be very low rather than very high.

An alternative possibility for the new scarce resource might be institutions to encourage AI-led production, such as maximally secure property rights. In that case, public choice factors would become a more significant determinant of national and regional outcomes. If "good government" is a public good of sorts, that would benefit nations and regions with especially effective norms for governance, for instance Singapore.

15.2   International Effects of an AI Revolution

Information technology also interacts with international trade. One effect of smart software is to enable more factor price equalization. It helps successful businesses become larger and also branch out internationally; for instance, it would be harder for Apple to finish off the iPhone in China if it only had the communications technologies of a few decades ago. These days, company leadership can manage an international empire by cell phone, email, and other technologies, and arguably that has led to higher investment in Chinese workers and lower investment in American and other developed country workers, especially at the lower-skilled end of the distribution.

That said, if you imagine artificial intelligence and other technologies progressing further, wage differentials might cease to be a reason to locate abroad at all. Why should the wage differential matter if the company is hardly employing any labor? As a result, there might be a reshoring of American or Western European manufacturing.

This could boost the demand for janitors here in the United States and also increase their wages, even though the number of such janitors might be small. Possibly the big income distribution effect is that artificial intelligence will be much worse for the poorer countries that can no longer industrialize through wage differentials; Dani Rodrik has labeled this phenomenon "premature deindustrialization." At the same time, AI may be just fine for people who have the lowest wages, namely, pure manual labor jobs that can't be outsourced at all. Information technology might be progressive at the lower end of the income distribution while hollowing out the middle, arguably a phenomenon we have seen in the United States. The biggest effects for income distribution might be across borders rather than within nations. Or, to put it another way, Africa may never have the chance to follow in the footsteps of Japan and South Korea with respect to industrialization.

From an egalitarian point of view, these distributional effects may be hard to address, precisely because they cross borders. Citizens are often willing to support income redistribution within their nations, but they are much less likely to favor significant investments in foreign aid, especially when it is to distant nations rather than to neighbors or major trading partners.

15.3 The Political Economy of Artificial Intelligence and Income Redistribution

Discussions of artificial intelligence sometimes postulate large numbers of unemployed or underemployed people, possibly living off a guaranteed annual income or some other form of massive redistribution. On one hand, I can see the reason for considering a shift to larger cash payments. Yet the economics, politics, and sociology of guaranteed income may create problems.

If you ask which are the countries today where citizens hardly do any work, Brunei and Qatar, two resource-rich monarchies, come to mind. In each country people get a lot of money from the government, and foreign workers do much of the labor. From an analytical point of view, that is not so different from relying on robots.

The recent histories of those countries indicate that redistribution is a politically tricky concept. Imagine for instance a polity where virtually the entire gross domestic product is in some way recycled or redistributed. I expect the resulting political economy would not resemble that of Norway, as Norway without oil still would have a living standard close to that of Sweden or Denmark. Brunei or Qatar without fossil fuels likely would be *much* poorer. Given that reality, when so much of the gross domestic product (GDP) is being redistributed through politics, I wonder if this is compatible with American or Western notions of democracy. For instance, the oligarchic political forces that control the oil might make upfront offers to the interest groups that might oppose them and cement their control. Indeed those monarchies do seem to be stable, and it is far from obvious that they are evolving toward democracy. Their governments are partially benevolent toward the citizenry, but they also use a lot of the surplus to achieve their own ends, which may be religious or ideological. It seems countries that rely on fossil fuels for their GDP don't end up with the thick middle class that in the West at least partially controls the government, and is also a dominant force in our civic society and social capital. Possibly oil-rich countries do not have the economic base to sustain a version of Western-style liberal democracy, and that has something to do with so much of the GDP being recycled and redistributed. That is correlated with having a politically weak middle class and an opposition that is too easily bought off; at least that is what we observed to date in some of fossil-fuel-rich small states.

The experience of Brunei and Qatar also raises the question of what the governmental authority should be redistributing. In simple economic models, cash is redistributed to those who typically need it most. But in more comfortable settings with a lot of resource wealth, it also may be necessary to redistribute status. That's harder to do; for the social scientist, it is also harder to model. We may need to redistribute the notion of having a meaningful job because although Qatar and Brunei have high per capita incomes, including at the median, it is not obvious to all outside observers that their citizens are happy and fulfilled.

It's possible that government "make-work" jobs will supply status to people, but there is also a danger the make-work component will be too obvious, and the resulting jobs will bring low rather than high status. In the last US presidential campaign, Hillary Clinton spoke more of redistribution and Donald Trump talked more of jobs; Trump's message seemed to be the more effective of the two.

Some desired redistributions may cross gender lines. For instance, as the population ages there will be a greater care burden for women than men, as women seem to put more time and effort into caring for their aging parents. Redistribution of money toward women may help, but at its core the problem may be one of stress rather than money per se. A change in social norms may produce a better and more effective redistribution than simply sending around checks.

If we think of caring for the elderly as a potential job with a lot of growth potential, on average women may be better at this than men, which in the labor market context serves as a penalty on being male, again to speak of the averages only. More generally, the shift toward service-sector jobs may favor women more than unskilled men. The public policies needed for many men may differ from those needed for women once again, and cash is not always the appropriate tool for recognizing those distinctions.

The general idea that in these stranger futures, what redistribution is, or has to be, is something quite different from what it is in the simple Paretian model. That is a frontier issue where we economists haven't done much work at all, but the ongoing progress of AI may make those questions all the more relevant.

Machine Learning and Regulation

Artificial Intelligence, Economics, and Industrial Organization

Hal Varian

16.1 Introduction

Machine learning (ML) and artificial intelligence (AI) have been around for many years. However, in the last five years, remarkable progress has been made using multilayered neural networks in diverse areas such as image recognition, speech recognition, and machine translation. Artificial intelligence is a general purpose technology that is likely to impact many industries. In this chapter I consider how machine learning availability might affect the industrial organization of both firms that *provide* AI services and industries that *adopt* AI technology. My intent is not to provide an extensive overview of this rapidly evolving area, but instead to provide a short summary of some of the forces at work and to describe some possible areas for future research.

16.2 Machine-Learning Overview

Imagine we have a set of digital images along with a set of labels that describe what is depicted in those images—things like cats, dogs, beaches, mountains, cars, or people. Our goal is to use this data to train a computer

Hal Varian is an emeritus professor at the University of California, Berkeley, and chief economist at Google.

Carl Shapiro and I started drafting this chapter with the goal of producing a joint work. Unfortunately, Carl became very busy and had to drop out of the project. I am grateful to him for the time he was able to put in. I also would like to thank Judy Chevalier and the participants of the NBER Economics of AI conference in Toronto, Fall 2017. For acknowledgments, sources of research support, and disclosure of the author's material financial relationships, if any, please see http://www.nber.org/chapters/c14017.ack.

to learn how to predict labels for some new set of digital images. (For a nice demonstration, see cloud.google.com/vision where you can upload a photo and retrieve a list of labels appropriate for that photo.)

The classical approach to machine vision involved creating a set of rules that identified pixels in the images with human-recognizable features such as color, brightness, and edges and then use these features to predict labels. This "featurization" approach had limited success. The modern approach is to work directly with the raw pixels using layered neural networks. This has been remarkably successful, not only with image recognition but also with voice recognition, language translation, and other traditionally difficult machine-learning tasks. Nowadays computers can outperform humans in many of these tasks.

This approach, called *deep learning*, requires (a) labeled data for training, (b) algorithms for the neural nets, and (c) special-purpose hardware to run the algorithms. Academics and tech companies have provided training data and algorithms for free, and compute time in cloud-computing facilities is available for a nominal charge.

1. Training data. Examples are OpenImages, a 9.5 million data set of labeled images and the Stanford Dog Data set, 20,580 images of 120 breeds of dogs.

2. Algorithms. Popular open-source packages include TensorFlow, Caffe, MXNet, and Theano.

3. Hardware. CPUs (central processing units), GPUs (graphical processing units), and TPUs (Tensor processing units), are available via cloud-computing providers. These facilities allow the user to organize vast amounts of data, which can be used to train machine-learning models.

Of course, it is also important to have experts who can manage the data, tune the algorithms, and nurture the entire process. These skills are, in fact, the main bottleneck at the moment, but universities are rapidly rising to the challenge of providing the education and training necessary to create and utilize machine learning.

In addition to machine vision, the deep learning research community has made dramatic advances in speech recognition and language translation. These areas also have been able to make this progress without the sorts of feature identification that had been required for previous ML systems.

Other types of machine learning are described in the Wikipedia entry on this topic. One important form of machine learning is *reinforcement learning*. This is a type of learning where a machine optimizes some task such as winning at chess or video games. One example of reinforcement learning is a multiarmed bandit, but there are many other tools used, some of which involve deep neural nets.

Reinforcement learning is a type of sequential experimentation and is therefore fundamentally about causality: moving a particular chess piece from one position to another *causes* the probability of a win to increase. This is unlike passive machine-learning algorithms that use only observational data.

Reinforcement learning can also be implemented in an adversarial context. For example, in October 2017 DeepMind announced a machine-learning system, Alpha Go 0, that developed a highly effective strategy by playing Go games against itself!

The model of "self-taught machine learning" is an interesting model for game theory. Can deep networks learn to compete and/or learn to cooperate with other players entirely their own? Will the learned behavior look anything like the equilibria for game-theoretic models we have built? So far these techniques have been applied primarily to full information games. Will they work in games with incomplete or asymmetric information?

There is a whole subarea of AI known as *adversarial AI* (or *adversarial ML*) that combines themes from AI, game theory, and computer security that examines ways to attack and defend AI systems. Suppose, for example, that we have a trained image recognition system that performs well, on average. What about its worst-case performance? It turns out that there are ways to create images that appear innocuous to humans that will consistently fool the ML system. Just as "optical illusions" can fool humans, these "ML illusions" can fool machines. Interestingly, the optimal illusions for humans and machines are very different. For some examples, see Goodfellow et al. (2017) for illustrative examples and Kurakin, Goodfellow, and Bengio (2016) for a technical report. Computer science researchers have recognized the connections with game theory; in my opinion, this area offers many interesting opportunities for collaboration. (See, e.g., Sreevallabh and Liu 2017).

16.2.1   What Can Machine Learning Do?

The example of machine learning presented in the popular press emphasizes novel applications, such as winning at games such as chess, Go, and Pong. However, there are also many practical applications that use machine learning to solve real-world business problems. A good place to see what kinds of problem ML can solve is Kaggle. This company sets up machine-learning competitions. A business or other organization provides some data, a problem statement, and some prize money. Data scientists then use the data to solve the problem posed. The winners get to take home the prize money. There are well over 200 competitions on the site. Here are a few of the most recent.

- Passenger Threats. Improve accuracy of Homeland Security threat recognition: $1,500,000.
- Home Prices. Improve accuracy of Zillow's home-price prediction: $1,200,000.

- Traffic to Wikipedia Pages. Forecast future traffic to Wikipedia pages: $25,000.
- Personalized Medicine. Predict effect of genetic variants to enable personalized medicine: $15,000.
- Taxi Trip Duration. Predict total ride duration of taxi trips in New York: $30,000.
- Product Search Relevance. Predict relevance of search results on homedepot.com: $40,000.
- Clustering Questions. Can you identify question pairs that have the same intent?: $25,000.
- Cervical cancer screening. Which cancer treatments will be most effective?: $100,000.
- Click Prediction. Can you predict which recommended content each user will click?: $25,000.
- Inventory Demand. Maximize sales and minimize returns of bakery goods: $25,000.

What is nice is that these are real questions and real money from organizations that want real answers for real problems. Kaggle gives concrete examples of how machine learning can be applied for practical business questions.[1]

16.2.2   What Factors Are Scarce?

Suppose you want to deploy a machine-learning system in your organization. The first requirement is to have a data infrastructure that collects and organizes the data of interest—a *data pipeline*. For example, a retailer would need a system that can collect data at point of sale, and then upload it to a computer that can then organize the data into a database. This data would then be combined with other data, such as inventory data, logistics data, and perhaps information about the customer. Constructing this data pipeline is often the most labor intensive and expensive part of building a data infrastructure, since different businesses often have idiosyncratic legacy systems that are difficult to interconnect.

Once the data has been organized, it can be collected together to in a data warehouse. The data warehouse allows easy access to systems that can manipulate, visualize, and analyze the data.

Traditionally, companies ran their own data warehouses that required not only purchase of costly computers, but also required human system administrators to keep everything functioning properly. Nowadays, it is more and more common to store and analyze the data in a cloud-computing facility

---

1. Disclosure: I was an angel investor in Kaggle up till mid-2017 when it was acquired by Google. Since then, I have had no financial interest in the company.

such as Amazon Web Services, Google Cloud Platform, or Microsoft Azure Cloud.

The cloud provider takes care of managing and updating the hardware and software necessary to host the databases and tools for data analysis. From an economic point of view, what is interesting is that what was previously a fixed cost to the users (the data center) has now turned into a variable cost (renting time on the data center). An organization can purchase virtually any amount of cloud services, so even small companies can start at a minimal level and be charged based on usage. Cloud computing is much more cost effective than owning your own data center, since compute and data resources can be purchased on an as-needed basis. Needless to say, most tech start-ups today use a cloud provider for their hardware, software, and networking needs.

Cloud providers also offer various machine-learning services such as voice recognition, image recognition, translation, and so on. These systems are already trained by the vendor and can be put to immediate use by the customer. It is no longer necessary for each company to develop its own software for these tasks.

Competition among the cloud providers is intense. Highly detailed and specific image recognition capabilities are offered at a cost of a tenth-of-a-cent per image or less, with volume discounts on top of that price.

A user may also have idiosyncratic data relevant to its own business like the point-of-sale data mentioned above. The cloud provider also provides up-to-date, highly optimized hardware and software than implements popular machine-learning algorithms. This allows the use immediate access to high-powered tools . . . providing that they have the expertise to use them.

If the hardware, software, and expertise are available, all that is needed is the labeled data. There are a variety of ways to acquire such data.

- As By-Product of Operations. Think of a chain of restaurants where some perform better than others, and management may be interested in factors that are associated with performance. Much of the data in the Kaggle competitions mentioned above are generated as a byproduct of day-to-day operations.
- Web Scraping. This is a commonly used way to extract data from websites. There is a legal debate about what exactly is permitted with respect to both the collection of data and how it is used. The debate is too complex to discuss here, but the Wikipedia entry on Web scraping is good. An alternative is to use data that others have scraped. For example, the Common Crawl database contains petabytes of data compiled over eight years of Web crawling.
- Offering a Service. When Google started its work on voice recognition, it had no expertise and no data. It hired the expertise and they came up

with the idea of a voice-input telephone directory as a way to acquire data. Users would say "Joe's Pizza, University Avenue, Palo Alto" and the system would respond with a phone number. The digitized question and the resulting user choices were uploaded to the cloud and machine learning was used to evaluate the relationship between Google's answer and the user action—for example, to call the suggested number. The ML training used data from millions of individual number requests and learned rapidly. ReCAPTCHA applies a similar model where humans label images to prove they are human and not a simple bot.

- Hiring Humans to Label Data. Mechanical Turk and other systems can be used to pay people to label data (see Hutson 2017).
- Buying Data from Provider. There are many providers of various sorts of data such as mail lists, credit scores, and so on.
- Sharing Data. It may be mutually advantageous to parties to share data. This is common among academic researchers. The Open Images Data set contains about nine million labeled images contributed by universities and research labs. Sharing may be mandated for a variety reasons, such as concerns for public safety. Examples are black boxes from airplanes or medical data on epidemics.
- Data from Governments. There are vast amounts of data available from governments, universities, research labs, and nongovernmental agencies.
- Data from Cloud Providers. Many cloud providers also provide public data repositories. See, for example, Google Public Data sets, Google Patents Public Data set, or AWS Public Data sets.
- Computer-Generated Data. The Alpha Go 0 system mentioned earlier generated its own data by playing Go games against itself. Machine-vision algorithms can be trained using "synthetic images," which are actual images that have been shifted, rotated, and scaled in various ways.

16.2.3   Important Characteristics of Data

Information science uses the concept of a "data pyramid" to depict the relationship between data, information, and knowledge. Some system has to collect the raw data, and subsequently organize and analyze that data in order to turn it into information—something such as a textual document image that can be understood by humans. Think of the pixels in an image being turned into human-readable labels. In the past this was done by humans; in the future more and more of this will be done by machines. (See figure 16.1.)

This insights from the information can then turned into knowledge, which generally is embodied in humans. We can think of data being stored in bits, information stored in documents, and knowledge stored in humans. There are well-developed markets and regulatory environments for information

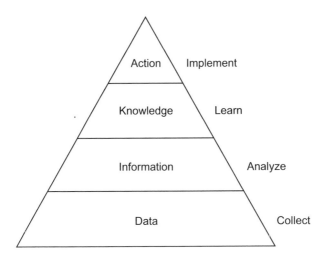

Fig. 16.1 **The information pyramid**

(books, articles, web pages, music, videos) and for knowledge (labor markets, consultants). Markets for data—in the sense of unorganized collections of bits—are not as developed. Perhaps this is because raw data is often heavily context dependent and is not very useful until it is turned into information.

Data Ownership and Data Access

It is said that "data is the new oil." Certainly, they are alike in one respect: both need to be refined in order to be useful. But there is an important distinction: oil is a private good and consumption of oil is *rival*: if one person consumes oil, there is less available for someone else to consume. But data is *nonrival:* one person's use of data does not reduce or diminish another person's use.

So instead of focusing on data "ownership"—a concept appropriate for private goods—we really should think about data access. Data is rarely "sold" in the same way private goods are sold, rather it is licensed for specific uses. Currently there is a policy debate in Europe about "who should own autonomous vehicle data?" A better question is to ask "who should have access to autonomous vehicle data and what can they do with it?" This formulation emphasizes that many parties can simultaneously access autonomous vehicle data. In fact, from the viewpoint of safety it seems very likely that multiple parties should be allowed to access autonomous vehicle data. There could easily be several data collection points in a car: the engine, the navigation system, mobile phones in rider's pockets, and so on. Requiring exclusivity without a good reason for doing so would unnecessarily limit what can be done with the data.

Ross Anderson's description of what happens when there is an aircraft crash makes an important point illustrating why it may be important to allow several parties to access data.

> When an aircraft crashes, it is front page news. Teams of investigators rush to the scene, and the subsequent enquiries are conducted by experts from organisations with a wide range of interests—the carrier, the insurer, the manufacturer, the airline pilots' union, and the local aviation authority. Their findings are examined by journalists and politicians, discussed in pilots' messes, and passed on by flying instructors. In short, the flying community has a strong and institutionalised learning mechanism. (Anderson 1993)

Should we not want the same sort of learning mechanism for autonomous vehicles? Some sorts of information can be protected by copyright. But in the United States, raw data such as a telephone directory is not protected by copyright. (See Wikipedia entry on the legal case *Feist Publications, Inc v. Rural Telephone Service Co.*)

Despite this, data providers may compile some data and offer to license on certain terms to other parties. For example, there are several data companies that merge US census data with other sorts of geographic data and offer to license this data. These transactions may prohibit resale or relicensing. Even though there is no protectable intellectual property, the terms of the contract form a private contract that can be enforced by courts, as with any other private contract.

Decreasing Marginal Returns

Finally, it is important to understand that data typically exhibits decreasing returns to scale like any other factor of production. The same general principle applies for machine learning. Figure 16.2 shows how the accuracy of the Stanford dog breed classification behaves as the amount of training data increases. As one would expect, accuracy improves as the number of training images increases, but it does so at a decreasing rate.

Figure 16.3 shows how the error rate in the ImageNet competition has declined over the last several years. An important fact about this competition is that the number of training and test observations has been fixed during this period. This means that the improved performance of the winning systems cannot depend on sample size since it has been constant. Other factors such as improved algorithms, improved hardware, and improved expertise have been much more important than the number of observations in the training data.

16.3   Structure of ML-Using Industries

As with any new technology, the advent of machine learning raises several economic questions.

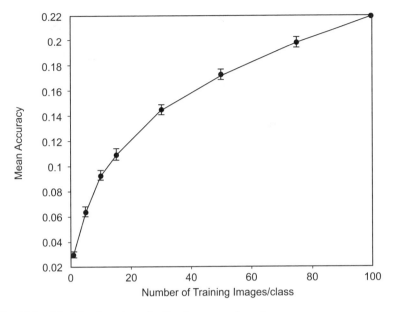

Fig. 16.2 Machine-learning adoption by economic sector
Source: http://vision.stanford.edu/aditya86/ImageNetDogs/.

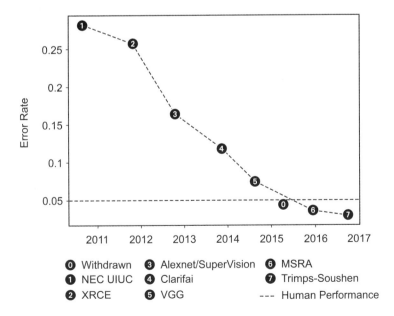

Fig. 16.3 Imagenet image recognition
Source: Eckersley and Nasser (2017).

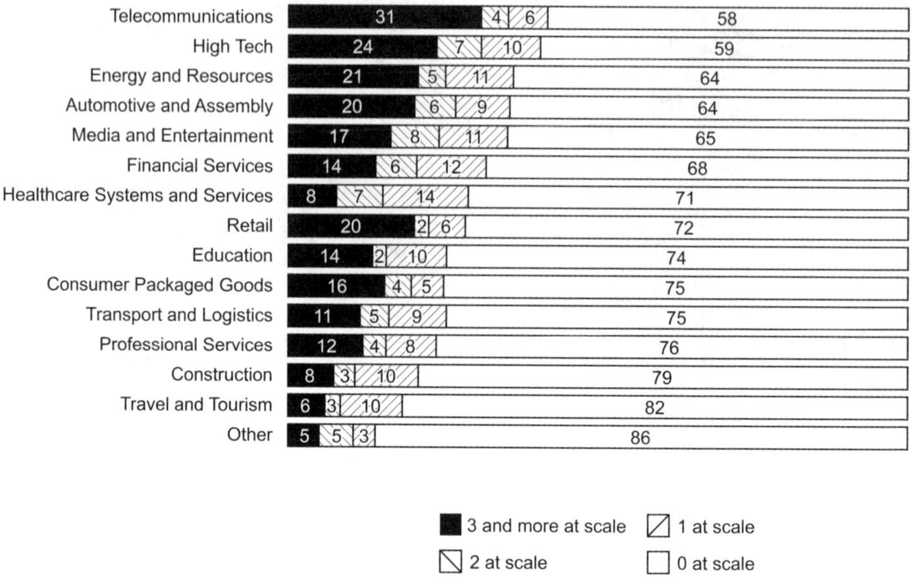

Telecommunications	31	4 6	58
High Tech	24	7 10	59
Energy and Resources	21	5 11	64
Automotive and Assembly	20	6 9	64
Media and Entertainment	17	8 11	65
Financial Services	14	6 12	68
Healthcare Systems and Services	8	7 14	71
Retail	20	2 6	72
Education	14	2 10	74
Consumer Packaged Goods	16	4 5	75
Transport and Logistics	11	5 9	75
Professional Services	12	4 8	76
Construction	8	3 10	79
Travel and Tourism	6	3 10	82
Other	5	5 3	86

■ 3 and more at scale   ▨ 1 at scale
◩ 2 at scale   ☐ 0 at scale

Fig. 16.4   Number of AI-related technologies adopted at scale or in a core part of the business
Source: McKinsey (2017).

- Which firms and industries will successfully adopt machine learning?
- Will we see heterogeneity in the timing of adoption and the ability to use ML effectively?
- Can later adopters imitate early adopters?
- What is the role of patents, copyright, and trade secrets?
- What is the role of geography in adoption patterns?
- Is there a large competitive advantage for early, successful adopters?

Bughin and Hazan (2017) recently conducted a survey of 3,000 "AI Aware" C-level executives about adoption readiness. Of these executives, 20 percent are "serious adopters," 40 percent are "experimenting," and 28 percent feel their firms "lack the technical capabilities" to implement ML. McKinsey identifies key enablers of adoption to be leadership, technical ability, and data access. Figure 16.4 breaks down how ML adoption varies across economic sectors. Not surprisingly, sectors such as telecom, tech, and energy are ahead of less tech-savvy sectors such as construction and travel.

16.3.1   Machine Learning and Vertical Integration

A key question for industrial organization is how machine-learning tools and data can be combined to create value. Will this happen within or across corporate boundaries? Will ML users develop their own ML capabilities or purchase ML solutions from vendors? This is the classic make versus buy question that is the key to understanding much of real-world industrial organization.

As mentioned earlier, cloud vendors provide integrated hardware and software environments for data manipulation and analysis. They also offer access to public and private databases, provide labeling services, consulting, and other related services that enable one-stop shopping for data manipulation and analysis. Special-purpose hardware provided by cloud providers such as GPUs and TPUs have become key technologies for differentiating provider services.

As usual there is a tension between standardization and differentiation. Cloud providers are competing intensely to provide standardized environments that can be easily maintained. At the same time, they want to provide services that differentiate their offerings from competitors.

Data manipulation and machine learning are natural areas to compete with respect to product speed and performance.

16.3.2   Firm Size and Boundaries

Will ML increase or decrease minimum efficient scale? The answer depends on the relationship between fixed costs and variable costs. If firms have to spend significant amounts to develop customized solutions to their problems, we might expect that fixed costs are significant and firm size must be large to amortize those costs. On the other hand, if firms can buy off-the-shelf services from cloud vendors, we would expect that fixed costs and minimum efficient scale to be small.

Suppose, for example, that an oil change service would like to greet returning customers by name. They can accomplish this using a database that joins license plate numbers with customer names and service history. It would be prohibitively expensive for a small provider to write the software to enable this, so only the large chains could provide such services. On the other hand, a third party might develop a smartphone app that could provide this service for a nominal cost. This service might allow minimum efficient scale to decrease. The same considerations apply for other small service providers such as restaurants, dry cleaners, or convenience stores.

Nowadays new start-ups are able to outsource a variety of business processes since there are a several providers of business services. Just as fast-food providers could perfect a model with a single establishment and then go national, business service companies can build systems once and replicate them globally.

Here is a list of how a start-up might outsource a dozen business processes.

- Fund your project on Kickstarter.
- Cloud cloud computing and network from Google, Amazon, or Micro-Soft.
- Use open-source software like Linux, Python, Tensorflow, and so forth.

- Manage your software using GitHub.
- Become a micromultinational and hire programmers from abroad.
- Set up a Kaggle competition for machine learning.
- Use Skype, Hangouts, Google Docs, and so forth for team communication.
- Use Nolo for legal documents (company, patents, NDAs).
- Use QuickBooks for accounting.
- Use AdWords, Bing, or Facebook for marketing.
- Use ZenDesk for user support.

This is only a partial list. Most start-ups in Silicon Valley and SOMA avail themselves of several of these business-process services. By choosing standardizing business processes, the start-ups can focus on their core competency and purchases services as necessary as they scale. One would expect to see more entry and more innovation as a result of the availability of these business-process services.

16.3.3   Pricing

The availability of cloud computing and machine learning offers lots of opportunities to adjust prices based on customer characteristics. Auctions and other novel pricing mechanisms can be implemented easily. The fact that prices can be so easily adjusted implies that various forms of differential pricing can be implemented. However, it must be remembered that customers are not helpless; they can also avail themselves of enhanced search capabilities. For example, airlines can adopt strategies that tie purchase price to departure date. But services can be created that reverse-engineer the airline algorithms and advise consumers about when to purchase (see, e.g., Etzioni et al. (2003). See Acquisti and Varian (2005) for a theoretical model of how consumers might respond to attempts to base prices on consumer history and how the consumers can respond to such attempts.

16.3.4 Price Differentiation

Traditionally, price differentiation has been classified into three categories:

1. First degree (personalized),
2. second degree (versioning: same price menu for all consumers, but prices vary with respect to quantity or quality), and
3. third degree (group pricing based on membership).

Fully personalized pricing is unrealistic, but prices based on fine-grained features of consumers may well be feasible, so the line between third degree and first degree is becoming somewhat blurred. Shiller (2013) and Dubé and Misra (2017) have investigated how much consumer surplus can be extracted using ML models.

Second-degree price discrimination can also be viewed as pricing by group membership, but recognizing the endogeneity of group membership and behavior. Machine learning using observational data will be of limited help in designing such pricing schemes. However, reinforcement learning techniques such as multiarmed bandits may also be helpful.

According to most noneconomics, the only thing worse than price differentiation is price discrimination! However, most economists recognize that price differentiation is often beneficial from both an efficiency and an equity point of view. Price differentiation allows markets to be served that would otherwise not be served and often those unserved markets involve low-income consumers.

DellaVigna and Gentzkow (2017) suggest that "the uniform pricing we document significantly increases the prices paid by poorer households relative to the rich." This effect can be substantial. The authors show that "consumers of [food] stores in the lowest income decile pay about 0.7 percent higher prices than they would pay under flexible pricing, but consumers of stores in the top income decile pay about 9.0 percent lower prices than under flexible pricing."

16.3.5 Returns to Scale

There are at least three types of returns to scale that could be relevant for machine learning.

1. Classical supply-side returns to scale (decreasing average cost).
2. Demand-side returns to scale (network effects).
3. Learning by doing (improvement in quality or decrease in cost due to experience).

Supply-Side Marginal Returns

It might seem like software is the paradigm case of supply-side returns to scale: there is a large fixed cost of developing the software, and a small variable cost of distributing it. But if we compare this admittedly simple model to the real world, there is an immediate problem.

Software development is not a one-time operation; almost all software is updated and improved over time. Mobile phone operating systems are a case in point: there are often monthly releases of bug fixes and security improvements coupled with yearly releases of major upgrades.

Note how different this is from physical goods—true, there are bug fixes for mechanical problems in a car, but the capabilities of the car remain more or less constant over time. A notable exception is the Tesla brand, where new updated operating systems are released periodically.

As more and more products become network enabled we can expect to see this happen more often. Your TV, which used to be a static device, will be able to learn new tricks. Many TVs now have voice interaction, and we can expect that machine learning will continue to advance in this area. This means that your TV will become more and more adept at communication and likely will become better at discerning your preferences for various sorts of content. The same goes for other appliances—their capabilities will no longer be fixed at time of sale, but will evolve over time.

This raises interesting economic questions about the distinction between goods and services. When someone buys a mobile phone, a TV, or a car, they are not just buying a static good, but rather a device that allows them to access a whole panoply of services. This, in turn, raises a whole range of questions about pricing and product design.

Demand-Side Returns to Scale

Demand-side economies of scale, or network effects, come in different varieties. There are *direct network effects*, where the value of a product or service to an incremental adopter depends on the total number of other adopters, and there are *indirect network effects* where there are two or more types of complementary adopters. Users prefer an operating system with lots of applications and developers prefer operating systems with lots of users.

Direct network effects could be relevant to choices of programming languages used in machine-learning systems, but the major languages are open source. Similarly, it is possible that prospective users might prefer cloud providers that have a lot of other users. However, it seems to me that this is no different than many other industries. Automobile purchasers may well have a preference for popular brands since dealers, repair shops, parts, and mechanics are readily available.

There is a concept that is circulating among lawyers and regulators called "data network effects." The model is that a firm with more customers can collect more data and use this data to improve its product. This is often true—the prospect of improving operations is what makes ML attractive—but it is hardly novel. And it is certainly not a network effect! This is essentially a supply-side effect known as "learning by doing" (also known as the "experience curve" or "learning curve"). The classical exposition is Arrow (1962); Spiegel and Hendel (2014) contain some up-to-date citations and a compelling example.

Learning by Doing

Learning by doing is generally modeled as a process where unit costs decline (or quality increases) as cumulative production or investment increases. The rough rule of thumb is that a doubling of output leads to a unit cost decline of 10 to 25 percent. Though the reasons for this efficiency increase are not firmly established, the important point is that learning by doing requires intention and investment by the firm and described in Stiglitz and Greenwald (2014).

This distinguishes learning by doing from demand-side or supply-side network effects that are typically thought to be more or less automatic.

This is not really true either; entire books have been written about strategic behavior in the presence of network effects. But there is an important difference between learning by doing and so-called "data network effects." A company can have huge amounts of data, but if it does nothing with the data it produces no value.

In my experience the problem is not lack of resources but lack of skills. A company that has data but no one to analyze it is in a poor position to take advantage of that data. If there is no existing expertise internally, it is hard to make intelligent choices about what skills are needed and how to find and hire people with those skills. Hiring good people has always been a critical issue for competitive advantage. But since the widespread availability of data is comparatively recent, this problem is particularly acute. Automobile companies can hire people who know how to build automobiles, since that is part of their core competency. They may or may not have sufficient internal expertise to hire good data scientists, which is why we can expect to see heterogeneity in productivity as this new skill percolates through the labor markets. Bessen (2016, 2017) has written perceptively about this issue.

16.3.6   Algorithmic Collusion

It has been known for decades that there are many equilibrium in repeated games. The central result in this area is the so-called "folk theorem," which says that virtually any outcome can be achieved as an equilibrium in a repeated game. For various formulations of this result, see the surveys by Fudenberg (1992) and Pierce (1992).

Interaction of oligopolists can be viewed as a repeated game, and in this case particular attention is focused on collusive outcomes. There are very simple strategies that can be used to facilitate collusion.

Rapid Response Equilibrium. For example, consider the classic example of two gas stations across the street from each other who can change prices quickly and serve a fixed population of consumers. Initially, they are both pricing above marginal cost. If one drops its price by a penny, the other quickly matches the price. In this case, both gas stations do worse off because they are selling at a lower price. Hence, there is no reward to price cutting and high prices prevail. Strategies of this sort may have been used in online competition, as described in Varian (2000). Borenstein (1997) documents related behavior in the context of airfare pricing.

Repeated Prisoner's Dilemma. In the early 1980s, Robert Axelrod (1984) conducted a prisoner's dilemma tournament. Researches submitted algorithmic strategies that were played against each other repeatedly. The winner by a large margin was a simple strategy submitted by Anatol Rapoport called "tit for tat." In this strategy, each side starts out cooperating (charging high prices). If either player defects (cuts its price), the other player matches. Axelrod then constructed a tournament where strategies reproduced according to their payoffs in the competition. He found that the best-performing strategies were very similar to tit for tat. This suggests that artificial agents might learn to play cooperative strategies in a classic duopoly game.

NASDAQ Price Quotes. In the early 1990s, price quotes in the NASDAQ were made in eighths of a dollar rather than cents. So if a bid was three-eighths and an ask was two-eighths, a transaction would occur with the buyer paying three-eighths and the seller receiving two-eighths. The difference between the bid and the ask was the "inside spread," which compensated the traders for risk bearing and maintaining the capital necessary to participate in the market. Note that the bigger the inside spread, the larger the compensation to the market makers doing the trading.

In the mid-1990s two economists, William Christie and Paul Schultz, examined trades for the top seventy listed companies in NASDAQ and found to their surprise that there were virtually no transactions made at odd-eighth prices. The authors concluded that "our results most likely reflected an understanding or implicit agreement among the market makers to avoid the use of odd-eighth price fractions when quoting these stocks" (Christie and Schultz 1995, 203).

A subsequent investigation was launched by the Department of Justice (DOJ), which was eventually settled by a $1.01 billion fine that, at the time, was the largest fine ever paid in an antitrust case.

As these examples illustrate, it appears to be possible for implicit (or perhaps explicit) cooperation to occur in the context of repeated interaction—what Axelrod refers to as the "evolution of cooperation."

Recently, issues of these sort have reemerged in the context of "algorithmic collusion." In June 2017, the Organisation for Economic Co-operation and Development (OECD) held a roundtable on algorithms and collusion as a part of their work on competition in the digital economy. See OECD (2017) for a background paper and Ezrachi and Stucke (2017) for a representative contribution to the roundtable.

There are a number of interesting research questions that arise in this context. The folk theorem shows that collusive outcomes can be an equilibrium of a repeated game, but does not describe a specific algorithm that leads to such an outcome. It is known that very simplistic algorithms, such as finite automata with a small number of states cannot discover all equilibria (see Rubinstein 1986).

There are auction-like mechanisms that can be used to approximate monopoly outcomes; see Segal (2003) for an example. However, I have not seen similar mechanisms in an oligopoly context.

16.4   Structure of ML-Provision Industries

So far we have looked at industries that *use* machine learning, but it is also of interest to look at companies that *provide* machine learning.

As noted above, it is likely that ML vendors will offer several related services. One question that immediately rises is how easy it will be to switch among providers. Technologies such as containers have been developed specifically make it easy to port applications from one cloud provider to another. Open-source implementation such as dockers and kubernetes are readily available. Lock in will not be a problem for small- and medium-size applications, but of course, there could be issues involving large and complex applications that involve customized applications.

Computer hardware also exhibits at least constant returns to scale due to the ease of replicating hardware installations at the level of the chip, motherboard, racks, or data centers themselves. The classic replication argument for constant returns applies here since the basic way to increase capacity is to just replicate what has been done before: add more core to the processors, add more boards to racks, add more racks to the data center, and build more data centers.

I have suggested earlier that cloud computing is more cost effective for most users than building a data center from scratch. What is interesting is that companies that require lots of data processing power have been able to replicate their existing infrastructure and sell the additional capacity to other, smaller entities. The result is an industry structure somewhat different than an economist might have imagined. Would an auto company build excess capacity that it could then sell off to other companies? This is not unheard of, but it is rare. Again it is the general purpose nature of computing that enables this model.

16.4.1   Pricing of ML Services

As with any other information-based industry, software is costly to produce and cheap to reproduce. As noted above, computer hardware also exhibits at least constant returns to scale due to the ease of replicating hardware installations at the level of the chip, motherboard, racks, or data centers themselves.

If services become highly standardized, then it is easy to fall into Bertrand-like price cutting. Even in these early days, machine pricing appears to be intensely competitive. For example, image recognition services cost about a tenth-of-a-cent per image at all major cloud providers. Presumably, we will see vendors try to differentiate themselves along dimensions of speed and capabilities. Those firms that can provide better services may be able to provide premium prices, to the extent that users are willing to pay for premium service. However, current speeds and accuracy are very high and it is unclear how users value further improvement in these dimensions.

16.5   Policy Questions

We have already discussed issues involving data ownership, data access, differential pricing, returns to scale, and algorithmic collusion, all of which have significant policy aspects. The major policy areas remaining are security and privacy. I start with a few remarks about security.

16.5.1   Security

One important question that arises with respect to security is whether firms have appropriate incentives in this regard. In a classic article, Anderson (1993) compares US and UK policy with respect to automatic teller machines (ATMs). In the United States, the user was right unless the bank could prove them wrong, while in the United Kingdom, the bank was right unless the user could prove them wrong. The result of this liability assignment was that US banks invested in security practices such as security cameras, while the UK banks didn't bother with such elementary precautions.

This industry indicates how important liability assignment is in creating appropriate incentives for investment in security. The law and economics analysis of tort law is helpful in understanding the implications of different liability assignments and what optimal assignments might look like.

One principle that emerges is that of the "due care" standard. If a firm follows certain standard procedures such as installing security fixes within a few days of their being released, implementing two-factor authentication, educating their workforce about security practices, and so on, they have a safe harbor with respect to liability for costs associated with security incidents.

But where does the due care standard come from? One possibility is from the government, particularly from military or law enforcement practices. The Orange Book and its successor, the Common Criteria standard, are good examples. Another possibility is that insurance agencies offer insurance to parties that implement good practices security. Just as an insurer may require a sprinkler system to offer fire insurance, cyber insurance may only be offered to those companies that engage in best practices (see Varian 2000 for more discussion).

This model is an appealing approach to the problem. However, we know that there are many issues involving insurance such as adverse selection and moral hazard that need to be addressed. See the archives of the Workshop on the Economics of Information Security for more work in this area, and Anderson (2017) for an overview.

16.5.2   Privacy

Privacy policy is a large and sprawling area. Acquisti, Taylor, and Wagman (2016) provide a comprehensive review of the economic literature.

There are several policy questions that arise in the machine-learning area. For example, do firms have appropriate incentives to provide appropriate levels of privacy? What is the trade-off between privacy and economic performance? It is widely recognized that privacy regulations may limit ability of ML vendors to combine data from multiple sources and there may be limits on transfer of data across corporate boundaries and/or sale of data. There is a tendency to promulgate regulation in this area that leads to unintended consequences. An example is the Health Insurance Portability and Accountability Act of 1996, commonly known as HIPAA. The original intent of the legislation was to stimulate competition among insurers by establishing standards for medical record keeping. However, many researchers argue that it has had a significant negative impact on the quantity and quality of medical research.

16.5.3 Explanations

European regulators are examining the idea of a "right to an explanation." Suppose information about a consumer is fed into a model to predict whether or not he or she will default on a loan. If the consumer is refused the loan, are they owed an "explanation" of why? If so, what would count as an explanation? Can an organization keep a predictive model secret because if it were revealed it could be manipulated? A notable example is the Discriminant Inventory Function, better known as the DIF function that the IRS uses to trigger audits. Is it legitimate to reverse engineer the DIF function? See CAvQM (2011) for a collection of links on the DIF function.

Can we demand more of an ML model than we can of a person? Suppose we show you a photo and that you correctly identify it as a picture of your spouse. Now we ask, "how do you know?" The best answer might be "because I've seen a lot of pictures that I know are pictures of my spouse, and that photo looks a lot like those pictures!" Would this explanation be satisfactory coming from a computer?

16.6 Summary

This chapter has only scratched the surface of how AI and ML might impact industrial structure. The technology is advancing rapidly, with the main bottleneck now being analysts who can implement these machine-learning systems. Given the huge popularity of college classes in this area and the wealth of online tutorials, we expect this bottleneck will be alleviated in the next few years.

References

Acquisti, Alessandro, Curtis R. Taylor, and Liad Wagman. 2016. "The Economics of Privacy." *Journal of Economic Literature* 52 (2).
Acquisti, Alessandro, and Hal Varian. 2004. "Conditioning Prices on Purchase History." *Marketing Science* 24 (4): 367–81.

Anderson, Ross. 1993. "Why Cryptosystems Fail." *Proceedings of the 1st ACM Conference on Computer and Communtications Security.* https://dl.acm.org/citation .cfm?id=168615.

————. 2017. "Economics and Security Resource Page." Working paper, Cambridge University. http://www.cl.cam.ac.uk/~rja14/econsec.html.

Arrow, Kenneth J. 1962. "The Economic Implications of Learning by Doing." *Review of Economic Studies* 29 (3): 155–73.

Axelrod, Robert. 1984. *The Evolution of Cooperation.* New York: Basic Books.

Bessen, James. 2016. *Learning by Doing: The Real Connection between Innovation, Wages, and Wealth.* New Haven, CT: Yale University Press.

————. 2017. "Information Technology and Industry." Law and Economics Research Paper no. 17-41, Boston University School of Law.

Borenstein, Severin. 1997. "Rapid Communication and Price Fixing: The Airline Tariff Publishing Company Case." Working paper. http://faculty.haas.berkeley .edu/borenste/download/atpcase1.pdf.

Bughin, Jacques, and Erik Hazan. 2017. "The New Spring of Artificial Intelligence." Vox CEPR Policy Portal. https://voxeu.org/article/new-spring-artificial -intelligence-few-early-economics.

CavQM. 2011. "Reverse Engineering The IRS DIF-Score." Comparative Advantage via Quantitative Methods blog, July 10. http://cavqm.blogspot.com/2011/07 /reverse-engineering-irs-dif-score.html.

Christie, William G., and Paul H. Schultz. 1995. "Did Nasdaq Market Makers Implicitly Collude?" Journal of Economic Perspectives 9 (3): 199–208.

DellaVigna, Stefano, and Matthew Gentzkow. 2017. "Uniform Pricing in US Retail Chains." NBER Working Paper no. 23996, Cambridge, MA.

Dubé, Jean-Pierre, and Sanjog Misra. 2017. "Scalable Price Targeting." NBER Working Paper no. 23775, Cambridge, MA.

Eckersley, Peter, and Yomna Nassar. 2017. "Measuring the Progress of AI Research." Electronic Frontier Foundation. https://eff.org/ai/metrics.

Etzioni, Oren, Rattapoom Tuchinda, Craig Knoblock, and Alexander Yates. 2003. "To Buy or Not to Buy: Mining Airfare Data to Minimize Ticket Purchase Price." *Proceedings of the Ninth ACM SIGKDD International Conference on Knowledge Discovery and Data Mining.* www.doi.org/10.1145/956750.956767.

Ezrachi, A., and M. E. Stucke. 2017. "Algorithmic Collusion: Problems and Counter-Measures—Note." OECD Roundtable on Algorithms and Collusion. https://www.oecd.org/officialdocuments/publicdisplaydocumentpdf/?cote=DAF /COMP/WD%282017%2925&docLanguage=En.

Fudenberg, Drew. 1992. "Explaining Cooperation and Commitment in Repeated Games." In *Advances in Economic Theory: Sixth World Congress*, Econometric Society Monographs, edited by Jean-Jacques Laffont. Cambridge, MA: Cambridge University Press.

Goodfellow, Ian, Nicolas Papernot, Sandy Huang, Yan Duan, Pieter Abbeel, and Jack Clark. 2017. "Attacking Machine Learning with Adversarial Examples." OpenAI blog, Feb. 26. https://blog.openai.com/adversarial-example-research/.

Hutson, Matthew. 2017. "Will Make AI Smarter for Cash." *Bloomberg Business Week*, Sept. 11.

Kurakin, Alexy, Ian Goodfellow, and Samy Bengio. 2016. "Adversarial Examples in the Physical World." Cornell University Library, ArXiv 1607.02533. https://arxiv .org/abs/1607.02533.

Organisation for Economic Co-operation and Development (OECD). 2017. "Algorithms and Collusion: Competition Policy in the Digital Age." www.oecd.org /competition/algorithms-collusion-competition-policy-in-the-digital-age.htm.

Pierce, David G. 1992 "Repeated Games: Cooperation and Rationality." In *Advances in Economic Theory: Sixth World Congress*, Econometric Society Monographs, edited by Jean-Jacques Laffont. Cambridge, MA: Cambridge University Press.

Rubinstein, Arial. 1986. "Finite Automata Play the Repeated Prisoner's Dilemma." *Journal of Economic Theory* 39:83–96.

Segal, Ilya. 2003. "Optimal Pricing Mechanisms with Unknown Demand." *American Economic Review* 93 (3): 509–29.

Shiller, Benjamin Reed. 2013. "First Degree Price Discrimination Using Big Data." Working Paper no. 58, Department of Economics and International Business School, Brandeis University.

Spiegel, Yossi, and Igal Hendel. 2014. "Small Steps for Workers, A Giant Leap for Productivity." *American Economic Journal: Applied Economics* 6 (1): 73–90.

Sreevallabh, Chivukula, and Wei Liu. 2017. "Adversarial Learning Games with Deep Learning Models." International Joint Conference in Neural Networks. www.doi.org/10.1109/IJCNN.2017.7966196.

Stiglitz, Joseph E., and Bruce C. Greenwald. 2014. *Creating a Learning Society*. New York: Columbia University Press.

Varian, H. 2000. "Managing Online Security Risks." *New York Times*, June 1.

Comment   Judith Chevalier

Varian provides an excellent overview of industrial organization issues arising out of the adoption of machine learning and artificial intelligence. A number of these issues have potential competition policy implications. For example, exploitation of AI technologies may either increase or decrease economies of scale, leading potentially to situations of market power. Ownership of data, if crucial to competition in a specific industry, may create barriers to entry. The potential for algorithmic collusion clearly leads to antitrust enforcement concerns. Here, I briefly address one of these issues, data ownership, and highlight some potential antitrust policy responses. While I focus here on data ownership as a barrier to entry, some of the policy trade-offs I discuss are germane to the other potential market structure changes highlighted in Varian.

Artificial intelligence and machine-learning processes often use raw data as an input. As Varian points out, it is not at all clear that data defies our usual expectation that a scarce asset or resource will eventually face decreasing returns to scale. Nonetheless, one can certainly imagine circumstances where exclusive ownership of a body of data will create a nearly insurmountable advantage to a market incumbent. While the concern that access to a

Judith Chevalier is the William S. Beinecke Professor of Finance and Economics at the Yale School of Management and a research associate of the National Bureau of Economic Research.

For acknowledgments, sources of research support, and disclosure of the author's material financial relationships, if any, please see http://www.nber.org/chapters/c14033.ack.

scarce asset creates entry barriers may be relatively new as it applies to data, the underlying fundamental economic issue is not new. Antitrust authorities in all jurisdictions have long wrestled with optimal policy toward firms for which the ownership of scarce assets creates barriers to entry. In the United States, analysis of this issue dates back at least to *United States v. Terminal Railroad Association* (224 US 383 (1912), a case in which consortia of railroads denied rival access to the only railroad bridges traversing the St. Louis River. In that case and subsequent ones, courts have occasionally articulated a duty to deal for a firm with market power that controls access to an asset (or facility) that is essential to competition and for which it is impractical for rivals to duplicate the asset. However, determining the precise circumstances under which a monopolist has an affirmative duty to deal with a rival remains an unsettled area of antitrust law.

In principle, this very kind of antitrust essential facilities doctrine could be applied to data ownership. Indeed, while Varian remains silent on the issue of remedies, recent legal literature in the United States has shown some enthusiasm for essential facilities doctrine as applied to data (see, e.g., Meadows 2015; Abrahamson 2014). Further, European antitrust authorities have begun to articulate principles for the control of big data that suggest an essential facilities doctrine. For example, Margrethe Vesteger (2016), the EU Commissioner for Competition, recently stated in a speech "it's true that we shouldn't be suspicious of every company which holds a valuable set of data. But we do need to keep a close eye on whether companies control unique data, which no one else can get hold of, and can use it to shut their rivals out of the market." In the speech, she highlighted a 2014 case in which the French competition authority required a French energy producer, GDF Suez, to share a customer list with industry rivals.

Despite enthusiasm in some quarters, the application of essential facilities doctrine to data sharing creates both important trade-offs and important practical concerns. I begin with the trade-offs. In evaluating antitrust policies in innovative industries, it is important to recognize that consumer benefits from new technologies arise not just from obtaining goods and services at competitive prices, but also from the flow of new and improved products and services that arise from innovation. Thus, antitrust policy should be evaluated not just in terms of its effect on prices and outputs, but also on its effect on the speed of innovation. Indeed, in high-technology industries, it seems likely that these dynamic efficiency considerations dwarf the static efficiency considerations. In the case of an application of the essential facilities doctrine to data, the trade-offs are numerous and they are directionally unclear.

An often-cited criticism of essential facilities doctrine is that creating an ex post duty to share diminishes the incentive to invest in the essential facility in the first place (see, e.g., Pate 2006). In this case, creating an ex post duty to share data could diminish the incumbent incentive to invest in data creation, thus slowing the pace of innovation. However, the overall incentive trade-offs are not as simple as that. In circumstances in which new entrants are an important source of potential innovation, exclusionary conduct by incumbents that reduces the incentive of entrants to invest in R&D can slow the pace of innovation. That is, in the case of data, if particular data is an essential complement to an AI innovation, exclusive ownership of the data by an incumbent can slow the pace of innovation by entrants. Issues of the impact of antitrust enforcement on the pace of innovation remains a nascent area of research, but is explored theoretically in, for example, Segal and Whinston (2007). Thus, in sum, while a broad application of the essential facilities doctrine to proprietary data may be tempting from an ex post static efficiency perspective, caution about ex ante incentives is warranted.

In addition to the trade-offs already discussed, any application of an essential facilities doctrine to data sharing also implies a host of practical considerations. As in any essential facilities scenario, once a court or antitrust authority establishes a duty to deal, it must also articulate terms of trade. Clearly, absent some articulation of terms, an incumbent can de facto refuse to deal by establishing transaction terms that are unattractive to any potential rival user of the data. Given that market conditions are continually changing, an ongoing regulation of the terms of trade will become unavoidable. There are certainly instances in which US courts have become ongoing regulators of the transactions of companies for which a court has imposed a duty to deal. The continuing oversight of the contracts of the music licensing firms ASCAP and BMI are good examples of a duty to deal leading to de facto regulation by the courts. However, the creation of such an ongoing regulatory structure brings with it costs to both the regulatory entity and the regulated firms. Essential facilities is not a quick fix.

Finally, while essential facilities doctrine may not always be the best tool for addressing data whose ownership has become concentrated, the potential for mergers to create importantly concentrated data should be considered in merger analysis, just as merger analysis considers the potential for mergers to substantially concentrate some other element of productive capacity.

Clearly, there are important trade-offs in implementing antitrust solutions to the problems potentially created by exclusive ownership of key data. This raises at least a few other public policy avenues to be explored. For example, given the public goods nature of data, there may be circumstances in which public investment in data creation and public ownership of the data thus created is worth exploring, particularly in circumstances when private creation of such data would lead to antitrust concerns.

References

Abrahamson, Zachary. 2014. "Comment: Essential Data." *Yale Law Journal* 124 (3): 867–68.

Meadows, Maxwell. 2014. "The Essential Facilities Doctrine in Information Econo-mies: Illustrating Why the Antitrust Duty to Deal is Still Necessary in the New Economy." *Fordham Intellectual Property, Media, and Entertainment Law Journal* 25 (3): 795–830.

Pate, R. Hewitt. 2006. "Refusals to Deal and Essential Facilities." Testimony of R. Hewitt Pate, DOJ/FTC Hearings on Single-Firm Conduct, Washington DC, July 18. https://www.justice.gov/atr/refusals-deal-and-essential-facilities-r -hewitt-pate-statement.

Segal, I., and M. Whinston. 2007. "Antitrust in Innovative Industries." *American Economic Review* 97 (5): 1703–30.

Vesteger, Margrethe. 2016. "Making Data Work for Us." Speech at the Data Ethics event on Data as Power, Copenhagen, Sept. 9. https://ec.europa.eu/commission /commissioners/2014–2019/vestager/announcements/making-data-work-us_en.

17
Privacy, Algorithms, and Artificial Intelligence

Catherine Tucker

Imagine the following scenario. You are late for a hospital appointment and searching frantically for a parking spot. You know that you often forget where you parked your car, so you use an app you downloaded called "Find my Car." The app takes a photo of your car and then geocodes the photo, enabling you to easily find the right location when you come to retrieve your car. The app accurately predicts when it should provide a prompt. This all sounds very useful. However, this example illustrates a variety of privacy concerns in a world of artificial intelligence.

1. Data Persistence: This data, once created, may potentially persist longer than the human that created it, given the low costs of storing such data.

2. Data Repurposing: It is not clear how such data could be used in the future. Once created, such data can be indefinitely repurposed. For example, in a decade's time parking habits may be part of the data used by health insurance companies to allocate an individual to a risk premium.

3. Data Spillovers: There are potential spillovers for others who did not take the photo. The photo may record other people and they may be identifiable through facial recognition, or incidentally captured cars may be identifiable through license plate databases. These other people did not choose to create the data, but my choice to create data may have spillovers for them in the future.

Catherine Tucker is the Sloan Distinguished Professor of Management Science at MIT Sloan School of Management and a research associate of the National Bureau of Economic Research.

For acknowledgments, sources of research support, and disclosure of the author's material financial relationships, if any, please see http://www.nber.org/chapters/c14011.ack.

This article will discuss these concerns in detail, after considering how the theory of the economics of privacy relates to artificial intelligence (AI).

17.1   The Theory of Privacy in Economics and Artificial Intelligence

17.1.1   Current Models of Economics and Privacy and Their Flaws

The economics of privacy has long being plagued by a lack of clarity about how to model privacy over data. Most theoretical economic models model privacy as an intermediate good (Varian 1996; Farrell 2012). This implies that an individual desire for data privacy will depend on how they anticipate that data's effect on future economic outcomes. If, for example, this data leads a firm to charge higher prices based on the behavior they observe in the data, a consumer may desire privacy. If a datum may lead a firm to intrude on their time, then again a consumer may desire privacy.

However, this contrasts with, or at the very least has a different emphasis on, how many policymakers and even consumers think about privacy policy and choice.

First, much of the policy debate involves whether or not consumers are capable of making the right choice surrounding the decision to provide data, and whether "notice and consent" provides sufficient information to consumers so they make the right choice. Work such as McDonald and Cranor (2008) emphasizes that even ten years ago it was unrealistic to think that consumers would have time to properly inform themselves about how their data may be used, as reading through privacy policies would take an estimated 244 hours each year. Since that study, the amount of devices (thermostats, smart phones, apps, cars) collecting data has increased dramatically, suggesting that it is, if anything, more implausible now that a consumer has the time to actually understand the choice they are making in each of these instances.

Relatedly, even if customers are assumed to have been adequately informed, a new "behavioral" literature on privacy shows that well-documented effects from behavioral economics, such as the endowment effect or "anchoring," may also distort the ways customers make decisions surrounding their data (Acquisti, Taylor, and Wagman 2016). Such distortions may allow for policy interventions of the "nudge" type to allow consumers to make better decisions (Acquisti 2010).

Third, this theory presupposes that customers will only desire privacy if their data is actually used for something, rather than experiencing distaste at the idea of their data being collected. Indeed, in some of the earliest work on privacy in the internet era, Varian (1996) states, "I don't really care if someone has my telephone number as long as they don't call me during dinner and try to sell me insurance. Similarly, I don't care if someone has my address, as long as they don't send me lots of official-looking letters offering to refinance my house or sell me mortgage insurance."

However, there is evidence to suggest that people do care about the mere fact of collection of their data to the extent of changing their behavior, even if the chance of their suffering meaningfully adverse consequences from that collection is very small. Empirical analysis of people's reactions to the knowledge that their search queries (Marthews and Tucker 2014) had been collected by the US National Security Agency (NSA), shows a significant shift in behavior even when that data was not going to be used by the government to identify terrorists, as it was simply personally embarrassing. Legally speaking, the Fourth Amendment of the US Constitution covers the "unreasonable seizure" as well as the "unreasonable search" of people's "papers and effects," suggesting that governments, and firms acting on government's behalf, cannot entirely ignore seizure of data and focus only on whether a search is reasonable. Consequently, a growing consumer market has emerged for "data-light" and "end-to-end encrypted" communications and software solutions, where the firm collects much less or no data about their consumers' activities on their platform. These kinds of concern suggest that the fact of data collection may matter as well as how the data is used.

Last, often economic theory assumes that while customers desire firms to have information that allows them to better match their horizontally differentiated preferences, they do not desire firms to have information that might inform their willingness to pay (Varian 1996). However, this idea that personalization in a horizontal sense may be sought by customers goes against popular reports of consumers finding personalization repugnant or creepy (Lambrecht and Tucker 2013). Instead, it appears that personalization of products using horizontally differentiated taste information is only acceptable or successful if accompanied by a sense of control or ownership over the data used, even where such control is ultimately illusory (Tucker 2014; Athey, Catalini, and Tucker 2017).

17.1.2   Artificial Intelligence and Privacy

Like "privacy," artificial intelligence is often used loosely to mean many things. This article follows (Agrawal, Gans, and Goldfarb 2016) and focuses on AI as being associated with reduced costs of prediction. The obvious effect that this will have on the traditional model of privacy is that more types of data will be used to predict a wider variety of economic objectives.

Again, the desire (or lack of desire) for privacy will be a function of an individual's anticipation of the consequences of their data being used in a predictive algorithm. If they anticipate that they will face worse economic outcomes if the AI uses their data, they may desire to restrict their data sharing or creating behavior.

It may be that the simple dislike or distaste for data collection will transfer to the use of automated predictive algorithms to process their data. The creepiness that leads to a desire for privacy that is attached to the use of data would be transferred to algorithms. Indeed, there is some evidence of a similar behavioral process where some customers only accept algorithmic prediction if it is accompanied by a sense of control (Dietvorst, Simmons, and Massey 2016).

In this way, the question of AI algorithms seems simply a continuation of the tension that has plagued earlier work in the economics of privacy. So, a natural question is whether AI presents new or different problems. This article argues that many of the questions of AI and privacy choices will constrain the ability of customers in our traditional model of privacy to make choices regarding the sharing of their data. I emphasize three themes that I think may distort this process in important and economically interesting ways.

17.2   Data Persistence, AI, and Privacy

Data persistence refers to the fact that once digital data is created, it is difficult to delete completely. This is true from a technical perspective (Adee 2015). Unlike analog records, which can be destroyed with reasonable ease, the intentional deletion of digital data requires resources, time, and care.

17.2.1   Unlike in Previous Eras, Data Created Now Is Likely to Persist

Cost constraints that used to mean that only the largest firms could afford to store extensive data, and even then for a limited time, have essentially disappeared.

Large shifts in the data-supply infrastructure have rendered the tools for gathering and analyzing large swaths of digital data commonplace. Cloud-based resources such as Amazon, Microsoft, and Rackspace make these tools not dependent on scale,[1] and storage costs for data continue to fall, so that some speculate they may eventually approach zero.[2] This allows ever-smaller firms to have access to powerful and inexpensive computing resources. This decrease in costs suggests that data may be stored indefinitely and can be used in predictive exercises should it be thought of as a useful predictor.

The chief resource constraint on the deployment of big data solutions is a lack of human beings with the data-science skills to draw appropriate conclusions from analysis of large data sets (Lambrecht and Tucker 2017). As time and skills evolve, this constraint may become less pressing.

Digital persistence may be concerning from a privacy point of view because privacy preferences may change over time. The privacy preference

1. http://betanews.com/2014/06/27/comparing-the-top-three-cloud-storage-providers/.
2. http://www.enterprisestorageforum.com/storage-management/can-cloud-storage-costs-fall-to-zero-1.html.

that an individual may have felt when they created the data may be inconsistent with the privacy preference of their older self. This is something we documented in Goldfarb and Tucker (2012). We showed that while younger people tended to be more open with data, as they grew older their preference for withholding data grew. This was a stable effect that persisted across cohorts. It is not the case that young people today are unusually casual about data; all generations when younger are more casual about data, but this pattern was simply less visible previously because social media, and other ways of sharing and creating potentially embarrassing data, did not yet exist.

This implies that one concern regarding AI and privacy is that it may use data that was created a long time in the past, which in retrospect the individual regrets creating.

Data that was created at $t = 0$ may have seemed innocuous at the time, and in isolation may still be innocuous at $t = t + 1$, but increased computing power may be able to derive much more invasive conclusions from aggregations of otherwise innocuous data at $t + 1$ relative to t. Second, there is a whole variety of data generated on individuals that individuals do not necessarily consciously choose to create. This not only includes incidental collection of the data such as being photographed by another party, but also data generated by the increased passive surveillance of public spaces, and the use of cellphone technology without full appreciation of how much data about an individual and location it discloses to third parties, including the government.

Though there has been substantial work in bringing in the insights of behavioral economics into the study of the economics of privacy, there has been less work on time-preference consistency, despite the fact that it is one of the oldest and most studied (Strotz 1955; Rubinstein 2006) phenomena in behavioral economics. Introducing the potential for myopia or hyperbolic discounting into the way we model privacy choices over the creation of data seems, therefore, an important step. Even if the economist concerned rejects behavioral economics or myopia as an acceptable solution, at the very least it is useful to emphasize that privacy choices should be modeled not as something where the time between the creation of the data and the use of the data is trivial, but instead is more acceptably modeled as a decision that may be played out over an extended amount of time.

17.2.2   How Long Will Data's Predictive Power Persist?

If we assume that any data created will probably persist, given low storage costs, it may be that the more important question for understanding the dynamics of privacy is the question of how long data's predictive power persists.

It seems reasonable to think that much of the data created today does not have much predictive power tomorrow. This is something we investigated in

Chiou and Tucker (2014) where we showed that the length of the data retention period that search engines were restricted to by the European Union (EU) did not appear to affect the success of their algorithm at generating useful search results. This is where the success of a search result was measured by whether or not the user felt compelled to search again. This may make sense in the world of search engines where many searches are either unique or focused on new events. On August 31, 2017, for example, the top trending search on Google was "Hurricane Harvey," something that could not have been predicted on the basis of search behavior from more than a few weeks prior.[3]

However, there are some forms of data where it is reasonable to think that their predictive power will persist almost indefinitely. The most important example of this is the creation of genetic digital data. As Miller and Tucker (2017) point out, companies such as 23andme.com are creating large repositories of genetic data spanning more than 1.2 million people. As pointed out by Miller and Tucker (2017), genetic data has the unusual quality that it does not change over time.

While the internet browsing behavior of a twenty-year-old may not prove to be good for predicting their browsing behavior at age forty, the genetic data of a twenty-year-old will almost perfectly predict the genetic data of that person when they turn forty.[4]

17.3   Data Repurposing, AI, and Privacy

The lengthy time frame that digital persistence of data implies increases uncertainty surrounding how the data will be used. This is because once created, a piece of data can be reused an infinite number of times. As prediction costs are lower, this generally expands the number of circumstances and occasions where data may be used. If an individual is unable to reasonably anticipate how their data may be repurposed or what the data may predict in this repurposed setting, modeling their choices over the creation of their data becomes more difficult and problematic than in our current very deterministic models, which assume certainty over how data will be used.

17.3.1   Unanticipated Correlations

There may be correlations in behavior across users that may not be anticipated when data is created, and it is in these kinds of spillovers that the largest potential consequences for privacy of AI may be found.

One famous example of this is that someone liking (or disliking) curly fries on Facebook would have been unable to reasonably anticipate it would be

---

3. https://trends.google.com/trends/.
4. As discussed in articles such as http://www.nature.com/news/2008/080624/full/news.2008.913.html, DNA does change somewhat over time, but that change is itself somewhat predictable.

predictive of intelligence (Kosinski, Stillwell, and Graepel 2013) and therefore potentially used as a screening device by algorithms aiming to identify desirable employees or students.[5]

17.3.2   Unanticipated Distortions in Correlations

In these cases, an algorithm could potentially make a projection based on a correlation in the data, using data that was created for a different purpose. The consequences for models of economics of privacy are that they assume a singular use of data, rather than allowing for the potential of reuse in unpredictable contexts.

However, even supposing that individuals were able to reasonably anticipate the repurposing of their data, there are incremental challenges with thinking about their ability to project distortions that might come about as a result of the repurposing of their data.

The potential for distortions based on correlations in data is something we investigate in new research.[6]

In Miller and Tucker (2018) we document the distribution of advertising by an advertising algorithm that attempts to predict a person's ethnic affinity from their data online. We ran multiple parallel ad campaigns targeted at African American, Asian American, and Hispanic ethnic affinities. We also ran an additional campaign targeted at those judged to not have any of these three ethnic affinities. These campaigns highlighted a federal program designed to enhance pathways to a federal job via internships and career guidance.[7] We ran this ad for a week and collected data on how many people the ad was shown to in each county. We found that relative to what would be predicted by the actual demographic makeup of that county given the census data, the ad algorithm tended to predict that more African American people are in states where there is a historical record of discrimination against African Americans. This pattern is true for states that allowed slavery at the time of the American Civil War, and also true for states that restricted the ability of African Americans to vote in the twentieth century. In such states, it was only the presence of African Americans that was over predicted, not people with Hispanic or Asian American backgrounds.

We show that this cannot be explained by the algorithm responding to behavioral data in these states, as there was no difference in click-through patterns across different campaigns across states, with or without this history of discrimination.

---

5. This study found that the best predictors of high intelligence include Thunderstorms, *The Colbert Report*, *Science*, and Curly Fries, whereas low intelligence was indicated by Sephora, I Love Being A Mom, Harley Davidson, and Lady Antebellum.

6. This new research will be the focus of my presentation at the NBER meetings.

7. For details of the program, see https://www.usajobs.gov/Help/working-in-government/unique-hiring-paths/students/.

We discuss how this can be explained by four facts about how the algorithm operates:

1. The algorithm identifies a user as having a particular ethnic affinity based on their liking of cultural phenomena such as celebrities, movies, TV shows, and music.
2. People who have lower incomes are more likely to use social media to express interest in celebrities, movies, TV shows, and music.
3. People who have higher incomes are more likely to use social media to express their thoughts about the politics and the news.[8]
4. Research in economics has suggested that African Americans are more likely to have lower incomes in states that have exhibited historic patterns of discrimination (Sokoloff and Engerman 2000; Bertocchi and Dimico 2014).

The empirical regularity that an algorithm predicting race is more likely to predict someone is black in geographies that have historic patterns of discrimination matters because it highlights the potential for historical persistence in algorithmic behavior. It suggests that dynamic consequences of earlier history may affect how artificial intelligence makes predictions. When that earlier history is repugnant, it is even more concerning. In this particular case the issue is using a particular piece of data to predict a trait when the generation of that data is endogenous.

This emphasizes that privacy policy in a world of predictive algorithms is more complex than in a straightforward world where individuals make binary decisions about their data. In our example, it would seem problematic to bar low-income individuals from expressing their identities via their affinity with musical or visual arts. However, their doing so could likely lead to a prediction that they belong to a particular ethnic group. They may not be aware ex ante of the risk that disclosing a musical preference may cause Facebook to infer an ethnic affinity and advertise to them on that basis.

17.3.3 Unanticipated Consequences of Unanticipated Repurposing

In most economic models, a consumer's prospective desire for privacy in the data depends here on the consumer being able to accurately forecast the uses to which the data is put. One problem with data privacy is that AI/algorithmic use of existing data sets may be reaching a point where data can be used and recombined in ways that people creating that data in, say, 2000 or 2005, could not reasonably have foreseen or incorporated into their decision-making at the time.

Again, this brings up legal concerns where an aggregation, or mosaic, of data on an individual is held to be sharply more intrusive than each datum considered in isolation. In *United States v. Jones* (2012), Justice Sotomayor wrote in a well-known concurring opinion, "It may be necessary to

---

8. One of the best predictors of high income on social media is a liking of Dan Rather.

reconsider the premise that an individual has no reasonable expectation of privacy in information voluntarily disclosed to third parties [. . .]. This approach is ill suited to the digital age, in which people reveal a great deal of information about themselves to third parties in the course of carrying out mundane tasks." Artificial intelligence systems have shown themselves as able to develop very detailed pictures of individuals' tastes, activities, and opinions based on analysis of aggregated information on our now digitally intermediated mundane tasks. Part of the risk in a mosaic approach for firms is that data previously considered not personally identifiable or personally sensitive—such as ZIP Code, gender, or age to within ten years—when aggregated and analyzed by today's algorithms, may suffice to identify you as an individual.

This general level of uncertainty surrounding the future use of data, coupled with certainty that it will be potentially useful to firms, affects the ability of a consumer to be able to clearly make a choice to create or share data. With large amounts of risk and uncertainty surrounding how private data may be used, this has implications for how an individual may process their preferences regarding privacy.

17.4 Data Spillovers, AI, and Privacy

In the United States, privacy has been defined as an individual right, specifically an individual's right to be left alone (Warren and Brandeis 1890) (in this specific case, from journalists with cameras).

Economists' attempts to devise a utility function that reflects privacy have reflected this individualistic view. A person has a preference for keeping information secret (or not) because of the potential consequences for their interaction with a firm. So far, their privacy models have not reflected the possibility that another person's preferences or behavior could have spillovers on this process.

17.5 Some Types of Data Used by Algorithms
May Naturally Generate Spillovers

For example, in the case of genetics, the decision to create genetic data has immediate consequences for family members, since one individual's genetic data is significantly similar to the genetic data of their family members. This creates privacy spillovers for relatives of those who upload their genetic profile to 23andme. Data that predicts I may suffer from bad eyesight or macular degeneration later in life could be used to reasonably predict that those who are related to me by blood may also be more likely to share a similar risk profile.

Of course, one hopes that an individual would be capable of internalizing the potential externalities on family members of genetic data revelation, but it does not seem far-fetched to imagine situations of estrangement where such internalizing would not happen and there would be a clear externality.

Outside the realm of binary data, there are other kinds of data that by their nature may create spillovers. These include photo, video, and audio data taken in public places. Such data may be created for one purpose such as the result of a recreational desire to use video to capture a memory or to enhance security, but may potentially create data about other individuals whose voices or images are captured without them being aware that their data is being recorded. Traditionally, legal models of privacy have distinguished between the idea of a private realm where an individual has an expectation of privacy and a public realm where an individual can have no reasonable expectation of privacy. For example, in the Supreme Court case *California v. Greenwood* (1988), the court refused to accept that an individual had a reasonable expectation of privacy in garbage he had left on the curb.

However, in a world where people use mobile devices and photo capture extensively, facial recognition allows accurate identification of any individual while out in public, and individuals have difficulty avoiding such identifications. Encoded in the notion that we do not have a reasonable expectation of privacy in the public realm are two potential errors: that one's presence in a public space is usually transitory enough to not be recorded, and that the record of one's activities in the public space will not usually be recorded, parsed, and exploited for future use. Consequently, the advance of technology muddies the allocation of property rights over the creation of data. In particular, it is not clear how video footage of my behavior in public spaces, which can potentially accurately predict economically meaningful outcomes such as health outcomes, can be clearly dismissed as being a context where I had no expectation of privacy, or at least no right to control the creation of data. In any case, these new forms of data, due in some sense to the incidental nature of data creation seem to undermine the clear-cut assumption of easily definable property rights over the data that is integral to most economic models of privacy.

17.5.1   Algorithms Themselves Will Naturally Create Spillovers across Data

One of the major consequences of AI and its ability to automate prediction is that there may be spillovers between individuals and other economic agents. There may also be spillovers across a person's decision to keep some information secret, if such secrecy predicts other aspects of that individual's behavior that AI might be able to project from.

Research has documented algorithmic outcomes that appear to be discriminatory, and has argued that such outcomes may occur because the algorithm itself will learn to be biased on the basis of the behavioral data that feeds it (O'Neil 2017). Documented alleged algorithmic bias spans charging more to Asians for test-taking prep software[9] to black names being more likely to produce criminal record check ads (Sweeney 2013) to women being less likely to seeing ads for an executive coaching service (Datta, Tschantz, and Datta 2015).

Such data-based discrimination is often held to be a privacy issue (Custers et al. 2012). The argument is that it is abhorrent for a person's data to be used to discriminate against them—especially if they did not explicitly consent to its collection in the first place. However, though not often discussed in the legally orientated data-based discrimination literature, there are many links between the fears expressed for the potential of data-based discrimination and the earlier economics literature on statistical discrimination literature. In much the same way that some find it distasteful when an employer extrapolates from general data on fertility decisions and consequences among females to project similar expectations of fertility and behavior onto a female employee, an algorithm making similar extrapolations is equally distasteful. Such instances of statistical discrimination by algorithms may reflect spillovers of predictive power across individuals, which in turn may not be necessarily internalized by each individual.

However, as of yet there have been few attempts to try to understand why ad algorithms can produce apparently discriminatory outcomes, or whether the digital economy itself may play a role in the apparent discrimination. I argue that above and beyond the obvious similarity to the statistical discrimination literature in economics, sometimes apparent discrimination can be best understood as spillovers in algorithmic decision-making. This makes the issue of privacy not just one of the potential that an individual's data can be used to discriminate against them.

In Lambrecht and Tucker (forthcoming), we discuss a field study into apparent algorithmic bias. We use data from a field test of the display of an ad for jobs in the science, technology, engineering, and math fields (STEM). This ad was less likely to be shown to women. This appeared to be a result of an algorithmic outcome, as the advertiser had intended the ad to be gender neutral. We explore various ways that might explain why the algorithm acted in an apparently discriminatory way. An obvious set of explanations is ruled out. For example, it is not because the predictive algorithm has fewer women to show the ad to, and it is not the case that the predictive algorithm learns that women are less likely are to click the ad, since women are more likely to click on it—conditional on being shown the ad—than men. In other words, this is not simply statistical discrimination. We also show it is not that

---

9. https://www.propublica.org/article/asians-nearly-twice-as-likely-to-get-higher-price-from-princeton-review. In this case, the alleged discrimination apparently stemmed from the fact that Asians are more likely to live in cities that have higher test prep prices.

the algorithm learned from local behavior that may historically have been biased against women. We use data from 190 countries and show that the effect we measure does not appear to be influenced by the status of women in that country. Instead, we present evidence that the algorithm is reacting to spillovers across advertisers. Women are a prized demographic among advertisers, both because they are often more profitable and because they control much of the household expenditure. Therefore, profit-maximizing firms pay more to show ads to female eyeballs than male eyeballs, especially in younger demographics. These spillovers across advertisers and the algorithms' attempts to cost-minimize given these spillovers explain the effect we measure. Women are less likely to see an intended gender-neutral ad due to crowding out effects.

To put it simply, our results are the result of these factors:

1. The ad algorithm is designed to minimize cost so that advertisers' advertising dollars will stretch further.

2. Other advertisers consider female eyeballs to be more desirable and deliver a higher return on investment and therefore are willing to pay more to have their ads shown to women than men.

Lambrecht and Tucker (forthcoming) explore apparent algorithmic bias, which is the consequence of clear economic spillovers between the value of a pair of eyeballs for one organization compared to another. Beyond ensuring that, for example, firms advertising for jobs are aware of the potential consequences, it is difficult to know what policy intervention is needed or the extent to which this should be thought of as a privacy issue rather than analyzed through the already established policy tools set up to address discrimination.

This kind of spillover, though, is another example of how in an interconnected economy, models of privacy that stipulate privacy as an exchange between a single firm and a single consumer may no longer be appropriate for a connected economy. Instead, the way any piece of data may be used by a single firm may itself be subject to spillovers from other entities in the economy, again in ways that may not be easily foreseen at the time of data creation.

17.6 Implications and Future Research Agenda

This chapter is a short introduction into the relationship between artificial intelligence and the economics of privacy. It has emphasized three themes: data persistence, data repurposing, and data spillovers. These three areas may present some new challenges for the traditional treatment of privacy within an individual's utility function as they suggest challenges for the ways we model how an individual may make choices about the creation of personal data that can later be used to inform an algorithm. At the highest level, this suggests that future work on privacy in economics may focus on the dynamics of privacy considerations amid data persistence and repurposing, and the spillovers that undermine the clarity of property rights over data, rather than the more traditional atomistic and static focus of our economic models of privacy.

17.6.1   Future Research Agenda

To conclude this chapter, I highlight specific research questions that fall under these three areas:

- Data Persistence

1. What causes consumers' privacy preferences to evolve over time? How stable are these preferences and for how long?
2. Are consumers able to correctly predict the evolution of their privacy preferences as they get older?
3. Would regulations designed to restrict the length of time that companies can store data be welfare enhancing or reducing?
4. What influences the persistence of the value of data over the long run? Are there some types of data that lose their value to algorithms quickly?

- Data Reuse

1. Do consumers appreciate the extent to which their data can be reused and are they able to predict what their data may be able to predict?
2. What kind of regulations restricting data reuse may be optimal?
3. Do approaches to data contracting based on the blockchain or other transaction cost-reducing technologies enable sufficiently broad contracts (and the establishment of property rights) over data?
4. Are there any categories of data where reuse by algorithms should be explicitly restricted?

- Data Spillovers

1. Are there any mechanisms (either theoretical or practical) that could be used to ensure that people internalized the consequences of their creation of data for others?
2. What is the best mechanism by which individuals may be able to assert their right to exclusion from some types of data that are being broadly collected (genetic data, visual data, surveillance data, etc.)?
3. Is there any evidence for the hypothesis of biased AI programmers, leading to biased AI algorithms? Would efforts to improve diversity in the technology community reduce the potential for bias?
4. How much more biased are algorithms that appear to engage in data-based discrimination than the counterfactual human process?

References

Acquisti, A. 2010. "From the Economics to the Behavioral Economics of Privacy: A Note." In *Ethics and Policy of Biometrics*, edited by A. Kumar and D. Zhang, 23–26. Lecture Notes in Computer Science, vol. 6005. Berlin: Springer.

Acquisti, A., C. R. Taylor, and L. Wagman. 2016. "The Economics of Privacy." *Journal of Economic Literature*, 52 (2): 442–92.

Adee, S. 2015. "Can Data Ever Be Deleted? *New Scientist* 227 (3032): 17.

Agrawal, A., J. Gans, and A. Goldfarb. 2016. "The Simple Economics of Machine Intelligence." *Harvard Business Review*, Nov. 17. https://hbr.org/2016/11/the -simple-economics-of-machine-intelligence.

Athey, S., C. Catalini, and C. Tucker. 2017. "The Digital Privacy Paradox: Small Money, Small Costs, Small Talk." Technical Report, National Bureau of Economic Research.

Bertocchi, G., and A. Dimico. 2014. "Slavery, Education, and Inequality." *European Economic Review* 70:197–209.

Chiou, L., and C. E. Tucker. 2014. "Search Engines and Data Retention: Implications for Privacy and Antitrust." MIT Sloan Research Paper no. 5094-14, Massachusetts Institute of Technology.

Custers, B., T. Calders, B. Schermer, and T. Zarsky. 2012. "Discrimination and Privacy in the Information Society." In *Volume 3 of Studies in Applied Philosophy, Epistemology and Rational Ethics* Berlin: Springer.

Datta, A., M. C. Tschantz, and A. Datta. 2015. "Automated Experiments on Ad Privacy Settings." *Proceedings on Privacy Enhancing Technologies* 2015 (1): 92–112.

Dietvorst, B. J., J. P. Simmons, and C. Massey. 2016. "Overcoming Algorithm Aversion: People Will Use Imperfect Algorithms If They Can (Even Slightly) Modify Them." *Management Science* https://doi.org/10.1287/mnsc.2016.2643.

Farrell, J. 2012. "Can Privacy Be Just Another Good?" *Journal on Telecommunications and High Technology Law* 10:251.

Goldfarb, A., and C. Tucker. 2012. "Shifts in Privacy Concerns." *American Economic Review: Papers and Proceedings* 102 (3): 349–53.

Kosinski, M., D. Stillwell, and T. Graepel. 2013. "Private Traits and Attributes are Predictable from Digital Records of Human Behavior." *Proceedings of the National Academy of Sciences* 110 (15): 5802–05.

Lambrecht, A., and C. Tucker. Forthcoming. "Algorithmic Discrimination? Apparent Algorithmic Bias in the Serving of Stem Ads." *Management Science*.

———. 2013. "When Does Retargeting Work? Information Specificity in Online Advertising." *Journal of Marketing Research* 50 (5): 561–76.

———. 2017. "Can Big Data Protect a Firm from Competition?" *CPI Antitrust Chronicle*, Jan. 2017. https://www.competitionpolicyinternational.com/can-big -data-protect-a-firm-from-competition/.

Marthews, A., and C. Tucker. 2014. "Government Surveillance and Internet Search Behavior." Unpublished manuscript, Massachusetts Institute of Technology.

McDonald, A. M., and L. F. Cranor. 2008. "The Cost of Reading Privacy Policies." *Journal of Law and Policy for the Information Society* 4 (3): 543–68.

Miller, A., and C. Tucker. 2017. "Privacy Protection, Personalized Medicine and Genetic Testing." *Management Science*. https://doi.org/10.1287/mnsc.2017.2858.

———. 2018. "Historic Patterns of Racial Oppression and Algorithms." Unpublished manuscript, Massachsetts Institute of Technology.

O'Neil, C. 2017. *Weapons of Math Destruction: How Big Data Increases Inequality and Threatens Democracy*. Portland, OR: Broadway Books.

Rubinstein, A. 2006. "Discussion of 'Behavioral Economics.'" Unpublished manuscript, School of Economics, Tel Aviv University, and Department of Economics, New York University.

Sokoloff, K. L., and S. L. Engerman. 2000. "Institutions, Factor Endowments, and Paths of Development in the New World." *Journal of Economic Perspectives* 14 (3): 217–32.

Strotz, R. H. 1955. "Myopia and Inconsistency in Dynamic Utility Maximization." *Review of Economic Studies* 23 (3): 165–80.

Sweeney, L. 2013. "Discrimination in Online Ad Delivery." *ACM Queue* 11 (3): 10.

Tucker, C. 2014. "Social Networks, Personalized Advertising, and Privacy Controls." *Journal of Marketing Research* 51 (5): 546–62.

Varian, H. R. 1996. "Economic Aspects of Personal Privacy." Working paper, University of California, Berkeley.

Warren, S. D., and L. D. Brandeis. 1890. "The Right to Privacy." *Harvard Law Review* 4 (5): 193–220.

18

Artificial Intelligence and Consumer Privacy

Ginger Zhe Jin

Thanks to big data, artificial intelligence (AI) has spurred exciting innovations. In the meantime, AI and big data are reshaping the risk in consumer privacy and data security. In this chapter, I first define the nature of the problem and then present a few facts about the ongoing risk. The bulk of the chapter describes how the US market copes with the risk in current policy environment. It concludes with key challenges facing researchers and policymakers.

18.1 Nature of the Problem

In early 1980s, economists tended to think of consumer privacy as an information asymmetry *within* a focal transaction: for example, consumers want to hide their willingness to pay just as firms want to hide their real marginal cost, and buyers with less favorable information (say a low credit score) prefer to withhold it just as sellers want to conceal poor product quality (Posner 1981; Stigler 1980). Information economics suggests that both buyers and sellers have an incentive to hide or reveal private information, and these incentives are crucial for market efficiency. In the context of a single transaction, less privacy is not necessarily bad for economic efficiency. Data technology that reveals consumer type could facilitate a better match

Ginger Zhe Jin is professor of economics at the University of Maryland and a research associate of the National Bureau of Economic Research.

I am grateful to Ajay Agrawal, Joshua Gans, and Avi Goldfarb for inviting me to contribute to the 2017 NBER Conference on the Economics of Artificial Intelligence, and to Catherine Tucker, Andrew Stivers, and conference participants for inspiring discussion and comments. All errors are mine. For acknowledgments, sources of research support, and disclosure of the author's material financial relationships, if any, please see http://www.nber.org/chapters /c14034.ack.

between product and consumer type, and data technology that helps buyers to assess product quality could encourage high-quality production.

New concerns arise because technological advances, which have enabled radical decline in the cost of collecting, storing, processing, and using data in mass quantities, extend information asymmetry *far beyond* a single transaction. These advances are often summarized by the terms "big data" and "AI." By big data, I mean large volume of transaction-level data that could identify individual consumers by itself or in combination with other data sets. The most popular AI algorithms take big data as an input in order to understand, predict, and influence consumer behavior. Modern AI, used by legitimate companies, could improve management efficiency, motivate innovations, and better match demand and supply. But AI in the wrong hands also allows the mass production of fraud and deception.

Since data can be stored, traded, and used long after the transaction, future data use is likely to grow with data processing technology such as AI. More important, future data use is *obscure to both* sides of the transaction when the buyer decides whether to give away personal data in a focal transaction. The seller may be reluctant to restrict data use to a particular purpose, a particular data-processing method or a particular time horizon in light of future data technology. Even if it does not plan to use any data technology itself, it can always sell the data to those that will use it. These data markets motivate the seller to collect as much information as consumers are willing to give.

Sophisticated consumers may anticipate the uncertainty and hesitate to give away personal data. However, in many situations, identity and payment information are crucial (or made crucial) to complete the focal transaction, leaving even the most sophisticated consumers to trade off between immediate gains from the focal transaction and potential loss from future data use. One may argue that future data use is simply a new attribute of the product traded in the focal transaction; as long as the attribute is clearly conveyed between buyer and seller (say via a well-written privacy policy), sellers in a competitive market will respect buyer preference for limited data use. Unfortunately, this attribute is not currently well defined at the time of the focal transaction, and it can evolve over time in ways that depend on the seller's data policy but are completely out of the buyer's view, control, ability to predict, or ability to value. This ongoing information asymmetry, if not addressed, could lead to a lemon's market (with respect to future data use).

Incomplete information about future data use is not the only problem lurking in the interaction between AI and consumer privacy. There are at least two other problems related to the uncertainty about future data use and value: one is externality and the other is commitment.

To be clear, future data use can be beneficial or detrimental to consumers, thus rational consumers may prefer to share personal data to some extent (Varian 1997). However, benefits from future data use—for example, better consumer classification, better demand prediction, or better product design—can usually be internalized by the collector of the information via internal data use or through the sale of data to third parties. In contrast, damages from future misuse—for example, identity theft, blackmail, or fraud—often accrue not to the collector but to the consumer. Because it is often hard to trace back consumer harm to a particular data collector, these damages may not be internalized by either the data collector or by consumers in their choices about how to interact with the collector. This is partly because the victim consumer may have shared the same information with hundreds of sellers, and she has no control over how each piece of information may get into the wrong hands. The asymmetry between accruable benefits and nonaccountable damages amounts to negative externality from sellers to buyers.[1] If there is no way to track back to the origin, sellers have an incentive to overcollect buyer information.[2]

This difficulty in tracing damages back to actions by the data collector, together with uncertainty about future use and ongoing information asymmetry about collector practices, also triggers a commitment problem. Assuming consumers care about data use, every seller has an incentive to boast about having the most consumer-friendly data policy in the focal transaction, but will also retain the option to renege after data collection. There might be some room to enforce declared data policy-specific promises, if the seller's actual practice is revealed to the public and found to contradict its promise. However, it is often difficult to discover the real data practice. It is even more difficult to rectify consumer damage from a misrepresented data policy, as a court often requires a "body on the ground"—that is, evidence of a harmful outcome—as well as some confidence that there is a causal link between that outcome and the data collector's practices.[3]

1. There could be positive externality from one player to another. For example, a data set that tracks an infectious disease nationwide can generate enormous public health benefits for everyone. But if each data collector accesses only part of the data and there is no way for him to benefit from the final product based on nationwide data, he may have an incentive to under-collect and undershare the data. Here I focus on negative externality, in order to highlight the risk of overcollecting and oversharing.

2. The argument of negative externality has been discussed in multiple papers, including Swire and Litan (1998) and Odlyzko (2003). See Acquisti, Taylor, and Wagman (2016) for a more comprehensive summary.

3. The Court's emphasis on tangible harm is best illustrated in an ongoing battle between the Federal Trade Commission (FTC) and LabMD. LabMD is a medical testing laboratory that collects sensitive personal and medical information from consumers. The FTC alleged that LabMD violated the FTC Act by failing to employ reasonable and appropriate measures to prevent unauthorized access to consumers' personal information. In November 2015, the Administrative Judge of the FTC dismissed the FTC complaint, arguing that complaint counsel failed to prove that LabMD's data security conduct caused or was likely to cause substantial injury to consumers (https://www.ftc.gov/news-events/press-releases/2015/11/administrative-law-judge-dismisses-ftc-data-security-complaint). This decision was reversed in July 2016, by an Opinion and Final Order from the FTC commissioners (https://www.ftc.gov/news-events/press-releases/2016/07/commission-finds-labmd-liable-unfair-data-security-practices). In November 2016, the 11th US Circuit Court of Appeals granted LabMD's request to tempo-

Information asymmetry, externality, and commitment concerns can all be exacerbated by AI. More specifically, by potentially increasing the scope and value of consumer data use, AI can increase the expected benefits and costs of big data. But since the benefits are more internalized to the owner of the data and AI than consumer risks, AI could encourage intrusive use of data despite higher risks to consumers. For the same reason, new benefits enabled by AI—say cost savings or better sales—could entice a firm to (secretly) abandon its promise in privacy or data security.

In short, big data introduces three "new" problems for consumer privacy: (a) sellers initially have more information about future data use than buyers after the focal transaction; (b) sellers need not fully internalize potential harms to consumers because of the inability to trace harm back to a data collector; and (c) sellers may promise consumer-friendly data policy at the time of data collection but renege afterward, as it is difficult to detect and penalize it ex post.[4] All three encourage irresponsible data collection, data storage, and data use.

All three problems could be aggravated by AI and other data technologies. Later in the chapter, I will describe a few AI-powered techniques that aim to *alleviate* the risk to consumer privacy and data security. Hence, the net impact of AI on privacy needs to take both sides into account.

18.2   Ongoing Risk in Consumer Privacy and Data Security

The risk associated with privacy and data security is real. Fundamentally data driven, the risk can be directly or indirectly related to AI and other data technologies. For example, since AI enhances the expected value of data, firms are encouraged to collect, store, and accumulate data, regardless of whether they will use AI themselves. The ever-growing big data storehouses become a prime target to hackers and scammers.

18.2.1   Data at Risk

According to the Privacy Rights Clearinghouse, 7,859 data breaches have been made public since 2005, exposing billions of records with personal identifiable information (PII) to potential abuse.[5] A closer look at the data is even more alarming: not only do we observe mega breaches that affect millions at once, but also the information lost in a single breach spreads to all

---

rarily stop enforcing the FTC order (while the appeals court considers the case), on the grounds that mere emotional harm and actions causing only a low likelihood of consumer harm may not meet the legal definition of unfair practice, even when the exposed data is highly sensitive. The court opinion can be found at http://f.datasrvr.com/fr1/016/73315/2016_1111.pdf. What type of consumer harm is needed for a data security practice to be unfair and illegal remains an open question.

4. Jin and Stivers (2017) elaborate on the three information problems in more details, but they do not associate them with AI or other data technology.

5. https://www.privacyrights.org/data-breaches, accessed on December 18, 2017.

kinds of PII. When Target lost 40 million records in December 2013, hackers got mostly debit and credit card numbers. But the recent Equifax breach (September 2017) affected 145 million people, with Social Security number, whole credit history, and even driver's license and transaction dispute data stolen from the same database. More concerning is the fact that data breaches occur disproportionally to organizations that accumulate massive PII data, including retailers, information aggregators, financial institutions, and nonprofit organizations such as governments, schools, and hospitals.

Causes of data breaches have evolved as well. A decade ago, most data losses were driven by human errors such as unshredded records left in the trash, lost laptops without encrypted data, or data inadvertently uploaded to the open Web. Recent breaches are often the result of targeted hacking and ransomware attack. If we view a malicious hacker as a thief sneaking in to steal, a ransomware attacker is a kidnapper who takes control of your data system and demands ransom immediately. For instance, the ransomware attack in May 2017 has infected computers in ninety-nine countries (including the United States), bringing down transportation, banking, nuclear, and hospital systems in many places.[6]

Thomas et al. (2017) follow the dark web from March 2016 to March 2017, passively monitoring forums that trade credential leaks exposed via data breaches, phishing kits that deceive users into submitting their credentials to fake login pages, and off-the-shelf keyloggers that harvest passwords from infected machines. They identify large numbers of potential victims, including 788,000 of off-the-shelf keyloggers, 12.4 million of phishing kits, and 1.9 billion usernames and passwords exposed via data breaches. After matching these exposed credentials to Google's internal database, they find that 7 to 25 percent of exposed passwords match a victim's Google account. More alarmingly, they observe "a remarkable lack of external pressure on bad actors, with phishing kit playbooks and keylogger capabilities remaining largely unchanged since the mid-2000s."

18.2.2   Consumers at Risk

The most concrete harm that could arise from a data breach is identity theft. According to the Bureau of Justice Statistics (BJS), identity theft affects 17.6 million (7 percent) of all US residents age sixteen and older (Harrell 2014). Consistently, identity theft is one of the biggest consumer-complaint categories—first in 2014, second in 2015, and third in 2016 (FTC 2014, 2015, 2016). In 2016, identity theft accounted for 13 percent of consumer complaints, trailing behind debt collection (28 percent) and imposter scam (13 percent), all of which could feed on lost personal data (FTC 2016).

Of course, not all identity thefts are driven by inadequate privacy protection or insufficient data security. Scammers practiced their creative art long

6. http://www.bbc.com/news/technology-39901382, accessed on October 20, 2017.

before big data and AI existed. However, loss from identity theft is likely a function of data misuse. As reported by BJS (Harrell 2014), 86 percent of identity theft victims experienced fraudulent use of existing account information and 64 percent reported a direct financial loss from the identity theft incident. Among those who reported direct financial loss, victims of personal information fraud lost an average of $7,761 (with a median of $2,000) and victims of existing bank fraud lost an average of $780 (with a median of $200).[7]

Researchers have attempted to draw a statistical link between data misuse and consumer harm. Romanosky, Acquisti, and Telang (2011) explore differences among state data breach notification laws and find that adoption of data breach disclosure laws reduces identity theft caused by data breaches by an average 6.1 percent. Romanosky, Hoffman, and Acquisti (2014) further examine federal data breach lawsuits from 2000 to 2010. They show that the odds of a firm being sued are 3.5 times greater when individuals suffer financial harm but 6 times lower when the firm provides free credit monitoring. Telang and Somanchi (2017) look at a more indirect consequence of data misuse. Using detailed transaction data from a US bank, they find that consumers are 3 percentage points more likely to leave the bank if they have experienced an unauthorized fraudulent transaction within six months. While the unauthorized transaction could be a result of previous data breaches, it is difficult to attribute the fraud to a particular data breach. In other words, the bank and the consumer may both suffer from a data breach, but the breached firm has virtually zero shares in this suffering.

Tax fraud offers another peek into the harm of data misuse. Through the Government Accounting Office (GAO 2015), the US Internal Revenue Service (IRS) reported a point estimate of attempted identity theft refund fraud (as of 2013). Although the IRS was able to prevent or recover $24.2 billion in fraudulent refunds, it paid out $5.8 billion in tax refunds that were later flagged as identity theft frauds. In May 2015, the IRS disclosed a data breach where 100,000 taxpayer accounts were compromised through its Get Transcript application. This breach exposes sensitive information such as taxpayers' prior-year tax filings. More important, it is compromised not because hackers broke a digital backdoor of the IRS, but because hackers were able to clear a multistep authentication process that required prior personal knowledge of the taxpayer's Social Security number, date of birth, tax filing status, and street address.[8] In other words, hackers got in the front door of the IRS, using information they already had or could readily guess. Such information is likely from previous data breaches or data available on the black market. This suggests that data breaches could have a ripple

---

7. Direct financial loss is not necessarily equal to the actual out-of-pocket loss to identity theft victims, as some financial loss may be reimbursed.

8. https://www.irs.gov/newsroom/irs-statement-on-the-get-transcript-application, accessed on October 19, 2017.

effect: a small vulnerability in one database could undermine data security in a completely unrelated organization.

In some situations, data in the wrong hands could cause damage much bigger than fraudulent charges. For instance, the breach of AshleyMadison .com was said to be linked to multiple suicides.[9] The ransomware attack in May 2017 was reported to have shut down work in sixteen UK hospitals,[10] crippled medical devices,[11] and delayed at least one surgery in a US hospital.[12] As more medical devices get connected to the internet, compromised data security could generate disruption in surgeries and life support. It is not difficult to imagine similar risks in connected cars and the "internet of things."

One may argue that the ongoing wave of data breaches is more driven by data availability than by data-processing technology. This could be true at the moment, but recent trends suggest that criminals are getting sophisticated and are ready to exploit data technology.

For instance, robocalls—the practice of using a computerized autodialer to deliver a prerecorded message to many telephones at once—has become prevalent because of relatively standard advances in information technology. But improved methods of pattern recognition and delivery appear to have increased the efficacy, and thus prevalence, of these calls. For example, by pretending the call is from a local number that looks familiar to the receiver, it tricks the receiver into listening to unwanted telemarketing. Similarly, phishing emails have long strived to target people vulnerable to financial and other frauds. Because the phishing attempt can be much more effective if it appears to come from a familiar email address and contains personal information that is supposedly only known to family and friends, effective phishing attempts have been limited by the labor needed to customize each email. This danger can be easily magnified when scammers mass produce PII-customized phishing emails with individualized targeting, appeals, and mass delivery.

Ironically, the same data technology that giant tech firms use for legitimate business can be converted into a tool for data misuse; AI is no exception. On September 6, 2017, Facebook admitted that it received approximately $100,000 in ad revenue from roughly 3,000 ads connected to 470 inauthentic accounts and pages that are affiliated with each other and likely operated out

9. http://www.dailymail.co.uk/news/article-3208907/The-Ashley-Madison-suicide-Texas -police-chief-takes-life-just-days-email-leaked-cheating-website-hack.html, http://money .cnn.com/2015/08/24/technology/suicides-ashley-madison/index.html, accessed on October 26, 2017.

10. https://www.theverge.com/2017/5/12/15630354/nhs-hospitals-ransomware-hack -wannacry-bitcoin, accessed on October 20, 2017.

11. https://www.forbes.com/sites/thomasbrewster/2017/05/17/wannacry-ransomware -hit-real-medical-devices/#7666463e425c, accessed on October 20, 2017.

12. https://www.recode.net/2017/6/27/15881666/global-eu-cyber-attack-us-hackers-nsa -hospitals, accessed on October 20, 2017.

of Russia.[13] Such information was estimated to reach as many as 126 million US users.[14] Similar discoveries followed from Twitter and Google. The ongoing investigation suggests that these Russian-backed accounts chose their content strategically so that the algorithms embedded in the platforms—including search rank, ad targeting, and post recommendation—helped to broadcast the message to specific demographics.[15]

It is not going to be long before the same algorithms get exploited for stalking, blackmail, and other shady use. According to Vines, Roesner, and Kohno (2017), one can spend as low as $1,000 to track someone's location with mobile ads. This is achieved by exploiting the ad tracking and ad targeting algorithms widely used in mobile platforms and mobile apps. We do not know whether this trick has been used in the real world, but it sends two chilling messages. First, personal data is not only available to giant consumer-facing companies that can use AI for mass, individualized *but impersonal*, marketing but is also within the reach of small, nonmarket parties who can exploit that data for *personalized* targeting of the consumer. Arguably, the latter is more dangerous to a targeted individual, as small nonmarket parties face less reputation constraint, they are invisible to consumers, and they may be interested in causing more harm than simply getting a consumer to purchase an unwanted product. Second, these bad actors may be able to take advantage of the key algorithms that are designed to reap the benefits of AI for legitimate purposes. As these algorithms are further developed, they could also empower data misuse.

Even if we can keep all data tightly secured and limit AI to its intended use, there is no guarantee that the intended use is harm free to consumers. Predictive algorithms often assume there is a hidden truth to learn, which could be the consumer's gender, income, location, sexual orientation, political preference, or willingness to pay. However, sometimes the to-be-learned "truth" evolves and is subject to external influence. In that sense, the algorithm may intend to *discover* the truth but end up *defining* the truth. This could be harmful, as algorithm developers may use the algorithms to serve their own interest, and their interests—say earning profits, seeking political power, or leading cultural change—could conflict with the interest of consumers.

The danger of misleading algorithms is already seen in the controversy about how Russia-sponsored posts got disseminated in social media during the 2016 US presidential election. In the congressional hearings held on October 31 and November 1, 2017, lawmakers expressed the concern that

13. https://newsroom.fb.com/news/2017/09/information-operations-update/, accessed on October 19, 2017.

14. https://www.nytimes.com/2017/10/30/technology/facebook-google-russia.html, accessed on December 18, 2017.

15. https://www.nytimes.com/2017/09/07/us/politics/russia-facebook-twitter-election.html, accessed on October 19, 2017. http://money.cnn.com/2017/09/28/media/blacktivist-russia-facebook-twitter/index.html, accessed on October 19, 2017.

the business model of Facebook, Twitter, and Google, which depends on advertising revenue from a large user base, may hamper their willingness to identify or restrict misinformation from problematic users.[16] Because social media users are more likely to consume information that platform algorithms push to them, they may end up consuming information that hurts them in the future.[17]

The same conflict of interest has sparked concerns in price discrimination. This argument is that if AI enables a firm to predict a consumer's willingness to pay, it could use that information to squeeze out every penny in consumer surplus. This argument is plausible in theory, but needs to be evaluated with at least three considerations: first, if more than one firm can use AI to discover the same consumer willingness to pay, competition among them will ease the concern of perfect price discrimination; second, the economics literature has long demonstrated the ambiguous welfare effect of price discrimination. As long as price discrimination is imperfect (i.e., firms cannot charge every consumer's willingness to pay), some consumers may benefit from the practice (via lower price) while other consumers suffer. From a social planner's point of view, whether to encourage or punish AI-enabled price discrimination depends on the weights it assigns to different parts of society. Third, in the long run, AI may reduce the operational costs within the firm (e.g., via a more cost-effective inventory management system) and foster product innovations that better fit consumer demand. These changes could be beneficial to both the firm and its consumers.

A somewhat opposite concern is that AI and other predictive technology are not 100 percent accurate in their intended use. It may not introduce much inefficiency or wasteful effort if Netflix cannot precisely predict the next movie I want to watch, but it could be much more consequential if the US National Security Agency (NSA) flags me as a future terrorist based on some AI algorithm. As Solove (2013) has argued, it is almost impossible for someone to prove that they will not be a terrorist *in the future*. But at the same time, they may be barred from air travel, have personal conversation with friends monitored, and be restricted from work, trade, and leisure activities. If this AI algorithm applies to a large population, it could do a lot of harm even if the probability of error is close to zero.

To summarize, there is a real risk in privacy and data security. The magni-

---

16. The full video and transcript of these hearings are available at c-span.org (https://www
.c-span.org/video/?436454–1/facebook-google-twitter-executives-testify-russia-election-ads,
and https://www.c-span.org/video/?436360–1/facebook-google-twitter-executives-testify
-russias-influence-2016-election&live).

17. Note that a predicative algorithm is not necessarily more biased than human judgment.
For example, Hoffman, Kahn, and Li (2018) study job-testing technologies in fifteen firms.
They find that hires made by managers against test recommendations are worse on average.
This suggests that managers often overrule test recommendations because they are biased
or mistaken.

tude of the risk, and its potential harm to consumers, will likely depend on AI and other data technologies.

18.3   How Does the US Market Cope with the Risk in Privacy and Data Security?

Before we jump into a regulatory conclusion, we must ask how the market copes with the risk in privacy and data security. Unfortunately, the short answer is that we do not know much. Below I describe what we know on the demand and supply sides, along with a summary of existing public policies in the United States. Admittedly, the literature cited below is more about privacy and data security than about AI. This is not surprising, as AI has just started to find its way into e-commerce, social media, national security, and the internet of things. However, given the ongoing risk and the potential interaction of AI and that risk, it is important to keep in mind the big picture.

18.3.1   Consumer Attitude

On the demand side, consumer attitude is heterogeneous, evolving, and sometimes self-conflicting.

When surveyed, consumers often express serious concerns about privacy, although self-reported value of privacy covers a wild range (see the summary in Acquisti, Taylor, and Wagman [2016]). However in real transactions, many consumers are willing to give away personal data in exchange for a small discount, free services, or a small incentive such as a pizza (Athey, Catalini, and Tucker 2017). This conflict, which some referred to as a "privacy paradox," suggests that we have yet to comprehend the link between consumer attitude and consumer behavior. Furthermore, researchers have found that privacy preference varies by age (Goldfarb and Tucker 2012), by time (Stutzman, Gross, and Acquisti 2012), and by context (Acquisti, Brandimarte, and Loewenstein 2015). Although old data are shown to add little value to search results (Chiou and Tucker 2014), biometric data such as fingerprint, facial profiles, and genetic profiles can be much longer lasting (Miller and Tucker, forthcoming). Hence, consumers may have a different preference on biometric data than on the data that gets obsolete fast. These heterogeneities make it even harder to paint a complete picture of consumer attitude and consumer behavior about privacy.

A similar puzzle exists for attitudes toward data security. A recent survey by the Pew Research Center suggests that many people are concerned about the safety and security of their personal data in light of numerous high-profile data breaches (Pew Research Center 2016). However, according to Ablon et al. (2016), only 11 percent stopped dealing with the affected company and 77 percent were highly satisfied with the company's postbreach response.

It is hard to tell why consumers are willing to give away data in real transactions. One possibility is that consumers have a large or even hyperbolical discount for the future, which motivates them to value the immediate gains from the focal transaction more than the potential risk of data misuse in the distant future. Other behavioral factors can be at play as well. Small incentives, small navigation costs, and irrelevant but privacy-reassuring information can all persuade people to relinquish personal data, according to a recent field experiment (Athey, Catalini, and Tucker 2017).

It is also possible that news coverage—on data breaches and privacy problems—raises consumer concern about the overall risk, but they do not know how to evaluate the risk specific to a transaction. Despite heavy news coverage, people may have an illusion that hacking will not happen to them. This illusion could explain why John Kelly, the former Secretary of Homeland Security and White House chief of staff, used a compromised personal phone for months.[18]

The third explanation is that consumers are fully aware of the risk, but given the fact that their personal data has been shared with many firms and has likely already been breached somewhere, they believe the extra risk of sharing the data with one more organization is small. Survey evidence seems to lend some support to this conjecture. According to the Pew Research Center (2016), few are confident that the records of their activities maintained by various companies and organizations will remain private and secure. A vast majority (91 percent) of adults agree that consumers have lost control of how PII is collected and used by companies, though most think personal control is important. Moreover, 86 percent of internet users have taken steps to remove or mask their digital footprints, and many say they would like to do more or are unaware of tools they could use.[19]

Consumer anxiety may explain why identity theft protection service has become a $3 billion industry (according to IBISWorld).[20] However, a market review by the Government Accounting Office (GAO 2017) shows that identity theft services offer some benefits, but generally do not prevent identity theft or address all of its variations. For instance, these services typically do not address medical identity theft or identity theft refund fraud. In fact, a number of identity theft service providers were caught making deceptive marketing claims,[21] casting doubt on whether such "insurance-like" services are the best way to safeguard consumers from identity theft.

18. https://www.wired.com/story/john-kelly-hacked-phone/, accessed on October 15, 2017.

19. "The state of privacy in post-Snowden America" by the Pew Research Center, source: http://www.pewresearch.org/fact-tank/2016/09/21/the-state-of-privacy-in-america/.

20. https://www.ibisworld.com/industry-trends/specialized-market-research-reports /technology/computer-services/identity-theft-protection-services.html, accessed on October 26, 2017.

21. For example, in September 2012, Discover settled with the Consumer Financial Protection Bureau (CFPB) and the Federal Deposit Insurance Corporation (FDIC) with $200 million refund to consumers and $14 million penalty. The CFPB and FDIC alleged that Discover engaged in misleading telemarketing on identity theft protection, credit score tracking, wallet

18.3.2   Supply Side Actions

Statistics from the supply side are mixed, too.

Thales (2017b) conducted a global survey of 1,100+ senior security executives, including 100+ respondents in key regional markets in the United States, United Kingdom, Germany, Japan, Australia, Brazil, and Mexico, and in key segments such as federal government, retail, finance, and health care. It finds that 68 percent of survey respondents have ever experienced a breach, while 26 percent experienced one last year. Both numbers rose from 2016 (61 percent and 22 percent).

For financial services in particular, Thales (2017a) finds that firms are aware of the cyber risk they face but tend to deploy new technology (e.g., cloud, big data, internet of things) *before* adopting security measures to protect them. Only 27 percent of US financial services organizations said to feel "very" or "extremely" vulnerable to data threats (the global average is 30 percent), despite the fact that 42 percent of US financials had been breached in the past (the global average is 56 percent). Consistently, both US and global financials rank data security at the bottom of their spending plans, citing institutional inertia and complexity as the main reasons. These numbers should be concerning because the financial sector has the highest cost of cyber crime according to the latest report from Accenture (2017). To add a little comfort, Thales (2017a) also reports that security spending, which includes but is not limited to data security, continues to trend up: 78 percent of US financials reported higher spending than last year, trailing only US health care (81 percent) and ahead of the overall global average (73 percent).

Firms' willingness to invest in data security is partially driven by the cost they suffer directly from data breaches. A strand of literature has studied the stock market's response to data breach. While results differ across studies, the general finding is that the financial market response is small and temporary, if negative at all (Campbell et al. 2003; Cavusoglu et al. 2004; Telang and Wattal 2007; Ko and Dorantes 2006). A couple of studies have provided an absolute estimate of the cost. According to Ponemon (2017), who surveyed 419 organizations in thirteen countries and regions, the average consolidated total cost of a data breach is $3.62 million. Ponemon (2017) further finds that data breaches are most expensive in the United States, with the average per capita cost of data breach as high as $225. In contrast, Romanosky (2016) examines a sample of 12,000 cyber events, including but

---

protection, and payment protection (http://money.cnn.com/2012/09/24/pf/discover-penalty -telemarketing/index.html). In December 2015, LifeLock agreed to pay $100 million to settle FTC contempt charges for order violation. The 2010 court order requires the company to secure consumers' personal information and prohibits the company from deceptive advertising in identity theft protection services (https://www.ftc.gov/news-events/press-releases/2015 /12/lifelock-pay-100-million-consumers-settle-ftc-charges-it-violated).

not limited to data breaches. He finds that the cost of a typical cyber incident (to the affected firm) is less than $200,000, roughly 0.4 percent of the firm's estimated annual revenues.

Thousands or millions, these estimates only reflect the direct cost of the cyber event to *the firm*, not all the consequential harm *to consumers*. For example, most breached firms offer one year of free credit monitoring service for affected consumers, but data misuse can occur after a year. Either way, consumers have to spend time, effort, and money to deal with identity theft, reputation setback, fraud, blackmail, or even unemployment as a result of a data breach. The lawsuit between the Federal Trade Commission (FTC) and Wyndham Hotel and Resort gives a concrete example. Wyndham was breached multiple times in 2008 and 2009, affecting more than 619,000 consumers. Before reaching a settlement, the FTC alleged that fraudulent charges attributable to the Wyndham breaches exceeded $10.6 million.[22] Although the final settlement involves no money, this case suggests that harm to consumers—via an increased risk of identity theft and the costs to mediate the risk—can be much more substantial than the direct loss suffered by the breached firm. Arguably, it is this difference that motivates firms to overcollect data or use lax data security, despite the real risk of data breach.

The good news is that market forces do push firms to respect consumer demand for privacy and data security. For instance, Facebook profiles expand over time and therefore the same default privacy setting tends to reveal more personal information to larger audiences.[23] In September 2014, Facebook adjusted its default setting of privacy from public posting to friend-only posting, which limits third party access to new users' Facebook posts. In the meantime, Facebook made it easier for existing users to update their privacy settings, block out ads, and edit their ad profiles.[24] We do not know the exact reason behind the change, but it could be related to a few things: for example, user willingness to share data on Facebook dropped significantly from 2005 to 2011 (Stutzman, Gross, and Acquisti 2012), academic research shows that it is very easy to identify strangers based on photos publicly posted on Facebook (Acquisti, Gross, and Stutzman 2014), and it costs Facebook $20 million to settle a class action lawsuit regarding its "sponsored stories" (an advertising feature alleged to misappropriate user profile pictures and likenesses without user consent).[25]

Similarly, a privacy scare prompted Samsung to change its privacy policy. In February 2015, CNN quoted a paragraph of Samsung's privacy policy,

22. https://www.washingtonpost.com/business/economy/2012/06/26/gJQATDUB5V_story .html?utm_term=.1ab4fedd7683, accessed October 19, 2017.

23. Matt McKeon gives a graphical account of how Facebook privacy evolves from 2005 to 2010, at http://mattmckeon.com/facebook-privacy/, accessed on October 24, 2017.

24. http://60secondmarketer.com/blog/2014/09/21/facebook-tightens-privacy-controls -affect-marketing/, accessed October 24, 3017.

25. https://www.wired.com/2013/08/judge-approves-20-million-facebook-sponsored -stories-settlement/, accessed October 24, 2017.

which stated that words spoken in front of a Samsung Smart TV are captured and transmitted to a third party through use of voice recognition.[26] In response to the intense fear that smart TVs "spy" in a private living room, Samsung later changed its privacy policy.[27] Samsung also clarified that voice recognition can be disabled and it uses industry standard encryption to secure the data.

The privacy competition in the smartphone market is even more interesting. In 2015, Google launched Android Marshmallow in Android 6.0,[28] which prompts users to grant or deny individual permissions (e.g., access to the camera) to a mobile app when it is needed for the first time, rather than automatically grant apps all of their specified permissions at installation. It also allows users to change the permissions at any time. Similar features were made available earlier in Apple iOS 8.[29] Apple's commitment to privacy protection was also highlighted when Apple refused to unlock the iPhone from one of the shooters in the December 2015 terrorist attack in San Bernardino, California.

As a pioneer in biometric authentication, Apple recently announced Face ID in its next smartphone launch (iPhone X). Using infrared cameras, Face ID uniquely identifies a user's face and utilizes that information to unlock the smartphone and authorize Apple Pay. Though it is meant to enhance convenience and security, Face ID has stirred a number of privacy concerns including exposing consumer privacy to Apple employees and allowing the police to forcefully unlock a phone using the owner's face. Whether this AI-powered technology will reduce or enhance privacy protection is an open question.

Note that market mechanisms can also work *against* consumer privacy and data security. Dina Florêncio and Cormac Herley (2010) examined the password policy of seventy-five websites and found that password strength is *weaker* for some of the largest, most attacked sites that should have greater incentives to protect their valuable database. Compared to security demand, it seems that competition is more likely to drive websites to adopt a weaker password requirement as they need to compete for users, traffic, and advertising. The sample size of this study is too small to represent the whole market, but the message is concerning: consumer demand in privacy and data

---

26. According to CNN (http://money.cnn.com/2015/02/09/technology/security/samsung-smart-tv-privacy/index.html), Samsung's privacy policy said "Please be aware that if your spoken words include personal or other sensitive information, that information will be among the data captured and transmitted to a third party through your use of Voice Recognition." The article further points out that, Samsung SmartTV has a set of pre-programmed commands that it recognizes even if you opt out of voice recognition.

27. https://www.cnet.com/news/samsung-changes-smarttv-privacy-policy-in-wake-of-spying-fears/, accessed on October 24, 2017.

28. Android Mashmellow was first released as a beta on May 28, 2015, followed by the official release on October 5, 2015. Its new model of app permission was received positively: https://fpf.org/2015/06/23/android-m-and-privacy-giving-users-control-over-app-permissions/.

29. https://fpf.org/2014/09/12/ios8privacy/, accessed on October 24, 2017.

security may compete with the same consumers' demand for convenience, usability, and other attributes (such as lower price). When these demands conflict with each other, firms may have a stronger incentive to accommodate the attributes that are more visible and easier to evaluate. Probably the same reason explains why only a small fraction of firms adopt multifactor authentication,[30] despite its ability to reduce data risk.

So far, we have considered AI as an external factor that potentially increases the risk of privacy violation and data breach. It is important to recognize that AI could also serve as *a tool to mitigate* the risk. Recently, AI has demonstrated super intelligence in games such as Go, even without the help of any human knowledge (Silver et al. 2017). Imagine what data risk would look like if the same AI power is used to grant data access to authorized personnel, to detect data attack when (or even before) it materializes, and to precisely predict whether a user-generated posting is authentic or fake. In fact, the technology frontier is moving this direction, though its net benefits remain to be seen.

Take differential privacy as an example. It was invented more than ten years ago (Dwork et al. 2006) and claimed by Apple as a key feature to protect consumer identity in some of its data collection since 2016. The basic logic goes as follows: the data collecting firm adds random noise to an individual user's information before uploading it to the cloud. That way, the firm can still use the collected data for meaningful analysis without knowing each user's secret. The effectiveness of this technology depends on how much noise to add, a parameter under the control of the data-collecting firm.

To evaluate how Apple implements differential privacy in practice, Tang et al. (2017) reverse-engineered Apple's MacOS and iOS operating systems. They find that the daily privacy loss permitted by Apple's differential privacy algorithm exceeds values acceptable by the theoretical community (Hsu et al. 2014), and the overall privacy loss per device may be unbounded. Apple disputes the results and argues that its differential privacy feature is subject to user opt-in. Google is another user of differential privacy (in its web browser Chrome). The "noise" parameter that Google uses—as estimated by Erlingsson, Pihur and Korolova (2014)—seems to be more privacy-protective than what is claimed to be used in Apple, but still falls outside the most acceptable range.[31] These debates cast doubt on the promise of differential privacy, especially on its real use relative to its theoretical potential.

Another promising technology is blockchain. In plain English, blockchain is an ever-growing list of records (blocks) that are linked with timestamp and transaction data. Secured by cryptography, blockchain is designed to

---

30. Multifactor authentication is a security measure that requires two or more independent credentials to verify the identity of the user. https://twofactorauth.org/ allows one to search whether a firm uses multi-factor authentication in various types of products or services.

31. https://www.wired.com/story/apple-differential-privacy-shortcomings/, accessed on October 24, 2017.

be verifiable, permanent, and resistant to data modification. Its successful application in Bitcoin suggests that similar technology could trace identities in data trade and data use, thus reducing the risk in privacy and data security (Catalini and Gans 2017). Ironically, a ransomware attacker in May 2017 demanded Bitcoin instead of traditional money, probably for a similar security reason.

18.3.3   Policy Landscape

Any market description is incomplete without a summary of the policy background. In the United States, there is no overarching legislation on consumer privacy or data security. So far, the policy landscape is a patchwork of federal and local regulations.

Only a few federal laws are explicit on privacy protection and they all tend to be industry specific. For example, the Gramm-Leach-Bliley Act (GLBA) controls the ways that financial institutions deal with personal data, the Health Insurance Portability and Accountability Act of 1996 (HIPAA) provides data privacy and security provisions for medical records, and the Children's Online Privacy Protection Act of 1998 (COPPA) disciplines online services directed to children under the age of thirteen. In accordance, privacy is subject to federal regulation by sectors: the Department of Health & Human Resources (DHHS) enforces HIPAA in health care, the Federal Communication Commission (FCC) regulates telecommunication services, the federal reserve systems monitors the financial sector, the Security and Exchange Commission (SEC) focuses on public firms and financial exchanges, and the Department of Homeland Security (DHS) deals with terrorism and cybercrimes related to national security.

Two exceptions are worth mentioning. First, the Federal Trade Commission (FTC) can address privacy violations and inadequate data security as deceptive and unfair practice, following the 1914 FTC Act. This enforcement authority covers almost every industry and overlaps with many sector-specific regulators.

More specifically, FTC's privacy enforcement focuses on "notice and choice," which emphasizes how firms' actual data practice deviates from the privacy notice they disclose to the public. For industries not subject to GLBA, HIPAA, or COPPA, there is no legislation that mandates privacy notice, but many firms provide it voluntarily and seek consumer consent before purchase or consumption. Some industries also adopt self-regulatory programs to encourage certain privacy practices.[32] This background allows the FTC to obtain privacy notice of the targeted firm and enforce it under the FTC Act.

---

32. For example, Digital Advertising Alliance (DAA), a nonprofit organization led by advertising and marketing trade associations, establishes and enforces privacy practices for digital advertising.

The FTC has published a number of guidelines on privacy,[33] but the best way to understand its enforcement is through cases. For example, the FTC alleged that Practice Fusion misled consumers by first soliciting reviews for their doctors and then publicly posting these reviews on the internet without adequate consumer notice. The case eventually settled in June 2016.[34] In another case against Vizio, FTC alleged Vizio captured second-by-second information about video displayed on its smart TV, appended specific demographic information to the viewing data, and sold this information to third parties for targeted ads and other purposes. According to the complaint, VIZIO touted its "Smart Interactivity" feature that "enables program offers and suggestions," but failed to inform consumers that the settings also enabled the collection of consumers' viewing data.[35] The case is joint with New Jersey Attorney General and settled for $2.2 million in February 2017. The third case is against Turn, a digital advertising company that tracks consumers in online browser and mobile devices and uses that information to target digital advertisements. The FTC alleged that Turn used unique identifiers to track millions of Verizon consumers even after they choose to block or delete cookies from websites, which is inconsistent with Turn's privacy policy. Turn settled with FTC in December 2016.[36]

While privacy notice is something that consumers can access, read (whether they read them is another question) and consent to, most data security practices are not visible until someone exposes the data vulnerability (via data breach or white-hat discovery). Accordingly, FTC enforcement on data security focuses on whether a firm has adequate data security, not whether the firm has provided sufficient information to consumers. Following this logic, the FTC has settled with Ashley Madison, Uber, Wyndham Hotel and Resorts, Lenovo, and TaxSlayer, but is engaged in litigation with LabMD and D-Link.[37]

The second exception relates to government access to personal data. Arguably, the US Constitution, in particular the First and Fourth Amendments, has already covered individual rights in free speech and limited government ability to access and acquire personal belongings. However, exactly how the Constitution applies to electronic data is subject to legal debate (Solove 2013).

---

33. The most comprehensive FTC guideline is its 2012 privacy report (FTC 2012). A list of privacy-related press releases can be found at https://www.ftc.gov/news-events/media -resources/protecting-consumer-privacy/ftc-privacy-report.

34. https://www.ftc.gov/news-events/press-releases/2016/06/electronic-health-records -company-settles-ftc-charges-it-deceived, accessed on October 24, 2017.

35. https://www.ftc.gov/news-events/press-releases/2017/02/vizio-pay-22-million-ftc-state -new-jersey-settle-charges-it, accessed on October 25, 2017.

36. https://www.ftc.gov/news-events/press-releases/2016/12/digital-advertising-company -settles-ftc-charges-it-deceptively, accessed on October 25, 2017.

37. For a list of FTC cases in data security, see https://www.ftc.gov/enforcement/cases -proceedings/terms/249.

Beyond the Constitution, a series of federal laws—the Electronic Communications Privacy Act of 1986 (ECPA), the Stored Communications Act (1986), the Pen Register Act (1986), and the 2001 USA Patriot Act—stipulate when and how the government can collect and process electronic information of individuals. But many of these laws were enacted in the wake of the Watergate scandal, long before the use of the internet, email, search engines, and social media. It is unclear how they apply to real cases. The legal ambiguity is highlighted in three events: first, as exposed by Edward Snowden, the NSA has secretly harvested tons of personal information for its global surveillance programs. The exposure generates an outcry for privacy and a hot debate in the balance between individual privacy and national security. Second, the Microsoft email case, regarding whether the US government has the right to access emails stored by Microsoft overseas, has reached the US Supreme Court. In March 2018, the CLOUD Act clarified how US law enforcement orders issued under the Stored Communication Act may reach data in other countries and how data hosting companies may challenge such law enforcement requests.[38] Third, Apple refused to unlock the iPhone of one of the shooters in the 2015 San Bernardino terrorist attack. Since the FBI was able to unlock the phone before the court hearing, it remains unknown whether Apple has the legal obligation to help the FBI.[39]

At the local level, all fifty states have enacted data breach notification laws, but no federal law has been passed on this topic.[40] According to the National Conference of State Legislatures, at least seventeen states have also passed some law on privacy. For example, the California Consumer Privacy Act was enacted in June 2018 and set to be effective on January 1, 2020. These local laws tend to vary greatly in content, coverage, and remedy.[41] From the

38. http://techcrunch.com/2018/04/17/supreme-court-dismisses-warrant-case-against-microsoft-after-cloud-act-renders-it-moot/, accessed January 13, 2019. The CLOUD Act was enacted in March 2018 and stands for the Clarifying Lawful Overseas Use of Data Act.

39. http://www.latimes.com/local/lanow/la-me-ln-fbi-drops-fight-to-force-apple-to-unlock-san-bernardino-terrorist-iphone-20160328-story.html, accessed October 25, 2017.

40. There have been multiple efforts towards a federal data breach notification law. In 2012, Senator Jay Rockefeller advocated for a cyber security legislation that strengthens the requirement to report cybercrimes. In January 2014, the Senate Commerce, Science, and Transportation Committee (led by Senator Rockefeller) introduced a bill to create a federal requirement for data breach notification (S. 1976 Data Security and Breach Notification Act of 2014). In his 2015 State of the Union Speech, President Obama proposed new legislation to create a national data breach standard with a thirty-day notification requirement for data breach. A related bill was later introduced by the US House of Representatives (H.R. 1770L Data Security and Breach Notification Act of 2015). All of them failed. In the wake of the mega breaches in 2017, Congress has introduced Personal Data Notification and Protection Act of 2017 (H.R. 3806), the Data Protection Act of 2017 (H.R. 3904), the Market Data Protection Act of 2017 (H.R. 3973), Cyber Breach Notification Act (H.R. 3975), Data Broker Accountability and Transparency Act (S. 1815) and Data Security and Breach Notification Act (S. 2179). They are under committee review and likely consolidated.

41. The National Conference of State Legislatures collects information on these state laws. For data breach laws, see http://www.ncsl.org/research/telecommunications-and-information-technology/security-breach-notification-laws.aspx. For privacy laws, see http://www.ncsl.org/research/telecommunications-and-information-technology/state-laws-related-to-internet-privacy.aspx.

research point of view, these variations are useful for studying the impact of data breach laws on identity theft (Romanosky, Acquisti, and Telang 2011)[42] and data breach lawsuits (Romanosky, Hoffman, and Acquisti 2014), but they can be difficult to comply if a firm operates in multiple states. It is also difficult for consumers to form an expectation of privacy protection, especially if they transact with both in-state and out-of-state firms.

In short, the US system is piecemeal and multilayered, in contrast to the European Union's attempt to unify data protection via its General Data Protection Regulation (effective in 2018).[43] Which approach is better for society is subject to an ongoing debate.

18.4 Future Challenges

To summarize, there are pressing issues in consumer privacy and data security, many of which are likely to be reshaped by AI and other data technologies.

A number of big questions arise: shall we continue to let the market evolve under the current laws, or shall we be more aggressive in government regulation? How do firms choose data technology and data policy if consumers demand both convenience and privacy? How to balance AI-powered innovations against the extra risk that the same technology brings to privacy and data security? If action is needed from policymakers, shall we let local governments use trial and error, or shall we push for federal legislations nationwide? Shall we wait for new legislations to address standing loopholes, or shall we rely on the court system to clarify existing laws case by case? These questions deserve attention from researchers in many disciplines, including economics, computer science, information science, statistics, marketing, and law.

In my opinion, the leading concern is that firms are not fully accountable for the risk they bring to consumer privacy and data security.[44] To restore full accountability, one needs to overcome three obstacles, namely (a) the difficulty to observe firms' actual action in data collection, data storage, and data use; (b) the difficulty to quantify the consequence of data practice, especially before low-probability adverse events realize themselves; and (c) the difficulty to draw a causal link between a firm's data practice and its consequence.

These difficulties exist, not only because of technical limits, but also because of misaligned incentives. Even if blockchain can track every piece of data and AI can predict the likelihood of every adverse event, whether

---

42. Romanosky, Acquisti, and Telang (2011) explore differences among state data breach notification laws and link them to a FTC database of identity theft from 2002 to 2009. They find that adoption of data breach disclosure laws reduces identity theft caused by data breaches by an average 6.1 percent.

43. An overview of GDPR is available at http://www.eugdpr.org/.

44. The same problem applies to nonprofit organizations and governments.

to develop and adopt such technology is up to firms. In the current setting, firms may still have incentives to hide real data practice from the public, to obfuscate information disclosed to consumers, or to blame other random factors for consumer harm.

There is a case for further changes to instill more transparency into the progression from data practice to harmful outcomes, and to translate outcomes (realized or probabilistic) into incentives that directly affect firms' choice of data practice. These changes should not aim to slow down data technology or to break up big firms just because they are big and on the verge of an AI breakthrough. Rather, the incentive correction should aim to help consumer-friendly data practice stand out from lemons, which in turn fosters innovations that respect consumer demand for privacy and data security.

There might be multiple ways to address misaligned incentives, including new legislation, industry self-regulation, court ruling, and consumer protection. Below I comment on the challenges of a few of them.

First, it is tempting to follow the steps in safety regulation. After all, the information problems we encounter in privacy and data security—as highlighted in section 18.1—are similar to those in food, drug, air, car, or nuclear safety. In those areas, the consequence of inadequate quality control is random and noisy, just as identity thefts and refund frauds are. In addition, firm input and process choices—like ingredients and plant maintenance—are often unobservable to final consumers. A common solution is direct regulation on the firm's action: for example, restaurants must keep food at a certain temperature, nuclear plants must pass periodical inspections, and so forth. These regulations are based on the assumption that we know what actions are good and what actions are bad. Unfortunately, this assumption is not easy to come by in data practice. With fast evolving technology, are we sure that politicians in Washington, DC, are the best ones to judge whether multifactor authentication is better than a twenty-character password? How do we ensure that the regulation is updated with every round of technological advance?

The second approach relies on firm disclosure and consumer choice. "Notice and choice" is already the backbone of FTC enforcement (in privacy), and data breach notification laws follow a similar principle. For this approach to be effective, we assume consumers can make the best choice for themselves as long as they have adequate information at hand. This assumption is unlikely to hold in privacy and data security because most consumers do not read privacy notices (McDonald and Cranor 2008), many data-intensive firms may not have a consumer interface, and it could be difficult for consumers to choose as they do not have the ability to evaluate different data practices and do not know what choices are available to mitigate the potential harm. Furthermore, firms' data practice may change frequently in light of technological advance, thus delivering updated notices to consumers may be infeasible and overwhelming.

The third approach is industry self-regulation. Firms know more about data technology and data practice, and therefore are better positioned to identify best practices. However, can we trust firms to impose and enforce regulations on themselves? History suggests that industry self-regulation may not occur without the threat of government regulation (Fung, Graham, and Weil 2007). This suggests that efforts pushing for government action may be complementary rather than substitutable to industry attempts to self-regulate. Another challenge is technical: many organizations are trying to develop a rating system on data practice, but it is challenging to find comprehensive and updated information firm by firm. This is not surprising, given the information asymmetry between firms and consumers. Solving this problem is crucial for any rating system to work.

The fourth approach is defining and enforcing privacy and data use as "rights." Law scholars have long considered privacy as a right to be left alone, and debated whether privacy rights and property rights should be treated separately (Warren and Brandeis 1890). As summarized in Acquisti, Taylor, and Wagman (2016), when economists consider privacy and data use as rights, they tend to associate them with property rights. In practice, the European Union has followed the "human rights" approach, which curtails transfer and contracting rights that are often assumed under a "property rights" approach. The European Union recognized individual rights of data access, data processing, data rectification, and data erasure in the new legislation (GDPR, effective in May 2018). The impact of GDPR remains to be seen, but two challenges are worth mentioning: first, for many data-intensive products (say self-driving cars), data do not exist until the user interacts with the product, often under third-party support (say GPS service and car insurance). Should the data belong to the user, the producer, or third parties? Second, even if property rights over data can be clearly defined, it does not imply perfect compliance. Music piracy is a good example. Both challenges could deter data-driven innovations if the innovator has to obtain the rights to use data from multiple parties beforehand.

Apparently, no approach is challenge free. Given the enormous impact that AI and big data may have on the economy, it is important to get the market environment right. This environment should respect consumer demand for privacy and data security, encourage responsible data practices, and foster consumer-friendly innovations.

References

Ablon, Lilian, Paul Heaton, Diana Lavery, and Sasha Romanosky. 2016. *Consumer Attitudes Toward Data Breach Notifications and Loss of Personal Information.* Santa Monica, CA: RAND Corporation.
Accenture. 2017. *2017 Insights on the Security Investments That Make a Difference.*

https://www.accenture.com/t20170926T072837Z__w__/us-en/_acnmedia/PDF
-61/Accenture-2017-CostCyberCrimeStudy.pdf.

Acquisti, Alessandro, Laura Brandimarte, and George Loewenstein. 2015. "Privacy and Human Behavior in the Age of Information." *Science* 347 (6221): 509–14.

Acquisti, Alessandro, Ralph Gross, and Fred Stutzman. 2014. "Face Recognition and Privacy in the Age of Augmented Reality." *Journal of Privacy and Confidentiality* 6 (2): Article 1. http://repository.cmu.edu/jpc/vol6/iss2/1.

Acquisti, Alessandro, Curtis Taylor, and Liad Wagman. 2016. "The Economics of Privacy." *Journal of Economic Literature* 54 (2): 442–92.

Athey, Susan, Christian Catalini, and Catherine E. Tucker. 2017. "The Digital Privacy Paradox: Small Money, Small Costs, Small Talk." MIT Sloan Research Paper no. 5196-17, Massachusetts Institute of Techonolgy. https://ssrn.com /abstract=2916489.

Campbell, Katherine, Lawrence A. Gordon, Martin P. Loeb, and Lei Zhou. 2003. "The Economic Cost of Publicly Announced Information Security Breaches: Empirical Evidence from the Stock Market." *Journal of Computer Security* 11 (3): 431–48.

Catalini, Christian, and Joshua S. Gans. 2017. "Some Simple Economics of the Blockchain." Rotman School of Management Working Paper no. 2874598. https://ssrn.com/abstract=2874598.

Cavusoglu, Huseyin, Birendra Mishra, and Srinivasan Raghunathan. 2004. "The Effect of Internet Security Breach Announcements on Market Value: Capital Market Reactions for Breached Firms and Internet Security Developers." *International Journal of Electronic Commerce* 9 (1): 69–104.

Chiou, Lesley, and Catherine E. Tucker. 2014. "Search Engines and Data Retention: Implications for Privacy and Antitrust." MIT Sloan Research Paper no. 5094-14, Massachusetts Institute of Technology.

Dwork, Cynthia, Frank McSherry, Kobbi Nissim, and Adam Smith. 2006. "Calibrating Noise to Sensitivity in Private Data Analysis." In *Theory of Cryptography Conference*, Lecture Notes in Computer Science, vol. 3876, edited by S. Halevi and T. Rabin, 265–84. Berlin: Springer.

Erlingsson, Úlfar, Vasyl Pihur, and Aleksandra Korolova. 2014. "RAPPOR: Randomized Aggregatable Privacy-Preserving Ordinal Response." In *Proceedings of the ACM SIGSAC Conference on Computer and Communications Security* (CCS):1054–67.

Federal Trade Commission (FTC). 2012. *Protect Consumer Privacy in an Era of Rapid Change: Recommendations for Businesses and Policy Makers.* https://www .ftc.gov/sites/default/files/documents/reports/federal-trade-commission-report -protecting-consumer-privacy-era-rapid-change-recommendations/120326 privacyreport.pdf.

———. 2014. *Consumer Sentinel Network Data Book from January—December 2014.* https://www.ftc.gov/system/files/documents/reports/consumer-sentinel -network-data-book-january-december-2014/sentinel-cy2014–1.pdf.

———. 2015. *Consumer Sentinel Network Data Book from January—December 2015.* https://www.ftc.gov/system/files/documents/reports/consumer-sentinel -network-data-book-january-december-2015/160229csn-2015databook.pdf.

———. 2016. *Consumer Sentinel Network Data Book from January—December 2016.* https://www.ftc.gov/system/files/documents/reports/consumer-sentinel -network-data-book-january-december-2016/csn_cy-2016_data_book.pdf.

Florêncio, Dina, and Cormac Herley. 2010. "Where Do Security Policies Come From?" *Symposium on Usable Privacy and Security (SOUPS)*, July 14–16, Redmond, WA.

Fung, Archon, Mary Graham, and David Weil. 2007. *Full Disclosure: The Perils and Promise of Transparency.* Cambridge: Cambridge University Press.

Goldfarb, Avi, and Catherine E. Tucker. 2012. "Shifts in Privacy Concerns." *American Economic Review: Papers and Proceedings* 102 (3): 349–53.

Government Accountability Office (GAO). 2015. *Identity Theft and Tax Fraud: Enhanced Authentication Could Combat Refund Fraud, but IRS Lacks an Estimate of Costs, Benefits and Risks,* GAO-15-119, January. https://www.gao.gov/products/GAO-15-119.

———. 2017. *Identity Theft Services: Services Offer Some Benefits but Are Limited in Preventing Fraud,* GAO-17-254, March. http://www.gao.gov/assets/690/683842.pdf.

Harrell, Erika. 2014. *Victims of Identity Theft, 2014.* Bureau of Justice Statistics. https://www.bjs.gov/content/pub/pdf/vit14.pdf.

Hoffman, Mitchell, Lisa B. Kahn, and Danielle Li. 2018. "Discretion in Hiring*." *Quarterly Journal of Economics* 133 (2): 765–800.

Hsu, Justin, Marco Gaboardi, Andreas Haeberlen, Sanjeev Khanna, Arjun Narayan, Benjamin C. Pierce, and Aaron Roth. 2014. "Differential Privacy: An Economic Method for Choosing Epsilon." In *27th IEEE Computer Security Foundations Symposium (CSF)*:398–410.

Jin, Ginger Zhe, and Andrew Stivers. 2017. "Protecting Consumers in Privacy and Data Security: A Perspective of Information Economics." Working paper. https://ssrn.com/abstract=3006172.

Ko, Myung, and Carlos Dorantes. 2006. "The Impact of Information Security Breaches on Financial Performance of the Breached Firms: An Empirical Investigation." *Journal of Information Technology Management* 17 (2): 13–22.

McDonald, Aleecia, and Lorrie Faith Cranor. 2008. "The Cost of Reading Privacy Policies." *I/S: A Journal of Law and Policy for the Information Society* 4 (3): 540–65.

Miller, Amalia, and Catherine E. Tucker. Forthcoming. "Privacy Protection, Personalized Medicine and Genetic Testing." *Management Science.*

Odlyzko, Andrew. 2003. "Privacy, Economics, and Price Discrimination on the Internet." In *Economics of Information Security,* edited by L. Jean Camp and Stephen Lewis, 187–212. Norwell, MA: Kluwer Academic Publishers.

Pew Research Center. 2016. *The State of Privacy in Post-Snowden America.* http://www.pewresearch.org/fact-tank/2016/09/21/the-state-of-privacy-in-america/.

Ponemon. 2017. *2017 Ponemon Cost of Data Breach Study.* https://www.ibm.com/security/data-breach/index.html.

Posner, Richard A. 1981. "The Economics of Privacy." *American Economic Review* 71 (2): 405–09.

Romanosky, Sasha. 2016. "Examining the Costs and Causes of Cyber Incidents." *Journal of Cybersecurity* 2 (2): 121–35.

Romanosky, Sasha, Alessandro Acquisti, and Rahul Telang. 2011. "Do Data Breach Disclosure Laws Reduce Identity Theft?" *Journal of Policy Analysis and Management* 30 (2): 256–86.

Romanosky, Sasha, David Hoffman, and Alessandro Acquisti. 2014. "Empirical Analysis of Data Breach Litigation." *Journal of Empirical Legal Studies* 11 (1): 74–104.

Silver, David, Julian Schrittwieser, Karen Simonyan, Ioannis Antonoglou, Aja Huang, Arthur Guez, Thomas Hubert, Lucas Baker, Matthew Lai, Adrian Bolton, Yutian Chen, Timothy Lillicrap, Fan Hui, Laurent Sifre, George van den Driessche, Thore Graepel, and Demis Hassabis. 2017. "Mastering the Game of Go without Human Knowledge." *Nature* 550:354–59.

Solove, Daniel. 2013. *Nothing to Hide: The False Tradeoff between Privacy and Security*. New Haven, CT: Yale University Press.

Stigler, George J. 1980. "An Introduction to Privacy in Economics and Politics." *Journal of Legal Studies* 9 (4): 623–44.

Stutzman, Fred, Ralph Gross, and Alessandro Acquisti. 2012. "Silent Listeners: The Evolution of Privacy and Disclosure on Facebook." *Journal of Privacy and Confidentiality* 4 (2): 7–41.

Swire, Peter P., and Robert E. Litan. 1998. *None of Your Business: World Data Flows, Electronic Commerce, and the European Privacy Directive*. Washington, DC: Brookings Institution Press.

Tang, Jun, Aleksandra Korolova, Xiaolong Bai, Xueqiang Wang, and Xiaofeng Wang. 2017. "Privacy Loss in Apple's Implementation of Differential Privacy on MacOS 10.12." https://arxiv.org/pdf/1709.02753.pdf.

Telang, Rahul, and Sriram Somanchi. 2017. "Security, Fraudulent Transactions and Customer Loyalty: A Field Study." Working paper, Carnegie Mellon University.

Telang, Rahul, and Sunil Wattal. 2007. "An Empirical Analysis of the Impact of Software Vulnerability Announcements on Firm Stock Price." *IEEE Transactions on Software Engineering* 33 (8): 544–57.

Thales. 2017a. *2017 Thales Data Threat Report: Trends in Encryption and Data Security (Financial Services Edition)*. https://dtr-fin.thalesesecurity.com/.

Thales. 2017b. *2017 Thales Data Threat Report: Trends in Encryption and Data Security (Global Edition)*. https://dtr.thalesesecurity.com/.

Thomas, Kurt, Frank Li, Ali Zand, Jacob Barrett, Juri Ranieri, Luca Invernizzi, Yarik Markov, Oxana Comanescu, Vijay Eranti, Angelika Moscicki, Daniel Margolis, Vern Paxson, and Elie Bursztein. 2017. "Data Breaches, Phishing, or Malware? Understanding the Risks of Stolen Credentials." Proceedings of the 2017 ACM SIGSAC Conference on Computer and Communications Security, 1421–34. https://acmccs.github.io/papers/p1421-thomasAembCC.pdf.

Varian, Hal R. 1997. "Economics Aspects of Personal Privacy." In *Privacy and Self-Regulation in the Information Age*. Washington, DC: US Department of Commerce, National Telecommunications and Information Administration.

Vines, Paul, Franziska Roesner, and Tadayoshi Kohno. 2017. "Exploring ADINT: Using Ad Targeting for Surveillance on a Budget—or—How Alice Can Buy Ads to Track Bob." *The 16th ACM Workshop on Privacy in the Electronic Society* (WPES 2017).

Warren, Samuel, and Louis Brandeis. 1890. "The Right to Privacy." *Harvard Law Review* 4:191.

19

Artificial Intelligence and International Trade

Avi Goldfarb and Daniel Trefler

The last 200 years have produced a remarkable list of major innovations, not the least of which is artificial intelligence (AI). Like other major innovations, AI will likely raise average incomes and improve well-being, but it may also disrupt labor markets, raise inequality, and drive noninclusive growth. Yet, even to the extent that progress has been made in understanding the impact of AI, we remain largely uninformed about its international dimensions. This is to our great loss. A number of countries are currently negotiating international agreements that will constrain the ability of sovereign governments to regulate AI, such as the North American Trade Agreement (NAFTA) and the Trans-Pacific Partnership (TPP)-11. Likewise, governments around the world are freely spending public funds on new AI clusters designed to shift international comparative advantage toward their favored regions, including the Vector Institute in Toronto and the Tsinghua-Baidu deep-learning lab around Beijing. The international dimensions of AI innovations and policies have not always been well thought out. This work begins the conversation.

China has become the focal point for much of the international discussion. The US narrative has it that Chinese protection has reduced the ability

Avi Goldfarb holds the Rotman Chair in Artificial Intelligence and Healthcare and is professor of marketing at the Rotman School of Management, University of Toronto, and a research associate of the National Bureau of Economic Research. Daniel Trefler holds the J. Douglas and Ruth Grant Canada Research Chair in Competitiveness and Prosperity at the University of Toronto and is a research associate of the National Bureau of Economic Research.

The authors thank Dave Donaldson and Hal Varian for their thoughtful feedback. Trefler acknowledges the support of the "Institutions, Organizations and Growth" Program of the Canadian Institute for Advanced Research (CIFAR). For acknowledgments, sources of research support, and disclosure of the authors' material financial relationships, if any, please see http://www.nber.org/chapters/c14012.ack.

of dynamic US firms such as Google and Amazon to penetrate Chinese markets. This protection has allowed China to develop significant commercial AI capabilities, as evidenced by companies such as Baidu (a search engine like Google), Alibaba (an e-commerce web portal like Amazon), and Tencent (the developer of WeChat, which can be seen as combining the functions of Skype, Facebook, and Apple Pay). While no Chinese AI-intensive company has household recognition outside of China, everyone agrees that this will not last. Further, a host of behind-the-border regulatory asymmetries will help Chinese firms to penetrate Canadian and US markets.

Even the Pentagon is worried. Chinese guided-missile systems are sufficiently sophisticated that they may disrupt how we think of modern warfare; large and expensive military assets such as aircraft carriers are becoming overly vulnerable to smart weapons.[1] This may do more than transform the massive defense industry; these AI developments may radically shift the global balance of power.

As international economists, we are used to hype and are typically dismissive of it. Despite AI's short life—Agrawal, Gans, and Goldfarb (2018) date its commercial birth to 2012—AI's rapid insinuation into our daily economic and social activities forces us to evaluate the international implications of AI and propose best-policy responses. Current policy responses often rest on a US narrative of a zero-sum game in which either the United States or China will win.[2] Is this the right premise for examining AI impacts and for developing AI policies? Further, calls for immediate action by prominent experts such as Bill Gates, Stephen Hawking, and Elon Musk will likely encourage governments to loosen their pocketbooks, but will government subsidies be effective in promoting broad-based prosperity or will subsidies become yet another form of ineffective corporate welfare? What specific policies are likely to tip the balance away from ineffective corporate handouts?

Using comparative advantage theory, trade economists have thought long and hard about the right mix of policies for successfully promoting industry. Many of our theories imply a laissez-faire free-trade approach. However, since the early 1980s our theories have shown that certain types of government interventions may be successful, for example, Krugman (1980), Grossman and Helpman (1991), and the more informal theories of Porter (1990). These theories emphasize the role of scale and the role of knowledge creation and diffusion. Unfortunately, the precise policy prescriptions produced by these theories are very sensitive to the form of scale and the form

---

1. *New York Times*, Feb. 3, 2017. See also *Preparing for the Future of Artificial Intelligence*, Office of the President, Oct., 2016.

2. For example, https://www.economist.com/news/business/21725018-its-deep-pool-data -may-let-it-lead-artificial-intelligence-china-may-match-or-beat-america and http://www .reuters.com/article/us-usa-china-artificialintelligence/u-s-weighs-restricting-chinese -investment-in-artificial-intelligence-idUSKBN1942OX?il=0.

of knowledge creation/diffusion. And competition can play an important role too, for example, in Aghion et al. (2001, 2005) and Lim, Trefler and Yu (2017).

We therefore start in section 19.2 by identifying the key features of AI technology in regard to scale and knowledge. To date there are no models that feature the particular scale and knowledge characteristics that are empirically relevant for AI. In section 19.3 we use these features (a) to offer some suggestions for what an appropriate model might look like, and (b) to draw implications for policy. This leads to high-level thinking about policy. For example, it provides a foundation for assessing recent proposals put forward by AI researcher Geoff Hinton and others on the potential benefit of public investments in AI.[3] However, these models are not sufficiently fine-grained to directly capture existing regulatory issues that "go behind the border" such as privacy policy, data localization, technology standards, and industrial regulation. In section 19.4 we therefore review the many behind-the-border policies that already impact AI and discuss their implications for comparative advantage and the design of trade agreements. We begin with a factual overview of the international dimensions of AI.

19.1   From Hype to Policy

Statistics about where AI is being done internationally and how it is diffusing can be tracked in a number of ways, for example, the number of basic research articles, patents and patent citations produced in a region; the number of start-ups established in a region; or the market capitalization of publicly traded AI-based companies in a region. We look at two of these indicators: basic research and market capitalization. For the former, we collected time-series data on the institutional affiliation of all authors of papers presented at a major AI research conference, namely, the Association for the Advancement of Artificial Intelligence (AAAI) Conference on Artificial Intelligence. In table 19.1, we compare the 2012 and 2017 conferences. In 2012, 41 percent of authors were at US institutions, but by 2017 this was down to 34 percent. The two other largest declines were recorded by Canada and Israel. While these countries all increased their absolute number of participants, in relative terms they all lost ground to China, which leapt from 10 percent in 2012 to 23 percent in 2017.

We have not examined patent numbers, but suggestive work by Fujii and Managi (2017) points to weaker international diffusion of AI: US technology giants such as IBM and Microsoft remain far and away the world's dominant patent applicants.

Another indication of the economic future of AI comes from the largest

---

3. "Artificial Intelligence is the Future, and Canada Can Seize It" by Jordan Jacobs, Tomi Poutanen, Richard Zemel, Geoffrey Hinton, and Ed Clark. *Globe and Mail*, Jan. 7, 2017.

Table 19.1   Participants at a major AI conference

Country	2012 (%)	2017 (%)	Change (%)
United States	41	34	−6
China	10	23	13
United Kingdom	5	5	0
Singapore	2	4	2
Japan	3	4	1
Australia	6	3	−2
Canada	5	3	−3
India	1	2	1
Hong Kong	3	2	−1
Germany	4	2	−1
France	4	2	−2
Israel	4	2	−3
Italy	2	2	−1
Other	10	10	0

Notes: Participation rates at the Association for the Advancement of Artificial Intelligence (AAAI) Conference on Artificial Intelligence. For example, of the papers presented at the 2017 conference, 34 percent of authors had a US affiliation.

public companies in the world by market capitalization. Table 19.2 lists the twelve largest companies worldwide. What is striking about the table is the number of companies that might subjectively be described as "AI intensive." Seven of the twelve companies are heavily engaged in AI (such as Alphabet/ Google), three are in finance (where the use of AI is growing rapidly), and one has a substantial pharmaceutical presence (where AI is likely to soon be reducing development costs). What makes table 19.2 relevant for international trade is the fact that two of the largest companies worldwide are now Chinese AI-intensive firms (Tencent and Alibaba). It is truly remarkable that two high-tech companies based out of China—private companies, not state-owned enterprises—are among the largest companies in the world. While we had to move beyond the round number of ten to make this point, it is striking nonetheless. It points to the major global shake-up that is coming.

Some would conclude from tables 19.1 and 19.2 that almost all of the world's largest companies will soon be competing directly against Chinese companies when—not if—these Chinese companies go global. In 2000, Robin Li signaled his agreement by moving to China to establish Baidu. The flood of US-trained talent returning to China has continued. This year, former Microsoft executive Qi Lu joined Baidu as chief operating officer (COO). In describing China, Lu writes, "We have an opportunity to lead in the future of AI."[4] Not everyone agrees. Some have argued that China's AI-intensive companies will not be globally competitive until they compete head-on in China with global leaders such as Google. This flies in the face of

4. *The Economist,* July 15, 2017.

Table 19.2   World's largest public companies and AI exposure

Company	Market value ($)	AI exposure
1. Apple	754	High
2. Alphabet	579	High
3. Microsoft	509	High
4. Amazon	423	High
5. Berkshire Hathaway	411	Rising
6. Facebook	411	High
7. ExxonMobil	340	Low
8. Johnson & Johnson	338	Rising
9. JPMorgan Chase	314	Rising
10. Wells Fargo	279	Rising
11. Tencent Holdings	272	High
12. Alibaba	269	High

Notes: Market capitalization of the largest public companies as of March 31, 2017, from PWC (2017). "AI exposure" is our subjective assessment of the role of AI in company performance.

a long history of Chinese export successes in other fields. Indeed, Sutton and Trefler (2016) describe both theoretically and empirically how developing countries such as China initially enter new markets at a low level of quality, but over time develop the capabilities to deliver high-quality, internationally competitive goods and services.

Many experts are weighing in on how to counter the "Chinese threat" and, more generally, how to enrich local economies through cluster policies that support sustained competitive advantage in AI-based market segments. Geoff Hinton and collaborators have convinced Canadian governments to develop a major AI institute that would "graduate the most machine-learning PhDs and master's students globally" and "become the engine for an AI supercluster that drives the economy of Toronto, Ontario, and Canada."[5] Hinton also emphasizes the importance of access to data. "Why? Because for a machine to 'think' intelligently, it must be trained with lots of data."

While there are potential benefits from Hinton's initiative, it raises two important points that loom large in our thinking. First, economists who specialize in clusters are deeply skeptical about the efficacy of cluster policies (e.g., Duranton 2011). Such policies have failed more often than not, and the theoretical justification for cluster policies is highly sensitive to assumptions about knowledge diffusion. For example, will Hinton's PhDs stay in Canada and will the knowledge they generate be commercialized in Canada? Second, a host of behind-the-border regulations on privacy, data localization, technology standards, and industrial policy will affect the ability of Canadian firms to access data relative to their competitors in larger markets such as the

5. *Globe and Mail*, Jan. 7, 2017.

United States, Europe, and China. What is the current state of these domestic data regulations, how do they effect trade patterns, do they serve a public interest, are they being used as disguised protection to generate comparative advantage, and should they be covered by international trade agreements (as some would have been in the TPP e-commerce chapter)?

The following sections help answer these questions and move us toward better policies for promoting AI and preventing both corporate welfare and welfare-reducing disguised protection.

19.2   The Technological Backdrop: Scale, Scope, Firm Size, and Knowledge Diffusion

The Oxford English Dictionary defines AI as "the theory and development of computer systems able to perform tasks normally requiring human intelligence." This has meant different things at different times. In the 1960s and 1970s, computer scientists approached this using rules, if-then statements, and symbolic logic. It worked well for factory robots and for playing chess. By the 1980s, it became clear that symbolic logic could not deal with the complexities of nonartificial settings, and AI research slowed substantially. Various approaches continued to be supported in a small number of locations, including by the Canadian Institute for Advanced Studies (CIFAR).

The recent resurgence in AI research is driven by one such approach: the insight that computers can "learn" from example. This approach is often called "machine learning" and is a field of computational statistics. The algorithm that has received the most attention is back propagation in neural networks, most notably through "deep learning," but there is a large suite of relevant technologies including deep learning, reinforcement learning, and so forth. Because the current excitement about AI is driven by machine learning, we focus on this particular set of algorithms here.

For our purposes, we need to zero in on those aspects of AI technology that are central to thinking about the economics of AI. We identify four aspects: economies of scale associated with data, economies of scale associated with an AI research team, economies of scope in the use of the team for multiple applications, and knowledge externalities.

19.2.1   Economies of Scale from Data

Statistical predictions improve with the quantity and quality of data. Recall from statistics 101 that the quality of prediction increases with N (or, more precisely with root N). All else being equal, this means that companies that have more observations will generate more accurate predictions. It is in this sense that economies of scale matter. Still, because predictions increase in root N, then, while scale matters, there are decreasing returns to scale in terms of the accuracy of prediction.

It is subtler than this, however. Google and Microsoft both operate search engines. Google has claimed their search engine has higher market share because it has better quality.[6] Microsoft has claimed the higher quality is a direct consequence of scale. By having more data, Google can predict what people want in their search results more accurately. Google responds that Microsoft has billions of search results. While Google has more data, surely the law of large numbers applies before one billion results. And so, more data does not give a meaningful advantage. Microsoft's response is the essence of where economies of scale bind. While they have billions of searches, many search queries are extremely rare. Microsoft may only see two or three, and so Google can predict those rare queries much better. If people choose search engines based on quality differences in rare searches, then Google's better data will lead to a substantial increase in market share. Having a larger share gives Google more data, which in turn improves quality and supports an even larger share.

The source of economies of scale here is therefore in the form of direct network externalities. More customers generate more data, which in turn generates more customers. This is different from the literature on two-sided markets and indirect network externalities. The network externalities resemble the phone network, rather than externalities between buyers and sellers on a marketplace like Ebay. This is significant in a trade context because the trade literature has emphasized two-sided matching, for example, in Rauch (1999) and McLaren (2000). This is also different from all of the trade and market structure literature, which emphasize economies of scale that are driven by fixed costs, so trade theory does not currently have models that are applicable to the AI technology environment.

The direct network externalities environment leads to a core aspect of competition in AI: competition for data. The companies that have the best data make better predictions. This creates a positive feedback loop so that they can collect even more data. In other words, the importance of data leads to strong economies of scale.

19.2.2   Economies of Scale from the Overhead of Developing AI Capabilities

Another source of economies of scale in AI involves the fixed cost of building an AI capability within a firm. The main cost is in personnel. Much of the software is open source, and in many cases hardware can be purchased as a utility through cloud services. The uses of AI need to be big enough to justify the substantial cost of building a team of AI specialists. World leaders in AI command very high pay, often in the millions or tens of millions.

---

6. There is a chicken and egg problem, whether good algorithms drive market share or whether market share drives hiring that leads to better algorithms. For one point of view, see https://www.cnet.com/news/googles-varian-search-scale-is-bogus/.

Top academic researchers have been hired to join Google (Hinton), Apple (Salakhutdinov), Facebook (LeCunn), and Uber (Urtasun). So far, there has been a meaningful difference between employing the elite researchers and others in terms of the capabilities of the AI being developed.

19.3.3 Economies of Scope

Perhaps more than economies of scale, the fixed cost of building an AI capacity generates economies of scope. It is only worth having an AI team within a company if there are a variety of applications for them to work on. Many of the currently leading AI firms are multiproduct firms. For example, Google parent Alphabet runs a search engine (Google), an online video service (YouTube), a mobile device operating system (Android), an autonomous vehicle division (Waymo), and a variety of other businesses. In most cases, the economies of scope happen on the supply side through AI talent, better hardware, and better software.

Another important source of economies of scope is the sharing of data across applications. For example, the data from Google's search engine might be valuable in helping determine the effectiveness of YouTube advertising, or its mapping services might be needed for developing autonomous vehicles. The sharing of data is a key source of international friction on disguised protection behind the border. Differences in privacy policies mean that it is easier to share data across applications in some countries compared to others. For example, when Ebay owned PayPal, it faced different restrictions for using the PayPal data in Canada compared to the United States. We will return to this subject later.

This contrasts with the main emphasis in the trade literature on economies of scope, which emphasizes the demand side. Economies of scope in AI do not seem to be about demand externalities in brand perception or in sales channels. Instead, they appear to be driven by economies of scope in innovation. A wider variety of potential applications generates greater incentives to invest in an AI research team, and it generates more benefits to each particular AI project due to the potential to share data across applications.

19.3.4 Knowledge Externalities

There is a tension in discussing knowledge diffusion in the AI sphere. On the one hand, the spectacular scientific advances are often taught at universities and published in peer-reviewed journals, providing businesses and government personnel with quick and easy access to frontier research. Further, there is the migration of personnel across regions and countries as the above examples of Robin Li and Qi Lu show. This suggests that knowledge externalities are global in scope.

On the other hand, AI expertise has also tended to agglomerate in several narrowly defined regions globally. As with other information technologies, much of the expertise is in Silicon Valley. Berlin, Seattle, London, Boston,

Shanghai, and to some extent Toronto and Montreal can all claim to be hubs of AI innovation. This suggests that AI involves a lot of tacit knowledge that is not easily codified and transferred to others.

In fact, the traditional discussion of knowledge externalities takes on a more nuanced hue in the context of AI. Can these researchers communicate long distance? Do they have to be together? How important are agglomeration forces in AI? As of 2017, AI expertise remains surprisingly rooted in the locations of the universities that invented the technologies. Google's Deep-Mind is in London because that is where the lead researcher lived. Then the first expansion of DeepMind outside the United Kingdom was to Edmonton, Alberta, because Richard Sutton, a key inventor of reinforcement learning, lives in Edmonton. Uber opened an AI office in Toronto because it wanted to hire Raquel Urtasun, a University of Toronto professor.

Generally, there are a small number of main AI research departments: Stanford, Carnegie Mellon University, the University of Toronto, and several others. Their location is often surprisingly disconnected from headquarters, and so companies open offices where the talent is rather than forcing the talent to move to where the company is.

As we shall see, the exact nature of knowledge externalities is terribly important for understanding whether cluster and other policies are likely to succeed. The nature of these externalities also has some unexpected implications such as the implications of noncompete clauses (Saxenian 1994) and the asymmetries in access to knowledge created by asymmetries in who can speak English versus who can speak Chinese versus who can speak both.

19.3 Trade Theory and the Case for Industrial and Strategic Trade Policies

There are many voices in the industrialized world arguing for industrial policies and strategic trade policies to promote rising living standards. Many of these voices point to the achievements of China as an example of what is possible. Much of what is claimed for China, and what was once claimed for Japan, is of dubious merit. China has redirected vast resources from the rural poor and urban savers toward state-owned enterprises that have massively underperformed. Those firms continue to be major players in the economy and a major drag on economic growth (Brandt and Zhu 2000). It is thus significant that China's greatest commercial successes in AI have come from private companies. So if we are to make the case for industrial and strategic trade policies, we cannot blithely appeal to Chinese state-directed successes. Rather, we must understand the characteristics of industries that increase the likelihood that government policy interventions will be successful.

To this end, we start with a vanilla-specific factors model of international trade (Mussa 1974; Mayer 1974) in which the case for departures from free trade is weak. We then add on additional elements and examine which of these is important for policy success. The first conclusion is that scale and knowledge externalities are critical. The second is that these two elements alone are not enough: their precise form also matters.

19.3.1   Scientists, Heterogeneous Scientists, and Superstar Scientists

Many factors enter into the location decisions of AI firms including access to local talent, local financing/management, and local markets. In this section, we focus on the role of university-related talent. Among the participants of this conference are three head researchers at top AI companies: Geoffrey Hinton (University of Toronto and Google), Russ Salakhutdinov (Carnegie Mellon University and Apple), and Yann LeCun (New York University and Facebook). Each joined his company while retaining his academic position, and each continues to live near his university rather than near corporate headquarters. These three examples are not exceptional, as indicated by the above examples of DeepMind and Richard Sutton, and Raquel Urtasun and Uber.

Scientists. We begin with the simplest model of trade that allows for two types of employees, scientists, and production workers. There are two industries, search engines and clothing. Production workers are employed in both industries and move between them so that their wages are equalized across industries. Scientists are "specific" to the search engine industry in that they are very good at AI algorithms and useless at sewing. We also assume that scientists and workers cannot migrate internationally. Then it is immediately obvious that the more scientists a country has, the larger will be both the size and service exports of the search engine industry.

We start with this benchmark model because, in this setting, without scale or externalities there is no scope for market failure and hence *there is no simple case for any trade policy other than free trade*. For example, consider a policy of restricting imports of search engine services, as China has done with Google. This restriction helps Chinese scientists but can hurt Chinese production workers and consumers (Ruffin and Jones 1977).

There are several departures from this benchmark model that lead to welfare-enhancing export subsidies and other departures from free trade. As we shall see, the two most important are economies of scale and knowledge creation. However, we start instead with profits because profits are at the core of arguments supporting strategic trade policies (Krugman 1986). Since there are no profits in the specific factors model, we introduce profits by introducing scientists of heterogeneous quality.

Heterogeneous Scientists. Consider an industry in which firms provide a search engine and generate advertising revenue. There is a continuum of scientists distinguished by their "quality" q. A firm is distinguished by the quality of its chief scientist and hence firms are also indexed by q. A higher-quality scientist produces a better search engine. A firm engages in activity a that increases advertising revenues $r(a)$ where $r_a > 0$. Let $p(q)$ be the proportion of consumers who choose firm q's search engine. It is natural to assume that $p_q > 0$ that is, a better scientist produces a more desirable search engine. The firm's profit before payments to the scientist is $\pi(a,q) = p(q)r(a) - c(a)$ where $c(a)$ is the cost of the firm's ad-generating activity. In this model the firm is essentially the scientist, but we can delink the two by assuming that the scientist is paid with stock options and so receives a fraction $(1 - \mu)$ of the profits. It is straightforward to show that profit $\pi(a,q)$ is supermodular in (a,q). This implies positive assortative matching; firms with better scientists engage in more ad-generating activity. This means that firms with better scientists will also have more users ($p_q > 0$), more revenues [$\partial r(a(q),q)/\partial q > 0$], and higher profits [$\partial \pi(a(q),q)/\partial q > 0$]. Putting these together, better scientists anchor bigger and more profitable firms.[7]

To place this model into an international-trade setting, we assume that there are multiple countries, a second constant-returns-to-scale industry (clothing), and no international migration of scientists or workers. Because there are profits in the search engine industry, policies that expand that industry generate higher profits. This is the foundation of *strategic trade policy*. In its simplest form, if there are supernormal profits then tariffs and other trade policies can be used to shift profits away from the foreign country and to the domestic country.

Strategic trade policy was first developed by Brander and Spencer (1981) and variants of it have appeared in many of the models discussed below. Unfortunately, the case for strategic trade policy is not as clear as it might seem. Its biggest logical problem is the assumption of positive profits: if there is free entry, then entry will continue until profits are driven to zero.[8] This means that any government policy that encourages entry of firms or training of scientists will be offset by inefficient entry of firms or scientists. Put simply, strategic trade policies only work if there are profits, but with free entry there are no profits (see Eaton and Grossman 1986). The conclusion we draw from this is that the model needs enriching before it can be used to justify trade policy.

Before enriching the model, we note that there are two other compelling

---

7. The first-order condition for advertising activities is $\mu\pi_a = \mu(pr_a - c_a) = 0$. We assume that the second-order condition is satisfied: $\mu\pi_{aa} < 0$. Supermodularity is given by $\partial^2\mu\pi(a,q)/\partial a\partial q = p_q r_a > 0$. The result that advertising activity levels $a(q)$ are increasing in q comes from differentiating the first-order condition: $\mu p_q r_a + \mu\pi_{aa}a_q = 0$ or $a_q = -p_q r_a/\pi_{aa} > 0$. The result that average revenues $p(q)r(a)$ are increasing in q follows from $\partial p(q)r(a(q))/\partial q = p_q r + pr_a a_q > 0$. The result that profits $\pi(a(q),q)$ are increasing in q follows from $\partial\mu\pi(a,q)/\partial q = \mu\pi_a a_q + \mu p_q r(a) = \mu p_q r(a) > 0$ where we have used the first-order condition ($\pi_a = 0$).

8. Free entry implies that ex ante profits are zero. Of course, ex post profits (operating profits of survivors) are always positive; otherwise, survivors would exit.

reasons for being skeptical about the efficacy of strategic trade policy. First, such policies set up political economy incentives for firms to capture the regulatory process used to determine the amount and form of government handouts. Second, the logic of strategic trade policy fails if there is retaliation on the part of the foreign government. Retaliation generates a trade war in which both countries lose. Artificial intelligence meets all the conditions that Busch (2001) identifies as likely to lead to a trade war. We now turn to enriching our model.

Superstar Scientists.[9] Strategic trade policies are more compelling in settings where scale and/or knowledge creation and diffusion are prevalent. To this end we follow section 19.2 in assuming that there are economies of scale in data. This will cause the market to be dominated by a small number of search engine firms; that is, it will turn our model into something that looks like a superstar model. To be more precise, it is a little different from standard superstar models that make assumptions on the demand side (Rosen 1981). The superstar assumptions here are on the supply side.

Modifying our model slightly, we introduce scale in data by assuming that the share of consumers choosing a search engine ($p(q)$) is increasing at an increasing rate ($p_{qq} > 0$);[10] $p_{qq} > 0$ implies that profits and scientist earnings increase at an increasing rate, that is, they are convex in q.[11] This, in turn, implies that the distribution of firm size becomes highly skewed toward large firms. It also implies that the shareholders of large firms will make spectacular earnings, that is, the 1 percent will pull away from the rest of society.

In this setting we expect that a small number of large firms will capture most of the world market for search engines. Further, these firms will be hugely profitable. We have in mind a situation like that found empirically in the search engine market. The top five leaders are (billions of monthly visitors in parentheses): Google (1.8), Bing (0.5), Yahoo (0.5), Baidu (0.5), and Ask (0.3).[12] If the Chinese government subsidizes Baidu or excludes Google from China, then Baidu captures a larger share of the market. This generates higher profits and higher earnings for shareholders within China, making China better off both absolutely and relatively to the United States. Depending on the details of the model, the United States may or may not be absolutely worse off.

This example is very similar to the mid-1980s discussions about commercial jet production. At a time when it was understood that there was room for only two players in the industry (Boeing and McDonnell Douglas were the leaders), the European Union (EU) heavily subsidized Airbus and ultimately

---

9. To our knowledge there are no superstar-and-trade models beyond Manasse and Turrini (2001), which deals with trade and wage inequality.

10. This is an ad hoc assumption, but to the extent that it has the flavor of scale economies, we will see less ad hoc variants in the models reviewed below.

11. From a previous footnote, $\partial \pi(a(q),q)/\partial q = p_q r(a)$. Hence $\partial^2 \pi(a(q),q)/\partial q^2 = p_{qq} r + p_q r_a a_q > 0$.

12. Source: http://www.ebizmba.com/articles/search-engines, July, 2017.

forced McDonnell Douglas to exit. These EU subsidies were enormous, but may nevertheless have been valuable for EU taxpayers.[13]

Our superstars model provides a more compelling case for government intervention because scale in data acts as a natural barrier to entry that prevents the free-entry condition from offsetting the impacts of government policies. Thus, the government can beneficially subsidize the education of AI scientists and/or subsidize the entry of firms, for example, by offering tax breaks, subsidies, expertise, incubators, and so forth. This establishes that scale economies and the supernormal profits they sometimes imply strengthen the case for strategic trade policy.

There is, however, one more assumption we have made that is essential to the argument for strategic trade policy, namely, that there are no international knowledge spillovers. In the extreme, if all the knowledge created, for example, by Canadian scientists, moved freely to the United States or China, then a Canadian subsidy would help the world, but would not differentially help Canada. This establishes the critical role of knowledge diffusion (in addition to scale) for thinking about government policies that promote AI.

Empirics. What do we know about superstar effects empirically? Nothing from the trade literature. We know that superstars matter for the rate and direction of innovation in academic research. We know that universities have played a key role in developing AI expertise and that a small number of university-affiliated chief scientists have played a key role in developing new technologies. We also have some evidence of a knowledge externality. Azoulay, Graff Zivin, and Wang (2010) show that the death of a superstar scientist in a field slows progress in the research area of the superstar. The field suffers as scientists associated with the deceased superstar produce less research. While Azoulay, Graff Zivin, and Wang do not consider AI, their work points to the existence of knowledge spillovers that are local rather than global.

Inequality. This discussion has not had much to say about inequality. In our superstars model, industrial policy and strategic trade policies are successful precisely because they promote large and highly profitable firms. We know that these firms account for an increasing share of total economic activity and that they are likely major contributors both to falling labor shares (Autor et al. 2017) and to rising top-end inequality. Thus, the policies being supported by our model do not lead to broad-based prosperity. This cannot be ignored.

Extensions. While the above model of AI science superstars is useful, it

---

13. The subsidies have continued unabated for over four decades. In 2016, the World Trade Organization (WTO) found that WTO-noncompliant EU subsidies were $10 billion. This does not include the WTO-compliant subsidies. Likewise, the WTO found comparable numbers for WTO-noncompliant US subsidies of Boeing. See Busch (2001) for a history. This raises the possibility that subsidies that are intended to get a firm "on its feet" become permanent, which is yet another reason to be skeptical about strategic trade policies.

has a number of other problems. It is beyond the scope of this chapter to resolve these problems through additional modeling. Instead, we highlight each problem and review the related international trade and growth literatures in order to provide insights into how the model might be improved and what the implications of these improvements are for thinking about trade and trade policy. The problems we cover are the following.

1. The scale assumption $p_{qq} > 0$ is ad hoc. In subsection B below, we consider scale returns that are external to the firm and show that the form of the scale returns matters for policy.

2. In our model, there is no knowledge creation within firms and no knowledge diffusion across firms and borders. In subsection C below, we review endogenous growth models and show that the form of knowledge diffusion, whether it is local or global, matters for policy.

3. Our model ignores the geography of the industry and so does not speak to economic geography and "supercluster" policies. We review the economic geography literature in subsection D below.

4. In section E below we discuss the implications for supercluster policies.

19.3.2   Increasing Returns to Scale External to the Firm—A Basic Trade Model

We start with a simple trade model featuring economies of scale whose geographic scope is variable, that is, regional, national, or international. The model captures the core insights of richer models developed by Ethier (1982), Markusen (1981), and Helpman (1984), along with more recent developments by Grossman and Rossi-Hansberg (2010, 2012).

Firm i produces a homogeneous good using a production function

$$q_i = Q^\alpha F(L_i, K_i),$$

where L_i is employment of labor, K_i is employment of capital, F displays constant returns to scale, Q is industry output ($Q = \Sigma_i q_i$), and $0 < \alpha < 1$; Q^α is like a Solow residual in that it controls productivity. The idea is that a firm's productivity depends on the output of all firms.[14] If Q is *world* output of the industry, then productivity Q^α is common to all firms internationally and scale has no implications for comparative advantage. On the other hand if Q is *national* output of the industry, then the country with the larger output Q will have higher productivity Q^α and hence will capture the entire world market.

Artificial intelligence as an industry has a technology that lies somewhere between national returns to scale (Q is national output) and international returns to scale (Q is international output). With national returns

---

14. Each firm ignores the impact of its output decision on Q so that returns to scale can be treated as external to the firm.

to scale, a government policy such as tariffs or production subsidies that increases domestic output will increase national welfare because the policy raises average productivity at home and also drive exports. Whether it helps or hurts the foreign country depends on a number of factors such as the strength of the scale returns (the size of a) and the size of the countries (Helpman 1984). Most important, the domestic benefits of industrial and trade policies depend on the geographic extent of scale, that is, how much of it is national versus international.

Whether scale operates at the national or international level is not easy to assess and has not been attempted for AI. For the DRAM market in the 1980s, Irwin and Klenow (1994) show that external economies of scale were entirely international rather than national. Other evidence that AI economies are international is the fact that AI algorithms have been disseminated internationally via scientific journals and teaching, and research and development (R&D)-based AI knowledge has diffused internationally via imitation and reverse engineering. On the other hand, the colocation of AI researchers in Silicon Valley and a handful of other technology hubs is suggestive of national and even subnational returns to scale. Azoulay, Graff Zivin, and Wang (2010) also suggests the existence of subnational returns to scale. Clearly, more research is needed on the extent of national versus international returns to scale in AI.

19.3.3   Knowledge Creation and Diffusion: Endogenous Growth

In the previous section, scale was external to the firm and, relatedly, firms did no research. We now introduce firm-level research. Conveniently, some of the key implications of firm-level innovation are similar to those from the previous section, namely, that trade policy depends in large part on the extent to which knowledge spillovers are national or international. To see this, we review the main endogenous growth models that feature international trade. These are Grossman and Helpman (1989, 1990, 1991), Rivera-Batiz and Romer (1991), and Aghion and Howitt (2009, ch. 15). In these models, firms conduct costly R&D and there is an externality that affects these costs. The dominant model in the trade literature features quality ladders (Grossman and Helpman 1991) featuring vertical (quality) differentiation. The highest-quality firm takes the entire market and earns profits.[15]

Innovation improves the quality of the frontier firm by a constant proportion λ. At date $t > 0$, let $n(t)$ be the number of quality improvements during the time interval $(0,t)$ so that the frontier quality is $\lambda^{n(t)}$. Firms invest an amount r in R&D and this generates an endogenous probability $p(r)$ of becoming the quality leader (with quality $\lambda^{n(t)+1}$).

A key feature of the R&D process is an externality: innovators stand

---

15. Ex post profits are needed in order to justify R&D expenses. However, these models have a free-entry condition that drives ex ante profits to zero.

on the shoulders of giants in the sense that they improve on the frontier level of quality. Had they improved on their own quality, there would be no externality. A two-sector, two-country quality ladder model appears in Grossman and Helpman (1991). Grossman and Helpman assume that there is a standard constant-returns-to-scale sector and a quality sector.[16]

Another popular approach is Romer's (1990) expanding-varieties model. Final goods producers combine varieties of intermediates using a constant elasticity of substitution (CES) production function so that there is love of variety. At any date t there is a measure $N(t)$ of varieties. The marginal returns to new varieties are positive, but diminishing. The key "building on the shoulders of giants" externality is that the cost of developing a new variety is inversely proportional to the measure of varieties. As a result, innovation costs fall over time, generating endogenous growth. A one-sector, two-country extension appears in Rivera-Batiz and Romer (1991). A two-sector, two-country extension appears in Grossman and Helpman (1991).

This brief review leads to a number of observations. As in the previous section, the benefit of trade policy depends on whether the externality operates at the national or international levels; Q of the previous section is replaced here by either $\lambda^{n(t)}$ or $N(t)$. Hence, if each firm builds on the *international* frontier $\lambda^{n(t)}$ or the *international* number of varieties $N(t)$, then there are no implications for comparative advantage; however, if each firm builds on its national $\lambda^{n(t)}$ or national $N(t)$ then the frontier country will develop an increasingly strong comparative advantage in the quality or expanding-varieties sector. With national-level externalities one country will capture the lion's share of the quality/varieties sector. Further, a country can capture this sector by using R&D and trade policies.

Endogenous growth models provide important insights into the details of R&D and trade policies. Research and development policies directly target the knowledge externality and so are preferred to (second-best) trade policies. One R&D policy avenue is to promote *knowledge diffusion*. This can be done through subsidies to nonprofit organizations targeting local within-industry interactions and industry-university collaborations. A second R&D policy avenue is to promote *knowledge creation* through R&D subsidies that are available to all firms, universities, and students. There is a tension between these two avenues; knowledge diffusion can discourage knowledge creation since knowledge diffusion to competitors reduces the returns to innovation. However, the tension is sometimes constructive: Silicon Valley emerged from the shadows of Massachusetts' Route 128 partly because of an "open-source attitude" (Saxenian 1994) and Califor-

---

16. Placing endogenous growth into a two-sector model so as to facilitate a discussion of comparative advantage is not easy because the sector with improving quality slowly takes over the entire economy unless other price or nonprice "congestion" forces prevent this.

nian restrictions on noncompete clauses (Marx and Fleming 2012). It is less likely that diffusion of knowledge to foreign countries will be as beneficial domestically.

This class of models discourages policies that target individual firms or that "pick winners." To understand why industry leaders should *not* be advantaged by policy, note that counterintuitively, industry leaders will be the least innovative firms due to the "market-stealing" effect. If an entrant innovates, it steals the market from the leader. If a leader innovates, it cannibalizes itself. Leaders therefore have *less* of an incentive to innovate. Aghion et al. (2001, 2005) address this counterintuitive result by developing a model in which leaders innovate in order to escape the competition. Aghion et al. (2017) and Lim, Trefler, and Yu (2017) are currently developing international trade models featuring escape the competition.

In the context of AI, none of the above endogenous growth models is ideal, leading us to conjecture about what an appropriate model might look like. The advantage of endogenous growth models is that they emphasize knowledge creation and diffusion. Thinking more deeply about AI development and commercialization, it is useful to distinguish two aspects of what is done in the AI research departments of large firms. First, they improve AI algorithms, which have the flavor of quality ladders. (Recall that quality can be something that is perceived by consumers *or*, as is relevant here, something that reduces marginal costs.) Second, AI research departments develop new applications of existing AI; for example, Google uses AI for its search engine, autonomous vehicles, YouTube recommendations, advertising network, energy use in data centers, and so forth. This suggests an expanding-varieties model, but one that operates *within* the firm. We are unaware of any endogenous growth models that have both these features. Grossman and Helpman (1991) have the first and Klette and Kortum (2004) have the second. Combining them in one model is not trivial and analytic results would likely have to be replaced with calibration.

19.3.4   New Economic Geography and Agglomeration

The discussion in the previous section points to the possibility that knowledge spillovers are subnational, and this leads naturally to a theory of regional clusters such as Silicon Valley. New economic geography or NEG (Krugman 1980) does not typically consider knowledge spillovers, but it does consider other local externalities that drive regional clusters. Three mechanisms have been particularly prominent: (a) demand-side "home-market effects," (b) upstream-downstream linkages, and (c) labor-market pooling. All of these theories feature two key elements: costs of trading across regions (e.g., tariffs) and increasing returns to scale at the firm level (which can be thought of as the fixed costs of developing a new product). We explain the role of these two elements in the context of home-market effects.

Consider a model with CES monopolistic competition and two regions ($j = 1, 2$). There are varieties of machines and the larger the set of machines to choose from, the more productive are the producers. Let N_j be the measure of machine varieties available in region j. Then with CES production functions, productivity is proportional to N_j.[17] The fundamental factor pushing for agglomeration is the strength of this love-of-variety/productivity externality. (This is related to the externality in Romer's expanding varieties model, which is also proportional to N_j.) As in previous models, the externality operates at the local level rather than at the international level. This externality encourages firms to colocate or agglomerate since the agglomeration of firms drives up N_j and productivity. The fundamental factor pushing against this agglomeration is trade costs: a firm can avoid trade costs by locating close to consumers rather than close to other producers. The main insight of this model is that in equilibrium a disproportionate share of the world's firms will locate in a single region, and this region will thus have higher productivity. As a result, this region will be richer. Notice that firms are choosing to set up where the competition is greatest and where wages and property values are the highest.

The above model of agglomeration has been extended in countless ways (e.g., Krugman and Venables 1995; Fajgelbaum, Grossman, and Helpman 2011; Duranton and Puga 2001) and it is easy to think of applications where the force for agglomeration is not the variety of machines, but the variety of knowledge held by firms. If this knowledge is tacit (meaning it cannot be codified and transmitted in a document), then knowledge spillovers are only transmitted locally via face-to-face interactions. In this case, knowledge externalities lead firms to agglomerate. The result is regions like Silicon Valley.

19.3.5   Cluster Policies

Cluster policies have long been the politician's best friend, yet economists remain highly critical of them. In surveying the evidence for the success of these policies, Uyarra and Ramlogan (2012) write "There is no clear and unambiguous evidence that over the long term clusters are able to generate strong and sustainable impacts in terms of innovation, productivity or employment." One of the world leaders in the economics of clusters, Gilles Duranton, titled his 2011 survey "'California Dreamin': The Feeble Case for Cluster Policies." Yet clusters remain fashionable.

In light of what we have described, the first question is: When are cluster policies likely to succeed? The answer is that they are most likely to succeed when there is clear evidence of scale economies and of knowledge creation together with local knowledge diffusion. Artificial intelligence displays these

---

17. More precisely, productivity is proportional to $N^{1/(\sigma-1)}$ where $\sigma > 1$ is the elasticity of substitution between varieties.

characteristics, though the extent of international knowledge diffusion cannot be ignored.

The second question is: What policies are likely to work? To answer this question we turn to the insights of Ajay Agrawal, Director of Rotman's Creative Destruction Lab (CDL), and Michael Porter, the business guru of cluster policies. We start with Agrawal. Agrawal identifies two problems with developing AI in the Canadian context. First, there is a shortage of people with the skills to scale up companies. Agrawal calls these people 1000Xers. Second, the cost of information about a start-up's quality is so high that capital markets cannot identify the best and the brightest start-ups. Agrawal's CDL addresses both of these problems by linking start-ups with serial entrepreneurs who can identify a good start-up, tap into 1000Xers for growth, and pass on valuable information about start-up quality to investors globally.

Another approach to the question of what policies are likely to work utilizes Porter's (1990) diamond, which emphasizes four features of clusters: (*a*) factor conditions such as universities and an abundant supply of AI scientists, (*b*) home-market-demand externalities for AI, (*c*) externalities flowing from suppliers of specialized intermediate inputs into AI such as financial services, and (*d*) a competitive environment. Items *b–d* involve effects that have already been described in our discussion of knowledge spillovers and lie at the heart of local agglomeration. Item *a* is a more conventional economic factor, that is, drive down the price of the key input by subsidizing its supply. Yet Porter's research shows that many clusters are driven primarily by *a*. That is to say, the single most important policy in practice is simple: follow Hinton's advice in training a large number of AI scientists locally.

Our models also suggest two difficulties with Hinton's advice that must be shored up. First, there is international rather than national knowledge diffusion due to the fact that, for example, Canadian-trained scientists are likely to leave Canada for Silicon Valley, China, and other AI hotspots. This suggests value in programs like those used successfully in Singapore that require student loans to be repaid if the student does not work in Singapore for a minimum number of years.

Second, scale in data is a huge problem for a small country like Canada. To understand appropriate solutions for this, we now turn to the details of national regulatory environments that affect data and the use of AI.

19.4   Behind-the-Border Trade Barriers: The Domestic Regulatory Environment

Given these models, we next turn to the specific regulatory issues that are likely to impact trade policy. Many of the core trade issues around AI involve access to data. Data is a key input into AI, and there are a number of government policies that affect data access and data flows. To the extent these regulations vary across countries, they can advantage some countries' AI industries. The models above suggest that this advantage can have consequences if there are economies of scale, local externalities, and/or rents.

We highlight five policies in particular. The first three involve data: domestic privacy policy, data localization rules, and access to government data. The others are development of the regulation of AI application industries (such as autonomous vehicles) and protection of source code. Privacy policy, data localization, and source code access have already become significant trade issues. For example, the TPP addresses all three of these, as do the US Trade Representative's NAFTA renegotiation objectives. The US position is that strong Canadian and Mexican privacy rules, localization requirements, and access to foreign source code are all impediments to US exports of AI-related goods. In other words, the emphasis on trade policy in these areas is that regulation could be disguised protection that helps domestic firms and hurts foreign firms. In the discussion below, we explore the extent to which this starting assumption is appropriate.

Privacy Regulation. Privacy regulation involves policies that restrict the collection and use of data. Such regulation differs across locations. Privacy policy has the power to limit or expand the ability of firms to use AI effectively. Restrictions on the use of data mean restrictions on the ability to use AI given the data available; however, restrictions on the use of data may also increase the supply of data available if it leads consumers to trust firms that collect the data. Although the theory is ambiguous, thus far, the empirical evidence favors the former effect on balance. Stricter privacy regulations reduce the ability of firms and nonprofits to collect and use data and therefore leads to less innovative use of data (Goldfarb and Tucker 2012). Thus, firms in some countries may benefit from favorable privacy policy.

We believe the most useful analogies for privacy policy in trade relate to labor and environmental regulations. Such regulations also differ across countries for a variety of reasons. They could reflect differences in preferences across countries, or could be perceived as normal goods that wealthier countries are willing to pay for but poorer countries are not (Grossman and Krueger 1995). There is room for reasonable disagreement on how data might be collected or used. Some countries will restrict the information used in prediction while others will not. For example, for insurance, the data that can be used varies by state, with different states providing a variety of restrictions on the use of race, religion, gender, and sexual orientation in insurance.[18] Even with such restrictions, if other variables provide surrogates for such categories, it is possible that firms may be forced to abandon AI methods entirely for more transparent prediction technologies. In terms of

18. http://repository.law.umich.edu/cgi/viewcontent.cgi?article=1163&context=law_econ _current.

privacy policy, we think it is useful to take as given that there are differences across countries in their preferences for policies that restrict the collection and use of data.

Given these differences in preferences, what are the implications for trade? Suppose that the optimal privacy policy for growing an AI industry involves relatively few restrictions on data. Artificial intelligence requires data, and so the fewer government restrictions on data collection, the more rapidly the industry grows.[19] To the extent that young firms tend to grow by focusing on the domestic market, this will advantage the growth of AI firms in some countries relative to others. Thus, lax privacy policies may help domestic industry relative to countries with strict policies just as lax labor and environmental regulation may help the domestic industry.

This suggests the potential of a "race to the bottom" in privacy policy. Evidence for such races has been found in enforcement of labor policies (e.g., Davies and Vadlamannati 2013) and in environmental policies (e.g., Beron, Murdoch, and Vijverberg 2003; Fredriksson and Milliment 2002). There is evidence that privacy regulation does disadvantage jurisdictions with respect to their advertising-supported software industries. In particular, Goldfarb and Tucker (2011) examined a change in European privacy regulation (implemented in 2004) that made it more difficult for European internet firms to collect data about their online customers. This regulatory change was particularly likely to reduce the effectiveness of advertising on websites that relied on customer-tracking data. Using a consistent measure of the effectiveness of thousands of online advertising campaigns, the results showed that European online advertising became about 65 percent less effective after the regulation took effect, compared to before the regulation and compared to advertising in other jurisdictions, mainly the United States. In other words, privacy regulation seemed to reduce the ability of companies to use data effectively. In a different context, Miller and Tucker (2011) show that state-level privacy restrictions can reduce the quality of health care. While this evidence does not pertain to AI, just like AI, online advertising and health care use data as a key input. In other words, the same forces will likely be at play for privacy regulation that restricts the ability of AI to operate.

Under strategic trade models, such races to the bottom are likely to matter if there are rents to be gained from AI. Under endogenous growth models with local spillovers and various agglomeration models, this could create an equilibrium in which the AI industry moves to the country with the most lax policies. Currently, privacy policies are much stricter in Europe than in the

---

19. Importantly, this is not a statement about the optimal privacy policy from the point of view of a firm. If consumers have a preference for privacy, the private sector can provide it even in the absence of regulation. For a richer debate on this point, see Goldfarb and Tucker (2012) and Acquisti, Taylor, and Wagman (2016).

United States or China.[20] Furthermore, there are a number of differences in such policies between the United States and China. This may give the United States and China an advantage over Europe in this industry.

If stricter privacy policy is likely to hamstring domestic firms in favor of foreign ones, we would expect policy to emphasize avoiding such a race to the bottom; however, recent trade negotiations have instead focused on privacy regulation as disguised protection. For example, this argument is at odds with the current US trade negotiation objectives, which want to weaken Canadian privacy laws. Based on the existing evidence from other data-driven industries, we believe this will help the Canadian industry relative to the US industry in the long run, even if it benefits American companies that already do business in Canada in the short run. In addition, TPP's chapter 14 on Electronic Commerce contains provisions that attempt to limit disguised protection, but contains almost no language that encourages harmonization in privacy policies beyond a request in Article 14.8.5 to "endeavor to exchange information on any such [personal information protection] mechanisms . . . and explore ways to extend these or other suitable arrangements to promote compatibility between them." The words "endeavor" and "explore" are what are known in the trade policy literature as "aspirational" language and generally have no force. The CETA agreement is even more vague with respect to electronic commerce generally. The electronic commerce section, chapter 16, says little but "recognize the importance of" electronic commerce regulation and interoperability and that "the Parties agree to maintain a dialogue on issues raised by electronic commerce."[21]

It is important to note that this is not a statement about company strategy. The market may discipline and provide consumer protection with respect to privacy. Apple, in particular, has emphasized the protection of the personal information of its customers as it has rolled out AI initiatives, and it is an open question whether this strategy will pay off in terms of consumer loyalty and access to better quality, if limited, data.

We also want to emphasize that we do not have a position on the optimal amount of privacy as enforced by regulation. In fact, we think this is a difficult question for economists to answer. Given that the empirical evidence suggests that privacy regulation, on balance and as implemented thus far, seems to reduce innovation, the determination of the optimal amount of privacy should not focus on maximizing innovation (through, as the TPP

20. Canada sits somewhere in the middle. Europe is strict on both data collection and its uses. Canada's core restrictions involve use for a purpose different from the collection context. The United States emphasizes contracts, and so as long as the privacy policy is clear, companies can collect and use data as they wish (at least outside of certain regulated industries like health and finance).

21. https://ustr.gov/sites/default/files/TPP-Final-Text-Electronic-Commerce.pdf, http://www.international.gc.ca/trade-commerce/trade-agreements-accords-commerciaux/agr-acc/ceta-aecg/text-texte/16.aspx?lang=eng.

emphasizes in article 14.8.1, "the contribution that this [privacy protection] makes to enhancing consumer confidence in electronic commerce"). Instead, it is a balance of the ethical value of (or even right to) privacy and the innovativeness and growth of the domestic AI industry.

To reiterate, privacy regulation is different from many other regulations because privacy (perhaps disproportionately) hamstrings domestic firms. Therefore, trade negotiations should not start with the assumption that privacy regulation is disguised protection. Instead, discussions should start with the public policy goal of the "social benefits of protecting the personal information of users of electronic commerce" that is also mentioned in article 14.8.1 of the TPP. Then, if needed, discussions can move to any particular situation in which a privacy regulation might really be disguised protection. As we hope is clear from the above discussion, domestic privacy regulations that restrict how firms can collect and use data are unlikely to be disguised protection. We next turn to two other regulations that might use privacy as an excuse to favor, rather than hamstring, domestic firms.

Data Localization. Data localization rules involve restrictions on the ability of firms to transmit data on domestic users to a foreign country. Such restrictions are often justified by privacy motivations. Countries may want data to stay domestic for privacy and (related) national security reasons. In particular, the argument for data localization emphasizes that governments want the data of their citizens to be protected by the laws of the domestic country. Foreign national security agencies should not have access to data that occurs within a country, and foreign companies should be bound by the laws of the country where the data were collected. The argument against such localization (at least in public) is technical: such localization imposes a significant cost on foreign companies wanting to do business. They need to establish a presence in every country, and they need to determine a system that ensures that the data is not routed internationally (something that is technically costly, particularly for integrated communications networks such as within Europe or within North America). US-based companies have lobbied against such requirements.[22]

On the technical side, consider two parties, A and B, who reside in the same country. Internet traffic between A and B cannot be confined within national borders without specific technical guidance (and some cost to quality) because the internet may route data indirectly. In addition, data on a transaction between A and B may be stored on a server located in a different country. Furthermore, if A and B reside in different countries, then the data on that transaction will likely be stored in both countries.[23]

Data localization is an issue for AI because AI requires data. And it often involves merging different data sources together. The quality of aggregate

22. https://publicpolicy.googleblog.com/2015/02/the-impacts-of-data-localization-on.html.
23. Dobson, Tory, and Trefler (2017).

predictions from AI will be lower if the scale of data is limited to within a country. In other words, localization is a way to restrict the possible scale of any country in AI, but at the cost of lower quality overall.

Put differently, data localization is a privacy policy that could favor domestic firms. Unlike the consumer protection privacy policies highlighted above, it can favor domestic over foreign firms because the foreign-firm AI experts may not have access to the data. The TPP recognizes this and explicitly restricts it in Article 14.11.3a, which states that the cross-border transfer of information should not be restricted in a manner that would constitute "a disguised restriction on trade."[24]

Privileged Access to Government Data. Another potential restriction on trade that might be justified by privacy concerns involves access to government data. Governments collect a great deal of data. Such data might be valuable to training AIs and improving their predictions. Such data include tax and banking data, education data, and health data. For example, as the only legal provider of most health care services in Ontario, the Ontario government has unusually rich data on the health needs, decisions, and outcomes of 14 million people. If domestic firms are given privileged access to that data, it would create an indirect subsidy to the domestic AI industry.

We think the most useful analogy in the current trade literature is the perennial softwood lumber trade dispute between Canada and the United States. In the softwood lumber case, most timber in Canada is on government-owned land, while in the United States, most timber is on privately owned land. The US complaints allege that Canadian timber is priced too low, and is therefore a government subsidy to the Canadian lumber industry. While there have been various agreements over the years, the disagreement has not been fully resolved. The superficial issue is what a fair price should be for access to government resources. The real issue is whether legitimate regulatory differences can be argued to convey unfair advantage and therefore constitute a trade-illegal subsidy.

Government data can be seen similarly. Links between the state and the corporation vary by country, and this might help some corporations more than others. What is a fair price for access to the data? Importantly, governments may not want to give foreign firms access to such data for the same privacy and national security issues that underlie motivations for data local-

---

24. Related to the issue of data localization is the question of who owns data collected on domestic individuals by foreign individuals or firms. For example, consider an American company that uses Peruvians' cell phones to gather data on agriculture and climate. Who owns the rights to that data? Are the Americans allowed to profit from that data? Are contracts between the individual actors enough, or is there a need for international laws or norms? The data might not be collected if not for the private companies, but the companies use the data in their own interest rather than in the public interest or in the interest of the Peruvians who provided the data. The recent attempts at a joint venture between Monsanto and John Deere, along with the US Department of Justice antitrust concerns that scuttled the deal, highlight how tangible this issue is.

ization. Thus, seemingly reasonable differences across countries in their data access policies can end up favoring the domestic industry.

Industrial Regulation. Most international agreements have a section on competition policy and industrial regulation. This is because regulation can be a source of unfair comparative advantage or disadvantage. In AI applications, this list is long. In addition to the points around data and privacy highlighted above, many applications of AI involve complementary technologies in which standards might not yet exist and the legal framework might still be evolving.

For example, in autonomous vehicles, a variety of standards will need to be developed around vehicle-to-vehicle communication, traffic signals, and many other aspects of automotive design. Most of these standards will be negotiated by industry players (Simcoe 2012), perhaps with some government input. As in other contexts, national champions can try to get their governments to adopt standards that raise costs for foreign competition. This leads to the possibility of international standards wars. This is particularly true of standards that are likely to involve a great deal of government input. For example, suppose governments require that the AI behind autonomous vehicles be sufficiently transparent that investigators are able to determine what caused a crash. Without international standards, different countries could require information from different sensors, or they could require access to different aspects of the models and data that underlie the technology. For companies, ensuring that their AI is compatible with multiple regulatory regimes in this manner would be expensive. Such domestic regulations could be a way to favor domestic firms. In other words, domestic technology standards around how AI interacts with the legal regime is a potential tool for disguised restriction on trade.

The autonomous vehicle legal framework is evolving, with different countries (and even states within the United States) allowing different degrees of autonomy on their public roads. Drones are another example where, in the United States, the Federal Aviation Administration (FAA) strictly regulates American airspace, while China and some other countries have fewer restrictions. This may have allowed China's commercial drone industry to be more advanced than the industry in the United States.[25] Thus, regulation can also impact the rate of innovation and therefore comparative advantage.

Source Code. To the extent that AI may discriminate, governments may demand information about the algorithms that underlie the AI's predictions under antidiscrimination laws. More generally with respect to software, including AI, governments may demand access to source code for security reasons, for example, to reduce fraud or to protect national security. Thus, using consumer protection or national security as an excuse, governments

---

25. https://www.forbes.com/sites/sarahsu/2017/04/13/in-china-drone-delivery-promises -to-boost-consumption-especially-in-rural-areas/#47774daf68fe.

could reduce the ability of foreign firms to maintain trade secrets. Furthermore, cyber espionage of such trade secrets may be widespread, but that is beyond the scope of this chapter.[26] Broadly, this issue has been recognized in the TPP negotiations, with Article 14.17 emphasizing that access to source code cannot be required unless that source code underlies critical infrastructure or unless the source code is needed to obey other domestic regulations that are not disguised restrictions on trade.

Other policies that might affect the size of domestic AI industries include intellectual property, antitrust, R&D subsidies, and national security. If AI is the next important strategic industry, then all of the standard questions arise with respect to trade policies in these industries. We do not discuss these in detail because we think the trade-specific issues with respect to these policies are not distinct to AI, but are captured more generally by the discussion of innovation and trade. The main point for these other aspects of domestic policy with respect to AI and trade is that there are economies of scale in AI at the firm level. Furthermore, we expect some of the externalities from the AI industry to remain local.

19.5 AI and International Macroeconomics

Before concluding, it is important to recognize that AI will have implications for international macroeconomics. For example, suppose that China does succeed in building a large AI industry. This will likely increase its trade surplus with the rest of the world, particularly in services. Furthermore, suppose that China manages to control wage inflation through promoting migration from rural to urban areas, and by relaxing the one-child policy. Then, this is likely to put upward pressure on the renminbi (RMB) and downward pressure on the dollar.

This will have implications for US labor markets. At the low end of the market, a weakening dollar might repatriate manufacturing jobs. At the high end of the market, skilled US workers will for the first time be exposed to competition from a low-wage country. In isolation, this would reduce one dimension of domestic US inequality.

If the Chinese market becomes open to US technology giants (and vice versa), both the Melitz (2003) model and the Oberfield (2018) model of trade predict that the giants will grow even larger. In the context in which these companies have already absorbed one-fifth of US value added, and may have contributed to US top-end inequality, the impact of international trade in further growing these impacts may increase top-end inequality.

---

26. https://obamawhitehouse.archives.gov/sites/default/files/omb/IPEC/admin_strategy _on_mitigating_the_theft_of_u.s._trade_secrets.pdf.

19.6 Conclusion

How will artificial intelligence affect the pattern of trade? How does it make us think differently about trade policy? In this article we have tried to highlight some key points.

First, the nature of the technology suggests that economies of scale and scope will be important. Furthermore, as a knowledge-intensive industry, knowledge externalities are likely to be important. Prior literature on other industries suggests that such externalities are often local, but more evidence is needed. Second, the trade models that are likely to be most useful in understanding the impact of AI are those that account for these points, specifically, scale, knowledge creation, and the geography of knowledge diffusion. These models suggest that whether AI-focused trade policies (or AI-focused investments in clusters) are optimal will depend very much on the presence of scale and the absence of rapid international knowledge diffusion. Third, we discussed whether and how regulation might be used to favor domestic industry. We highlighted that privacy policy that targets consumer protection is unlike many other regulations in that it is likely to hamstring domestic firms, even relative to foreign ones. So, rather than focusing trade discussions on how privacy policy might be used as a disguised restriction on trade, such discussions should emphasize regulatory harmonization so as to avoid a race to the bottom. In contrast, several other policies may be used to favor domestic firms including data localization rules, limited access to government data, industry regulations such as those around the use of drones, and forced access to source code.

Generally, this is an exciting new area for trade research and policy. There is still much to learn before we have a comprehensive understanding of these questions.

References

Acquisti, Alessandro, Curtis Taylor, and Liad Wagman. 2016. "The Economics of Privacy." *Journal of Economic Literature* 54 (2): 442–92.

Aghion, Philippe, Antonin Bergeaud, Matthieu Lequien, and Marc Melitz. 2017. "The Impact of Exports on Innovation: Theory and Evidence." Working paper, Harvard University.

Aghion, Philippe, Nick Bloom, Richard Blundell, Rachel Griffith, and Peter Howitt. 2005. "Competition and Innovation: An Inverted-U Relationship." *Quarterly Journal of Economics* 120 (2): 701–28.

Aghion, Philippe, Christopher Harris, Peter Howitt, and John Vickers. 2001. "Competition, Imitation and Growth with Step-by-Step Innovation." *Review of Economic Studies* 68 (3): 467–92.

Aghion, Philippe, and Peter Howitt. 2009. *The Economics of Growth*. Cambridge, MA: MIT Press.

Agrawal, Ajay, Joshua Gans, and Avi Goldfarb. 2018. *Prediction Machines: The Simple Economics of Artificial Intelligence*. Boston, MA: Harvard Business Review Press.

Autor, David, David Dorn, Lawrence F. Katz, Christina Patterson, and John Van Reenen. 2017. "Concentrating on the Fall of the Labor Share." NBER Working Paper no. 23108, Cambridge, MA.

Azoulay, Pierre, Joshua S. Graff Zivin, and Jialan Wang. 2010. "Superstar Extinction." *Quarterly Journal of Economics* 125 (2): 549–89.

Beron, Kurt J., James C. Murdoch, and Wim P. M. Vijverberg. 2003. "Why Cooperate? Public Goods, Economic Power, and the Montreal Protocol." *Review of Economics and Statistics* 85 (2): 286–97.

Brander, James A., and Barbara J. Spencer. 1981. "Tariffs and the Extraction of Foreign Monopoly Rents under Potential Entry." *Canadian Journal of Economics* 14 (3): 371–89.

Brandt, Loren, and Xiaodong Zhu. 2000. "Redistribution in a Decentralized Economy: Growth and Inflation in Reform China." *Journal of Political Economy* 108 (2): 422–39.

Busch, Marc L. 2001. *Trade Warriors: States, Firms, and Strategic-Trade Policy in High-Technology Competition*. Cambridge: Cambridge University Press.

Davies, Ronald B., and Krishna Chaitanya Vadlamannati. 2013. "A Race to the Bottom in Labor Standards? An Empirical Investigation." *Journal of Development Economics* 103:1–14.

Dobson, Wendy, Julia Tory, and Daniel Trefler. 2017. "Modernizing NAFTA: A Canadian Perspective." In *A Positive NAFTA Renegotiation*, edited by Fred Bergsten, 36–49. Washington, DC: Petersen Institute for International Economics.

Duranton, Gilles. 2011. "California Dreamin': The Feeble Case for Cluster Policies." *Review of Economic Analysis* 3 (1): 3–45.

Duranton, Gilles, and Diego Puga. 2001. "Nursery Cities: Urban Diversity, Process Innovation, and the Life Cycle of Products." *American Economic Review* 91 (5): 1454–77.

Eaton, Jonathan, and Gene M. Grossman. 1986. "Optimal Trade and Industrial Policy under Oligopoly." *Quarterly Journal of Economics* 101 (2): 383–406.

Ethier, Wilfred J. 1982. "National and International Returns to Scale in the Modern Theory of International Trade." *American Economic Review* 72 (3): 389–405.

Fajgelbaum, Pablo, Gene M. Grossman, and Elhanan Helpman. 2011. "Income Distribution, Product Quality, and International Trade." *Journal of Political Economy* 119 (4): 721–65.

Fredriksson, Per G., and Daniel L. Millimet. 2002. "Strategic Interaction and the Determination of Environmental Policy across U.S. States." *Journal of Urban Economics* 51 (1): 101–22.

Fujii, Hidemichi, and Shunsuke Managi. 2017. "Trends and Priority Shifts in Artificial Intelligence Technology Invention: A Global Patent Analysis." RIETI Discussion Paper Series no. 17-E066, Research Institute of Economy, Trade, and Industry, May.

Goldfarb, Avi, and Catherine Tucker. 2011. "Privacy Regulation and Online Advertising." *Management Science* 57 (1): 57–71.

———. 2012. "Privacy and Innovation." In *Innovation Policy and the Economy*, vol. 12, edited by Josh Lerner and Scott Stern, 65–89. Chicago: University of Chicago Press.

Grossman, Gene M., and Elhanan Helpman. 1989. "Product Development and International Trade." *Journal of Political Economy* 97 (6): 1261–83.

———. 1990. "Trade, Innovation, and Growth." *American Economic Review Papers and Proceedings* 80 (2): 86–91.

———. 1991. *Innovation and Growth in the Global Economy.* Cambridge, MA: MIT Press.

Grossman, Gene M., and Alan B. Krueger. 1995. "Economic Growth and the Environment." *Quarterly Journal of Economics* 110 (2): 353–77.

Grossman, Gene M., and Esteban Rossi-Hansberg. 2010. "External Economies and International Trade Redux." *Quarterly Journal of Economics* 125 (2): 829–58.

———. 2012. "Task Trade between Similar Countries." *Econometrica* 80 (2): 593–629.

Helpman, Elhanan. 1984. "Increasing Returns, Imperfect Markets, and Trade Theory." In *Handbook of International Economics*, edited by Peter B. Kenen and Ronald W. Jones, 325–65. Amsterdam: North-Holland.

Irwin, Douglas A., and Peter J. Klenow. 1994. "Learning-by-Doing Spillovers in the Semiconductor Industry." *Journal of Political Economy* 102 (6): 1200–27.

Klette, Tor Jakob, and Samuel Kortum. 2004. "Innovating Firms and Aggregate Innovation." *Journal of Political Economy* 112 (5): 986–1018.

Krugman, Paul R. 1980. "Scale Economies, Product Differentiation, and the Pattern of Trade." *American Economic Review* 70 (5): 950–59.

———. 1986. *Strategic Trade Policy and the New International Economics.* Cambridge, MA: MIT Press.

Krugman, Paul R., and Anthony J. Venables. 1995. "Globalization and the Inequality of Nations." *Quarterly Journal of Economics* 110 (4): 857–80.

Lim, Kevin, Daniel Trefler, and Miaojie Yu. 2017. "Trade and Innovation: The Role of Scale and Competition Effects." Working paper, University of Toronto.

Manasse, Paolo, and Alessandro Turrini. 2001. "Trade, Wages, and Superstars." *Journal of International Economics* 54 (1): 97–117.

Markusen, James R. 1981. "Trade and the Gains from Trade with Imperfect Competition." *Journal of International Economics* 11 (4): 531–51.

Marx, M., and L. Fleming. 2012. "Non-compete Agreements: Barriers to Entry . . . and Exit?" In *Innovation Policy and the Economy*, vol. 12, edited by J. Lerner and S. Stern. Chicago: University of Chicago Press.

Mayer, Wolfgang. 1974. "Short-Run and Long-Run Equilibrium for a Small Open Economy." *Journal of Political Economy* 82 (5): 955–67.

McLaren, John. 2000. "'Globalization' and Vertical Structure." *American Economic Review* 90 (5): 1239–54.

Melitz, Marc J. 2003. "The Impact of Trade on Intra-Industry Reallocations and Aggregate Industry Productivity." *Econometrica* 71 (6): 1695–725.

Miller, A. R., and C. Tucker. 2011. "Can Healthcare IT Save Babies?" *Journal of Political Economy* 119 (2): 289–332.

Mussa, Michael L. 1974. "Tariffs and the Distribution of Income: The Importance of Factor Specificity, Substitutability, and Intensity in the Short and Long Run." *Journal of Political Economy* 82 (6): 1191–203.

Oberfield, Ezra. 2018. "A Theory of Input-Output Architecture." *Econometrica* 86:559–89.

Porter, Michael E. 1990. "The Competitive Advantage of Nations." *Harvard Business Review* 68 (2): 73–93.

PWC. 2017. "Global Top 100 Companies by Market Capitalisation." March 31, 2017, update. https://www.pwc.com/top100. Accessed August 17, 2017.

Rauch, James E. 1999. "Networks versus Markets in International Trade." *Journal of International Economics* 48 (1): 7–35.

Rivera-Batiz, Luis A., and Paul M. Romer. 1991. "Economic Integration and Endogenous Growth." *Quarterly Journal of Economics* 106 (2): 531–55.

Romer, Paul M. 1990. "Endogenous Technological Change." *Journal of Political Economy* 98 (5): S71–102.

Rosen, Sherwin. 1981. "The Economics of Superstars." *American Economic Review* 71 (5): 845–58.

Ruffin, Roy J., and Ronald W. Jones. 1977. "Protection and Real Wages: The Neoclassical Ambiguity." *Journal of Economic Theory* 14 (2): 337–48.

Saxenian, AnnaLee. 1994. *Regional Advantage Culture and Competition in Silicon Valley and Route 128*. Cambridge, MA: Harvard University Press.

Simcoe, Timothy. 2012. "Standard Setting Committees: Consensus Governance for Shared Technology Platforms." *American Economic Review* 102 (1): 305–36.

Sutton, John, and Daniel Trefler. 2016. "Capabilities, Wealth and Trade." *Journal of Political Economy* 124 (3): 826–78.

Uyarra, Elvira, and Ronnie Ramlogan. 2012. "The Effects of Cluster Policy on Innovation Compendium of Evidence on the Effectiveness of Innovation Policy Intervention." Technical Report, Manchester Institute of Innovation Research Manchester Business School, March.

Punishing Robots
Issues in the Economics of Tort Liability and Innovation in Artificial Intelligence

Alberto Galasso and Hong Luo

20.1 Introduction

A tort is an action that causes harm or loss, resulting in legal liability for the person who commits the act. The role of the tort system is to deter people from injuring others and to compensate those who are injured. Two important classes of tort law are product liability law that protects customers from defective or dangerous products, and medical malpractice law that governs professional negligence by physicians. Tort suits often make the headlines because of their large damages awards. For example, General Motors recently paid about $2.5 billion in penalties and settlements in a case involving faulty ignition switches linked to 124 deaths.[1]

Rapid advancements in the field of artificial intelligence and robotics have led to lively debates over the application of tort law to these technologies. For example, the diffusion of autonomous vehicles is expected to shift the focus of motor vehicle accident litigation from driver liability to product (i.e., manufacturer) liability. Similar shifts are expected in health care because of advances in robot-assisted surgery and robot assistance for the elderly and disabled. These changes in the technological and economic landscape are also seen as an opportunity to redesign regulatory and liability rules. For

Alberto Galasso is associate professor of strategic management at the University of Toronto and a research associate of the National Bureau of Economic Research. Hong Luo is the James Dinan and Elizabeth Miller Associate Professor of Business Administration at Harvard Business School.

For acknowledgments, sources of research support, and disclosure of the authors' material financial relationships, if any, please see http://www.nber.org/chapters/c14035.ack.

1. https://ca.reuters.com/article/businessNews/idCAKBN19E25A-OCABS and Del Rossi and Viscusi (2010) document one hundred cases with punitive damages awards of at least $100 million as of the end of 2008.

example, in February 2017 the European Parliament adopted—by a large majority—a resolution containing recommendations for EU-wide legislation to regulate "sophisticated robots, bots, androids and other manifestations of artificial intelligence" and to establish legislative instruments related to the liability for their actions (European Parliament 2017). An effective design and implementation of these policy changes require an understanding of how liability risk affects firms' strategies and shapes future technological progress.

In an influential book, Porter (1990) concludes that "product liability is so extreme and uncertain as to retard innovation," and he recommends a systematic overhaul of the US product liability system. A number of legal scholars share this view and warn about a potential "chilling effect" on innovation; that is, high damages awards may reduce firms' willingness to develop new and riskier technologies, even if they are potentially superior to customary products (e.g., Huber 1989; Parchomovsky and Stein 2008). This idea that excessive liability may retard innovation also shaped high-profile legal cases such as the 2008 *Riegel v. Medtronic* Supreme Court decision and is a key argument for tort reforms currently discussed in the US Congress.

Despite the fundamental relevance of this issue, empirical work on the relationship between liability and innovation is scarce. Huber and Litan (1991) brought together a broad set of experts on five sectors of the economy where the liability system would have had the largest impacts. Based mostly on surveys and historical case studies, the authors were far from reaching a consensus. What were commonly agreed upon, however, were the dearth of data and systematic evidence, and a call for future research.

This chapter reviews the handful of empirical studies on the links between liability and innovation using a large sample of data. It aims to provide some insights into the potential impacts that liability laws and likely changes in the system may have on the rate and direction of innovation in robots and artificial intelligence, and to identify areas and questions for future research.[2]

20.2   Liability and Innovation: An Illustrative Theoretical Model

This section presents a simple, stylized model that explores the effects of liability risk on innovation incentives. Technologies are characterized by multidimensional heterogeneity. Specifically, a technology, i, is characterized by two parameters: $b_i \in [0,1]$ and $r_i \in [0,1]$; b_i is the expected profit from incorporating technology i into the firm's product, and r_i is the probability

---

2. It is important to note that this chapter focuses solely on the likely impacts on innovation and the direction of technological change. We refer interested readers to Hay and Spier (2005) and Polinsky and Shavell (2010) for an overall welfare discussion of the liability system and its features, and to Marchant and Lindor (2012) and Hubbard (2015) and the references within for details of tort law and an exploration of their applications to autonomous vehicles and sophisticated robots.

that the use of the product will result in personal injuries. The expected liability cost given that injury happens is H, which captures the (conditional) probability that a liability suit will be filed and the expected cost that the firm will face if involved in such a suit. We expect H to be positive even if the firm is fully insured against claims for monetary damages because liability suits also invariably result in opportunity costs of employee time and firm resources, as well as in reputational damage.

The firm's expected profit, net of liability risk from selling a product incorporating technology i, is

$$\Pi_i = b_i - r_i H.$$

We denote the technology that the firm currently uses as O and consider the firm's decision to develop a new technology, which we denote as N. We assume a simple R&D process such that successful development takes place with probability $p(x) = x$ if the innovator incurs a research cost $C(x) = x^2/2$. As in Aghion et al. (2016), we refer to x as the "innovation intensity," which captures the likelihood of successfully developing a new technology. In this setting, the problem for the innovating firm is

$$\max_x x\Pi_N + (1-x)\Pi_O - \frac{x^2}{2}$$

which yields the following:

(1) $$x^* = \Pi_N - \Pi_O = b_N - b_O + (r_O - r_N)H.$$

Formula (1) provides some basic insights into the relationship between liability and innovation. First, at the intensive margin, the sign of the derivative of x^* with respect to H captures the directional effect of an increase in liability risk on innovation intensity. Thus, an increase in liability risk suppresses innovation incentives for new technologies that are riskier than the current technology ($r_N > r_O$) but encourages new technologies that are safer ($r_N < r_O$). In other words, changes in liability risk affect the type of technologies in which a firm invests and influence the direction of innovation. Second, investment in innovation takes place if the profit potential of the new technology is greater than its liability risk, relative to the old technology—that is, $x^* > 0$ only if $b_N - b_O > (r_N - r_O)H$. Thus, at the extensive margin, marginal changes in liability risk will not affect whether the firm develops the new technology if it is expected to be highly profitable relative to the existing one (i.e., $b_N - b_O$ is very large) unless it is extremely risky. In contrast, liability concerns will matter more for technologies "at the margin" (i.e., the improvement in expected profitability is modest).

Galasso and Luo (2017) extend this stylized model to the medical setting, in which physicians (i.e., the direct users of technologies) face malpractice liability risk. Changes in their liability exposure affect innovation incentives in medical technologies through the demand channel. Assuming that ideas for new technologies (b_N, r_N) are random draws from a bivariate distribution (as in Scotchmer 1999), they show that the overall effect of tort reforms that reduce physicians' liability risk on innovation incentives is ambiguous and depends on the characteristics of the existing technology $(b_N - r_O)$.

The main message of this illustrative model is that the link between liability and innovation is more complex and nuanced than the simple view of "liability chills innovation," which ignores the potential encouraging effect of liability risk on a potentially broad set of innovations that help firms and their customers manage risk.

20.3   Empirical Evidence on Liability and Innovation

In a pioneering study, Viscusi and Moore (1993) examine the relationship between product-liability insurance costs and firms' research and development (R&D) investments, using a data set covering large US manufacturing firms in multiple industries between 1980 and 1984. They document a significant positive correlation between the expected liability insurance costs and firms' R&D intensity when such costs are low or moderate. Only when liability costs are very high the correlation is negative. Furthermore, the liability-innovation link is driven mainly by product rather than by process R&D. They interpret these results as evidence that, on average, product liability, rather than discouraging innovation, promotes firm investment in product safety (likely through product design).

Galasso and Luo (2017) examine whether tort reforms that reduce physicians' liability exposure to medical malpractice litigation affect incentives to develop new medical technologies. Different from the focus on product liability in Viscusi and Moore (2017), they examine how liability costs that users (physicians) face affect upstream research investment. It is worth noting that such a perspective broadens the scope of innovation from product safety design to include a wide variety of complementary technologies that help physicians manage risk, such as monitoring and diagnostic devices and devices used in complex procedures to reduce the likelihood of adverse events. Because these technologies are not themselves subject to product liability claims, they are more likely to be influenced by changes in user liability through the demand channel than by product liability.

Using a panel data set for the period of 1985–2005, Galasso and Luo (2017) find that, on average, the introduction of noneconomic damage caps in a state is associated with a 15 percent reduction in medical device patenting. The effect is, however, highly heterogeneous: tort reforms have the largest negative impact in medical fields in which the probability of a malpractice claim is the highest, and they do not seem to affect patenting of the highest or the lowest quality. These results are consistent with the idea that the decline in innovation is driven primarily by the reduced demand from physicians for safer technologies or complementary technologies that help them manage risk. The welfare loss from such a large decline in quantity, however, appears not as worrying because patents with the highest impacts are not negatively affected.

Galasso and Luo (2018) study the medical implant industry in the early 1990s, during which the liability risk faced by raw material suppliers significantly increased relative to the risk faced by downstream producers. Vitek was a leading producer of jaw (temporomandibular joint) implants in the 1980s. Its Food and Drug Administration (FDA)-approved products were considered state of the art and safe for use by oral surgeons across the United States (Schmucki 1999). In the late 1980s, unexpected and widespread problems arose with Vitek's products. Vitek filed for bankruptcy in 1990 under a deluge of lawsuits. Following Vitek's bankruptcy, implant patients started to file a large number of lawsuits against DuPont, a raw material supplier for Vitek's implants and a large firm with "deep pockets."[3]

The consensus among industry observers is that these events generated a substantial increase in the perceived liability risk faced by firms that supplied materials to producers of permanent implants, many of which had withdrawn from this market. This view is well summarized in a 1994 report on the status of the biomaterial market (Aronoff 1995), which links this fear of product liability suits to the jaw implant litigation. Eventually, DuPont won all the lawsuits, but the process took ten years and cost over $40 million (House of Representatives 1997). In contrast, DuPont's revenue from these implants totaled only a few thousand dollars.

Galasso and Luo (2018) compare the rate of patenting in implant devices—excluding technologies involved in these litigations—to patenting in a control group of nonimplant medical technologies whose suppliers were not affected by the heightened litigation risk. The difference-in-differences (DID) results show, overall, a substantial decrease in the number of new patents for implants in the five years after Vitek's bankruptcy in 1990. Time-specific effects show that implant and nonimplant technologies exhibited parallel increasing trends before 1990, and that the negative effect on implant technologies was immediate after 1990 and increased in magnitude over time. The significant drop in innovation in medical implants appears to have been largely driven by device producers' expectation of a supply shortage of material inputs.

To address this problem, in 1998 the US Congress passed the Biomaterial Access Assurance Act (BAAA), which exempts biomaterial suppliers for medical implants from liabilities as long as they do not engage in the design,

---

3. In parallel, problems also surfaced with silicone breast implants. Also in this case, a leading implant manufacturer filed for bankruptcy, and silicone suppliers were named as defendants in numerous lawsuits (Feder 1994).

production, testing, and distribution of the implants. The BAAA is one of the few federal liability reforms, an area of legislation typically reserved for the states (Kerouac 2001).[4]

Together, the empirical evidence in Viscusi and Moore (1993) and Galasso and Luo (2017, 2018) challenges the simple view that "liability chills innovation." All three papers suggest that the link between liability and innovation depends on the context, including the nature of the innovation, the level of the liability risk, and the value of the technology. Furthermore, liability risk affecting one area may impact innovation incentives in other, vertically related segments. More research is needed to understand the complex and nuanced links between liability and innovation, and whether targeted policies can address these issues.

20.4   Tort Liability and the Development of AI Technologies

The liability system may affect innovation incentives of AI technologies and sophisticated robots in multiple ways, and the development of these technologies may, in turn, demand adjustments to the law. Below, we focus on a number of areas and highlight some of the economic trade-offs that deserve further examination, both theoretically and empirically.[5]

20.4.1   Allocation of Liability Risk between Producers and Consumers

A central question in designing a liability system for AI technologies is how liability risk should be allocated between producers and consumers, and how this allocation might affect innovation. Effective policies would require a basic understanding of the relationship between humans and AI technologies—for example, whether they are substitutes or complements (Agrawal, Gans, and Goldfarb, chapter 3, this volume).

A key promise of AI technologies is to achieve autonomy. With less room for consumers to take precautions, the relative liability burden is likely to shift toward producers, especially in situations in which producers are in a better position than individual users to control risk. For example, the operator of a fleet of self-driving cars would have the data and predictive capability to provide instantaneous warnings of an adverse event. The cost

---

4. Examples of such federal policies include the General Aviation Revitalization Act of 1994, which exempts makers of small aircraft from liability for planes after eighteen years, and the National Childhood Vaccine Injury Act of 1986, which limits liability for drug companies and creates a no-fault compensation system for those injured by vaccines.

5. It is important to note that the likely impacts on innovation incentives would also depend on firms' ability to write contracts and the development of the insurance markets (Schwartz 1988). We leave the discussion of these important topics and the interplay between liability law and contract law for future work. In situations in which externality (harm to third parties) is high and in the early stage of AI technologies, during which the insurance market may not be well developed or even exist, the roles of these systems are likely to be more limited than for mature technologies.

of observing systematic, hazardous user behaviors may also become sufficiently low such that it would be more efficient for producers to take precautions through product redesign. How such a shift might affect innovation incentives would depend on how producer liability is specified, especially whether the long-term social benefits are included in the analysis of the producer's liability.

On the other hand, during the transitional period of an AI technology, substantial human supervision may still be required. Such interaction between AI and humans may not be obvious and difficult to predict. For example, it may actually be more difficult for drivers to sustain a safe degree of concentration levels and reaction speed when they are not actively engaged in driving.[6] Human-machine interactions may also become more extensive and span increasingly complex domains as technologies are developed to enhance human skills. In the case of robot-assisted surgeries, for example, physicians may not have enough incentive to obtain sufficient training or to be sufficiently prepared for back-up options if the machine were to malfunction.

In many of these situations, it may be impractical or too costly for producers to monitor individual users and to intervene. Therefore, it would be important to maintain consumer liability to the extent that users of AI technologies have sufficient incentives to take precautions and invest in training, thus internalizing potential harm to others. When negative externalities are sufficiently high, regulators may find it necessary to mandate such investment. For example, a special driver's license may be required to operate a self-driving car. Similarly, doctors may be required to take a minimum number of training sessions with the robotic system before being allowed to perform certain types of procedures on patients.[7]

Consumer liability may incentivize users themselves to innovate in ways that help them take more effective precautions (Von Hippel 2005). For example, hospitals may redesign the operating room process or reorganize physicians' training and work schedules. Furthermore, consumer liability may also incentivize producer innovation because users would demand safer and easier-to-use design features (Hay and Spier 2005), and mandatory training would favor "easier to teach" designs in order to reduce adoption costs.

20.4.2   Federal Regulation

Another key issue is whether Congress should pass federal regulations on the safety of AI and robotic technologies that preempts state laws and how such regulation would affect innovation. This would involve the creation of

---

6. The National Transportation Safety Board determined that the 2016 fatal Tesla crash was partly due to the driver's inattention and overreliance on vehicle automation despite manufacturer safety warnings.

7. Some expert robotic surgeons and many surgical societies have voiced the need for basic, standardized training and certification in robotic surgery skills (O'Reilly 2014).

a centralized regulatory system similar to the FDA for drugs and high-risk medical devices: federal regulatory bodies would specify the safety standards, and approved products would be exempted from state liability claims under certain conditions.[8] For autonomous vehicles, the House passed a version of such a regulation with bipartisan support in September 2017 (the SELF DRIVE Act, H.R. 3388).

From the perspective of innovation, a centralized AI regulatory system presents a number of trade-offs. On the one hand, relative to tort laws that examine liability cases ex post through judges and juries, ex ante regulations and safety preemption would significantly reduce the degree of uncertainty regarding liability risk.[9] Reduction in uncertainty, in general, increases R&D and other complementary investment. Furthermore, harmonizing different, slow-moving state-wide regulations could also speed up experimentation and adoption. In the case of autonomous vehicles, as of September 2017, some testing was explicitly allowed in less than half of the states with different degrees of restriction and safety standards.

On the other hand, federal regulation could trade off certainty with flexibility. With the fast-changing landscape of AI technologies, federal agencies may not have sufficient information in the early development stage to set effective standards.[10] If such regulations were hard to change, they could influence the rate and direction of innovation in undesirable ways.

20.4.3   Allocation of Liability Risk across the Vertical Chain

Artificial intelligence and sophisticated robotics are often complex technologies that involve multiple suppliers of software and hardware and that may require high degrees of integration between different components. Furthermore, AI technologies, like other general purpose technologies (such as polymers), once developed for the first few areas, may later be developed for a wide variety of applications at a lower cost.

Current laws, such as component parts and sophisticated purchaser doctrines, stipulate that component suppliers are not liable unless the component per se is defective or the process of integrating the component has caused the adverse effect (Hubbard 2015). In practice, however, these laws may be inadequate in certain circumstances and may expose component

---

8. Federal preemption of state laws may be explicit or implicit, with the former providing significantly greater clarity. In the case of FDA preemption in *Riegel v. Medtronic, Inc.* (2008), the US Supreme Court ruled that manufacturers of FDA-approved devices that went through the pre-market approval process are protected from liability claims under state laws. In *Wyeth v. Levine* (2009), however, the US Supreme Court ruled that Vermont tort law was not preempted.

9. Kaplow (1992) provides a general economic analysis of rules versus standards; that is, whether laws should be given content ex ante or ex post. The basic trade-offs depend on factors including the frequency and the degree of heterogeneity of adverse events, as well as the relative costs of individuals in learning and applying the law.

10. For example, for autonomous vehicles state regulators currently differ in their opinions about whether cars without steering wheels or brake pedals should be allowed on public roads for testing and operation purposes.

suppliers to disproportionately high liability risk relative to their expected revenue. Evidence from Galasso and Luo (2018) suggests that in such situations, downstream innovation may suffer. It would be interesting for future research to examine how liability costs should be allocated across component producers and its impacts on innovation, and under what conditions policymakers should consider applying exemption regulations, such as the BAAA enacted in the medical implants industry.

It would also be interesting to examine how liability rules, apart from their direct impacts on innovation, influence firm boundaries, which, in turn, could affect innovation. For example, rules such as the BAAA may discourage vertical integration because its exemption applies only to component material suppliers sufficiently removed from downstream activities. Similarly, liability rules may also influence how products and services are designed. For example, they may encourage more modular designs to better insulate liability risk across different components.

20.4.4   Liability Risk and Market Structure

Relatedly, it would be interesting to better understand the interplay between liability risk and industry market structure and whether changes in market structure driven by liability risk have long-term consequences for innovation (Agrawal et al. 2014).

How liability risk affects firms of different sizes is likely to depend on the empirical context. Plaintiffs may be more likely to target larger and cash-rich firms (Cohen, Gurun, and Kominers [2014] find this pattern in patent litigation cases). At the same time, larger firms are better at withstanding high liability risk because they have greater resources both to self-insure and to provide more generous indemnification contracts to suppliers.

One may argue that liability insurance could insulate producers from potential liability concerns. However, in the early stages of AI technologies the market for liability insurance may not be fully developed, or even exist, due to insufficient data on adverse events of a particular nature and their damages. Even with well-developed insurance markets, high liability risk may result in high premiums, which can be prohibitively expensive for smaller firms and, thus, deter entry.

20.4.5   Liability Litigation

An important feature of an effective liability system is that disputes are resolved quickly. Longer settlement delays are typically associated with higher transaction costs for the negotiating parties. More importantly, delays and uncertainty in the process mean slower diffusion of the AI technology at the center of the dispute.

It is not obvious whether liability suits related to AI technologies will be easier to settle than those involving other technologies. In particular, the complexity of these new technologies and certain types of human-machine interactions may reduce the litigants' ability to find a compromise. That said, classic models of pretrial negotiations predict a higher likelihood of settlement when information asymmetries between litigating parties are reduced (Spier 2007). Manufacturers of AI technologies may find it in their own interest to design the machine's data-recording capability in ways that facilitate the discovery process and speed up settlement. In cases where manufacturers lack such incentives, mandates of certain designs may be necessary if they are clearly efficiency enhancing. Once again, how effective these data capabilities of AI technologies are in facilitating dispute resolution would also depend on the ability of the court system to understand and interpret data, on private incentives for data sharing, and on whether policies are in place to discourage misrepresentation and manipulation of data.

20.4.6   Liability Risk and Intellectual Property Protection

The likely impacts of liability risk on innovation would also depend on the strength of intellectual property (IP) rights. Intuitively, when IP rights are strong, firms can invest in safer products and recover their investments by charging a price premium. However, if competitors can easily copy and sell these products or features, the incentive to innovate in the first place would decrease. The above considerations may be different, however, if consumers cannot easily distinguish between safer and less safe products, and their fears about dangerous products suppress their demand for the entire product category. For example, Jarrell and Pelzman (1985) show that one firm's product recalls may have negative reputational impacts on competitors and producers of related products. When such negative spillover is strong, firms with other means of extracting rents (e.g., larger firms) may have the incentive to invest in safety features and share them with firms in the industry so as to maintain consumer demand for the whole industry.

Finally, in a cumulative innovation environment, as Green and Scotchmer (1995) have shown, the allocation of IP rights among sequential innovators may have important effects on their respective innovation incentives. Related trade-offs are likely to also emerge for the allocation of liability damages among sequential innovators.

20.5   Conclusion

This chapter has examined some of the basic economic trade-offs linking liability risk with innovation incentives and the direction of technological progress in the context of artificial intelligence and sophisticated robots. Features of the liability system, such as the allocation of risk between producers and consumers and the level of centralization in regulation, may have a significant impact on the development and diffusion of these new technologies, as well as on the products and services that apply them. The extent of these effects is likely to also depend on the market structure and the organization of the vertical chain of innovation.

More broadly, our analysis supports the idea that the liability system and its reforms can affect the rate and the direction of technological change, indicating that these policies have dynamic effects on innovation incentives that go beyond their short-term impact on the safety of the users and others. As Finkelstein (2004) stresses, recognizing and estimating these dynamic effects is crucial to evaluating the costs and benefits of policy reforms.

References

Aghion, P., A. Dechezleprêtre, D. Hemous, R. Martin, and J. Van Reenen. 2016. "Carbon Taxes, Path Dependency, and Directed Technical Change: Evidence from the Auto Industry." *Journal of Political Economy* 124:1–51.

Agrawal, A., I. Cockburn, A. Galasso, and A. Oettl. 2014. "Why Are Some Regions More Innovative Than Others? The Role of Small Firms in the Presence of Large Labs." *Journal of Urban Economics* 81:149–65.

Aronoff, M. 1995. "Market Study: Biomaterials Supply for Permanent Medical Implants." *Journal of Biomaterials Applications* 9:205–60.

Cohen, L., U. Gurun, and S. D. Kominers. 2014. "Patent Trolls: Evidence from Targeted Firms." NBER Working Paper no. 20322, Cambridge, MA.

Del Rossi, A., and K. Viscusi. 2010. "The Changing Landscape of Blockbuster Punitive Damages Awards." *American Law and Economics Review* 12:116–61.

European Parliament. 2017. Civil Law Rules on Robotics 2015/2103(INL)—16/02/2017.

Feder, Barnaby. 1994. "Implant Industry Is Facing Cutback by Top Suppliers." *New York Times*, Apr. 25. https://www.nytimes.com/1994/04/25/us/implant-industry-is-facing-cutback-by-top-suppliers.html.

Finkelstein, A. 2004. "Static and Dynamic Effects of Health Policy: Evidence from the Vaccine Industry." *Quarterly Journal of Economics* 119:527–64.

Galasso, A., and H. Luo. 2017. "Tort Reform and Innovation." *Journal of Law and Economics* 60:385–412.

———. 2018. "How Does Product Liability Risk Affect Innovation? Evidence from Medical Implants." Working paper, Harvard Business School.

Green, J., and S. Scotchmer. 1995. "On the Division of Profit in Sequential Innovation." *RAND Journal of Economics* 26:20–33.

Hay, B. and K. Spier. 2005. "Manufacturer Liability for Harms Caused by Consumers to Others." *American Economic Review* 95:1700–11.

House of Representatives. 1997. Subcommittee on Commercial And Administrative Law.

Hubbard, F. 2015. "Allocating the Risk of Physical Injury from 'Sophisticated Robots': Efficiency, Fairness, and Innovation." In *Robot Law*, edited by R. Calo, A. Froomkin, and I. Kerr. Cheltenham, UK: Edward Elgar Publishing.

Huber, P. 1989. *Liability: The Legal Revolution and Its Consequences*. New York: Basic Books.

Huber, P., and R. Litan, eds. 1991. *The Liability Maze: The Impact of Liability Law on Safety and Innovation*. Washington, DC: Brookings Institution.

Jarrell, G., and S. Peltzman. 1985. "The Impact of Product Recalls on the Wealth of Sellers." *Journal of Political Economy* 93:512–36.

Kaplow, L. 1992. "Rules versus Standards: An Economic Analysis." *Duke Law Journal* 42:557–629.

Kerouac, J. 2001. "A Critical Analysis of the Biomaterials Access Assurance Act of 1998 as Federal Tort Reform Policy." *Boston University Journal of Science and Technology Law* 7:327–45.

Marchant, G., and R. Lindor. 2012. "The Coming Collision between Autonomous Vehicles and the Liability System." *Santa Clara Law Review* 52:1321–40.

O'Reilly, B. 2014. "Patents Running Out: Time to Take Stock of Robotic Surgery." *International Urogynecology Journal* 25:711–13.

Parchomovsky, G., and A. Stein. 2008. "Torts and Innovation." *Michigan Law Review* 107:285–315.

Polinsky, M., and S. Shavell. 2010. "The Uneasy Case for Product Liability." *Harvard Law Review* 123:1437–92.

Porter, M. 1990. *The Competitive Advantage of Nations.* New York: Free Press.

Schwartz, A. 1988. "Products Liability Reform: A Theoretical Synthesis." *Yale Law Journal* 97:353–419.

Schmucki, R. 1999. "Final Status Report on History of TMJ Litigation." DuPont, unpublished communication.

Scotchmer, S. 1999. "On the Optimality of the Patent Renewal System." *RAND Journal of Economics* 30:181–96.

Spier, K. 2007. "Litigation." In *Handbook of Law and Economics*, edited by A. M. Polinsky and S. Shavell. Amsterdam: North-Holland.

Viscusi, K., and M. Moore. 1993. "Product Liability, Research and Development, and Innovation." *Journal of Political Economy* 101:161–84.

Von Hippel, E. 2005. *Democratizing Innovation.* Cambridge, MA: MIT Press.

IV

Machine Learning and Economics

21

The Impact of Machine Learning on Economics

Susan Athey

21.1 Introduction

I believe that machine learning (ML) will have a dramatic impact on the field of economics within a short time frame. Indeed, the impact of ML on economics is already well underway, and so it is perhaps not too difficult to predict some of the effects.

The chapter begins by stating the definition of ML that I will use in this chapter, describing its strengths and weaknesses, and contrasting ML with traditional econometrics tools for causal inference, which is a primary focus of the empirical economics literature. Next, I review some applications of ML in economics where ML can be used off the shelf: the use case in economics is essentially the same use case that the ML tools were designed and optimized for. I then review "prediction policy" problems (Kleinberg et al. 2015), where prediction tools have been embedded in the context of economic decision-making. Then, I provide an overview of the questions considered and early themes of the emerging literature in econometrics and statistics combining machine learning and causal inference, a literature that is providing insights and theoretical results that are novel from the perspective of both ML and statistics/econometrics. Finally, I step back and

Susan Athey is the Economics of Technology Professor at Stanford University Graduate School of Business and a research associate of the National Bureau of Economic Research.

I am grateful to David Blei, Guido Imbens, Denis Nekipelov, Francisco Ruiz, and Stefan Wager, with whom I have collaborated on many projects at the intersection of machine learning and econometrics and who have shaped my thinking, as well as to Mike Luca, Sendhil Mullainathan, and Hal Varian, who have also contributed to my thinking through their writing, lecture notes, and many conversations. For acknowledgments, sources of research support, and disclosure of the author's material financial relationships, if any, please see http://www.nber.org/chapters/c14009.ack.

describe the implications of the field of economics as a whole. Throughout, I make reference to the literature broadly, but do not attempt to conduct a comprehensive survey or reference every application in economics.

The chapter highlights several themes.

A first theme is that ML does not add much to questions about identification, which concerns when the object of interest, for example, a causal effect, can be estimated with infinite data, but rather yields great improvements when the goal is semiparametric estimation or when there are a large number of covariates relative to the number of observations. Machine learning has great strengths in using data to select functional forms flexibly.

A second theme is that a key advantage of ML is that ML views empirical analysis as "algorithms" that estimate and compare many alternative models. This approach constrasts with economics, where (in principle, though rarely in reality) the researcher picks a model based on principles and estimates it once. Instead, ML algorithms build in "tuning" as part of the algorithm. The tuning is essentially model selection, and in an ML algorithm that is data driven. There are a whole host of advantages of this approach, including improved performance as well as enabling researchers to be systematic and fully describe the process by which their model was selected. Of course, cross-validation has also been used historically in economics, for example, for selecting the bandwidth for a kernel regression, but it is viewed as a fundamental part of an algorithm in ML.

A third, closely related theme is that "outsourcing" model selection to algorithm works very well when the problem is "simple"—for example, prediction and classification tasks, where performance of a model can be evaluated by looking at goodness of fit in a held-out test set. Those are typically not the problems of greatest interest for empirical researchers in economics, who instead are concerned with causal inference, where there is typically not an unbiased estimate of the ground truth available for comparison. Thus, more work is required to apply an algorithmic approach to economic problems. The recent literature at the intersection of ML and causal inference, reviewed in this chapter, has focused on providing the conceptual framework and specific proposals for algorithms that are tailored for causal inference.

A fourth theme is that the algorithms also have to be modified to provide valid confidence intervals for estimated effects when the data is used to select the model. Many recent papers make use of techniques such as sample splitting, leave-one-out estimation, and other similar techniques to provide confidence intervals that work both in theory and in practice. The upside is that using ML can provide the best of both worlds: the model selection is data driven, systematic, and a wide range of models are considered; yet, the model-selection process is fully documented, and confidence intervals take into account the entire algorithm.

Finally, the combination of ML and newly available data sets will change economics in fairly fundamental ways ranging from new questions, to new approaches, to collaboration (larger teams and interdisciplinary interaction), to a change in how involved economists are in the engineering and implementation of policies.

21.2   What Is Machine Learning and What Are Early Use Cases?

It is harder than one might think to come up with an operational definition of ML. The term can be (and has been) used broadly or narrowly; it can refer to a collections of subfields of computer science, but also to a set of topics that are developed and used across computer science, engineering, statistics, and increasingly the social sciences. Indeed, one could devote an entire article to the definition of ML, or to the question of whether the thing called ML really needed a new name other than statistics, the distinction between ML and AI, and so on. However, I will leave this debate to others and focus on a narrow, practical definition that will make it easier to distinguish ML from the most commonly used econometric approaches used in applied econometrics until very recently.[1] For readers coming from a machine-learning background, it is also important to note that applied statistics and econometrics have developed a body of insights on topics ranging from causal inference to efficiency that have not yet been incorporated in mainstream machine learning, while other parts of machine learning have overlap with methods that have been used in applied statistics and social sciences for many decades.

Starting from a relatively narrow definition of machine learning, machine learning is a field that develops algorithms designed to be applied to data sets, with the main areas of focus being prediction (regression), classification, and clustering or grouping tasks. These tasks are divided into two main branches, supervised and unsupervised ML. Unsupervised ML involves finding clusters of observations that are similar in terms of their covariates, and thus can be interpreted as "dimensionality reduction"; it is commonly used for video, images, and text. There are a variety of techniques available for unsupervised learning, including k-means clustering, topic modeling, community detection methods for networks, and many more. For example, the Latent Dirichlet Allocation model (Blei, Ng, and Jordan 2003) has frequently been applied to find "topics" in textual data. The output of a typical unsupervised ML model is a partition of the set of observations, where observations within each element of the partition are similar according to some metric, or, a vector of probabilities or weights that describe a mixture of topics or groups that an observation might belong to. If you read in the

---

1. I will also focus on the most popular parts of ML; like many fields, it is possible to find researchers who define themselves as members of the field of ML doing a variety of different things, including pushing the boundaries of ML with tools from other disciplines. In this chapter I will consider such work to be interdisciplinary rather than "pure" ML, and will discuss it as such.

newspaper that a computer scientist "discovered cats on YouTube," that might mean that they used an unsupervised ML method to partition a set of videos into groups, and when a human watches the the largest group, they observe that most of the videos in the largest group contain cats. This is referred to as "unsupervised" because there were no "labels" on any of the images in the input data; only after examining the items in each group does an observer determine that the algorithm found cats or dogs. Not all dimensionality reduction methods involve creating clusters; older methods such as principal components analysis can be used to reduce dimensionality, while modern methods include matrix factorization (finding two low-dimensional matrices whose product well approximates a larger matrix), regularization on the norm of a matrix, hierarchical Poisson factorization (in a Bayesian framework) (Gopalan, Hofman, and Blei 2015), and neural networks.

In my view, these tools are very useful as an intermediate step in empirical work in economics. They provide a data-driven way to find similar newspaper articles, restaurant reviews, and so forth, and thus create variables that can be used in economic analyses. These variables might be part of the construction of either outcome variables or explanatory variables, depending on the context. For example, if an analyst wishes to estimate a model of consumer demand for different items, it is common to model consumer preferences over characteristics of the items. Many items are associated with text descriptions as well as online reviews. Unsupervised learning could be used to discover items with similar product descriptions in an initial phase of finding potentially related products, and it could also be used to find subgroups of similar products. Unsupervised learning could further be used to categorize the reviews into types. An indicator for the review group could be used in subsequent analysis without the analyst having to use human judgement about the review content; the data would reveal whether a certain type of review was associated with higher consumer perceived quality, or not. An advantage of using unsupervised learning to create covariates is that the outcome data is not used at all; thus, concerns about spurious correlation between constructed covariates and the observed outcome are less problematic. Despite this, Egami et al. (2016) have argued that researchers may be tempted to fine-tune their construction of covariates by testing how they perform in terms of predicting outcomes, thus leading to spurious relationships between covariates and outcomes. They recommend the approach of sample splitting, whereby the model tuning takes place on one sample of data, and then the selected model is applied on a fresh sample of data.

Unsupervised learning can also be used to create outcome variables. For example, Athey, Mobius, and Pál (2017) examine the impact of Google's shutdown of Google News in Spain on the types of news consumers read. In this case, the share of news in different categories is an outcome of interest. Unsupervised learning can be used to categorize news in this type of analysis; that paper uses community detection techniques from network theory. In the absence of dimensionality reduction, it would be difficult to meaningfully summarize the impact of the shutdown on all of the different news articles consumed in the relevant time frame.

Supervised machine learning typically entails using a set of features or covariates (X) to *predict* an outcome (Y). When using the term prediction, it is important to emphasize that the framework focuses not on forecasting, but rather on a setting where there are some labeled observations where both X and Y are observed (the training data), and the goal is to predict outcomes (Y) in an independent test set based on the realized values of X for each unit in the test set. In other words, the goal is to construct $\hat{\mu}(x)$, which is an estimator of $\mu(x) = E[Y|X = x]$, in order to do a good job predicting the true values of Y in an independent data set. The observations are assumed to be independent, and the joint distribution of X and Y in the training set is the same as that in the test set. These assumptions are the only substantive assumptions required for most machine-learning methods to work.

In the case of classification, the goal is to accurately classify observations. For example, the outcome could be the animal depicted in an image, the "features" or covariates are the pixels in the image, and the goal is to correctly classify images into the correct animal depicted. A related but distinct estimation problem is to estimate $Pr(Y = k|X = x)$ for each of $k = 1, \ldots, K$ possible realizations of Y.

It is important to emphasize that the ML literature does not frame itself as solving estimation problems—so estimating $\mu(x)$ or $Pr(Y = k|X = x)$ is not the primary goal. Instead, the goal is to achieve goodness of fit in an independent test set by minimizing deviations between actual outcomes and predicted outcomes. In applied econometrics, we often wish to understand an object like $\mu(x)$ in order to perform exercises like evaluating the impact of changing one covariate while holding others constant. This is not an explicit aim of ML modeling.

There are a variety of ML methods for supervised learning, such as regularized regression (LASSO, ridge and elastic net), random forest, regression trees, support vector machines, neural nets, matrix factorization, and many others, such as model averaging. See Varian (2014) for an overview of some of the most popular methods and Mullainathan and Spiess (2017) for more details. (Also note that White [1992] attempted to popularize neural nets in economics in the early 1990s, but at the time they did not lead to substantial performance improvements and did not become popular in economics.) What leads us to categorize these methods as ML methods rather than traditional econometric or statistical methods? First is simply an observation: until recently, these methods were neither used in published social science research, nor taught in social science courses, while they were widely studied in the self-described ML and/or "statistical learning" literatures. One exception is ridge regression, which received some attention in economics, and LASSO had also received some attention. But from a more functional perspective, one common feature of many ML methods is that they use data-driven model selection. That is, the analyst provides the list of covariates or features, but the functional form is at least in part determined as a function of the data, and rather than performing a single estimation (as is done, at least in theory, in econometrics), so that the method is better described as an algorithm that might estimate many alternative models and then select among them to maximize a criterion.

There is typically a trade-off between expressiveness of the model (e.g., more covariates included in a linear regression) and risk of overfitting, which occurs when the model is too rich relative to the sample size. (See Mullainathan and Spiess [2017] for more discussion of this.) In the latter case, the goodness of fit of the model when measured on the sample where the model is estimated is expected to be much better than the goodness of fit of the model when evaluated on an independent test set. The ML literature uses a variety of techniques to balance expressiveness against overfitting. The most common approach is cross-validation whereby the analyst repeatedly estimates a model on part of the data (a "training fold") and then evaluates it on the complement (the "test fold"). The complexity of the model is selected to minimize the average of the mean-squared error of the prediction (the squared difference between the model prediction and the actual outcome) on the test folds. Other approaches used to control overfitting include averaging many different models, sometimes estimating each model on a subsample of the data (one can interpret the random forest in this way).

In contrast, in much of cross-sectional econometrics and empirical work in economics, the tradition has been that the researcher specifies one model, estimates the model on the full data set, and relies on statistical theory to estimate confidence intervals for estimated parameters. The focus is on the estimated effects rather than the goodness of fit of the model. For much empirical work in economics, the primary interest is in the estimate of a causal effect, such as the effect of a training program, a minimum wage increase, or a price increase. The researcher might check robustness of this parameter estimate by reporting two or three alternative specifications. Researchers often check dozens or even hundreds of alternative specifications behind the scenes, but rarely report this practice because it would invalidate the confidence intervals reported (due to concerns about multiple testing and searching for specifications with the desired results). There are many disadvantages to the traditional approach, including but not limited to the fact that researchers would find it difficult to be systematic or comprehensive in checking alternative specifications, and further because researchers were not honest about the practice, given that they did not have a way to correct for the specification search process. I believe that regularization and systematic model selection have many advantages over traditional approaches, and for this reason will become a standard part of empirical practice in economics. This will particularly be true as we more frequently encounter data sets with many covariates, and also as we see the advantages of being systematic about model selection. As I discuss later, however, this practice must be modified from traditional ML and in general "handled with care" when the researcher's ultimate goal is to estimate a causal effect rather than maximize goodness of fit in a test set.

To build some intuition about the difference between causal effect estimation and prediction, it can be useful to consider the widely used method of instrumental variables. Instrumental variables are used by economists when they wish to learn a causal effect, for example, the effect of a price on a firm's sales, but they only have access to observational (nonexperimental) data. An instrument in this case might be an input cost for the firm that shifts over time, and is unrelated to factors that shift consumer's demand for the product (such demand shifters can be referred to as "confounders" because they affect both the optimal price set by the firm and the sales of the product). The instrumental variables method essentially projects the observed prices onto the input costs, thus only making use of the variation in price that is explained by changes in input costs when estimating the impact of price on sales. It is very common to see that a predictive model (e.g., least squares regression) might have very high explanatory power (e.g., high R^2), while the causal model (e.g., instrumental variables regression) might have very low explanatory power (in terms of predicting outcomes). In other words, economists typically abandon the goal of accurate prediction of outcomes in pursuit of an unbiased estimate of a causal parameter of interest.

Another difference derives from the key concerns in different approaches, and how those concerns are addressed. In predictive models, the key concern is the trade-off between expressiveness and overfitting, and this trade-off can be evaluated by looking at goodness of fit in an independent test set. In contrast, there are several distinct concerns for causal models. The first is whether the parameter estimates from a particular sample are spurious, that is, whether estimates arise due to sampling variation so that if a new random sample of the same size was drawn from the population, the parameter estimate would be substantially different. The typical approach to this problem in econometrics and statistics is to prove theorems about the consistency and asymptotic normality of the parameter estimates, propose approaches to estimating the variance of parameter estimates, and finally to use those results to estimate standard errors that reflect the sampling uncertainty (under the conditions of the theory). A more data-driven approach is to use bootstrapping and estimate the empirical distribution of parameter estimates across bootstrap samples. The typical ML approach of evaluating performance in a test set does not directly handle the issue of the uncertainty over parameter estimates, since the parameter of interest is not actually observed in any test set. The researcher would need to estimate the parameter again in the test set.

A second concern is whether the assumptions required to "identify" a causal effect are satisfied, where in econometrics we say that a parameter is identified if we can learn it eventually with infinite data (where even in the limit, the data has the same structure as in the sample considered). It is well known that the causal effect of a treatment is not identified without making assumptions, assumptions that are generally not testable (that is, they cannot be rejected by looking at the data). Examples of identifying assumptions include the assumption that the treatment is randomly assigned, or that treatment assignment is "unconfounded." In some settings, these assumptions require the analyst to observe all potential "confounders" and control for them adequately; in other settings, the assumptions require that an instrumental variable is uncorrelated with the unobserved component of outcomes. In many cases it can be proven that even with a data set of infinite size, the assumptions are not testable—they cannot be rejected by looking at the data, and instead must be evaluated on substantive grounds. Justifying assumptions is one of the primary components of an observational study in applied economics. If the "identifying" assumptions are violated, estimates may be biased (in the same way) in both training data and test data. Testing assumptions usually requires additional information, like multiple experiments (designed or natural) in the data. Thus, the ML approach of evaluating performance in a test set does not address this concern at all. Instead, ML is likely to help make estimation methods more credible, while maintaining the identifying assumptions: in practice, coming up with estimation methods that give unbiased estimates of treatment effects requires flexibly modeling a variety of empirical relationships, such as the relationship between the treatment assignment and covariates. Since ML excels at data-driven model selection, it can be useful in systematizing the search for the best functional forms when implementing an estimation technique.

Economists also build more complex models that incorporate both behavioral and statistical assumptions in order to estimate the impact of counterfactual policies that have never been used before. A classic example is McFadden's methodological work in the early 1970s (e.g., McFadden 1973) analyzing transportation choices. By imposing the behavioral assumption that consumers maximize utility when making choices, it is possible to estimate parameters of the consumer's utility function and estimate the welfare effects and market share changes that would occur when a choice is added or removed (e.g., extending the BART transportation system), or when the characteristics of the good (e.g., price) are changed. Another example with more complicated behavioral assumptions is the case of auctions. For a data set with bids from procurement auctions, the "structural" approach involves estimating a probability distribution over bidder values, and then evaluating the counterfactual effect of changing auction design (e.g., Laffont, Ossard, and Vuong 1995; Athey, Levin, and Seira 2011; Athey, Coey, and Levin 2013; or the review by Athey and Haile 2007). For further discussions of the contrast between prediction and parameter estimation, see the recent review by Mullainathan and Spiess (2017). There is a small literature in ML referred to as "inverse reinforcement learning" (Ng and Russell 2000) that has a similar approach to the structural estimation literature economics; this ML literature has mostly operated independently without much reference to the earlier econometric literature. The literature attempts to learn "reward functions" (utility functions) from observed behavior in dynamic settings.

There are also other categories of ML models; for example, anomaly detection focuses on looking for outliers or unusual behavior and is used, for example, to detect network intrusion, fraud, or system failures. Other categories that I will return to are reinforcement learning (roughly, approximate dynamic programming) and multiarmed bandit experimentation (dynamic experimentation where the probabiity of selecting an arm is chosen to balance exploration and exploitation). These literatures often take a more explicitly causal perspective and thus are somewhat easier to relate to economic models, and so my general statements about the lack of focus on causal inference in ML must be qualified when discussing the literature on bandits.

Before proceeding, it is useful to highlight one other contribution of the ML literature. The contribution is computational rather than conceptual, but it has had such a large impact that it merits a short discussion. The technique is called stochastic gradient descent (SGD), and it is used in many different types of models, including the estimation of neural networks as well as large scale Bayesian models (e.g., Ruiz, Athey, and Blei [2017], discussed in more detail below). In short, stochastic gradient descent is a method for optimizing an objective function, such as a likelihood function or a generalized method of moments objective function, with respect to parameters. When the objective function is expensive to compute (e.g., because it requires numerical integration), stochastic gradient descent can be used. The main idea is that if the objective is the sum of terms, each term corresponding to a single observation, the gradient can be approximated by picking a single data point and using the gradient evaluated at that observation as an approximation to the average (over observations) of the gradient. This estimate of the gradient will be very noisy, but unbiased. The idea is that it is more effective to "climb a hill" taking lots of steps in a direction that is noisy but unbiased, than it is to take a small number of steps, each in the right direction, which is what happens if computational resources are focused on getting very precise estimates of the gradient of the objective at each step. Stochastic gradient descent can lead to dramatic performance improvements, and thus enable the estimation of very complex models that would be intractable using traditional approaches.

21.3   Using Prediction Methods in Policy Analysis

21.3.1   Applications of Prediction Methods to Policy Problems in Economics

There have already been a number of successful applications of prediction methodology to policy problems. Kleinberg et al. (2015) have argued that there is a set of problems where off-the-shelf ML methods for prediction are the key part of important policy and decision problems. They use examples like deciding whether to do a hip replacement operation for an elderly patient; if you can predict based on their individual characteristics that they will die within a year, then you should not do the operation. Many Americans are incarcerated while awaiting trial; if you can predict who will show up for court, you can let more out on bail. Machine-learning algorithms are currently in use for this decision in a number of jurisdictions. Another natural example is credit scoring; an economics paper by Bjorkegren and Grissen (2017) uses ML methods to predict loan repayment using mobile phone data.

In other applications, Goel, Rao, and Shroff (2016) use ML methods to examine stop-and-frisk laws, using observables of a police incident to predict the probability that a suspect has a weapon, and they show that blacks are much less likely than whites to have a weapon conditional on observables and being frisked. Glaeser, Hillis, et al. (2016) helped cities design a contest to build a predictive model that predicted health code violations in restaurants in order to better allocate inspector resources. There is a rapidly growing literature using machine learning together with images from satellites and street maps to predict poverty, safety, and home values (see, e.g., Naik et al. 2017). As Glaeser, Kominers, et al. (2015) argue, there are a variety of applications of this type of prediction methodology. It can be used to compare outcomes over time at a very granular level, thus making it possible to assess the impact of a variety of policies and changes, such as neighborhood revitalization. More broadly, the new opportunities created by large-scale imagery and sensors may lead to new types of analyses of productivity and well-being.

Although prediction is often a large part of a resource allocation problem—there is likely to be agreement that people who will almost certainly die soon should not receive hip replacement surgery, and rich people should not receive poverty aid—Athey (2017) discusses the gap between identifying units that are at risk and those for whom intervention is most beneficial. Determining which units should receive a treatment is a causal inference question, and answering it requires different types of data than prediction. Either randomized experiments or natural experiments may be needed to estimate heterogeneous treatment effects and optimal assignment policies. In business applications, it has been common to ignore this distinction and focus on risk identification; for example, as of 2017, the Facebook advertising optimization tool provided to advertisers optimizes for consumer clicks, but not for the causal effect of the advertisement. The distinction is often not emphasized in marketing materials and discussions in the business world, perhaps because many practitioners and engineers are not well versed in the distinction between prediction and causal inference.

21.3.2 Additional Topics in Prediction for Policy Settings

Athey (2017) summarizes a variety of research questions that arise when prediction methods are taken into policy applications. A number of these have attracted initial attention in both ML and the social sciences, and interdisciplinary conferences and workshops have begun to explore these issues.

One set of questions concerns interpretability of models. There are discussions of what interpretability means, and whether simpler models have advantages. Of course, economists have long understood that simple models can also be misleading. In social sciences data, it is typical that many attributes of individuals or locations are positively correlated—parents' education, parents' income, child's education, and so on. If we are interested in a conditional mean function, and estimate $\hat{\mu}(x) = E[Y_i \mid X_i = x]$, using a simpler model that omits a subset of covariates may be misleading. In the simpler model, the relationship between the omitted covariates and outcomes is loaded onto the covariates that are included. Omitting a covariate from a model is not the same thing as controlling for it in an analysis, and it can sometimes be easier to interpret a partial effect of a covariate controlling for other factors than it is to keep in mind all of the other (omitted) factors and how they covary with those included in a model. So, simpler models can sometimes be misleading; they may seem easy to understand, but the understanding gained from them may be incomplete or wrong.

One type of model that typically is easy to interpret and explain is a causal model. As reviewed in Imbens and Rubin (2015), the causal inference framework typically makes the estimand very precise—for example, the average effect if a treatment were applied to a particular population, the conditional average treatment effect (conditional on some observable characteristics of individuals), or the average effect of a treatment on a subpopulation such as "compliers" (those whose treatment adoption is affected by an instrumental variable). Such parameters by definition give the answer to a well-defined question, and so the magnitudes are straightforward to interpret. Key parameters of "structural" models are also straightforward to interpret—they represent parameters of consumer utility functions, elasticities of demand curves, bidder valuations in auctions, marginal costs of firms, and so on. An area for further research concerns whether there are other ways to mathematically formalize what it means for a model to be interpretable, or to analyze empirically the implications of interpretability. Yeomans, Shah, and

Kleinberg (2016) study empirically a related issue of how much people trust ML-based recommender systems, and why.

Another area that has attracted a lot of attention is the question of fairness and nondiscrimination, for example, whether algorithms will promote discrimination by gender or race when used in settings like hiring, judicial decisions, or lending. There are a number of interesting questions that can be considered. One is, how can fairness constraints be defined? What type of fairness is desired? For example, if a predictive model is used to allocate job interviews based on resumes, there are two types of errors, Type I and Type II. It is straightforward to show that it is in general impossible to equalize both Type I and Type II errors across two different categories of people (e.g., men and women), so the analyst must choose which to equalize (or both). See Kleinberg, Mullainathan, and Raghaven (2016) for further analysis and development of the inherent trade-offs in fairness in predictive algorithms. Overall, the literature on this topic has grown rapidly in the last two years, and we expect that as ML algorithms are deployed in more and more contexts, the topic will continue to develop. My view is that it is more likely that ML models will help make resource allocation more rather than less fair; algorithms can absorb and effectively use a lot more information than humans, and thus are less likely than humans to rely on stereotypes. To the extent that unconstrained algorithms do have undesirable distributional consequences, it is possible to constrain the algorithms. Generally, algorithms can be trained to optimize objectives under constraints, and thus it may be easier to impose societal objectives on algorithms than on subjective decisions by humans.

A third issue that arises is stability and robustness, for example, in response to variations in samples or variations in the environment. There are a variety of related ideas in machine learning, including domain adaptation (how do you make a model trained in one environment perform well in another environment), "transfer learning," and others. The basic concern is that ML algorithms do exhaustive searches across a very large number of possible specifications looking for the best model that predicts Y based on X. The models will find subtle relationships bewteen X and Y, some of which might not be stable across time or across environments. For example, for the last few years there may be more videos of cats with pianos than dogs with pianos. The presence of a piano in a video may thus predict cats. However, pianos are not a fundamentnal feature of cats that holds across environments, and so if a fad arises where dogs play pianos, performance of an ML algorithm might suffer. This might not be a problem for a tech firm that reestimates its models with fresh data daily, but predictive models are often used over much longer time periods in industry. For example, credit-scoring models may be held fixed, since changing them makes it hard to assess the risk of the set of consumers who accept credit offers. Scoring models used in medicine might be held fixed over many years. There are many interesting methodological issues involved in finding models that have stable performance and are robust to changing circumstances.

Another issue is that of manipulability. In the application of using mobile data to do credit scoring, a concern is that consumers may be able to manipulate the data observed by the loan provider (Bjorkegren and Grissen 2017). For example, if certain behavioral patterns help a consumer get a loan, the consumer can make it look like they have these behavioral patterns, for example, by visiting certain areas of a city. If resources are allocated to homes that look poor via satellite imagery, homes or villages can possibly modify the aerial appearance of their homes to make them look poorer. An open area for future research concerns how to constrain ML models to make them less prone to manipulability; Athey (2017) discusses some other examples of this.

There are also other considerations that can be brought into ML when it is taken to the field, including computational time, the cost of collecting and maintaining the "features" that are used in a model, and so on. For example, technology firms sometimes make use of simplified models in order to reduce the response time for real-time user requests for information.

Overall, my prediction is that social scientists (and computer scientists at the intersection with social science), particularly economists and other social scientists, will contribute heavily to defining these types of problems and concerns formally, and proposing solutions to them. This will not only provide for better implementations of ML in policy, but will also provide rich fodder for interesting research.

21.4   A New Literature on Machine Learning and Causal Inference

Despite the fascinating examples of "off-the-shelf" or slightly modified prediction methods, in general ML prediction models are solving fundamentally different problems from much empirical work in social science, which instead focuses on causal inference. A prediction I have is that there will be an active and important literature combining ML and causal inference to create new methods, methods that harness the strengths of ML algorithms to solve causal inference problems. In fact, it is easy to make this prediction with confidence because the movement is already well underway. Here I will highlight a few examples, focusing on those that illustrate a range of themes, while emphasizing that this is not a comprehensive survey or a thorough review.

To see the difference between prediction and causal inference, imagine that you have a data set that contains data about prices and occupancy rates of hotels. Prices are easy to obtain through price comparison sites, but occupancy rates are typically not made public by hotels. Imagine first that a hotel chain wishes to form an estimate of the occupancy rates of competitors, based on publicly available prices. This is a prediction problem:

the goal is to get a good estimate of occupancy rates, where posted prices and other factors (such as events in the local area, weather, and so on) are used to predict occupancy. For such a model, you would expect to find that higher posted prices are predictive of higher occupancy rates, since hotels tend to raise their prices as they fill up (using yield management software). In contrast, imagine that a hotel chain wishes to estimate how occupancy would change if the hotel raised prices across the board (that is, if it reprogrammed the yield management software to shift prices up by 5 percent in every state of the world). This is a question of causal inference. Clearly, even though prices and occupancy are positively correlated in a typical data set, we would not conclude that raising prices would increase occupancy. It is well known in the causal inference literature that the question about price increases cannot be answered simply by examining historical data without additional assumptions or structure. For example, if the hotel previously ran randomized experiments on pricing, the data from these experiments can be used to answer the question. More commonly, an analyst will exploit natural experiments or instrumental variables where the latter are variables that are unrelated to factors that affect consumer demand, but that shift firm costs and thus their prices. Most of the classic supervised ML literature has little to say about how to answer this question.

To understand the gap between prediction and causal inference, recall that the foundation of supervised ML methods is that model selection (through, e.g., cross-validation) is carried out to optimize goodness of fit on a test sample. A model is good if and only if it predicts outcomes well in a test set. In contrast, a large body of econometric research builds models that substantially reduce the goodness of fit of a model in order to estimate the causal effect of, say, changing prices. If prices and quantities are positively correlated in the data, any model that estimates the true causal effect (quantity goes down if you change price) will not do as good a job fitting a test data set that has the same joint distribution of prices and quantities as the training data. The place where the econometric model with a causal estimate would do better is at fitting what happens if the firm actually changes prices at a given point in time at doing counterfactual predictions when the world changes. Techniques like instrumental variables seek to use only some of the information that is in the data the clean or exogenous or experiment-like variation in price sacrificing predictive accuracy in the current environment to learn about a more fundamental relationship that will help make decisions about changing price.

However, a new but rapidly growing literature is tackling the problem of using ML methods for causal inference. This new literature takes many of the strengths and innovations of ML methods, but applies them to causal inference. Doing this requires changing the objective function, since the ground truth of the causal parameter is not observed in any test set. Also as a consequence of the fact that the truth is not observed in a test set, statistical theory plays a more important role in evaluating models, since it is more difficult to directly assess how well a parameter estimates the truth, even if the analyst has access to an independent test set. Indeed, this discussion highlights one of the key ways in which prediction is substantially simpler than parameter estimation: for prediction problems, a prediction for a given unit (given its covariates) can be summarized in a single number, the predicted outcome, and the quality of the prediction can be evaluated on a test set without further modeling assumptions. Although the average squared prediction error of a model on a test set is a noisy estimate of the expected value of the mean squared error on a random test set (due to small sample size), the law of large numbers applies to this average and it converges quickly to the truth as the test set size increases. Since the standard deviation of the prediction error can also be easily estimated, it is straightforward to evaluate predictive models without imposing additional assumptions.

There are a variety of different problems that can be tackled with ML methods. An incomplete list of some that have gained early attention is given as follows. First, we can consider the type of identification strategy for identifying causal effects. Some that have received attention in the new ML/causal inference literature include:

1. Treatment randomly assigned (experimental data).
2. Treatment assignment unconfounded (conditional on covariates).
3. Instrumental variables.
4. Panel data settings (including difference-in-difference designs).
5. Regression discontinuity designs.
6. Structural models of individual or firm behavior.

In each of those settings, there are different problems of interest:

1. Estimating average treatment effects (or a low-dimensional parameter vector).
2. Estimating heterogeneous treatment effects in simple models or models of limited complexity.
3. Estimating heterogeneous treatment effects nonparametrically.
4. Estimating optimal treatment assignment policies.
5. Identifying groups of individuals that are similar in terms of their treatment effects.

Although the early literature is already too large to summarize all of the contributions to each combination of identification strategty and problem of interest, it is useful to observe that at this point there are entries in almost all of the "boxes" associated with different identification strategies, both for average treatment effects and heterogeneous treatment effects. Here, I will provide a bit more detail on a few leading cases that have received a lot of attention, in order to illustrate some key themes in the literature.

It is also useful to observe that even though the last four problems seem closely related, they are distinct, and the methods used to solve them as well as the issues that arise are distinct. These distinctions have not traditionally been emphasized as much in the literature on causal inference, but they matter more in environments with data-driven model selection because each has a different objective and the objective function can make a big difference in determining the selected model in ML-based models. Issues of inference are also distinct, as we will discuss further below.

21.4.1   Average Treatment Effects

A large and important branch of the literature on causal inference focuses on estimation of average treatment effects under the unconfoundedness assumption. This assumption requires that potential outcomes (the outcomes a unit would experience in alternative treatment regimes) are independent of treatment assignment, conditional on covariates. In other words, treatment assignment is as good as random after controlling for covariates.

From the 1990s through the first decade of the twenty-first century, a literature emerged about using semiparametric methods to estimate average treatment effects (e.g., Bickel et al. [1993], focusing on an environment with a fixed number of covariates that is small relative to the sample size). The methods are semiparametric in the sense that the goal is to estimate a low-dimensional parameter—in this case, the average treatment effect—without making parametric assumptions about the way in which covariates affect outcomes (e.g., Hahn 1998). (See Imbens and Wooldridge [2009] and Imbens and Rubin [2015] for reviews.) In the middle of the first decade of the twenty-first decade, Mark van der Laan and coauthors introduced and developed a set of methods called "targeted maximum likelihood" (van der Laan and Rubin 2006). The idea is that maximum likelihood is used to estimate a low-dimensional parameter vector in the presence of high-dimensional nuisance parameters. The method allows the nuisance parameters to be estimated with techniques that have less well-established properties or a slower convergence rate. This approach can be applied to estimate an average treatment effect parameter under a variety of identification assumptions, but importantly, it is an approach that can be used with many covariates.

An early example of the application of ML methods to causal inference in economics (see Belloni, Chernozhukov, and Hansen 2014 and Chernozhukov, Hansen, and Spindler 2015 for reviews) uses regularized regression as an approach to deal with many potential covariates in an environment where the outcome model is "sparse," meaning that only a small number of covariates actually affect mean outcome (but there are many observables, and the analyst does not know which ones are important). In an environment with unconfoundedness, since some covariates are correlated with both the treatment assignment and the outcome, if the analyst does not condition on them the omission of the confounder will lead to a biased estimate of the treatment effect. Belloni, Chernozhukov, and Hansen propose a double-selection method based on the LASSO. The LASSO is a regularized regression procedure where a regression is estimated using an objective function that balances in-sample goodness of fit with a penalty term that depends on the sum of the magnitude of regression coefficients. This form of penalty leads many covariates to be assigned a coefficient of zero, effectively dropping them from the regression. The magnitude of the penalty parameter is selected using cross-validation. The authors observe that if LASSO is used in a regression of the outcome and both the treatment indicator and other covariates, the coefficient on the treatment indicator will be a biased estimate of the treatment effect because confounders that have a weak relationship with the outcome but a strong relationship with the treatment assignment may be zeroed out by an algorithm whose sole objective is to select variables that predict outcomes.

A variety of other methods have been proposed for combining machine learning and traditional econometric methods for estimating average treatment effects under the unconfoundedness assumption. Athey, Imbens, and Wager (2016) propose using a method they refer to as "residual balancing," building on work on balancing weights by Zubizarreta (2015). Their approach is similar to a "doubly-robust" method for estimating average treatment effects that proceeds by taking the average of the efficient score, which involves an estimate of the conditional mean of outcomes given covariates as well as the inverse of the estimated propensity score; however, the residual balancing replaces inverse propensity score weights with weights obtained using quadratic programming, where the weights are designed to achieve balance between the treatment and control group. The conditional mean of outcomes is estimated using LASSO. The main result in the paper is that this procedure is efficient and achieves the same rate of convergence as if the outcome model was known, under a few key assumptions. The most important assumption is that the outcome model is linear and sparse, although there can be a large number of covariates and the analyst does not need to have knowledge of which ones are important. The linearity assumption, while strong, allows the key result to hold in the absence of any assumptions about the structure of the process mapping covariates to the assignment, other than overlap (propensity score bounded strictly between 0 and 1, which is required for identification of average treatment effects). No other approach has been proposed that is efficient without assumptions on the assignment model. In settings where the assignment model is complex, simulations show that the method works better than alternatives, without sacrificing much in terms of performance on simpler models. Complex assignment rules with many weak confounders arise commonly in technology firms, where complex models are used to map from a user's observed history to assignments of recommendations, advertisements, and so on.

More recently, Chernozhukov et al. (2017) propose "double machine learning," a method analogous to Robinson (1988), using a semiparametric residual-on-residual regression as a method for estimating average treatment effects under unconfoundedness. The idea is to run a nonparametric regression of outcomes on covariates, and a second nonparametric regression of the treatment indicator on covariates; then, the residuals from the first regression are regressed on the residuals from the second regression. In Robinson (1988), the nonparametric estimator was a kernel regression; the more recent work establishes that any ML method can be used for the nonparametric regression, so long as it is consistent and converges at the rate $n^{1/4}$.

A few themes are common to the latter two approaches. One is the importance of building on the traditional literature on statistical efficiency, which provides strong guidance on what types of estimators are likely to be successful, as well as the particular advantages of doubly robust methods for average treatment effect estimation. A second theme is that orthogonalization can work very well in practice—using machine learning to estimate flexibly the relationship between outcomes and treatment indicators and covariates—and then estimating average treatment effects using residualized outcomes and/or residualized treatment indicators. The intuition is that in high dimensions, mistakes in estimating nuisance parameters are likely, but working with residualized variables makes the estimation of the average treatment effect orthogonal to errors in estimating nuisance parameters. I expect that this insight will continue to be utilized in the future literature.

21.4.2   Heterogeneous Treatment Effects and Optimal Policies

Another area of active research concerns the estimation of heterogeneity in treatment effects, where here we refer to heterogeneity with respect to observed covariates. For example, if the treatment is a drug, we can be interested in how the drug's efficacy varies with individual characteristics. Athey and Imbens (2017) provides a more detailed review of a variety of questions that can be considered relating to heterogeneity; we will focus on a few here.

Treatment effect heterogeneity can be of interest either for basic scientific understanding (that can be used to design new policies or understand mechanisms), or as a means to the end of estimating treatment assignment policies that map from a user's characteristics to a treatment.

Starting with basic scientific understanding of treatment effects, another question concerns whether we wish to discover simple patterns of heterogeneity, or whether a fully nonparametric estimator for how treatment effects vary with covariates is desired. One approach to discovering simpler patterns is provided by Athey and Imbens (2016). This paper proposes to create a partition of the covariate space, and then estimate treatment effects in each element of the partition. The splitting rule optimizes for finding splits that reveal treatment effect heterogeneity. The paper also proposes sample splitting as a way to avoid the bias inherent in using the same data to discover the form of heterogeneity, and to estimate the magnitude of the heterogeneity. One sample is used to construct the partition, while a second sample is used to estimate treatment effects. In this way, the confidence intervals built around the estimates on the second sample have nominal coverage no matter how many covariates there are. The intuition is that since the partition is created on an independent sample, the partition used is completely unrelated to the realizations of outcomes in the second sample. In addition, the procedure used to create the partition penalizes splits that increase the variance of the estimated treatment effects too much. This, together with cross-validation to select tree complexity, ensures that the leaves don't get too small, and thus the confidence intervals have nominal coverage.

There have already been a wide range of applications of "causal trees" in applications ranging from medicine to economic field experiments. The methods allow the researcher to discover forms of heterogeneity that were not specified in a preanalysis plan without invalidating confidence intervals. The method is also easily "interpretable," in that for each element of the partition the estimator is a traditional estimate of a treatment effect. However, it is important for researchers to recognize that just because, say, three covariates are used to describe an element of a partition (e.g., male individuals with income between $100,000 and $120,000 and fifteen to twenty years of schooling), the average of all values of covariates will vary across partition elements. So, it is important not to draw conclusions about what covariates are not associated with treatment effect heterogeneity. This chapter builds on earlier work on "model-based recursive partitioning" (Zeileis, Hothorn, and Hornik 2008), which looked at recursive partitioning for more complex models (general models estimated by maximum likelihood), but did not provide statistical properties (nor suggest the sample splitting, which is a focus of Athey and Imbens 2016). Asher et al. (2016) provide another related example of building classification trees for heterogeneity in GMM models.

In some contexts, a simple partition of the covariate space is most useful. In other contexts, it is desirable to have a fully nonparametric estimate of how treatment effects vary with covariates. In the traditional econometrics literature, this could be accomplished through kernel estimation or matching techniques; these methods have well-understood statistical properties. However, even though they work well in theory, in practice matching methods and kernel methods break down when there are more than a handful of covariates.

In Wager and Athey (forthcoming), we introduce the idea of a "causal forest." Essentially, a causal forest is the average of a lot of causal trees, where trees differ from one another due to subsampling. Conceptually, a causal forest can be thought of as a version of a nearest neighbor matching method, but one where there is a data-driven approach to determine which dimensions of the covariate space are important to match on. The main technical results in this chapter establish the first asymptotic normality results for random forests used for prediction; this result is then extended to causal inference. We also propose an estimator for the variance and prove its consistency, so that confidence intervals can be constructed.

A key requirement for our results about random forests is that each individual tree is "honest"; that is, we use different data to construct a partition of the covariate space from the data used to estimate treatment effects within the leaves. That is, we use sample splitting, similar to Athey and Imbens (2016). In the context of a random forest, all of the data is used for both "model selection" and estimation, as an observation that is in the partition-building subsample for one tree may be in the treatment effect estimation sample in another tree.

Athey, Tibshirani, and Wager (2017) extended the framework to analyze nonparametric parameter heterogeneity in any model where the parameter of interest can be estimated via GMM. The idea is that the random forest is used to construct a series of trees. Rather than estimating a model in the leaves of every tree, the algorithm instead extracts the weights implied by the forest. In particular, when estimating treatment effects for a particular value of X, we estimate a "local GMM" model, where observations close to X are weighted more heavily. How heavily? The weights are determined by the fraction of time an observation ended up in the same leaf during the forest creation stage. A subtlety in this project is that it is difficult to design general purpose, computationally lightweight "splitting rules" for constructing partitions according to the covariates that predict parameter heterogeneity. We provide a solution to that problem and also provide a proof of asymptotic normality of estimates, as well as an estimator for confidence intervals. The paper highlights the case of instrumental variables, and how the method can be used to find heterogeneity in treatment effect parameters estimated with instrumental variables. An alternative approach to estimating parameter heterogeneity in instrumental variables models was proposed by Hartford, Lewis, and Taddy (2016), who use an approach based on neural nets. General nonparametric theory is more challenging for neural nets.

The method of Athey, Tibshirani, and Wager (2017), "generalized random forests," can be used as an alternative to "traditional" methods such as local generalized method of moments or local maximum likelihood (Tibshirani and Hastie 1987). Local methods such as local linear regression typically target a particular value of covariates, and use a kernel-weighting function to weight nearby observations more heavily when running a regression. The insight in Athey, Tibshirani, and Wager (2017) is that the random forest can be reinterpreted as a method to generate a weighting function, and the forest-based weighting function can substitute for the kernel-weighting function in a local linear estimation procedure. The advantages of the forest-weighting function are that it is data adaptive as well as model adaptive. It is data adaptive in that covariates that are important for heterogeneity in parameters of interest are given more importance in determining what observations are "nearby." It is model adaptive in that it focuses on heterogeneity in parameter estimates in a given model, rather than hetereogeneity in predicting the conditional mean of outcomes as in a traditional regression forest.

The insight of Athey, Tibshirani, and Wager (2017) is more general and I expect it to reappear in other papers in this literature: anyplace in traditional econometrics where a kernel function might have been used, ML methods that perform better than kernels in practice may be substituted. However, the statistical and econometric theory for the new methods needs to be established in order to ensure that the ML-based procedure has desired properties such as asymptotic normality of parameter estimates. Athey, Tibshirani, and Wager (2017) does this for their generalized random forests for estimating heterogeneity in parameter estimates, and Hartford, Lewis, and Taddy (2016) use neural nets instead of kernels for semiparametric instrumental variables; Chernozhukov et al. (2017) does this for their generalization of Robinson (1988) semiparametric regression models.

There are also other possible approaches to estimating conditional average treatment effects when the structure of the heterogeneity is assumed to take a simple form, or when the analyst is willing to understand treatment effects conditioning only on a subset of covariates rather than attempting to condition on all relevant covariates. Targeted maximum likelihood (van der Laan and Rubin 2006) is one approach to this; more recently, Imai and Ratkovic (2013) proposed using LASSO to uncover heterogeneous treatment effects, while Künzel et al. (2017) proposes an ML approach using "metalearners." It is important to note, however, that if there is insufficient data to estimate the impact of all relevant covariates; a model such as LASSO will tend to drop covariates (and their interactions) that are correlated with other included covariates, so that the included covariates "pick up" the impact of omitted covariates.

Finally, a motivating goal for understanding treatment effects is estimating optimal policy functions; that is, functions that map from the observable covariates of individuals to policy assignments. This problem has been recently studied in economics by, for example, Kitagawa and Tetenov (2015), who focus on estimating the optimal policy from a class of potential policies of limited complexity. The goal is to select a policy function to minimize the loss from failing to use the (infeasible) ideal policy, referred to as the "regret" of the policy. Despite the general lack of research about causal inference in the ML literature, the topic of optimal policy estimation has received some attention. However, most of the ML literature focuses on algorithmic innovations, and does not exploit insights from the causal inference literature. An exception is that a line of research has incorporated the idea of propensity score weighting or doubly robust methods, although often without much reference to the statistics and econometrics literature. Examples of papers from the ML literature focused on policy learning include Strehl et al.

(2010), Dudik, Langford, and Li (2011), Li et al. (2012), Dudik et al. (2014), Li et al. (2014), Swaminathan and Joachims (2015), Jiang and Li (2016), Thomas and Brunskill (2016), and Kallus (2017). One type of result in that literature establishes bounds on the regret of the algorithm. In Athey and Wager (2017), we show how bringing in insights from semiparametric efficiency theory allows us to establish a tighter "regret bound" than the existing literature, thus narrowing down substantially the set of algorithms that might achieve the regret bound. This highlights the fact that the econometric theory literature has added value that has not been fully exploited in ML. Another unrelated observation is that, perhaps surprisingly, the econometrics of the problem of estimating optimal policy functions within a class of potential policies of limited complexity is quite different from the problem of estimating conditional average treatment effects, although of course, the problems are related.

21.4.3   Contextual Bandits: Estimating Optimal Policies Using Adaptive Experimentation

Previously, I reviewed methods for estimating optimal policies mapping from individual covariates to treatment assignments. A growing literature based primarily in ML studies the problem of "bandits," which are algorithms that actively learn about which treatment is best. Online experimentation work yields large benefits when the setting is such that it is possible to quickly measure outcomes, and when there are many possible treatments. In the basic bandit problem when all units have identical covariates, the problem of "online experimentation," or "multiarmed bandits," asks the question of how experiments be designed to assign individuals to treatments as they arrive, using data from earlier individuals to determine the probabilities of assigning new individuals to each treatment, balancing the need for exploration against the desire for exploitation. That is, bandits balance the need to learn against the desire to avoid giving individuals suboptimal treatments. This type of online experimentation has been shown to yield reliable answers orders of magnitude faster than traditional randomized controlled trials in cases where there are many possible treatments (see, e.g., Scott 2010); the gain comes from the fact that treatments that are doing badly are effectively discarded, so that newly arriving units are instead assigned to the best candidates. When the goal is to estimate an optimal policy, it is not necessary to continue to allocate units to treatments that are fairly certain not to be optimal. Further, it is also not important from the perspective of expected payoffs to statistically distinguish two very similar treatments. The literature has developed a number of heuristics for managing the explore-exploit trade-off; for example, "Thompson sampling" allocates units to treatment arms in proportion to the estimated probability that each treatment arm is the best.

There is much less known about the setting where individuals have observed attributes, in which case the goal is to construct and evaluate personalized treatment assignment policies. This problem has been termed the "contextual bandit" problem, since treatment assignments are sensitive to the "context" (in this case, user characteristics). At first, the problem seems very challenging because the space of possible policies is large and complex (each policy maps from user characteristics to the space of possible treatments). However, if the returns to each of the actions can be estimated as a function of individual attributes, a policy can be constructed by finding the action whose return is estimated to be highest, balanced against the need for exploration. Although there are a number of proposed methods for the contextual bandit problem in the literature already, there is relatively little known about how to select among methods and which ones are likely to perform best in practice. For example, the literature on optimal policy estimation suggests that particular approaches to policy estimation may work better than others.

In particular, there are a variety of choices a researcher must make when selecting a contextual bandit algorithm. These include the choice of the model that maps user characteristics to expected outcomes (where the literature has considered alternatives such as Ridge regression, Li et al. [2010]; ordinary least squares (OLS) Goldenshluger and Zeevi [2013]; generalized linear model (GLM) Li, Lu, and Zhou [2017]; LASSO, [Bastani and Bayati 2015]; and random forests, Dimakopoulou, Athey, and Imbens [2017]; Feraud et al. [2016]). Another choice concerns the heuristic used to balance exploration versus exploitation, with leading choices Thompson Sampling and Upper Confidence Bounds (UCB) (Chapelle and Li 2011).

Dimakopoulou, Athey, and Imbens (2017) highlights some issues that arise uniquely in the contextual bandit and that relate directly to the estimation issues that have been the focus of the literature on estimation of treatment effects (Imbens and Rubin 2015). For example, the paper highlights the comparison between noncontextual bandits, where there will be many future individuals arriving with exactly the same context (since they all share the same context), and contextual bandits, where each unit is unique. The assignment of a particular individual thus contributes to learning for the future indirectly indirectly, since the future individuals will have different contexts (characteristics). The fact that the exploration benefits the future through a model of how contexts relates to outcomes changes the problem.

This discussion highlights a further theme for the connection between ML and causal inference: estimation considerations matter even more in the "small sample" settings of contextual bandits, where the assumption is that there is not enough data available to the policymaker to estimate perfectly the optimal assignment. However, we know from the econometrics literature that the small sample properties of different estimators can vary substantially across settings (Imbens and Rubin 2015), making it clear that the best contextual bandit approach is likely to also vary across settings.

21.4.4   Robustness and Supplementary Analysis

In a recent review paper, Athey and Imbens (2017) highlights the importance of "supplementary analyses" for establishing the credibility of causal estimates in environments where crucial assumptions are not directly testable without additional information. Examples of supplementary analyses include placebo tests, whereby the analyst assses whether a given model is likely to find evidence of treatment effects even at times where no treatment effect should be found. One type of supplementary analysis is a robustness measure. Athey and Imbens (2015) proposes to use ML-based methods to develop a range of different estimates of a target parameter (e.g., a treatment effect), where the range is created by introducing interaction effects between model parameters and covariates. The robustness measure is defined as the standard deviation of parameter estimates across model specifications. This paper provides one possible approach to ML-based robustness measures, but I predict that more approaches will develop over time as ML methods become more popular.

Another type of ML-based supplementary analysis, proposed by Athey, Imbens, et al. (2017), uses ML-based methods to construct a measure of how challenging the confounding problem is in a particular setting. The proposed measure constructs an estimated conditional mean function for the outcome as well as an estimated propensity score, and then estimates the correlation between the two.

There is much more potential for supplementary analyses to be further developed; the fact that ML has well-defined, systematic algorithms for comparing a wide range of model specifications makes ML well suited for constructing additional robustness checks and supplementary analyses.

21.4.5   Panel Data and Difference-in-Difference Models

Another commonly used approach to identifying causal effects is to exploit assumptions about how outcomes vary across units and over time in panel data. In a typical panel-data setting, units are not necessarily assigned to a treatment randomly, but all units are observed prior to some units being treated; the identifying assumption is that one or more untreated units can be used to provide an estimate of the counterfactual time trend that would have occurred for the treated units in the absence of the treatment. The simplest "difference-in-difference" case involves two groups and two time periods; more broadly, panel data may include many groups and many periods. Traditional econometric models for the panel-data case exploit functional form assumptions, for example, assuming that a unit's outcome in a particular time period is an additive function of a unit effect, a time effect, an independent shock. The unit effect can then be inferred for treated units in the pretreatment period, while the time effect can be inferred from the untreated units in the periods where some units receive the treatment. Note that this structure implies that the matrix of mean outcomes (with rows associated with units and columns associated with time) has a very simple structure: it has rank two.

There have been a few recent approaches bringing ML tools to the panel data setting. Doudchenko and Imbens (2016) develop an approach inspired by synthetic controls (pioneered by Abadie, Diamond, and Hainmueller 2010), where a weighted average of control observations is used to construct the counterfactual untreated outcomes for treated units in treated periods. Doudchenko and Imbens (2016) propose using regularized regression to determine the weights, with the penalty parameter selected via cross-validation.

Factor Models and Matrix Completion

Another way to think about causal inference in a panel-data setting is to consider a matrix completion problem; Athey, Bayati, et al. (2017) propose taking such a perspective. In the ML literature, a matrix completion problem is one where there is an observed matrix of data (in our case, units and time periods), but some of the entries are missing. The goal is to provide the best possible prediction of what those entries should be. For the panel-data application, we can think of the units and time periods where the units are treated as the missing entries, since we don't observe the counterfactual outcomes of those units in the absence of the treatment (this is the key bit of missing information for estimating the treatment effect).

Athey, Bayati, et al. (2017) propose using a matrix version of regularized regression to find a matrix that well approximates the matrix of untreated outcomes (a matrix that has missing elements corresponding to treated units and periods). Recall that LASSO regression minimizes sum of squared errors in sample, plus a penalty term that is proportional to the sum of the magnitudes of the coefficients in the regression. We propose matrix regression that minimizes the sum of squared errors of all elements of the matrix, plus a penalty term proportional to the nuclear norm of the matrix. The nuclear norm is the sum of absolute values of the singular values of the matrix. A matrix that has a low nuclear norm is well approximated by a low rank matrix.

How do we interpret the idea that a matrix can be well approximated by a low-rank matrix? A low-rank matrix can be "factored" into the product of two matrices. In the panel-data case, we can interpret such a factorization as incorporating a vector of latent characteristics for each unit and a vector of latent characteristics of each period. The outcome of a particular unit in a particular period, if untreated, is approximately equal to the inner product of the unit's characteristics and the period characteristics. For example, if the data concerned employment at the county level, we can think of the counties as having outcomes that depend on the share of employment in different industries, and then each industry has common shocks in each period.

So a county's latent characteristic would be the vector of industry shares, and the time characteristics would be industry shocks in a given period.

Athey, Bayati, et al. (2017) show that the matrix completion approach reduces to commonly employed techniques in the econometrics literature when the assumptions needed for those approaches hold, but the matrix completion approach is able to model more complex patterns in the data, while allowing the data (rather than the analyst) to indicate whether time-series patterns within units, or cross-sectional patterns within a period, or a more complex combination, are more useful for predicting counterfactual outcomes.

The matrix completion approach can be linked to a literature that has grown in the last two decades in time-series econometrics on factor models (see, e.g., Bai and Ng 2008 for a review). The matrix-factorization approach is similar, but rather than assuming that the true model has a fixed but unknown number of factors, the matrix-completion approach simply looks for the best fit while penalizing the norm of the matrix. The matrix is well approximated by one with a small number of factors, but does not need to be exactly represented that way. Athey, Bayati, et al. (2017) describe a number of advantages of the matrix completion approach, and also show that it performs better than existing panel-data causal inference approaches in a range of settings.

21.4.6   Factor Models and Structural Models

Another important area of connection between machine learning and causal inference concerns more complex structural models. For decades, scholars working at the intersection of marketing and economics have built structural models of consumer choice, sometimes in dynamic environments, and used Bayesian estimation to estimate the model, often Markov Chain Monte Carlo. Recently, the ML literature has developed a variety of techniques that allow similar types of Bayesian models to be estimated at larger scale. These have been applied to settings such as textual analysis and consumer choices of, for example, movies at Netflix. (See, for example, Blei, Ng, and Jordan [2003] and Blei [2012]). I expect to see much closer synergies between these two literatures in the future. For example, Athey, Blei, et al. (2017) builds on models of hierarchical Poisson factorization to create models of consumer demand, where a consumer's preference over thousands of products are considered simultaneously, but the consumer's choices in each product category are independent of one another. The model reduces the dimensionality of this problem by using a lower-dimensional factor representation of a consumer's mean utility as well as the consumer's price sensitivity for each product. The paper establishes that substantial efficiency gains are possible by considering many product categories in parallel; it is possible to learn about a consumer's price sensitivity in one product using behavior in other products. The paper departs from the pure prediction literature in ML by evaluating and tuning the model based on how it does at predicting consumer responses to price changes, rather than simply on overall goodness of fit. In particular, the paper highlights that different models would be selected for the "goodness of fit" objective as opposed to the "counterfactual inference" objective. In order to achieve this goal, the paper analyzes goodness of fit in terms of predicting changes in demand for products before and after price changes, after providing evidence that the price changes can be treated as natural experiments after conditioning on week effects (price changes always occur mid-week). The paper also demonstrates the benefits of personalized prediction, versus more standard demand estimation methods. Thus the paper again highlights the theme that for causal inference, the objective function differs from standard prediction.

With more scalable computational methods, it becomes possible to build much richer models with much less prior information about products. Ruiz, Athey, and Blei (2017) analyzes consumer preferences for bundles selected from over 5,000 items in a grocery store, without incorporating information about which items are in the same category. Thus, the model uncovers whether items are substitutes or complements. Since there are $2^{5,000}$ bundles when there are 5,000 products, in principle each individual consumer's utility function has $2^{5,000}$ parameters. Even if we restrict the utility function to have only pairwise interaction effects, there are still millions of parameters of a consumer's utility function over bundles. Ruiz, Athey, and Blei (2017) uses a matrix-factorization approach to reduce the dimensionality of the problem, factorizing the mean utilities of the items, the interaction effects among items, and the user's price sensitivity for the items. Price and availability variation in the data allows the model to distinguish correlated preferences (some consumers like both coffee and diapers) from complementarity (tacos and taco shells are more valuable together). In order to further simplify the analysis, the model assumes that consumers are boundedly rational when they make choices, and consider the interactions among products as the consumer sequentially adds items to the cart. The alternative—that the consumer considers all $2^{5,000}$ bundles and optimizes among them—does not seem plausible. Incorporating human computational constraints into structural models thus appears to be another potential fruitful avenue at the intersection of ML and economics. In the computational algorithm for Ruiz, Athey, and Blei (2017), we rely on a technique called variational inference to approximate the posterior distribution, as well as the technique stochastic gradient descent (described in detail above) to find the parameters that provide the best approximation.

In another application of similar methodology, Athey et al. (2018) analyzes consumer choices over lunchtime restaurants using data from a sample of several thousand mobile phone users in the San Francisco Bay Area. The data is used to identify users' typical morning location, as well as their choices of lunchtime restaurants. We build a model where restaurants have latent characteristics (whose distribution may depend on restaurant observables, such as star ratings, food category, and price range), and each user has preferences for these latent characteristics, and these preferences are heterogeneous across users. Similarly, each item has latent characteristics that describe users' willingness to travel to patronize the restaurant, and each user has individual-specific preferences for those latent characteristics. Thus, both users' willingness to travel and their base utility for each restaurant vary across user-item pairs. To make the estimation computationally feasible, we build on the methods of Ruiz, Athey, and Blei (2017). We show that our model performs better than more standard competing models such as multinomial logit and nested logit models, in part due to the personalization of the estimates. We demonstrate in particular that our model performs better when predicting consumer responses to restaurant openings and closings, and we analyze how consumers reallocate their demand after a restaurant closes to nearby restaurants versus more distant restaurants with similar characteristics. Since there are several hundred restaurant openings and closings in the data, we are able to use the large number of "natural experiments" in the data to assess performance of the model. Finally, we show how the model can be used to analyze questions involving counterfactuals such as what type of restaurant would attract the most consumers in a given location.

Another recent paper that makes use of factorization in the context of a structural model of consumer demand is Wan et al. (2017). This paper builds a model of consumer choice that includes choices over categories, purchases within a category, and quantity to purchase. The model allows for individual heterogeneity in preferences, and uses factorization techniques to estimate the model.

21.5   Broader Predictions about the Impact of Machine Learning on Economics

My prediction is that there will be substantial changes in how empirical work is conducted; indeed, it is already happening, and so this prediction already can be made with a high degree of certainty. I predict that a number of changes will emerge, summarized as follows:

1. Adoption of off-the-shelf ML methods for their intended tasks (prediction, classification, and clustering, e.g., for textual analysis).

2. Extensions and modifications of prediction methods to account for considerations such as fairness, manipulability, and interpretability.

3. Development of new econometric methods based on machine learning designed to solve traditional social science estimation tasks.

4. No fundamental changes to theory of identification of causal effects.

5. Incremental progress to identification and estimation strategies for causal effects that exploit modern data settings including large-panel data sets and environments with many small experiments.

6. Increased emphasis on model robustness and other supplementary analysis to assess credibility of studies.

7. Adoption of new methods by empiricists at large scale.

8. Revival and new lines of research in productivity and measurement.

9. New methods for the design and analysis of large administrative data, including merging these sources and privacy-preserving methods.

10. Increase in interdisciplinary research.

11. Changes in organization, dissemination, and funding of economic research.

12. Economist as engineer engages with firms, government to design, and implement policies in digital environment.

13. Design and implementation of digital experimentation, both one-time and as an ongoing process, including multiarmed bandit experimentation algorithms, in collaboration with firms and government.

14. Research on developing high-quality metrics that can be measured quickly, in order to facilitate rapid incremental innovation and experimentation.

15. Increased use of data analysis in all levels of economics teaching; increase in interdisciplinary data science programs.

16. Research on the impact of AI and ML on the economy.

This chapter has discussed the first three predictions in some detail; I will now discuss each of the remaining predictions in turn.

First, as emphasized in the discussion about the benefits from using ML, ML is a very powerful tool for data-driven model selection. Getting the best flexible functional form to fit data is very important for many reasons; for example, when the researcher assumes that treatment assignment is unconfounded, it is still crucial to flexibly control for covariates, and a vast literature has documented that modeling choices matter. A theme highlighted in this chapter is that ML can be used any time that semiparametric methods might have been used in the traditional econometrics literature. However, finding the best functional form is a distinct concern from whether an economic parameter would be identified with sufficient data. Thus, there is no obvious benefit from ML in terms of thinking about identification issues.

However, the types of data sets that are becoming widely available due to digitization suggest new identification questions. For example, it is common for there to be frequent changes in algorithms in ecommerce platforms. These changes in algorithms create variation in user experiences (as well as in seller experiences in platforms and marketplaces). Thus, a typical user or seller may experience a large number of changes, each of which has modest effects. There are open questions about what can be learned in such environments. From an estimation perspective, there is also room to develop ML-inspired algorithms that take advantage of the many sources of variation experienced by market participants. In my 2012 Fisher Schultz lecture, I illustrated the idea of using randomized experiments conducted by technology firms as instruments for estimating position effects for sponsored search advertisements. This idea has since been exploited more fully by others (e.g., Goldman and Rao 2014), but many open questions remain about the best ways to use the information in such data sets.

Digitization is also leading to the creation of many panel data sets that record individual behavior at relatively high frequency over a period of time. There are many open questions about how to make the best use of rich panel data. Previously, we discussed several new papers at the intersection of ML and econometrics that made use of panel data (e.g., Athey, Bayati, et al. 2017), but I predict that this literature will grow dramatically over the next few years.

There are many reasons that empiricists will adopt ML methods at scale. First, many ML methods simplify a variety of arbitrary choices analysts needed to make. In larger and more complex data sets, there are many more choices. Each choice must be documented, justified, and serves at a potential source of criticism of a paper. When systematic, data-driven methods are available, research can be made more principled and systematic, and there can be objective measures against which these choices can be evaluated. Indeed, it would really be impossible for a researcher using traditional empirical methods to fully document the process by which the model specification was selected; in contrast, algorithmic selection (when the algorithm is given the correct objective for the problem) has superior performance while simultaneously being reproducible. Second, one way to conceptualize ML algorithms is that they perform like automated research assistants—they work much faster and more effectively than traditional research assistants at exploring modeling choices, yet the methods that have been customized for social science applications also build in protections so that, for example, valid confidence intervals can be obtained. Although it is crucial to consider carefully the objective that the algorithms are given, in the end they are highly effective. Thus, they help resolve issues like "p-value hacking" by giving researchers the best of both worlds—superior performance as well as correct p-values that take into account the specification-selection process. Third, in many cases, new results can be obtained. For example, if an author has run a field experiment, there is no reason not to search for heterogeneous treatment effects using methods such as those in Athey and Imbens (2016). The method ensures that valid confidence intervals can be obtained for the resulting estimates of treatment effect heterogeneity.

Alongside the adoption of ML methods for old questions, new questions and types of analyses will emerge in the fields of productivity and measurement. Some examples of these have already been highlighted, such as the ability to measure economic outcomes at a granular level over a longer period of time, through, for example, imagery. Glaeser et al. (2018) provides a nice overview of how big data and ML will affect urban economics as a field, as well as the operational efficiency of cities. More broadly, as governments begin to absorb high-frequency, granular data, they will need to grapple with questions about how to maintain the stability of official statistics in a world where the underlying data changes rapidly. New questions will emerge about how to architect a system of measurement that takes advantage of high-frequency, noisy, unstable data, but yields statistics whose meaning and relationship with a wide range of economic variables remains stable. Firms will face similar problems as they attempt to forecast outcomes relevant to their own businesses using noisy, high-frequency data. The emerging literature in academics, government, and industry on "nowcasting" in macroeconomics (e.g., Banbura et al. [2013] and ML begins to address some, but not all, of these issues). We will also see the emergence of new forms of descriptive analysis, some inspired by ML. Examples of these include techniques for describing association, for example, people who do A also do B; as well as interpretations and visualizations of the output of unsupervised ML techniques such as matrix factorization, clustering, and so on. Economists are likely to refine these methods to make them more directly useful quantiatively, and for business and policy decisions.

More broadly, the ability to use predictive models to measure economic outcomes at high granularity and fidelity will change the types of questions we can ask and answer. For example, imagery from satellites or Google's street view can be used in combination with survey data to train models that can be used to produce estimates of economic outcomes at the level of the individual home, either within the United States or in developing countries where administrative data quality can be problematic (e.g., Jean et al. 2016; Engstrom, Hersh, and Newhouse 2017; Naik et al. 2014).

Another area of transformation for economics will be in the design and analysis of large-scale administrative data sets. We will see attempts to bring together disparate sources to provide a more complete view of individuals and firms. The behavior of individuals in the financial world, the physical world, and the digital world will be connected, and in some cases ML will be needed simply to match different identities from different contexts onto the same individual. Further, we will observe behavior of individuals over time, often with high-frequency measurements. For example, children will leave digital footprints throughout their education, ranging from how often they check their homework assignments, the assignments themselves, comments from teachers, and so on. Children will interact with adaptive systems that change the material they receive based on their previous engagement and performance. This will create the need for new statistical methods, building on existing ML tools, but where the methods are more tailored to a panel-data setting with significant dynamic effects (and possibly peer effects as well; see, for some recent statistical advances designed around analyzing large scale network data, Ugander et al. 2013; Athey, Eckles, and Imbens 2015; Eckles et al. 2016).

Another area of future research concerns how to analyze personal data without compromising user privacy. There is a literature in computer science around querying data while preserving privacy; the literature is referred to as "differential privacy." Some recent research has brought together the computer science literature with questions about estimating statistical models (see, e.g., Komarova, Nekipelov, and Yakovlev 2015).

I also predict a substantial increase in interdisciplinary work. Computer scientists and engineers may remain closer to the frontier in terms of algorithm design, computational efficiency, and related concerns. As I will expand on further in a moment, academics of all disciplines will be gaining a much greater ability to intervene in the environment in a way that facilitates measurement and caual inference. As digital interactions and digital interventions expand across all areas of society, from education to health to government services to transportation, economists will collaborate with domain experts in other areas to design, implement, and evaluate changes in technology and policy. Many of these digital interventions will be powered by ML, and ML-based causal inference tools will be used to estimate personalized treatment effects of the interventions and design personalized treatment assignment policies.

Alongside the increase in interdisciplinary work, there will also be changes to the organization, funding, and dissemination of economics research. Research on large data sets with complex data creation and analysis pipelines can be labor intensive and also require specialized skills. Scholars who do a lot of complex data analysis with large data sets have already begun to adopt a "lab" model more similar to what is standard today in computer science and many natural sciences. A lab might include a postdoctoral fellow, multiple PhD students, predoctoral fellows (full-time research assistants between their bachelor's and PhD), undergraduates, and possibly full-time staff. Of course, labs of this scale are expensive, and so the funding models for economics will need to adapt to address this reality. One concern is inequality of access to resources required to do this type of research, given that it is expensive enough that it cannot be supported given traditional funding pools for more than a small fraction of economists at research universities.

Within a lab, we will see increased adoption of collaboration tools such as those used in software firms; tools include GitHub (for collaboration, version control, and dissemination of software), as well as communication tools (e.g., my generalized random-forest software is available as an open source package on Github at http://github.com/swager/grf, and users report issues through the GitHub, and can submit request to pull in proposed changes or additions to the code).

There will also be an increased emphasis on documenation and reproducibility, which are necessary to make a large lab function. This will happen even as some data sources remain proprietary. "Fake" data sets will be created that allow others to run a lab's code and replicate the analysis (except not on the real data). As an example of institutions created to support the lab model, both Stanford GSB and the Stanford Institute for Economic Policy Research have "pools" of predoctoral fellows that are shared among faculty; these programs provide mentorship, training, the opportunity to take one class each quarter, and they also are demographically more diverse than graduate student populations. The predoctoral fellows have a special form of student status within Stanford. Other public- and private-sector research groups have also adopted similar programs, with Microsoft Research-New England an early innovator in this area, while individual researcheres at universities like Harvard and MIT have also been making use of predoctoral research assistants for a number of years.

We will also see changes in how economists engage with government, industry, education, and health. The concept of the "economist as engineer" promoted by market-design experts including Robert Wilson, Paul Milgrom, and Al Roth (Roth 2002), and even "economist as plumber" (Duflo 2017) will move beyond the fields of market design and development. As digitization spreads across application areas and sectors of the economy, it will bring opportunities for economists to develop and implement policies that can be delivered digitially. Farming advice, online education, health information and information, government-service provision, government collections, and personalized resource allocation—all of these create opportunities for economists to propose policies, design the delivery and implementation of the policy including randomization or staggered roll-outs to enable evaluation, and to remain involved through successive rounds of incremental improvement for adopted policies. Feedback will come more quickly and there will be more opportunities to gather data, adapt, and adjust. Economists will be involved in improving operational efficiency of government and industry, reducing costs, and improving outcomes.

Machine-learning methods, when deployed in practice in industry, government, education, and health, lend themselves to incremental improvement. Standard practice in the technology industry is to evaluate incremental improvements through randomized controlled trials. Firms like Google and Facebook do 10,000 or more randomized controlled trials of incremental improvements to ML algorithms every year. An emerging trend is to build the experimentation right into the algorithm using bandit techniques. As described in more detail earlier, multiarmed bandit is a term for an algorithm that balances exploration and learning against exploiting information that is already available about which alternative treatment is best. Bandits can be dramatically faster than standard randomized controlled experiments (see, e.g., the description of bandits on Google's web site: https://support.google.com/analytics/answer/2844870?hl=en) because they have a different goal: the goal is to learn what the best alternative is, not to accurately estimate the average outcome for each alternative, as in a standard randomized controlled trial.

Implementing bandit algorithms requires the statistical analysis to be embedded in the system that delivers the treatments. For example, a user might arrive at a web site. Based on the user's characteristics, a contextual bandit might randomize among treatment arms in proportion to the current best estimate of the probability that each arm is optimal for that user. The randomization would occur "on the fly" and thus the software for the bandit needs to be integrated with the software for delivering the treatments. This requires a deeper relationship between the analyst and the technology than a scenario where an analyst analyzes historical data "offline" (that is, not in real time).

Balancing exploration and exploitation involves fundamental economic concepts about optimization under limited information and resource constraints. Bandits are generally more efficient and I predict they will come into much more widespread use in practice. In turn, that will create opportunities for social scientists to optimize interventions much more effectively, and to evaluate a large number of possible alternatives faster and with less inefficiency. More broadly, statistical analysis will come to be commonly placed in a longer-term context where information accumulates over time.

Beyond bandits, other themes include combining experimental and observational data to improve precison of estimates (see, e.g., Peysakhovich and Lada 2016), and making use of large numbers of related experiments when drawing conclusions.

Optimizing ML algorithms require an objective or an outcome to optimize for. In an environment with frequent and high-velocity experimentation, measures of success that can be obtained in a short time frame are needed. This leads to a substantively challenging problem: what are good measures that are related to long-term goals, but can be measured in the short term, and are responsive to interventions? Economists will get involved in helping define objectives and constructing measures of success that can be used to evaluate incremental innovation. One area of research that is receiving renewed attention is the topic of "surrogates," a name for intermediate measures that can be used in place of long-term outcomes (see, e.g., Athey et al. 2016). Economists will also place renewed interest on designing incentives that counterbalance the short-term incentives created by short-term experimentation.

All of these changes will also affect teaching. Anticipating the digital transformation of industry and government, undergraduate exposure to programming and data will be much higher than it was ten years ago. Within ten years, most undergraduates will enter college (and most MBAs will enter business school) with extensive coding experience obtained from elementary through high school, summer camps, online education, and internships. Many will take coding and data analysis in college, viewing these courses as basic preparation for the workforce. Teaching will need to change to complement the type of material covered in these other classes. In the short run, more students may arrive at econometrics classes thinking about data analysis from the perspective that all problems are prediction or classification problems. They may have a cookbook full of algorithms, but little intuition for how to use data to solve real-world problems or answer business or public policy questions. Yet, such questions are prevalent in the business world: firms want to know the return on investment on advertising campaigns,[2] the impact of changing prices or introducing products, and so on. Economic education will take on an important role in educating students in how to use data to answer questions. Given the unique advantages economics as a discipline has at these methods and approaches, many of the newly created data science undergraduate and graduate programs will bring in economists and other social scientists, creating an increased demand for teaching from empirical economists and applied econometricians. We will also see more interdisciplinary majors; Duke and MIT both recently announced joint degrees between computer science and economics. There are too many newly created data science master's programs to mention, but a key observation is that while early programs most commonly have emerged from computer science and engineering, I predict that these programs will over time incorporate more social science, or else adopt and teach social science empirical methods themselves. Graduates entering the workforce will need to know basic empirical strategies like difference-in-differences that often arise in the business world (e.g., some consumers or areas are exposed to a treatment and not others, and there are important seasonality effects to control for).

A final prediction is that we will see a lot more research into the societal impacts of machine learning. There will be large-scale, very important regulatory problems that need to be solved. Regulating the transportation infrastructure around autonomous vehicles and drones is a key example. These technologies have the potential to create enormous efficiency. Beyond that, reducing transportation costs substantially effectively increases the supply of land and housing in commuting distance of cities, thus reducing housing costs for people who commute into cities to provide services for wealthier people. This type of reduction in housing cost would be very impactful for the cost of living for people providing services in cities, which could reduce effective inequality (which may otherwise continue to rise). But there are a plethora of policy issues that need to be addressed, ranging from insurance

2. For example, several large technology companies employ economists with PhDs from top universities who specialize in evaluating and allocating advertising spend for hundreds of millions of dollars of expenditures; see Lewis and Rao (2015) for a description of some of the challenges involved.

and liability, to safety policy, to data sharing, to fairness, to competition policy, and many others. Generally, the problem of how regulators approach algorithms that have enormous public impact is not at all worked out. Are algorithms regulated on outcomes, or on procedures and processes? How should regulators handle equilibrium effects, for example, if one autonomous vehicle system makes a change to its driving algorithms, and how is that communicated to others? How can we avoid problems that have plagued personal computer software, where bugs and glitches are common following updates? How do we deal with the fact that having an algorithm used by 1 percent of cars does not prove it will work when used by 100 percent of cars, due to interaction effects?

Another industry where regulation of ML is already becoming problematic is financial services. Financial-service regulation traditionally concerned processes, rules, and regulations. There is not currently a framework for cost-benefit analysis, or deciding how to test and evaluate algorithms, and determining an acceptable error rate. For algorithms that might have an effect on the economy, how do we assess systematic risks? These are fruitful areas for future research as well. And of course, there are crucial questions about how ML will affect the future of work, as ML is used across wider and wider swaths of the economy.

We will also see experts in the practice of machine learning and AI collaborate with different subfields of economics in evaluating the impact of AI and ML on the economy.

Summarizing, I predict that economics will be profoundly transformed by AI and ML. We will build more robust and better-optimized statistical models, and we will lead the way in modifying the algorithms to have other desirable properties, ranging from protection against overfitting and valid confidence intervals, to fairness or nonmanipulability. The kinds of research we do will change; in particular, a variety of new research areas will open up, with better measurement, new methods, and different substantive questions. We will grapple with how to reorganize the research process, which will have increased fixed costs and larger-scale research labs, for those who can fund it. We will change our curriculum and take an important seat at the table in terms of educating the future workforce with empirical and data science skills. And, we will have a whole host of new policy problems created by ML and AI to study, including the issues experienced by parts of the workforce who need to transition jobs when their old jobs are eliminated due to automation.

21.6 Conclusions

It is perhaps easier than one might think to make predictions about the impact of ML on economics, since many of the most profound changes are well underway. There are exciting and vibrant research areas emerging, and dozens of applied papers making use of the methods. In short, I believe there will be an important transformation. At the same time, the automation of certain aspects of statistical algorithms does not change the need to worry about the things that economists have always worried about: is a causal effect really identified from the data, are all confounders measured, what are effective strategies for identifying causal effects, what considerations are important to incorporate in a particular applied setting, defining outcome metrics that reflect overall objectives, constructing valid confidence intervals, and many others. As ML automates some of the routine tasks of data analysis, it becomes all the more important for economists to maintain their expertise at the art of credible and impactful empirical work.

References

Abadie, A., A. Diamond, and J. Hainmueller. 2010. "Synthetic Control Methods for Comparative Case Studies: Estimating the Effect of California's Tobacco Control Program." *Journal of the American Statistical Association* 105 (490): 493–505.

Asher, S., D. Nekipelov, P. Novosad, and S. Ryan. 2016. "Classification Trees for Heterogeneous Moment-Based Models." NBER Working Paper no. 22976, Cambridge, MA.

Athey, S. 2017. "Beyond Prediction: Using Big Data for Policy Problems." *Science* 355 (6324): 483–85.

Athey, S., M. Bayati, N. Doudchenko, G. Imbens, and K. Khosravi. 2017. "Matrix Completion Methods for Causal Panel Data Models." Cornell University Library. arXiv preprint arXiv:1710.10251.

Athcy, S., D. Blei, R. Donnelly, and F. Ruiz. 2017. "Counterfactual Inference for Consumer Choice across Many Product Categories." Working paper.

Athey, S., D. M. Blei, R. Donnelly, F. J. Ruiz, and T. Schmidt. 2018. "Estimating Heterogeneous Consumer Preferences for Restaurants and Travel Time Using Mobile Location Data." *AEA Papers and Proceedings* 108:64–67.

Athey, S., R. Chetty, G. Imbens, and H. Kang. 2016. "Estimating Treatment Effects Using Multiple Surrogates: The Role of the Surrogate Score and the Surrogate Index." Cornell University Library. preprint arXiv:1603.09326.

Athey, S., D. Coey, and J. Levin. 2013. "Set-Asides and Subsidies in Auctions." *American Economic Journal: Microeconomics* 5 (1): 1–27.

Athey, S., D. Eckles, and G. W. Imbens. 2015. "Exact P-Values for Network Interference." NBER Working Paper no. 21313, Cambridge, MA.

Athey, S., and P. A. Haile. 2007. "Nonparametric Approaches to Auctions." *Handbook of Econometrics* 6:3847–965.

Athey. S., and G. Imbens. 2015. "A Measure of Robustness to Misspecification." *American Economic Review* 105 (5): 476–80.

———. 2016. "Recursive Partitioning for Heterogeneous Causal Effects." *Proceedings of the National Academy of Sciences* 113 (27): 7353–60.

———. 2017. "The State of Applied Econometrics: Causality and Policy Evaluation." *Journal of Economic Perspectives* 31 (2): 3–32.

Athey, S., G. Imbens, T. Pham, and S. Wager. 2017. "Estimating Average Treatment Effects: Supplementary Analyses and Remaining Challenges." *American Economic Review* 107 (5): 278–81.

Athey, S., G. W. Imbens, and S. Wager. 2016. "Approximate Residual Balancing: De-Biased Inference of Average Treatment Effects in High Dimensions." Cornell University Library. preprint arXiv:1604.07125.

Athey, S., J. Levin, and E. Seira. 2011. "Comparing Open and Sealed Bid Auctions: Evidence from Timber Auctions." *Quarterly Journal of Economics* 126 (1): 207–57.

Athey, S., M. M. Mobius, and J. Pál. 2017. "The Impact of Aggregators on Internet News Consumption." Working Paper no. 3353, Stanford Graduate School of Business.

Athey, S., J. Tibshirani, and S. Wager. 2017. "Generalized Random Forests." Cornell University Library. https://arxiv.org/abs/1610.01271.

Athey, S., and S. Wager. 2017. "Efficient Policy Estimation." Cornell University Library. https://arxiv.org/abs/1702.02896.

Bai, J., and S. Ng. 2008. "Large Dimensional Factor Analysis." *Foundations and Trends® in Econometrics* 3 (2): 89–163.

Banbura, M., D. Giannone, M. Modugno, and L. Reichlin. 2013. "Now-Casting and the Real-Time Data Flow." ECB Working Paper no. 1564, European Central Bank.

Bastani, H., and M. Bayati. 2015. "Online Decision-Making with High-Dimensional Covariates." *SSRN Electronic Journal*. https://www.researchgate.net/publication/315639905_Online_Decision-Making_with_High-Dimensional_Covariates.

Belloni, A., V. Chernozhukov, and C. Hansen. 2014. "High-Dimensional Methods and Inference on Structural and Treatment Effects." *Journal of Economic Perspectives* 28 (2): 29–50.

Bickel, P. J., C. A. Klaassen, Y. Ritov, J. Klaassen, J. A. Wellner, and Y. Ritov. 1993. *Efficient and Adaptive Estimation for Semiparametric Models*. Baltimore: Johns Hopkins University Press.

Bjorkegren, D., and D. Grissen. 2017. "Behavior Revealed in Mobile Phone Usage Predicts Loan Repayment." *SSRN Electronic Journal*. https://www.researchgate.net/publication/321902459_Behavior_Revealed_in_Mobile_Phone_Usage_Predicts_Loan_Repayment.

Blei, D. M. 2012. "Probabilistic Topic Models." *Communications of the ACM* 55 (4): 77.

Blei, D. M., A. Y. Ng, and M. I. Jordan. 2003. "Latent Dirichlet Allocation." *Journal of Machine Learning Research*, 3 (Jan): 993–1022.

Chapelle, O., and L. Li. 2011. "An Empirical Evaluation of Thompson Sampling." *Proceedings of the Conference on Neural Information Processing Systems*. https://papers.nips.cc/paper/4321-an-empirical-evaluation-of-thompson-sampling.

Chernozhukov, V., D. Chetverikov, M. Demirer, E. Duo, C. Hansen, and W. Newey. 2017. "Double/Debiased/Neyman Machine Learning of Treatment Effects. January. Cornell University Library. http://arxiv.org/abs/1701.08687.

Chernozhukov, V., C. Hansen, and M. Spindler. 2015. "Valid Post-Selection and Post- Regularization Inference: An Elementary, General Approach." January. www.doi.org/10.1146/annurev-economics-012315-015826.

Dimakopoulou, M., S. Athey, and G. Imbens. 2017. "Estimation Considerations in Contextual Bandits." Cornell University Library. https://arxiv.org/abs/1711.07077.

Doudchenko, N., and G. W. Imbens. 2016. "Balancing, Regression, Difference-in-Differences and Synthetic Control Methods: A Synthesis." Technical report, National Bureau of Economic Research.

Dudik, M., D. Erhan, J. Langford, and L. Li. 2014. "Doubly Robust Policy Evaluation and Optimization." *Statistical Science* 29 (4): 485–511.

Dudik, M., J. Langford, and L. Li. 2011. "Doubly Robust Policy Evaluation and Learning." *International Conference on Machine Learning.*

Duflo, E. 2017. "The Economist as Plumber." NBER Working Paper no. 23213, Cambridge, MA.

Eckles, D., B. Karrer, J. Ugander, L. Adamic, I. Dhillon, Y. Koren, R. Ghani, P. Senator, J. Bradley, and R. Parekh. 2016. "Design and Analysis of Experiments in Networks: Reducing Bias from Interference." *Journal of Causal Inference* 1–62. www.doi.org/10.1515/jci-2015-0021.

Egami, N., C. Fong, J. Grimmers, M. Roberts, and B. Stewart. 2016. "How to Make Causal Inferences Using Text." Working paper. https://polmeth.polisci.wisc.edu /Papers/ais.pdf.

Engstrom, R., J. Hersh, and D. Newhouse. 2017. "Poverty from Space: Using High-Resolution Satellite Imagery for Estimating Economic Well-Being (English)." Policy Research Working Paper no. WPS 8284, Washington, DC, World Bank Group.

Feraud, R., R. Allesiardo, T. Urvoy, and F. Clerot. 2016. "Random Forest for the Contextual Bandit Problem." *Proceedings of Machine Learning Research* 51:93–101.

Glaeser, E. L., A. Hillis, S. D. Kominers, and M. Luca. 2016. "Predictive Cities Crowdsourcing City Government: Using Tournaments to Improve Inspection Accuracy." *American Economic Review* 106 (5): 114–18.

Glaeser, E. L., S. D. Kominers, M. Luca, and N. Naik. 2015. "Big Data and Big Cities: The Promises and Limitations of Improved Measures of Urban Life." NBER Working Paper no. 21778, Cambridge, MA.

Glaeser, E. L., S. D. Kominers, M. Luca, and N. Naik. 2018. "Big Data and Big Cities: The Promises and Limitations of Improved Measures of Urban Life." *Economic Inquiry* 56 (1): 114–37.

Goel, S., J. M. Rao, and R. Shroff. 2016. "Precinct or Prejudice? Understanding Racial Disparities in New York City's Stop-and-Frisk Policy." *Annals of Applied Statistics* 10 (1): 365–94.

Goldenshluger, A., and A. Zeevi. 2013. "A Linear Response Bandit Problem." *Stochastic Systems* 3 (1): 230–61.

Goldman, M., and J. M. Rao. 2014. "Experiments as Instruments: Heterogeneous Position Effects in Sponsored Search Auctions." The Third Conference on Auctions, Market Mechanisms and Their Applications. www.doi.org/10.4108 /eai.8-8-2015.2261043.

Gopalan, P., J. M. Hofman, and D. M. Blei. 2015. "Scalable Recommendation with Hierarchical Poisson Factorization." Proceedings of the Thirty-First Conference on Uncertainty in Artificial Intelligence, 326–35.

Hahn, J. 1998. "On the Role of the Propensity Score in Efficient Semiparametric Estimation of Average Treatment Effects." *Econometrica*:315–31.

Hartford, J., G. Lewis, and M. Taddy. 2016. "Counterfactual Prediction with Deep Instrumental Variables Networks." Working paper. https://arxiv.org/pdf /1612.09596.pdf.

Imai, K., and M. Ratkovic. 2013. "Estimating Treatment Effect Heterogeneity in Randomized Program Evaluation." *Annals of Applied Statistics* 7 (1): 443–70.

Imbens, G. W., and D. B. Rubin. 2015. *Causal Inference in Statistics, Social, and Biomedical Sciences.* Cambridge: Cambridge University Press.

Imbens, G. W., and J. M. Wooldridge. 2009. "Recent Developments in the Econometrics of Program Evaluation." *Journal of Economic Literature* 47 (1): 5–86.

Jean, N., M. Burke, M. Xie, W. M. Davis, D. B. Lobell, and S. Ermon. 2016. "Combining Satellite Imagery and Machine Learning to Predict Poverty." *Science* 353 (6301): 790–94.

Jiang, N., and L. Li. 2016. "Doubly Robust Off-Policy Value Evaluation for Reinforcement Learning." *Proceedings of the 33rd International Conference on Machine Learning*, vol. 48, 652–61.

Kallus, N. 2017. "Balanced Policy Evaluation and Learning." Cornell University Library. https://arxiv.org/abs/1705.07384.

Kitagawa, T., and A. Tetenov. 2015. "Who Should Be Treated? Empirical Welfare Maximization Methods for Treatment Choice." Technical report, Centre for Microdata Methods and Practice, Institute for Fiscal Studies.

Kleinberg, J., J. Ludwig, S. Mullainathan, and Z. Obermeyer. 2015. "Prediction Policy Problems." *American Economic Review* 105 (5): 491–95.

Kleinberg, J., S. Mullainathan, and M. Raghavan. 2016. "Inherent Trade-Offs in the Fair Determination of Risk Scores." Cornell University Library. https://arxiv.org/abs/1609.05807.

Komarova, T., D. Nekipelov, and E. Yakovlev. 2015. "Estimation of Treatment Effects from Combined Data: Identification versus Data Security." In *Economic Analysis of the Digital Economy*, edited by A. Goldfarb, S. M. Greenstein, and C. Tucker, 279–308. Chicago: University of Chicago Press.

Künzel, S., J. Sekhon, P. Bickel, and B. Yu. 2017. "Meta-Learners for Estimating Heterogeneous Treatment Effects Using Machine Learning." Cornell University Library. https://arxiv.org/abs/1706.03461.

Laffont, J.-J., H. Ossard, and Q. Vuong. 1995. "Econometrics of First-Price Auctions." *Econometrica: Journal of the Econometric Society* 63 (4): 953–80.

Lewis, R. A., and J. M. Rao. 2015. "The Unfavorable Economics of Measuring the Returns to Advertising." *Quarterly Journal of Economics* 130 (4): 1941–73.

Li, L., S. Chen, J. Kleban, and A. Gupta. 2014. "Counterfactual Estimation and Optimization of Click Metrics for Search Engines." Cornell University Library. https://arxiv.org/abs/1403.1891.

Li, L., W. Chu, J. Langford, T. Moon, and X. Wang. 2012. "An Unbiased Offline Evaluation of Contextual Bandit Algorithms with Generalized Linear Models." *Journal of Machine Learning Research Workshop and Conference Proceedings* 26:19–36.

Li, L., W. Chu, J. Langford, and R. Schapire. 2010. "A Contextual-bandit Approach to Personalized News Article Recommendation." *International World Wide Web Conference.* https://dl.acm.org/citation.cfm?doid=1772690.1772758.

Li, L., Y. Lu, and D. Zhou. 2017. "Provably Optimal Algorithms for Generalized Linear Contextual Bandits." *International Conference on Machine Learning.* https://arxiv.org/abs/1703.00048.

McFadden, D. 1973. "Conditional Logit Analysis of Qualitative Choice Behavior." In *Frontiers in Econometrics*, edited by P. Zarembka. New York: Wiley.

Mullainathan, S., and J. Spiess. 2017. "Machine Learning: An Applied Econometric Approach." *Journal of Economic Perspectives* 31 (2): 87–106.

Naik, N., S. D. Kominers, R. Raskar, E. L. Glaeser, and C. A. Hidalgo. 2017. "Computer Vision Uncovers Predictors of Physical Urban Change." *Proceedings of the National Academy of Sciences* 114 (29): 7571–76.

Naik, N., J. Philipoom, R. Raskar, and C. Hidalgo. 2014. "Streetscore-Predicting the Perceived Safety of One Million Streetscapes." In *Proceedings of the IEEE Conference on Computer Vision and Pattern Recognition Workshops*, 779–85.

Ng, A. Y., and S. J. Russell. 2000. "Algorithms for Inverse Reinforcement Learning."

In *Proceedings of the Seventeenth International Conference on Machine Learning*, 663–70. https://dl.acm.org/citation.cfm?id=657801.

Peysakhovich, A., and A. Lada. 2016. "Combining Observational and Experimental Data to Find Heterogeneous Treatment Effects." Cornell University Library. http://arxiv.org/abs/1611.02385.

Robinson, P. M. 1988. "Root-n-Consistent Semiparametric Regression." *Econometrica: Journal of the Econometric Society* 56 (4): 931–54.

Roth, A. E. 2002. "The Economist as Engineer: Game Theory, Experimentation, and Computation as Tools for Design Economics." *Econometrica* 70 (4): 1341–78.

Ruiz, F. J., S. Athey, and D. M. Blei. 2017. "Shopper: A Probabilistic Model of Consumer Choice with Substitutes and Complements." Cornell University Library. https://arxiv.org/abs/1711.03560.

Scott, S. L. 2010. "A Modern Bayesian Look at the Multi-Armed Bandit." *Applied Stochastic Models in Business and Industry* 26 (6): 639–58.

Strehl, A., J. Langford, L. Li, and S. Kakade. 2010. "Learning from Logged Implicit Exploration Data." *Proceedings of the 23rd International Conference on Neural Information Processing Systems*, vol. 2, 2217–25.

Swaminathan, A., and T. Joachims. 2015. "Batch Learning from Logged Bandit Feedback through Counterfactual Risk Minimization." *Journal of Machine Learning Research* 16 (Sep.): 1731–55.

Thomas, P., and E. Brunskill. 2016. "Data-Efficient Off-Policy Policy Evaluation for Reinforcement Learning." *Proceedings of the 33rd International Conference on Machine Learning*, vol. 48, 2139–48.

Tibshirani, R., and T. Hastie. 1987. "Local Likelihood Estimation." *Journal of the American Statistical Association* 82 (398): 559–67.

Ugander, J., B. Karrer, L. Backstrom, and J. Kleinberg. 2013. "Graph Cluster Randomization." In *Proceedings of the 19th ACM SIGKDD International Conference on Knowledge Discovery and Data Mining—KDD '13*, 329. New York: ACM Press. ISBN 9781450321747. doi: 10.1145/2487575.2487695. http://dl.acm.org/citation.cfm?doid=2487575.2487695

van der Laan, M. J., and D. Rubin. 2006. "Targeted Maximum Likelihood Learning." Working Paper no. 213, UC Berkeley Division of Biostatistics.

Varian, H. R. 2014. "Big Data: New Tricks for Econometrics." *Journal of Economic Perspectives* 28 (2): 3–27.

Wager, S., and S. Athey. Forthcoming. "Estimation and Inference of Heterogeneous Treatment Effects Using Random Forests." *Journal of the American Statistical Association.*

Wan, M., D. Wang, M. Goldman, M. Taddy, J. Rao, J. Liu, D. Lymberopoulos, and J. McAuley. 2017. "Modeling Consumer Preferences and Price Sensitivities from Large-Scale Grocery Shopping Transaction Logs." In *Proceedings of the 26th International Conference on World Wide Web*, 1103–12.

White, H. 1992. *Artificial Neural Networks: Approximation and Learning Theory.* Hoboken, NJ: Blackwell Publishers.

Yeomans, M., A. K. Shah, and J. Kleinberg. 2016. "Making Sense of Recommendations." Working paper, Department of Economics, Harvard University. https://scholar.harvard.edu/files/sendhil/files/recommenders55.pdf.

Zeileis, A., T. Hothorn, and K. Hornik. 2008. "Model-Based Recursive Partitioning." *Journal of Computational and Graphical Statistics* 17 (2): 492–514.

Zubizarreta, J. R. 2015. "Stable Weights That Balance Covariates for Estimation with Incomplete Outcome Data." *Journal of the American Statistical Association* 110 (511): 910–22.

Comment   Mara Lederman

Athey provides a comprehensive, accessible, and exciting summary of the impact that machine learning (ML) is having—and will continue to have—on the field of economics. It is a thorough, thoughtful, and optimistic chapter that makes clear the unique strengths of ML and the unique strengths of traditional econometrics-based techniques for causal inference and highlights both the opportunities to combine these approaches as well as the sorts of tasks and problems that are likely to remain in each domain. The chapter contains several useful and practical examples that illustrate the application of ML techniques to questions and problems that are of interest to economists including allocating health care procedures, pricing, and measuring the impact of advertising.

At a broad level, the chapter has four main sections. The chapter begins by offering straightforward definitions of unsupervised and supervised ML. Athey puts it quite simply: unsupervised ML uses algorithms to identify observations that are similar in their covariates, while supervised ML uses algorithms to predict an outcome variable from observations on covariates. It is important to emphasize, and I will return to this, that the observations and variables that ML algorithms can handle often do not look like the typical quantitative data that economists use in empirical analysis. Both unsupervised and supervised machine-learning techniques can be applied to text, images, and video. For example, unsupervised ML algorithms can be used to identify similar videos (without needing to specify in advance what makes these videos similar) or similar restaurant reviews (again, without needed to specify which reviews are positive or negative or what words or phrases makes a review positive or negative). Supervised ML algorithms can be used to predict variables such as the sentiment of a tweet or the slant of a newspaper article, without having to specify ex ante what the relevant covariates are.

The chapter then discusses a number of ways in which off-the-shelf ML techniques can be directly integrated into traditional economics research. For example, both unsupervised and supervised ML can be used to create variables that can be used in standard econometric analyses. In addition, ML techniques can be directly applied to what Kleinberg et al. (2015) call "prediction policy problems." These are policy problems or decisions that inherently involve a prediction component and, in these cases, ML techniques may be superior to other statistical methodologies. These problems may involve novel sources of so-called "big data"—such as satellite image data used in Glaeser et al. (2018)—but need not. They are simply policy

Mara Lederman is associate professor of strategic management at Rotman School of Management, University of Toronto.

For acknowledgments, sources of research support, and disclosure of the author's material financial relationships, if any, please see http://www.nber.org/chapters/c14036.ack.

problems in which the predicted value of an unknown variable acts an input into a decision.

The third and most substantial section of the chapter discusses the growing literature at the intersection of machine learning, statistics, and econometrics. As Athey puts it, this literature is developing novel methodologies that "harass the strengths of ML algorithms to solve causal inference problems." Athey provides details on a number of recent contributions in this area, highlighting the parts of the estimation approaches that are improved by ML and the parts that continue to rely on traditional econometric approaches and assumptions. Athey predicts that these techniques will soon become commonly used in applied empirical work in economics.

Finally, the chapter concludes with a discussion of some of the broader effects that ML might have on the economics profession, beyond the impact on the way we do empirical research, including the types of questions economists will ask, the degree of cross-disciplinary collaboration, the production function for research and the emergence of the "economist as an engineer," working with business and government to implement policies, and experiments in a digital environment.

Athey's chapter lays out an exciting future for empirical work in economics. It makes clear that there are real complementarities between ML techniques and econometric techniques and she and others are working to develop the relevant methodological tools and make them available to applied researchers. Athey also points out that the growth of ML and ML-based decision-making raises a number of new questions—such as, how to avoid "gaming" of the algorithms as they become known and how to ensure algorithms are fair and nondiscriminatory—and that economists and other social scientists seem particularly well-suited to shed light on these types of issues.

While Athey discusses the current opportunities for economists to utilize "off-the-shelf" ML methodologies in their research—for example, to systematize model selection and robustness checks, to create variables, or to carry-out prediction exercises—I believe this point deserves even greater emphasis. The opportunities for researchers to integrate ML techniques into traditional reduced-form or structural empirical work seem enormous. This is because ML, at a fundamental level, takes inputs that do not look like data and turns them into an output that looks very much like the type of data that we can include in traditional econometric analyses. Machine learning is a machinery for prediction. Sometimes that prediction exercise looks like the kind of prediction exercise we might carry out with a simple logit or probit model. For example, we might have data on which students graduate college along with a number of their attributes upon admission, and we might use this data to develop a model that predicts that probability of graduation for each new college applicant.

However, much of the excitement around ML algorithms is that they can handle data sets that are "unstructured"—that do not contain a set of neatly labeled covariates in a series of columns. Indeed, ML does not even require the covariates to be specified or labeled. The algorithm determines what the relevant covariates are. Consider text. Text doesn't look like data. We cannot easily put text—whether long bodies of texts or short fragments of text—into regression models. But what ML can do is take text as an input and predict a variety of things about that text—its content, its sentiment, its political leaning—and these can be used as variables in traditional empirical analyses. As a very simple example, in Gans, Goldfarb, and Lederman (2017), we use a sentiment analysis algorithm to classify the sentiment of over four million unique tweets to or about a major US airline. This allows us to construct a variety of variables that measure not only the quantity, but also the sentiment of "voice" to an airline on a given day that can be used in our empirical analysis. Absent the algorithm we would be able to count up the number of tweets, but would have a much harder time classifying the sentiment of the tweet for anything other than a sample small enough to code by hand.

Tweets are only one example. There are many potentially interesting and informative sources of text that, with ML, can be now be exploited in empirical research. For example, other types of social media posts, online reviews, patent applications, job descriptions, newspaper articles, commercial contracts, court transcripts, research papers, email communications, customer service logs, performance evaluations, and financial filings to name just a few. Indeed, some of these examples have been discussed by others in this volume. Machine-learning technologies literally open the door to novel sources of data that economists can use to answer important questions in a variety of fields.

Finally, in addition to thinking about how we as researchers might integrate ML techniques into our own work, it seems critical to also think about how organizations' integration of ML into their decision-making may impact our research. Despite the growing use of randomized experiments, most research in applied economics still relies on observational data. Observational data, of course, creates challenges for causal identification because the data-generating process is unlikely to be random. We believe that observed equilibrium prices are the result of the interaction of supply and demand and we therefore cannot regress quantity on price to estimate the slope of a demand curve. Or, to use an example from organizational economics, we believe that organizational forms are chosen optimally to maximize performance, including economizing on transaction costs, and therefore we cannot simply regress performance on organizational form in order to estimate the performance implications of firm boundary decisions. We develop theoretical models to help us understand the data-generating process which, in turn, informs both our concerns about causality as well as the identification strategies that we develop.

As organizations increasingly allocate decisions to ML-based algorithms we need to ask what implications this will have for the variation we observe and exploit in the data we use for research. There are a number of factors to consider. First, ML-based decisions are generally opaque. Thus, even the organizations deploying the ML may not be able to explain how certain decisions were made and so we may not be to understand the data-generating process in some cases. Second, to the extent that organizations use ML to optimize decisions—for example, to target advertising toward those for which it will have the largest impact or to admit the MBA students who are predicted to be the most successful upon graduation—the use of ML may exacerbate selection problems. The treated and nontreated groups that we observe in our data may be even more different on unobservables when those two groups are the result of ML-based decisions. On the other hand, in some instances ML-based decisions may come closer to the behavioral models we specify. For example, many structural papers in industrial organization specify complicated pricing or entry models. Machine-earning-based algorithms may come closer to solving these problems than individual decision-makers within a firm. Finally, as ML and other artificial intelligence technologies diffuse across organizations, they are likely to diffuse at different rates. This means that, at least in some data sets, we are likely to observe a mix of ML-based and traditional decision-making that creates another potentially important source of unobserved heterogeneity. Overall, as applied researchers working with real-world data sets, we need to recognize that increasingly the data we are analyzing is going the be the result of decisions that are made by algorithms in which the decision-making process may or may not resemble the decision-making processes we model as social scientists.

References

Gans, Joshua S., Avi Goldfarb, and Mara Lederman. 2017. "Exit, Tweets and Loyalty." NBER Working Paper no. 23046, Cambridge, MA.

Glaeser, Edward L., Scott Duke Kominers, Michael Luca, and Nikhil Naik. 2018."Big Data and Big Cities: The Promises and Limitations of Improved Measures of Urban Life." *Economic Inquiry* 56 (1) 114–37.

Kleinberg, Jon, Jens Ludwig, Sendhil Mullainathan, and Ziad Obermeyer. 2015. "Prediction Policy Problems." *American Economic Review* 105 (5): 491–95.

Artificial Intelligence, Labor, Productivity, and the Need for Firm-Level Data

Manav Raj and Robert Seamans

22.1 Introduction

There have recently been dramatic increases in the technical capabilities of artificial intelligence (AI).[1] For example, in February 2016, Google's Deep-Mind used its AI to beat Korean Go master Lee Se-dol,[2] and in January 2017, an AI system called DeepStack beat humans at the complex poker game Texas Hold 'Em.[3] The Electronic Frontier Foundation (EFF) has tracked the rapid progress of AI in performing tasks at human-like levels of capability in domains including voice recognition, translation, visual image recognition, and others.[4] These advancements have led to both excitement about the capability of new technology to boost economic growth and concern about the fate of human workers in a world in which computer algorithms can perform many of the functions that a human can (e.g., Frey and Osborne 2017; Furman 2016b).

Indicative of this excitement and interest in the area, recent academic research, using national-level data on worldwide robotics shipments, suggests that robotics may have been responsible for about one-tenth of the

Manav Raj is a PhD student in the Management and Organizations Department at the Stern School of Business, New York University. Robert Seamans is associate professor of management and organizations at the Stern School of Business, New York University.

For acknowledgments, sources of research support, and disclosure of the authors' material financial relationships, if any, please see http://www.nber.org/chapters/c14037.ack.

1. Artificial intelligence is a loose term used to describe a range of advanced technologies that exhibit human-like intelligence, including machine learning, autonomous robotics and vehicles, computer vision, language processing, virtual agents, and neural networks.

2. https://www.nytimes.com/2016/03/10/world/asia/google-alphago-lee-se-dol.html.

3. https://www.scientificamerican.com/article/time-to-fold-humans-poker-playing-ai-beats-pros-at-texas-hold-rsquo-em/.

4. https://www.eff.org/ai/metrics.

increase in the gross domestic product (GDP) between 1993 and 2007 (Graetz and Michaels 2015). Moreover, according to the 2016 *Economic Report of the President*, worldwide demand for robotics has nearly doubled between 2010 and 2014, and the number and share of robotics-oriented patents have also increased (CEA 2016). Thus, robots may now be contributing even more to GDP growth than in the past.

However, even as these technologies may be contributing to GDP growth at a national level, we lack an understanding about how and when they contribute to firm-level productivity, what conditions they complement or substitute for labor, how they affect new firm formation, and how they shape regional economies. We lack an understanding of these issues because, to date, there is a lack of firm-level data on the use of robotics and AI. Such data will be important to collect to answer these questions and to inform policymakers about the role of these new technologies in our economy and society.

This chapter describes high-level findings about the effects of robotics on the economy while highlighting the few articles addressing the impact of AI, describes shortcomings of the existing data, and argues for more systematic data collection at the firm level. We echo a recent National Academies of Science Report (NAS 2017) calling for more data collection on the effects of automation, including both artificial intelligence and robotics, on the economy. More generally, collection of and access to granular data allows for better analysis of complex questions, and provides a "scientific safeguard" via replication work done by multiple sets of researchers (Lane 2003).

22.2   Existing Empirical Work

While there is little empirical work on the effects of either AI or robots, there are comparably more studies on robots, likely owing to their physical nature, which makes them easier to track over time and location. Initial studies of the effect of robots on productivity and labor provide a mixed view. Using robot shipment data at the country, industry, and year level from the International Federation of Robotics (IFR), Graetz and Michaels (2015) find large effects on productivity growth. Looking at national-level data on robot shipments across seventeen countries, Graetz and Michaels show that robots may be responsible for roughly one-tenth of the increases in the gross domestic product of these countries between 1993 and 2007 and may have increased productivity growth by more than 15 percent. This is a significant effect; according to the authors, it is comparable to the impact of the adoption of steam engines on British labor productivity in the nineteenth century. They also find evidence that, on average, wages increase with robot use, but hours worked drops for low-skilled and middle-skilled workers.

In another study using IFR data, Acemoglu and Restrepo (2017) examine the impact of the increase in industrial robot usage on regional US labor markets between 1990 and 2007. Using the distribution of robots at the industry level in other advanced countries as an instrument, the authors find that industrial robot adoption in the United States was negatively correlated with employment and wages during this time period. They estimate that each additional robot reduced employment by six workers and that one new robot per thousand workers reduced wages by 0.5 percent. The authors note that the effects are most pronounced in manufacturing, particularly in routine manual and blue-collar occupations, and for workers without a college degree. Further, they find no positive effects on employment due to the adoption of robotics in any industry.

The European Commission Report on Robotics and Employment (EC 2016) examined the use of industrial robots in Europe. The report relies on robotics data from the European Manufacturing Survey, a sample of 3,000 manufacturing firms in seven European countries, which has been periodically administered since 2001, most recently in 2012. Using this data, the authors find that the use of industrial robots is likelier in larger companies, firms utilizing batch production, and firms that are export oriented. The study finds no evidence that the use of industrial robots has any direct effect on employment, though firms utilizing robotics do have significantly higher levels of labor productivity.

More broadly, existing work on automation and employment has suggested that automation can either substitute for or complement labor. Frey and Osborne (2017) argue that almost half of the total US employment is at risk of being automated over the next two decades. Similarly, Brynjolfsson, and McAfee (2014) suggest that, due to the automation of cognitive tasks, new technologies may increasingly serve as substitutes rather than complements. On the other hand, other research has found that positive technology shocks have historically increased job opportunities and employment overall (e.g., Alexopoulos and Cohen 2016).

Regardless of the effect of automation on employment in the directly impacted industry, technology adoption may have positive upstream and downstream effects on labor. Autor and Salomons (2017) show that, while employment seems to fall within an industry as industry-specific productivity increases, positive spillovers to other sectors more than offset the negative own-industry employment effect. Further, Bessen (2017) finds that new technologies should have a positive effect on employment if they improve productivity in markets where there is a large amount of unmet demand. In the context of robotics and automation, Bessen suggests that new computer technology is associated with employment declines in manufacturing, where demand has generally been met, but is correlated with employment growth in less saturated, nonmanufacturing industries. Similarly, Mandel (2017), studying the effects of e-commerce, finds that job losses at brick-and-mortar department stores were more than made up for by new opportunities at fulfillment and call centers. Dauth et al. (2017) combines German labor market data with IFR robot shipment data and finds that, while each additional industrial robot leads to the loss of two manufacturing jobs, enough new jobs are created in the service industry to offset and in some cases overcompensate for the negative employment effect in manufacturing.

There has been less systematic work on the effect of AI on the economy. Two notable exceptions are studies by Frey and Osborne (2017) and the McKinsey Global Institute (MGI). Frey and Osborne (2017) attempt to determine what jobs may be particularly susceptible to automation and to provide an idea of how large an impact automation could have on the US labor force. The authors focus particularly on machine learning and its application to mobile robotics, and propose a model to predict the extent of computerization's impact on nonroutine tasks, noting potential engineering bottlenecks at tasks involving high levels of perception or manipulation, creative intelligence, and social intelligence. After categorizing tasks by their susceptibility to automation, Frey and Osborne map these tasks to the O*NET job survey, which provides open-ended descriptions of skills and responsibilities involved in an occupation over time. Integrating this data set with employment and wage data from the Bureau of Labor Statistics (BLS) allows the authors to propose certain subsets of the labor market that may be at high, medium, or low risk of automation. The study finds that 47 percent of US employment is at high risk of computerization. It should be noted that this study is at an aggregate level and does not examine how firms may react, any labor saving innovations that could arise, or potential productivity or economic growth.

Frey and Osborne's work has also been applied by researchers in other countries—mapping Frey and Osborne's occupation-level findings to German labor market data, Brzeski and Burk (2015) suggest that 59 percent of German jobs may be highly susceptible to automation, while conducting that same analysis in Finland, Pajarinen and Rouvinen (2014) suggest that 35.7 percent of Finnish jobs are at high risk to automation.

The Organisation for Economic Co-operation and Development (OECD) similarly set out to estimate the automatability of jobs across twenty-one OECD countries applying Frey and Osborne to a task-based approach. The OECD report argues that certain tasks will be displaced and that the extent that bundles of tasks differ within occupations and across countries may make certain occupations less prone to automation than Frey and Osborne predicted. Relying upon the task categorization done by Frey and Osborne, the authors map task susceptibility to automation to US data from the Programme for the International Assessment of Adult Competencies (PIAAC), a microlevel data source containing indicators on socioeconomic characteristics, skills, job-related information, job tasks, and competencies at the individual level. They then construct a model using the PIAAC to create a predicted susceptibility to automation based off of the observables in the PIAAC data to mirror the automatability score that Frey and Osborne created. This model is then applied at the worker level across all the PIAAC data to predict how susceptible occupations may be to automation. By conducting the analysis at the individual level, the OECD argues that it is better able to account for task variation between individuals within the same occupation. As a result, the report suggests that Frey and Osborne overestimated the extent to which occupations would be susceptible to automation. The OECD Report argues that only 9 percent of jobs in the United States and across OECD countries will be highly susceptible to automation. The report continues to discuss variations across OECD countries, suggesting that the percent can range from 6 percent (in Korea) up to 12 percent (in Austria).

Mann and Püttmann (2017) take a different approach to analyze the effects of automation on employment. In their study, the authors rely on information provided from granted patents. They apply a machine-learning algorithm to all US patents granted from 1976 to 2014 to identify patents related to automation (an automation patent is defined as a "device that operates independently from human intervention and fulfills a task with reasonable completion"). They then link the automation patents to the industries they are likely to be used in, and identify which areas in the United States that these industries are related in. By examining economic indicators in comparison to the density of automation patents used in an area, Mann and Puttman find that though automation causes manufacturing employment to fall, it increases employment in the service sector, and overall has a positive impact on employment.

In June 2017, the McKinsey Global Institute published an independent discussion paper examining trends in investment in artificial intelligence, the prevalence of AI adoption, and how AI is being deployed by companies that have started to use the technology (MGI Report 2017). For the purpose of their report, the authors adopted a fairly narrow definition of AI, focusing only on AI technology that is programmed to conduct one set task. The MGI report conducted their investigation with a multifaceted approach: it surveyed executives at over 3,000 international firms, interviewed industry experts, and analyzed investment flows using third-party venture capital, private equity, and mergers and acquisitions data. Using the data collected, the MGI report attempts to answer questions regarding adoption by sector, size, and geography; to look at performance implications of adoption; and to examine potential impacts to the labor market. Though the findings are presented at an aggregate level, much of the data, particularly the survey of executives, were collected at the firm level, allowing for further inquiry if one had access.

In addition to these published works, other researchers have begun to examine the effect of AI on occupations by looking at its impact on individual abilities and skills. Brynjolfsson, Mitchell, and Rock (forthcoming) apply a rubric from Brynjolfsson and Mitchell (2017) that evaluates the potential for applying machine learning to tasks to the set of work activities and tasks in the Bureau of Labor Statistics' O*NET occupational database. With this analysis, they create a "Suitability for Machine Learning" for labor inputs in the United States. Similar research by Felten, Raj, and Seamans (forthcoming) uses data-tracking progress in artificial intelligence aggregated by the Electronic Frontier Foundation (EFF) across a variety of different artificial intelligence metrics and the set of fifty-two abilities in the O*NET occupational database to identify the impact of artificial intelligence on each of the abilities, and create an occupation-level score measuring the potential impact of AI on the occupation. Because the data from the EFF is separated by AI metric, this work allows for the investigation and simulation of progress in different kinds of AI technology, such as image recognition, speech recognition, and ability to play abstract strategy games among others.

The current body of empirical literature surrounding robotics and AI adoption is growing, but is still thin, and despite often trying to answer similar questions, different studies have found disparate results. These discrepancies highlight the need for further inquiry, replication studies, and more complete and detailed data.

22.3   The Need for Firm-Level Data

While there is generally a paucity of data examining the adoption, use, and effects of both AI and robotics, there is currently less information available regarding AI. There are no public data sets on the utilization or adoption of AI at either the macro or micro level. The most complete source of information, the MGI study, is proprietary and inaccessible to the general public or the academic community.

The most comprehensive and widely used data set examining the diffusion of robotics is the International Federation of Robotics Robot Shipment Data. The IFR has been recording information regarding worldwide robot stock and shipment figures since 1993. The IFR collects this data from its members, who are typically large robot manufacturers such as FANUC, KUKA, and Yaskawa. The data are broken up by country, year, industry, and technological application, which allows for analysis of the industry-specific impacts of technology adoption. However, the IFR data set has shortcomings. The IFR defines an industrial robot as an "automatically controlled, reprogrammable, multipurpose manipulator, programmable in three or more axes, which can be either fixed in place or mobile for use in industrial automation applications."[5] This definition limits the set of industrial robots and ensures that the IFR does not collect any information on dedicated industrial robots that serve one purpose. Further, some of the robots are

---

5. https://ifr.org/standardization.

not classified by industry, detailed data is only available for industrial robots (and not robots in service, transportation, warehousing, or other sectors), and geographical information is often aggregated (e.g., data exist for North America as a category rather than the United States, or an individual state within the United States).

Another issue with the IFR data is the difficulty of integrating it with other data sources. The IFR utilizes its own industry classifications when organizing the data, rather than relying on broadly used identifiers such as the North American Industry Classification System (NAICS). Mapping IFR data to other data sets (such as BLS or census data) first requires cross-referencing IFR classifications to other identifiers. Industry-level data also cannot be used to answer micro-oriented questions about the impacts and reaction to technology adoption at the firm level.

While the IFR data are useful for some purposes, particularly examining the adoption of robotics by industry and country, its aggregated nature obscures differences occurring within industries and across regions, making it difficult to uncover when and how robots might serve as substitutes or complements to labor, and obscuring the differential effects of adoption within industries or countries. Additional data is needed to answer the issues raised above and to replicate existing studies. In particular, the National Academy of Sciences Report (NAS 2017) highlights the need for computer capital broken down at the firm and occupation level, skill changes over time by field, and data on organizational processes as they relate to technology adoption.

The European Manufacturing Survey (EMS) has been organized and executed periodically by a number of research organizations and universities across Europe since 2001, and is currently one of the only firm-level data sets examining the adoption of robotics. The overall objective of the EMS is to provide empirical evidence regarding the use and impact of technological innovation in manufacturing at the firm level. The EMS accomplishes this via a survey of a random sample of manufacturing firms with at least twenty employees across seven European countries (Austria, France, Germany, Spain, Sweden, Switzerland, and the Netherlands). While some aspects of the survey vary across countries, the core set of questions inquire about whether the firm uses robots, the intensity of robot usage, and reinvestment in new robot technology. Data currently exists for five survey rounds: 2001–2002, 2003–2004, 2006–2007, 2009–2010, and 2012–2013, and has been used in reports created by the European Commission to analyze the use of robotics and its impact on labor patterns, including wages, productivity, and offshoring.

As of now, the EMS appears to be one of the few data sources that are capturing the use of robots and automation at the firm level. This provides opportunities to analyze microeffects of robotics technology on firm productivity and labor, and to analyze firm decision-making following adoption. However, the EMS has its own limitations. The survey only considers industrial robots, and the core questionnaire only asks three questions regarding the use of robots in a factory setting. The survey is performed at the firm rather than establishment level, and the sample size of 3,000 is quite small. In contrast, the Census's Annual Survey of Manufacturers (ASM) surveys 50,000 establishments annually and 300,000 every five years.[6] Finally, similar to many other existing data sets, the EMS is purely focused on the manufacturing industry and does not address technology adoption at smaller firms with less than twenty employees.

22.4   Additional Firm-Level Research Questions

Firm-level data on the use of AI would allow researchers to address a host of questions including, but not limited to: the extent to which, and under what conditions, AI complement or substitute for labor; how AI affect firm- or establishment-level productivity; which types of firms are more or less likely to invest in AI; how market structure affects a firm's incentives to invest in AI; and how adoption is effecting firm strategies. As the nature of work itself changes with increased adoption, researchers can also investigate how firm management has been affected, particularly at the lower and middle level.

Additionally, there are many important policy questions that cannot be answered without disaggregated data. Some of these questions are related to the need to reevaluate how individuals are trained prior to entering the workforce. Without an understanding of the changes in worker experience resulting from technology adoption, it will be difficult to craft appropriate worker education, job training, and retraining programs. Further, issues related to inequality could be examined, particularly with relation to the "digital divide" and the effects of technology adoption on different demographics. There are also unanswered questions regarding the differential effects of adoption on regional economies. For example, the effects of AI on labor may be pronounced in some regions because industries, and even occupations within those industries, tend to be geographically clustered (Feldman and Kogler 2010). Thus, to the extent that AI or robots substitute for labor in certain industries or occupations, regions that rely heavily on those industries and occupations for jobs and local tax revenue may suffer. Moreover, following the recent financial crisis, unemployment insurance reserves in some states have been slow to recover (Furman 2016a). Data on the regional adoption of AI could be used to simulate the extent to which future adoption may increase unemployment and whether unemployment insurance reserves are adequately funded.

---

6. The census surveys all 300,000 manufacturing establishments every five years, and a rotating subsample of about 50,000 every year. See: https://www.census.gov/programs-surveys/asm /about.html.

Finally, these new technologies may have implications for entrepreneurs. Entrepreneurs may lack knowledge of how best to integrate robotics with a workforce and often face financing constraints that make it harder for them to adopt capital-intensive technologies. In the case of AI, entrepreneurs may lack data sets on customer behavior, which are needed to train AI systems. Firm-level surveys on the use of AI will help us develop a better understanding of these and related issues.

22.5   Strategies for Collecting More Data

Micro-level data regarding the adoption of AI, robots, and other types of automation can be created in a variety of ways, the most comprehensive of which would be via a census. Census data would provide information for the entire population of relevant establishments, and while the information provided would be narrow, quality is likely to be high. Additionally, data from the Census Bureau would be highly integrable with other government data sources, such as employment or labor statistics from the BLS. Data could be collected as a stand-alone inquiry, similar to the Management and Organizational Practices (MOPS) survey (see Bloom et al. 2017), or by adding questions to existing surveys, similar to work done by Brynjolfsson and McElheran (2016), which involved adding questions on data-driven decision-making to an existing census survey.

Data can also be created via a survey of firms. Survey data allows for more detailed inquiry than a census and can be carried out in a quicker and less expensive fashion. Further, a variety of organizations, both private and public, may have the interest and ability to conduct a survey regarding the adoption of AI or robotic technology. However, surveys introduce issues regarding sample selection and response rates, and depending on what organization is administering the survey, access to data can be limited or expensive.

Collecting survey data regarding the adoption of technology is not an entirely new concept. The Survey of Manufacturing Technology (SMT) was conducted by the Census Bureau in collaboration with the Department of Defense in 1988, 1991, and 1993 to measure the diffusion, use, and planned future use of new technologies in the manufacturing sector of the United States. The SMT surveyed 10,000 establishments to learn about plant characteristics and adoption of seventeen established technologies grouped into five categories: design and engineering, fabricated machining and assembly, automated material handling, automated sensors, and communication and control. Because the survey was administered by the Census Bureau, data from the SMT could easily be integrated with other firm-level data from the BLS or Census Bureau. The survey also allowed for panel analysis, as a subset of firms within the sample were respondents in multiple editions. Following the 1993 SMT, the Census Bureau discontinued the survey for funding reasons.

The Department of Defense used the SMT data to assess the diffusion of technology, and other federal agencies used the data to gauge competitiveness of the US manufacturing sector. The data were also used by the private sector in market analysis, competitiveness assessments, and planning. Multiple academic studies, including Dunne (1994), Mcguckin, Streitwieser, and Doms (1998), Doms, Dunne, and Troske (1997) and Lewis (2011) analyzed the SMT data to address questions related to productivity growth, skill-biased technical change, earnings, and capital-labor substitution, among others.

In many ways, the SMT could serve as a model for future inquiry into the adoption of robotics technology. It provided a broad look at the manufacturing industry in the United States and allowed for the examination of effects over time and for firm- and individual-level analysis when integrated with other data from the BLS or Census Bureau. However, any updated version of the SMT would need to redefine the relevant technologies, examine the intensity of use, and investigate what tasks different technologies are used for.

Private data collected at individual firms can also be a useful tool. Internal data from a firm exacerbates both the strengths and weaknesses of survey data. Data collected at a single establishment can provide an unmatched level of detail and richness compared to data created by either a census or a survey. For example, Cowgill (2016) uses detailed individual-level skill and performance data from a single establishment to assess the returns to machine-learning algorithms used in hiring decisions. However, with a sample size of one, selection on firm is a highly salient issue and generalizability may be low. Further, any data produced will almost certainly be proprietary and difficult to get access to by other researchers, making reproducibility difficult (Lane 2003).

22.6   Conclusion

The recent dramatic increases in technological capabilities we have seen in the fields of robotics and artificial intelligence provide society with a myriad of opportunities and challenges. To effectively take advantage of these technologies, we must have a complete and thorough understanding of the impacts of these technologies on growth, productivity, labor, and equality. Systematic data on the adoption and use of these technologies, particularly at the establishment level, is necessary to understand the effects of these technologies on the economy and society as a whole. The creation and aggregation of these data sets through the census, surveys conducted by public or private organizations, and internal data collected at individual firms, would provide researchers and policymakers with the tools needed to empirically investigate the impact of these technologies, and craft appropriate responses to this phenomenon.

Finally, the need for high-quality data in this area is also linked with national competitiveness, particularly in relation to crafting appropriate policy responses. Mitchell and Brynjolfsson (2017) argue that the lack of information on AI could cripple our ability to prepare for the effects of technological advancement, leading to missed opportunities and potentially disastrous consequences. For example, decisions regarding whether to tax or subsidize AI or robots rely on understanding whether or not the particular technology serves as a substitute or complement to labor. These decisions can affect adoption patterns, and if made with an incomplete understanding of the effect of these technologies on labor markets, can lead to lower economic growth, less hiring, and lower wages. In addition, data must also be utilized to properly respond to consequences stemming from technology adoption. Identifying which populations may be most vulnerable to job displacement and effectively structuring job retraining programs requires a comprehensive understanding of the microlevel impacts of adoption of these technologies.

References

Acemoglu, Daron, and Pascual Restrepo. 2017. "Robots and Jobs: Evidence from US Labor Markets." NBER Working Paper no. 23285, Cambridge, MA.

Alexopoulos, Michelle, and Jon Cohen. 2016. "The Medium Is the Measure: Technical Change and Employment, 1909–1949." *Review of Economics and Statistics* 98 (4): 792–810.

Autor, David, and Anna Salomons. 2017. "Robocalypse Now—Does Productivity Growth Threaten Employment?" Working paper, Massachusetts Institute of Technology.

Bessen, James. 2017. "Automation and Jobs: When Technology Boosts Employment." Law and Economics Paper no. 17-09, Boston University School of Law.

Bloom, Nicholas, Erik Brynjolfsson, Lucia Foster, Ron Jarmin, Megha Patnaik, Itay Saporta-Eksten, and John Van Reenen. 2017. "What Drives Differences in Management?" NBER Working Paper no. 23300, Cambridge, MA.

Brynjolfsson, Erik, and Andrew McAfee. 2014. *The Second Machine Age: Work, Progress, and Prosperity in a Time of Brilliant Technologies.* New York: W. W. Norton.

Brynjolfsson, Erik, and Kristina McElheran. 2016. "The Rapid Adoption of Data-Driven Decision-Making." *American Economic Review* 106 (5): 133–39.

Brynjolfsson, Erik, and Tom Mitchell. 2017. "What Can Machine Learning Do? Workforce Implications." *Science* 358 (6370): 1530–34.

Brynjolfsson, Erik, Tom Mitchell, and Daniel Rock. Forthcoming. "What Can Machines Learn, and What Does It Mean for Occupations and the Economy?" *American Economic Association Papers and Proceedings.*

Brzeski, Carsten, and Inga Burk. 2015. "Die Roboter Kommen." ("The Robots Come.") ING DiBa Economic Research. https://www.ing-diba.de/binaries /content/assets/pdf/ueber-uns/presse/publikationen/ing-diba-economic-analysis _roboter-2.0.pdf.

Council of Economic Advisers (CEA). 2016. "Economic Report of the President." https://obamawhitehouse.archives.gov/administration/eop/cea/economic-report -of-the-President/2016.

Cowgill, Bo. 2016. "The Labor Market Effects of Hiring through Machine Learning." Working paper, Columbia University.

Dauth, Wolfgang, Sebastian Findeisen, Jens Südekum, and Nicole Wößner. 2017. "German Robots—The Impact of Industrial Robots on Workers." IAB Discussion Paper, Institut für Arbeitsmarkt- und Berufsforschung. https://www.iab.de /en/publikationen/discussionpaper.aspx.

Doms, Mark, Timothy Dunne, and Kenneth R. Troske. 1997. "Workers, Wages and Technology." *Quarterly Journal of Technology* 62 (1): 253–90.

Dunne, Timothy. 1994. "Plant Age and Technology Use in U.S. Manufacturing Industries." *RAND Journal of Economics* 25 (3): 488–99.

European Commission (EC). 2016. "Analysis of the Impact of Robotic Systems on Employment in the European Union—2012 Data Update."

Feldman, Maryann P., and Dieter F. Kogler. 2010. "Stylized Facts in the Geography of Innovation." *Handbook of the Economics of Innovation* 1:381–410.

Felten, Ed, Manav Raj, and Rob Seamans. Forthcoming. "Linking Advances in Artificial Intelligence to Skills, Occupations, and Industries." *American Economics Association Papers & Proceedings.*

Frey, Carl B., and Michael A. Osborne. 2017. "The Future of Employment: How Susceptible Are Jobs to Computerisation?" *Technological Forecasting and Social Change* 114:254–80.

Furman, Jason. 2016a. "The Economic Case for Strengthening Unemployment Insurance." Remarks at the Center for American Progress, Washington DC, July 11. https://obamawhitehouse.archives.gov/sites/default/files/page/files /20160711_furman_uireform_cea.pdf.

———. 2016b. "Is This Time Different? The Opportunities and Challenges of Artificial Intelligence." Remarks at AI Now: The Social and Economic Implications of Artificial Intelligence Technologies in the Near Term, New York University, July 7. https://obamawhitehouse.archives.gov/sites/default/files/page/files /20160707_cea_ai_furman.pdf.

Graetz, Georg, and Guy Michaels. 2015. "Robots at Work." CE P Discussion Paper no. 1335, Centre for Economic Performance.

Lane, Julia. 2003. "Uses of Microdata: Keynote Speech." In *Statistical Confidentiality and Access to Microdata: Proceedings of the Seminar Session of the 2003 Conference of European Statisticians,* 11–20. Geneva.

Lewis, Ethan. 2011. "Immigration, Skill Mix, and Capital Skill Complementarity." *Quarterly Journal of Economics* 126 (2): 1029–69.

Mandel, Michael. 2017. "How Ecommerce Creates Jobs and Reduces Income Inequality." Working paper, Progressive Policy Institute. http://www.progressive policy.org/wp-content/uploads/2017/09/PPI_ECommerceInequality-final.pdf.

Mann, Katja, and Lukas Püttmann. 2017. "Benign Effects of Automation: New Evidence from Patent Texts." Unpublished manuscript.

Mcguckin, Robert H., Mary L. Streitwieser, and Mark Doms. 1998. "The Effect of Technology Use on Productivity Growth." *Economics of Innovation and New Technology* 7 (1): 1–26.

McKinsey Global Institute (MGI). 2017. "Artificial Intelligence the Next Digital Frontier?" https://www.mckinsey.com/business-functions/mckinsey-analytics /our-insights/how-artificial-intelligence-can-deliver-real-value-to-companies.

Mitchell, Tom, and Erik Brynjolfsson. 2017. "Track How Technology Is Transforming Work." *Nature* 544 (7650): 290–92.

National Academy of Sciences (NAS). 2017. "Information Technology and the U.S. Workforce: Where Are We and Where Do We Go from Here?" https://www.nap .edu/catalog/24649/information-technology-and-the-us-workforce-where-are -we-and.

Pajarinen, Mike, and Petri Rouvinen. 2014. "Computerization Threatens One Third of Finnish Employment." ETLA Brief no. 22, Research Institute of the Finnish Economy.

How Artificial Intelligence and Machine Learning Can Impact Market Design

Paul R. Milgrom and Steven Tadelis

23.1 Introduction

For millennia, markets have played a key role in providing individuals and businesses with the opportunity to gain from trade. More often than not, markets require structure and a variety of intuitional support to operate efficiently. For example, auctions have become a commonly used mechanism to generate gains from trade when price discovery is essential. Research in the area now commonly referred to as market design, going back to Vickrey (1961), demonstrated that it is critical to design auctions and market institutions more broadly in order to achieve efficient outcomes (see, e.g., Milgrom 2017; Roth 2015).

Any market designer needs to understand some fundamental details of the transactions that are expected to be consummated in order to design the most effective and efficient market structure to support these transactions. For example, the National Resident Matching Program, which matches doctors to hospital residencies, was originally designed in an era when nearly all doctors were men and wives followed them to their residencies. It needed to be redesigned in the 1990s to accommodate the needs of couples, when men and women doctors could no longer be assigned jobs in different cities. Even

Paul R. Milgrom is the Shirley and Leonard Ely Professor of Humanities and Sciences in the Department of Economics at Stanford University and professor, by courtesy, at both the Department of Management Science and Engineering and the Graduate School of Business. Steven Tadelis holds the James J. and Marianne B. Lowrey Chair in Business and is professor of economics, business, and public policy at the University of California, Berkeley, and a research associate of the National Bureau of Economic Research.

For acknowledgments, sources of research support, and disclosure of the authors' material financial relationships, if any, please see http://www.nber.org/chapters/c14008.ack.

something as mundane as the sale of a farm when a farmer dies requires knowledge of the structure and decisions about whether to sell the whole farm as a unit, or to separate the house for sale as a weekend retreat while selling the land to neighboring farmers, or selling the forest separately to a wildlife preservation fund.

In complex environments, it can be difficult to understand the underlying characteristics of transactions, and it is challenging to learn enough about them in order to design the best institutions to efficiently generate gains from trade. For example, consider the recent growth of online advertising exchanges that match advertisers with online ads. Many ads are allocated to advertisers using real-time auctions. But how should publishers design these auctions in order to make the best use of their advertising space, and how can they maximize the returns to their activities? Based on the early theoretical auction design work of Myerson (1981), Ostrovsky and Schwartz (2017) have shown that a little bit of market design in the form of setting better reserve prices can have a dramatic impact on the profits an online ad platform can earn.

But how can market designers learn the characteristics necessary to set optimal, or at least better, reserve prices? Or, more generally, how can market designers better learn the environment of their markets? In response to these challenges, artificial intelligence (AI) and machine learning are emerging as important tools for market design. Retailers and marketplaces such as eBay, TaoBao, Amazon, Uber, and many others are mining their vast amounts of data to identify patterns that help them create better experiences for their customers and increase the efficiency of their markets. By having better prediction tools, these and other companies can predict and better manage sophisticated and dynamic market environments. The improved forecasting that AI and machine-learning algorithms provide help marketplaces and retailers better anticipate consumer demand and producer supply as well as help target products and activities to finer segmented markets.

Turning back to markets for online advertising, two-sided markets such as Google, which match advertisers with consumers, are not only using AI to set reserve prices and segment consumers into finer categories for ad targeting, but they also develop AI-based tools to help advertisers bid on ads. In April 2017 Google introduced "Smart Bidding," a product based on AI and machine learning that helps advertisers bid automatically on ads based on ad conversions so they can better determine their optimal bids. Google explained that the algorithms use vast amounts of data and continually refine models of users' conversion to better spend an advertiser's dollars to where they bring in the highest conversion.

Another important application of AI's strength in improving forecasting to help markets operate more efficiently is in electricity markets. To operate efficiently, electricity market makers such as California's Independent System Operator must engage in demand and supply forecasting. An inaccurate forecast in the power grid can dramatically affect market outcomes causing high variance in prices, or worse, blackouts. By better predicting demand and supply, market makers can better allocate power generation to the most efficient power sources and maintain a more stable market.

As the examples above demonstrate, the applications of AI algorithms to market design are already widespread and diverse. Given the infancy of the technology, it is a safe bet that AI will play a growing role in the design and implementation of markets over a wide range of applications. In what follows, we describe several less obvious ways in which AI has played a key role in the operation of markets.

23.2   Machine Learning and the Incentive Auction

In the first part of the twentieth century, the most important infrastructure projects for the United States related to transportation and energy infrastructure. By the early twenty-first century, however, it was not just people and goods that needed to be transported in high volumes, but also information. The emergence of mobile devices, WiFi networks, video on demand, the Internet of Things, services supplied through the cloud, and much more has already created the need for major investments in the communication network, and with 5G technologies just around the corner, more is coming.

Wireless communications, however, depend on infrastructure and other resources. The wireless communication rate depends on the channel capacity, which in turn depends jointly on the communication technology used and the amount of radio spectrum bandwidth devoted to it. To encourage growth in bandwidth and the rapid develop of new uses, the Obama White House in 2010 issued its National Broadband Plan. That plan set a goal of freeing a huge amount of bandwidth from older, less productive uses to be used instead as part of the modern data highway system.

In 2016–2017, the US Federal Communications Commission (FCC) designed and ran an auction market to do part of that job. The radio spectrum licenses that it sold in that auction raised about $20 billion in gross revenue. As part of the process of making room for those new licenses, the FCC purchased TV broadcast rights for about $10 billion, and incurred nearly $3 billion in costs to move other broadcasters to new TV channels. Some 84MHz of spectrum was made available in total, including 70MHz for wireless broadband and 14MHz for unlicensed uses. This section describes the processes that were used, and the role of AI and machine learning to improve the underlying algorithms that supported this market.

Reallocating spectrum from one use to another is, in general, neither easy nor straightforward, in either the planning or the implementation (Leyton-Brown, Milgrom, and Segal 2017). Planning such a change can involve surprisingly hard computational challenges, and the implementation requires high levels of coordination. In particular, the reallocation of a portion of the spectrum band that had been used for UHF broadcast television required deciding how many channels to clear, which stations would cease broadcasting (to make room for the new uses), what TV channels would be assigned to the remaining stations that continued to broadcast, how to time the changes to avoid interference during the transition, and to assure that the TV tower teams, which would replace the old broadcast equipment, had sufficient capacity, and so on. Several of the computations involved are, in principle, nondeterministic polynomial time (NP)-hard, making this a particularly complex market-design problem. One of the most critical algorithms used for this process—the "feasibility checker"—was developed with the aid of machine-learning methods.

But why reallocate and reassign TV stations at all? Broadcast television changed enormously in the late twentieth century. In the early days of television, all viewing was of over-the-air broadcasts using an analog technology. Over the decades that followed, cable and satellite services expanded so much that, by 2010, more than 90 percent of the US population was reached by these alternative services. Standard definition TV signals were replaced by high definition and, eventually, 4K signals. Digital television and tuners reduced the importance of channel assignments, so that the channel used by consumers/viewers did not need to match the channel used by the broadcaster. Digital encoding made more efficient use of the band and it became possible to use multiplexing, so that what was once a single standard-definition broadcast channel could carry multiple high-definition broadcasts. Marginal spectrum had fallen in value compared to the alternative uses.

Still, the reallocation from television broadcasting would be daunting and beyond what an ordinary market mechanism could likely achieve. The signal from each of thousands of TV broadcast towers across the United States can interfere with potential uses for about 200 miles in every direction, so all of the broadcasts in any frequency needed to be cleared to make the frequencies available for new uses. Not only would it be necessary to coordinate among different areas of the United States, but coordination with Canada and Mexico would improve the allocation, too; most of the population of Canada lives, and most of its TV stations operate, within 200 miles of the US border. Because a frequency is not usable until virtually all of the relevant broadcasters have ceased operation, efficiency would demand that these changes would need to be coordinated in time, too; they should be roughly simultaneous. In addition, there needed to be coordination *across* frequencies. The reason is that we need to know in advance which channels will be cleared before the frequencies can be efficiently divided between uplink uses and downlink uses.

Among the many issues to be resolved, one would be how to determine which stations would continue to broadcast after the transition. If the goal were efficiency, then the problem can be formulated as maximizing the total value of the TV stations that continue to broadcast after the auction. Let N

be the set of all currently broadcasting TV stations and let $S \subseteq N$ be a subset of those TV stations. Let C be the set of available channels to which to assign stations after the auction, and let $\emptyset$ denote the null assignment for a station that does not continue to broadcast. A channel assignment is a mapping $A : N \rightarrow C \cup \{\emptyset\}$. The constraints on the channels available for assignment are to ones that rule out interference between pairs of TV stations, taking the form: $A(n_1) = c_1 \Rightarrow A(n_2) \neq c_2$ for some $(c_1, c_2) \in C^2$. Each such constraint is described by a fourtuple: $(n_1, c_1 n_2, c_2)$. There were more than a million such constraints in the FCC's problem. A channel assignment is feasible if it satisfies all the interference constraints; let $\mathcal{A}$ denote the feasible set of assignments. A set of stations S' can be feasibly assigned to continue broadcasting, which we denote by $S' \in \mathcal{F}(C)$, if there exists some feasible channel assignment $A \in \mathcal{A}$ such that $\emptyset \notin A(S')$.

Most of the interference constraints took a special form. Those constraints assert that no two stations that are geographic neighbors can be assigned to the same channel. Let us call such stations "linked" and denote the relationship by $(n_1, n_2) \in L$. For such a pair of stations, the constraint can be written as: $A(n_1) = A(n_2) \Rightarrow A(n_1) = \emptyset$. These are the *cochannel interference constraints*. One can think of (N, L) as defining a graph with nodes N and arcs L. If the cochannel constraints were the only ones, then determining whether $S' \in \mathcal{F}$ would amount to deciding whether there exists a way to assign channels in C to the stations in N so that no two linked nodes are on the same channel.

Figure 23.1 shows the graph of the cochannel interference constraints for the United States and Canada. The constraint graph is most dense in the eastern half of the United States and along the Pacific Coast.

In the special case of cochannel constraints, the problem of checking the feasibility of a set of stations is a standard *graph-coloring* problem. The problem is to decide whether it is possible to assign a color (channel) to each node (station) in the graph so that no two linked nodes are given the same color. Graph-coloring is in the class of NP-complete problems, for which there is no known algorithm that is guaranteed to be fast, and for which it is commonly hypothesized[1] that worst-case solution time grows exponentially in the problem size. Since the general station assignment problem includes the graph coloring problem, it, too, is NP-complete, and can become intractable at scales such as that of the FCC's problem.

The problem that the FCC would ideally like to solve using an auction is to maximize the value of the stations that remain on-air to broadcast, given the reduced set of channels C. If the value of station j is v_j, the problem can be formulated as follows:

$$\max_{S \in \mathcal{F}(C)} \sum_{j \in S} v_j.$$

1. The standard computer science hypothesis that $P \neq NP$ implies that no fast algorithm exists for NP-complete problems.

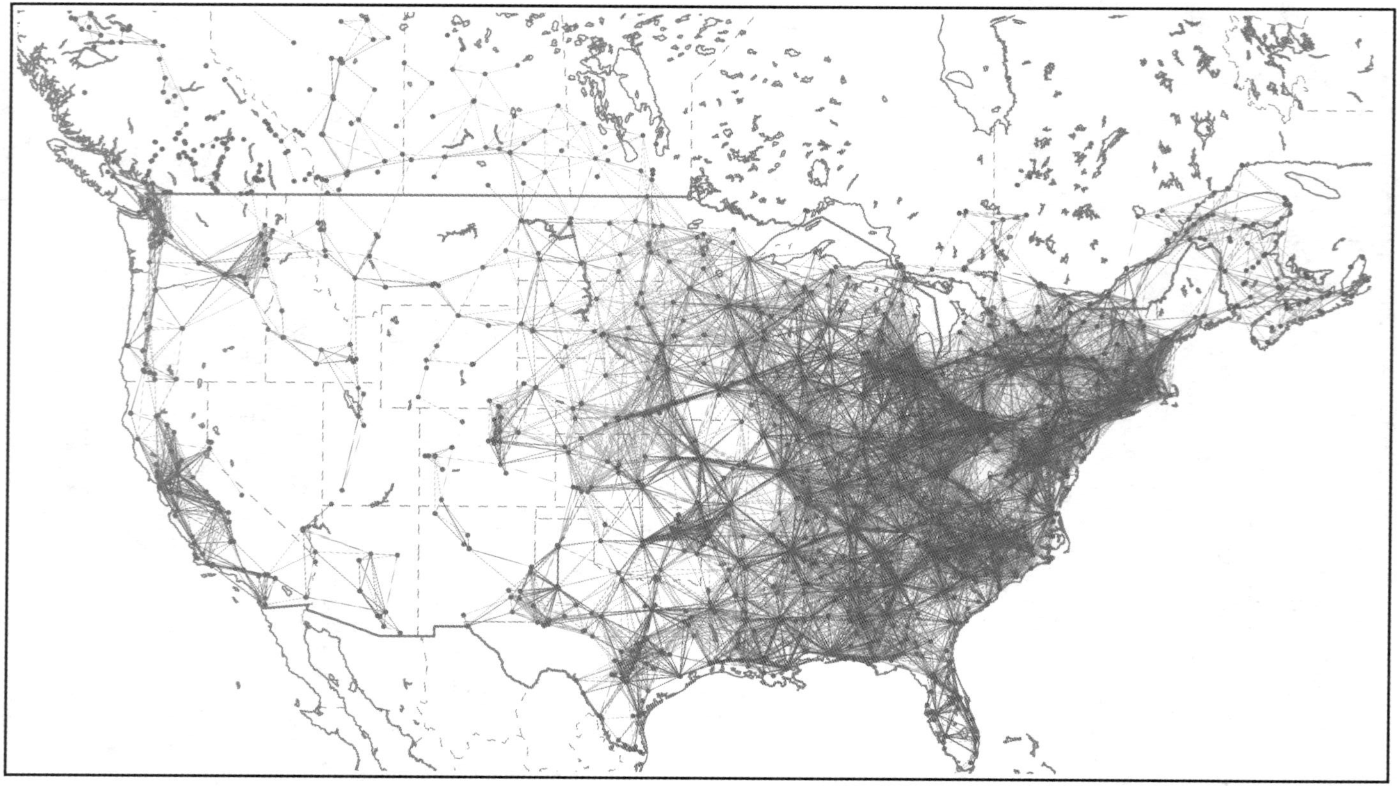

Fig. 23.1   Cochannel interference graph for spectrum reallocation

This problem is very hard. Indeed, as we have just argued, even checking the condition $S \in \mathcal{F}(C)$ is NP-complete, and solving exactly the related optimization is even harder in practice. Computational experiments suggest that with weeks of computation approximate optimization is possible, but with an optimization shortfall that can be a few percent.

For a TV station owner, it would be daunting to formulate a bid in an auction in which even the auctioneer, with all the bids in hand, would find it challenging to determine the winners. Faced with such a problem, some station owners might choose not to participate. That concern led the FCC staff to prefer a strategy-proof design, in which the optimal bid for the owner of a single station is relatively simple, at least in concept: compute your station's value and bid that amount. As is well known, there is a unique strategy-proof auction that optimizes the allocation and pays zero to the losers: the Vickrey auction. According to the Vickrey rules, if the auctioneer purchases the broadcast rights from station j, it must pay the owner this price:

$$p_i = \left(\max_{S \in \mathcal{F}(C)} \sum_{j \in S} v_j \right) - \left(\max_{\substack{S \in \mathcal{F}(C) \\ i \notin S}} \sum_{j \in S} v_j \right).$$

For a winning station i, the Vickrey price p_i will be larger than the station value. With roughly 2,000 stations to include in the optimization, a 1 percent error in either of the two maximizations would result in a pricing error for p_i equal to about 2,000 percent of the value of an average station. Such huge potential pricing errors would likely raise hackles among some of the potential bidders.

One way to put the problem of the Vickrey auction into sharp relief is to imagine the letter that the FCC might write to broadcasters to encourage their participation:

Dear Mr. Broadcaster:

We have heard your concerns about the complexity of the spectrum reallocation process. You may even be unsure about whether to participate or how much to bid. To make things as easy as possible for you, we have adopted a Nobel Prize–winning auction procedure called the "Vickrey auction." In this auction, all you need to do is to tell us what your broadcast rights are worth to you. We'll figure out whether you are a winner and, if so, how much to pay to buy your rights. The rules will ensure that it is in your interest to report truthfully. That is the magic of the Vickrey auction!

The computations that we do will be very hard ones, and we cannot guarantee that they will be exactly correct.

Such a letter would leave many stations owners uncomfortable and unsure about whether to participate. The FCC decided to adopt a different design.

What we describe here is a simplified version of the design, in which the broadcasters' only choices are whether to sell their rights or to reject the

FCC's offer and continue to broadcast. Each individual broadcaster was comforted by the assurance that it could bid this way, even if it had additional options, too. [2]

In the simplified auction, each bidder i was quoted a price $p_i(t)$ at each round t of the auction that decreased from round-to-round. In each round, the bidder could "exit," rejecting the current price and keeping its broadcast rights, or it could accept the current price. After a round t of bidding, stations were processed one at a time. When station i was processed, the auction software would use its *feasibility checker* to attempt to determine whether it could feasibly assign station i to continue broadcasting, given the other stations that had already exited and to which a channel must be assigned. This is the generalized graph-coloring problem, mentioned earlier. If the software timed out, or if it determined that it is impossible to assign the station, then the station would become a winner and be paid $p_i(t-1)$. Otherwise, its price would be reduced to $p_i(t)$ and it would exit or continue, according to the bidder's instructions. It would be obvious to a station owner that, regardless of the pricing formula and of how the software performed, its optimal choice when its value is v_i is to exit if $p_i(t) < v_i$ and otherwise to continue. [3]

The theory of clock auctions of this sort for problems with hard computations has been developed by Milgrom and Segal (2017), who also report simulations showing high performance in terms of efficiency and remarkably low costs of procuring TV broadcast rights.

The performance of this descending auction design depends deeply on the quality of the feasibility checker. Based on early simulations, our rough estimate was the each 1 percent of failures in feasibility checking would add about 1.5 percent—or about $150 million—to the cost of procuring the broadcast rights. So, solving most of the problems very fast became a high priority for the auction-design team.

As a theoretical proposition, any known algorithm for feasibility checking in the spectrum-packing problem has worst-case performance that grows exponentially in the size of the problem. Nevertheless, if we know the distribution of likely problems, there can still be algorithms that are fast with

---

2. In the actual auction, some broadcasters also had the option to switch from a UHF TV channel to a channel in the high VHF band, or one in the low VHF band (the so-called HVHF and LVHF options).

3. The pricing formula that the FCC used for each station was $p_i(t) = (\text{Pop}_i \text{Links}_i)^{0.5} q(t)$. In this formula, $q(t)$ is the "base clock price" that scaled the price offers to all the bidders. This price began at a high level $q(0)$ to encourage participation, and it declined round-by-round during the auction; Pop_i denotes the population of the area served by the station, which stands in for the value of the station. By linking prices to population served, the auctioneer is able to offer higher prices to valuable stations in high-population areas that it might need to acquire for a successful auction; Links_i measured the number of other stations to which station i was linked in the interference graph. It was hoped that, by including this term in the pricing formula, the auction would be able to offer higher prices to and buy the rights of stations that pose particularly difficult problems by interfering with many other stations.

high probability. But how can we know the distribution and how can such an algorithm be found?

The FCC auction used a feasibility checker developed by a team of Auctionomics researchers at the University of British Columbia, led by Professor Kevin Leyton-Brown. There were many steps in the development, as reported by Newman, Fréchette, and Leyton-Brown (forthcoming), but here we emphasize the role of machine learning. Auctionomics' goal was to be able to solve 99 percent of the problem instances in one minute or less.

The development effort began by simulating the planned auction to generate feasibility problems like those that might be encountered in a real auction. Running many simulations generated about 1.4 million problem instances that could be used for training and testing a feasibility-checking algorithm. The first step of the analysis was to formulate the problem as mixed integer programs and test standard commercial software—CPLEX and Gurobi—to see how close those could come to meeting the performance objectives. The answer was: not close. Using a 100-seconds cutoff, Gurobi could solve only about 10 percent of the problems and CPLEX only about 25 percent. These were not nearly good enough for decent performance in a real-time auction.

Next, the same problems were formulated as satisfiability problems and tested using seventeen research solvers that had participated in recent SAT-solving tournaments. These were better, but none could solve as many as two-thirds of the problems within the same 100-second cutoff. The goal remained 99 percent in sixty seconds.

The next step was to use automated algorithm configuration, a procedure developed by Hutter, Hoos, and Leyton-Brown (2011) and applied in this setting by Leyton-Brown and his students at the University of British Columbia. The idea is to start with a highly parameterized algorithm for solving satisfiability problems[4] and to train a random forest model of the algorithm performance, given the parameters. To do that, we first ran simulated auctions with what we regarded as plausible behavior by the bidders to generate a large data set of representative problems. Then, we solved those problems using a variety of different parameter settings to determine the distribution of solution times for each vector of parameters. This generated a data set with parameters and performance measures. Two of the most interesting performance characteristics were the median run time and

---

4. There are no known algorithms for NP-complete problems that are guaranteed to be fast, so the best existing algorithms are all heuristics. These algorithms weight various characteristics of the problem to decide about such things as the order in which to check different branches of a search tree. These weights are among the parameters that can be set and adapted to work well for a particular class of problems, such as those that arise in the incentive auction application. The particular software algorithm that we used was CLASP, which had more than 100 exposed parameters that could be modified.

the fraction of instances solved within one minute. Then, using a Bayesian model, we incorporated uncertainty in which the experimenter "believes" that the actual performance is normally distributed with a mean determined by the random forest and a variance that depends on the distance of the parameter vector from the nearest points in the data set. Next, the system identifies the parameter vector that maximizes the expected improvement in performance, given the mean and variance of the prior and the performance of the best-known parameter vector. Finally, the system tests the actual performance for the identified parameters and adds that as an observation to the data set. Proceeding iteratively, the system identifies more parameters to test, investigates them, and adds them to the data to improve the model accuracy until the time budget is exhausted.

Eventually, this machine-learning method leads to diminishing returns to time invested. One can then create a new data set from the instances on which the parameterized algorithm was "slow," for example, taking more than fifteen seconds to solve. By training a new algorithm on those instances, and running the two parameterized algorithms in parallel, the machine-learning techniques led to dramatic improvements in performance.

For the actual auction, several other problem-specific tricks were also applied to contribute to the speed-up. For example, to some extent it proved possible to decompose the full problem into smaller problems, to reuse old solutions as starting points for a search, to store partial solutions that might help guide solutions of further problems, and so on. In the end, the full set of techniques and tricks resulted in a very fast feasibility checker that solved all but a tiny fraction of the relevant problems within the allotted time.

23.3   Using AI to Promote Trust in Online Marketplaces

Online marketplaces such as eBay, Taobao, Airbnb, and many others have grown dramatically since their inception just over two decades ago, providing businesses and individuals with previously unavailable opportunities to purchase or profit from online trading. Wholesalers and retailers can market their goods or get rid of excess inventory; consumers can easily search marketplaces for whatever is on their mind, alleviating the need for businesses to invest in their own e-commerce website; individuals transform items they no longer use into cash; and more recently, the so called "gig economy" is comprised of marketplaces that allow individuals to share their time or assets across different productive activities and earn extra income.

The amazing success of online marketplaces was not fully anticipated, primarily because of the hazards of anonymous trade and asymmetric information. Namely, how can strangers who have never transacted with one another, and who may be thousands of miles apart, be willing to trust each other? Trust on both sides of the market is essential for parties to be willing to transact and for a marketplace to succeed. The early success of eBay is often attributed to the innovation of introducing its famous feedback and reputation mechanism, which was adopted in one form or another by practically every other marketplace that came after eBay. These online feedback and reputation mechanisms provide a modern-day version of more ancient reputation mechanisms used in the physical marketplaces that were the medieval trade fairs of Europe (see Milgrom, North, and Weingast 1990).

Still, recent studies have shown that online reputation measures of marketplace sellers, which are based on buyer-generated feedback, don't accurately reflect their actual performance. Indeed, a growing literature has shown that user-generated feedback mechanisms are often biased, suffer from "grade inflation," and can be prone to manipulation by sellers.[5] For example, the average percent positive for sellers on eBay is about 99.4 percent, with a median of 100 percent. This causes a challenge to interpret the true levels of satisfaction on online marketplaces.

A natural question emerges: Can online marketplaces use the treasure trove of data it collects to measure the quality of a transaction and predict which sellers will provide a better service to their buyers? It has become widely known that all online marketplaces, as well as other web-based services, collect vast amounts of data as part of the process of trade. Some refer to this as the "exhausts data" generated by the millions of transactions, searches, and browsing that occur on these marketplaces daily. By leveraging this data, marketplaces can create an environment that would promote trust, not unlike the ways in which institutions emerged in the medieval trade fairs of Europe that helped foster trust. The scope for market design goes far beyond the more mainstream application like setting rules of bidding and reserve prices for auctions or designing tiers of services, and in our view, includes the design of mechanisms that help foster trust in marketplaces. What follows are two examples from recent research that show some of the many ways that marketplaces can apply AI to the data they generate to help create more trust and better experiences for their customers.

23.3.1   Using AI to Assess the Quality of Sellers

One of the ways that online marketplaces help participants build trust is by letting them communicate through online messaging platforms. For example, on eBay buyers can contact sellers to ask them questions about their products, which may be particularly useful for used or unique products for which buyers may want to get more refined information than is listed. Similarly, Airbnb allows potential renters to send messages to hosts and ask questions about the property that may not be answered in the original listing. Using Natural Language Processing (NLP), a mature area in AI, market-

---

5. On bias and grade inflation see, for example, Nosko and Tadelis (2015), Zervas, Proserpio, and Byers (2015), and Filippas, Horton, and Golden (2017). On seller manipulation of feedback scores see, for example, Mayzlin, Dover, and Chevalier (2014) and Xu et al. (2015).

places can mine the data generated by these messages in order to better predict the kind of features that customers value. However, there may also be subtler ways to apply AI to manage the quality of marketplaces. The messaging platforms are not restricted to pretransaction inquiries, but also offer the parties to send messages to each other *after* the transaction has been completed. An obvious question then emerges: How could a marketplace analyze the messages sent between buyers and sellers post the transaction to infer something about the quality of the transaction that feedback doesn't seem to capture?

This question was posed and answered in a recent paper by Masterov, Mayer, and Tadelis (2015) using internal data from eBay's marketplace. The analysis they performed was divided into two stages. In the first stage, the goal was to see if NLP can identify transactions that went bad when there was an independent indication that the buyer was unhappy. To do this, they collected internal data from transactions in which messages were sent from the buyer to the seller after the transaction was completed, and matched it with another internal data source that recorded actions by buyers indicating that the buyer had a poor experience with the transactions. Actions that indicate an unhappy buyer include a buyer claiming that the item was not received, or that the item was significantly not as described, or leaves negative or neutral feedback, to name a few.

The simple NLP approach they use creates a "poor-experience" indicator as the target (dependent variable) that the machine-learning model will try to predict, and uses the messages' content as the independent variables. In its simplest form and as a proof of concept, a regular expression search was used that included a standard list of negative words such as "annoyed," "dissatisfied," "damaged," or "negative feedback" to identify a message as negative. If none of the designated terms appeared, then the message was considered neutral. Using this classification, they grouped transactions into three distinct types: (a) no posttransaction messages from buyer to seller, (b) one or more negative messages, or (c) one or more neutral messages with no negative messages.

Figure 23.2, which appears in Masterov, Mayer, and Tadelis (2015), describes the distribution of transactions with the different message classifications together with their association with poor experiences. The x-axis of figure 23.1 shows that approximately 85 percent of transactions fall into the benign first category of no posttransaction messages. Buyers sent at least one message in the remaining 15 percent of all transactions, evenly split between negative and neutral messages. The top of the y-axis shows the poor experience rate for each message type. When no messages are exchanged, only 4 percent of buyers report a poor experience. Whenever a neutral message is sent, the rate of poor experiences jumps to 13 percent, and if the message's content was negative, over one-third of buyers express a poor experience.

In the second stage of the analysis, Masterov, Mayer, and Tadelis (2015)

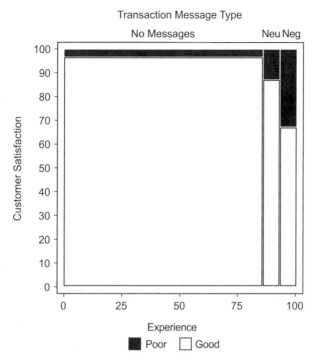

Fig. 23.2   Message content and poor experiences on eBay
Source: Masterov et al. 2015. ©2015 Association for Computing Machinery, Inc. Reprinted by permission. https://doi.org/10.1145/2764468.2764499.

used the fact that negative messages are associated with poor experiences to construct a novel measure of seller quality based on the idea that sellers who receive a higher frequency of negative messages are worse sellers. For example, imagine that seller A and seller B both sold 100 items and that seller A had five transactions with at least one negative message, while seller B had eight such transactions. The implied quality score of seller A is then 0.05 while that of seller B is 0.08, and the premise is that seller B is a worse seller than seller A. Masterov, Mayer, and Tadelis (2015) show that the relationship between this ratio, which is calculated for every seller at any point in time using aggregated negative messages from past sales, and the likelihood that a current transaction will result in a poor experience, is monotonically increasing.

This simple exercise is a proof of concept that shows that by using the message data and a simple natural language processing AI procedure, they were able to better predict which sellers will create poor experiences than one can infer from the very inflated feedback data. eBay is not unique in allowing the parties to exchange messages and the lessons from this research are easily generalizable to other marketplaces. The key is that there is information in communication between market participants, and past communication can help identify and predict the sellers or products that will cause buyers poor experiences and negatively impact the overall trust in the marketplace.

23.2.2 Using AI to Create a Market for Feedback

Aside from the fact that feedback is often inflated as described earlier, another problem with feedback is that not all buyers choose not to leave feedback at all. In fact, through the lens of mainstream economic theory, it is surprising that a significant fraction of online consumers leave feedback. After all, it is a selfless act that requires time, and it creates a classic free-rider problem. Furthermore, because potential buyers are attracted to buy from sellers or products that already have an established good track record, this creates a "cold-start" problem: new sellers (or products) with no feedback will face a barrier-to-entry in that buyers will be hesitant to give them a fair shot. How could we solve these free-rider and cold-start problems?

These questions were analyzed in a recent paper by Li, Tadelis, and Zhow (2016) using a unique and novel implementation of a market for feedback on the huge Chinese marketplace Taobao where they let sellers pay buyers to leave them feedback. Naturally, one may be concerned about allowing sellers to pay for feedback as it seems like a practice in which they will only pay for good feedback and suppress any bad feedback, which would not add any value in promoting trust. However, Taobao implemented a clever use of NLP to solve this problem: it is the platform, using an NLP AI model, that decides whether feedback is relevant and not the seller who pays for the feedback. Hence, the reward to the buyer for leaving feedback was actually managed by the marketplace, and was handed out for informative feedback rather than for positive feedback.

Specifically, in March 2012, Taobao launched a "Rebate-for-Feedback" (RFF) feature through which sellers can set a rebate value for any item they sell (cash back or store coupon) as a reward for a buyer's feedback. If a seller chooses this option, then Taobao guarantees that the rebate will be transferred from the seller's account to a buyer who leaves high-quality feedback. Importantly, feedback quality only depends on how informative it is, rather than whether the feedback is positive or negative. Taobao measures the quality of feedback with a NLP algorithm that examines the comment's content and length and finds out whether key features of the item are mentioned. Hence, the marketplace manages the market for feedback by forcing the seller to deposit at Taobao a certain amount for a chosen period, so that funds are guaranteed for buyers who meet the rebate criterion, which itself is determined by Taobao.[6]

---

6. According to a Taobao survey (published in March 2012), 64.8 percent of buyers believed that they will be more willing to buy items that have the RFF feature, and 84.2 percent of buyers believed that the RFF option will make them more likely to write detailed comments.

Taobao's motivation behind the RFF mechanism was to promote more informative feedback, but as Li, Tadelis, and Zhow (2016) noted, economic theory offers some insights into how the RFF feature can act as a potent signaling mechanism that will further separate higher- from lower-quality sellers and products. To see this, recall the literature launched by Nelson (1970) who suggested that advertising acts as a signal of quality. According to the theory, advertising—which is a form of burning money—acts as a signal that attracts buyers who correctly believe that only high-quality sellers will choose to advertise. Incentive compatibility is achieved through repeat purchases: buyers who purchase and experience the products of advertisers will return in the future only if the goods sold are of high enough quality. The cost of advertising can be high enough to deter low-quality sellers from being willing to spend the money and sell only once because those sellers will not attract repeat customers, and still low enough to leave profits for higher-quality sellers. Hence, ads act as signals that separate high-quality sellers, and in turn attract buyers to their products.

As Li, Tadelis, and Zhow (2016) argue, the RFF mechanism plays a similar signaling role as ads do. Assuming that consumers express their experiences truthfully in written feedback, any consumer who buys a product and is given incentives to leave feedback will leave positive feedback only if the buying experience was satisfactory. Hence, a seller will offer RFF incentives to buyers only if the seller expects to receive positive feedback, and this will happen only if the seller will provide high quality. If a seller knows that their goods and services are unsatisfactory, then paying for feedback will generate negative feedback that will harm the low-quality seller. Equilibrium behavior then implies that RFF, as a signal of high quality, will attract more buyers and result in more sales. The role of AI was precisely to reward buyers for information, not for positive feedback.

Li, Tadelis, and Zhou (2016) proceeded to analyze data from the period where the RFF mechanism was featured and confirmed that first, as expected, more feedback was left in response to the incentives provided by the RFF feature. More important, the additional feedback did not exhibit any biases, suggesting that the NLP algorithms used were able to create the kind of screening needed to select informative feedback. Also, the predictions of the simple signaling story were borne out in the data, suggesting that using NLP to support a novel market for feedback did indeed solve both the free-rider problem and the cold-start problem that can hamper the growth of online marketplaces.

23.4   Using AI to Reduce Search Frictions

An important application of AI and machine learning in online marketplaces is the way in which potential buyers engage with the site and proceed to search for products or services. Search engines that power the search of products online are based on a variety of AI algorithms that are trained to maximize what the provider believes to be the right objective. Often this boils down to conversion, under the belief that the sooner a consumer converts a search to a purchase, the happier the consumer is both in the short and the long run. The rationale is simply that search itself is a friction, and hence, maximizing the successful conversion of search activity to a purchase reduces this friction.

This is not inconsistent with economic theory that has modeled search as an inevitable costly process that separates consumers from the products they want. The canonical search models in economics either build on the seminal work of Stigler (1961), who assumes that consumers sample a fixed number of stores and choose to buy the lowest priced item, or more often, on the models of McCall (1970) and Mortensen (1970), who posit that a model of sequential search is a better description of consumer search behavior. In both modeling approaches consumers know exactly what they wish to buy.

However, it turns out that unlike the simplistic models of search employed in economic theory, where consumers know what they are looking for and the activity of search is just a costly friction, in reality, people's search behavior is rich and varied. A recent paper by Blake, Nosko, and Tadelis (2016) uses comprehensive data from eBay to shed light on the search process with minimal modeling assumptions. Their data show that consumers search significantly more than other studies—which had limited access to search behavior over time—have suggested.

Furthermore, search often proceeds from the vague to the specific. For example, early in a search a user may use the query "watch," then refine it to "men's watch," and later add further qualifying words such as color, shape, strap type, and more. This suggests that consumers often learn about their own tastes, and what product characteristics exist, as part of the search process. Indeed, Blake et al. (2016) show that the average number of terms in the query rises over time, and the propensity to use the default-ranking algorithm declines over time as users move to more focused searches like price sorting.

These observations suggest that marketplaces and retailers alike could design their online search algorithms to understand search intent so as to better serve their consumers. If a consumer is in the earlier, exploratory phases of the search process, then offering some breadth will help the consumer better learn their tastes and the options available in the market. But when the consumer is driven to purchase something particular, offering a narrower set of products that match the consumer's preferences would be better. Hence, machine learning and AI can play an instrumental role in recognizing customer intent.

Artificial intelligence and machine learning cannot only help predict a customer's intent, but given the large heterogeneity on consumer tastes, AI can help a marketplace or retailer better segment the many customers into groups that can be better served with tailored information. Of course, the idea of using AI for more refined customer segmentation, or even personalized experiences, also raises concerns about price discrimination. For example, in 2012 the *Wall Street Journal* reported that "Orbitz Worldwide Inc. has found that people who use . . . Mac computers spend as much as 30% more a night on hotels, so the online travel agency is starting to show them different, and sometimes costlier, travel options than Windows visitors see. The Orbitz effort, which is in its early stages, demonstrates how tracking people's online activities can use even seemingly innocuous information—in this case, the fact that customers are visiting Orbitz.com from a Mac—to start predicting their tastes and spending habits."[7]

Whether these practices of employing consumer data and AI will help or harm consumers is not obvious, as it is well known from economic theory that price discrimination can either increase or reduce consumer welfare. If, on average, Mac users prefer staying at fancier and more expensive hotels because owning a Mac is correlated with higher income and tastes for luxury, then the Orbitz practice is beneficial because it shows people what they want to see and reduces search frictions. However, if this is just a way to extract more surplus from consumers who are less price sensitive, but do not necessarily care for the snazzier hotel rooms, then it harms these consumers.

There is currently a lot of interest in policy circles regarding the potential harms to consumers from AI-based price discrimination and market segmentation. McSweeny and O'Dea (2017) suggest that once AI is used to create more targeted market segments, this may not only have implications only for consumer welfare, but for antitrust policy and market definitions for mergers. But, as Gal and Elkin-Koren (2017) suggest, the same AI-targeting tools used by retailers and marketplaces to better segment consumers may be developed into tools for consumers that will help them shop for better deals and limit the ways in which marketplaces and retailers can engage in price discrimination.

23.5 Concluding Remarks

In its early years, classical economic theory paid little attention to market frictions and treated information and computation as free. That theory led to conclusions about efficiency, competitive prices for most goods, and full employment of valuable resources. To address the failures of that theory, economists began to study models with search frictions, which predicted that price competition would be attenuated, that some workers and resources

---

7. See "On Orbitz, Mac Users Steered to Pricier Hotels," Dana Mattioli, *The Wall Street Journal*, Aug. 23, 2012. https://www.wsj.com/articles/SB10001424052702304458604577488882 2667325882.

could remain unemployed, and that it could be costly to distinguish reliable trading partners from others. They also built markets for complex resource-allocation problems in which computations and some communications were centralized, lifting the burden of coordination from individual market participants.

With these as the key frictions in the traditional economy, AI holds enormous potential to improve efficiency. In this chapter, we have described some of the ways that AI can overcome computational barriers, reduce search frictions, and distinguish reliable partners. These are among the most important causes of inefficiency in traditional economies, and there is no longer any question that AI is helping to overcome them, with the promise of widespread benefits for all of us. As Roth (2002) noted, market designers "cannot work only with the simple conceptual models used for theoretical insights into the general working of markets. Instead, market design calls for an engineering approach." Artificial intelligence has already proven to be a valuable tool in the economist-as-engineer tool box.

References

Blake, T., C. Nosko, and S. Tadelis. 2016. "Returns to Consumer Search: Evidence from eBay."*17th ACM Conference on Electronic Commerce* (EC 2016), 531–45.

Filippas, A., J. J. Horton, and J. M. Golden. 2017. "Reputation in the Long-Run." Working paper, Stern School of Business, New York University.

Gal, M. S., and N. Elkin-Koren. 2017. "Algorithmic Consumers." *Harvard Journal of Law & Technology* 30:1–45.

Hutter, F., H. Hoos, and K. Leyton-Brown. 2011. "Sequential Model-Based Optimization for General Algorithm Configuration." Conference paper, International Conference on Learning and Intelligent Optimization. https://link.springer.com /chapter/10.1007/978-3-642-25566-3_40.

Leyton-Brown, K., P. R. Milgrom, and I. Segal. 2017. "Economics and Computer Science of a Radio Spectrum Reallocation." *Proceedings of the National Academy of Sciences* 114 (28): 7202–09. www.pnas.org/cgi/doi/10.1073/pnas.1701997114.

Li, L. I., S. Tadelis, and X. Zhou. 2016. "Buying Reputation as a Signal of Quality: Evidence from an Online Marketplace." NBER Working Paper no. 22584, Cambridge, MA.

Masterov, D. V., U. F. Mayer, and S. Tadelis. 2015. "Canary in the E-commerce Coal Mine: Detecting and Predicting Poor Experiences Using Buyer-to-Seller Messages." In *Proceedings of the Sixteenth ACM Conference on Economics and Computation*, EC '15, 81–93.

Mayzlin, D., Y. Dover, and J. Chevalier. 2014. "Promotional Reviews: An Empirical Investigation of Online Review Manipulation." *American Economic Review* 104 (8): 2421–55.

McCall, J. J. 1970. "Economics of Information and Job Search." *Quarterly Journal of Economics* 84 (1): 113–26.

McSweeny, T., and B. O'Dea. 2017. "The Implications of Algorithmic Pricing for

Coordinated Effects, Analysis and Price Discrimination Markets in Antitrust Enforcement." *Antitrust* 32 (1): 75–81.

Milgrom, P. R. 2017. *Discovering Prices: Auction Design in Markets with Complex Constraints.* New York: Columbia University Press.

Milgrom, P. R., D. C. North, and B. R. Weingast. 1990. "The Role of Institutions in the Revival of Trade: The Law Merchant, Private Judges, and the Champagne Fairs." *Economics and Politics* 2 (1): 1–23.

Milgrom, P. R., and I. Segal. 2017. "Deferred Acceptance Auctions and Radio Spectrum Reallocation." Working paper.

Mortensen, D. T. 1970. "Job Search, the Duration of Unemployment and the Phillips Curve." *American Economic Review* 60 (5): 847–62.

Myerson, R. B. 1981. "Optimal Auction Design." *Mathematics of Operations Research* 6 (1): 58–73.

Nelson, P. 1970. "Information and Consumer Behavior." *Journal of Political Economy* 78 (2): 311–29.

Newman, N., A. Fréchette, and K. Leyton-Brown. Forthcoming. "Deep Optimization for Spectrum Repacking." *Communications of the ACM* (CACM).

Nosko, C., and S. Tadelis. 2015. "The Limits of Reputation in Platform Markets: An Empirical Analysis and Field Experiment." NBER Working Paper no. 20830, Cambridge, MA.

Ostrovsky, M., and M. Schwartz. 2017. "Reserve Prices in Internet Advertising: A Field Experiment." Working paper.

Stigler, G. J. 1961. "The Economics of Information." *Journal of Political Economy* 69 (3): 213–25.

Roth, A. E. 2002. "The Economist as Engineer: Game Theory, Experimentation, and Computation as Tools for Design Economics." *Econometrica* 70 (4): 1341–78.

Roth, A. E. 2015. *Who Gets What—and Why: The New Economics of Matchmaking and Market Design.* New York: Houghton Mifflin Harcourt.

Vickrey, W. 1961. "Counterspeculation, Auctions, and Competitive Sealed Tenders." *Journal of Finance, American Finance Association* 16 (1): 8–37.

Xu, H., D. Liu, H. Wang, and A. Stavrou. 2015. "E-commerce Reputation Manipulation: The Emergence of Reputation-Escalation-as-a-Service." *Proceedings of 24th World Wide Web Conference* (WWW 2015):1296–306.

Zervas, G., D. Proserpio, and J. W. Byers. 2015. "A First Look at Online Reputation on Airbnb, Where Every Stay Is Above Average." Working paper, Boston University.

24

Artificial Intelligence and Behavioral Economics

Colin F. Camerer

24.1 Introduction

This chapter describes three highly speculative ideas about how artificial intelligence (AI) and behavioral economics may interact, particular in future developments in the economy and in research frontiers. First note that I will use the terms AI and machine learning (ML) interchangeably (although AI is broader) because the examples I have in mind all involve ML and prediction. A good introduction to ML for economists is Mullainathan and Spiess (2017), and other chapters in this volume.

The first idea is that ML can be used in the search for new "behavioral"-type variables that affect choice. Two examples are given, from experimental data on bargaining and on risky choice. The second idea is that some common limits on human prediction might be understood as the kinds of errors made by poor implementations of machine learning. The third idea is that it is important to study how AI technology used in firms and other institutions can both overcome and exploit human limits. The fullest understanding of this tech-human interaction will require new knowledge from behavioral economics about attention, the nature of assembled preferences, and perceived fairness.

24.2 Machine Learning to Find Behavioral Variables

Behavioral economics can be defined as the study of natural limits on computation, willpower, and self-interest, and the implications of those

Colin F. Camerer is the Robert Kirby Professor of Behavioral Finance and Economics at the California Institute of Technology.

For acknowledgments, sources of research support, and disclosure of the author's material financial relationships, if any, please see http://www.nber.org/chapters/c14013.ack.

limits for economic analysis (market equilibrium, IO, public finance, etc.). A different approach is to define behavioral economics more generally, as simply being open-minded about what variables are likely to influence economic choices.

This open-mindedness can be defined by listing neighboring social sciences that are likely to be the most fruitful source of explanatory variables. These include psychology, sociology (e.g., norms), anthropology (cultural variation in cognition), neuroscience, political science, and so forth. Call this the "behavioral economics trades with its neighbors" view.

But the open-mindedness could also be characterized even more generally, as an invitation to machine-learn how to predict economic outcomes from the largest possible feature set. In the "trades with its neighbors" view, features are constructs that are contributed by different neighboring sciences. These could be loss aversion, identity, moral norms, in-group preference, inattention, habit, model-free reinforcement learning, individual polygenic scores, and so forth.

But why stop there?

In a general ML approach, predictive features could be—and *should* be—*any* variables that predict. (For policy purposes, variables that could be controlled by people, firms, and governments may be of special interest.) These variables can be measurable properties of choices, the set of choices, affordances and motor interactions during choosing, measures of attention, psychophysiological measures of biological states, social influences, properties of individuals who are doing the choosing (SES, wealth, moods, personality, genes), and so forth. The more variables, the merrier.

From this perspective, we can think about what sets of features are contributed by different disciplines and theories. What features does textbook economic theory contribute? Constrained utility maximization in its most familiar and simple form points to only three kinds of variables—prices, information (which can inform utilities), and constraints.

Most propositions in behavioral economics add some variables to this list of features, such as reference-dependence, context-dependence (menu effects), anchoring, limited attention, social preference, and so forth.

Going beyond familiar theoretical constructs, the ML approach to behavioral economics specifies a very long list of candidate variables (= features) and include *all* of them in an ML approach. This approach has two advantages: First, simple theories can be seen as bets that only a small number of features will predict well; that is, some effects (such as prices) are hypothesized to be first-order in magnitude. Second, if longer lists of features predict better than a short list of theory-specified features, then that finding establishes a plausible upper bound on how much potential predictability is left to understand. The results are also likely to create raw material for theory to figure out how to consolidate the additional predictive power into crystallized theory (see also Kleinberg, Liang, and Mullainathan 2015).

If behavioral economics is recast as open-mindedness about what variables might predict, then ML is an ideal way to do behavioral economics because it can make use of a wide set of variables and select which ones predict. I will illustrate it with some examples.

Bargaining. There is a long history of bargaining experiments trying to predict what bargaining outcomes (and disagreement rates) will result from structural variables using game-theoretic methods. In the 1980s there was a sharp turn in experimental work toward noncooperative approaches in which the communication and structure of bargaining was carefully structured (e.g., Roth 1995 and Camerer 2003 for reviews). In these experiments the possible sequence of offers in the bargaining are heavily constrained and no communication is allowed (beyond the offers themselves). This shift to highly structured paradigms occurred because game theory, at the time, delivered sharp, nonobvious new predictions about what outcomes might result depending on the structural parameters—particularly, costs of delay, time horizon, the exogenous order of offers and acceptance, and available outside options (payoffs upon disagreement). Given the difficulty of measuring or controlling these structural variables in most field settings, experiments provided a natural way to test these structured-bargaining theories.[1]

Early experiments made it clear that concerns for fairness or outcomes of others influenced utility, and the planning ahead assumed in subgame perfect theories is limited and cognitively unnatural (Camerer et al. 1994; Johnson et al. 2002; Binmore et al. 2002). Experimental economists became wrapped up in understanding the nature of apparent social preferences and limited planning in structured bargaining.

However, most natural bargaining is *not* governed by rules about structure as simple as those theories, and experiments became focused from 1985 to 2000 and beyond. Natural bargaining is typically "semi-structured"—that is, there is a hard deadline and protocol for what constitutes an agreement, and otherwise there are no restrictions on which party can make what offers at what time, including the use of natural language, face-to-face meetings or use of agents, and so on.

The revival of experimental study of unstructured bargaining is a good idea for three reasons (see also Karagözoğlu, forthcoming). First, there are now a lot more ways to measure what happens during bargaining in laboratory conditions (and probably in field settings as well). Second, the large number of features that can now be generated are ideal inputs for ML to predict bargaining outcomes. Third, even when bargaining is unstructured it is possible to produce bold, nonobvious precise predictions (thanks to the revelation principle). As we will see, ML can then test whether the features

---

1. Examples include Binmore, Shaked, and Sutton (1985, 1989); Neelin, Sonnenschein, and Spiegel (1988); Camerer et al. (1994); and Binmore et al. (2002).

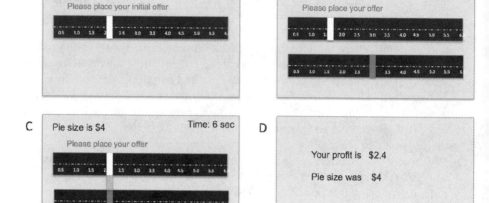

Fig. 24.1 *A*, **initial offer screen (for informed player *I*, white bar); *B*, example cursor locations after three seconds (indicating amount offered by *I*, white, or demanded by *U*, dark gray); *C*, cursor bars match which indicates an offer, consummated at six seconds; *D*, feedback screen for player *I*. Player *U* also receives feedback about pie size and profit if a trade was made (otherwise the profit is zero).**

predicted by game theory to affect outcomes actually do, and how much predictive power other features add (if any).

These three properties are illustrated by experiments of Camerer, Nave, and Smith (2017).[2] Two players bargain over how to divide an amount of money worth $1–$6 (in integer values). One informed (*I*) player knows the amount; the other, uninformed (*U*) player, doesn't know the amount. They are bargaining over how much *the uninformed U player* will get. But both players know that *I* knows the amount.

They bargain over ten seconds by moving cursors on a bargaining number line (figure 24.1). The data created in each trial is a time series of cursor locations, which are a series of step functions coming from a low offer to higher ones (representing increases in offers from *I*) and from higher demands to lower ones (representing decreasing demands from *U*).

Suppose we are trying to predict whether there will be an agreement or not based on all variables that can be observed. From a theoretical point of view, efficient bargaining based on revelation principle analysis predicts an exact rate of disagreement for each of the amounts $1–6, based only on the different amounts available. Remarkably, this prediction is process-free.

2. This paradigm builds on seminal work on semistructured bargaining by Forsythe, Kennan, and Sopher (1991).

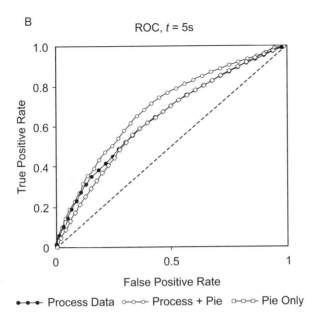

Fig. 24.2   ROC curves showing combinations of false and true positive rates in predicting bargaining disagreements

Notes: Improved forecasting is represented by curves moving to the upper left. The combination of process (cursor location features) and "pie" (amount) data are a clear improvement over either type of data alone.

However, from an ML point of view there are lots of features representing what the players are doing that could add predictive power (besides the process-free prediction based on the amount at stake). Both cursor locations are recorded every twenty-five msec. The time series of cursor locations is associated with a huge number of features—how far apart the cursors are, the time since last concession (= cursor movement), size of last concession, interactions between concession amounts and times, and so forth.

Figure 24.2 shows an ROC curve indicating test-set accuracy in predicting whether a bargaining trial ends in a disagreement (= 1) or not. The ROC curves sketch out combinations of true positive rates, P(disagree|predict disagree) and false positive rates P(agree|predict disagree). An improved ROC curve moves up and to the left, reflecting more true positives and fewer false positives. As is evident, predicting from process data only is about as accurate as using just the amount ("pie") sizes (the ROC curves with black circle and empty square markers). Using both types of data improves prediction substantially (curve with empty circle markers).

Machine learning is able to find predictive value in details of how the bargaining occurs (beyond the simple, and very good, prediction based only on the amount being bargained over). Of course, this discovery is the beginning of the *next* step for behavioral economics. It raises questions that include: What variables predict? How do emotions,[3] face-to-face communication, and biological measures (including whole-brain imaging)[4] influence bargaining? Do people consciously understand why those variables are important? Can ML methods capture the effects of motivated cognition in unstructured bargaining, when people can self-servingly disagree about case facts?[5] Can people constrain expression of variables that hurt their bargaining power? Can mechanisms be designed that record these variables and then create efficient mediation, into which people will voluntarily participate (capturing all gains from trade)?[6]

Risky Choice. Peysakhovich and Naecker (2017) use machine learning to analyze decisions between simple financial risks. The set of risks are randomly generated triples ($\$y$, $\$x$, 0) with associated probabilities (p_x, p_y, p_0). Subjects give a willingness-to-pay (WTP) for each gamble.

The feature set is the five probability and amount variables (excluding the $0 payoff), quadratic terms for all five, and all two- and three-way interactions among the linear and quadratic variables. For aggregate-level estimation this creates $5 + 5 + 45 + 120 = 175$ variables.

Machine learning predictions are derived from regularized regression with a linear penalty (LASSO) or squared penalty (ridge) for (absolute) coefficients. Participants were $N = 315$ MTurk subjects who each gave ten useable responses. The training set consists of 70 percent of the observations, and 30 percent are held out as a test set.

They also estimate predictive accuracy of a one-variable expected utility model (EU, with power utility) and a prospect theory (PT) model, which adds one additional parameter to allow nonlinear probability weighting (Tversky and Kahneman 1992) (with separate weights, not cumulative ones). For these models there are only one or two free parameters per person.[7]

The aggregate data estimation uses the same set of parameters for all subjects. In this analysis, the test set accuracy (mean squared error) is almost exactly the same for PT and for both LASSO and ridge ML predictions, even though PT uses only two variables and the ML methods use 175 variables. Individual-level analysis, in which each subject has their own parameters has about half the mean squared error as the aggregate analysis. The PT and ridge ML are about equally accurate.

The fact that PT and ML are equally accurate is a bit surprising because the ML method allows quite a lot of flexibility in the space of possible

---

3. Andrade and Ho (2009).

4. Lohrenz et al. (2007) and Bhatt et al. (2010).

5. See Babcock et al. (1995) and Babcock and Loewenstein (1997).

6. See Krajich et al. (2008) for a related example of using neural measures to enhance efficiency in public good production experiments.

7. Note, however, that the ML feature set does not exactly nest the EU and PT forms. For example, a weighted combination of the linear outcome X and the quadratic term X^2 does not exactly equal the power function X^{α}.

predictions. Indeed, the authors' motivation was to use ML to show how a model with a huge amount of flexibility could fit, possibly to provide a ceiling in achievable accuracy. If the ML predictions were more accurate than EU or PT, the gap would show how much improvement could be had by more complicated combinations of outcome and probability parameters. But the result, instead, shows that much busier models are not more accurate than the time-tested two-parameter form of PT, for this domain of choices.

Limited Strategic Thinking. The concept of subgame perfection in game theory presumes that players look ahead in the future to what other players might do at future choice nodes (even choice nodes that are unlikely to be reached), in order to compute likely consequences of their current choices. This psychological presumption does have some predictive power in short, simple games. However, direct measures of attention (Camerer at al. 1994; Johnson et al. 2002) and inference from experiments (e.g., Binmore et al. 2002) make it clear that players with limited experience do not look far ahead.

More generally, in simultaneous games, there is now substantial evidence that even highly intelligent and educated subjects do not all process information in a way that leads to optimized choices given (Nash) "equilibrium" beliefs—that is, beliefs that accurately forecast what other players will do. More important, two general classes of theories have emerged that can account for deviations from optimized equilibrium theory. One class, quantal response equilibrium (QRE), are theories in which beliefs are statistically accurate but noisy (e.g., Goeree, Holt, and Palfrey 2016). Another type of theory presumes that deviations from Nash equilibrium result from a cognitive hierarchy of levels of strategic thinking. In these theories there are levels of thinking, starting from nonstrategic thinking, based presumably on salient features of strategies (or, in the absence of distinctive salience, random choice). Higher-level thinkers build up a model of what lower-level thinkers do (e.g., Stahl and Wilson 1995; Camerer, Ho, and Chong 2004; Crawford, Costa-Gomes, and Iriberri 2013). These models have been applied to hundreds of experimental games with some degree of imperfect cross-game generality, and to several field settings.[8]

Both QRE and CH/level-k theories extend equilibrium theory by adding parsimonious, precise specifications of departures from either optimization (QRE) or rationality of beliefs (CH/level-k) using a small number of behavioral parameters. The question that is asked is: Can we add predictive power in a simple, psychologically plausible[9] way using these parameters?

A more general question is: Are there structural features of payoffs and

---

8. For example, see Goldfarb and Xiao 2011, Östling et al. 2011, and Hortacsu et al. 2017.

9. In the case of CH/level-k theories, direct measures of visual attention from Mouselab and eyetracking have been used to test the theories using a *combination* of choices and visual attention data. See Costa-Gomes, Crawford, and Broseta 2001; Wang, Spezio, and Camerer 2010; and Brocas et al. 2014. Eyetracking and moused-based methods provide huge data

strategies that can predict even more accurately than QRE or CH/level-k? If the answer is "Yes" then the new theories, even if they are improvements, have a long way to go.

Two recent research streams have made important steps in this direction. Using methods familiar in computer science, Wright and Leyton-Brown (2014) create a "meta-model" that combines payoff features to predict what the nonstrategic "level 0" players seem to, in six sets of two-player 3×3 normal form games. This is a substantial improvement on previous specifications, which typically assume random behavior or some simple action based on salient information.[10]

Hartford, Wright, and Leyton-Brown (2016) go further, using deep learning neural networks (NNs) to predict human choices on the same six data sets. The NNs are able to outpredict CH models in the hold-out test sample in many cases. Importantly, even models in which there is no hierarchical iteration of strategic thinking ("layers of action response" in their approach) can fit well. This result—while preliminary—indicates that prediction purely from hidden layers of structural features can be successful.

Coming from behavioral game theory, Fudenberg and Liang (2017) explore how well ML over structural properties of strategies can predict experimental choices. They use the six data sets from Wright and Leyton-Brown (2014) and also collected data on how MTurk subjects played 200 new 3×3 games with randomly drawn payoffs. Their ML approach uses eighty-eight features that are categorical structural properties of strategies (e.g., Is it part of a Nash equilibrium? Is the payoff never the worst for each choice by the other player?).

The main analysis creates decision trees with k branching nodes (for k from 1 to 10) that predict whether a strategy will be played or not. Analysis uses tenfold test validation to guard against overfitting. As is common, the best-fitting trees are simple; there is a substantial improvement in fit going from $k = 1$ to $k = 2$, and then only small improvements for bushier trees. In the lab game data, the best $k = 2$ tree is simply what is called level 1 play in CH/level-k; it predicts the strategy that is a best response to uniform play by an opponent. That simple tree has a misclassification rate of 38.4 percent. The best $k = 3$ tree is only a little better (36.6 percent) and $k = 5$ is very slightly better (36.5 percent).

The model classifies rather well, but the ML feature-based models do a

---

sets. These previous studies heavily filter (or dimension-reduce) those data based on theory that requires consistency between choices and attention to information necessary to execute the value computation underlying the choice (Costa-Gomes, Crawford, and Broseta 2001; Costa-Gomes and Crawford 2006). Another approach that has never been tried is to use ML to select features from the huge feature set, combining choices and visual attention, to see which features predict best.

10. Examples of nonrandom behavior by nonstrategic players include bidding one's private value in an auction (Crawford and Iriberri 2007) and reporting a private state honestly in a sender-receiver game (Wang, Spezio, and Camerer 2010; Crawford 2003).

Table 24.1   **Frequency of prediction errors of various theoretical and ML models for new data from random-payoff games (from Fudenberg and Liang 2017)**

	Error	Completeness
Naïve benchmark	0.6667	1
Uniform Nash	0.4722	51.21%
	(0.0075)	
Poisson cognitive hierarchy model	0.3159	92.36%
	(0.0217)	
Prediction rule based on game features	0.2984	96.97%
	(0.0095)	
"Best possible"	0.2869	0

little better. Table 24.1 summarizes results for their new random games. The classification by Poisson cognitive hierarchy (PCH) is 92 percent of the way from random to "best possible" (using the overall distribution of actual play) in this analysis. The ML feature model is almost perfect (97 percent).

Other analyses show less impressive performance for PCH, although it can be improved substantially by adding risk aversion, and also by trying to predict different data set-specific τ values.

Note that the FL "best possible" measure is the same as the "clairvoyant" model upper bound used by Camerer, Ho, and Chong (2004). Given a data set of actual human behavior, and assuming that subjects are playing people chosen at random from that set, the best they can do is to have somehow accurately guessed what those data would be and chosen accordingly.[11] (The term "clairvoyant" is used to note that this upper bound is unlikely to be reached except by sheer lucky guessing, but if a person repeatedly chooses near the bound it implies they have an intuitive mental model of how others choose, which is quite accurate.)

Camerer, Ho, and Chong (2004) went a step further by also computing the expected *reward value* from clairvoyant prediction and comparing it with how much subjects actually earn and how much they could have earned if they obeyed different theories. Using reward value as a metric is sensible because a theory could predict frequencies rather accurately, but might not generate a much higher reward value than highly inaccurate predictions (because of the "flat maximum" property).[12] In five data sets they studied, Nash equilibrium added very little marginal value and the PCH approach

11. In psychophysics and experimental psychology, the term "ideal observer" model is used to refer to a performance benchmark closely related to what we called the clairvoyant upper bound.

12. This property was referred to as the "flat maximum" by von Winterfeldt and Edwards (1973). It came to prominence much later in experimental economics when it was noted that theories could badly predict, say, a distribution of choices in a zero-sum game, but such an inaccurate theory might not yield much less earnings than an ideal theory.

added some value in three games and more than half the maximum achievable value in two games.

24.3 Human Prediction as Imperfect Machine Learning

24.3.1 Some Pre-History of Judgment Research and Behavioral Economics

Behavioral economics as we know it and describe it nowadays, began to thrive when challenges to simple rationality principles (then called "anomalies") came to have rugged empirical status and to point to natural improvements in theory (?). It was common in those early days to distinguish anomalies about "preferences" such as mental accounting violations of fungibility and reference-dependence, and anomalies about "judgment" of likelihoods and quantities.

Somewhat hidden from economists, at that time and even now, was the fact that there was active research in many areas of judgment and decision-making (JDM). The JDM research proceeded in parallel with the emergence of behavioral economics. It was conducted almost entirely in psychology departments and some business schools, and rarely published in economics journals. The annual meeting of the S/JDM society was, for logistical efficiency, held as a satellite meeting of the Psychonomic Society (which weighted attendance toward mathematical experimental psychology).

The JDM research was about general approaches to understanding judgment processes, including "anomalies" relative to logically normative benchmarks. This research flourished because there was a healthy respect for simple mathematical models and careful testing, which enabled regularities to cumulate and gave reasons to dismiss weak results. The research community also had one foot in practical domains too (such as judgments of natural risks, medical decision-making, law, etc.) so that generalizability of lab results was always implicitly addressed.

The central ongoing debate in JDM from the 1970s on was about the cognitive processes involved in actual decisions, and the quality of those predictions. There were plenty of careful lab experiments about such phenomena, but also an earlier literature on what was then called "clinical versus statistical prediction." There lies the earliest comparison between primitive forms of ML and the important JDM piece of behavioral economics (see Lewis 2016). Many of the important contributions from this fertile period were included in the Kahneman, Slovic, and Tversky (1982) edited volume (which in the old days was called the "blue-green bible").

Paul Meehl's (1954) compact book started it all. Meehl was a remarkable character. He was a rare example, at the time, of a working clinical psychiatrist who was also interested in statistics and evidence (as were others at Minnesota). Meehl had a picture of Freud in his office, and practiced clinically for fifty years in the Veteran's Administration.

Meehl's mother had died when he was sixteen, under circumstances which apparently made him suspicious of how much doctors actually knew about how to make sick people well.

His book could be read as pursuit of such a suspicion scientifically: he collected all the studies he could find—there were twenty-two—that compared a set of clinical judgments with actual outcomes, and with simple linear models using observable predictors (some objective and some subjectively estimated).

Meehl's idea was that these statistical models could be used as a benchmark to evaluate clinicians. As Dawes and Corrigan (1974, 97) wrote, "the statistical analysis was thought to provide a floor to which the judgment of the experienced clinician could be compared. The floor turned out to be a ceiling."

In every case the statistical model outpredicted or tied the judgment accuracy of the average clinician. A later meta-analysis of 117 studies (Grove et al. 2000) found only six in which clinicians, on average, were more accurate than models (and see Dawes, Faust, and Meehl 1989).

It is possible that in any one domain, the distribution of clinicians contains some stars who could predict much more accurately. However, later studies at the individual level showed that only a minority of clinicians were more accurate than statistical models (e.g., Goldberg 1968, 1970). Kleinberg et al.'s (2017) study of machine-learned and judicial detention decisions is a modern example of the same theme.

In the decades after Meehl's book was published, evidence began to mount about *why* clinical judgment could be so imperfect. A common theme was that clinicians were good at measuring particular variables, or suggesting which objective variables to include, but were not so good at combining them consistently (e.g., Sawyer 1966). In a recollection Meehl (1986, 373) gave a succinct description of this theme:

> Why should people have been so surprised by the empirical results in my summary chapter? Surely we all know that the human brain is poor at weighting and computing. When you check out at a supermarket, you don't eyeball the heap of purchases and say to the clerk, "Well it looks to me as if it's about $17.00 worth; what do you think?" The clerk adds it up. There are no strong arguments, from the armchair or from empirical studies of cognitive psychology, for believing that human beings can assign optimal weights in equations subjectively or that they apply their own weights consistently, the query from which Lew Goldberg derived such fascinating and fundamental results.

Some other important findings emerged. One drawback of the statistical prediction approach, for practice, was that it requires large samples of high-quality outcome data (in more modern AI language, prediction required labeled data). There were rarely many such data available at the time.

Dawes (1979) proposed to give up on estimating variable weights through a criterion-optimizing "proper" procedure like ordinary least squares (OLS),[13] using "improper" weights instead. An example is equal-weighting of standardized variables, which is often a very good approximation to OLS weighting (Einhorn and Hogarth 1975).

An interesting example of improper weights is what Dawes called "boot-strapping" (a completely distinct usage from the concept in statistics of bootstrap resampling). Dawes's idea was to regress clinical judgments on predictors, and use those estimated weights to make prediction. This is equivalent, of course, to using the predicted part of the clinical-judgment regression and discarding (or regularizing to zero, if you will) the residual. If the residual is mostly noise then correlation accuracies can be improved by this procedure, and they typically are (e.g., Camerer 1981a).

Later studies indicated a slightly more optimistic picture for the clinicians. If bootstrap-regression residuals are pure noise, they will also lower the test-retest reliability of clinical judgment (i.e., the correlation between two judgments on the same cases made by the same person). However, analysis of the few studies that report both test-retest reliability and bootstrapping regressions indicate that only about 40 percent of the residual variance is unreliable noise (Camerer 1981b). Thus, residuals do contain reliable subjective information (though it may be uncorrelated with outcomes). Blattberg and Hoch (1990) later found that for actual managerial forecasts of product sales and coupon redemption rate, residuals are correlated about .30 with outcomes. As a result, averaging statistical model forecasts and managerial judgments improved prediction substantially over statistical models alone.

24.3.2 Sparsity Is Good for You but Tastes Bad

Besides the then-startling finding that human judgment did reliably worse than statistical models, a key feature of the early results was how well small numbers of variables could fit. Some of this conclusion was constrained by the fact that there were not huge feature sets with truly large number of variables in any case (so you couldn't possibly know, at that time, if "large numbers of variables fit surprisingly better" than small numbers).

A striking example in Dawes (1979) is a two-variable model predicting marital happiness: the rate of lovemaking minus the rate of fighting. He reports correlations of .40 and .81 in two studies (Edwards and Edwards 1977; Thornton 1977).[14]

In another more famous example, Dawes (1971) did a study about admitting students to the University of Oregon PhD program in psychology from 1964 to 1967. He compared and measured each applicant's GRE, undergraduate GPA, and the quality of the applicant's undergraduate school. The

13. Presciently, Dawes also mentions using ridge regression as a proper procedure to maximize out-of-sample fit.

14. More recent analyses using transcribed verbal interactions generate correlations for divorce and marital satisfaction around .6–.7. The core variables are called the "four horsemen" of criticism, defensiveness, contempt, and "stonewalling" (listener withdrawal).

variables were standardized, then weighted equally. The outcome variable was faculty ratings in 1969 of how well the students they had admitted succeeded. (Obviously, the selection effect here makes the entire analysis much less than ideal, but tracking down rejected applicants and measuring their success by 1969 was basically impossible at the time.)

The simple three-variable statistical model correlated with later success in the program more highly (.48, cross-validated) than the admissions committee's quantitative recommendation (.19).[15] The bootstrapping model of the admissions committee correlated .25.

Despite Dawes's evidence, I have never been able to convince any graduate admissions committee at two institutions (Penn and Caltech) to actually compute statistical ratings, even as a way to filter out applications that are likely to be certain rejections.

Why not?

I think the answer is that the human mind rebels against regularization and the resulting sparsity. We are born to overfit. Every AI researcher knows that including fewer variables (e.g., by giving many of them zero weights in LASSO, or limiting tree depth in random forests) is a useful all-purpose prophylactic for overfitting a training set. But the same process seems to be unappealing in our everyday judgment.

The distaste for sparsity is ironic because, in fact, the brain is built to do a massive amount of filtering of sensory information (and does so remarkably efficiently in areas where optimal efficiency can be quantified, such as vision; see Doi et al. [2012]). But people do not like to *explicitly* throw away information (Einhorn 1986). This is particularly true if the information is already in front of us—in the form of a PhD admissions application, or a person talking about their research in an AEA interview hotel room. It takes some combination of willpower, arrogance, or what have you, to simply ignore letters of recommendation, for example. Another force is "illusory correlation," in which strong prior beliefs about an association bias encoding or memory so that the prior is maintained, incorrectly (Chapman and Chapman 1969; Klayman and Ha 1985).

The poster child for misguided sparsity rebellion is personal short face-to-face interviews in hiring. There is a mountain of evidence that such interviews do not predict anything about later work performance, if interviewers are untrained and do not use a structured interview format, that isn't better predicted by numbers (e.g., Dana, Dawes, and Peterson 2013).

A likely example is interviewing faculty candidates with new PhDs in hotel suites at the ASSA meetings. Suppose the goal of such interviews is to predict which new PhDs will do enough terrific research, good teaching,

---

15. Readers might guess that the quality of econometrics for inference in some of these earlier papers is limited. For example, Dawes (1971) only used the 111 students who had been admitted to the program and stayed enrolled, so there is likely scale compression and so forth. Some of the faculty members rating those students were probably also initial raters, which could generate consistency biases, and so forth.

and other kinds of service and public value to get tenure several years later at the interviewers' home institution.

That predictive goal is admirable, but the brain of an untrained interviewer has more basic things on its mind. Is this person well dressed? Can they protect me if there is danger? Are they friend or foe? Does their accent and word choice sound like mine? Why are they stifling a yawn?—they'll *never* get papers accepted at *Econometrica* if they yawn after a long tense day slipping on ice in Philadelphia rushing to avoid being late to a hotel suite!

People who do these interviews (including me) **say** that we are trying to probe the candidate's depth of understanding about their topic, how promising their new planned research is, and so forth. But what we really are evaluating is probably more like "Do they belong in my tribe?"

While I do think such interviews are a waste of time,[16] it is *conceivable* that they generate valid information. The problem is that interviewers may weight the wrong information (as well as overweighting features that should be regularized to zero). If there is valid information about long-run tenure prospects and collegiality, the best method to capture such information is to videotape the interview, combine it with other tasks that more closely resemble work performance (e.g., have them review a difficult paper), and machine learn the heck out of that larger corpus of information.

Another simple example of where ignoring information is counterintuitive is captured by the two modes of forecasting that Kahneman and Lovallo (1993) wrote about. They called the two modes the "inside" and "outside" view. The two views were in the context of forecasting the outcome of a project (such as writing a book, or a business investment). The inside view "focused only on a particular case, by considering the plan and its obstacles to completion, by constructing scenarios of future progress" (25). The outside view "focuses on the statistics of a class of cases chosen to be similar in relevant respects to the current one" (25).

The outside view deliberately throws away most of the information about a specific case at hand (but keeps some information): it reduces the relevant dimensions to *only* those that are present in the outside view reference class. (This is, again, a regularization that zeros out all the features that are not "similar in relevant respects.")

In ML terms, the outside and inside views are like different kinds of cluster analyses. The outside view parses all previous cases into K clusters; a current case belongs to one cluster or another (though there is, of course, a degree of cluster membership depending on the distance from cluster centroids). The inside view—in its extreme form—treats each case, like fingerprints and snowflakes, as unique.

---

16. There are many caveats, of course, to this strong claim. For example, often the school is pitching to attract a highly desirable candidate, not the other way around.

24.3.3   Hypothesis: Human Judgment Is Like Overfitted Machine Learning

The core idea I want to explore is that some aspects of everyday human judgment can be understood as the type of errors that would result from badly done machine learning.[17] I will focus on two aspects: overconfidence and how it increases, and limited error correction.

In both cases, I have in mind a research program that takes data on human predictions and compares them with machine-learned predictions. Then *deliberately* re-do the machine learning badly (e.g., failing to correct for overfitting) and see whether the impaired ML predictions have some of the properties of human ones.

Overconfidence. In a classic study from the early days of JDM, Oskamp (1965) had eight experienced clinical psychologists and twenty-four graduate and undergraduate students read material about an actual person, in four stages. The first stage was just three sentences giving basic demographics, education, and occupation. The next three stages were one and a half to two pages each about childhood, schooling, and the subject's time in the army and beyond. There were a total of five pages of material.

The subjects had to answer twenty-five personality questions about the subject, each with five multiple-choice answers[18] after each of the four stages of reading. All these questions had correct answers, based on other evidence about the case. Chance guessing would be 20 percent accurate.

Oskamp learned two things: First, there was no difference in accuracy between the experienced clinicians and the students.

Second, all the subjects were barely above chance, and accuracy did not improve as they read more material in the three stages. After just the first paragraph, their accuracy was 26 percent; after reading all five additional pages across the three stages, accuracy was 28 percent (an insignificant difference from 26 percent). However, the subjects' subjective *confidence* in their accuracy rose almost linearly as they read more, from 33 percent to 53 percent.[19]

This increase in confidence, combined with no increase in accuracy, is reminiscent of the difference between training set and test set accuracy in AI. As more and more variables are included in a training set, the (unpenalized) accuracy will always increase. As a result of overfitting, however, test-set accuracy will *decline* when too many variables are included. The

---

17. My intuition about this was aided by Jesse Shapiro, who asked a well-crafted question pointing straight in this direction.

18. One of the multiple choice questions was "Kid's present attitude toward his mother is one of: (a) love and respect for her ideals, (b) affectionate tolerance for her foibles," and so forth.

19. Some other results comparing more and less experienced clinicians, however, have also confirmed the first finding (experience does not improve accuracy much), but found that experience tends to *reduce* overconfidence (Goldberg 1959).

resulting gap between training- and test-set accuracy will grow, much as the overconfidence in Oskamp's subjects grew with the equivalent of more "variables" (i.e., more material on the single person they were judging).

Overconfidence comes in different flavors. In the predictive context, we will define it as having too narrow a confidence interval around a prediction. (In regression, for example, this means underestimating the standard error of a conditional prediction $P(Y|X)$ based on observables X.)

My hypothesis is that human overconfidence results from a failure to winnow the set of predictors (as in LASSO penalties for feature weights). Overconfidence of this type is a consequence of not anticipating overfitting. High training-set accuracy corresponds to confidence about predictions. Overconfidence is a failure to anticipate the drop in accuracy from training to test.

Limited Error Correction. In some ML procedures, training takes place over trials. For example, the earliest neural networks were trained by making output predictions based on a set of node weights, then back-propagating prediction errors to adjust the weights. Early contributions intended for this process to correspond to human learning—for example, how children learn to recognize categories of natural objects or to learn properties of language (e.g., Rumelhart and McClelland 1986).

One can then ask whether some aspects of adult human judgment correspond to poor implementation of error correction. An invisible assumption that is, of course, part of neural network training is that output errors are recognized (if learning is supervised by labeled data). But what if humans do not recognize error or respond to it inappropriately?

One maladaptive response to prediction error is to add features, particularly interaction effects. For example, suppose a college admissions director has a predictive model and thinks students who play musical instruments have good study habits and will succeed in the college. Now a student comes along who plays drums in the Dead Milkmen punk band. The student gets admitted (because playing music is a good feature), but struggles in college and drops out.

The admissions director could back-propagate the predictive error to adjust the weights on the "plays music" feature. Or she could create a new feature by splitting "plays music" into "plays drums" and "plays nondrums" and ignore the error. This procedure will generate too many features and will not use error-correction effectively.[20]

Furthermore, note that a *different* admissions director might create two different subfeatures, "plays music in a punk band" and "plays nonpunk music." In the stylized version of this description, both will become convinced that they have improved their mental models and will retain high confidence about future predictions. But their inter-rater reliability will have

---

20. Another way to model this is as the refinement of a prediction tree, where branches are added for new feature when predictions are incorrect. This will generate a bushy tree, which generally harms test-set accuracy.

gone *down*, because they "improved" their models in different ways. Inter-rate reliability puts a hard upper bound on how good average predictive accuracy can be. Finally, note that even if human experts are mediocre at feature selection or create too many interaction effects (which ML regular-izes away), they are often more rapid than novices (for a remarkable study of actual admissions decisions, see Johnson 1980, 1988). The *process* they use is rapid, but the predictive *performance* is not so impressive. But AI algorithms are even faster.

24.4   AI Technology as a Bionic Patch, or Malware, for Human Limits

We spend a lot of time in behavioral economics thinking about how po-litical and economic systems either exploit bad choices or help people make good choices. What behavioral economics has to offer to this general discus-sion is to specify a more psychologically accurate model of human choice and human nature than the caricature of constrained utility-maximization (as useful as it has been).

Artificial intelligence enters by creating better tools for making inferences about what a person wants and what a person will do. Sometimes these tools will hurt and sometimes they will help.

Artificial Intelligence Helps. A clear example is recommender systems. Recommender systems use previous data on a target person's choices and ex post quality ratings, as well as data on many other people, possible choices, and ratings, to predict how well the target person will like a choice they have not made before (and may not even know exists, such as movies or books they haven't heard of). Recommender systems are a behavioral prosthetic to remedy human limits on attention and memory and the resulting incom-pleteness of preferences.

Consider Netflix movie recommendations. Netflix uses a person's viewing and ratings history, as well as opinions of others and movie properties, as inputs to a variety of algorithms to suggest what content to watch. As their data scientists explained (Gomez-Uribe and Hunt 2016):

> a typical Netflix member loses interest after perhaps 60 to 90 seconds of choosing, having reviewed 10 to 20 titles (perhaps 3 in detail) on one or two screens. . . . The recommender problem is to make sure that on those two screens each member in our diverse pool will find something compel-ling to view, and will understand why it might be of interest.

For example, their "Because You Watched" recommender line uses a video-video similarity algorithm to suggest unwatched videos similar to ones the user watched and liked.

There are so many interesting implications of these kinds of recom-mender systems for economics in general, and for behavioral economics in particular. For example, Netflix wants its members to "understand *why* it (a recommended video) might be of interest." This is, at bottom, a question about interpretability of AI output, how a member learns from recommender successes and errors, and whether a member then "trusts" Netflix in general. All these are psychological processes that may also depend heavily on design and experience features (UD, UX).

Artificial Intelligence "Hurts."[21] Another feature of AI-driven personalization is price discrimination. If people do know a lot about what they want, and have precise willingness-to-pay (WTP), then companies will quickly develop the capacity to personalize prices too. This seems to be a concept that is emerging rapidly and desperately needs to be studied by industrial economists who can figure out the welfare implications.

Behavioral economics can play a role by using evidence about how people make judgments about fairness of prices (e.g., Kahneman, Knetsch, and Thaler 1986), whether fairness norms adapt to "personalized pricing," and how fairness judgments influence behavior.

My intuition (echoing Kahneman, Knetsch, and Thaler 1986) is that people can come to accept a high degree of variation in prices for what is essentially the same product as long as there is either (a) very minor product differentiation[22] or (b) firms can articulate why different prices are fair. For example, price discrimination might be framed as cross-subsidy to help those who can't afford high prices.

It is also likely that personalized pricing will harm consumers who are the most habitual or who do not shop cleverly, but will help savvy consumers who can hijack the personalization algorithms to look like low WTP consumers and save money. See Gabaix and Laibson (2006) for a carefully worked-out model about hidden ("shrouded") product attributes.

24.5 Conclusion

This chapter discussed three ways in which AI, particularly machine learning, connect with behavioral economics. One way is that ML can be used to mine the large set of features that behavioral economists think *could* improve prediction of choice. I gave examples of simple kinds of ML (with much smaller data sets than often used) in predicting bargaining outcomes, risky choice, and behavior in games.

The second way is by construing typical patterns in human judgment as the output of implicit machine-learning methods that are inappropriately applied. For example, if there is no correction for overfitting, then the gap

---

21. I put the word "hurts" in quotes here as a way to conjecture, through punctuation, that in many industries the AI-driven capacity to personalize pricing will harm consumer welfare overall.

22. A feature of their fairness framework is that people do not mind price increases or surcharges if they are even partially justified by cost differentials. I have a recollection of Kahneman and Thaler joking that a restaurant could successfully charge higher prices on Saturday nights if there is some enhancement, such as a mariachi band—even if most people don't like mariachi.

between training set accuracy and test-set accuracy will grow and grow if more features are used. This could be a model of human overconfidence.

The third way is that AI methods can help people "assemble" preference predictions about unfamiliar products (e.g., through recommender systems) and can also harm consumers by extracting more surplus than ever before (through better types of price discrimination).

References

Andrade, E. B., and T.-H. Ho. 2009. "Gaming Emotions in Social Interactions." *Journal of Consumer Research* 36 (4): 539–52.

Babcock, L., and G. Loewenstein. 1997. "Explaining Bargaining Impasse: The Role of Self-Serving Biases." *Journal of Economic Perspectives* 11 (1): 109–26.

Babcock, L., G. Loewenstein, S. Issacharoff, and C. Camerer. 1995. "Biased Judgments of Fairness in Bargaining." *American Economic Review* 85 (5): 1337–43.

Bhatt, M. A., T. Lohrenz, C. F. Camerer, and P. R. Montegue. 2010. "Neural Signatures of Strategic Types in a Two-Person Bargaining Game." *Proceedings of the National Academy of Sciences* 107 (46): 19720–25.

Binmore, K., J. McCarthy, G. Ponti, A. Shaked, and L. Samuelson. 2002. "A Backward Induction Experiment." *Journal of Economic Theory* 184:48–88.

Binmore, K., A. Shaked, and J. Sutton. 1985. "Testing Noncooperative Bargaining Theory: A Preliminary Study." *American Economic Review* 75 (5): 1178–80.

———. 1989. "An Outside Option Experiment." *Quarterly Journal of Economics* 104 (4): 753–70.

Blattberg, R. C., and S. J. Hoch. 1990. "Database Models and Managerial Intuition: 50% Database + 50% Manager." *Management Science* 36 (8): 887–99.

Brocas, Isabelle, J. D. Carrillo, S. W. Wang, and C. F. Camerer. 2014. "Imperfect Choice or Imperfect Attention? Understanding Strategic Thinking in Private Information Games." *Review of Economic Studies* 81 (3): 944–70.

Camerer, C. F. 1981a. "General Conditions for the Success of Bootstrapping Models." *Organizational Behavior and Human Performance* 27:411–22.

———. 1981b. "The Validity and Utility of Expert Judgment." Unpublished PhD diss., Center for Decision Research, University of Chicago Graduate School of Business.

———. 2003. *Behavioral Game Theory, Experiments in Strategic Interaction*. Princeton, NJ: Princeton University Press.

Camerer, C. F., T.-H. Ho, and J.-K. Chong. 2004. "A Cognitive Hierarchy Model of Games." *Quarterly Journal of Economics* 119 (3): 861–98.

Camerer, C., E. Johnson, T. Rymon, and S. Sen. 1994. "Cognition and Framing in Sequential Bargaining for Gains and Losses. In *Frontiers of Game Theory*, edited by A. Kirman, K. Binmore, and P. Tani, 101–20. Cambridge, MA: MIT Press.

Camerer, C. F., G. Nave, and A. Smith. 2017. "Dynamic Unstructured Bargaining with Private Information and Deadlines: Theory and Experiment." Working paper.

Chapman, L. J., and J. P. Chapman. 1969. "Illusory Correlation as an Obstacle to the Use of Valid Psychodiagnostic Signs." *Journal of Abnormal Psychology* 46:271–80.

Costa-Gomes, M. A., and V. P. Crawford. 2006. "Cognition and Behavior in Two-Person Guessing Games: An Experimental Study." *American Economic Review* 96 (5): 1737–68.

Costa-Gomes, M. A., V. P. Crawford, and B. Broseta. 2001. "Cognition and Behavior in Normal-Form Games: An Experimental Study." *Econometrica* 69 (5): 1193–235.

Crawford, V. P. 2003. "Lying for Strategic Advantage: Rational and Boundedly Rational Misrepresentation of Intentions." *American Economic Review* 93 (1): 133–49.

Crawford, V. P., M. A. Costa-Gomes, and N. Iriberri. 2013. "Structural Models of Nonequilibrium Strategic Thinking: Theory, Evidence, and Applications." *Journal of Economic Literature* 51 (1): 5–62.

Crawford, V. P., and N. Iriberri. 2007. "Level-k Auctions: Can a Nonequilibrium Model of Strategic Thinking Explain the Winner's Curse and Overbidding in Private-Value Auctions?" *Econometrica* 75 (6): 1721–70.

Dana, J., R. Dawes, and N. Peterson. 2013. "Belief in the Unstructured Interview: The Persistence of an Illusion." *Judgment and Decision Making* 8 (5): 512–20.

Dawes, R. M. 1971. "A Case Study of Graduate Admissions: Application of Three Principles of Human Decision Making." *American Psychologist* 26:180–88.

———. 1979. "The Robust Beauty of Improper Linear Models in Decision Making." *American Psychologist* 34 (7): 571.

Dawes, R. M., and B. Corrigan. 1974. "Linear Models in Decision Making." *Psychological Bulletin* 81, 97.

Dawes, R. M., D. Faust, and P. E. Meehl. 1989. "Clinical versus Actuarial Judgment." *Science* 243:1668–74.

Doi, E., J. L. Gauthier, G. D. Field, J. Shlens, A. Sher, A. Greschner, T. A. Machado, et al. 2012. "Efficient Coding of Spatial Information in the Primate Retina." *Journal of Neuroscience* 32 (46): 16256–64.

Edwards, D. D., and J. S. Edwards. 1977. "Marriage: Direct and Continuous Measurement." *Bulletin of the Psychonomic Society* 10:187–88.

Einhorn, H. J. 1986. "Accepting Error to Make Less Error." *Journal of Personality Assessment* 50:387–95.

Einhorn, H. J., and R. M. Hogarth. 1975. "Unit Weighting Schemas for Decision Making." *Organization Behavior and Human Performance* 13:171–92.

Forsythe, R., J. Kennan, and B. Sopher. 1991. "An Experimental Analysis of Strikes in Bargaining Games with One-Sided Private Information." *American Economic Review* 81 (1): 253–78.

Fudenberg, D., and A. Liang. 2017. "Predicting and Understanding Initial Play." Working paper, Massachusetts Institute of Technology and the University of Pennsylvania.

Gabaix, X., and D. Laibson. 2006. "Shrouded Attributes, Consumer Myopia, and Information Suppression in Competitive Markets." *Quarterly Journal of Economics* 121 (2): 505–40.

Goeree, J., C. Holt, and T. Palfrey. 2016. *Quantal Response Equilibrium: A Stochastic Theory of Games*. Princeton, NJ: Princeton University Press.

Goldberg, L. R. 1959. "The Effectiveness of Clinicians' Judgments: The Diagnosis of Organic Brain Damage from the Bender-Gestalt Test." *Journal of Consulting Psychology* 23:25–33.

———. 1968. "Simple Models or Simple Processes?" *American Psychologist* 23:483–96.

———. 1970. "Man versus Model of Man: A Rationale, Plus Some Evidence for a Method of Improving on Clinical Inferences." *Psychological Bulletin* 73:422–32.

Goldfarb, A., and M. Xiao. 2011. "Who Thinks about the Competition? Managerial Ability and Strategic Entry in US Local Telephone Markets." *American Economic Review* 101 (7): 3130–61.

Gomez-Uribe, C., and N. Hunt. 2016. "The Netflix Recommender System: Algorithms, Business Value, and Innovation." *ACM Transactions on Management Information Systems (TMIS)* 6 (4): article 13.

Grove, W. M., D. H. Zald, B. S. Lebow, B. E. Snits, and C. E. Nelson. 2000. "Clinical vs. Mechanical Prediction: A Meta-analysis." *Psychological Assessment* 12:19–30.

Hartford, J. S., J. R. Wright, and K. Leyton-Brown. 2016. "Deep Learning for Predicting Human Strategic Behavior." *Advances in Neural Information Processing Systems*. https://dl.acm.org/citation.cfm?id=3157368.

Hortacsu, A., F. Luco, S. L. Puller, and D. Zhu. 2017. "Does Strategic Ability Affect Efficiency? Evidence from Electricity Markets." NBER Working Paper no. 23526, Cambridge, MA.

Johnson, E. J. 1980. "Expertise in Admissions Judgment." Unpublished PhD diss., Carnegie-Mellon University.

Johnson, E. J. 1988. "Expertise and Decision under Uncertainty: Performance and Process." In *The Nature of Expertise*, edited by M. T. H. Chi, R. Glaser, and M. I. Farr, 209–28. Hillsdale, NJ: Erlbaum.

Johnson, E. J., C. F. Camerer, S. Sen, and T. Rymon. 2002. "Detecting Failures of Backward Induction: Monitoring Information Search in Sequential Bargaining." *Journal of Economic Theory* 104 (1): 16–47.

Kahneman, D., J. L. Knetsch, and R. Thaler. 1986. "Fairness as a Constraint on Profit Seeking: Entitlements in the Market." *American Economic Review*: 728–41.

Kahneman, D., and D. Lovallo. 1993. "Timid Choices and Bold Forecasts: A Cognitive Perspective on Risk Taking." *Management Science* 39 (1): 17–31.

Kahneman, D., P. Slovic, and A. Tversky, eds. 1982. *Judgment under Uncertainty: Heuristics and Biases*. Cambridge: Cambridge University Press.

Karagözoğlu, E. Forthcoming. "On 'Going Unstructured' in Bargaining Experiments." *Studies in Economic Design by Springer, Future of Economic Design*.

Klayman, J., and Y. Ha. 1985. "Confirmation, Disconfirmation, and Information in Hypothesis Testing." *Psychological Review*: 211–28.

Kleinberg, J., H. Lakkaraju, J. Leskovec, J. Ludwig, and S. Mullainathan. 2017. "Human Decisions and Machine Predictions." NBER Working Paper no. 23180, Cambridge, MA.

Kleinberg, J., A. Liang, and S. Mullainathan. 2015. "The Theory is Predictive, But Is It Complete? An Application to Human Perception of Randomness." Unpublished manuscript..

Krajbich, I., C. Camerer, J. Ledyard, and A. Rangel. 2009. "Using Neural Measures of Economic Value to Solve the Public Goods Free-Rider Problem." *Science* 326 (5952): 596–99.

Lewis, M. 2016. *The Undoing Project: A Friendship That Changed Our Minds*. New York: W. W. Norton.

Lohrenz, T., J. McCabe, C. F. Camerer, and P. R. Montague. 2007. "Neural Signature of Fictive Learning Signals in a Sequential Investment Task." *Proceedings of the National Academy of Sciences* 104 (22): 9493–98.

Meehl, P. E. 1954. *Clinical versus Statistical Prediction: A Theoretical Analysis and a Review of the Evidence*. Minneapolis: University of Minnesota Press.

———. 1986. "Causes and Effects of My Disturbing Little Book." *Journal of Personality Assessment* 50 (3): 370–75.

Mullainathan, S., and J. Spiess. 2017. "Machine Learning: An Applied Econometric Approach." *Journal of Economic Perspectives* 31 (2): 87–106.

Neelin, J., H. Sonnenschein, and M. Spiegel. 1988. "A Further Test of Noncooperative Bargaining Theory: Comment." *American Economic Review* 78 (4): 824–36.

Oskamp, S. 1965. "Overconfidence in Case-Study Judgments." *Journal of Consulting Psychology* 29 (3): 261.

Östling, R., J. Wang, E. Chou, and C. F. Camerer. 2011. "Strategic Thinking and Learning in the Field and Lab: Evidence from Poisson LUPI Lottery Games." *American Economic Journal: Microeconomics* 23 (3): 1–33.

Peysakhovich, A., and J. Naecker. 2017. "Using Methods from Machine Learning to Evaluate Behavioral Models of Choice under Risk and Ambiguity." *Journal of Economic Behavior & Organization* 133:373–84.

Roth, A. E. 1995. "Bargaining Experiments." In *Handbook of Experimental Econom-*

ics, edited by J. Kagel and A. Roth, 253–348. Princeton, NJ: Princeton University Press.

Rumelhart, D. E., and J. L. McClelland. 1986. "On Learning the Past Tenses of English Verbs." In *Parallel Distributed Processing*, vol. 2, edited by D. Rumelhart, J. McClelland, and the PDP Research Group, 216–71. Cambridge, MA: MIT Press.

Sawyer, J. 1966. "Measurement and Prediction, Clinical and Statistical." *Psychological Bulletin* 66:178–200.

Stahl, D. O., and P. W. Wilson. 1995. "On Players' Models of Other Players: Theory and Experimental Evidence." *Games and Economic Behavior* 10 (1): 218–54.

Thornton, B. 1977. "Linear Prediction of Marital Happiness: A Replication." *Personality and Social Psychology Bulletin* 3:674–76.

Tversky, A., and D. Kahneman. 1992. "Advances in Prospect Theory: Cumulative Representation of Uncertainty." *Journal of Risk and Uncertainty* 5 (4): 297–323.

von Winterfeldt, D., and W. Edwards. 1973. "Flat Maxima in Linear Optimization Models." Working Paper no. 011313-4-T, Engineering Psychology Lab, University of Michigan, Ann Arbor.

Wang, J., M. Spezio, and C. F. Camerer. 2010. "Pinocchio's Pupil: Using Eyetracking and Pupil Dilation to Understand Truth Telling and Deception in Sender-Receiver Games." *American Economic Review* 100 (3): 984–1007.

Wright, J. R., and K. Leyton-Brown. 2014. "Level-0 Meta-models for Predicting Human Behavior in Games." In *Proceedings of the Fifteenth ACM Conference on Economics and Computation*, 857–74.

Comment   Daniel Kahneman

Below is a slightly edited version of Professor Kahneman's spoken remarks.

During the talks yesterday, I couldn't understand most of what was going on, and yet I had the feeling that I was learning a lot. I will have some remarks about Colin (Camerer) and then some remarks about the few things that I noticed yesterday that I could understand.

Colin had a lovely idea that I agree with. It is that if you have a mass of data and you use deep learning, you will find out much more than your theory is designed to explain. And I would hope that machine learning can be a source of hypotheses. That is, that some of these variables that you identify are genuinely interesting.

At least in my field, the bar for successful publishable science is very low. We consider theories confirmed even when they explain very little of the variance so long as they yield statistically significant predictions. We treat the residual variance as noise, so a deeper look into the residual variance, which machine learning is good at, is an advantage. So as an outsider, actu-

Daniel Kahneman is professor emeritus of psychology and public affairs at the Woodrow Wilson School and the Eugene Higgins Professor of Psychology emeritus, Princeton University, and a fellow of the Center for Rationality at the Hebrew University in Jerusalem.

For acknowledgments, sources of research support, and disclosure of the author's material financial relationships, if any, please see http://www.nber.org/chapters/c14016.ack.

ally, I was surprised not to hear more about that aspect of the superiority of artificial intelligence (AI) compared to what people can do. Perhaps, as a psychologist, this is what interests me most. I'm not sure that new signals will always be interesting, but I suppose that some may lead to new theory and that would be useful.

I do not fully agree with Colin's second idea: that it is useful to view human intelligence as a weak version of artificial intelligence. There certainly are similarities, and certainly you can model some of human overconfidence in that way. But I do think that the processes that occur in human judgment are quite different than the processes that produce overconfidence in software.

Now I turn to some general remarks of my own based on what I learned yesterday. One of the recurrent issues, both in talks and in conversations, was whether AI could eventually do whatever people can do. Will there be anything that is reserved for human beings?

Frankly, I don't see any reason to set limits on what AI can do. We have in our heads a wonderful computer. It is made of meat, but it's a computer. It's extremely noisy, but it does parallel processing. It is extraordinarily efficient, but there is no magic there. So, it is difficult to imagine that, with sufficient data in the future, there will remain things that only humans can do.

The reason that we see so many limitations, I think, is that this field is really at the very beginning. I mean we are talking about developments (i.e., deep learning) that took off eight years ago. That is nothing. You have to imagine what it might be like in fifty years. Because the one thing that I find extraordinarily surprising in what is happening in AI these days is that everything is happening faster than we expected. People were saying that it will take ten years for AI to beat Go. The interesting thing is it took less by an order of magnitude. This excess of speed at which this thing is developing and accelerating, I think, is very remarkable. So, setting limits is certainly premature.

One point that was made yesterday was about the uniqueness of humans when it comes to evaluations. It was called judgment, but in my jargon it is "evaluation." Evaluations of outcomes are, basically, the utility side of the decision function. I do not see why that should be reserved for humans. On the contrary, I would like to make the following argument: the main characteristic of people is that they are very noisy. You show them the same stimulus twice and they do not give you the same response twice. We have stochastic choice theory because there is so much variability in people's choices conditional on the same stimuli. What can be done with AI is to create a program that observes an individual's choices. That program will be better than people at a wide variety of things. In particular, it will make better choices for the individual. Why? Because it will be noise free. We know from the literature that Colin cited on predictions that there is an interesting tidbit. Take some clinicians and have them predict some criterion a large number of times. Then develop a simple equation that predicts, not the outcome, but each clinician's judgment. That model does better in predicting the outcome than the clinicians themselves.

That is fundamental. It is telling you that one of the major limitations on human performance is not bias, it is just noise. I may be partly responsible for this as, when people now talk about error, they tend to think of bias as an explanation. That's the first thing that comes to mind when there is an error in human performance.

In fact, most of the errors that people make are better viewed as random noise, and there is an awful lot of it. Admitting the existence of noise has implications for practice. One implication is obvious. You should replace humans by algorithms whenever possible. Even when the algorithm does not do very well, humans do so poorly and are so noisy that, just by removing the noise, you can do better than people. The other is that when you cannot replace the human by an algorithm, you try to have human simulate an algorithm. The idea is that, by enforcing regularity, process and discipline on judgment and on choice, you reduce the noise, and you improve performance because noise is so pernicious.

Yann LeCun said yesterday that humans would always prefer emotional contact with other humans. That strikes me as probably wrong. It is extremely easy to develop stimuli to which people will respond emotionally. An expressive face that changes expressions, especially if it's baby-shaped, gives cues that will make people feel very emotional. Robots will have these cues. Furthermore, it is already the case that AI reads faces better than people do. Undoubtedly, robots will be able to predict emotions and development in emotions far better than people can.

I really can imagine that one of the major uses of robots will be taking care of the old. I can imagine that many old people will prefer to be taken care of by friendly robots that have a name, have a personality, and are always pleasant. They will prefer that to being taken care of by their children.

I want to end on a story. A well-known novelist wrote me some time ago that he's planning a novel. The novel is about a love triangle between two humans and a robot. What he wanted to know is how the robot would be different from the people.

I proposed three main differences. One is obvious: the robot will be much better at statistical reasoning and less enamored with stories and narratives than people are. The other is that the robot would have a much higher emotional intelligence. The third is that the robot would be wiser. Wisdom is breadth. Wisdom is not having too narrow a view. That is the essence of wisdom; it's broad framing. A robot will be endowed with broad framing. I say that when it has learned enough, it will be wiser than we people because we do not have broad faming. We are narrow thinkers, we are noisy thinkers, and it is very easy to improve upon us. I do not think that there is very much that we can do that computer will not eventually be programmed to do.

Contributors

Daron Acemoglu
Department of Economics
Massachusetts Institute of
    Technology
50 Memorial Drive
Cambridge, MA 02142-1347

Philippe Aghion
Collège de France
3 Rue D'Ulm
75005 Paris, France

Ajay Agrawal
Rotman School of Management
University of Toronto
105 St. George Street
Toronto, ON M5S 3E6, Canada

Susan Athey
Graduate School of Business
Stanford University
655 Knight Way
Stanford, CA 94305

James Bessen
Technology & Policy Research
    Initiative
Boston University School of Law
765 Commonwealth Avenue
Boston, MA 02215

Erik Brynjolfsson
MIT Sloan School of Management
100 Main Street, E62-414
Cambridge, MA 02142

Colin F. Camerer
Department of Economics
California Institute of Technology
1200 East California Boulevard
Pasadena, CA 91125

Judith Chevalier
Yale School of Management
135 Prospect Street
New Haven, CT 06520

Iain M. Cockburn
School of Management
Boston University
595 Commonwealth Avenue
Boston, MA 02215

Tyler Cowen
Department of Economics
George Mason University
4400 University Drive
Fairfax, VA 22030

Patrick Francois
Vancouver School of Economics
University of British Columbia
IONA Building, 6000 Iona Drive
Vancouver, BC V6T 2E8, Canada

Jason Furman
Harvard Kennedy School
79 John F. Kennedy Street
Cambridge, MA 02138

Alberto Galasso
Rotman School of Management
University of Toronto
105 St. George Street
Toronto, ON M5S 3E6, Canada

Joshua Gans
Rotman School of Management
University of Toronto
105 St. George Street
Toronto, ON M5S 3E6, Canada

Avi Goldfarb
Rotman School of Management
University of Toronto
105 St. George Street
Toronto, ON M5S 3E6, Canada

Austan Goolsbee
University of Chicago Booth School
   of Business
5807 S. Woodlawn Avenue
Chicago, IL 60637

Rebecca Henderson
Harvard Business School
Morgan Hall 445
Soldiers Field Road
Boston, MA 02163

Ginger Zhe Jin
Department of Economics
University of Maryland
3115F Tydings Hall
College Park, MD 20742-7211

Benjamin F. Jones
Department of Management and
   Strategy
Kellogg School of Management
Northwestern University
2211 Campus Drive
Evanston, IL 60208

Charles I. Jones
Graduate School of Business
Stanford University
655 Knight Way
Stanford, CA 94305-4800

Daniel Kahneman
Woodrow Wilson School
Princeton University
Princeton, NJ 08544-1013

Anton Korinek
University of Virginia
Monroe Hall 246
248 McCormick Road
Charlottesville, VA 22904

Mara Lederman
Rotman School of Management
University of Toronto
105 St. George Street
Toronto, Ontario M5S 3E6, Canada

Hong Luo
Harvard Business School
Morgan Hall 241
Soldiers Field Road
Boston, MA 02163

John McHale
108 Cairnes Building
School of Business and Economics
National University of Ireland
Galway H91 TK33, Ireland

Paul R. Milgrom
Department of Economics
Stanford University
579 Serra Mall
Stanford, CA 94305-6072

Matthew Mitchell
Rotman School of Management
University of Toronto
105 St. George Street
Toronto, ON M5S 3E6, Canada

Alexander Oettl
Scheller College of Business
Georgia Institute of Technology
800 West Peachtree Street NW
Atlanta, GA 30308

Andrea Prat
Columbia Business School
Uris Hall 624
3022 Broadway
New York, NY 10027-6902

Manav Raj
Stern School of Business
New York University
44 West Fourth Street
New York, NY 10012

Pascual Restrepo
Department of Economics
Boston University
270 Bay State Road
Boston, MA 02215

Daniel Rock
MIT Sloan School of Management
100 Main Street, E62-365
Cambridge, MA 02142

Jeffrey D. Sachs
Center for Sustainable Development,
    Earth Institute
Columbia University
535 West 116th Street, MC 4327
New York, NY 10027

Robert Seamans
Stern School of Business
New York University
44 West 4th Street, KMC 7-58
New York, NY 10012

Scott Stern
MIT Sloan School of Management
100 Main Street, E62-476
Cambridge, MA 02142

Betsey Stevenson
Gerald R. Ford School of Public Policy
University of Michigan
5224 Weill Hall
735 South State Street
Ann Arbor, MI 48109-3091

Joseph E. Stiglitz
Columbia University
Uris Hall 212
3022 Broadway
New York, NY 10027

Chad Syverson
University of Chicago Booth School of
    Business
5807 S. Woodlawn Avenue
Chicago, IL 60637

Matt Taddy
University of Chicago Booth School of
    Business
5807 S. Woodlawn Avenue
Chicago, IL 60637

Steven Tadelis
Haas School of Business
University of California, Berkeley
545 Student Services Building
Berkeley, CA 94720

Manuel Trajtenberg
Eitan Berglas School of Economics
Tel Aviv University
Tel Aviv 69978, Israel

Daniel Trefler
Rotman School of Management
University of Toronto
105 St. George Street
Toronto, ON M5S 3E6, Canada

Catherine Tucker
MIT Sloan School of Management
100 Main Street, E62-536
Cambridge, MA 02142

Hal Varian
School of Information
University of California, Berkeley
102 South Hall
Berkeley, CA 94720-4600

Author Index

Subject Index